AN INTRODUCTION TO

THEORIES
OF
PERSONALITY

AN INTRODUCTION TO

THEORIES
OF
PERSONALITY

Sixth Edition

Robert B. Ewen

LEA

LAWRENCE ERLBAUM ASSOCIATES, PUBLISHERS

2003   Mahwah, New Jersey   London

Senior Editor:	Debra Riegert
Textbook Marketing Manager:	Marisol Kozlovski
Editorial Assistant:	Jason Planer
Cover Design:	Kathryn Houghtaling Lacey
Textbook Production Manager:	Paul Smolenski
Full-Service Compositor:	TechBooks
Text and Cover Printer:	Hamilton Printing Company

This book was typeset in 10/12 pt. Times, Italic, Bold, and Bold Italic.
The heads were typeset in Gill Sans Extra Bold.

Lawrence Erlbaum Associates, Inc., Publishers
10 Industrial Avenue
Mahwah, New Jersey 07430

Library of Congress Cataloging-in-Publication Data

Ewen, Robert B., 1940-
   An introduction to theories of personality / Robert B. Ewen.—6th ed.
     p. cm.
Includes bibliographical references (p.   ) and index.
  ISBN 0-8058-4356-6 (casebound)
  1. Personality.   I. Title.
BF698.E87 2003
155.2—dc21

                                  2002152190

CONTENTS

PREFACE

This book is an introduction to the field of personality theory. The goals are to provide a foundation for further study, to stimulate enthusiasm for this important and provocative area, and to promote interest in the primary sources on which this secondary one is based. I have tried to achieve these objectives in the following ways:

First-hand Quotations. To familiarize students with the writings of the famous theorists, numerous quotations have been integrated within the text. Also, paperback reprints are cited as well as more standard editions. Paperbacks make it possible to acquire a scholarly library at moderate cost, and my hope is that the somewhat awkward referencing system will facilitate comparisons with (and promote interest in) the original sources.

Capsule Summaries. Most personality theorists are fond (perhaps too fond) of neologisms. To help students learn the many definitions presented in each chapter, Capsule Summaries of these concepts are included throughout the text.

Theoretical Applications. In my opinion, some knowledge of the major applications of a personality theory helps to clarify its more abstruse concepts. I have therefore included an introduction to such applications as dream interpretation, psychopathology, psychotherapy, work, religion, education, literature, and areas of importance to a particular psychologist (e.g., Allport and prejudice).

Common Framework. To facilitate comparisons among the various theories, each chapter follows a common framework (described in chapter 1), and important similarities and differences among the theories are emphasized throughout the book. Each chapter stands on its own, however, so the instructor may select virtually any combination for inclusion in a given course.

Coverage. The coverage of this text was influenced by two polls of those who teach theories of personality. According to these polls ($N = 38$), this book includes the 11 most important theorists plus 4 of the following 5.

Interest and Readability. I have tried to maintain a readable and interesting style, without sacrificing accuracy or scholarliness. I have begun most chapters with a significant anecdote from the theorist's life, and used this to lead into his or her theory.

I have avoided the use of "he" to refer to people in general. But I do not feel justified in rewriting history, so I have left such pronouns intact in the firsthand quotations. At times I have made minor changes in the quotations, such as adding or deleting a comma or interchanging a capital and a small letter, without inserting an ellipsis or brackets. However, more major alterations have been so denoted.

Study Questions.   Study questions are presented at the end of each chapter dealing with a personality theory (that is, chapters 2–16). These questions are designed to encourage critical thinking about the material, and to stimulate discussion and debate about important issues. To make these questions more user-friendly, case material has been placed in a brief Appendix for ready reference, whereas comments and suggestions appear in a "help" section that immediately follows the study questions in each chapter.

Updating the Sixth Edition.   Two goals have guided the preparation of this sixth edition: to make the text more accessible to undergraduate students, and to bring the format more in line with the current status of psychology. The changes include:

— The text is now organized according to five major perspectives: psychodynamic, humanistic, trait, behaviorist, and cognitive. This new organization clarifies the major approaches to personality for the student, while retaining the theorist-organized approach that users of previous editions (and I) prefer.
— A glossary of terms has been added at the end of the book, with page references that indicate where the concept is first discussed, to make it easier for students to look up definitions.
— While I am reluctant to make major changes that may alienate previous users, two (low-rated) theories that were included in previous editions have been deleted: Murray's, and Dollard and Miller's. There are a great many ideas and terms in this book for students to learn, and I find it difficult to maintain that beginning personality theory students should be asked to study in detail these historically less important (and in Murray's case, rather abstruse) theories. The space saved by deleting these theories can be put to better use by including more student aids and additional information about the major theories, while keeping the size of the text within reasonable bounds. Rather than totally exclude these theorists, however, I have made some mention of them in a new glossary of theorists that follows the glossary of terms.
— New student aids have been added, including tables that provide an overview of the theorists who belong to a given perspective at the beginning of that perspective, a section at the beginning of each chapter that outlines what that theorist was seeking to accomplish with his/her theory, and scales comparing theorists at the conclusion of each perspective.
— More material has been included dealing with social-cognitive theory and cognitive constructs.
— More applications that deal with everyday life have been included, so students can better appreciate the material by making it personally meaningful. For example, questions about terrorism and deception by corporate executives have been added to the study questions. Therefore, the study questions should be regarded as an integral part of each chapter.
— As always, the text has been thoroughly reviewed to improve readability without losing scholarly accuracy.

One thorny issue involves a sixth perspective: the biological perspective. This is an important perspective in psychology, but it is less important as an aspect of personality theory. Here again, I find it difficult to believe that beginning personality theory students should be asked to study in detail neurons, synapses, lobes of the brain, parts of the nervous system, et cetera. I have therefore mentioned this perspective in the concluding chapter and noted that students can (and should) learn more about it in courses that deal with more general aspects of psychology.

Thanks are due once again to those who helped in various ways with the preparation of previous editions of this book: Dr. Eugene Sachs, Dr. Olaf W. Millert, Dr. Ronald Tikofsky, Joan Goldstein, Jack Burton, and James Anker. A special vote of thanks goes to Larry Erlbaum for making the present edition possible, and to Debra Riegert for her assistance.

The Psychodynamic Perspective

Overview	Psychodynamic theories emphasize the unconscious: Many important aspects of personality are beyond our awareness and can be brought to consciousness only with great difficulty, if at all.
Sigmund Freud	Devised the first theory of personality (and the first psychotherapy), psychoanalysis. Most of personality is unconscious: we hide many unpleasant truths about ourselves from ourselves by using defense mechanisms, and we are driven by wishes, beliefs, fears, conflicts, and memories of which we are totally unaware. Human nature is entirely malignant, our only instincts are sexual and aggressive, and these inborn impulses include powerful desires for the parent of the opposite sex and intense jealousy toward the parent of the same sex (the Oedipus complex). Personality is often a house divided against itself, torn by conflicting wishes and goals, and this is best explained by using the concepts of id, ego, and superego. Personality develops through a series of psychosexual stages and is firmly established by about age 5 to 6 years. Dreams are a "royal road" to understanding the unconscious. Psychopathology occurs when we can't find ways to channel (sublimate) our malignant instincts into behavior that society will accept.
Carl Jung	At first a supporter of psychoanalysis, then broke with Freud to establish his own theory. Believed that the unconscious is extremely important but disagreed with Freud in many respects: Human nature is both good and bad. There are important instincts in addition to sexuality and aggressiveness (including individuation, the forerunner of the humanistic concept of self-actualization). There is a collective unconscious that contains archetypes, or inherited predispositions to perceive the world in certain ways. Introversion–extraversion is a major aspect of personality. Psychopathology occurs when personality becomes too one-sided, as when we fail to develop important aspects of personality or overemphasize aspects that are contrary to our true (inborn) nature.
Alfred Adler	Adler's inclusion among the psychodynamic theorists is controversial because he did not believe that the unconscious is important. Personality is shaped by the child's relationship with his/her parents and by our consciously chosen life goals, rather than by instincts. The most important motive is striving for self-perfection

(superiority). Cooperation with others is essential for our survival, and we have an inborn tendency to do so. Psychopathology occurs when pathogenic parenting causes the child to develop an inferiority complex and refuse to cooperate with others.

Karen Horney	Combined Freud's belief that the unconscious is extremely important with Adler's belief that personality is shaped by the child's relationship with his/her parents. Psychopathology involves a personality that is torn by inner conflicts (but concepts such as the id, ego, and superego are not necessary to explain this); self-hate, which is often concealed by an idealized self-image; and painful anxiety that causes the healthy quest for personal growth to be replaced by an all-out drive for safety and a compulsive desire to be protected, to dominate others, or to be alone.
Erich Fromm	Because humans don't have inborn instincts that program our behavior, we are more isolated and anxious than any other species, and we find freedom and independence desirable but threatening. Psychopathology is caused by pathogenic parenting and by our poorly designed society, of which Fromm was severely critical, and it occurs when we use our freedom to choose unwisely (as by being selfish instead of loving others). Devised important methods of dream interpretation.
Harry Stack Sullivan	Defined personality in terms of our relationships with other people. Stages beyond early childhood, including adolescence, are important for personality development. Psychopathology is caused by pathogenic parenting that leads to intense anxiety and damaged interpersonal relationships. Made significant contributions to our understanding of the causes and treatment of schizophrenia.
Erik Erikson	Became the leader of the psychoanalytic movement after Freud because he was able to revise psychoanalytic theory in ways that did not offend the establishment. Corrected some of Freud's major errors: Human nature is both good and bad, and the rational ego is stronger than Freud believed. Personality is shaped much more by the child's relationship with his/her parents than by instincts and sexuality, and it develops through a series of psychosocial stages that go from infancy to old age. These stages include adolescence and the identity crisis, and there are criteria for determining whether development is successful at each stage. Devised techniques of play therapy for use with children.

CHAPTER 1

INTRODUCTION
Theories of Personality

This book is about one of the most fascinating of all topics: the human personality. There is as yet no one best theory of personality, and the great psychologists whose views we will examine frequently disagree with one another, so any reader who is seeking a field with clear-cut answers will be disappointed. But if you are intrigued by the challenge of trying to understand human nature, and by comparing and evaluating different and thought-provoking ideas, you should find this field to be highly rewarding.

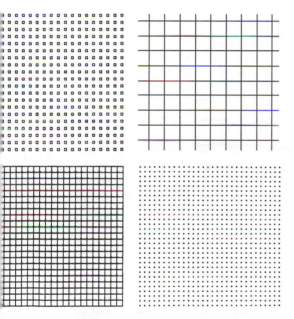

THE MEANING OF PERSONALITY

Personality refers to *important* and *relatively stable* aspects of behavior. Consider a young woman whose personality includes the trait of "painfully shy." She will behave shyly in many different situations, and over a significant period of time. There are likely to be exceptions: She may be more outgoing with her family or a close friend, or at her own birthday party. But she will often have difficulty dealing with other people, which will continue for months or even years and will have a significant effect on her general well-being.

Some theorists contend that personality can be studied only by observing external, social behavior. However, the majority of psychologists define personality as originating *within the individual*. These theorists emphasize that personality may exist in the absence of other people, and may have aspects that are not visible.

Personality deals with a *wide range of human behavior*. To most theorists, personality includes virtually everything about a person—mental, emotional, social, and physical. Some aspects of personality are *unobservable*, such as thoughts, memories, and dreams, whereas others are *observable*, such as overt actions. Personality also includes aspects that are concealed from yourself, or *unconscious*, as well as those that are *conscious* and well within your awareness.

THEORIES OF PERSONALITY

Theories and Constructs

A **theory** is an *unproved speculation* about reality. Established facts are often lacking in scientific work, and a theory offers guidelines that will serve us in the absence of more precise information.

A theory consists of *a set of terms and principles constructed or applied by the theorist*, which are referred to as **constructs**. Like the author or inventor, the theorist is a creator (of constructs); and like creators in other disciplines, the theorist borrows from and builds upon the work of his or her predecessors.

Finally, constructs must be *interrelated* so that a theory is logically consistent. In addition to defining and explaining the terms and principles, the theorist must show how they fit together into a coherent whole.

Dimensions for Comparing Theories of Personality

Ideally, there are four criteria that a theory of personality should satisfy: description, explanation, prediction, and control.

Human behavior can be bewilderingly complicated, and a useful theory helps bring order out of chaos. It provides convenient *descriptions*, establishes a framework for organizing substantial amounts of data, and focuses attention on matters that are of greater importance. In addition, a good personality theory *explains* the phenomena under study. It offers answers to such significant questions as the causes of individual differences in personality, why some people are more pathological than others, and so forth. A theory should also generate *predictions*, so that it may be evaluated and improved (or discarded). To many psychologists, the acid test of any theory is its ability to predict future events. Finally, a valuable theory usually leads to important practical applications. It facilitates *control* and change of the environment—for example, by bringing about better techniques of parenting, education, or psychotherapy.

CAPSULE SUMMARY
Some Important Basic Terminology

Construct	A term or principle that is created (or adopted) by a theorist. A theory consists of a set of constructs that are related to each other in a logical and consistent way.
Personality	Important and relatively stable characteristics within a person that account for consistent patterns of behavior. Aspects of personality may be observable or unobservable, and conscious or unconscious.
Theory	An unproved speculation about certain phenomena, which provides us with descriptions and explanations when more factual information is not available.
Theory of personality	An "educated guess" about important aspects of human behavior, which may be based on clinical observation or empirical research (or both).

These criteria may seem unambiguous, yet there is often considerable disagreement about how to apply them. Some psychologists emphasize that a scientific theory should generate formal, objective predictions that can be tested under the controlled conditions of the research laboratory. By these lights, a theory with many constructs that are difficult to evaluate empirically (such as the Freudian id, ego, and superego), or one that does not stimulate a considerable amount of research, would be regarded as inferior. Other psychologists view the research laboratory as artificial. They prefer to derive their theories of personality from informal clinical observations, an approach they regard as scientific:

> In point of fact psychoanalysis is a method of research, an impartial instrument, like the infinitesimal calculus. . . . The use of analysis for the treatment of the neuroses is only one of its applications; the future will perhaps show that it is not the most important one. . . . It is only by carrying on our analytic pastoral work that we can deepen our dawning comprehension of the human mind. This prospect of scientific gain has been the proudest and happiest feature of analytic work. (Freud, 1927/1961c, p. 36; 1926/1969b, pp. 97, 109–110.)[1]

If laboratory research methods in psychology were as effective as those of other sciences, this approach might well be superior. Clinical observation is subjective and uncontrolled, and the power of suggestion may influence the patient's behavior in ways that support the therapist's theory of personality. Or the therapist may more readily perceive evidence that supports the theory, and disregard contradictory data. Therefore, the prospect of objective validation through laboratory research is highly appealing.

Unfortunately, psychology is a much younger science than physics or chemistry, its subject matter is quite different, and its techniques are less well refined. Practical and financial limitations often require the use of small and/or atypical samples, such as college students, laboratory animals, or volunteers. Experimental procedures are often too insensitive to measure unobservable or unconscious processes with any accuracy, or to ensure that the effects intended by the experimenter are created within the minds of the participants. And human

---

[1]Where two dates appear separated by a slash (such as 1927/1961c), the first is that of the original publication, whereas the second refers to a paperback reprint of the same work. Although awkward, this notation should prove helpful to readers who do not have ready access to the standard edition (or who would like to build an inexpensive library of their own).

beings differ significantly from chemical elements or inert physical objects. For these reasons, the insights available from experiences of real importance to people (such as psychotherapy) are extremely valuable, and both approaches are essential to present-day psychology:

> [In our study, we found that] clinical judgments provided information about mental health that was, apparently, not available from "objective" mental health scales. Qualitative clinical methods have long ago fallen into disfavor among many psychological researchers, and much has been published about the inadequacies of clinical judgment. Indeed, a culture has developed among many academic psychologists in which it is considered acceptable and even laudable to disparage clinical [insight]. . . . Perhaps it is time for researchers to attempt to understand not just the weaknesses but also the strengths of clinical judgment. (Shedler, Mayman, & Manis, 1993, p. 1129; see also Oppenheimer, 1956; Sechrest, 1976; Silverman, 1975; Wachtel, 1980.)

Since psychological theorizing is not yet advanced enough for the usual criteria to be applied in a universally acceptable way, we will compare the theories along the following content-oriented dimensions:

The Basic Nature of Human Beings.   Personality is a comprehensive construct, and motivation is a fundamental aspect of behavior. Therefore, theories of personality are in large part theories of motivation, and must (directly or indirectly) make crucial assumptions about the basic nature of human beings. Are we selfish and willful? Socially oriented and considerate of others? Devoted to maximizing our innate positive potentials in constructive ways? Are we motivated primarily by prior causes, or by our intentions for the future? By conscious or unconscious aspects of personality? Such important issues provide a useful basis for comparing the various theories.

The Structure of Personality.   The constructs that are used to explain the structure of personality also facilitate comparisons among the theories. Freudian theory is well-known for its concepts of id, ego, and superego; Jungian theory is denoted by such ideas as the collective unconscious and archetypes; and so forth.

The Development of Personality.   Some theories posit specific stages of growth that delineate the development of personality. The characteristics of these stages (e.g., sexual in Freudian theory), and of the corresponding character types (e.g., oral, anal, phallic, and genital), also highlight important theoretical similarities and differences.

Further Applications.   A theory of personality can be better understood by examining its important applications. These may include such areas as dream interpretation, psychopathology, psychotherapy, education, work, religion, and literature.

Evaluation.   Although it is difficult to evaluate a theory of personality, it would be remiss not to make some educated guesses about the usefulness of its major constructs.

THE PRE-FREUDIAN ERA

Although personality theory begins with Sigmund Freud, we must first back up a bit in order to set the stage—and to avoid some potentially serious misconceptions.

Freud Versus Wundt

In the year 1879, Wilhelm Wundt founded the first psychological laboratory at Leipzig, Germany. Psychology grew out of two well-established fields, philosophy and experimental physiology; and so the early efforts of the fledgling science dealt with such objective issues as measuring the speed of the nerve impulse, and searching for specific locations of the brain that controlled various organic functions.

At about this time, Freud was viewing his medical training with some skepticism and beginning to study human beings from a different direction—the treatment of people suffering from disorders that could *not* be traced to physical causes. Academic Wundtian psychology had little to say about such matters, and Freud and his followers were understandably loath to wait. Their patients needed immediate help, and their own thirst for knowledge demanded satisfaction. Thus they organized their research in ways more suitable to the study of psychopathology. They dealt with the whole person (symptoms, childhood causes, thoughts, wishes, dreams, and so forth), rather than with physiological details. They evolved techniques to help their suffering patients, and theories to explain the origin and dynamics of the psychological disorders that they confronted. They disdained the psychological laboratory in favor of natural observation in the clinical setting, provoking a controversy that persists today (as we have seen). And they even extended their findings to people in general, arguing that the intensive searchlight provided by psychotherapy illuminated universal truths:

> The source of our findings [i.e., sick people] does not seem to me to deprive them of their value. . . . If we throw a crystal to the floor, it breaks; but not into haphazard pieces. It comes apart along its lines of cleavage into fragments whose boundaries, though they were invisible, were predetermined by the crystal's structure. Mental patients are split and broken structures of this same kind. Even we cannot withhold from them something of the reverential awe which peoples of the past felt for the insane. They have turned away from external reality, but for that very reason they know more about internal, psychical reality and can reveal a number of things to us that would otherwise be inaccessible to us. . . . Pathology has always done us the service of making discernible by isolation and exaggeration conditions which would remain concealed in a normal state. (Freud, 1933/1965b, pp. 59, 121; 1926/1969b, p. 14.)

The perspective of history explains the emphasis of early personality theories on psychopathology. It also accounts for their complexity, since a theory that deals with the totality of human behavior will be more involved than one that concentrates on specific details. It was not until some years later that psychologists raised the question of approaching personality theory through the study of healthy and well-adjusted individuals, or tried to extend the applications of academic laboratory research to such issues as psychopathology and dreams.

The Unconscious Before Freud

A common misconception is that Freud invented such ideas as the unconscious and dream analysis out of a clear sky, filling in what had been a complete void in our knowledge. Not even a genius operates in a vacuum; he or she draws on the work of those who have gone before. The quest to understand the basic nature of human beings is as old as time, and many of Freud's theories existed in some form well before he appeared on the scene.

The idea of unconscious determinants of behavior was clearly in evidence some 100 years prior to Freud (Ellenberger, 1970). Hypnotism was used to gain access to the unknown mind as early as 1784, starting with such pioneers as Franz Anton Mesmer and James Braid and continuing with Jean-Martin Charcot, with whom Freud studied briefly. Certain German philosophers of the early nineteenth century, notably Gotthilf Heinrich von Schubert, Carl Gustav Carus, and Arthur Schopenhauer, anticipated many of Freud's theories. Von Schubert developed a tripartite theory somewhat similar to the Freudian id, ego, and superego, as well as concepts much like narcissism and the death instinct. Carus argued that the key to knowledge of conscious life lay in the realm of the unconscious. Schopenhauer's statement, "The Will's opposition to let what is repellent to it come to the knowledge of the intellect is the spot through which insanity can break through the spirit," closely parallels Freud's later ideas of the id (Will), ego (intellect), and repression.

Toward the latter half of the 19th century, the philosopher Friedrich Nietzsche discussed the self-deceiving and self-destructive nature of human beings, the active inhibition of threatening thoughts, and the need to unmask unconscious materials so as to remove self-deceptions. Nietzsche was also the first to use the term *id,* and is regarded by some as the true founder of modern psychology. A noted French contemporary of Freud's, Pierre Janet, theorized that traumatic events caused ideas to become fixed in the subconscious (a word that he coined) and to be replaced by neurotic symptoms. And Gustav Theodor Fechner, the "father of experimental psychology" and Wundt's immediate predecessor, recognized the possibility of unconscious perception and supplied Freud with such principles as mental energy and pleasure–unpleasure. (Despite his reservations about academic psychology, Freud [1920/1961a, p. 2; 1900/1965a, p. 574] was quite complimentary about Fechner.)

Similarly, attempts to interpret the meaning of dreams can be traced back to medieval times (Ellenberger, 1970; Freud, 1900/1965a). Some ancient theories were quite farfetched, such as the belief that a person's soul left the body and performed the actions of the dream. Others contained elements of truth, as with Plato's claim that there are strong impulses within us that emerge more readily during sleep. According to Plato, these impulses include desires for "intercourse with a mother or anyone else," and they emerge in our dreams "when the reasonable and humane part of us is asleep and its control relaxed, and our bestial nature . . . wakes and has its fling"—ideas which are remarkably similar to Freud's concepts of Oedipal conflicts, the id, and the relaxing of the ego's defenses during sleep.

By the nineteenth century, there was increasingly accurate knowledge about dreams. Von Schubert emphasized the symbolic nature of dream language, and observed that dream symbols may combine many concepts in a single picture (what Freud later called condensation). Karl Albert Scherner designated elongated objects (towers, the mouthpiece of a pipe) as symbols of the male genitals, and a slippery courtyard footpath as symbolic of the female genitals. Alfred Maury studied the effects of sensory stimulation on dreams, and drew attention to the role of forgotten memories in dream formation. The Marquis Hervey de Saint-Denis, who developed the remarkable technique of learning to become aware that he was dreaming and then waking himself at will in order to make appropriate notes, published an extremely thorough study of his own dreams and anticipated the Freudian concepts of condensation and displacement. Yves Delage concluded that dreams originate from unfinished acts or thoughts, primarily those of the preceding day. And still other investigators were adding important theories and insights.

It should also be noted that Freud was by no means the first theorist to concentrate on sexuality, or to relate it to psychopathology. Schopenhauer argued that sexuality was the most important of all instincts, whereas Richard von Krafft-Ebing published his famous *Psychopathia Sexualis* in 1886, coined the terms *sadism* and *masochism,* and even used the term *libido* 6 years prior to Freud in an 1889 article.

This brief sketch hardly does justice to a long and painstaking search for knowledge, and the interested reader will want to consult Ellenberger (1970) for additional information. It does support the contention made previously that theorists do not work in isolation, but draw on the contributions of others. However, this in no way argues against Freud's genius. He made many original and important contributions, and he is the first person identified as a psychologist to develop a theory of personality. Therefore, we will begin our investigation of personality theories with a study of his work.

A SUGGESTED APPROACH TO THE STUDY OF PERSONALITY THEORY

You will probably find that some of the theories presented in this book are more to your liking than others. Possibly, one theory will seem superior to the rest. There are modern psychologists who consider themselves to be strict Freudians, or Jungians, or Adlerians, and who adamantly reject the ideas and constructs of any other theorist. So you are within your rights if you choose to follow in their footsteps.

Nevertheless, I urge you *not* to adopt such a rigid point of view. Theoretical constructs (e.g., the Freudian id, ego, and superego) are not undeniable truths, nor are they concrete entities. They are concepts that have been created (or adopted) by the theorist to describe, explain, predict, and control human behavior. Any theory of personality represents but one possible way of interpreting psychological phenomena. No one of these alternative conceptions has proved to be completely without fault; each has significant virtues and defects. Therefore, if you understand and make use of constructs from a variety of personality theories, you will have at your disposal more useful tools (and a more flexible approach) for unraveling the mysteries of human behavior (Ewen, 2001).

When you study any of the theories in this book, I recommend doing so with a wholly accepting attitude—at least at first. For example, when you read Chapter 2, become a Freudian (if only for the moment) and try to see the functioning of personality strictly from his point of view. As we have seen, personality theorists must interrelate their constructs and fit them together into a coherent whole. So if you are too quick to criticize and discard certain aspects of a theory, this may make it impossible for you to appreciate the overall design of the theory and those concepts that are more palatable. If you find some aspect of a theory that you cannot accept, make a note of this and put it aside. When you complete the evaluation section, *then* decide on your opinions about the theory.

By following this approach, you may well find (as I did) that some theories that at first glance seem absurdly complicated (or even farfetched) contain pearls of wisdom about human behavior. At the very least, you will better appreciate what the theorists were trying to accomplish with their constructs and principles. And you are much more likely to avoid the trap of rejecting (or even ridiculing) good and useful ideas and constructs simply because they were devised by a theorist other than your particular favorite.

SUMMARY

1. **PERSONALITY.** Personality refers to long-lasting and important characteristics within an individual, ones that continue to exert a strong influence on behavior. Aspects of personality may be observable or unobservable, and conscious or unconscious.

2. **THEORIES AND CONSTRUCTS.** A theory is an unproved speculation about reality. It consists of a set of interrelated terms and principles, called *constructs*, that are created or applied by the theorist. Ideally, a useful theory should provide accurate descriptions, comprehensive

explanations, predictions that allow us to verify or discard the theory, and applications that enable us to control and change our environment. Both formal laboratory research and informal clinical observation have important advantages and serious drawbacks, and both are essential sources of information for present-day psychology.

3. THE PRE-FREUDIAN ERA. The first academic psychology dealt primarily with physiological and organic issues. Therefore Freud and his followers, who were concerned with the treatment of psychopathology, developed clinically oriented theories of personality to explain the phenomena that they encountered. Although Freud is properly regarded as the first psychologist to develop a theory of personality, many of his ideas (the unconscious, dream analysis, the id, repression, the sexual nature of psychopathology, and so forth) can be traced back to philosophers and other theorists who preceded him by many years.

CHAPTER 2

SIGMUND FREUD
Psychoanalysis

Throughout the course of history, scientists have dealt three great shocks to our feelings of self-importance. Nicolaus Copernicus demonstrated that the Earth is not the center of all creation, but merely one of several planets that rotate around the sun. Charles Darwin showed that humans are not a unique and privileged life form, but just one of many animal species that have evolved over millions of years. Sigmund Freud emphasized that we are not even the masters of our own minds, but are driven by many powerful unconscious processes (wishes, fears, beliefs, conflicts, emotions, memories) of which we are totally unaware. (See Freud, 1917a; 1916–1917/1966, pp. 284–285.)

Theories that minimize our role in the general scheme of things, and attack widely held beliefs, will not find ready acceptance. Galileo, a follower of Copernicus, was forced to recant his beliefs about the solar system in order to avoid being burned at the stake; while John Thomas Scopes was fired in 1925 for daring to teach evolutionary theory in an American high school, precipitating the famous "Monkey Trial." Freud's theory of personality has also provoked strong resistance, but here there are additional reasons for controversy. Early in Freud's career, three men whom he admired gave him similar (and startling) bits of information. Josef Breuer, with whom Freud later coauthored the landmark *Studies on Hysteria* (Freud & Breuer, 1895/1966),
remarked that neurotic behaviors were always concerned with secrets of the marital bed. Jean-Martin Charcot emphatically proclaimed to an assistant that certain nervous disorders were "always a question of the genitals," a conversation Freud overheard. And the distinguished gynecologist Rudolf Chrobak advised Freud that the only cure for a female patient with severe anxiety and an impotent husband could not be prescribed:
"Rx: A normal penis, dose to be repeated" (Freud, 1914/1967, pp. 13–15; E. Jones,

1953/1963a, p. 158). Although Freud was somewhat shocked by these radical notions and dismissed them from his mind, they later emerged from his preconscious to form the cornerstone of this theory—one that attributes virtually all human behavior to the erotic instinct.

OBJECTIVES

- *To devise the first theory of personality and the first psychotherapy, which he needed to treat his patients (and himself).*
- *To explore the unconscious, a vast hidden realm within every personality, so he could better understand his patients (and himself).*
- *To show that we do not want to understand important aspects of our own personality, and to explain how and why we conceal such information from ourselves.*
- *To devise methods for bringing unconscious material to consciousness, including the interpretation of dreams.*
- *To explain why personality often becomes a house divided against itself, torn by severe intrapsychic conflicts.*
- *To show that sexuality underlies virtually all human behavior, and the failure to resolve the Oedipus complex is the primary cause of psychopathology.*
- *To emphasize that childhood is extremely important for personality development, and is when psychopathology originates.*
- *To warn that we are born with malignant instincts, which we must learn to sublimate into socially acceptable (but less satisfying) behaviors.*
- *To urge us to know ourselves and discover our hidden wishes, fears, beliefs, and conflicts, difficult though this may be.*
- *To apply psychoanalytic theory to many areas, including religion, work, and literature.*

BIOGRAPHICAL SKETCH

Sigmund Freud was born on May 6, 1856, at Freiberg, Moravia (now Czechoslovakia). His father was a wool merchant, his parents Jewish. Freud spent nearly all of his life in Vienna, where his family moved in 1860, and gradually rose from the lower middle class to the heights of society and world fame—though not without considerable physical and psychological suffering.

Freud was an excellent student throughout his academic career, receiving his medical degree from the University of Vienna in 1881. He was not overly enthusiastic about becoming a practicing physician, a slow route to economic security in those days, and longed for the brilliant discovery that would bring rapid fame. After graduation he continued to work in the physiology laboratory of his teacher, Ernst Brücke, and performed some high-quality research in microscopic neuroanatomy. Ironically, Freud narrowly missed out on the renown that he sought by failing to appreciate the full significance of some of his findings.

Freud's future at this time was highly uncertain. His finances were meager, his job did not pay well, and two senior assistants blocked his chances for advancement. When he became engaged to Martha Bernays in 1882, he accepted Brücke's friendly advice to seek his fortune elsewhere. He spent the next 3 years as an assistant to two noted medical scientists, Hermann Nothnagel and Theodor Meynert, won a travel grant to study for a few months with Charcot in Paris, and at last ended a 4 year courtship by marrying Martha on September 30, 1886. Freud's letters to his betrothed show him to have been an ardent and devoted lover, if at times jealous and possessive, and the marriage was for some time a happy one. The Freuds had six children, three boys and three girls, with the youngest (Anna) becoming a prominent child psychoanalyst and ultimately assuming the leadership of the Freudian movement. Interestingly, the man who emphasized sexuality so heavily in his theories was in all probability celibate until his marriage at age 30. Also, while Freud normally declined to practice his psychological ideas on his wife and children, he did create a rather bizarre Oedipal situation by psychoanalyzing Anna himself; and no doubt due in part to this unusual emotional involvement with her father, she never married, devoted her life to the cause of psychoanalysis, and eventually replaced Martha as the most important woman in Sigmund's life (Roazen, 1975/1976b, pp. 58–59, 63, 439–440).

Freud's own life provided him with a great deal of psychological data. He was himself Oedipal, had powerful unconscious hostility toward his father, and was quite close to his mother (who was some nineteen years younger than her husband and devoted to her "golden Sigi"). Freud suffered from a severe neurosis during the 1890s yet did strikingly original work during this time, as though the pressure of his own emerging psychopathology drove him to new heights (E. Jones, 1953/1963a, p. 194). Ellenberger (1970, pp. 447ff.) has described this syndrome as a "creative illness." The sufferer undergoes agonizing symptoms that alternately worsen and improve, exaggerated feelings of isolation, and intense self-absorption, and emerges from this ordeal with a permanently transformed personality and the conviction of having discovered profound new truths. During this period Freud also began his self-analysis (1897), probing the depths of his own mind with the psychological techniques that he developed. Though his creative illness ended by 1900, he continued the self-analysis for the remainder of his life and reserved the last half-hour of each day for this purpose.

Personally, Freud was highly moral and ethical—even puritanical. Some found him cold, bitter, rejecting, the kind of man who does not suffer fools gladly, and more interested in the discoveries to be made from his patients than in themselves. Others depicted him as warm, humorous, profoundly understanding, and extremely kind. (See, for example, Ellenberger, 1970, pp. 457–469; E. Jones, 1953/1963a; 1955/1963b; 1957/1963c; Reik, 1948/1964, p. 258;

Rieff, 1959/1961; Roazen, 1975/1976b; Schur, 1972.) Some colleagues remained devotedly loyal to Freud throughout their lives, whereas others (including Josef Breuer, Wihelm Fliess, Carl Jung, and Alfred Adler) engaged in acrimonious partings because of Freud's adamant emphasis on sexuality as the prime mover of human behavior.

Freud's professional life had many interesting highlights, and also a few major blunders. In 1884, his friend Ernst Fleischl von Marxow suffered an extremely painful illness and became addicted to morphine, which he took as medication. Freud recommended a "harmless" substitute—cocaine—and even published an article praising the new drug. Unfortunately, cocaine also proved to be highly addictive, and Freud was justifiably criticized. In 1896, Freud announced that most of his psychoanalytic patients had been seduced by immoral adults during their childhood. A year later he concluded to his chagrin that these incidents were imaginary, and that the unconscious cannot distinguish between memory and fantasy.

However, successes far outnumbered failures. Freud and Breuer culminated a decade of work by publishing *Studies on Hysteria* in 1895, which described the psychological treatment of behavior disorders (paralyses, headaches, loss of speech, and so forth) that had no physical cause. *The Interpretation of Dreams*, the cornerstone of Freud's theory, appeared in 1900. Fame was far from instant, and this classic took 8 years to sell all of 600 copies. By now Freud had completed his break with official medicine, however, and was more self-assured as the leader of an established movement. There were some vitriolic accusations that psychoanalysts were obscene sexual perverts, and Freud clearly identified with the role of the lonely hero struggling against insuperable odds, but the belief that he was ostracized by Vienna is one of the unfounded legends that surround his life. Rather, his position and fame continued to improve. (See Ellenberger, 1970, p. 450; Freud, 1927/1961c, p. 36; 1925/1963a, pp. 44, 91; 1933/1965b, pp. 8, 60, 137; E. Jones, 1955/1963b, pp. 237, 291.)

In 1909, Freud received an invitation to visit the United States and deliver a series of lectures at Clark University. They were well received, but he left with the impression that "America is a mistake; a gigantic mistake, it is true, but none the less a mistake" (E. Jones, 1955/1963b, p. 263). World War I impressed on him the importance of aggression as a basic human drive, and the ensuing runaway inflation cost him his life savings (about $30,000). Fortunately his reputation was sufficient to attract English and American patients, who paid in a more stable currency, but his hardships were not over.

During the last 16 years of his life, Freud was afflicted with an extremely serious cancer of the mouth and jaw. This required no fewer than thirty-three operations, forced him to wear an awkward prosthesis to fill the resulting gap between what had been the nasal and oral cavities, and prevented him at times from speaking and swallowing, yet he bore this ordeal with his customary stoic courage. Nor did he curtail his prolific and literate writings, which fill twenty-three volumes and won the Goethe Prize in 1930. Still one more trial was in store: the Nazi invasion of Vienna in 1938, during which Anna was detained by the Gestapo but eventually released. Freud and his family successfully escaped to London, where he was received with great honor. There he finally succumbed to the cancer on September 23, 1939. Freud's death took the currently controversial form of an assisted suicide: he reluctantly decided that his suffering had reached the point where going on made no sense, and his doctor administered a dose of morphine that produced a peaceful sleep from which Freud never awoke (Schur, 1972).

THE BASIC NATURE OF HUMAN BEINGS

Freud named his theory **psycho-analysis**. (Most modern writers omit the hyphen.) This term is also used to denote the form of psychotherapy that Freud originated.

Instincts and Psychic Energy

Drive Reduction.   Freud concludes that human beings are motivated by powerful innate forces (**instincts**). An instinct becomes activated when your body requires sustenance, such as food or water. The activated instinct (*need*) produces a psychological state of increased tension or arousal (**drive**) that you experience as unpleasant, such as hunger or thirst.

According to Freud, the goal of all behavior is to obtain pleasure and avoid unpleasure or pain (the *pleasure principle*, to be discussed later in this chapter). So you take action to reduce the unpleasant tension (the drive), as by eating or drinking, which satisfies your body's need. **Drive reduction** restores the body to a previous state of equilibrium where no needs are active (*homeostasis*), and is our primary way of achieving pleasure. (See Freud, 1911/1963c, p. 22; 1916–1917/1966, p. 356; 1926/1969b, pp. 25–26.) Freud does concede that drive *increases* may sometimes be pleasurable, as in the case of excitement during sexual intercourse, but he regards this as an awkward contradiction that cannot readily be reconciled with his theory (1924/1963h, p. 191).

Insofar as the specific nature of instincts is concerned, Freud changed his mind several times. At one point he distinguished between sexuality and those instincts that serve the goal of self-preservation (such as hunger and thirst). However, the ultimate version of his theory states that we are motivated by two instincts: sexual and destructive (aggressive).

The Sexual Instinct (Eros).   In Freudian theory, sexuality has an unusually wide meaning: it signifies the whole range of erotic, pleasurable experience. In addition to the genitals, the body has many parts capable of producing sexual gratification (**erotogenic zones**); "in fact, the whole body is an erotogenic zone" (Freud, 1940/1969a, p. 8; see also Freud, 1905/1965d, pp. 58ff).

To emphasize that sexuality refers to far more than intercourse and reproduction, Freud frequently uses the name **Eros** (the ancient Greek god of love) as a synonym for this instinct. Such self-preservative behavior as eating and drinking involves the sexual instinct because the mouth is one of the major erotogenic zones, and because we preserve ourselves out of self-love (**narcissism**) and the wish to continue gaining erotic pleasure.

The Destructive Instinct.   One of Freud's more radical conclusions (reached toward the latter part of his career) is that life itself aims at returning to its previous state of nonexistence, with all human beings driven by a "death instinct" (Freud, 1920/1961a, pp. 30ff; see also Freud, 1923/1962, pp. 30–37). The concept of a death instinct remains controversial even among psychoanalysts, however, since it is incompatible with the accepted evolutionary principle of survival of the fittest.

A more widely accepted interpretation of Freud's later ideas is that there are two primary human drives, sexual (Eros) and destructive or aggressive (e.g., Brenner, 1973/1974). These two types of instincts are fused together, though not necessarily in equal amounts. Thus any erotic act, even sexual intercourse, is also partly aggressive, whereas any aggressive act, even murder, is partly erotic. Both the sexual and destructive instincts are present at birth.

External and Internal Conflict.   Freud (1927/1961c, p. 10) is extremely pessimistic about human nature. He argues that we are inherently uncivilized, and that the sexual and destructive instincts include the desire for incest and the lust for killing. Since other people will not tolerate such behavior, conflict between the individual and society is inevitable. And this also implies that intrapsychic conflict is unavoidable, for we must reluctantly learn to channel these strong but forbidden impulses into compromise activities that are socially acceptable (**sublimate** them). For example, destructive and sadistic impulses may be sublimated by becoming a football player.

Although we may try to make these compromises and substitutes as close to the original goal as society will permit, they are not as satisfying. We are all left with some unpleasant psychological tension, which is the price we must pay for living in a civilized society (Freud, 1908b; 1930/1961b).

Psychic Energy (Libido) and Cathexis.   Just as overt actions are powered by physical energy, mental activity involves constant expenditures of **psychic energy**. Psychic energy is unobservable and has no known physical correlates, despite Freud's belief that underlying neurological functions would ultimately be discovered. It should be considered a hypothetical construct, rather than an actual entity.

Each of us possesses a more or less fixed supply of psychic energy. If a relatively large amount is usurped by one component of personality, or is expended in pathological forms of behavior, less will be available for other components or for healthy activities.

Freud refers to the psychic energy associated with the sexual instinct as **libido**, but offers no name for aggressive energy. Since virtually all behavior involves a fusion of sexuality and destructiveness, however, libido may be considered to refer to both varieties of psychic energy (Brenner, 1973/1974, p. 30). Libido is wholly intrapsychic, and never flows out of the mind into the outside world. It attaches itself to mental representations of objects that will satisfy instinctual needs, a process known as **cathexis** (plural, *cathexes*).

For example, an infant soon learns that its mother is an important source of such instinctual satisfactions as feeding, oral stimulation, and physical contact. The infant therefore develops a strong desire for her and invests a great deal of psychic energy (libido) in thoughts, images and fantasies of her. In Freudian terminology, the infant forms a strong cathexis for its mother. Conversely, a visiting stranger is not greatly desired and is only weakly (if at all) cathected with libido. The hungrier you are, the more libido you expend in thoughts of food. And an individual who devotes more libido to unresolved Oedipal desires will have less available to fuel such activities as finding a suitable wife or husband.

Psychic Determinism and Parapraxes

Psychoanalytic theory states that nothing in the psyche happens by chance; *all* mental (and physical) behavior is determined by prior causes. Apparently random thoughts, the inability to recall a familiar word or idea, saying or writing the wrong words, self-inflicted injuries, and dreams all have underlying reasons, which are usually unconscious. This principle is known as **psychic determinism**, and Freud (1901/1965c) presents many examples of such **parapraxes** (erroneous actions; singular, *parapraxis*).

One famous illustration of motivated forgetting (**repression**) occurred when a friend tried to convince Freud that their generation was doomed to dissatisfaction. The friend wished to conclude his argument by quoting a phrase from Virgil that he knew well, "Exoriar(e) aliquis nostris ex ossibus ultor" ("Let someone arise from my bones as an avenger"), but could not recall the word "aliquis" and became hopelessly confused. After supplying the correct quotation, Freud advised his friend to think freely and uninhibitedly about the "forgotten" word (the technique of **free association**). This led to the discovery of numerous unconscious connections—the division of the word into "a" and "liquis," liquidity and fluid, blood and ritual sacrifices, and a miracle of flowing blood alleged to have taken place at Naples—and eventually to the friend's fear that a woman with whom he had enjoyed a romantic affair in Naples had become pregnant (that is, her menstrual blood had stopped flowing). The word "aliquis" was deliberately forgotten (repressed) because it was a threatening reminder of an important inner conflict: a wish for (avenging) descendants, as indicated by the Virgil quotation, and a stronger opposing desire not to be embarrassed by any out-of-wedlock offspring (Freud, 1901–1965c, pp. 9–11, 14).

Forgetting (or arriving late at) an appointment or college examination happens for definite reasons. The explanation of these parapraxes may be fairly simple, such as anger at the person to be met or fear of failing the exam. The causes of important psychic phenomena, however, are usually numerous (**overdetermined**) and more complicated. For example, the forgetful student may also be motivated by an unconscious wish to punish parents who are applying too much pressure to excel—and to punish herself because she feels guilty about her strong hostility toward them.

"Freudian slips" of the tongue or pen are also parapraxes that reflect unconscious motivation. A politician who expected little good from a meeting began it with the statement, "Gentlemen: I take notice that a full quorum of members is present and herewith declare the sitting *closed!*" Only when the audience burst into laughter did he become aware of his error. A German professor, intending a modest observation that he was not *geeignet* (qualified) to describe an illustrious rival, exposed his true jealousy by declaring that he was not *geneigt* (inclined) to talk about him. Another expert with an exaggerated sense of self-importance declaimed that the number of real authorities in his field could be "counted *on one finger*—I mean on the fingers of one hand." A young man who wished to escort (*begleiten*) a lady acquaintance, but feared that she would regard his offer as an insult (*beleidigen*), revealed his true feelings by unconsciously condensing the two words and offering to "insort" (*begleitdigen*) her (Freud, 1901/1965c, pp. 59, 68–69, 79).

Self-inflicted injuries are likely to be caused by unconscious guilt that creates a need for punishment. A member of Freud's family who bit a tongue or pinched a finger did not get sympathy, but instead the question: "Why did you do that?" (Freud, 1901/1965c, p. 180). Brenner (1973/1974, p. 139) relates the case of a female patient who was driving her husband's car in heavy traffic, and stopped so suddenly that the car behind crashed into and crumpled one of the rear fenders. Her free associations indicated that this parapraxis was due to three related, unconscious motives: anger toward her husband because he mistreated her (expressed by smashing up his car), a desire to be punished for such unwifely hostility (which was certain to be satisfied once her husband learned of the accident), and powerful repressed sexual desires that her husband was unable to satisfy (which were symbolically gratified by having someone "bang into her tail"). Thus apparently bungled actions may prove to be quite skillful displays of unconscious motivation.

The Unconscious

The common occurrence of parapraxes implies that much of personality is beyond our immediate awareness. Freud concludes that most of personality and mental activity is **unconscious** and cannot be called to mind even with great effort. Information that is not conscious at a given moment, but which can readily become so, is described as **preconscious**. The preconscious is much closer to the conscious than to the unconscious because it is largely within our control. (See Freud, 1923/1962, pp. 5, 10; 1915/1963g, pp. 116–150.)

THE STRUCTURE OF PERSONALITY

Freud originally defined the structure of personality in terms of the unconscious, preconscious, and conscious (the *topographic* model). However, he found that this straightforward approach left much to be desired.

The topographic model states that the act of relegating material to the unconscious (repression) originates from the preconscious or conscious, and should therefore be accessible to awareness. Yet Freud found that his patients often engaged in repression without having any conscious knowledge that they were doing so. He was therefore forced to conclude that "all that is repressed is unconscious, but not all that is unconscious is repressed" (1923/1962, p. 8; see also Freud, 1915/1963f, pp. 104–115; 1916–1917/1966, pp. 294ff).

To overcome such difficulties, Freud developed a revised theory (the *structural* model) that describes personality in terms of three constructs: the **id**, the **ego**, and the **superego** (Freud, 1923/1962). These concepts, and their relationship to the topographic model, are illustrated in Figure 2.1. ("Pcpt.-cs." refers to the "perceptual-conscious," which is the outermost layer of consciousness.) Freud emphasizes that the id, ego, and superego are not separate compartments within the mind. They blend together, like sections of a telescope or colors in a painting. For purposes of discussion, however, it is necessary to treat these interrelated constructs one at a time.

The Id

The **id** (*das Es*; literally, the "it") is the only component of personality that is present at birth. It therefore includes all of the instincts, and the total supply of psychic energy. The id is entirely unconscious and represents "the dark, inaccessible part of our personality... a chaos, a cauldron full of seething excitations" (Freud, 1933/1965b, p. 73).

The id transforms biological needs into psychological tension (drives). Its only goal is to gain pleasure by reducing these drives (the aforementioned **pleasure principle**). The id is totally illogical and amoral, however, and has no conception of reality or self-preservation. Its only resource is to form mental images of what it wants, a process called **wish-fulfillment**. The id is like an impulsive child that wants pleasure right away, so it demands an immediate

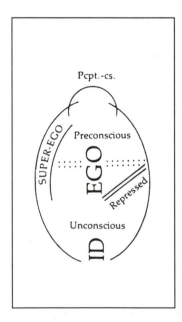

FIG. 2.1.   Freud's structural model of personality. "The space occupied by the unconscious id ought to have been incomparably greater than that of the ego or the preconscious. I must ask you to correct it in your thoughts." (Freud; 1933/1965b, pp. 78–79.)

substitute if its initial choice is frustrated. For example, an infant deprived of the bottle may cathect its thumb and discharge tension by sucking.

The id's irrational, impulsive, and image-producing mode of thought is known as the **primary process** (Freud, 1911/1963c). The primary process permits opposites to coexist side by side, represents ideas by parts that stand for the whole, and condenses related concepts into a single entity. It has no sense of time and is not affected by experience, so childhood instinctual impulses and repressions exist in the adult id as strongly as though they had just occurred. The primary process plays a prominent role in parapraxes, such as the word "insort" produced by condensation or the association of opposites by the chairman who began a meeting by declaring it "closed." (See Freud, 1933/1965b, pp. 15–16; 1940/1969a, p. 29.)

The Ego

Starting at about age 6 to 8 months, the **ego** (*das Ich*; literally, the "I") begins to develop out of the id. The formation of the ego is aided by experiences that help the infant to differentiate between self and not-self, notably those concerning its own body. When the infant touches itself, it also experiences the sensation of being touched, which does not happen with other objects. And the infant's body is a source of pleasure (and pain) that cannot be taken away, unlike the bottle at feeding time.

The images produced by the id cannot reduce drives or satisfy biological needs, since these images are only mental pictures of what the infant wants. However, the maturing child makes an important discovery: the environment contains objects that can satisfy the demands of the id. Mental representations of these objects are incorporated in the ego, and the growth of the ego increases the child's capacity to deal with reality.

The ego is "a kind of facade of the id ... like an external, cortical, layer of it" (Freud, 1926/1969b, pp. 18–19). Unlike the id, however, the ego spans the conscious, preconscious, and unconscious. The ego is the only component of personality that can interact with the environment. It is logical and rational, and forms realistic plans of action designed to satisfy the needs of the id. Although the ego is also interested in pleasure, it suspends the pleasure principle in favor of the **reality principle** and delays the discharge of tension until a suitable object can be found. This makes it possible to avoid errors, such as drinking from a bottle of bleach when you are thirsty; to avoid punishment, like a parental slap for trying to eat a forbidden object; and to increase pleasure, as by rejecting an edible but unappetizing object and waiting for a tastier one. The rational, pleasure-delaying, problem-solving, and self-preservative mode of thought representative of the ego is known as the **secondary process** (Freud, 1911/1963c; see also Freud, 1940/1969a, p. 55).

The relationship between the ego and the id is intimate and complex. The ego may be servile and try at all costs to remain on good terms with the id. Or the ego's concern with self-preservation may cause it to contest the impulsive id:

> . . . in its relation to the id [the ego] is like a man on horseback, who has to hold in check the superior strength of the horse; with this difference, that the rider tries to do so with his own strength while the ego uses borrowed forces. The analogy may be carried a little further. Often a rider, if he is not to be parted from his horse, is obliged to guide it where it wants to go; so in the same way the ego is in the habit of transforming the id's will into action as if it were its own. (Freud, 1923/1962, p. 15. See also Freud, 1923/1962, p. 46; 1933/1965b, p. 77)

Freud regards decisions about when to bridle the id's passions and bow before reality, and when to side with them and take arms against the external world, as "the ego's highest function.... such decisions make up the whole essence of worldly wisdom" (1926/1969b, p. 27).

Anxiety.   The ego's task is a difficult one because it is "a poor creature owing service to three masters and consequently menaced by three dangers: from the external world, from the libido of the id, and from the severity of the superego" (Freud, 1923/1962, p. 46; see also Freud, 1933/1965b, p. 77). The ego responds to such threats with **anxiety,** a highly unpleasant emotion that is similar to intense nervousness. Anxiety does serve a self-preservative function, however: it readies the individual for appropriate action, so a limited amount is both normal and desirable.

Freud identifies anxiety by its source, or which of the ego's three masters is responsible. **Realistic** (or **objective**) **anxiety** is caused by danger in the environment, such as an ominous-looking individual coming your way on a deserted street. In addition to such immediate threats, memories of previous traumatic experiences may enable the ego to respond with anxiety as a signal of future danger. A knowledgeable sailor may react with signal anxiety to a cloud on the horizon because it indicates the approach of a hurricane, or a satiated infant may grow upset at the mother's departure because it has learned that becoming hungry in her absence will mean frustration and discomfort (Freud, 1926/1963j, pp. 76–77; 1916–1917/1966, p. 394). Such realistic anxiety may cause the pedestrian to flee or call for help, the sailor to batten down the hatches, and the child to try to get its mother to stay by crying.

Neurotic anxiety concerns the harm that will result from yielding to a powerful and dangerous id impulse. **Moral anxiety** is caused by acts or wishes that violate one's standards of right and wrong (the superego, discussed later) and includes feelings of shame and guilt. These two sources of anxiety are more difficult to deal with because they are intrapsychic, and cannot be escaped by such simple physical actions as running away.

The Defense Mechanisms.   To cope with severe threats from the id (or from the superego or external world) and with the associated anxiety, the ego may resort to various **defense mechanisms**. Perhaps the most important of these is **repression** (Freud, 1915/1963f), which (as we have seen) consists of unconsciously eliminating threatening material from awareness and being unable to recall it on demand.

We are not aware of using repression because it originates from the unconscious part of the ego, which expends psychic energy in order to prevent a dangerous id impulse from surfacing (a process called **anticathexis** or **countercathexis**, since it opposes a cathexis of the id). So long as the ego's anticathexis is stronger than the id's cathexis, repression succeeds and the dangerous material does not reach consciousness. Therefore, repressed material cannot be brought to consciousness simply by trying to do so; special methods are needed (as we will see). During sleep, however, the ego's anticathexes weaken and allow repressed material to emerge in the form of dreams. This may also happen during such waking states as alcohol intoxication or extreme temptation.

All important repressions occur during early childhood, when the immature and relatively powerless ego needs special methods to cope with danger (Freud, 1926/1963j, pp. 97–99;

CAPSULE SUMMARY
Some Important Psychoanalytic Terminology (I)

Anticathexis (counter-cathexis)	Psychic energy that is used by the ego to oppose a dangerous or immoral cathexis.
Anxiety	A highly unpleasant emotion similar to intense nervousness. The three types are realistic or objective anxiety (related to threats in the external world), neurotic anxiety (related to powerful id impulses), and moral anxiety (related to the superego's standards of right and wrong).

Castration anxiety	The boy's fears that his sexual organ will be removed as punishment for his Oedipal wishes.
Cathexis	Psychic energy that is invested in a mental representation of an object. The stronger the cathexis, the greater the amount of psychic energy and the more the object is desired.
Conscious	The part of personality that includes material of which one is aware.
Drive	(1) A psychological state of tension and discomfort that is caused by a physiological (bodily) need. (2) Sometimes used as a synonym for instinct.
Drive reduction	Eliminating or decreasing the discomfort and tension of a drive, which satisfies the underlying physiological need. To Freud, the major source of pleasure.
Eros	A synonym for the sexual instinct.
Erotogenic zone	An area of the body that is capable of producing erotic gratification when stimulated.
Instinct	An innate motivating force that is activated by a need. The two types are sexual and destructive (aggressive).
Libido	The psychic energy associated with the sexual instinct; sometimes used to refer to both sexual and destructive energy.
Narcissism	Self-love; the investment of one's own self with libido.
Object	Whatever will satisfy an activated instinct. May be an inanimate entity, a person, or even something fanciful and irrational.
Oedipus complex	Powerful feelings of love for the parent of the opposite sex and hostile jealousy for the parent of the same sex, together with powerful feelings of love for the parent of the same sex and hostile jealousy for the parent of the opposite sex. The former set of attitudes is usually, but not always, the stronger.
Overdetermination	A term referring to the numerous, complicated causes of most behavior.
Parapraxis	An apparent accident that is caused by unconscious mental processes, and therefore indicates one's real feelings and beliefs; a "Freudian slip."
Penis envy	The girl's jealousy of the boy's protruding sexual organ.
Pleasure principle	The goal underlying all human behavior, to achieve pleasure and avoid unpleasure (pain).
Preconscious	The part of personality that includes material that is not within one's awareness, but can readily be brought to mind.
Primal scene	Observing one's parents' sexual intercourse.
Primary process	The chaotic, irrational mode of thought representative of the id.
Psychic determinism	The principle that nothing in the psyche happens by chance; all mental activity has a prior cause.
Psychic energy	The "fuel" that powers all mental activity; an unobservable, abstract construct.
Psychoanalysis	(1) The name Freud gave to his theory of personality. (2) The method of psychotherapy devised by Freud.
Reality principle	Delaying the discharge of tension until a suitable object has been found; a function of the ego.
Secondary process	The logical, self-preservative, problem-solving mode of thought representative of the ego.
Unconscious	The part of personality that includes material that is not within one's awareness and cannot readily be brought to mind. To Freud, most of personality is unconscious.
Wish-fulfillment	Forming a mental image of an object that will satisfy a need; a function of the id.

1926/1969b, pp. 30–31). Although repression can help to keep the id under control, it often creates more problems than it solves. Fleeing from an external threat can be a wise choice, but there is no good way to escape one's own psyche. The id impulses continue to demand satisfaction, forcing the ego to use some of its limited supply of psychic energy in order to maintain the anticathexis. Repressed material is not affected by experience, since it is under the aegis of the id. So it remains at a childish level, which makes immature behavior more likely (such as a temper tantrum by an adult). And since repressions operate unconsciously, they cannot be undone when they are no longer needed. Self-deception provides relief, but at a price: an inability to perceive that the danger has disappeared, or that one is now old enough to deal with it effectively. Childhood repressions therefore persist into adolescence and adulthood, where they prevent true self-knowledge and may even lead to the development of troublesome neurotic symptoms.

Repression often occurs in combination with other defense mechanisms. One of these is **reaction formation** (Freud, 1926/1963j, p. 30; 1905/1965d, pp. 72–73), where threatening emotions, beliefs, or motives are repressed and are unconsciously replaced by their opposites. A child who is afraid to confront an all-powerful parent may repress her intense anger, and feel only constant affection. Or a man may repress strong feelings of self-hate that originated in childhood, and believe that he is superior to everyone else. In each case, overemphasizing the opposite emotion (love) reduces anxiety and helps to maintain the repression of the true but threatening emotion (hate). Similarly, an extremist may crusade against sexual immorality in order to conceal his own deviant sexual desires from himself. Although reaction formations may seem sincere, they can usually be identified by their extreme and compulsive nature. This defense mechanism also operates unconsciously, making possible the primary goal of self-deception.

The defense mechanism of **displacement** involves the transfer of feelings or behaviors from a dangerous object to one that is less threatening. A person who is angry with the boss may maintain a discreet silence, then go home and shout at a family member. Or aggressive impulses may be unconsciously diverted from a frightening object (such as a parent) to oneself, which may lead to self-inflicted injuries or even to suicide. Anxiety may also be displaced, as when a child who is victimized by abusive parents shies away from people in general.

In contrast, the defense mechanism of **projection** conceals dangerous impulses by unconsciously attributing them to other people or things (Freud, 1912–1913/1950, pp. 61ff; 1922/1963m). For example, projected anger may lead to the belief that you are disliked, hated, or being persecuted by other people. In displacement, you know that you are angry and choose a safer target; in projection, you repress your anger and believe that other people are angry at you. Also, projection always operates unconsciously, whereas some displacements may be conscious. Although projection plays a significant role in the development of paranoid behavior, it is a normal way for very young children to deny their mistakes (A. Freud, 1936/1966, p. 123).

The ego may also protect itself by refusing to face an unpleasant truth (**denial of reality**). Denial differs from repression in that the threat occurs in the external world, rather than within your own psyche (A. Freud, 1936/1966, p. 109). For example, a child who resents the birth of a sibling may keep repeating "no baby, no baby." Or parents who are confronted with evidence that their son has committed a serious crime may refuse to believe it and insist that "he is a good boy." The terrifying specter of death is a frequent cause of denial, for it is very difficult to accept the fact that we and our loved ones will someday be gone (Becker, 1973).

Denial is often accompanied by another defense mechanism, **fantasy**, where unfulfilled needs are gratified in one's imagination. A child may deny weakness not only by playing with reassuring symbols of strength like toy guns or dolls, but also by daydreaming about being a famous general or worthy parent (A. Freud, 1936/1966, pp. 69ff). Virtually everyone daydreams to some extent. As with denial, however, an excessive amount of fantasy prevents the ego from fulfilling its main function—perceiving and dealing with reality.

CAPSULE SUMMARY
Some Important Psychoanalytic Terminology (II)

Defense mechanism	A method used by the ego to ward off threats from the id, superego, or external world, and to reduce the corresponding anxiety. Most defense mechanisms operate unconsciously, making possible the primary goal of self-deception.
Denial of reality	Refusing to believe, or even to perceive, some threat in the external world; a defense mechanism.
Displacement	Transferring behaviors or emotions, often unconsciously, from one object to another that is less threatening; a defense mechanism.
Fantasy (daydreaming)	Gratifying unfulfilled needs by imagining situations in which they are satisfied; a defense mechanism.
Identification	(1) Reducing painful feelings of self-contempt by becoming like objects that are illustrious and admired, such as idols, aggressors, or lost loves; a defense mechanism that may be partly or wholly unconscious. (2) The healthy desire to become like one's parents.
Intellectualization	Unconsciously separating threatening emotions from the associated thoughts or events and reacting on only an intellectual level; a defense mechanism.
Introjection	Unconsciously incorporating someone else's values or personal qualities into one's own personality.
Projection	Unconsciously attributing one's own threatening impulses, emotions, or beliefs to other people or things; a defense mechanism.
Rationalization	Using and believing superficially plausible explanations in order to justify illicit behavior and reduce feelings of guilt; a defense mechanism.
Reaction formation	Repressing threatening beliefs, emotions, or impulses and unconsciously replacing them with their opposites; a defense mechanism.
Regression	(1) Unconsciously adopting behavior typical of an earlier and safer time in one's life; a defense mechanism. (2) A reverse flow of libido to an object previously abandoned, or to an earlier psychosexual stage.
Repression	Unconsciously eliminating threatening material from consciousness and using anticathexes to prevent it from regaining consciousness, thus being unable to recall it; a defense mechanism.
Sublimation	Unconsciously channeling illicit instinctual impulses into socially acceptable behavior. A form of displacement, but one that represents ideal behavior.
Undoing	Unconsciously adopting ritualistic behaviors that symbolically negate previous actions or thoughts that cause feelings of guilt; a defense mechanism.

Rationalization consists of using and believing superficially plausible explanations in order to justify unacceptable behavior (E. Jones, 1908). Unlike excuses, which are designed to persuade someone else, rationalizations reduce anxiety by concealing the truth from the person who uses them. For example, a man who abuses his wife may convince himself that he is in some way the real victim. A poorly prepared student who fails an examination may decide that the grading system was unfair. An inferior teacher may conclude that the students lack ability. Or a politician who spends tax money on personal vacations, engages in sexual harassment, or accepts favors from businesses that his committee regulates may believe that his august position entitles him to bend the rules.

Threatening emotions may unconsciously be separated from related thoughts or memories, a defense mechanism known as **intellectualization**. Some patients in psychotherapy seek relief by repressing their pain and talking unemotionally about their problems, thereby failing to make progress because they do not feel what they are saying. Another defense mechanism, **undoing**, involves rituals that symbolically negate a previous act or thought that causes feelings of guilt (Freud, 1926/1963j, pp. 53ff). A well-known literary example is that of Lady Macbeth, who murders the king and later tries to undo this heinous act ("get the blood off her hands") with compulsive handwashing gestures.

It is normal for children to identify with their parents and want to become like them. However, **identification** can also be used as a defense mechanism. A child upset by the death of a beloved pet kitten may alleviate her pain by becoming like the lost object, claiming to be a cat, and crawling around on all fours. Or a student criticized by a domineering instructor may try to gain some feelings of strength by unconsciously adopting his aggressor's facial expressions (A. Freud, 1936/1966, p. 110; S. Freud, 1921/1959, p. 41). Teenagers who dress like their favorite rock stars, and adults who wear jerseys with the names of famous athletes, feel more positive about themselves by identifying with people whom they admire.

The defense mechanism of **regression** involves a return to behavior that is typical of an earlier and safer time in one's life. The birth of a sibling may cause a child to resume actions long since discarded, like thumb sucking or bed wetting, as a reassuring reminder of the time when no threatening rivals were present. Or an adult faced with a traumatic divorce may regress to childish behavior and become dependent on her parents.

Finally, **sublimation** serves defensive purposes by unconsciously channeling illicit impulses (such as murder) into more socially acceptable outlets (like contact sports). However, sublimation differs from true defense mechanisms in that it cannot be used to excess. Sublimation represents ideal behavior—the solution to our having inborn illicit and antisocial instincts, yet also needing the benefits of society.

The defensive capacities of the ego are fortunate in view of the dangers that it faces. But since self-deception is beyond our conscious control, defense mechanisms can all too easily become excessive and self-defeating:

> … the news that reaches your consciousness is incomplete and often not to be relied on…. Even if you are not ill, who can tell all that is stirring in your mind of which you know nothing or are falsely informed? You behave like an absolute ruler who is content with the information supplied him by his highest officials and never goes among the people to hear their voice. Turn your eyes inward, look into your own depths, learn first to know yourself! (Freud, 1917a, p. 143.)

The Superego

According to psychoanalytic theory, infants have no sense of right and wrong. (Recall that only the amoral id is present at birth.) At first this function is carried out by the parents, on whom the helpless child must depend for many years. They reward certain behaviors, a gratifying reassurance of their presence and affection. But they also punish other actions, a threatening sign that the child has lost their love and is now at the mercy of an awesome and dangerous environment.

Partly to protect itself from such disasters, and partly because it identifies with the all-powerful parents, the ego begins to internalize (**introject**) their standards. This leads to the formation of the **superego** (*das Überich*; literally, the "over I"), a special part of the ego that observes and sits in judgment above the rest. The superego is partly conscious and partly unconscious. It starts to develop out of the ego during the third to fifth year of life and continues to introject characteristics of teachers, teenage idols, and other authority figures, though these usually remain of secondary importance. Since the parents indirectly reflect the demands of society, the superego helps perpetuate the status quo (Freud, 1923/1962, p. 25; 1940/1969a, p. 3).

The superego includes two components: the *conscience* punishes illicit thoughts and actions, and the *ego ideal* rewards desirable behavior. A person who refuses to cheat or steal even though no one else is watching, or who strives to do the best possible job without being supervised, is responding to the dictates of the superego. For behaving in such acceptable ways, the superego rewards the ego with feelings of pride and virtue.

Unfortunately, psychic life is rarely this pleasant. Much of the superego lies in the unconscious, where it is intimately related to the id. It condemns the id's illicit impulses as severely as actual misdeeds, but can directly influence only the ego. Therefore, both forbidden impulses and unacceptable behaviors cause tension to be generated between the superego and the

CAPSULE SUMMARY
The Structure of Personality (Freud)

Id	Ego	Superego
Present at birth.	Develops out of the id at about age 6–8 months. Results from experience with one's body and with the outside world.	Develops out of the ego at about age 3–5 years. Results from introjections of parental standards and the resolution of the Oedipus complex.
Entirely unconscious.	Partly conscious, partly preconscious, partly unconscious.	Partly conscious, partly unconscious.
Operates by the primary process: Is chaotic, irrational, amoral, has no sense of time or logic, is capable only of producing wish-fulfilling images.	Operates by the secondary process: Is logical, self-preservative, problem-solving.	Operates by introjected moral imperatives. May or may not be realistic and self-preservative.
Motivated entirely by the pleasure principle. Transforms biological needs into psychological tensions.	Motivated by the reality principle. Delays the discharge of tension until a suitable object is found in order to avoid errors, dangers, punishment.	Motivated by the energy bound in its formation. Enforces its standards by stimulating the ego's feelings of guilt or pride.
Contains all innate instincts, which differ in strength from person to person.	The locus of all emotions, including anxiety. Uses defense mechanisms.	Includes the ego ideal (standards of what is right) and the conscience (standards of what is wrong.)
May be too powerful and cruel (or too weak), resulting in psychopathology.	The stronger the ego, the healthier the personality.	May be too powerful and cruel (or too weak), resulting in psychopathology.
In a sense, the biological component of personality.	In a sense, the psychological executive of personality.	In a sense, the social component of personality.

ego, and this is experienced by the ego as guilt or moral anxiety. (Thus Freudian theory regards the idea of a "guilty conscience" as a misnomer. Emotions occur only in the ego, so the conscience causes the ego to feel guilty.) You feel guilty and anxious not only when you do something wrong, but also when you want to do something wrong, even if your illicit wishes are beyond your awareness.

Even though the ego may be unaware of the reasons for these unpleasant feelings, it is obliged to do something about them. It can obtain relief by substituting more acceptable thoughts or actions, or by resorting to defense mechanisms.

It is possible for the superego to be underdeveloped, leaving the individual without effective inner guidelines. Children brought up without love do not introject proper standards, lack appropriate tension between the ego and superego, and have few qualms about aggressing against others (Freud, 1930/1961b, p. 77n). More often, however, the superego proves to be a harsh master—and another potential source of danger. It may become so perfectionistic and unrealistic that genuine achievements seem worthless. For example, a student who gives an excellent speech before a large group may feel little satisfaction because she made a few minor errors. Or the superego may overstep its bounds and punish legitimate behavior:

> ... the superego ... can be supermoral and then become as cruel as only the id can be.... [It then] becomes over-severe, abuses the poor ego, humiliates it and ill-treats it, threatens it with the direst punishments, [and] reproaches it for actions in the remotest past which had been taken lightly at the time.... (Freud, 1923/1962, p. 44; 1933/1965b, p. 61.)

Intense unconscious guilt can be the cause of illicit or self-destructive behavior, rather than the result. A person may commit a crime, suffer an injurious parapraxis, fail at work or school, or take a turn for the worse when praised by the psychoanalyst in order to gain relief by being punished (Freud, 1923/1962, pp. 39ff).

The superego may become relentless even though the parental upbringing was relatively mild and kindly. One reason is that the formation of the superego is a complicated process. It involves not only the introjection of parental standards, but also the resolution of the child's Oedipus complex—a major Freudian construct that will be discussed in the following section.

THE DEVELOPMENT OF PERSONALITY

Psychosexual Stages

To Freud, personality development consists of a series of **psychosexual stages**. Each stage is characterized by a particular erotogenic zone that serves as the primary source of pleasure.

The Oral Stage.   During the first 12 to 18 months of life, the infant's sexual desires center around the oral region (mouth, tongue, and lips). Sucking at the breast or bottle provides not only nourishment, but erotic pleasure as well:

> Primarily, of course, [oral] satisfaction serves the purpose of self-preservation by means of nourishment; but physiology should not be confused with psychology. The baby's obstinate persistence in sucking gives evidence at an early stage of a need for satisfaction which... strives to obtain pleasure independently of nourishment and for that reason may and should be termed *sexual*.... No one who has seen a baby sinking back satiated from the breast and falling asleep with flushed cheeks and a blissful smile can escape the reflection that this picture persists as a prototype of the expression of sexual satisfaction in later life. (Freud, 1905/1965d, pp. 76–77; 1940/1969a, p. 11.)

Pleasure is only part of the story, however. Frustration and conflict are inevitable because food does not always appear when the child is hungry, and because the child must eventually be weaned from the breast and taught to stop sucking its thumb. These are the first of many lessons about the need to sublimate instinctual urges and satisfy the demands of society. Toward the latter part of this stage, orality takes an aggressive turn when the teeth emerge and biting becomes possible.

The Anal Stage.   At about age 1 to $1^1/_2$ years, the infant gains some control over its anal expulsions. Most of the libido detaches from the oral zone and cathects the anus, with the child gaining erotic gratification from the bodily sensations involved in excretion. In addition, the child can now exert control over the environment by contributing or withholding the feces. The former becomes an expression of compliance, similar to the giving of a gift, whereas the latter is a form of disobedience. Frustration and conflict center about the issue of toilet training, a difficult exercise in self-control. Once again, the child must learn to sacrifice pleasure in order to meet parental demands. (See Freud, 1908a; 1917b; 1933/1965b, pp. 99–102; 1905/1965d, pp. 81–83, 96.)

The Urethral Stage.   The urethral stage is not clearly distinct from the anal stage, and Freud has relatively little to say about it. The canal carrying urine from the bladder now becomes an erotogenic zone, the child must learn to control urinary urges, and conflict arises from the problem of bed wetting. (See Freud, 1908a; 1905/1965d, pp. 104 n. 2, 144 n. 1.)

The Phallic Stage.   At about age 2 to 3 years, the boy learns to produce pleasurable sensations by manually stimulating his sexual organ. This has a powerful effect on his cathexis for his mother:

> He becomes his mother's lover. He wishes to possess her physically in such ways as he has divined from his observations and intuitions about sexual life, and he tries to seduce her by showing her the male organ which he is proud to own. In a word, his early awakened masculinity seeks to take his father's place with her; his father has hitherto in any case been an envied model to the boy, owing to the physical strength he perceives in him and the authority with which he finds him clothed. His father now becomes a rival who stands in his way and whom he would like to get rid of. (Freud, 1940/1969a, p. 46.)

The boy also displays affection for his father, together with jealousy toward his mother. This double set of attitudes toward both parents constitutes the **Oedipus complex**, named after the legendary Greek king who unknowingly killed his father and married his mother.

Oedipal feelings are extremely powerful. They include all the aspects of a true love affair: heights of passion, jealous rages, and desperate yearnings. However, the Oedipus complex ultimately leads to severe conflicts. The boy fears that his illicit wishes will cost him his father's love and protection, a child's strongest need (Freud, 1930/1961b, p. 19; see also Freud, 1909; 1924/1963o; 1905/1965d, p. 92.) He also discovers the physical differences between the sexes, and draws a terrifying conclusion: that girls originally possessed a penis but had it taken away as punishment, and the same fate will befall his own prized organ if he persists in his Oedipal wishes.

To alleviate this intense **castration anxiety**, the boy abandons his Oedipal strivings and replaces them with a complicated set of attitudes. He intensifies his identification with his father, wishing to be like him rather than replace him. The boy also recognizes that he may not do certain things that his father does (such as enjoy special privileges with his mother), and learns to defer to authority. This reduces castration anxiety by eliminating the need for punishment, while identifying with his father also provides some vicarious gratification of his incestuous wishes for his mother.

These identifications and prohibitions are incorporated into the superego and help bring about its formation, with the prevention of Oedipal sexuality and hostility becoming its primary function (albeit an unconscious one). Thus a severe superego may result from an unusually strong Oedipus complex that requires powerful countermeasures. The whole issue is so frightening that it is thoroughly repressed, making it impossible to recall Oedipal experiences without the aid of psychoanalytic therapy. The effects of the Oedipus complex may be more obvious, however, as when a man chooses a wife who strongly resembles his mother.

The fear of castration cannot apply to girls, so Freud must find another way to explain the female Oedipus complex. (Some writers refer to this as the Electra complex, but Freud rejected this term [1920/1963l, p. 141n; 1931/1963q, p. 198].) Like the boy, the girl first forms a strong cathexis for her nurturing mother. The girl also has twofold attitudes (love and jealousy) for both parents. However, the discovery that she does not have a penis causes intense feelings of inferiority and jealousy (**penis envy**). Typically, the girl responds by resenting the mother who shares her apparent defect. She intensifies the envious attachment to her father, regards her mother as a rival, and develops an unconscious desire to compensate for her supposed physical deficiency by having her father's baby:

> In males... the threat of castration brings the Oedipus complex to an end; in females we find that, on the contrary, it is their lack of a penis that forces them into their Oedipus complex.... Not until the emergence of the wish for a penis does the doll-baby [that the girl plays with] become a baby from the girl's father, and thereafter the aim of the most powerful feminine wish. Her happiness is great if later on this wish for a baby finds ful-fillment in reality, and quite especially so if the baby is a little boy who brings the longed-for penis with him. (Freud, 1933/1965b, p. 128; 1940/1969a, p. 51. See also Freud, 1923/1963n, pp. 171–175; 1924/1963o, p. 181; 1925/1963p, p. 191.)

Because the girl lacks the vital and immediate threat of castration anxiety, her superego is weaker, she has more difficulty forming effective sublimations, and she is more likely to become neurotic. Freud also regards the clitoris as an inferior possession that has permanent negative effects on a woman's character, and concludes that a woman's place is in the home (Freud, 1930/1961b, p. 50; 1926/1963j, p. 83; 1933/1965b, p. 65; 1940/1969a, pp. 12, 50; see also Rieff, 1959/1961, pp. 191ff). Freud does admit to great difficulty in understanding the feminine psyche, and ruefully concedes an inability to answer the "great question" of what a woman wants (E. Jones, 1955/1963b, p. 368). However, he has no doubts about the importance of the Oedipal theory:

> I venture to say that if psychoanalysis could boast of no other achievement than the discovery of the repressed Oedipus complex, that alone would give it claim to be included among the precious new acquisitions of mankind. (Freud, 1940/1969a, pp. 49–50.)

The Latency Period.   By age 5 to 6 years, personality is firmly established. From this time until puberty (age 12 or later), the child's erotic drives become deemphasized. Oedipal storms subside, sexuality yields to safer forms of expression (such as affection and identification), amnesia clouds unsettling memories of infantile sexuality, and reaction formation may lead the child to spurn members of the opposite sex. The latency period is not a true psycho-sexual stage, however, and may even be largely or entirely absent in some instances.

The Genital Stage. The genital stage is the goal of normal development and represents psychological maturity. (The prior oral, anal, urethral, and phallic stages are therefore referred to as **pregenital**.) Narcissism now yields to a more sincere interest in other people, and the woman's primary erotogenic zone shifts from the (pregenital) clitoris to the vagina. Thus "the female genital organ for the first time meets with the recognition which the male one acquired long before" (Freud, 1933/1965b, p. 99).

So long as the majority of libido successfully reaches this last stage, there is sufficient psychic energy to cathect appropriate heterosexual objects and form satisfactory relationships. Freud's emphasis on sexuality does not blind him to the importance of love and affection, however, and he regards an attachment based solely on lust as doomed to eventual failure because there is little to keep the parties together once instinctual cathexes have been discharged.

The preceding age limits cannot be specified precisely because the psychosexual stages blend together, with no clear-cut point at which one gives way to the next. These stages deal primarily with the erotic drive, and there are no corresponding "psychodestructive stages" (just as there is no destructive analogue of libido). The emphasis on infantile and childhood sexuality may seem radical, but psychoanalysts regard this as a fact that is both obvious and proven (e.g., Brenner, 1973/1974, p. 22; Fenichel, 1945, p. 56; Freud, 1926/1969b, p. 39).

Fixation and Character Typology

Because human nature is inherently malignant, we have no inborn wish to change for the better, and parents must pressure the reluctant child to proceed through the various stages of development. This task is fraught with difficulties, and some libido inevitably remains attached (**fixated**) to the pregenital erotogenic zones.

So long as most of the libido reaches the genital stage, no great harm is done. But if traumatic events occur during a pregenital stage, such as harsh attempts at weaning or overly severe punishment during toilet training, excessive amounts of libido will become fixated at that stage. The child will reject further development, and will demand the satisfactions that have been withheld. Excessive fixations can also be caused by overindulgence, as by allowing the child to engage in too much thumb sucking. Such intense gratification is undesirable because it is difficult to abandon and remains a source of yearning. So the parents must be careful not to allow either too little or too much gratification during any pregenital stage (Fenichel, 1945, pp. 65–66).

Fixation may leave too little libido available for mature heterosexuality and result in serious psychological disturbances. However, it is also possible for a personality to be marked by characteristics of a pregenital stage without being classified as pathological.

Oral Characteristics. The oral stage primarily involves the passive incorporation of food, so the fixation of excessive libido at this stage is likely to cause dependence on other people. The oral individual also tends to be gullible (liable to "swallow anything"), and to overdo such pleasures as eating or smoking. It is possible for the defense mechanism of reaction formation to convert these characteristics into their opposites, however, leading to pronounced independence or suspiciousness. Thus psychoanalytic theory typically describes behavior patterns in terms of polarities, such as gullible–suspicious, with the ideal falling somewhere between the two extremes.

CAPSULE SUMMARY
The Psychosexual Stages, Fixation, and Regression

Stage	Erotogenic Zone	Duration; Description	Source of Conflict	Personality Characteristics
Oral	Mouth, lips, tongue	About age 0–1$^1/_2$ years. Primarily involves passive incorporation, but becomes aggressive when the teeth emerge and biting is possible.	Feeding	Oral behavior such as smoking and eating; passivity and gullibility (and the opposites).
Anal	Anus	About age 1–3 years. Some control over the environment is provided by expelling or withholding the feces.	Toilet training	Orderliness, parsimoniousness, obstinacy (and the opposites).
Urethral	Urethra (canal carrying urine from the bladder)	Not clearly distinct from the anal stage.	Bed wetting	Ambition (and the opposite).
Phallic	Penis, clitoris	About age 2–5 years.	Oedipus complex	Vanity, recklessness (and the opposites).

[Sexual impulses become deemphasized during the latency period, which occurs at about age 5–12 years and is not a true psychosexual stage.]

Stage	Erotogenic Zone	Duration; Description	Source of Conflict	Personality Characteristics
Genital	Penis, vagina	Adulthood; the goal of normal development.	The inevitable difficulties of life	A more sincere interest in others, effective sublimations, realistic enjoyments.

Fixation: Occurs when libido remains attached to one or more of the pregenital erotogenic zones. A certain amount is inevitable, but too much will result in psychopathology.

Regression: The reverse flow of libido back to an earlier psychosexual stage or object-choice. As with fixation, a certain amount is normal. The most likely objects of regression are ones that were strongly fixated.

Anal Characteristics.   Three traits result from excessive fixation at the anal stage: orderliness, parsimoniousness, and obstinacy (Freud, 1908a; 1933/1965b, p. 102). In bipolar terms, anal characteristics include miserliness–overgenerosity, stubbornness–acquiescence, and orderliness–sloppiness. Miserliness and stubbornness are related to a rebellion against toilet training, whereas orderliness represents obedient cleanliness following evacuation. These characteristics are sometimes referred to as *anal-retentive*, and the opposite extremes as *anal-expulsive*.

Urethral Characteristics. Fixation at the urethral stage is related to ambition, which represents a reaction formation against the shame of childhood bed wetting. Ambition may have other causes, however, such as parental pressures (Fenichel, 1945, pp. 69, 493).

Phallic Characteristics. The characteristics of phallic fixation depend on how the Oedipus complex is resolved. An excessive concern with sexual activity and self-love may lead to promiscuity, or to a chaste preoccupation with one's attractiveness. Other common phallic characteristics include vanity–self-contempt and recklessness–timidity.

The concept of fixation does not apply to the latency period (which is not a psychosexual stage), or to the genital stage (which is the ideal and is denoted by effective sublimations, realistic enjoyments, and mature sexuality). However, it is possible to become fixated on an object as well as a stage of development. For example, a person who has failed to resolve the Oedipus complex may be unable to develop rewarding heterosexual relationships because of a fixation on the parent of the opposite sex.

Regression

As we have seen, the defense mechanism of **regression** involves a return to behavior that is typical of an earlier and safer time in one's life. More precisely, regression refers to a reverse flow of libido back to an earlier psychosexual stage, or to the cathexis of an object that has long since been abandoned.

As with fixation, a limited amount of regression is a normal aspect of mental life. However, severe frustration or stress may lead to regressions that are excessive and harmful. A child in the phallic stage may regress to thumb sucking or bed wetting at the birth of a sibling, with large quantities of libido returning to a cathexis of the oral or urethral zone because of the appearance of a threatening rival for the parents' attention. Or an adult or adolescent may become childishly stubborn in a crisis, thereby regressing to the anal stage.

We tend to regress to objects or stages that were strongly fixated during childhood. Thus another disadvantage of powerful fixations is that they make damaging regressions more likely:

> … if a people which is in movement has left strong detachments behind at the stopping-places on its migration, it is likely that the more advanced parties will be inclined to retreat to these stopping-places if they have been defeated or have come up against a superior enemy. But they will also be in the greater danger of being defeated, the more of their number they have left behind on their migration. (Freud, 1916–1917/1966, p. 341.)

FURTHER APPLICATIONS OF PSYCHOANALYTIC THEORY

Dream Interpretation

Psychoanalytic theory presents a formidable difficulty: the most important part of personality, the unconscious, is also the most inaccessible. During sleep, however, the ego relaxes its defenses and allows repressed material to emerge, and id impulses that were blocked during waking hours find gratification in the form of dreams. It is as though the ego says to the id, "It's all right, no great harm can happen now, so enjoy yourself." However, the ego recognizes that an overly threatening dream will cause the sleeper to awaken prematurely. So it censors the repressed material in various ways and limits the id to only partial fulfillment, and the resulting compromise between the pleasure-seeking id and the sleep-preserving ego is what the dreamer experiences.

In accordance with the principle of psychic determinism, no dream is accidental or trivial. But to understand the true meaning, it is necessary to unravel the disguises imposed by the ego and reveal the unconscious thoughts that lie beneath (**interpret** the dream). This is likely to be a difficult task, partly because the language of dreams is an unusual one and also because repression returns to full force immediately upon awakening. Nevertheless, having analyzed hundreds of dreams (including many of his own), Freud concludes that "the interpretation of dreams is the royal road to a knowledge of the unconscious activities of the mind" (1900/1965a, p. 647).

Manifest Content, Latent Dream-thoughts, and the Dream-work.

The part of a dream that you remember (or could remember) upon awakening is the **manifest** content. The unconscious impulses, beliefs, emotions, conflicts, and memories concealed behind the façade of manifest content are the **latent** dream-thoughts. And the **dream-work** is the process that converts latent thoughts into manifest content (Freud, 1901/1952, p. 27; 1900/1965a, pp. 168, 211, 311ff; 1933/1965b, pp. 9–10; 1916–1917/1966, pp. 120, 170; 1940/1969a, p. 22).

The goal of the dream-work is to conceal threatening material that is likely to awaken the sleeper. For example, the dream-work may change troublesome latent Oedipal thoughts into manifest content wherein the dreamer enjoys a romantic affair with an attractive stranger, defeating a serious rival in the process. If the ego decides that greater deception is necessary, perhaps because the Oedipus complex is still a source of considerable conflict, the dream-work may turn love into anger and alter the sex (or even the species) of the romantic object. Now the manifest content will have the dreamer fighting with a person of the same sex. Alternatively, the dream-work may attribute the romantic or aggressive impulses to someone else. And countless other distortions are possible.

Dreams as Wish-fulfillments.

Dreams are triggered by memories of the preceding day that involve important frustrations (**day's residues**). According to Freud, the purpose of dreams is to fulfill the dreamer's wishes. A child forbidden to eat a delectable dish of cherries gained some satisfaction by dreaming of consuming them all, a woman who was pregnant but didn't want to be dreamed of having her period, and a group of explorers in the icy wilderness had frequent dreams of tempting meals and the comforts of home. Adult dreams are usually more complicated, however, and involve repressed childhood impulses that are frequently of a sexual nature. (See Freud, 1901/1952, pp. 32–37; 105ff; 1925/1963a, p. 88; 1900/1965a, pp. 159–164, 431–435; 1933/1965b, p. 8; 1916–1917/1966, pp. 126ff.)

Although some dreams may appear to be disappointing, frightening, or self-punishing, closer analysis usually reveals some form of (or attempt at) wish-fulfillment. (Freud [1920/1961a, pp. 26–27] does recognize one exception: the tendency to have repeated dreams about a previous traumatic physical injury.) A lawyer once heard Freud lecture about dream interpretation, and then dreamed about losing all of his cases. He argued that psychoanalytic theory must be wrong, since he didn't want to be a failure. This man had been a former classmate of Freud's, with grades that were quite inferior. He was jealous and wanted to embarrass Freud, and he fulfilled this wish by having a dream that made Freud's theories look absurd. "Considering that for eight whole years I sat on the front bench at the top of the class while he drifted about somewhere in the middle, he could hardly fail to nourish a wish, left over from his school days, that some day *I* would come a complete cropper" (Freud, 1900/1965a, p. 185).

A woman patient of Freud's dreamed that she was unable to give a supper party because all of the stores were closed. "My wish was not fulfilled," she told him. "How do you fit that in with your theory?" During the preceding day, a female friend had asked to be invited to dinner. The dreamer's husband greatly admired this friend, but thought she was much too skinny. This dream satisfied the dreamer's wish to keep a dangerous rival from becoming more attractive. As Freud explained: "It is as though, when your friend made this suggestion, you said to yourself: 'A likely thing! I'm to ask you to come and eat in my house so that you may get stout and attract my husband still more! I'd rather never give another supper party'" (Freud, 1900/1965a, p. 182).

Frightening dreams indicate that the ego's disguises are about to fail and allow dangerous material to emerge. Awakening the dreamer now becomes the lesser of two evils, and the dream-work behaves.

> like a conscientious night watchman, who first carries out his duty by suppressing distur-
> bances so that the townsmen may not be waked up, but afterward continues to do his duty
> by himself waking the townsmen up, if the causes of the disturbance seem to him serious
> and of a kind that he cannot cope with alone. (Freud, 1901/1952, p. 102. See also Freud,
> 1900/1965a, p. 267; 1933/1965b, p. 17; 1916–1917/1966, p. 217; 1940/1969a, p. 28.)

Self-punishment dreams satisfy a wish of the superego. An illicit id impulse strives for gratification, and the superego responds by causing the ego to feel guilty. The punishment dream alleviates this unpleasant emotion, thereby serving as an extraordinary sort of compromise between the three components of personality (Freud, 1900/1965a, pp. 514 n. 1, 596ff; 1933/1965b, pp. 27–28).

The Language of Dreams.   Dreams are expressed in **symbols**, a device also found in myths, legends, jokes, and literature. For example, a stranger who appears in the manifest content may actually represent a parent, spouse, or even the dreamer. Freud attributes a sexual meaning to most symbols, with the male organ represented by elongated and potent objects (sticks, rifles, knives, umbrellas, neckties, snakes, plows) and the female organ denoted by containers (cupboards, caves, bottles, rooms, jewel cases). Staircases, going upstairs or downstairs, and being run over stand for the sexual act, whereas decapitation or the loss of teeth reflects castration (Freud, 1901/1952, pp. 107ff; 1900/1965a, pp. 385ff; 1916–1917/1966, pp. 149ff).

However, dream interpretation requires far more than a list of symbols and their meanings. Some symbols are used in an idiosyncratic way known only to the dreamer, and some elements are just what they seem and are not symbolic at all. Therefore, as was the case with parapraxes, free association must be used to reveal the underlying thoughts:

> … we ask the dreamer… to free himself from the impression of the manifest dream, to
> divert his attention from the dream as a whole on to the separate portions of its content
> and to report to us in succession everything that occurs to him in relation to each of these
> portions—what associations present themselves to him if he focuses on each of them
> separately…. A knowledge of dream symbolism will never do more than enable us to
> translate certain constituents of the dream content…. It will, however, afford the most
> valuable assistance to interpretation precisely at points at which the dreamer's
> associations are insufficient or fail altogether. (Freud, 1901/1952, pp. 110–111;
> 1933/1965b, pp. 10–11.)

The dream-work disguises threatening material in various ways. It may cause important aspects of the latent dream-thoughts to become minor parts of the manifest content (or vice versa), move the end of a series of latent thoughts to the beginning of the manifest content (or vice versa), or convert hate into love (or vice versa). The dream-work may **condense** several related ideas into a single symbol whose meaning is far from clear, or even eliminate some of the latent material altogether. Or it may attribute the dreamer's hostile impulses to someone else, resulting in manifest content wherein a parent scolds the dreamer.

Because of these complexities, and because the dreamer's free associations are likely to grind to a halt as they get closer to threatening material, not every dream can be interpreted (Freud, 1933/1965b, p. 13). Nevertheless, in the preface to the 1932 English edition of *The Interpretation of Dreams*, Freud concluded that

> this book... contains, even according to my present-day judgment, the most valuable of all the discoveries it has been my good fortune to make. Insight such as this falls to one's lot but once in a lifetime.

Psychopathology

The components of a well-adjusted adult personality work together in relative harmony, under the leadership of the ego, to achieve pleasurable yet safe discharges of tension. The majority of libido successfully reaches the genital stage, enabling the ego to deal with its three masters. The ego sublimates or blocks dangerous id impulses, but not those that are healthy. It heeds the moral dictates of the superego, but resists demands that are harsh and perfectionistic. And it takes the frustrations caused by the external world more or less in stride, forming appropriate plans and revising them as necessary. Though life is difficult and some unhappiness is inevitable, the healthy individual is able to do two things well: love and work (Freud, cited by Erikson, 1963, pp. 264–265).

In maladjustment, on the other hand, the ego is weakened by the loss of libido to strong childhood fixations. The ego may therefore respond to external frustration by allowing more libido to regress, resulting in childish behavior. It may be dominated by a stern and unyielding superego, enforce defense mechanisms too rigidly, and deprive the individual of healthy and socially acceptable satisfactions. Or, if the superego is also weak, illicit id impulses may lead to immoral and destructive behavior.

Although psychopathology may cause behavior that seems extreme or bizarre, there is no sharp borderline between the normal and abnormal personality. The distinction involves a difference in degree, not in kind. The painful difficulties of childhood can never be entirely avoided, with the result that "we are all a little neurotic" (Freud, 1901/1965c, p. 278).

Causes of Neurosis.   Neurosis invariably begins in infancy and childhood, though it may not become clearly evident until much later. One important cause is a lack of physical affection, which makes it difficult for the infant to distinguish self from not-self and seriously hinders the development of the ego. Overindulgence or too much frustration during a psychosexual stage will result in harmful fixations, as we have seen. The child may suffer such traumatic events as observing the parents' sexual intercourse (the **primal scene**), being seduced by an adult, or (in the case of the boy) being threatened with castration. This overwhelms the immature ego with more excitement than it can discharge, a painful condition, and creates the impression that sexuality is dangerous. During the phallic stage, lack of love may prevent the superego from introjecting proper standards. Or the superego may become overly severe, either because of introjects from stem parents or the need to overcome unusually powerful Oedipal conflicts.

The child who succumbs to neurosis enters the latency period with the Oedipus complex unresolved. For a while, the immature ego is able to achieve a state of balance by resorting to repression and other defense mechanisms. At puberty, however, when sexual activity heightens, this complicated and basically unstable adjustment begins to collapse. The instinctual impulses are now reinforced by an increased supply of libido, so they surge forth with renewed vigor.

A relatively healthy adolescent can sublimate these impulses by forming cathexes for members of the opposite sex. But the neurotic individual cannot do this, because he or she remains fixated on Oedipal desires and conflicts. The ego, influenced by the superego, blocks these dangerous wishes by using anticathexes and defense mechanisms. The only way that the dammed-up libido can gain a measure of discharge is by emerging in a form that is both disguised and distorted—namely, a neurotic symptom. (See Fenichel, 1945, p. 20; Freud, 1915/1963f, pp. 111–112.)

Neurotic Symptoms. Neurotic symptoms resemble dreams in several ways. A symptom reveals important information about the unconscious, and is expressed in symbols. Like dream symbols, a symptom usually has several meanings. And a symptom represents a compromise between the demands of the id, the regulations of the superego, and the defenses of the ego. However, a neurotic symptom is always caused by sexual impulses. And more powerful defensive measures are necessary, since the waking state is a source of potential danger to the individual. (See Freud, 1900/1965a, p. 608; 1905/1963b, p. 136; 1906/1963k; 1916–1917/1966, p. 360.)

As an illustration, let us consider one of Freud's less successful (but more instructive) cases. In *hysteria*, psychological difficulties are unconsciously converted into physical symptoms. An 18-year-old girl, given the pseudonym of Dora, suffered from hysterical nervous coughing and the occasional loss of her voice. Dora's unresolved Oedipal conflicts stemmed in part from an overindulgent father, who tried to compensate for an unhappy marriage by making her his confidante at an early age. Aided by two detailed dream interpretations, Freud concluded that Dora's symptoms had several meanings. They reflected a clash between an id impulse for oral sex and the defenses of a horrified ego, with coughing providing some disguised wish-fulfillment in the appropriate erotogenic zone. It also served as punishment for such an illicit wish. Dora had experienced a traumatic seductive embrace with an older married man when she was 14, and she unconsciously displaced this threatening genital stimulation to the oral zone. She spent some time in the company of this man, whose wife was having an affair with her father, and formed strong unconscious desires for him. Her vocal difficulties often occurred during his absences, and expressed a disguised wish not to talk at all unless she could speak to him. The coughing also resulted from an identification with her father, who had a similar mannerism (Freud, 1905/1963b; 1921/1959, p. 38).[1]

One patient successfully treated by Freud, the "Rat Man," was obsessed by horrifying (yet also unconsciously pleasing) thoughts that a pot containing hungry rats would be attached to the buttocks of his father and girlfriend. This distasteful symptom, which was based on a story that the Rat Man had heard while in military service, had at least three meanings. It reflected a powerful conflict between conscious love and unconscious hate for his father, a "gambling rat" who once disappointed his son by running up a debt that he did not repay. It indicated that

---

[1]Dora terminated treatment prematurely. As is common in psychotherapy, she unconsciously displaced the hostility that she felt for her aloof parents and elderly seductor onto the therapist (the phenomenon of transference, to be discussed later in this chapter). Freud felt that he blundered by not realizing the strength of these feelings in time, allowing Dora to act out her anger by depriving him of the chance to cure her. However, others have attributed the error to an excessive emphasis on sexuality. Freud apparently ignored the possibility that Dora's conscious distaste for her seductor was not so much a reaction formation against her own unconscious sexual desires, but justified resentment at being "a pawn in her elders' pathetic little end-games, her cooperation necessary in order for them to salvage something erotic for themselves in a loveless world" (Rieff, 1963, p. 16; see also Rieff, 1959/1961, pp. 88–92; Singer, 1970, p. 389).

CAPSULE SUMMARY
Some Important Psychoanalytic Terminology (III)

Condensation	The unconscious combination of various symbols or words into a single entity with several meanings.
Countertransference	An unconscious displacement of emotion or behavior, by the psychoanalyst, from some other person to the patient.
Day's residues	Memories of the preceding day that trigger a dream because they are related to important unconscious issues.
Dream-work	The unconscious process that converts latent dream-thoughts into manifest content.
Free association	Saying whatever comes to mind, no matter how silly or embarrassing it may seem. The "fundamental rule" of psychoanalytic therapy, used to bring unconscious material to consciousness.
Insight	An emotional and intellectual understanding of the causes and dynamics of one's behavior, achieved by bringing unconscious material to consciousness.
Interpretation	The psychoanalyst's explanation of the true meaning of the patient's free associations, resistances, dreams, or other behaviors.
Latent dream-thoughts	The unconscious motives, beliefs, emotions, conflicts, and memories that are concealed behind the manifest content of a dream; usually related to Oedipal issues.
Manifest content	The part of a dream that one remembers, or could remember, upon awakening.
Primary gain	The partial discharge of libido provided by neurotic symptoms.
Resistance	The patient's unconscious attempts to defeat the purpose of psychoanalytic therapy and preserve illicit id wishes. May take any form that violates the fundamental rule, such as long silences, refusing to talk about certain topics, and so forth.
Secondary gain	An incidental advantage provided by neurotic symptoms, such as avoiding unpleasant tasks or receiving sympathy from others.
Symbol	An entity that conveys a meaning that is not immediately apparent; the "language" in which dreams occur. According to Freud, most dream symbols have a sexual meaning.
Transference	An unconscious displacement of emotion or behavior, by the patient, from some other important person (such as a parent) to the psychoanalyst. Produces the attachment that makes positive therapeutic change possible, but may defeat the therapy if it becomes overly negative.
Transference neurosis	A major intensification of transference, wherein the relationship to the analyst becomes even more important than the problems that originally brought the patient into psychoanalytic therapy.
Working through	The process by which the patient in psychoanalytic therapy becomes convinced that formerly unconscious material is true, learns to avoid repressing it, and gradually refines this new knowledge into appropriate and effective behavior.

his conflict carried over into his relationship with his girlfriend. And it involved a regression to the anal stage, which is when the conflict originated (Freud, 1909/1963y).

Another famous case is that of the "Wolf Man," who suffered from a severe animal phobia. (A *phobia* is an intense fear of a specific object or situation that is not dangerous.) Through a detailed analysis of the patient's free associations and dreams, this symptom was traced to various traumatic childhood events: seeing a frightening picture of a wolf during his early childhood, observing either a primal scene or intercourse between animals that was similar to this picture, and threats of castration from a beloved nurse when his sister engaged him in sex play at the age of three (Freud, 1918/1963aa).

A child known as "Little Hans" suffered from an irrational fear (phobia) of horses. Hans often played horse-and-rider with his father and had once seen a horse fall. Freud attributed this phobia to Hans' Oedipal wishes that his father would suffer a painful fall and to displaced castration fears, expressed as anxiety about the horse biting him. This case is atypical, however, being analyzed primarily through correspondence with Hans' father (Freud, 1909; 1926/1963j, pp. 29–41, 59–68).

Freud actually reports very few case histories, opting instead to preserve the anonymity of his patients by presenting his findings in the form of theoretical arguments. He also has little to say about the problems caused by an overly lenient superego, preferring not to treat such "worthless" people as juvenile delinquents and criminals (Roazen, 1975/1976b, pp. 145–153). Among the other areas of interest to Freud are homosexuality and sexual perversions (1920/1963l; 1905/1965d). In a letter to the mother of a homosexual son, he wrote:

> Homosexuality is assuredly no advantage, but it is nothing to be ashamed of, no vice, no degradation, it cannot be classified as an illness; we consider it to be a variation of the sexual function produced by a certain arrest of sexual development.... It is a great injustice to persecute homosexuality as a crime, and cruelty too. (Jones, 1957/1963c, p. 502.)

Whatever the form, neurotic symptoms can be remarkably persistent. Since they represent a compromise between the id, ego, and superego, they are actively maintained by all three parties to the conflict. Neurosis often involves powerful feelings of guilt, and painful symptoms may fulfill an unconscious wish for relief through punishment. As in the case of Dora, not getting well may also be a (primarily unconscious) way of punishing other people. Finally, in addition to the **primary gain** provided by the partial discharge of libido, symptoms may be supported by **secondary gains** as well. The sufferer may receive outpourings of sympathy from others, or be relieved of such onerous tasks as working or going to war, with these fringe benefits making it still more difficult to relinquish the symptoms. (See Freud, 1923/1962, p. 39; 1905/1963b, pp. 60–61; 1933/1965b, pp. 109–110.) These strong reasons for *not* wanting to be cured conflict with the sufferer's wish for relief, making the task of psychotherapy an extremely challenging one.

Psychosis. In psychosis, the patient's severe withdrawal from reality is likely to make hospitalization necessary. Repressed material becomes so powerful that it overwhelms the ego, or the conflict between the ego and reality proves to be so traumatic that the ego surrenders and throws itself into the fantasy world of the id.

Freud's view of psychopathology as a difference in degree does extend to psychosis, but he regards a moderately well-functioning ego as essential for treatment and rejects the use of psychoanalytic therapy with psychotics. (See Freud, 1933/1965b, pp. 16, 154; 1916–1917/1966, p. 447; 1940/1969a, pp. 30, 58; 1926/1969b, pp. 31–32.) This view may well reflect some defensiveness on his part, and has been successfully challenged by later theorists (e.g., Fromm-Reichmann, 1950; Searles, 1965; Sullivan, 1962/1974).

Freud did analyze the autobiography of a psychotic named Daniel Schreber. He concluded that paranoia is inevitably related to underlying homosexuality: Love for people of the same sex is converted into hate by reaction formation, and is then projected onto others (Freud, 1922/1963m; 1911/1963z). However, modern theory also regards this idea as only partially correct at best (e.g., Arieti, 1974, p. 118).

Psychotherapy

During the years 1880 to 1882, Freud's noted friend Josef Breuer treated the 21-year-old hysterical patient known as "Anna O." Severe sexual and intellectual deprivation during her childhood and adolescence, followed by the fatal illness of her beloved father, produced a veritable museum of neurotic and psychotic symptoms: paralyzed limbs, hallucinations, a second personality that lived exactly one year in the past, nervous coughing, sleepwalking, and various speech disorders—and perhaps a hysterical pregnancy as well, although this has been disputed.

Breuer discovered a most unusual way to alleviate these formidable difficulties. He hypnotized Anna O., and had her relive each previous occurrence of a symptom in reverse chronological order! This procedure enabled her to release powerful emotions that she had been afraid to express at the time (the process of "catharsis"). Unfortunately, Breuer's sympathetic care aroused such powerful displaced love from his attractive patient that he became upset, his wife became even more upset, and he dropped the case with considerable embarrassment. But he had shown that the forces causing psychopathology were unconscious, and could be brought to light with words and ideas alone. (See Ellenberger, 1970, pp. 480–484; Ellenberger, 1972; Freud & Breuer, 1895/1966, pp. 55–82; E. Jones, 1953/1963a, pp. 142ff; Rieff, 1959/1961, pp. 10, 41.)

Freud was so impressed by this demonstration that he adopted the hypnotic method with his own patients. However, he soon found that it left much to be desired. Cures were likely to be only temporary, with the patient becoming dependent on the therapist and suffering a relapse as soon as treatment was discontinued. The cathartic removal of a symptom left the underlying causes and conflicts unresolved, free to create new difficulties. Thus hypnotic therapy acted more like a cosmetic coverup than successful surgery. (The reason, according to Freud, is that hypnosis immobilizes the ego. Since the ego is the rational and problem-solving part of personality, it must remain active and functioning for therapy to succeed.) And some of Freud's patients were unable to achieve a trance state, partly because he wasn't a particularly good hypnotist (Freud, 1916–1917/1966, pp. 450–451; Freud & Breuer, 1895/1966, pp. 145ff). For these reasons, Freud abandoned hypnosis (and catharsis) and gradually developed the form of psychotherapy that has become known as psychoanalysis.

Theoretical Foundation. Simply telling the patient about the causes and meanings of neurotic symptoms will not produce a cure, for the information will be deflected by the ego's defenses and appear to be irrelevant or incorrect (Freud, 1916–1917/1966, p. 281). A psyche dominated by unconscious forces from the past can be liberated in only one way: by bringing this unconscious material to consciousness, and enabling the patient to achieve an intellectual and emotional understanding (**insight**) about such issues as unresolved Oedipal conflicts and childhood fixations. These insights reeducate and strengthen the ego so that it may assume its proper role of leadership over the id and superego. As Freud puts it, "where id was, there ego shall be" (1933/1965b, p. 80).

Since the origin of neurosis lies in infancy and childhood, psychoanalysis strives to bring about a moderate amount of regression. This regression is therapeutic because it occurs in a favorable atmosphere, though there may well be a temporary turn for the worse as defense mechanisms are stripped away. Therapeutic regression is induced by carefully applied frustration, with the psychoanalyst remaining silent for considerable periods of time. This also avoids the error of excessive sympathy, which would add to the secondary gains of neurosis and make it harder for the patient to get well. Freud views the analyst's role as similar to the gardener, who removes weeds that impede growth but does not provide a direct cure (Ellenberger, 1970, p. 461). Yet the analyst must also give enough gratification to prevent excessive frustration and regression, which would lead to infantile behavior. Unlike some modern psychoanalysts, who refuse even a small Christmas present and then try to deduce the patient's unconscious motives for offering it, Freud would accept the gift of a book and might even respond in kind (Roazen, 1975/1976b, p. 125).

Therapeutic Procedures: Free Association, Resistance, Transference, and Others.

The patient in classical psychoanalytic therapy reclines on a couch while the analyst sits to the rear, out of view. This procedure, which has become a popular symbol of psychoanalysis, enables the patient to relax physically and devote more energy to the demanding mental tasks that are required. It also prevents the patient's regressions from being disrupted by the analyst's facial expressions and gestures. Finally, it allowed Freud to avoid the unpleasant experience of being stared at for hours on end (1913/1963t, p. 146). The patient attends therapy from four to six times per week, for approximately 50 minutes (and up to 100 dollars or more) per session, usually for several years. The heavy expense in money and time makes psychoanalysis inaccessible to most people, but an appropriately high fee is claimed to benefit the analysis (as well as the analyst) by providing an additional incentive to tear down one's psychological defenses and enter the frightening world of the unconscious (Menninger & Holzman, 1973, pp. 31–32).

While reclining on the couch, the patient is required to say whatever comes to mind (the aforementioned technique of **free association**). Nothing may be held back, no matter how silly, embarrassing, or trivial it may seem:

> Your talk with me must differ in one respect from an ordinary conversation. Whereas usually you rightly try to keep the threads of your story together and to exclude all intruding associations and side issues, so as not to wander too far from the point, here you must proceed differently. You will notice that as you relate things various ideas will occur to you which you feel inclined to put aside with certain criticisms and objections. You will be tempted to say to yourself: "This or that has no connection here, or it is quite unimportant, or it is nonsensical, so it cannot be necessary to mention it." Never give in to these objections, but mention it even if you feel a disinclination against it, or indeed just because of this.... Never forget that you have promised absolute honesty, and never leave anything unsaid because for any reason it is unpleasant to say it. (Freud, 1913/1963t, p. 147.)

The goal of free association is to evade the patient's defenses and bring important unconscious material to consciousness. This "fundamental rule" of psychoanalysis was suggested by one of Freud's patients ("Emmy von N."), who asked that he refrain from interrupting so she could say what was on her mind (Freud & Breuer, 1895/1966, pp. 97–98). While the patient free associates (or tries to), the analyst gives full attention and (in most cases) avoids such distractions as taking written notes.

Free association is a difficult task. The patient's conscious wishes to be cured by psychoanalysis conflict with strong unconscious drives to repress threatening material, not be in analysis, and remain ill. The ego's defenses cannot be eliminated just by an instruction to tell everything, and they intrude on the free associations in the form of **resistances**. These may include long silences, refusing to say something that seems silly or embarrassing, telling carefully planned stories, avoiding important topics, "forgetting" (i.e., repressing) insights or issues discussed previously, hiding emotion behind a façade of intellectualization, being late or absent from therapy, or a myriad of other devices that violate the fundamental rule and prevent the patient from producing material from the unconscious. (See Fenichel, 1945, p. 27; Freud, 1900/1965a, p. 555.) The analyst must then help the patient become aware that a resistance is taking place, the form in which it occurs, and (lastly) the underlying reason, thereby eliminating the resistance so free association can continue. Thus it is necessary to analyze not only the threatening Oedipal impulses and other unconscious residues from childhood, but also the obstacles unconsciously placed in the path of therapy by powerful defense mechanisms.

During those periods when free association is not impeded by resistances, the patient relives childhood conflicts in the analytic situation. Behaviors and emotions are unconsciously displaced from the past to the present, and from other important people in the patient's life (such as the parents) to the analyst. This process is known as **transference**. (See Freud, 1920/1961a, pp. 12–13; 1905/1963b, p. 138; 1914–1963u, pp. 160, 165; 1916–1917/1966, p. 455.)

Transference provides the analyst with firsthand evidence about the patient's problems. It also usually involves childhood love for the parents, and it is this transferred emotional attachment that makes the patient receptive to the analyst's influence. The analyst therefore tries to intensify this process and make the transference, rather than the original symptoms, the main focus of treatment (**transference neurosis**). However, this procedure has some potential pitfalls. A patient's transferred love may be intense and difficult to deal with, as Breuer discovered. Or the transference may be too negative, as when powerful distrust or obstinacy is displaced from a harsh parent to the analyst. In fact, "there are cases in which one cannot master the unleashed transference and the analysis has to be broken off" (Freud, 1937/1963w, p. 270; 1926/1969b, p. 66). Managing the transference is the most crucial aspect of psychoanalytic therapy, and Freud succeeded where Breuer failed partly because he was able to deal with this important phenomenon. (See Fenichel, 1945, pp. 29–31; Freud, 1925/1963a, pp. 79–81; 1915/1963v.)

Since free association is distorted by resistances and transferences, the psychoanalyst must deduce the true meaning of the patient's words and actions. Such an **interpretation** might relate a patient's present heterosexual difficulties to unresolved childhood Oedipal conflicts. However, interpretations must be withheld until the patient is only a few steps away from the repressed material and the related ego defenses are ready to crumble. Otherwise, even a correct interpretation is likely to produce resistance and rejection because it is too far beyond the patient's conscious knowledge. (See Freud, 1913/1963t, pp. 152–153; 1937/1963x; 1926/1969b, p. 56.)

As is the case with most learning, the insights gained through psychoanalytic therapy must be practiced in order to integrate them into one's life (the process of **working through**). Learning for the first time about an unconscious conflict, resistance, or self-defeating behavior usually does not produce change. The patient only gradually becomes convinced about the truth of formerly unconscious material, learns to avoid repressing it again, and refines the new knowledge into appropriate and effective behavior (Freud, 1914/1963u).

Psychoanalytic therapy also places considerable emphasis on **dream interpretation**. Dreams provide the analyst with important information because they usually involve a regression to infantile wishes and childhood sexuality.

A final aspect of Freudian psychotherapy concerns the psychoanalyst, who also has an unconscious tendency to displace emotions and behaviors from other important people (such as a parent or spouse) onto the patient, Such **countertransferences** may prevent the analyst from perceiving the patient accurately and responding appropriately (Freud, 1910/1963s, pp. 86–87). For example, a nagging patient might trigger the analyst's unconscious resentment toward a parent who behaved in the same way. Or the analyst might overlook important symptoms because they are frighteningly similar to his or her own serious problems. To help avoid such errors, and to provide a better understanding of psychoanalysis, psychoanalysts must undergo analysis themselves as part of their training. Many do not even begin private practice untill they are in their forties (Frenichel, 1945, pp. 30–31; Fine, 1973, p. 6; Freud, 1937/1963w, pp. 267–268).

Although Freud regards psychoanalysis as the premier method of psychotherapy, he does not recommend it for everyone or regard it as infallible, nor does he reject other approaches so long as they work (Freud, 1905/1963r, pp. 65–66, 69–72; 1937/1963w; 1933/1965b, p. 157). Psychoanalytic therapy strives to gain the best possible psychological conditions for the functioning of the ego, thereby enabling it to accept the challenge of living and loving. In a sense, the patient is freed from the extreme misery of neurosis in order to face the normal misery of everyday life. More optimistically, the patient leaves psychoanalytic therapy with feelings similar to those of an anonymous poet (cited by Menninger & Holzman, 1973, p. 182):

I asked for all things, that I might enjoy life;
I was given life, that I might enjoy all things.

Work

According to psychoanalytic theory, human behavior is governed by the pleasure principle. People seek to avoid the unpleasure of increased drives, and to obtain pleasure by discharging tension. But society rules out the greatest sources of pleasure by imposing restrictions against our wild and untamed instincts, such as incest and murder. We must therefore channel these illicit instincts into socially acceptable (albeit less satisfying) behavior, and work offers a good outlet for such sublimations.

For example, a young boy developed intense curiosity about the births of his brothers and sisters. These dramatic events took place in his farmhouse home, yet he was not allowed to watch. As an adult, he satisfied his wish to know about such matters by becoming an obstetrician. This profession required him to be kind and considerate toward the babies and mothers whom he treated, thereby strengthening his unconscious defenses against the murderous rage he had felt at the birth of each new sibling. And it enabled him to sublimate hostile Oedipal wishes by identifying with his mother's doctor, a superior figure who was treated with great deference by his father (Brenner, 1973/1974, p. 200).

Alternatively, a person may sublimate sadistic impulses by becoming a surgeon and cutting people up in a socially approved way. Or powerful Oedipal desires may be sublimated by becoming a photographer or painter of the opposite sex. Unfortunately, "the great majority of people only work under the stress of necessity [and have a] natural human aversion to work," thus overlooking an important source of potential satisfaction (Freud, 1930/1961b, p. 27 n. 1; see also Freud, 1927/1961c, p. 8).

Religion

Not even our modern civilization can conquer the superior forces of nature. Earthquakes, floods, hurricanes, and diseases exact their inevitable toll in lives and property, while the relentless specter of death awaits us all.

To alleviate such threatening reminders of human helplessness, certain religions preach a reassuring message: Life continues even after death, brings the perfection that we missed on earth, and ensures that all good is rewarded and all evil punished. Fate and nature only appear to be cruel, for the omnipotent and omniscient Providence that governs all creation is benevolent as well. The difficulties of life serve some higher purpose, so there is no reason to despair. Those who successfully subject their thinking to religion receive comfort in return, whereas those who may be skeptical are advised that these tenets have been handed down from the beginning of time, and that one does not question the highest Authority of all.

Freud regards such beliefs as extremely harmful to the individual and to society, and has authored some of the sharpest attacks on religion ever published (Freud, 1939; 1930/1961b, pp. 21–22, 28–32, 56–58; 1933/1965b, pp. 160–175; 1927/1961c.) He views religion as a regression to infancy, when the helpless baby desperately needed the protection of an all-powerful parent. These childhood wishes are unconsciously projected onto the environment, creating the image of an exalted deity who must be blindly obeyed:

> The whole thing is so patently infantile, so foreign to reality, that to anyone with a friendly attitude to humanity it is painful to think that the great majority of mortals will never be able to rise above this view of life. (Freud, 1930/1961b, p. 21.)

Thus religion is a collective neurosis, a shared fixation at a very early stage of development. It is an illusion that tries to master the real world with fantasized wish-fulfillments, which must fall before the onslaught of reason and intellect. The more intelligent must eventually realize that our ancestors were wrong about a great many things, and perhaps religion as well; that the prohibitions against questioning religious doctrines are a clear sign of weakness, designed to protect these ideas from critical examination; that tales of miracles contradict everything learned from sober observation; that earthquakes, floods, and diseases do not distinguish between believer and nonbeliever; that human evolution follows Darwinian principles rather than a divine plan; and that the promised afterlife of perfect justice is most unlikely ever to be delivered.

Furthermore, religion does not provide a good basis for social morality. "Thou shalt not kill," a commandment that was frequently violated even when the influence of religion was strongest, becomes meaningless if people do not believe that God will enforce it. Nor does it pay to "love thy neighbor" if the neighbor replies with hatred, and no omnipotent being is on hand to keep score and redress this injustice.[2] Civilization does require prohibitions against killing, but should base them on rational grounds: if one person may kill, so may everyone else. Ultimately all will be wiped out, for even the strongest individual cannot withstand the attack of a large group. If refusing to kill were properly recognized as a self-serving human principle, rather than a commandment of God, people would understand how such rules work to their own interests and strive to preserve them (Freud, 1930/1961b, pp. 56–58; 1927/1961c, pp. 37–44).

Freud concedes that his arguments will encounter powerful and emotional opposition. Since people are indoctrinated with religion during childhood, before they are able to apply reason to this issue, they become dependent on its narcotizing effects. Therefore, he recommends bringing children up without religion. This would force us to face the full extent of our insignificance in the universe, abandon the security blankets of childhood, learn to rely on our own resources, and grow from infantilism to maturity (Freud, 1927/1961c, pp. 49–50). Just as Freud took no more than an occasional aspirin during 16 painful years with cancer, he allows us no narcotics and no rationalizations. We must forgo illusions of ideal justice and happiness

---

[2] Freud did take a more positive approach to loving one's neighbor in a subsequent publication (1933).

in the hereafter, and be content to relieve the inevitable burdens of life. This will enable us to deal most effectively with reality:

> [Science attempts] to take account of our dependence on the real external world, while religion is an illusion and it derives its strength from its readiness to fit in with our instinctual wishful impulses…. Our science is no illusion. But an illusion it would be to suppose that what science cannot give us we can get elsewhere. (Freud, 1927/1961c, p. 56; 1933/1965b, pp. 174–175.)

Literature

According to psychoanalytic theory, Oedipal themes can be found throughout literature and the arts. The young hero who slays the fearsome giant in "Jack and the Beanstalk" is scoring a symbolic Oedipal triumph over a castration-threatening father, whereas Cinderella achieves a similar victory over her cruel stepmother and stepsisters by winning the heart of a handsome father-figure (the prince). To minimize the reader's guilt feelings about fulfilling such illicit wishes, the hero(ine) with whom the child identifies is depicted as honest and in the right, whereas the rivals are portrayed as evil villains or monsters.

In adult literature, Shakespeare's Hamlet cannot bring himself to avenge his father's murder because the behavior of his dastardly uncle is an all-too-threatening reminder of his own forbidden wish: to take his father's place with his mother. Parricide also plays a major role in many novels (e.g., Dostoevski's *Brothers Karamazov*) and in various myths and legends, notably the story of Oedipus that formed the basis for Freud's theories. Even in tales where the characters are loving or submissive, the manifest content can be interpreted as a defense against underlying illicit impulses. For example, the Homeric myth of immortal gods and goddesses disguises the issue of parricide by having a father-figure (Zeus) who cannot be killed (Brenner, 1973/1974, p. 206).

Freud regards jokes as of considerable psychological importance, and has devoted a monograph to this topic (1905/1963i). Many jokes allow the discharge of sexual or aggressive tension in a socially acceptable way, with a "joke-work" (similar to the dream-work) concealing the true meaning. Freud's analysis presents considerable difficulties for the modern American reader, however, and is probably the least read of all his works. Jokes that are funny in Freud's native German often require a lengthy explanation in English or involve a play on words that cannot be translated at all, whereas others are amusing only to those who are familiar with life in Vienna at the turn of the century.

EVALUATION

Sigmund Freud was a genius, with many brilliant insights about the human personality. There are significant errors in his theory, however, as well as aspects that remain highly controversial. To complicate matters, Freud changed his mind often and left more than a few loose ends. Conceding and correcting an error is in the best spirit of scientific integrity, but his many revisions have caused considerable difficulties for those trying to evaluate his theory.

Criticisms and Controversies

Female Sexuality. Freud's belief that women are inferior creatures with defective sexual organs, weaker superegos, and a greater predisposition to neurosis is regarded by virtually all modern psychologists as absurd—a truly major blunder. Freud apparently had sexist prejudices (as was common in his era), which made it difficult even for such a sensible and rational man to understand the feminine psyche. Today, of course, theorists stress the equality or even superiority of women (such as their greater longevity and ability to bear children).

The psychoanalytic belief that clitoral orgasm is an inferior and pregential form of sexuality, and that vaginal orgasm is the only mature version, has also been contradicted by modern research. Although sexual response is probably too complex to be attributed to any single factor, studies have indicated that women who experience orgasm through clitoral stimulation are as normal and well-adjusted as those who obtain it from vaginal penetration. To many observers, therefore, Freudian theory represents yet another expression of an age-old cultural bias against women. (See for example Breger, 1981; Fromm, 1973; 1980; Horney, 1923–1937/1967; Lewis, 1981; Masters & Johnson, 1966.)

Sexuality and Rigidity.   Freudian theory has been strongly attacked for its heavy emphasis on sexuality: the universality of the Oedipus complex, libido, the psychosexual stages, attributing all psychopathology to malfunctions of the sexual drive, regarding most dream symbols as sexual, and so forth. Even today, when sexuality is no longer so shocking, many find it hard to believe that this one drive explains nearly all human behavior. Psychoanalysts would argue that we have not yet come far enough along the path of freeing ourselves from our repressions, but there is also the possibility that Freud's personal life affected his theorizing to an excessive degree. For example, his frequent allusions to Oedipal parricide wishes may be related to an unusual degree of resentment toward his father (Ellenberger, 1970, pp. 451–452; Roazen, 1975/1976b, pp. 36–37). And although Freud was in many respects a fearless and objective investigator, he appears to have had an intense personal commitment to the issue of sexuality:

> There was no mistaking the fact that Freud was emotionally involved in his sexual theory to an extraordinary degree. When he spoke of it, his tone became urgent, almost anxious, and all signs of his normally critical and skeptical manner vanished. A strange, deeply moved expression came over his face, the cause of which I was at a loss to understand. I had a strong intuition that for him sexuality was a sort of *numinosum*. (Jung, 1961/1965, p. 150.)

Freud was in the difficult position of having the intelligence and sensitivity to fear death very strongly, yet not believing in religion. He hated helplessness and passivity, particularly the inevitable nonexistence and insignificance of death. Thus psychoanalysis may well have become the religion that would provide him with the immortality of lasting recognition. In fact, his harsh rejection of former colleagues who criticized libido theory (such as Jung and Adler) reflects an intolerance more suited to religion than to scientific controversy. (See Becker, 1973, pp. 100–101; Roazen, 1975/1976b, pp. 188, 209). Interestingly, Freud himself recognized this potential characteristic of a science:

> … every religion is … a religion of love for all those whom it embraces; while cruelty and intolerance towards those who do not belong to it are natural to every religion.… If another group tie takes the place of the religious one… then there will be the same intolerance towards outsiders … and if differences between scientific opinions could ever attain a similar significance for groups, the same result would again be repeated with this new motivation. (Freud, 1921/1959, pp. 30–31.)

Some modern analysts act like members of an exclusive ingroup, and invoke scathing criticisms against even the most respected psychologists of other persuasions. Fine (1973, pp. 8–10), for example, characterizes Adler's contributions to psychological theory as "negligible" and dismisses behavior therapy as a "gimmick." Challenging psychoanalytic theory, on the other hand, can be as difficult and frustrating as attacking a religion. If you cannot recall any Oedipal trauma, a psychoanalyst would reply that these events have been cloaked by repression. Similarly, a novel or dream that affords no obvious evidence of sexuality would be explained as the result of various defenses. Disagreement with a psychoanalyst's interpretation is almost always seen as a resistance, rather than an error by the analyst. When Freud told Dora that a jewel case in her dream symbolized the female genitals, and she replied with "I knew you would say that," Freud rejected the obvious conclusion (that she knew his theories well enough by then to predict his responses) and regarded her answer as a typical way of resisting the truth of his interpretation (Freud, 1905/1963b, p. 87). In fact, there is virtually no way to have a legitimate argument about sexuality with a Freudian.

To be sure, Freud's beliefs derived from a deep and passionate commitment to what he regarded as the truth. He spent a lifetime of hard work sharing his patients' deepest thoughts and most intimate feelings, and he was well aware that psychoanalysis has serious limitations. (See Freud, 1937/1963w; 1933/1965b, p. 144; 1916–1917/1966, p. 245.) Nor is professional arrogance limited to psychoanalysis, or even to psychology. Yet psychoanalysis would appear to suffer from an excessive rigidity, one that provokes public and professional disillusionment and risks losing the more valuable of Freud's hard-won insights (Strupp, 1971).

Pessimism and Drive Reduction. Freud's picture of the dark side of personality has also provoked strong criticism. No one can deny that people are capable of highly destructive and illicit acts, but can we really be inherently murderous and incestuous? Is adult pleasure limited to watered-down sublimations of our forbidden childhood desires? Is the belief in the goodness of human nature "one of those evil illusions by which mankind expect their lives to be beautified and made easier, while in reality they only cause damage?" (Freud, 1933/1965b, p. 104). Rather than accept such somber conclusions, some theorists have tried to recast Freudian psychoanalysis in more optimistic terms (e.g., Horney, Fromm, Erikson). Others have chosen to opt for Freud's "illusion" (e.g., Rogers, Maslow).

Freud's emphasis on drive reduction has also come under heavy fire. A wealth of experience suggests that people are also motivated by desires for increases in tension, and actively seek out excitation and stimulation. Children display an incessant and lively curiosity, some adults continue to work despite being financially secure, and many people take up a challenging project or hobby instead of remaining idle. This issue is deceptively complicated, however, and some of these criticisms seem to be based on misunderstandings of psychoanalytic theory. Work that appears to be unnecessary and drive-increasing may actually be due to the lash of a demanding superego, or it may provide an opportunity for effective sublimations. Psychoanalytic theory does regard boredom as an unpleasant state, where some tension whose aim is unconscious is blocked from discharge (Fenichel, 1945, p. 15). Some gratifying drive increases, such as sexual forepleasure, depend on the expectation of subsequent drive reduction and lose their appeal if this belief is shattered. And Freud himself conceded the existence of pleasurable drive increases (1924/1963h, p. 191), as we have seen. It is probably true, however, that he did not give this factor sufficient attention.

Psychic Energy. According to Freud, the fixation or regression of too much libido will lead to neurosis. But how much is excessive? Although Freud believed that neurological correlates of libido would ultimately be discovered, this has not happened, and it is impossible to measure the amount of psychic energy that is invested in a given cathexis, fixation, or regression. Therefore, some psychologists include the energy model among Freud's dramatic failures. (See, for example, Bieber, 1980; Carlson, 1975.)

Internal Consistency. Despite the fact that Freud's constructs are carefully and intricately interrelated, psychoanalytic theory does not quite hold together. Serious contradictions tear at the foundation and threaten to bring down the entire structure.

As an example, let us consider once again the nature of the instincts. Freud originally re-garded the sexual and self-preservative instincts as two separate categories. He also main-tained that all instincts have the conservative function of restoring matter to a previous state of existence (e.g., returning from hunger to satiation). In 1920, however, Freud made some sig-nificant theoretical changes. Partly because aggressive behavior was becoming increasingly difficult to explain in terms of his theory, he redefined the two major types of instincts as sex-ual and destructive, with self-preservation included as part of Eros. However, tinkering with one part of a theory is likely to affect other aspects as well. Freud continued to argue that all instincts are conservative, yet this now became a new source of difficulty. If nonexistence was our original condition, it is easy to see how the death instinct is conservative: it tries to bring us back to the inanimate state from which we started. But how, then, can the self-preserving Eros be conservative? If, on the other hand, our earliest condition was that of existence, then the death instinct cannot be conservative.

Freud finally indicated that perhaps Eros is not conservative (1940/1969a, p. 6), yet this creates a host of new difficulties. One gets the distinct impression of a man approaching the twilight of his life, confronting a majestic but weakening theoretical dam, and creating new leaks with every attempt to patch up old ones.

Methodology.   Some critics regard psychoanalysis as too subjective and uncontrolled. The psychoanalyst may be biased by preconceived theoretical notions and disregard contra-dictory evidence, or the patient may be influenced to behave in ways that support the analyst's beliefs. The analyst exerts a powerful effect on the patient despite the apparent passivity of the procedure (e.g., Strupp, 1972), and Freud's assertion (1937/1963x, pp. 278–279) that he never led a patient astray by suggestion seems highly improbable.

It has even been argued that Freud exaggerated the success of some of his cases, and distorted some of the facts in ways that would support his theory. For example, some critics contend that Freud tried to force interpretations on the "Rat Man" that were favorable to his theory by using the power of his intellect and personality, and that he lengthened the case report and changed the order of events to make therapy appear more orderly and effective. Although these issues are very troublesome, they do not necessarily mean that Freud was seriously lacking in integrity; they do suggest that he was considerably more prone to human failings than his legend allows. And there are historians of psychoanalysis who regard these criticisms as unfair, and as unlikely to have much effect on the prevailing view of Freud's work. (For a further discussion of these and related issues, see Eagle, 1988; the *New York Times* article by Goleman, 1990; Mahony, 1986.)

Freud's refusal to take notes during the analytic session, so that he could respond uncon-sciously and empathically to the patient, is questioned by those who distrust the vagaries of memory (Wallerstein & Sampson, 1971). Despite Freud's protestations, concentrating on neu-rotic people may have limited his understanding of the healthy and fulfilled personality. And there are no statistical analyses or hypothesis tests in Freud's writings, in contrast to the usual scientific emphasis on quantification and control. For example, his analysis of the "aliquis" parapraxis may not prove that it was motivated by the unconscious fear of having impregnated a woman, since free associations beginning with any other word might also have led to this all-important personal issue.

Other Issues.   Such psychoanalytically oriented theorists as Erikson, Fromm, Horney, and Sullivan believe that Freud overemphasized the biological determinants of personality, and underestimated social and environmental factors (as we will see in subsequent chapters). Jung, Sullivan, and Erikson are among those who contend that personality development con-tinues during adolescence and adulthood, rather than concluding at age 5–6 years. It has been argued that Freud overemphasized the negative aspects of religion, overlooked some of its advantages (and some of the disadvantages of science), and had a personal bias regarding the whole issue (Rieff, 1959/1961, pp. 325–328; Roazen, 1975/1976b, pp. 250–251).

It now appears that dreams are *not* the guardians of sleep, as Freud contended. It is sleep that serves to protect dreaming, a process that is apparently essential to our well-being. It is also doubtful that dreams are as sexually oriented as Freud thought, and it may well be that dream symbols are used more to reveal and express complicated ideas than to conceal illicit wishes. (See Dement, 1964; 1974; Fisher & Greenberg, 1977, pp. 21–79; Fromm, 1951/1957; C. S. Hall, 1966.)

Although a century has passed since the publication of *The Interpretation of Dreams*, few people today use their dreams as an aid to self-understanding. Even when one has the assistance of a psychotherapist, it is all too easy to forget a dream or have difficulty arriving at a valid interpretation. Therefore, Freud's belief that dreams represent the royal road to a knowledge of the unconscious aspects of the mind may well have been too optimistic.

Empirical Research

As would be expected of a science, psychology has tried to resolve the aforementioned controversies by turning to empirical research. However, this has not been an easy task.

Psychoanalytic Theory. A number of studies carried out between 1950 and 1970 focused on the defense mechanisms. Some investigators tried to induce adolescent or adult participants to repress previously learned material by persuading them that they had failed on an important task, such as a test of intelligence or a measure of sexual deviation. Other researchers studied the ability to remember fairly recent life events, hypothesizing that traumatic incidents should be more readily repressed than pleasurable ones. Still others concentrated on the perceptual aspects of defense, using a tachistoscope (a high-speed projection device) to flash a series of individual words on a screen for a brief instant. These investigators hypothesized that taboo words (e.g., "penis," "rape") should be more readily repressed, and hence more difficult to perceive, than neutral words (e.g., "apple," "stove").

Taken as a whole, the results appear to indicate little support for the existence of repression. That is, the experimental group (which underwent the unpleasant experience) usually did *not* demonstrate poorer recall than the control group (which did not). However, since Freud states that the decisive repressions all take place during early childhood, it is difficult to see how an experimenter can justifiably claim to have refuted psychoanalytic theory merely by failing to trigger this mechanism in older participants. Even though the taboo words in the perceptual defense experiments were sometimes readily identified, the existence of some people who do not deny this particular aspect of reality is hardly a major blow to psychoanalytic theory. Thus the clinical evidence in favor of repression and the defense mechanisms would appear to outweigh these negative, but flawed, research findings. (For specific references, see the first edition of this book [Ewen, 1980, p. 65] and Hilgard & Bower [1975, pp. 362–369].)

Silverman (1976) also concludes that research on psychoanalytic theory prior to the 1970s has been poorly designed, in part because it is difficult to study unconscious material without allowing it to become conscious. As a result, there has been a lack of convincing research support for the major propositions of psychoanalysis. To help remedy this defect, he reports on two independent research programs conducted over a 10-year period. Both programs dispensed with the metaphysical aspects of psychoanalysis (e.g., psychic energy and cathexes), and concentrated instead on basic clinical propositions. One program used subliminal tachistoscopic presentations of stimuli designed to intensify the participants' wishes, feelings, and conflicts about sex and aggression (and *not* to induce repression, as in the studies criticized above). The other program employed hypnotic suggestion to induce conflict, as by suggesting that the participant strongly desired a member of the opposite sex who was married, more experienced, and likely to treat any advances with ridicule. The results supported a fundamental contention of psychoanalytic theory, namely that psychopathology is causally related to unconscious conflicts about sex and aggression.

Fisher and Greenberg (1977) have reviewed a substantial amount of research dealing with psychoanalytic theory. The evidence indicates that dreams do *not* serve to preserve sleep, as noted in a previous section. Nor is the manifest content of a dream merely a meaningless camouflage. It may at times function defensively, but it also provides important information about the dreamer's personality and success in coping with important life issues. However, Freud was correct when he concluded that dreams provide an outlet for our internal, unconscious tensions. With regard to personality types, such oral characteristics as dependency, pessimism, and passivity do frequently cluster together. The same is true for the anal characteristics of orderliness, parsimoniousness, and obstinacy. Research on Oedipal issues supports Freud's belief that both sexes begin life with a closer attachment to the mother, that castration anxiety is a common occurrence among men, and that the boy goes through a phase of rivalry with his father. But the studies also indicate that Freud was wrong about female Oedipality: there is no evidence that women believe their bodies to be inferior because they possess a vagina instead of a penis, or that women have less severe superegos than men. The research findings also suggest that the boy resolves his Oedipus complex *not* to reduce castration anxiety, but because the father's friendliness and nurturance invite the boy to become like him. That is, the resolution of the boy's Oedipus complex is due to trust rather than fear.

Hunt (1979) reviewed literature dealing with the psychosexual stages, and concluded that Freudian theory is incorrect in certain respects. Although some support does exist for the anal character, there is no evidence that it derives from the management of toilet training. (See also Singer, 1997.) Also questionable is the Oedipal hypothesis that children regularly compete with the parent of the same sex for the attention and love of the parent of the opposite sex. However, the research results support Freud's general emphasis on experiences during early life as determinants of personality.

Recent research evidence also strongly supports two major aspects of Freudian theory. Anxiety is clearly harmful to one's physical and psychological health (e.g., Suinn, 2001). And unconscious defense mechanisms influence many kinds of behavior, including child development, prejudice and racism, self-esteem, memory, and decision making (e.g., Cramer, 2000; Cramer & Davidson, 1998; Paulhus et al., 1997). To cite just one example, children who report extremely high self-esteem are often denying or defending against underlying feelings of imperfection (Cassidy, 1988; Cramer & Block, 1998). Yet Freud often fails to receive the credit that he deserves, for all too many modern psychologists have devised and used new names for the defense mechanisms while ignoring his work.

Some animal studies appear to demonstrate the existence of pleasurable tension increases. Animals will explore the environment, learn to solve mechanical puzzles, and learn to open a door in an opaque cage just to see outside, without any biological drive reduction taking place. Insofar as learning theory is concerned, it has been concluded that the drive-reduction hypothesis is probably inadequate (Bower & Hilgard, 1981, p. 113). On the other hand, Freud's original theory about the seduction of children by adults may not have been as incorrect as he ultimately concluded. It has been suggested that incest is more prevalent than is generally believed, but is not publicized because of feelings of shame and guilt. The continuing interest in such Freudian issues is evidenced by the prominent coverage in such popular periodicals as *The New York Times* (Blumenthal, 1981a; 1981b; Goleman, 1990) and *Newsweek* (Gelman, 1981; 1991).

Finally, Shevrin and Dickman (1980) surveyed diverse fields of empirical research dealing with the unconscious. Although the results by no means always agree with Freudian theory, the authors conclude that no psychological model that seeks to explain human behavior can afford to ignore the concept of unconscious processes.

Psychoanalytic Therapy. Psychoanalytic therapy has also been subjected to the rigors of formal research, though there are serious methodological problems here also. (See, for example, Fisher & Greenberg, 1977; Seligman, 1995; Strupp & Howard, 1992; VandenBos, 1986; 1996.)

There is evidence that newer forms of psychotherapy may be more efficient and effective than psychoanalysis, at least for certain types of pathology (e.g., Corsini, 1973; Sloane et al., 1975; Fisher & Greenberg, 1996). Even Eysenck's polemical attacks on psychoanalysis (1952; 1965; 1966), which at one time appeared to have been convincingly refuted (Bergin, 1971; Meltzoff & Kornreich, 1970), have since met with some support (Erwin, 1980; Garfield, 1981). Nevertheless, a study of 20 behavior therapists who were themselves in personal therapy revealed that 10 opted for psychoanalysis (and none for behavior therapy!), with some freely conceding that analysis is the treatment of choice if one can afford it (Lazarus, 1971). And some analysts have sought to update their procedures by having the patient attend only once or twice per week, and by dispensing with the couch in favor of face-to-face interviews, while retaining many of the fundamental aspects of Freudian theory (e.g., Bieber, 1980).

Some theorists emphasize the common factors among the various forms of psychotherapy, arguing that the differences are more apparent than real (e.g., Bergin & Strupp, 1972; Luborsky, Singer, & Luborsky, 1975; Strupp, 1973). Others argue that those differences that do exist can and should be reconciled, so that psychologists can concentrate on advancing our knowledge rather than debating the merits of particular schools of thought. (See Goldfried, 1980; Marmor & Woods, 1980; Wachtel, 1977; 1987). At present, then, there are no simple answers regarding the relative effectiveness of psychoanalytic therapy.

Contributions

Despite the controversies that beset psychoanalysis, Freud deserves his lasting place in history. Although there are modern psychologists who would disagree, the following almost certainly represent major progress in our attempts to understand the human personality.

Freud emphasized the importance of the unconscious. Instead of naively assuming that behavior is what it seems on the surface, it is now widely accepted that part of every personality—and probably a very significant part—is below the level of awareness. The term *Freudian slip* and the various defense mechanisms have become part of our everyday language. Freud devised valuable techniques for interpreting dreams, and was the first to incorporate dream interpretation as a formal part of psychotherapy.

Freud developed the first method of psychotherapy, including procedures for bringing unconscious material to consciousness. He identified such fundamental issues as resistance and transference, and showed that many difficulties in adult life relate to childhood conflicts with one's parents. He pointed out the importance of early childhood for personality development. He stressed that psychopathology represents a difference in degree rather than kind, and showed that apparently incomprehensible neurotic symptoms have important meanings.

Freud called attention to the importance of anxiety, and emphasized that psychological pain can be as or more troublesome than physical pain. He showed that we may suffer from self-imposed commands and restrictions that are relentless and cruel, a concept accepted by many other theorists (albeit often presented using their own terminology rather than the super-ego). He analyzed himself and probed the terrors of his own unconscious without the aid of another analyst, because there were no others. And his theories about infantile sexuality and the inevitable conflict between the individual and society, although controversial, have triggered valuable discussions and rethinkings of these issues.

Despite many sharp attacks and incredulous critics, Freud is accorded great esteem throughout psychology and psychiatry. Textbooks in all areas of psychology pay him due respect, and many of the noted personality theorists whose views we will examine in subsequent chapters have used psychoanalytic theory as the foundation for their own work. Whatever Freud's errors may have been, this extraordinary and brilliant man opened new psychological vistas for all humanity. The ultimate personality theory must include, at the very least, the best of his ideas, and no one who claims an interest in human behavior can afford to be without a firsthand knowledge of his works.

Suggested Reading

The best way to approach Freud is by starting with his latest writings, which express his theory in its final form. *The Question of Lay Analysis* (1926/1969b) is a highly readable short monograph that summarizes many of the main points of psychoanalysis. The *New Introductory Lectures on Psychoanalysis* (1933/1965b), which was designed as a sequel to the *Introductory Lectures on Psychoanalysis* (1916–1917/1966), can stand in its own right as a well-written guide to various aspects of Freudian theory. *An Outline of Psychoanalysis* (1940/1969a) is a brief and highly condensed survey, whereas the *The Ego and the Id* (1923/1962) is the seminal work that introduced the structural model of personality. Many of Freud's views on religion and society will be found in *The Future of an Illusion* (1927/1961c) and *Civilization and its Discontents* (1930/1961b).

Among Freud's earlier works, *The Interpretation of Dreams* (1900/1965a) is probably his single most important effort. *The Psychopathology of Everyday Life* (1901/1965c) is the definitive work on parapraxes. *Beyond the Pleasure Principle* (1920/1961a), a difficult and challenging monograph, brought forth the concept of the death instinct. Freud's description of his treatment of Dora (1905/1963b), the Rat Man (1909/1963y), and the Wolf Man (1918/1963aa) are also readily available, as are many of his theoretical papers. Of the various alternatives, the standard edition of Freud's works (edited by James Strachey) is the most accurate.

The classic biography of Freud is by Ernest Jones (1953–1957/1963), though there are those who feel that it affords too favorable a picture of its subject. Other valuable sources of biographical information and critical evaluation are Ellenberger (1970), Gay (1988), Rieff (1959/1961), Roazen (1975/1976b), and Schur (1972). Freud also wrote a brief autobiographical sketch (1925/1963a). Useful secondary sources include Brenner (1973/1974) on psychoanalytic theory, Menninger and Holzman (1973) on psychoanalytic therapy, and Fenichel (1945) on both areas.

SUMMARY

1. THE BASIC NATURE OF HUMAN BEINGS. *The Instincts*: People are motivated by innate instincts that convert bodily needs into psychological tensions. We seek to gain pleasure by reducing these drives and to avoid unpleasure (the pleasure principle). The two types of instincts are sexual, which includes the whole range of pleasurable and self-preserving behavior, and destructive. These two types are fused together, though not necessarily in equal amounts, so that any behavior is at least partly erotic and partly aggressive. Our inherent nature is murderous and incestuous. Therefore, to enjoy the benefits of a civilized society, we must accept some frustration and sublimate our true illicit desires into socially acceptable (but less pleasurable) behavior. *Psychic Energy*: All mental activity is powered by psychic energy. The energy associated with the sexual instincts is called libido, whereas that related to the destructive instincts has no name. Mental representations of objects are cathected with varying quantities of psychic energy; the greater the amount, the stronger the cathexis and the more the object is desired. *Psychic Determinism*: All behavior has underlying causes. Apparent accidents (parapraxes), dreams, and seemingly irrelevant thoughts provide evidence about one's unconscious feelings and beliefs, which may well be different from their conscious counterparts. *The Unconscious*: The vast majority of mental activity is unconscious, and cannot be called to mind without the aid of such psychoanalytic techniques as free association and dream interpretation.

2. **THE STRUCTURE OF PERSONALITY.** *The Id*: The id is present at birth, is entirely unconscious, and includes all innate instincts. It operates in accordance with the irrational primary process, and is motivated entirely by the pleasure principle. It has no sense of logic, time, or self-preservation, and its only resource is to form wish-fulfilling mental images of desired objects. *The Ego*: The ego begins to develop out of the id at about age 6 to 8 months. The ego results from experience with one's own body and with the outside world, and spans the conscious, preconscious, and unconscious. It operates in accordance with the logical and self-preservative secondary process and is motivated by the reality principle, delaying pleasure until a suitable and safe object has been found. The ego is the locus of all emotions, including anxiety, and tries to keep the id under control by using various defense mechanisms. *The Superego*: The superego begins to develop out of the ego at about age 3 to 5 years. It is partly conscious and partly unconscious, and includes standards of right and wrong. The superego results from introjected parental standards and from the resolution of the Oedipus complex.

3. **THE DEVELOPMENT OF PERSONALITY.** *Psychosexual Stages*: Personality is determined primarily during the first 5 years of life. We proceed through a series of psychosexual stages: oral, anal, urethral, phallic, a latency period (usually), and genital. A different part of the body serves as the primary erotogenic zone during each stage, providing the main source of pleasure (and conflict). The Oedipus complex occurs during the phallic stage and consists of a double set of attitudes toward both parents, with love for the parent of the opposite sex and jealousy toward the parent of the same sex usually stronger than the reverse feelings. The boy eventually abandons his Oedipal strivings because of castration fears, whereas the girl ultimately seeks resolution by having children. *Fixation and Regression*: Normally, most libido eventually reaches the genital stage. The fixation of excessive amounts of libido at pregenital stages results in various character patterns, and perhaps in psychopathology. Libido may also regress to a previous psychosexual stage or to an object that was long since abandoned, usually one that was strongly fixated.

4. **FURTHER APPLICATIONS:** *Dream Interpretation*: Dreams serve as "the royal road to the unconscious." But they are expressed in a symbolic language that is difficult to understand, with the dream-work changing threatening latent dream-thoughts into more acceptable manifest content. Most dreams involve childhood sexual impulses, though some (especially those of children) are obvious and nonsexual. Virtually all dreams seek to fulfill some wish. *Psychopathology*: Neurosis invariably begins in infancy and childhood, though it may not become evident until much later. Failure to resolve the Oedipus complex results in an inability to form effective sublimations, so libido can be discharged only in the disguised and distorted form of neurotic symptoms. Like dreams, neurotic symptoms represent a compromise among the id, ego, and superego; and they have important underlying meanings, however strange they may appear on the surface. *Psychotherapy*: Psychoanalytic therapy strives to bring unconscious

material to consciousness, where it can be examined and corrected by the ego. These insights strengthen the ego, increase its control over the id and superego, and improve its ability to deal with the difficulties of everyday life. Psychoanalytic therapy is extremely expensive and time-consuming, uses the well-known couch, has the patient free-associate by saying whatever comes to mind, pays special attention to the patient's resistances and transferences, and emphasizes carefully timed interpretations by the analyst. *Other Applications*: Psychoanalysis has been applied to such areas as work, religion (of which Freud was extremely critical), and literature.

5. EVALUATION. Among the weaknesses of psychoanalysis are male chauvinism, internal inconsistencies, methodological problems, difficulties with the metaphysical energy model, a resilience to attack that borders on evasiveness, a lack of tolerance for other ideas and modern innovations, and (perhaps) an overemphasis on sexuality, drive reduction, and the biological determinants of personality. It has proved difficult to subject the propositions of psychoanalytic theory to empirical research. Nevertheless, Freud's contributions are monumental: the importance of the unconscious, dream interpretation, psychoanalytic therapy, resistance and transference, repression and the defense mechanisms, parapraxes, anxiety, the meaning of neurotic symptoms, and more.

STUDY QUESTIONS

Note: A set of study questions appears at the end of each chapter dealing with a theory of personality. It is important to understand that many of these questions do not have a single "right" answer. The questions are designed to encourage critical thinking about the material you have read, and to stimulate discussion and debate about important issues. They will also help you relate personality theory to the world in which we live.

Following the study questions, you will find a "help" section that includes comments and suggestions. However, try to devise your own answers before you consult the help section. Some questions deal with certain case material, which has been placed in an Appendix at the end of this book for ready reference.

Part I. Questions

1. It has been argued that the content of any theory of personality is strongly influenced by the theorist's own personality (e.g., Mindess, 1988). Why might a personality theorist want to believe that aspects of his or her personality are shared by everyone?

2. How might Freud's personality and life experiences have influenced: (a) his conclusions regarding the Oedipus complex? (b) his belief that nearly all of personality is unconscious?

3. Freud suffered from some of the same neurotic symptoms that he treated in his patients. Would a person who is psychologically healthy have Freud's intense desire to probe deeply within his or her own psyche?

4. (a) Did Freud regard at least some of his ideas and constructs as truths that deserved to remain unchallenged for a long time? (b) What is the difference between a construct and a fact? (c) Given this difference, is it likely that Freud's constructs would be as enduring as he hoped?

5. Give an example of a parapraxis from your own life, and suggest how Freud might interpret it. How would you interpret it?

6. Give an example from your own life, or from the life of someone you know well, which shows that anxiety can be just as painful as (or even more painful than) a physical injury.

7. (a) Give an example from your own life of the use of one or more defense mechanisms. (b) What purpose did the defense mechanism(s) serve? (c) Were there any harmful effects? (d) Since many of these mechanisms are used unconsciously, how can you (or anyone) know that they actually exist?

8. Give an example from your own life of an undesirable id impulse overcoming the ego's restrictions and defenses.

9. Give an example from your own life of the superego being overly demanding and cruel to the ego.

10. Why might a theorist use a construct such as libido, even though it cannot be observed or measured?

11. By today's standards, Freud's views of women were clearly biased. To what extent (if any) should criticism of Freud take into account the era in which he lived?

12. A young woman dreams that she rushes to catch a train but gets to the station too late, the train leaves without her, and there are no more trains to her destination for several weeks. On the surface, it appears that the dreamer has been disappointed. How might this dream be interpreted to support Freud's belief that virtually every dream fulfills some wish of the dreamer?

13. Consider the following quotes from Chapter 1: (a) "Psychoanalysis is a method of research, an impartial instrument, like the infinitesimal calculus." Do you agree? Why or why not? (b) "[Mental patients] have turned away from external reality, but for that very reason they know more about internal, psychical reality and can reveal a number of things to us that would otherwise be inaccessible to us." Do you agree that studies of mental patients can provide important information about personality in general? Why or why not?

14. Explain how the concept of resistance can be viewed both as a major contribution to our knowledge and as a way for Freud to protect his theory against attack.

15. A terrorist blows up a building in a hated foreign country. How might Freud use the concepts of id, ego, and superego to explain this behavior?

16. The chief executive officer of a major corporation lies to his coworkers and the public, thereby defrauding them of a great deal of money while making millions for himself. A religious leader conceals evidence of child abuse by his subordinates, thereby allowing such abuse to continue. When found out, both individuals steadfastly maintain that they did nothing wrong. (a) Is this an excuse or a rationalization? (b) How might Freud explain this behavior?

17. The author of a popular textbook on introductory psychology (which I use when I teach that course) concludes that the following evidence disproves Freud's construct of repression: "Shouldn't we expect children who have witnessed a parent's murder to repress the experience? A study of sixteen 5- to 10-year-old children who had this horrific experience found that not one repressed the memory. Shouldn't survivors of Nazi death camps have banished the atrocities from consciousness? With rare exceptions, they remember all too well." (Myers, 2001, p. 498) Why is the author's conclusion incorrect?

Part II. Comments and Suggestions

1. Suppose the theorist's introspections reveal that he or she has some highly undesirable (perhaps even shocking) personality characteristics. Suppose further that the theorist is a moral, ethical person. How might the theorist feel if these characteristics were possessed by very few people? If these characteristics could be attributed to human nature?

2. (a) Recall the family situation in which Freud grew up, and compare this with Jung's family situation (biographical sketch, Chapter 3). (b) If a person wishes to startle the world and achieve fame as an unraveler of great mysteries, what better way than to discover an immense, vitally important, but largely unexplored realm within every human being?

3. I don't think so. I concede that there are relatively well-adjusted psychologists who are interested in studying personality, possibly including their own. But insofar as Freud's intense self-analysis is concerned, I doubt if he would have undertaken this difficult and painful task had he not been afflicted with psychological problems that he needed to resolve.

4. (a) Consider Freud's statements about the merits of Oedipal theory and dream interpretation. (b) See Chapter 1. (c) Why is it necessary for a theorist to create constructs?

5. I am angry at my wife or daughter, and I am thinking quite unhusbandly or unfatherly thoughts. A few moments later I accidentally collide with a piece of furniture and sustain a painful bruise. Freud would argue that this is no accident; I am relieving my guilt over my hostile thoughts by punishing myself. He would also contend that this parapraxis indicates an underlying conflict, possibly the obvious one between love and anger toward my family and perhaps some deeper and more complicated ones as well. (Recall that the causes of behavior are usually overdetermined.) In this case, I'd be inclined to agree with him.

6. See section 1 of the case material in the Appendix.

7. (a) Denial of reality: A man's relationship with his father is a troubled one. When he is in his late twenties, and living a few thousand miles away form his parents, his mother phones to tell him that his father has just suffered a heart attack. When she says that she can handle everything, he is pleased that he doesn't have to disrupt his schedule and make a long trip. So he hangs up and goes about his business. He does not allow himself to understand that a heart attack is a serious matter, and that his father might need his help. (His father is an independent and dominating person who never seems to need his help.) Nor does it occur to him that in spite of her brave words, his mother might want some firsthand support. Instead he acts as though nothing very important has happened. (b) Denial helps him to conceal his painful feelings and inner conflicts involving love and hate for his father, so he doesn't have to face them and deal with them. (c) His behavior certainly didn't improve his relationship with his parents. (d) Everyone knows that a heart attack is extremely serious. He was not making excuses; he sincerely believed that this was a trivial matter. Only the operation of unconscious psychological defenses could lead to such a severe distortion of reality.

8. I don't like waiting in long lines at the supermarket or bank (or even short lines). I tell myself that I have more important things to do, and I don't want any delays in gratification. The checkout clerk or teller is working hard to satisfy everyone, and my ego should develop an anticathexis against these id impulses. But all too often the id impulses win out, and I become childishly impatient.

9. A young teacher is speaking in front of a large class. Most of what the teacher says is well thought out, instructive, and entertaining. But a few attempts at humor are inept and fall flat. Later, the teacher focuses on these failures and is very self-critical for not preparing more thoroughly, thereby depriving himself of the legitimate gratification that should have been derived from a good and effective presentation.

10. Consider an example from the world of sports. The Dallas Cowboys score two quick touchdowns against the San Francisco 49ers and lead, 14–0. They are driving for a third touchdown, which will seemingly turn the game into a rout, when disaster strikes: A pass is intercepted and returned for a touchdown. The 49ers appear revitalized, and the announcers proclaim that the "momentum" of the game has changed. Can momentum be seen or measured? Why do announcers and fans find this construct useful?

11. During much of the time in which Freud lived, women in the United States were treated as second-class citizens; for example, they were not allowed to vote. Should a theorist be able to rise above such prevailing standards?

12. You could argue that she didn't want to go where the train would take her; perhaps her spouse insisted on vacationing in a place that she didn't like. I would look more deeply,

however, and posit an underlying inner conflict. Suppose that the train trip represents her journey to psychological maturity. She partly wants to grow up and be her own woman (and catch the train), but is also afraid of surrendering her dependence on her parents and the protection that they provide. The latter wish is stronger at this moment, so she arranges in her dream to miss the train. Freud would presumably see an Oedipal conflict somewhere, perhaps with the train as a phallic symbol.

13. (a) I don't. Science is objective, and its procedures and results can be verified and reproduced by other people. Freud's procedures were subjective; he did not keep records during the psychoanalytic session, or allow the presence of outside observers (understandably, in view of the sensitive material being discussed). (b) I do. We all use defense mechanisms and experience anxiety to some extent, and these ideas (like all of Freud's) were derived from his work with his patients. Modern psychologists generally agree that at least some forms of psychopathology represent differences in degree from healthy adjustment, rather than differences in kind.

14. How does a resistance enable a patient to avoid having to confront threatening beliefs, emotions, and memories? How might the concept of resistance enable Freud to find fault with those attacking psychoanalytic theory?

15. Everyone's id contains such destructive impulses. Most of us are taught that blowing up buildings is wrong, we incorporate this standard into our superegos, and the superego tells the ego not to allow this behavior. But the terrorist's society approves of such violence, so parents in that society are likely to agree and to convey this belief to their children. Thus the terrorist's superego doesn't regard blowing up the building as wrong, so the ego has no reason to prohibit it. In fact, the superego causes the ego to feel pride and virtue for committing such a "desirable" act.

16. (a) Are the executive and the religious leader trying to mislead others in order to avoid punishment? Or are they trying to deceive themselves so they will feel less guilt? (b) The superego of the chief executive officer may be too weak, perhaps because appropriate standards of right and wrong were not taught by his parents. Or the executive's ego may be too weak to resist the selfish demands of the id, perhaps because he was severely frustrated (or overly gratified) during early childhood and there was too much fixation at a pregenital stage of development. The religious leader may be engaging in denial of reality by believing that the abusive subordinates will change their ways, and he may be accepting the "illusion" that some benevolent Deity will eventually intercede and make everything right.

17. What is the difference between repression and denial of reality? Where does the threat arise from in each case? According to Freud, when do virtually all important repressions occur? Does Freudian theory contend that people usually deny the reality of unpleasant events in the external world?

CHAPTER 3

CARL GUSTAV JUNG
Analytical Psychology

Early in 1909 Carl Jung, then a colleague and close friend of Freud's, expressed a keen interest in precognition and parapsychology. To Jung's dismay and irritation, Freud strongly denounced such beliefs as nonsensical. The rejection made Jung feel as though his diaphragm were made of red-hot iron, whereupon a strange loud noise issued from a nearby bookcase.

"There," Jung argued, "that is an example of a so-called catalytic exteriorization phenomenon."

"Bosh," retorted Freud.

"It is not," Jung replied. "And to prove my point I now predict that in a moment there will be another such loud report!"

No sooner had these words been spoken than a second inexplicable detonation went off in the bookcase. "To this day I do not know what gave me this certainty," Jung was to reflect years later, "but I knew beyond all doubt that the report would come again. Freud only stared aghast at me...." (Jung, 1961/1965, pp. 155–156.)[1]

Jung's quest for information about the human psyche led him to sources that many would regard as farfetched—the occult, studies of extrasensory perception, alchemy, the myth of flying saucers. Yet Jung regarded himself as an empirical researcher, possessed a fine mind, read voraciously and acquired an immense store of knowledge, traveled widely in order to study various races and classes, and was an esteemed psychotherapist; and some of his ideas have become part of the everyday language of psychology and life.

---

[1]Freud later took a more positive approach to the occult. See for example Freud, 1933/1965b, pp. 31–56; Roazen, 1975/1976b, pp. 232–241.

OBJECTIVES

- *To devise a theory of personality that greatly improves on Freud's ideas while continuing to emphasize the importance of the unconscious.*
- *To correct Freud's extreme pessimism about human nature by showing that we have both healthy and malignant instincts, and that one of our healthy instincts is individuation (the forerunner of the humanistic concept of self-actualization).*
- *To show that every personality includes a collective unconscious that contains archetypes, or inherited predispositions to perceive the world in certain ways, as well as a personal unconscious that contains repressed or forgotten material.*
- *To show that introversion–extraversion and the four ways in which we perceive the world (sensation, thinking, feeling, and intuition) are important aspects of every personality.*
- *To correct Freud's belief that mental illness usually has sexual causes by showing that every personality consists of various opposites, and that becoming too one-sided and ignoring the corresponding opposite aspect of personality is the major cause of psychopathology.*
- *To devise improved methods of dream interpretation and psychotherapy.*
- *To relate areas that most would regard as beyond the realm of personality theory, including the occult, extrasensory perception, and alchemy, to the study of personality.*

BIOGRAPHICAL SKETCH

Carl Gustav Jung was born on July 26, 1875, in Kesswil, a small village in Switzerland. His father was a Protestant country minister who was tormented by a lack of faith, and was unable to answer Jung's penetrating questions about religion and life. Jung's skepticism about the Oedipus complex may have been due in part to a mother who was a "kindly, fat old woman" troubled by marital difficulties (Jung, 1961/1965, p. 48), an influence quite different from that of Freud's beautiful, young doting mother. Like Freud, Jung rose from austere middle-class origins to the heights of world fame.

Jung was an introverted and lonely child, deeply preoccupied with his inner psychic world. From an early age he experienced visions of the supernatural, such as a faintly luminous figure with a detached head that appeared to emanate from his mother's bedroom. He soon came to regard himself as "a solitary, because I know things and must hint at things which other people do not know, and usually do not even want to know. . . . Loneliness does not come from having no people about one, but from being unable to communicate the things that seem important to oneself, or from holding certain views which others find inadmissible" (Jung, 1961/1965, pp. 42, 356; see also pp. 18–19).

Jung became attracted to the fledgling field of psychiatry during his medical studies at the University of Basel, where he received his degree in 1900. Some of his professors were amazed and disappointed by his choice, but Jung was convinced that he had found his true calling. He became absorbed with the occult, participated in experiments with mediums, and devoured books on parapsychology. In addition to his visions, various experiences appeared to confirm the existence of the supernatural: A solid table and a steel knife in his parents' home inexplicably shattered into pieces by themselves. He made up a supposedly imaginary story to entertain a group, only to find that he was clairvoyantly revealing true and intimate secrets about a man he did not know. And the morning after being awakened by a sharp headache, he discovered that one of his patients had that night shot himself in the back of the skull (Jung, 1961/1965, pp. 51, 105–106, 109, 137, 206).

Jung first worked at the famed Burghölzli Psychiatric Hospital in Zurich under the direction of Eugen Bleuler, who coined the term *schizophrenia* and was well known for his work on this disorder. There he developed the word association test and remained until 1909, when he departed to concentrate on his growing private practice. In 1903 he married Emma Rauschenbach, who also became his collaborator and learned to apply his psychotherapeutic methods. The marriage was basically successful, with the Jungs having four daughters and a son. But no one woman could make up for the emotional deprivations of Carl's childhood. During middle age he entered into a lengthy affair with a young, attractive, and well-educated former patient, Toni Wolff. He even drew Toni into his family life, making her a regular guest for Sunday dinner. Emma ultimately decided to accept this situation, and Carl kept both his mistress and his family. (See Stern, 1976/1977.)

Jung read *The Interpretation of Dreams* upon its publication in 1900, and he began what proved to be a lengthy correspondence with Freud in 1906. The two men met a year later, and were so captivated with each other that they talked continuously for 13 hours. Unfortunately, the union of the two giants was based on a fundamental misconception that eventually destroyed the relationship. Freud was seeking disciples who would carry forth the psychoanalytic banner and he saw Jung as his crown prince and successor. Jung, on the other hand, regarded his association with Freud as a collaboration that left both sides free to pursue their own ideas. It was inevitable that Jung would view Freud's insistence on the universality of the Oedipus complex and the sexual nature of libido as dogmatism, whereas Freud would see Jung's attempts to develop his own theory as a betrayal.

For some years, Jung did follow in Freud's footsteps. Jung defended Freud's ideas, accompanied him to the United States as an invited lecturer at Clark University in 1909, became a psychoanalyst and taught this subject at the University of Zurich, and served as the first president of the International Psychoanalytic Association. But Jung had to be his own man. His analysis of the delusions and hallucinations of psychotic patients at the Burghölzli had persuaded him of the frequent occurrence of universal archetypes, and he came to view the human personality quite differently from Freud. When Jung continued to argue for his own constructs, the breach with Freud became irreparable—a trying experience that occasioned two fainting spells on Freud's part, and more than a little anguish on Jung's. The formal parting came in 1913, with Jung also resigning from the International Psychoanalytic Association in 1914.

Jung now turned to the solitude of his home, a large and beautiful edifice of his own design in Küsnacht (a suburb of Zurich), where he was to live for the rest of his life. Here he spent the years from 1913 to 1919 in relative isolation, probing the depths of his own unconscious. He conversed with voices from within his psyche, including a female that he interpreted as his anima and a group of ghosts that he believed to be souls returning from the dead (Jung, 1961/1965, pp. 170–199). He observed many archetypes emerging into his consciousness, and felt that he was going through the process of individuation and discovering his self. He also suffered symptoms of emotional disturbance, suggesting that this experience was similar to the "creative illness" undergone by Freud (Ellenberger, 1970, p. 672). To avoid succumbing to psychosis, Jung forced himself to retain close ties with his family and patients and scrupulously fulfilled his commitments to the external world. He emerged from this period of introspection in 1919 with a firm belief in the universal validity of the constructs that he developed.

Jung was now widely admired as an unusually skilled psychotherapist, attracting patients from England and the United States. He was an active and vigorous man, over six feet tall and broad-shouldered, interested in sailing and mountain climbing as well as scholarly pursuits, a good listener and fine conversationalist, and a democratic man at ease with all types of people. Like Freud, however, Jung's personality was complex and multifaceted. Some saw him as wise, sensitive, and caring, whereas others viewed him as cantankerous, womanizing, sarcastic (even brutal), and highly critical and condescending toward others—especially those who failed to meet his high standards of scholarship. (See Brome, 1978; Stern, 1976/1977, pp. 181–182.)

In 1923, Jung built a primitive, towerlike house in nearby Bollingen, which served as a place for reflection and meditation. He also traveled extensively and observed a variety of peoples and cultures, including the Pueblo Indians of New Mexico and tribes in Tunis, Kenya, Uganda, and India. World War II sharpened his interest in world politics and mass psychoses and also brought charges that he was pro-Nazi and anti-Semitic, which ultimately proved to be unjustified. In 1944, Jung nearly died from a heart attack, had a vision of his soul leaving his body, and at first felt bitter disappointment upon returning to life. He also predicted that his doctor would die in his place, which actually happened shortly thereafter. Jung now became the "wise old man of Küsnacht," with people coming from all over the world to visit him. His many honors include the City of Zurich Award for literature and honorary doctorates from Harvard and Oxford, and his prolific writings fill some 20 volumes. Jung died in his Küsnacht home on June 6, 1961.

THE BASIC NATURE OF HUMAN BEINGS

Jung called his theory **analytical psychology**. Despite the similarity of names (and of some of the constructs), analytical psychology is substantially different from Freudian psychoanalysis.

Instincts and Psychic Energy

Libido and Value.   Jung agrees with Freud that humans are motivated by innate physiological urges (**instincts**), which he defines as inborn and regularly recurring modes of action and reaction (Jung, 1919/1971c, p. 54; 1921/1976, p. 376). He also concurs that mental activity is powered by psychic energy (**libido**). But Jung rejects Freud's emphasis on sexuality:

> I am no opponent of Freud's; I am merely presented in that light by his own short-sightedness and that of his pupils. No experienced psychiatrist can deny having met with dozens of cases whose psychology answers in all essentials to that of Freud. . . . I do not mean to deny the importance of sexuality in psychic life, though Freud stubbornly maintains that I do deny it. What I seek is to set bounds to the rampant terminology of sex which vitiates all discussion of the human psyche, and to put sexuality itself in its proper place. . . . Eros is certainly always and everywhere present. . . . but the psyche is not *just* [that] . . . [Therefore] I do not connect any specifically sexual definition with the word "libido." . . . [This term] is used by me in much wider sense. (Jung, 1928/1969a, p. 30; 1917/1972d, pp. 46, 52n.6; 1929/1975c, pp. 226, 230. See also Jung, 1911–1912; 1961/1965, pp. 168, 209.)

Jungian libido refers to the psychic energy that is invested in a mental event, regardless of the instinct(s) involved. The greater the amount of libido (**value**), the more the event is desired. Even a child readily begins to form different values, as by weighing whether the mother or the father is more preferred, what objects in the environment are liked or disliked more than others, and so forth. Jung's construct of "value" is therefore similar to Freud's concept of "cathexis," except that cathexes are invariably sexual (in one sense or another) although values need not be.

In an extremely competitive society like our own, some people may value power so highly that they direct most of their psychic energy toward professional success and become sexually impotent. Freud would take a dim view of such behavior, since (sexual) libido is denied its most satisfactory outlet. But Jungian libido includes energy from many sources, so discharging it in a quest for power is neither more nor less pathological than discharging it in sexual activity. "The shoe that fits one person pinches another; there is no universal recipe for living" (Jung, 1931/1933b, p. 41; see also Jung, cited by Evans, 1976, p. 46).

It is difficult to identify all of the human instincts, and to ascertain the exact nature of libido, because instinctual behavior is easily confused with our conscious motives. A partial list of instincts includes nutrition (hunger and thirst), sexuality, power, activity (including the love of change, the urge to travel, and play), becoming whole or one's true self (individuation), and creativity (Jung, 1917/1972d; 1919/1971c, p. 53; 1937). Jung also differs sharply with Freud by concluding that human beings have an inborn religious need, and the idea of God is absolutely necessary:

> Man positively needs general ideas and convictions that will give a meaning to his life and enable him to find a place for himself in the universe. He can stand the most incredible hardships when he is convinced that they make sense; he is crushed when, on top of all his misfortunes, he has to admit that he is taking part in a "tale told by an idiot." (Jung, 1964/1968, p. 76. See also Jung, 1957/1958b, p. 36; 1917/1972d, pp. 27, 71; 1929/1975c, p. 227.)

Complexes.   Psychic energy attracts constellations of related and emotionally charged ideas, or **complexes**. (See Jung, 1934a; 1938/1970a, pp. 19ff.) For example, the group of thoughts and feelings that concern "mother" cluster together to form the mother-complex, whereas the complex relating to "I" or "myself" constitutes the component of personality known as the ego.

The power of a complex to attract psychic material depends on the amount of libido at its disposal (its value). A weak mother-complex possesses little psychic energy (low value), includes only a small quantity of associated ideas, and has relatively little influence on behavior. Alternatively, a mother-complex may be so powerful that it dominates the psyche like a large electromagnet, attracting ideas that belong elsewhere. Such highly valued complexes can exert considerable control over one's personality. For example, a man ruled by his mother-complex may be unable to form satisfying heterosexual relationships because he is far more concerned about her wishes and opinions. He may also talk about his mother at length, make her the subject of various slips of the tongue, and constantly dream of mother-symbols. Complexes may be wholly or partly conscious, or they may be entirely within either of the two realms of the unconscious (personal and collective, to be discussed below). (See Jung, 1928/1969a, p. 11; Fordham, 1966, pp. 23–23.)

The Word Association Test.   Jung cautions that the construct of libido is useful only if quantitative differences in values can be estimated. Otherwise this approach can never become scientific and must be abandoned.

For a time Jung measured the power of a complex by using the **word association test**, wherein a list of single words is read one at a time and the subject must reply with the first word that comes to mind. (See Jung, 1910; 1928/1969a, p. 9; 1905/1974e). For example, the stimulus word "mother" might well evoke the response of "father." After the list has been completed, the participant goes through it once again and tries to recall the previous responses. If a series of related words in the list should cause such signs of disturbance as significant hes-itations, unusual responses (e.g. "mother"—"anger"), becoming pale or having a markedly increased pulse rate, or failing to recall the original responses during the retest, this would indicate the existence of an important (and probably troublesome) complex. Jung eventually abandoned this technique, however, concluding that

> anyone who wants to know the human psyche will learn next to nothing from experi-mental psychology. He would be better advised to abandon exact science, put away his scholar's gown, bid farewell to his study, and wander with human heart through the world. There, in the horrors of prisons, lunatic asylums and hospitals, in drab suburban pubs . . . he would reap richer stores of knowledge than textbooks a foot thick could give him, and he will know how to doctor the sick with real knowledge of the human soul. (Jung, 1912/1972f, pp. 246–247. See also Ellenberger, 1970, pp. 691–694; Jung, 1957/1958b, pp. 61–62.)

The Principle of Opposites

To Jung, life consists of "a complex of inexorable opposites": day and night, birth and death, happiness and misery, good and evil, introversion (inner-directedness) and extraversion (outer-directedness), consciousness and unconsciousness, thinking and feeling, love and hate, and so forth. Such contradictory ideas, emotions, and instincts exist simultaneously within the psyche, producing a tension that creates psychic energy and enables life to exist. "There is no energy unless there is a tension of opposites. . . . Life is born only of the spark of opposites" (Jung, 1917/1972d, pp. 53–54; see also Jung, 1964/1968, p. 75; 1928/1972e, p. 142).

When any extreme is primarily conscious, the unconscious **compensates** by emphasizing the other extreme. The psyche is for the most part a closed system, so libido withdrawn from one aspect of personality normally reappears somewhere else (the principle of **equivalence**). The psyche is also a self-regulating system wherein libido flows from a more intense to a less intense component, just as heat flows from a warmer to a colder body (the principle of **entropy**). Sooner or later, therefore, any overvalued component will yield psychic energy to its undervalued counterpart. Thus the (unconscious) opposite is likely to emerge in the course of time, a tendency Jung refers to as **enantiodromia**. For example, intense love may eventu-ally give way to profound hate, or a rational and skeptical scientist may turn to mysticism and the occult. Values are particularly likely to undergo radical changes as we grow from the morning of youth to the afternoon of middle age, with religious needs gaining ascendance while material and sexual urges become less important (Jung, 1917/1972d, pp. 74–75; see also Jung, 1928/1969a, pp. 18, 25; 1934/1974c, p. 101).

The principle of opposites and enantiodromia imply that no personality is ever truly one-sided. An individual who appears to be cold and lacking in sentiment will have warm and emotional characteristics, though these compensating tendencies may be unconscious and un-observable. "Extremes always arouse suspicion of their opposite" (Jung, 1917/1972d, p. 21). Furthermore, any extreme (introversion, extraversion, emotionality, rationality, or whatever) is harmful because it prevents the contradictory tendency from gaining satisfactory expression. The opposites must then waste libido in conflict with each other, as when the apparently unfeeling individual uses up psychic energy in a misguided attempt to suppress innate emotional instincts and repeal the principle of entropy.

In a mature and well-adjusted personality, the various opposites are united through some middle path. This concept is common in Eastern philosophies, as with the Taoist symbols of Yin and Yang; but it is a difficult one for our Western culture, which has never even devised a name for it. Jung proposes the term **transcendent function** for the process that unites the various opposing aspects of personality, particularly consciousness and unconsciousness, into a coherent middle ground. The transcendent function also provides us with guidelines for personal development that enable us to become our true selves—guidelines that cannot be found in the external world or opinions of other people. (See Jung, 1916/1971e, pp. 298, 300; 1921/1976, p. 449; 1928/1972e, p. 205.)

Teleology

Whereas Freud stressed the childhood determinants of personality (*causality*), Jung argues that behavior must also be understood in terms of its purpose or goal (*teleology*). Personality is shaped by our past and by our intentions and plans for the future:

> A man is only half understood when we know how everything in him came into being. . . . Life does not have only a yesterday, nor is it explained by reducing today to yesterday. Life has also a tomorrow, and today is understood only when we can add to our knowledge of what was yesterday the beginnings of tomorrow. (Jung, 1917/1972d, p. 46. See also Jung, 1921/1976, p. 431.)

Jung also rejects Freud's contention that psychic events can be reduced to physiological causes. Instincts have an organic aspect, but mental life follows "a specific law of its own which cannot be deduced from the known physical laws of nature" (Jung, 1947/1969b, p. 91; see also p. 90).

The Unconscious

Jung readily accepts the existence of parapraxes, even contributing some specimens to Freud's collection. (See Freud, 1901/1965c, p. 84; Jung, 1927/1971b, p. 28; 1916/1971e, p. 276; 1917/1972d, p. 115; 1928/1972e, pp. 177, 180.) In marked contrast to Freud, however, Jung concludes that the unconscious is relatively autonomous and speaks to us of its own accord. The messages and wishes that emanate from the unconscious are events that happen to us, and are *not* caused by any actions of our own.

Some people hear their unconscious as a voice within themselves and actually carry on a conversation with it, "as if a dialogue were taking place between two human beings with equal rights, each of whom gives the other credit for a valid argument." But most of us do not allow this invisible partner of ours to make itself heard, for "we are so in the habit of identifying ourselves with the thoughts that come to us that we invariably assume we have made them" (Jung, 1916/1971e, p. 297; 1928/1972e, p. 201).

Jung does agree with Freud about the importance of bringing unconscious material to consciousness, and about our reluctance to experience the dark side of our personality. So long as the unconscious strongly influences our behavior, we are not the masters of our own personality. Yet we turn away in fear from investigating our shadow-side, for it consists not just of minor weaknesses but of a "positively demonic dynamism" (Jung, 1917/1972d, p. 30; see also Jung, 1964/1968, p. 72; 1917/1972d, p. 26).

Unlike Freud, however, Jung does not regard the unconscious as a purely demoniacal monster. The unconscious includes wellsprings of creativity and sources of guidance that can suggest solutions when the conscious mind becomes hopelessly bogged down. "[The unconscious] has at its disposal . . . all those things which have been forgotten or over-looked, as well as the wisdom and experience of uncounted centuries" (Jung, 1917/1972d, p. 116; see also Jung, 1931/1933b, pp. 61–62; Jung, 1934/1974c, p. 100).

A substantial part of the unconscious is collective, and contains predispositions and guide-lines inherited from past generations. Only a smaller part results from repressions and other personal experiences unique to the individual.

THE STRUCTURE OF PERSONALITY

Jung's model of the psyche is considerably more chaotic than Freud's. Complexes originating in the unconscious can gravitate to consciousness and exert control over the personality for purposes of their own, and unconscious components may fuse together rather than remaining separate and distinct.

Consciousness

Consciousness in psychoanalytic theory is often depicted as the tip of a huge iceberg, with the un-conscious represented by the vast portion below the water. Similarly, consciousness in analytical psychology resembles a small island rising from the midst of a vast sea (Jung, 1928/1969d, p. 41).

The Ego.   The **ego** is a complex of conscious ideas that constitutes the center of aware-ness. It includes feelings of continuity and identity, and begins to develop at about the fourth year of life. Jung conceives of the ego as a relatively weak entity that is often at the mercy of more powerful forces, tossed like a shuttlecock between the demands of reality and those of the unconscious. However, it can consign threatening material to the (personal) unconscious by means of **repression**. (See Jung, 1951; 1928/1972e, p. 196; 1921/1976, p. 425; Jung, cited by Evans, 1976, pp. 60–61.)

The Persona.   We usually cannot afford to confront the world with our true feelings. Instead, we must fashion an outward appearance that will satisfy the demands of society. This protective façade is a complex of conscious material called the **persona**, after the masks worn by ancient actors to signify the roles that they played.

The persona helps us to deal with other people by indicating what may be expected from them. The doctor's professional role is validated in the patient's eyes by an appropriately reassuring manner, whereas the college professor is supposed to display a persona of expert-ise. If the doctor or professor violates these expectations by acting anxious and uncertain, this will provoke suspicion and resistance. In general, people with underdeveloped personas appear to be incompetent, boring, tactless, eternally misunderstood, and blind to the realities of the world. (See Jung, 1928/1972e, pp. 198–199; Jung, cited by Evans, 1976, p. 79.)

The persona may instead become overdeveloped and intrude on the ego. For example, a mediocre doctor with false visions of greatness may present a pompous persona of excellence. In such instances, the ego misguidedly identifies with the persona and becomes **inflated** with a sense of excess importance:

> *L'état c'est moi* is the motto for such people. . . . In vain would one look for a personal-ity behind the husk. Underneath all the padding one would find a very pitiable little crea-ture. That is why the office—or whatever this outer husk may be—is so attractive: it offers easy compensation for personal deficiencies. (Jung, 1928/1972e, pp. 143, 145; see also p. 156 n.1.)

As would be expected from the principle of opposites, this conscious arrogance is compensated for by unconscious feelings of inferiority that cannot find satisfactory expression. The conflict between these extreme aspects of personality wastes libido that could better be used in the pursuit of healthy activities.

The Personal Unconscious

The **personal unconscious** begins to form at birth, and contains material that is no longer (or is not yet) at the level of awareness. Some memories are simply forgotten because they are no longer important, many of which can easily be recalled to consciousness (such as the contents of last night's dinner). Other material in the personal unconscious is repressed because of its painful nature. For example, a secretary who is jealous of one of her employer's associates may habitually "forget" to invite this individual to meetings and never admit—not even to herself—the true reason for her omission. (See Jung, 1964/1968, p. 22; 1927/1971b, p. 38; 1917/1972d, pp. 64ff, 77; 1928/1972e, pp. 135ff.)

Other aspects of mental life remain in the personal unconscious because they lack sufficient psychic energy to enter awareness. We often see, hear, taste, and smell things without noticing them because the sensory impressions are not strong enough ("subliminal perceptions"). A professor who was walking in the country with a student noticed that his thoughts were invaded by memories of his early childhood. He could not account for this distraction until he retraced his steps and realized that they had recently passed some geese, whose odor provided a subliminal reminder of a farm where he had lived as a youth. Similarly, a young woman once developed a blinding headache. Without consciously noticing it, she had heard the foghorn of a distant ship, which reminded her of an unhappy parting with a loved one (Jung, 1964/1968, pp. 21–22).

The Shadow. The **shadow** is the primitive and unwelcome side of personality that derives from our animal forebears. (See Jung, 1951.) It consists of material that is repressed into the personal unconscious because it is shameful and unpleasant, and it plays a compensatory role to the more positive persona and ego. The shadow's power is evident when a person is overcome by violent and uncontrollable rage, a theme exemplified in literature by the dangerous Mr. Hyde underlying the implacable Dr. Jekyll.

As with any construct in analytical psychology, the shadow must be at least somewhat beneficial in order to have survived generations of evolution. Like the Freudian id, it provides us with vitality and strength. "Too much of the animal distorts the civilized man, [but] too much civilization makes sick animals" (Jung, 1917/1972d, p. 28). Just as it is impossible to have sunshine without shadow, the light of consciousness must always be accompanied by the dark side of our personality. Rather than turn away in disgust from our shadow, we must open this Pandora's box and accept its contents. Jung does not regard repression as actively maintained, so a person who honestly wishes to examine the shadow can do so, but this is a highly threatening task that most prefer to avoid.

The shadow, like all that is unconscious, is **projected** onto other people. We normally experience it in this indirect fashion, with the characteristics that we find most objectionable in others very likely to be those aspects of ourselves that we most dislike. Thus another unfortunate effect of denying our shadow is that the resulting deeper repressions will trigger more powerful projections of our undesirable characteristics, producing greater dislike of other people—and possibly, culminating in the sick system of social relationships that constitutes neurosis. (See Jung, 1931/1933c, p. 142; 1935b, p. 24; 1951; 1957/1958b, pp. 109–114; 1964/1968, p. 73; 1917/1972d, p. 26.)

The Collective Unconscious

Although the personal unconscious and the ego originate after birth, the newborn infant is far from a *tabula rasa*. Its psyche is a complicated, clearly defined entity consisting of the **collective** (or **transpersonal**) **unconscious**, a storehouse of archaic remnants ("primordial images" or **archetypes**) inherited from our ancestral past. (See Jung, 1938/1970a, p. 11; 1919/1971c, p. 52; 1917/1972d, pp. 65–66; 1921/1976, p. 376.)

Characteristics of Archetypes.   Archetypes result from the "deposits of the constantly repeated experiences of humanity" (Jung, 1917/1972d, p. 69). They differ from instincts in that they are modes of perception, rather than of action and reaction. That is, archetypes predispose us to perceive the world in certain ways.

Archetypes resemble poorly formed channels in the psyche that may predispose libido to follow a certain course, but are too roughly hewn to ensure that it will actually do so. They are only potentialities, *not* specific memories or facts, and will remain dormant unless strengthened by appropriate experiences. "I do not by any means assert the inheritance of ideas, but only of the possibility of such ideas, which is something very different" (Jung, 1917/1972d, p. 65; see also Jung, 1938/1970a, pp. 13–17). Everyone inherits a tendency to fear objects that our ancestors found to be potentially dangerous, such as snakes, so it will be easier to learn to fear snakes than to fear flowers. But an individual who grows up enjoying only pleasant encounters with snakes will not be greatly affected by this archetype.

The Persona and Shadow Archetypes.   The persona and shadow have existed in the human psyche throughout countless generations. This is reflected by corresponding archetypes in the collective unconscious, so that we all inherit tendencies to form these components of personality.

The Anima and Animus.   All males and females possess some characteristics of the opposite sex. Man's unconscious feminine disposition is due to the archetype known as the **anima**, whereas the male archetype in women is called the **animus**. The anima and animus develop from generations of exposure to the opposite sex, and imbue each sex with an innate understanding of the other. "The whole nature of man presupposes woman, both physically and spiritually. His system is tuned in to woman from the start" (Jung, 1928/1972e, p. 190; see also Jung, 1925/1971d; 1951).

Typically, the feminine anima compensates for the outward masculine persona of power. Trying to deny this aspect of personality will result in a one-sided and conflicted individual, as when a man who prides himself on an overly virile persona is beset by feelings of weakness and moodiness. The masculine animus, on the other hand, produces unshakable and arbitrary convictions. The woman who suppresses her animus in a misguided attempt to appear extremely feminine will be troubled by spells of intense stubbornness (Jung, 1928/1972e, p. 206). The well-adjusted personality integrates the male and female attributes by means of the transcendent function, allowing both to find satisfactory expression.

Other Archetypes.   Other archetypes include the wise old man, the mother, the father, the child, the parents, the wife, the husband, God, the hero, various animals, energy, the self (the ultimate goal of personality development), the trickster, rebirth or reincarnation, the spirit, the prophet, the disciple, and numerous archetypes representative of situations. (See Jung, 1934b; 1940; 1938/1970a; 1940/1970b; 1945/1970c; 1954/1970d; 1917/1972d, pp. 68, 95, 110; 1928/1972e, pp. 171, 178, 190.) However, Jung advises against trying to understand the

CAPSULE SUMMARY
Some Important Jungian Terminology (I)

Analytical psychology	The name given by Jung to his theory of personality.
Anima	The female archetype in man. Predisposes man to understand the nature of woman, is sentimental, and compensates for the powerful male persona.
Animus	The male archetype in woman. Predisposes woman to understand the nature of man, is powerful, and compensates for the sentimental female persona.
Archetype	A predisposition to perceive the world in certain ways that is inherited from past generations; *not* a specific idea or belief. Is much the same across different cultures (a "universal thought form") and is in the collective unconscious: Archetypes include the anima, animus, shadow, persona, mother, father, and many others.
Compensation	The tendency of one part of personality to balance or adjust for another part. For example, the unconscious will compensate for pronounced conscious introversion by emphasizing the quality of extraversion.
Complex	A constellation of related and emotionally charged thoughts, feelings, or ideas. A complex varies in strength according to the amount of psychic energy at its disposal (its value), and may be conscious or unconscious (or both).
Enantiodromia	The tendency of any characteristic to eventually turn into its opposite.
Inflation	Expansion of the ego beyond its proper limits, resulting in feelings of exaggerated self-importance. Usually compensated for by unconscious feelings of inferiority.
Instinct	An inborn physiological urge. The instincts include hunger, thirst, sexuality, power, individuation, activity, creativity, morality, and religious needs.
Libido	A synonym for psychic energy; *not* necessarily sexual.
Numinosum	A profoundly moving experience with spiritual, mystical, and religious aspects.
Principle of entropy	The tendency for psychic energy to flow from a more highly valued to a less highly valued part of personality, just as heat flows from a warmer to a colder body.
Principle of equivalence	The tendency for psychic energy that is withdrawn from one part of personality to reappear elsewhere within the psyche. Thus the psyche is for the most part a closed system.
Principle of opposites	The belief that personality consists of many contradictory ideas, emotions, and instincts, and the spark of life is created from the tension between these extremes.
Projection	Unconsciously attributing one's own threatening impulses, emotions, or beliefs to other people or things. Similar to Freud's use of the term.
Psychic energy	The "fuel" that powers all mental activity; an unobservable, abstract construct.
Repression	Unconsciously eliminating threatening material from consciousness and relegating it to the personal unconscious. *Not* actively maintained (as in Freudian theory), so repressed material may be recovered fairly easily.
Symbol	A representation of something vague and unknown, such as an archetype.
Transcendent function	A process that joins various opposing forces into a coherent middle ground, and furthers the course of individuation by providing personal lines of development that could not be reached by adhering to collective norms.
Value	The amount of psychic energy that is invested in a mental event. The greater the value, the more the event is preferred or desired.
Word association test	A procedure for determining the strength of a complex. The tester reads a list of words, one at a time, and the respondent answers with the first word that comes to mind. The stronger the complex, the more likely are unusual responses, hesitations, and physiological changes.

CAPSULE SUMMARY
The Structure of Personality (Jung)

	PERSONAL	*COLLECTIVE*
CONSCIOUS	*The ego*: a complex of conscious ideas that constitutes the center of awareness, and provides feelings of identity and continuity. Begins to develop at about the fourth year of life.	*The persona*: the outward face of personality; a protective façade that conceals one's true inner nature in order to meet the demands of society. Facilitates contacts with people by indicating what may be expected from them.
UNCONSCIOUS	*The personal unconscious*: includes material that has been forgotten, repressed, or perceived subliminally. The layer between the collective unconscious and consciousness; begins to form at birth. Includes the primitive, guilt-laden, unwelcome aspects of personality (the *shadow*).	*The collective (transpersonal) unconscious*: a storehouse of inherited predispositions to perceive the world in certain ways (*archetypes*); thus, present at birth. The deepest, most inaccessible layer of the psyche. Includes the persona and shadow archetypes (among others), which facilitate the development of the corresponding representations elsewhere in the personality.

nature of archetypes by memorizing such a list. Archetypes are autonomous events that come upon us like fate, and they must be experienced firsthand in order to be understood.

Unfortunately, Jung has no simple remedy for those who remain skeptical about analytical psychology because they have never enjoyed such enriching encounters with the collective unconscious. "You can only say that you have never had such an experience, and your opponent will say: 'Sorry, I have.' And there your discussion will come to an end" (Jung, 1938, p. 113). He does recommend learning more about one's personal unconscious, which will weaken the layer above the collective unconscious and make archetypal images more accessible to consciousness.

Archetypal Symbols.   We never become aware of archetypes themselves, which always remain within the inaccessible collective unconscious. But the collective unconscious is like the base of a volcano that extends to the core of personality and occasionally erupts, shooting archetypal images or **symbols** up to the surface.

Unlike such common signs as words and pictures, which merely denote the objects to which they are attached, archetypal symbols imply something that is hidden from us. Since they are produced entirely by the unconscious, they have a **numinous** or fascinating quality that clearly identifies them as something out of the ordinary. (See Jaffé, 1971/1975, p. 16; Jung, 1964/1968, pp. 3, 41; 1917/1972d, p. 70; Progoff, 1953/1973, p. 56.)

Symbols derived from the same archetype may differ in form and content, especially to the extent that they are influenced by racial, cultural, and even family differences. "There is also a collective psyche limited to race, tribe, and family over and above the 'universal' collective psyche" (Jung, 1928/1972e, pp. 147–148).[2] But such symbols all point back to one basic form, the underlying universal archetype. For this reason, the unconscious processes of widely separated races show a remarkable correspondence. The archetype of the universal creative mother is expressed in such varied cultural myths as Mother Nature, Greek and Roman goddesses, and the "Grandmother" of Native Americans. Jung was once advised by a psychotic patient that the sun possesses a phallus, whose movement creates the wind; and when he later encountered the same unusual symbology in an ancient Greek papyrus, which the patient could never have seen, he attributed the similar imagery to an unconscious universal archetype. He also cites the production of archetypal symbols by children as further support for his theory, since it often seems clear that they could not have had access to the relevant facts and must therefore have produced the images from their own psyche. (See Jung, 1964/1968, p. 61; 1938/1970a; 1927/1971b, pp. 36–37; 1917/1972d, p. 96; Progoff, 1953/1973, pp. 59–60.)

The collective unconscious is widely regarded as an extremely controversial construct. Yet even Freud, a staunch opponent of analytical psychology, accepted the idea of an "*archaic heritage* that a child brings with him into the world, before any experiences of his own, influenced by the experiences of his ancestors" (Freud, 1940/1969a, p. 24; see also Freud, 1916–1917/1966, p. 371; 1939; Rieff, 1959/1961, p. 220).

THE DEVELOPMENT OF PERSONALITY

Individuation and the Self

Although Jung does not posit specific stages of development, he does draw a sharp distinction between youth and middle age.

During childhood the ego, the personal unconscious, and other parts of personality gradually develop into separate entities. This process continues through puberty, which is when the sexual drive begins, and into young adulthood. Our early years are like the rising sun, which "gains continually in strength until it reaches the zenith-heat of high noon. Then comes the enantiodromia: the steady forward movement no longer denotes an increase, but a decrease, in strength" (Jung, 1917/1972d, p. 74; see also Jung, 1930–1931/1971a, pp. 14–15; 1913/1975a, pp. 35, 83). This "second puberty" occurs at about age 35 to 40 and serves as the gateway to the latter half of life, which is a time of considerable importance:

> A human being would certainly not grow to be seventy or eighty years old if this longevity had no meaning for the species. The afternoon of human life must also have a significance of its own, and cannot be merely a pitiful appendage to life's morning. (Jung, 1930–1931/1971a, p. 17.)

Middle age is highlighted by a shift from materialism, sexuality, and propagation to more spiritual and cultural values; by radical reversals in one's strongest convictions and emotions, often leading to changes of profession, divorces, and religious upheavals; and by the reconciliation of the various opposing forces of personality through the transcendent function. This gradual, lifelong unfolding of one's inherent and unique personality is known as **individuation**.

Individuation is a difficult and complicated journey of self-discovery, and many hazards along the way are likely to prevent a successful outcome. First of all, the formidable and often terrifying contents of the shadow must be brought to consciousness and experienced both intellectually and

---

[2]And therefore "it is a quite unpardonable mistake to accept the conclusions of a Jewish psychology [i.e., Freud's] as generally valid" (Jung, 1928/1972e, p. 152 n. 8).

emotionally. The persona must also be torn down, for this collectively oriented façade impedes true individuality. The libido freed by the destruction of these superstructures gravitates downward to the collective unconscious, and this additional energy enables archetypal symbols to rise to consciousness. Among these are the anima (animus), wise old man, and great mother. This creates yet another pitfall: These alluring archetypes may prove to be overwhelming, causing the individual to succumb to megalomanic beliefs of omniscience and omnipotence. (See Jung, 1928/1972e, pp. 227–241.)

If the process of individuation is able to avoid these pitfalls, the individual's increased knowledge of the collective unconscious liberates substantial amounts of libido that had been associated with the aforementioned archetypes. This libido comes to rest in a twilight zone between consciousness and unconsciousness and forms an entity known as the **self**, which represents the ultimate goal of personality development and serves as the new center of personality.

> The . . . purpose of [individuation] is the realization, in all its aspects, of the personality originally hidden away in the embryonic germplasm . . . Individuation means becoming an "in-dividual," and, insofar as "individuality" embraces our innermost, last, and incomparable uniqueness, it also implies becoming one's own self. We could therefore translate individuation as "coming to selfhood" or "self-realization." (Jung, 1917/1972d, p. 110; 1928/1972e, p. 173. See also Jung, 1929; Fordham, 1966, pp. 49–62, 77; Progoff, 1953/1973, pp. 124–132.)

CAPSULE SUMMARY
Psychological Types (Jung)

| Function | Attitude | |
	Extraversion	Introversion
Thinking	Tries to understand and interpret aspects of the external world. Is logical, practical, objective. May be a scientist (Darwin, Einstein) or public prosecutor. Unconscious emphasizes introversion and feeling.	Tries to understand and interpret own ideas. May be a philosopher, theorist like Freud, or absent-minded professor. Unconscious emphasizes extraversion and feeling.
Feeling	Makes judgments that conform to external standards. Conservative; enjoys popular trends. May seem emotional, flighty, capricious. Unconscious emphasizes introversion and thinking.	Makes judgments based on own standards. Nonconformist; views are often contrary to public opinion. May seem cold, reserved, inscrutable. Unconscious emphasizes extraversion and thinking.
Sensation	Interested in perceiving and experiencing the external world. Realistic, unimaginative; often sensual, pleasure-seeking. Unconscious emphasizes introversion and intuition.	Interested in perceiving and experiencing own inner self. May be modern artist or musician whose work is often misunderstood. Unconscious emphasizes extraversion and intuition.
Intuition	Seeks new possibilities in the external world. Easily bored; often unable to persist in one job or activity. May be a speculator or entrepreneur. Unconscious emphasizes introversion and sensation.	Seeks new possibilities within own inner self. May develop brilliant new insights or be a mystical dreamer, self-styled prophet, or "misunderstood genius." Unconscious emphasizes extraversion and sensation.

The emergence of the self is signaled by archetypal symbols that express wholeness, completeness, and perfection. Such a symbol often takes the form of a circle (**mandala**, after the Sanskrit word for "magic circle") and may appear in dreams, drawings, and paintings. (See Fordham, 1966, pp. 65–68; Jung, 1955/1972a; 1934/1972b; 1950/1972c.)

Although the self lies between consciousness and the unconscious, it is beyond our awareness. Every personality possesses the innate tendency to individuate and develop selfhood, but this ideal is rarely if ever achieved to the fullest. For some people, it remains totally out of reach; so they resort to imitating peers or eminent people, a faulty and ineffective way of seeking individuation. "To find out what is truly individual in ourselves, profound reflection is needed; and suddenly we realize how uncommonly difficult the discovery of individuality is" (Jung, 1928/1972e, p. 155).

Progression and Regression

Libido normally proceeds in a forward direction, furthering the development of personality. But if this **progression** is blocked by frustrations in the external world, or by the internal barrier of repression, libido turns back to early memories and archetypal images that reside within the depths of the psyche (**regression**).

In contrast to Freud, who conceptualized regression as a return to childhood fixations, Jung regards the backward flow of libido as a potentially creative process that can awaken neglected aspects of one's personality. "The patient's regressive tendency . . . is not just a relapse into infantilism, but a genuine attempt to get at something necessary. . . . His development was one-sided; it left important items of character and personality behind, and thus it ended in failure. That is why he has to go back" (Jung, 1930, pp. 32–33; see also Jung, 1935a, pp. 8–9). However, regression does involve one danger: The unconscious may use the additional psychic energy to overwhelm consciousness, producing neurotic or even psychotic behavior.

Character Typology: Functions and Attitudes

Jung attributes individual differences in personality to two processes: the typical way in which we perceive internal and external stimuli, and the characteristic direction (inward or outward) of libido movement. (See Jung, 1937; 1921/1976.)

There are four ways of perceiving stimuli, or **functions**: merely establishing what is there (**sensation**), interpreting and understanding the meaning of what we perceive (**thinking**), evaluating how desirable or pleasant it is (**feeling**), and forming apparently inexplicable hunches or conclusions without using any of the other functions (**intuition**). "*Sensation* tells you that something exists; *thinking* tells you what it is; *feeling* tells you whether it is agreeable or not; and *intuition* tells you whence it comes and where it is going" (Jung, 1964/1968, p. 49). Thinking and feeling are opposites, and are called "rational" functions because they involve acts of cognition and judgment. Sensation and intuition also oppose each other, and these more reflexive functions are referred to as "irrational" (meaning nonrational, *not* pathological). Although everyone has the ability to use all four functions, there is an inborn tendency for one of them to become dominant over the others.

There are also two directions of libido movement, or **attitudes**. The outward turning of libido toward the external world is known as **extraversion**, whereas the inward flow of libido toward the depths of the psyche is referred to as **introversion**. Extraverts are outgoing, venture forth with careless confidence into the unknown, and are particularly interested in people and events in the external world. Introversion is reflected by a keen interest in one's own psyche, and often preferring to be alone. (See Jung, 1917/1972d, p. 44; 1921/1976, p. 330.) As with the functions, there is an innate tendency for one attitude to become dominant over the other; and the dominant attitude combines with the dominant function to form the conscious personality. This yields a total of eight possible character types, which are shown in the Capsule Summary on page 70.

Jung's typology is often misunderstood and oversimplified. There are no pure introverts or extraverts, nor can people be classified into a mere eight categories. As with intelligence or mental health, the extent to which a person is introverted or extraverted, thinking or feeling, and sensing or intuitive is a matter of degree. Also, the unconscious compensates for the dominant attitude and function by emphasizing the opposite tendencies, whereas the remaining two functions waver between consciousness and the unconscious.

For example, a person with a dominant thinking function will often try to analyze information in a logical and objective way. If introversion is the dominant attitude, most of these thoughts will focus on ideas within the psyche (as with Freud, or an absent-minded professor). If extraversion is dominant, thinking will be directed toward the external world (as with a scientist like Darwin or Einstein). In either case, the opposite function (feeling) and the opposite attitude are repressed into the personal unconscious. The remaining two functions (here, sensation and intuition) may serve as conscious or unconscious auxiliaries, as when the scientist's attempts to think out new research hypotheses are aided by intuitive hunches. Thus the typological model for the extraverted-thinking type looks like this:

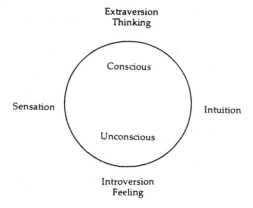

Extraversion
Thinking

Conscious

Sensation   Intuition

Unconscious

Introversion
Feeling

Similar reasoning applies to the remaining categories. (See also Progoff, 1953/1973, p. 90.) For example, an introverted–sensation type is unconsciously extraverted and intuitive, and may use thinking or feeling as conscious or unconscious auxiliaries:

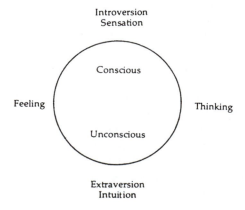

Introversion
Sensation

Conscious

Feeling   Thinking

Unconscious

Extraversion
Intuition

The function and attitude to which one is innately predisposed must become dominant in order for personality development to be successful. Since America strongly favors extraversion, parents and teachers in our society are likely to treat an introverted child with excessive concern and criticism. But extraversion and introversion are equally normal and healthy, and misguided attempts to alter a person's inherent nature will lead to later neurosis. (See Jung, 1921/1976, pp. 332, 375; Jung, cited by Evans, 1976, p. 94.)

Maladjustment will also occur if the inferior attitude and functions are repressed too strongly. A natural extravert may ignore inner warnings, become a "workaholic," and develop an ulcer or heart attack. A natural introvert may be blind to the demands of the external world, behave ineptly in social situations, and suffer painful rejections. Or a person who is inherently sensing or intuitive may be unable to deal with a problem that requires thinking, and make serious errors. Such behaviors are ineffective and self-defeating because they are governed by functions and attitudes that have not been sufficiently developed.

The remedy for an overly one-sided personality is a regression to the unconscious, possibly with the aid of Jungian psychotherapy. Ideally, this will enable any undervalued function or attitude to emerge in its own right. Some people do develop a second or even a third function, or strike a balance between introversion and extraversion. But individuation is a difficult process that is never completely achieved, and very few people are able to integrate all of the attitudes and functions into a coherent whole and allow each one its due expression.

FURTHER APPLICATIONS OF ANALYTICAL PSYCHOLOGY

Dream Interpretation

In analytical psychology, as in psychoanalysis, dreams provide important clues about the hidden realm of the unconscious. However, Jung's approach to dream interpretation differs significantly from that of Freud.

Personal and Collective Dreams. Dreams about one's family, friends, and everyday life arise from the personal unconscious. In contrast, the collective unconscious triggers archetypal dreams that are numinous and fascinating. Jung relates that this distinction is prominent among the Elgonyi natives of central Africa: A "little" (i.e., personal) dream is regarded as unimportant, but anyone who has a "big" (i.e., collective) dream summons the whole tribe and tells it to everybody (Jung, 1928/1972e, p. 178; see also Fordham, 1966, pp. 97ff).

The Purpose of Dreams. To Jung, a dream can serve many purposes other than wish-fulfillment. It may express a person's fears, mirror actual situations in the dreamer's life, anticipate the future (as by providing a warning of impending trouble), propose solutions to the dreamer's problems, or even result from telepathy. (See Ellenberger, 1970, p. 716; Jung, 1964/1968, p. 34; 1916/1974a.)

The majority of dreams are compensatory, and aim at restoring a state of psychological balance. Jung once dreamed of bending his head far back in order to see a patient in a high tower. He concluded that he must be looking down on her in reality, and this insight enabled a previously unsuccessful treatment to progress at a rapid pace. Similarly, a man with an inflated ego may dream of himself as a drunken tramp rolling in a ditch, or a person suffering from feelings of inferiority may dream of encountering such famous personages as Napoleon or

Alexander the Great (Jung, 1961/1965, p. 133; 1964/1968, pp. 51–52; 1917/1972d, p. 112; 1928/1972e, p. 179; 1934/1974c, pp. 102–103). Although it is possible to detect wish-fulfillments in some of these dreams, the primary goal is to compensate for a one-sided aspect of personality by emphasizing the opposite view.

Dream Symbols.   Whereas Freud believed that dream symbols disguise unpleasant truths in order to preserve sleep, Jung regards the manifest content as the true dream. The language of dreams is confusing only because it reflects the natural illogic of the unconscious:

> To me dreams are a part of nature, which harbors no intention to deceive, but expresses something as best it can. . . . What [Freud] called "disguise" is actually the shape all impulses naturally take in the unconscious. (Jung, 1961/1965, p. 161; 1964/1968, p. 53. See also Jung, 1930, p. 32; 1917/1972d, p. 100.)

Jung agrees that some dream symbols have sexual connotations, but emphasizes that there are many other possibilities. Inserting a key in a lock might symbolize sexual intercourse, or it could describe the hopeful opening of new possibilities in one's life. A passive female patient's dream of her energetic father's sword could be caused by childhood sexual fantasies and unconscious wishes for his "weapon" (phallus), or it might signify the need for some new source of strength that will enable her future dealings with the world to be more aggressive and effective.

According to Jung, every dream symbol has at least two meanings. Also, the identical symbol can mean different things to different people. Two of Jung's patients dreamed of leading a group of horsemen across a wide field and barely managing to jump a ditch, into which the other riders fell. To the first patient, a cautious introvert, the dream indicated that he ought to take more chances. The second patient was a pronounced extravert, and his dream warned that he was far too daring. Thus accurate interpretation requires the active cooperation of the dreamer, and "it is plain foolishness to believe in ready-made systematic guides to dream interpretation, as if one could simply buy a reference book and look up a particular symbol" (Jung, 1964/1968, p. 38). Instead Jung favors Freud's technique of free association, though he prefers to restrict the dreamer's train of thought to the context of the dream. (See Fordham, 1966, pp. 97–98; Jung, 1964/1968, pp. 12–15, 18, 42, 56; 1916/1971e, pp. 281–282; 1917/1972d, p. 25; 1945/1974b, pp. 69, 71–72; 1913/1975b, pp. 155–156).

Dream Series.   When possible, Jung bases his interpretations on a series of dreams from the same individual. Important themes and issues tend to recur in various dreams, so this approach facilitates accurate interpretations by providing more substantial data. The use of dream series, and the nondeceptive nature of dream symbols, have been accepted by some modern theorists in preference to Freudian theory (e.g., C. S. Hall, 1966).

Psychopathology

Jung shares Freud's view of psychopathology as a difference in degree, rather than in kind. The ideal of normality is rarely reached, and virtually every personality is at least somewhat one-sided:

> Neurotic phenomena are by no means the products exclusively of disease. They are in fact no more than pathological exaggerations of normal occurrences; it is only because they are exaggerations that they are more obvious than their normal counterparts. . . . At bottom we discover nothing new and unknown in the mentally ill; rather, we encounter the substratum of our own natures. (Jung, 1961/1965, p. 127; 1964/1968, p. 20. See also Jung, 1917/1972d, p. 55; 1928/1972e, pp. 143–144.)

CAPSULE SUMMARY
Some Important Jungian Terminology (II)

Attitude	Introversion or extraversion.
Extraversion	An outward flow of libido toward the external world. Extraverts are outgoing, venture forth with confidence into the unknown, and are particularly interested in people and events in the environment.
Function	A way of experiencing internal or external stimuli. *Sensation* establishes that something is there, *thinking* interprets what is perceived, *feeling* determines the desirability of what is perceived, and *intuition* forms hunches or conclusions without the aid of the other functions. Thinking and feeling are "rational" functions, whereas sensation and intuition are "irrational" functions.
Individuation	The unfolding of one's inherent and unique personality, aided by the transcendent function and leading to the formation of the self. A lifelong task that is rarely if ever completed.
Introversion	An inward flow of libido toward the depths of the psyche. Characterized by a keen interest in one's own inner world and often preferring to be alone.
Mandala	A circular symbol of wholeness and perfection, and therefore of the self.
Progression	A forward movement of libido, favoring personal growth and development.
Regression	A backward movement of libido to earlier memories or periods of development. Contrary to Freudian theory, Jungian regression may be a creative process that liberates neglected aspects of personality.
Self	The new center of personality that results from individuation, unifies the various opposites, and lies between consciousness and the unconscious. There is also a self archetype within the collective unconscious.
Synchronicity	A relationship between events that is based on meaningful coincidence, rather than cause and effect.

Causes of Neurosis.   The collective unconscious includes an innate tendency to be more introverted or extraverted, and to emphasize one of the four functions. For personality development to be successful, the favored attitude and function must become dominant, and they must be brought into harmony with the inferior opposites.

If this goal is frustrated by the external world, or if one misguidedly tries to make some other function or attitude dominant, the unconscious will come into conflict with consciousness. This inner cleavage may eventually become so severe as to constitute a neurosis, with the attempt to deny one's true nature causing the normal intrapsychic polarities to erupt into open warfare. Neurotic conflicts may occur between various components of personality, such as the ego versus the shadow, the dominant versus the inferior function or attitude, the persona versus the anima or animus, or the persona versus the shadow. (See Jung, 1932/1933d, p. 236; 1935a, p. 20; 1917/1972d, p. 19.)

Suppose that an inherently introverted child is pressured into becoming a pronounced extravert by the parents (or by society). This unwelcome external influence disrupts the individuation process, and causes the child's psyche to become a house divided against itself. The conscious mind now seeks conformity with the parental dictates by emphasizing extraverted behavior, and by banishing introverted wishes from awareness. But the introverted tendencies, which must remain within the closed system of the psyche, flourish within the unconscious and strongly oppose the conscious processes. Or neurosis might be caused by overemphasizing the inherent introversion and trying to exclude all traces of extraversion, for not even the inferior aspects of personality can or should be totally eliminated.

In contrast to psychoanalysis, analytical psychology prefers to concentrate on the neurotic's present attempts to maintain a pathological state of one-sidedness. To Jung, dwelling upon childhood memories is an evasion that may well do more harm than good:

> *The cause of the pathogenic conflict lies mainly in the present moment. . . .* We ask: . . . What is the task which the patient does not want to fulfill? What difficulty is he trying to avoid? . . . The task of psychotherapy is to correct the conscious attitude and not go chasing after infantile memories. Naturally you cannot do the one without paying attention to the other, but the main emphasis should be upon the attitude of the patient. There are extremely practical reasons for this, because there is scarcely a neurotic who does not love to dwell upon the evils of the past and to wallow in self-commiserating memories. Very often his neurosis consists precisely in his hanging back and constantly excusing himself on account of the past. (Jung, 1930, pp. 31–32; 1913/1975a, pp. 84, 100.)

Neurotic Symptoms.   The libido involved in neurotic conflicts cannot move in a forward direction, since the normal course of progression is disrupted by the inner war. Instead, the libido regresses toward the unconscious. This regression is not necessarily harmful (as we have seen), since it may help to awaken the neglected and undervalued aspects of personality. But it is all too easy to maintain the one-sided behaviors that caused the neurotic conflict, and to ignore the warnings sent by the collective unconscious in the form of dream symbols. (For example, a person who overuses the thinking function may keep trying to reason out solutions to his or her problems, instead of allowing the undervalued feeling function to emerge.) The regressing libido, deprived of a satisfactory outlet, will then constellate powerful unconscious complexes that express themselves in the form of neurotic symptoms. Thus a man who has stifled his anima in order to emphasize a persona of power and authority may develop a complex that indicates a damaged anima, project this complex onto women in general, and be attracted only to women who are physically or mentally disabled. (See Jung, 1934c.)

The neuroses of young adults usually concern power and sexuality. In marked contrast to Freud, however, Jung concludes that the neurotic symptoms of older adults often result from the denial of their inherent religious needs. Some two thirds of the patients seeking his services were past middle age, and the primary problem facing each one was that of finding a religious outlook on life. Only those who succeeded in this quest were truly healed (Jung, 1931/1933b, p. 61; 1932/1933d, p. 229). Jung also takes exception to Freud's literal interpretation of incestuous wishes, arguing instead that these are symbolic desires to achieve psychological rebirth and bring forth the undervalued aspects of personality from one's unconscious. Finally, Jung is not enthusiastic about using such terms as phobia and hysteria. He prefers to stress the need for understanding patients, rather than merely assigning them to preconceived categories. (See Jung, 1961/1965, p. 124; 1964/1968, p. 82; 1913/1975a, p. 86; Progoff, 1953/1973, pp. 110–114.)

Psychosis.   Unlike the neurotic, the psychotic is totally inundated by archetypal images. (See Jung, 1907/1974f; 1939/1974g, p. 160.) This gives psychosis a numinous and spellbinding quality, similar to a "big" dream. For this reason, exploring the depths of one's psyche requires a firm attachment to reality (as through work or marriage) and the guidance of a competent psychotherapist. If disinterring a neurosis will allow a latent psychosis to emerge, it may well be best to leave the neurosis alone.

> We are greatly mistaken if we think that [analyzing] the unconscious is something harmless that could be made into an object of entertainment, a parlor game. . . . Something

deeply buried and invisible may thereby be set in motion . . . as if one were digging an artesian well and ran the risk of stumbling on a volcano. (Jung, 1917/1972d, p. 114; see also Jung, 1961/1965, pp. 135–136.)

Jung's early psychological training included considerable experience with schizophrenia (then called "dementia praecox"). He soon recognized that psychotic symptoms, like those of neurosis, have important meanings. One of his schizophrenic patients who made the apparently senseless statement, "I am the Lorelei," was referring to the poor prognosis of her case. Her doctors often discussed her symptoms with the words "I know not what it means," which is the first line of Heine's famous poem "Die Lorelei" (Jung, 1961/1965, p. 126; 1907/1974f, p. 116). Jung was the first to apply psychoanalytic concepts to schizophrenia, and to recognize the possibility of psychosomatic mechanisms in this disorder (Arieti, 1974, pp. 22–25).

Psychotherapy

Jung's early attempts to explore the unconscious involved the use of hypnosis, but this technique soon proved to be unsatisfactory. At a demonstration before a group of 20 students, he informed a middle-aged woman patient suffering from paralysis of her left leg that he was going to hypnotize her. She obligingly fell into a deep trance without any hypnosis whatsoever and talked at length for half an hour, resisting Jung's attempts to awaken her. Upon finally being brought out of the trance she cried out that she was cured, threw away her crutches, and was able to walk! To cover his embarrassment, Jung announced: "Now you've seen what can be done with hypnosis!" Actually he had not the slightest idea what had happened (Jung, 1961/1965, pp. 118–120).

Such experiences led Jung to seek out more comprehensible and dependable methods, as by obtaining the patient's unconscious projections from dreams and drawings. The latter is generally credited as the forerunner of modern art therapy, whereas another suggestion of Jung's led indirectly to the establishment of Alcoholics Anonymous (Ellenberger, 1970, pp. 732–733; Roazen, 1975/1976b, p. 284).

Theoretical Foundation. Jungian psychotherapy strives to eliminate the sufferer's inner conflicts and bring the conscious and unconscious opposites into harmonious unity, thereby restoring the normal course of individuation. Through a confrontation or conversation with the unconscious, the patient learns that life is not a matter of being either introverted or extraverted, thinking or feeling, sensing or intuiting, good or evil. Rather, the undervalued components of personality must be accepted by the ego. Harmful projections also wane as greater knowledge of the unconscious is achieved, enabling the patient to perceive others more accurately and respond more appropriately. The therapist must be careful to avoid proceeding too quickly, however, lest an onslaught of archetypal material result in a psychosis. (See Ellenberger, 1970, pp. 713–719; Jung, 1961/1965, p. 135; 1917/1972d, pp. 111, 114.)

Therapeutic Procedures. Jung advocates a wide variety of therapeutic procedures. "There is no therapeutic technique or doctrine that is of general application, since every case that one receives for treatment is an individual in a specific condition" (Jung, 1964/1968, p. 54). Painting, modeling with clay, singing, and acting are not uncommon in Jungian therapy. When faced with a patient who had not slept for some time, Jung sang her a lullabye. In the case of a woman who was unable to tap her inner religiosity, he taught her the Scriptures and assigned regular homework (Whitmont & Kaufmann, 1973, p. 99). Upon being threatened with a slap by an imposing and arrogant female patient, Jung promptly rose to his full six-foot stature.

"Very well, you are the lady," he said. "You hit first—ladies first! But then I hit back!" The deflated patient fell back into her chair, and from that moment the treatment began to succeed (Jung, 1961/1965, p. 142). Nor was Jung averse to using psychoanalytic methods, even giving some of his more educated patients books by Freud and Adler and discovering from their reaction the approach that would be more suitable. (See Jung, 1935a, p. 20; 1961/1965, p. 131.)

In the early phase of treatment, the Jungian therapist sees the patient four times a week. The initial stage is one of catharsis and emotional cleansing, a period that often requires the utmost in confidentiality and compassion from the therapist. Jung once inferred from the word association test of an apparently psychotic woman patient that she had deliberately allowed one of her children to drink tainted water, which proved fatal. Her pathology dated from the moment she discovered that her true love, whose seeming disinterest had been the occasion of her marrying someone else, had actually cared for her all along. Jung confronted her with his conclusions, which he carefully concealed even from his colleagues, and 2 weeks later the patient was well enough to be discharged and never again required hospitalization (Jung, 1929/1933a, pp. 55, 57; 1961/1965, pp. 115–116).

The heartfelt outpourings of the cathartic stage bind the patient emotionally to the therapist, leading to the next stage of treatment. The patient examines the threatening contents of the shadow and learns to abandon immature and unrealistic fantasies, such as the transferential wish for an all-powerful provider, and "the road to a normally disillusioned life is now open" (Jung, 1929/1933a, p. 68). After this comes a stage of education about various aspects of life, designed to overcome the inevitable gaps in knowledge caused by the patient's pathology.

Some patients require a fourth stage of treatment. This uniquely Jungian approach is referred to as transformation, or as the synthetic-hermeneutic method (after Hermes, the god of revelation). It occurs after the persona, personal unconscious, and shadow have been explored, making the deeper layer of the collective unconscious more accessible and allowing archetypal symbols to emerge more readily. These symbols offer clues and guidelines for further individuation, and promote the formation of the self. (See Ellenberger, 1970, pp. 717–718; Fordham, 1966, pp. 59–60, 84–96.)

During the latter stages of therapy (or earlier in less severe cases), the patient is seen only once or twice a week. The patient and therapist sit face to face, and specific tasks and reading matter are often assigned. "In my experience the absolute period of cure is not shortened by too many sittings. It lasts a fair time in all cases requiring thorough treatment. . . . The patient must learn to go his own way" (Jung, 1935a, p. 20; 1935b, p. 27). This approach helps the patient develop independence, is less financially demanding, and allows the therapist more time for other cases.

Resistance, Transference, and Countertransference.   Jung does not regard transference as a necessary part of psychotherapy, though its emergence is almost inevitable. He criticizes the transference neurosis of psychoanalysis as a therapeutic blunder that encourages the patient to wallow in infantile fantasies, creating an extreme dependence that can be difficult to terminate:

> Apparently we are to fall back on some nebulous trust in fate: somehow or other the matter will settle itself. "The transference stops automatically when the patient runs out of money," as a slightly cynical colleague once remarked to me. (Jung, 1928/1972e, p. 131. See also Jung, 1946/1969f, pp. 8–9; 1917/1972d, pp. 62, n. 13, 66–67; 1913/1975a, pp. 112–118.)

Jung also argues that the patient's rejection of an interpretation is not necessarily a resistance. "Either the patient has not yet reached the point where he understands, or the interpretation does not fit" (Jung, 1964/1968, p. 50). And Jung stresses that the personality and psychological health of the therapist are more important than technique. Jung was the first to advocate that all analysts be analyzed themselves so as to reduce the likelihood of harmful countertransferences, a suggestion Freud readily accepted. (See Jung, 1934c, pp. 158–159; 1935a, pp. 5, 8; 1961/1965, p. 132; 1964/1968, p. 48.)

Jung does not regard the effects of psychotherapy as permanent. The difficulties and contradictions of life cannot be eliminated—nor should they be, since they provide an essential challenge—and periodic returns to therapy may well prove helpful (Jung, 1916/1971e, p. 278).

Work

Jung's prolific writings include relatively little about the psychology of work. As we have seen, an extraverted-thinking type would appear well suited for a career in the physical sciences, an extraverted-intuitive type would undoubtedly prefer an entrepreneurial profession, an introvert should probably be dissuaded from becoming a salesperson, and so forth. Such categorizations tend to be oversimplifications, since the inferior and auxiliary processes also affect personality to a significant degree. But in work, as elsewhere, successful adjustment requires that one follow the innate predispositions of the collective unconscious.

Religion

Although Jung takes a positive approach to religion, he does not advocate any particular denomination. Having extensively studied Eastern and Western religions, he concludes that people should follow their own path to individuation.

Jung is highly critical of religions that emphasize blind faith and minimize the importance of reason, for this devaluing of the thinking function is another form of pathological one-sidedness. He does concede that people need to form some conception of life after death, even though it is far from certain that aspects of the psyche continue beyond our physical demise. Nevertheless, the literal teaching of religious mythology is likely to present people with a most unpleasant choice: either to believe in impossibilities, or to reject religion entirely. (See Jung, 1957/1958b, pp. 49, 76; 1961–1965, pp. 94, 302, 322; 1964/1968, p. 84.)

Jung therefore recommends an analytical approach to religion. He postulates the existence of a God archetype, which can trigger intense religious feelings. He attributes contradictory aspects even to God, including kindness and cruelty. And he treats religious myths as symbolic representations of the human unconscious. For example, Christ dying for others epitomizes the internal crucifixion of an ego suspended between hostile forces (Jung, 1938; 1952/1973a; Progoff, 1953/1973, p. 115). Jung's ideas have generated more than a little controversy, yet many theologians regard them as major contributions to the development of religious thought (Ellenberger, 1970, pp. 688–689, 734–735).

Literature and Mythology

According to Jung, literature that has a clear and asymbolic meaning is determined primarily by the author's conscious intentions. Other creative impulses are triggered by autonomous unconscious complexes and archetypal images, which use the author to fulfill their own particular purpose. A work of this sort, typified by Wagner's *Ring* and the second part of *Faust*, has an enthralling quality that compels us to seek out its hidden significance. "Sublime, pregnant with meaning, yet chilling the blood with its strangeness, it arises from timeless depths: glamorous, daemonic, and grotesque, it bursts asunder our human standards of value and aesthetic form" (Jung, 1930/1971g, p. 90; see also Jung, 1922/1971f, pp. 72, 83; 1930/1971g, p. 104). Literature and art exert a broadening effect that helps society to compensate for its faulty, one-sided development.

Analytical psychology offers an interesting interpretation of the common fascination with flying saucers. We are threatened with disaster from such sources as nuclear weapons and increases in population, and the earth may well be becoming an overcrowded prison from which humanity would like to escape. Such unpleasant issues tend to be repressed, and create an unconscious desire for heavenly beings who will solve our problems. We project the aliens' mode of transportation in the form of a circle or mandala, which symbolizes the order and stability that we so urgently seek (Jung, 1958a).

Alchemy

Jung ascribes a symbolic meaning to the work of ancient alchemists, whose manifest concern was to transmute less valuable elements into gold. (See Fordham, 1966, p. 80–82; Jaffé, 1971/1975, pp. 50–52; Jung, 1944; 1955–1956; Rieff, 1959/1961, p. 16.) He argues that alchemical writings represent unconscious projections of inner experience, particularly the need to "transmute" the various components of personality into a new spiritual wholeness: "The secret of alchemy was in fact the transcendent function, the transformation of personality through the blending and fusion of the noble with the base components, of the differentiated with the inferior functions, of the conscious with the unconscious" (Jung, 1928/1972e, p. 220).

Synchronicity

Toward the end of his life, Jung developed the principle of **synchronicity**, which refers to events that are related to each other by meaningful coincidence rather than by cause and effect. When a clock stops at the moment of its owner's death, one event does not cause the other; the malfunction serves no known purpose; yet neither can Jung attribute this coincidence to pure chance. Similarly, one may dream of an unlikely event that shortly thereafter comes true, such as a chance meeting with a friend one has not seen for years. (See Jung, 1964/1968, p. 41; 1952/1973b; 1951/1973c.)

EVALUATION

Criticisms and Controversies

The Autonomy of the Psyche.   If sexuality was the "numen" that drove Freud to dogmatism, psychic autonomy may well have done the same to Jung. He regards our thoughts and fantasies as autonomous events that happen to us, triggered by complexes that have a purpose of their own. (See for example Jung, 1928/1972e, p. 201). Not only is it normal to hear voices originating from within your head, but this is *necessary* in order to learn from the collective unconscious and further the process of individuation! This unusual position differs radically from modern psychological standards, for a statement about hearing inner voices is in and of itself sufficient for an (actually healthy) individual to be admitted to a mental institution (Rosenhan, 1973).

This aspect of Jung's theory may well have been influenced by a personal bias. At an early age, he was besieged with thoughts so terrible that he developed intense anxiety. "Don't think of it, just don't think of it!" he would tell himself. He resolved his anguish by deciding that "God Himself had placed me in this situation. . . . God had also created Adam and Eve in such a way that they had to think what they did not at all want to think" (Jung, 1961/1965, pp. 36–40). Thus he attributed his distressing thoughts to an external, supernatural source, which would seem to be an unconscious projection designed to alleviate the accompanying guilt. Jung did regard it as ironical "that I, a psychiatrist, should at almost every step of my [self-analysis] have run into the same psychic material which is the stuff of psychosis and is found in the insane" (1961/1965, p. 188). Yet he apparently underestimated his need to disavow his own unpleasant thoughts, and the extent to which this personal consideration influenced his bizarre belief that auditory hallucinations are normal and healthy.

Literary and Conceptual Confusion. Although Jung's writing is at times strikingly clear and insightful, his usual literary style has been described as dreadful, confused, and lacking any semblance of logical order. His readers must frequently struggle through pages of abstruse ideas, often including lengthy citations from obscure and tedious sources. Some of Jung's terminology is also confusing: his definition of *instinct* includes habitual or learned responses as well as innate determinants of behavior, and *feeling* actually signifies something closer to *evaluating*.

Lack of Scientific Rigor. Jung's construct of the collective unconscious, and his belief in parapsychology, have been criticized as mystical and unscientific. Despite the differences in definition, Jung's model of libido is as vulnerable to attack as is Freud's. The quantity of psychic energy that is invested in any mental activity cannot be measured, so the concept of libido currently enjoys little use outside of strict Jungian and psychoanalytic circles.

The transcendent function does not explain the process to which it applies, whereas synchronicity is little more than a name for coincidences to which Jung arbitrarily assigns some grand design. The so-called law of averages does not necessarily apply in the short run, and even a fair coin or pair of dice is likely to yield some exceptional and apparently noteworthy series. A coincidence that seems meaningful or "synchronistic" may only reflect the fact that the laws of statistics do not always operate in accordance with common sense.

Psychology and Religion. Jung's emphasis of our spiritual and religious longings has provoked considerable controversy. Proponents claim that Jung has extended the scope of psychology by calling attention to a vital area of human functioning. Critics argue that a scientific psychology cannot deal with such arcane issues as the nature of God and the existence of the supernatural, or that Jung's approach is shallow and unsuccessful (e.g., Stern, 1976/1977).

Empirical Research

Research on analytical psychology has focused on the psychological types. The Myers-Briggs Type Indicator (Myers, 1962) is a pencil-and-paper inventory that measures four bipolar dimensions: introversion versus extraversion, thinking versus feeling, sensation versus intuition, and perception (simply experiencing events) versus judgment (evaluating these events in terms of a set of standards). Studies using this instrument have found that extraverts were more likely (and introverts less likely) to accept a group learning situation, as would be expected, and that social service volunteers tended to be extraverted–intuitive (Carlson & Levy, 1973; Kilmann & Taylor, 1974). The Myers-Briggs Type Indicator has also been widely used in vocational and educational counseling, as by advising extraverts who emphasize the thinking function to study such externally oriented sciences as astronomy or physics and students who are introverted-thinking to consider such inner-directed subjects as personality theory. (See for example Myers, 1993; Myers & Kirby, 1994; Myers & McCaulley, 1985.)

Factor-analytic research has consistently found introversion–extraversion to be one of the four or five most important human traits, as we will see in Chapter 13. And introversion–extraversion is determined to a considerable extent by heredity, which supports Jung's belief that each of us has an innate tendency to be more introverted or extraverted and that it is an error to force a child in the opposite direction. This issue will be discussed in the section in Chapter 17 that deals with the biological perspective.

Research findings also provide some support for Jung's construct of archetypes. We do appear to have an inborn predisposition to perceive the world in certain ways, as by being more afraid of objects that our ancestors found dangerous (such as snakes, spiders, heights, and tainted food). It is easy to condition and difficult to extinguish fears of such objects, and it is easier to learn to fear snakes and spiders than to fear flowers. (See, for example, Cook et al., 1986; Davey, 1995; Garcia & Koelling, 1966; Ohman, 1986.) These are only predispositions, as Jung emphasized, and a person who has only pleasant experiences with snakes or heights may well adopt a snake as a pet or become a tightrope walker. But we more easily fear those things that our ancestors had to avoid in order to survive, because those ancestors who did so lived long enough to transmit their genes to subsequent generations.

Contributions

Jung's concept of an inherent positive tendency for self-realization helps to correct Freud's extreme pessimism about human nature, and it anticipates the general outlook of such theorists as Horney, Allport, Rogers, and Maslow. Jung also departed from Freud by taking an active interest in psychosis, and made significant contributions to our understanding of schizophrenia. He emphasized that dream symbols may be neither sexual nor deceptive, and developed the dream series method. Introversion–extraversion is regarded as extremely important by modern psychologists and has become part of our everyday language, albeit in a more simplified way than Jung intended.

Jung's implicit or explicit suggestions led to such modern forms of treatment as art therapy and Alcoholics Anonymous. Some of his approaches to psychotherapy have gained widespread acceptance, such as the use of fewer than four sessions per week, face-to-face interviews, and required training analyses for psychoanalysts. Like Freud, Jung emphasized the importance of unconscious projections and the problems that they cause.

The concept of a collective unconscious suggests that something of us continues after death. Jung was acutely aware that we need our lives to have meaning, and his positive approach to religion has supporters as well as critics. Finally, many of Jung's practical guidelines make excellent sense: to follow our true inner nature yet not use this as an excuse to trample on the rights of others, to bring the shadow to light and accept the unpleasant aspects of our personality, to avoid the dangers of an excessive and stifling persona or one that is underdeveloped, and—above all—to beware of the extreme one-sidedness that constitutes pathology. To Jung as to Freud, extremism is surely a vice, and true self-knowledge is indeed a virtue.

Freud once tartly characterized Jung as crazy (Roazen, 1975/1976b, p. 261), and there are modern psychologists who would agree. Yet at the very least, Jung was an insightful psychotherapist and highly imaginative thinker who possessed unusually extensive knowledge about a wide variety of subjects. Many of the criticisms of Jungian theory are cogent and serious, but his writings offer considerable riches as well.

Suggested Reading

Perhaps the best place to begin a first-hand study of Jung is with his autobiography, *Memories, Dreams, Reflections* (1961/1965). Although there are apparently some contradictions and inaccuracies in his retrospections (Ellenberger, 1970, pp. 663, 667), this work provides a strikingly personal glimpse of the man and his theories. Jung's chapter in *Man and His Symbols* (1964/1968) ranks among his clearest expositions and includes substantial material on dream interpretation. Two of Jung's most important articles appear in *Two Essays on Analytical Psychology* (1917/1972d, 1928/1972e), and the basic introduction to the attitudes and functions is given in Chapter Ten of *Psychological Types* (1921/1976). The latter is also included in *The Portable Jung* (Viking Press, 1971), a collection of significant articles. The standard edition of Jung's work, translated or revised by R. F. C. Hull, is the definitive version.

Among the helpful secondary sources on Jung are those by Ellenberger (1970), Fordham (1966), Progoff (1953/1973), and a critical biography by Stern (1976/1977). Evans (1976) reports an interesting interview with Jung that took place toward the end of the latter's life. The extensive correspondence between Freud and Jung is also readily available (McGuire, 1974).

SUMMARY

1. The basic nature of human beings. *The Instincts*: We are motivated by such innate instincts as hunger, thirst, sexuality, individuation, power, activity, and creativity. Moral tendencies and a need for religion are also inborn. *Psychic Energy*: All mental activity is powered by psychic energy, which is called libido regardless of the instinct(s) involved. The greater the amount of libido (value) that is invested in a mental event, the more the event is desired. Psychic energy attracts complexes of related and emotionally charged ideas. Powerful conscious or unconscious complexes can exert considerable control over one's thoughts and behaviors. *The Principle of Opposites*: Psychic energy is created by the tension between such opposites as introversion–extraversion, thinking–feeling, sensation–intuition, good–evil, consciousness–unconsciousness, love–hate, and many others. When one extreme is primarily conscious, the unconscious compensates by emphasizing the opposite tendency. Successful adjustment requires uniting the various opposing forces through some middle ground. *Teleology*: Behavior is not only motivated by prior causes, but is also oriented toward a future purpose or goal. *The Unconscious*: The vast majority of the psyche is unconscious, and includes both destructive forces and positive wellsprings of creativity and guidance. The unconscious is divided into two parts, personal and collective.

2. The structure of personality. *The Ego*: The ego is an entirely conscious complex that constitutes the center of awareness and begins to develop at about the fourth year of life. The Jungian ego is a relatively weak component of personality. *The Persona*: The (conscious) persona is a protective façade, or social mask, that facilitates contacts with other people. An overdeveloped persona results in a state of pomposity or inflation, whereas an underdeveloped persona gives one the appearance of being incompetent, tactless, boring, and eternally misunderstood. *The Personal Unconscious*: The personal unconscious begins to form at birth. It includes material that is no longer (or is not yet) conscious, such as forgotten and unimportant memories, significant repressions, and stimuli that have been perceived subliminally. *The Shadow*: The shadow, located in the personal unconscious, is the primitive and unwelcome side of personality. However, it also provides a necessary ingredient of vitality. Like all that is unconscious, the shadow is often projected onto other people and experienced in this indirect fashion. *The Collective Unconscious*: The collective unconscious is a storehouse of archetypes inherited from our ancestral past. Archetypes result from the repeated experiences of past generations and predispose us to perceive the world in particular ways. Included among the many archetypes are the shadow, persona, anima, animus, self, wise old man, and great mother. We never become aware of the archetypes themselves, but experience them through the images or symbols that they produce and transmit to consciousness.

3. THE DEVELOPMENT OF PERSONALITY. *Individuation and the Self*: There are no formal stages of development in analytical psychology. During childhood the various components of personality develop, with sexuality not appearing until puberty. A "second puberty" occurs at about age thirty-five to forty, at which time interests in sexuality and power yield to more spiritual and cultural values. The lifelong unfolding of one's inherent potential, or individuation, results in the formation of a new center of personality (the self) that unifies the many opposites. Individuation can never be fully achieved, however, and may well be beyond the reach of many people. *Progression and Regression*: Libido normally proceeds in a forward direction, furthering the development of personality. If this progression is blocked by frustrations in the external world, or by internal repressions, libido turns back to earlier memories and archetypal images. Such regressions may result in infantile or pathological behavior, but they may also awaken undervalued and neglected aspects of one's personality. *Character Typology*: Individual differences in personality result from the characteristic direction of libido movement (introversion or extraversion), and from the typical way in which a person perceives the world (thinking, feeling, sensation, or intuition). The dominant or superior attitude and function are conscious, whereas the opposite (inferior) processes are primarily unconscious. A predisposition toward one attitude and function is inborn, and these are the ones that should become dominant for the personality to be well adjusted. However, the inferior processes must also be afforded satisfactory expression.

4. FURTHER APPLICATIONS. *Dream Interpretation*: Dreams provide important information about the personal and collective unconscious. They may serve as wish-fulfillments, anticipate the future, provide a warning, offer solutions to waking problems, or even result from telepathy. A dream symbol has at least two meanings, is not an attempt at deception, and often does not concern sexuality. *Psychopathology*: Psychopathology consists of an excessively one-sided personality, which brings the unconscious into conflict with consciousness. It may be caused by trying to go against one's true inner nature or by rejecting essential aspects of one's personality. The neuroses of the young usually concern sexuality and power, whereas those of older people are more likely to involve the denial of their inherent religious needs. Psychosis is also understandable and amenable to treatment, although the prognosis is poorer than for neurosis. *Psychotherapy*: Jungian psychotherapy uses a wide variety of procedures, often including face-to-face interviews and only one or two weekly sessions. The goal is to eliminate painful inner conflicts and pathological one-sidedness through a regression to the unconscious, thereby bringing the conscious and unconscious opposites into harmonious unity and allowing individuation to continue. The stages of treatment include catharsis, elucidation, education, and perhaps transformation, with transference kept to a much lower level than in psychoanalysis. *Other Applications*: Other applications of analytical psychology include work, religion (to which Jung is highly favorable but critical of many religious practices), literature, mythology, and the analysis of alchemical writings.

5. EVALUATION. Analytical psychology has been criticized for literary and conceptual confusions, a lack of scientific rigor, and overemphasizing the autonomy of the psyche. It is all too easy to misconstrue Jung's words as permission to be neurotic or psychotic, or to disavow the responsibility for one's thoughts and actions. Jung has made substantial contributions to the understanding and treatment of psychosis, to dream interpretation, to the development of psychotherapy, to more positive views of human nature, to religious thought, and to our understanding of such characteristics as introversion and extraversion.

STUDY QUESTIONS

Part I. Questions

1. What differences between the personalities of Jung and Freud might help to explain: (a) Jung's belief that many of our thoughts and fantasies are autonomous events that happen to us, rather than our own creations? (b) Jung's greater tolerance for and interest in psychosis?

2. "I know things and must hint at things which other people do not know, and usually do not even want to know. . . . Loneliness does not come from having no people about one, but from being unable to communicate the things that seem important to oneself, or from holding certain views which others find inadmissible." Do you think that this statement by Jung could just as easily have been made by Freud? Why or why not?

3. Compare Jung's list of human instincts with Freud's. Which better explains our behavior?

4. Give a real-life example to support Jung's contention that "extremes [in personality] always arouse suspicion of their [unconscious] opposite."

5. Give an example from your own life, or from the life of someone you know well, to illustrate: (a) enantiodromia; (b) an inflated persona.

6. Give an example from your own life, or from the life of someone you know well, to support Jung's contention that the characteristics we detest in other people often represent what we most dislike about ourselves.

7. "To find out what is truly individual in ourselves, profound reflection is needed; and suddenly we realize how uncommonly difficult the discovery of individuality is." Do you agree? Why or why not?

8. (a) Which attitude is dominant in your personality? (b) Which function is dominant in your personality? (c) Are the opposite attitude and function underdeveloped and difficult for you to express, as Jung would expect? (d) Based on the preceding answers, what job might you be well suited for?

9. If possible, provide an example from your own life of an archetypal symbol emerging into consciousness or of a "big dream."

10. (a) How might Freud criticize such Jungian therapeutic procedures as singing a lullabye to a woman who could not sleep, or teaching Scriptures to a patient who could not tap her inner religious feelings? (b) How might Jung reply?

11. Do you prefer Jung's approach to religion or Freud's? Why?

12. At the moment someone dies, the person's favorite picture falls off a wall and is shattered. How might this be understood as a mere coincidence, rather than as an example of synchronicity?

Part II. Comments and Suggestions

1. See the discussion of the autonomy of the psyche in the evaluation section. Also recall that Jung saw a luminous figure with a detached head emanating from his mother's bedroom, and that he conversed with voices in his head that he believed to be souls returning from the dead. Apparently Jung experienced psychotic ideation firsthand, whereas Freud did not.

2. I think so. The first sentence aptly represents Freud's view of Oedipal theory, while the remainder of the quote fits Freud's self-perception as an unraveler of great mysteries. Since

Jung saw himself in much the same way, it is hardly surprising that he ultimately broke with Freud; it was essential to find new mysteries and new explanations.

3. Ask a psychoanalyst and an analytical psychologist and you'll get two different answers. However, I prefer Jung's list. All too often I am reluctant to risk trying something new, preferring instead the safety of the familiar. So I have found that it is possible to be sexually satisfied, but dissatisfied with regard to what Jung calls activity (which includes the love of change, the urge to travel, and play). I therefore share Jung's belief that activity and sexuality are separate needs.

4. When I see a television evangelist crusading with great intensity and passion against sexual behavior (usually because I have accidentally tuned to the wrong channel), I suspect that these extremely negative conscious attitudes about sexuality conceal powerful repressed sexual urges, and that the crusade is a form of reaction formation. (Of course, there are other possibilities. But there are many other ways to make a living, yet the evangelist chose this one.) So I am not surprised when a scandal erupts because the evangelist is caught in a sexually compromising situation, as actually happened not long ago.

5. (a) In my teens, I became an avid bridge player. For some 25 years I participated in tournaments, read voraciously about bridge, discussed bridge with friends for hours on end, and even wrote numerous bridge books and articles. I also had no interest in religion. Some 15 years ago, however, enantiodromia set in. My interest in bridge yielded to almost complete disinterest; I hardly ever play, and I no longer read or write about it. (Some might say that I "burned out.") Also, I have become more involved with religion. I enjoy working with my religious organization, and studying religion from the point of view of modern psychology. This supports Jung's belief that middle age is highlighted by a shift in one's strongest convictions and interests. I find all this particularly striking because I'm not a Jungian. (b) Consider the late Howard Cosell, or any of the all too common professional athletes who are consistently arrogant and self-centered.

6. What might well be the true (albeit unconscious) feelings of a man who detests weakness in other people? A woman who detests those who are arrogant?

7. If you disagree because you have always known who you are and what you wanted, I envy you (though I suspect that you may not know yourself as well as you think). Having spent too much of my time obeying introjected parental demands (or what I thought were parental demands), I have experienced more than a little difficulty untangling my own wishes from these introjected standards and figuring out what I really want (as by finding work that I genuinely like). So I agree with Jung's statement. See also the quote that appears at the end of the section on criteria of maturity in the chapter on Allport, and Freud's quote at the end of the section on the ego in Chapter 2.

8. My answers: (a) Introversion. I am introspective, comfortable being by myself, and not wildly enthusiastic about seeking out new situations. (b) Thinking. I emphasize rationality and trying to solve problems by thinking out good answers. (c) Extraversion: yes. (See above.) Feeling: I usually don't have much difficulty evaluating the desirability of what I perceive, so here I disagree with Jung. But if this term were meant more literally (namely, the experiencing of emotion), I would agree. (d) A writer of textbooks on psychology.

9. I have never experienced an archetypal symbol emerging into consciousness, which makes it more difficult for me to appreciate Jung's theory. However, I have had one dream that might well fit the description of a "big dream:"

I dreamed that I was a physiological psychologist studying cell mechanisms. I was on the track of something unbelievably important, for I was going to be the first person to discover the true meaning of life. But then some invisible super-being put a message in my head: "They kill you if you find out too much. The secret of life is DEATH!" So I gave up my research and decided that it was safer not to know what life really meant. This was not a nightmare; the dream had an awesome quality, as though I were experiencing rare and profound wonders.

This dream may indicate that there were unpleasant aspects of my life that I was on the verge of discovering, but preferred not to know about. Or I could have been placing too much emphasis on raising my self-esteem by making brilliant discoveries and achieving lasting fame (like a Freud or Jung), and the dream might have been warning me that this was psychological suicide; I should instead be working on other issues, such as my relationships with important people in my life. (See also the section on dream interpretation in Chapter 6 and the dream of a writer driving up a mountain peak.) Jung might well see an emerging archetype somewhere.

10. (a) Consider Freud's views about secondary gains, managing the transference correctly in order to create a transference neurosis, and religion. (b) Consider Jung's views about transference neurosis, religion, and the purpose of the third stage of psychotherapy.

11. I find something useful in each approach. I agree with Freud that some people focus too heavily on a hereafter, and misguidedly sacrifice their responsibility for making decisions by conceiving of an all-powerful Being who will direct their behavior and solve their problems. Certainly many evils, such as wars, have been committed in the name of religion. But I also share Jung's belief that many people (including myself) need to believe that there is some greater meaning to life, and that it is not "a tale told by an idiot." Surely many evils have been committed because of a failure to follow important moral and ethical principles that are found in religion. And it has been shown that people who are religious are more likely to survive certain serious illnesses because they are reassured by a real and valuable faith.

12. Science emphasizes the importance of using predictions to verify a theory; after-the-fact reasoning is suspect. Consider that a great many other coincidences might have occurred at the time of the person's death: his clock might have stopped (as in Jung's example), his house might have been damaged by a storm, a stock he owned might have fallen, a friend might have had an accident. There are countless possibilities—so many, in fact, that it might be more surprising if nothing coincidental happened at the moment of the person's death. Also, we tend to forget the many times when no coincidence occurred. To find one specific coincidence like the falling picture and then argue after the fact that this event somehow shows the existence of "synchronicity" is unscientific—and, in my opinion, incorrect.

CHAPTER 4

ALFRED ADLER
Individual Psychology

Scientific inquiry is normally rational and objective, yet there are times when it resembles a bitter family feud. One such monumental uproar occurred in 1911, when it became apparent that the theories of Freud's colleague Alfred Adler were irreconcilably different from those of psychoanalysis. An irate Freud "forced the whole Adler gang" to resign from psychoanalytic circles, and forbade his followers to attend any of Adler's conferences. Long-standing friendships broke up, wives of the combatants stopped speaking to each other, and members of opposing factions refused to sit near each other at dinner parties. Psychoanalysts charged Adler with plagiarism, and were accused in turn of retaining his

ideas while expunging his name from their writings. Even Jung, a man known for his tolerance of all races and peoples, described Adler's group as an "insolent gang" of "impudent puppies." (See Ellenberger, 1970, pp. 638–645; McGuire, 1974, pp. 447, 534; Roazen, 1975/1976b, pp. 184–193.)

Although Freud's pungent attacks were excessive, he better understood the way to lasting fame. Today Freud is clearly recognized as the originator of psychoanalysis, whereas Adler's significant ideas have been widely subsumed, without credit, into the theories of other psychologists.

OBJECTIVES

- *To devise a theory of personality that can easily be understood and used because it is less metaphysical and complicated than Freud's or Jung's.*
- *To argue that instincts and heredity aren't important causes of human behavior.*
- *To emphasize the social aspects of personality: We must cooperate with others in order to survive, and everyone has an inborn tendency to do so (social interest).*
- *To show that striving for superiority over our formidable environment (striving for self-perfection) is the most important human motive.*
- *To reject Freud's emphasis on the depths of personality by showing that the unconscious is relatively unimportant, and that personality is determined by our consciously chosen goals and methods of achieving them (style of life).*
- *To argue that personality is an indivisible unity: Conscious and unconscious always work together, and personality is never torn by conflicting wishes and goals that set one part against another part.*
- *To emphasize that personality development is strongly influenced by the child's relationship with his/her parents and birth order.*
- *To correct Freud's belief that mental illness usually has sexual causes by showing that psychopathology most often occurs when pathogenic parenting (notably pampering and neglect) causes the child to develop an inferiority complex, abandon the desire to cooperate, and try to achieve superiority in selfish ways that hurt rather than help other people.*
- *To show that successful psychotherapy can be accomplished more easily and quickly than Freud believed.*

BIOGRAPHICAL SKETCH

Alfred Adler was born on February 7, 1870, in Rudolfsheim, a suburb of Vienna. His father was a Jewish grain merchant with a cheerful disposition and a particular fondness for Alfred, and his mother has been described as gloomy, rejecting, and self-sacrificing. Like Freud and Jung, Adler rose from lower middle-class origins to world fame; but unlike his illustrious counterparts, he remained emotionally attached to the lower classes and keenly concerned with their problems. Adler was a second-born (Ellenberger, 1970, p. 576) who grew up in the shadow of a gifted and successful older brother, and his family included an envious younger brother and three other siblings. Alfred never developed strong ties to his Jewish heritage, perhaps because his childhood was spent in liberal and heterogeneous surroundings, and he converted to Protestantism in 1904.

Adler studied medicine at the University of Vienna. Ironically, he never attended any of the lectures on hysteria given there by a relatively unknown psychologist, Sigmund Freud. Adler received his medical degree in 1895, though not with outstanding marks, and soon thereafter began private practice. In 1897 he married Raissa Epstein, an ardent socialist and independent thinker whom he met at a political convention. The Adlers were to have four children (three daughters and a son), two of whom became individual psychologists. His first publication, which appeared in 1898, stressed the pathogenic working conditions of independent tailors and the need of the poor for socialized medicine.

Adler first met Freud in 1902 under circumstances that are shrouded in legend (Ellenberger, 1970, p. 583). He remained active in psychoanalytic circles for some 10 years, and became the first president of the Viennese Psychoanalytic Society in 1910. Like Jung, however, Adler insisted on the freedom to pursue his own ideas. As he once remarked to Freud, "do you think it gives me such great pleasure to stand in your shadow my whole life long?" (Freud, 1914/1967, p. 51; Roazen, 1975/1976b, pp. 179–184.) Eventually Adler's theories became so different from psychoanalysis as to precipitate an acrimonious parting of the ways, with Freud accusing him of heresy and imposing the penalty of excommunication. Adler resigned from the Psychoanalytic Society in 1911 and founded his own organization, known first as the Society for Free Psychoanalysis and later as the Society for Individual Psychology.

Adler suffered a particularly painful rebuff in 1915, when he was denied a teaching position at the University of Vienna because his work was regarded as unscientific. During World War I, he engaged in psychiatric work with the Viennese Army. The postwar period was a difficult one, with the defeated Austria-Hungary suffering from poverty, famine, and epidemics. These trying times reinforced Adler's socialistic leanings, though he rejected any involvement with militant political activities.

Adler was a short and sturdy man. He was less handsome and charismatic than Freud or Jung, and he often presented an almost sloppy appearance. His style of life was simple and unpretentious, quite unlike the typical man of distinction. He possessed strong emotions that at times yielded to hypersensitivity, as well as the ability to make quick and accurate guesses about a patient's clinical disturbances, life problems, and birth order. He also impressed people as a witty and inspiring lecturer. Unfortunately, he could be highly impractical as well. Whereas psychoanalytic conferences were conducted in a formal and proper manner, Adler unwisely acquired a reputation for superficiality by meeting with followers and patients in various Viennese coffeehouses.

Adler's most significant achievements came during the years 1920–1933. He published numerous important books, and founded a series of child guidance clinics in Vienna. Adler visited the United States frequently from 1926 onward, participating in a symposium at Wittenberg College and teaching extension courses at Columbia University. In 1930 he was honored with the title of Citizen of Vienna, but the mayor unwittingly earned Adler's deep resentment by introducing him as "a deserving pupil of Freud." Adler foresaw the Nazi menace at an early date and moved permanently to the United States in 1934, where he taught at the Long Island College of Medicine and continued to strive for the establishment of individual psychology. There is no official standard edition of his works, which number perhaps a dozen volumes.

During his later years Adler developed a heart condition, but he enjoyed working too much to lead a limited life. While on a lecture tour in Aberdeen, Scotland, he suffered a fatal heart attack on May 28, 1937.

THE BASIC NATURE OF HUMAN BEINGS

Adler called his theory **individual psychology**, a name that is somewhat misleading. The term *individual* expresses his belief in the uniqueness and indivisibility of every human personality. It by no means precludes the social element, a factor he considers "all-important…. The individual becomes an individual only in a social context. Other systems of psychology make a distinction between what they call individual psychology and social psychology, but for us there is no such distinction" (Adler, 1929/1969, p. 95).

Individual psychology pays little attention to abstruse metaphysical constructs, or to speculations about the deepest layers of the psyche. Adler emphasizes practical recommendations for dealing with our problems, bringing up children, getting along with others, and upgrading the quality of life in general. (See Adler, 1927/1957, p. 1; 1929/1969, p. 1.)

Social Interest

Whereas psychoanalysis views life as an inevitable struggle between our selfish drives and the demands of society, Adler argues that we have an innate potential for relating to others. This **social interest** or **community feeling** (*Gemeinschaftsgefühl*) involves more than membership in a particular group. It refers to a sense of kinship with humanity, and it enables our physically weak species to survive through cooperation:

> Imagine a man alone, and without an instrument of culture, in a primitive forest! He would be more inadequate than any other living organism…. The community is the best guarantee of the continued existence of human beings… [and social interest] is the true and inevitable compensation for all [of their] natural weaknesses…. (Adler, 1927/1957, pp. 35–36; 1929/1964a, p. 31. See also Adler, 1933/1964b, pp. 98–99; 1931/1979e, pp. 210–211.)

It is social interest, rather than a superego or collective unconscious, that establishes the guidelines for proper personality development. The well-adjusted person learns at an early age to develop this inherent potential, and to assist the common good of present and future generations. Maladjustment is defined not as the failure to sublimate or individuate, as Freud or Jung would argue, but as the denial of one's social interest. A major task of psychology, therefore, is to understand and alleviate deficiencies in cooperation. "Society has no place for deserters" (Adler, 1927/1957, p. 194; see also Adler, 1933/1964b, p. 283; 1933/1979g).

Teleology, Feelings of Inferiority, and Striving for Superiority (Self-Perfection)

Life Goals and Teleology. Adler differs sharply from Freud and Jung by regarding the idea of inherited personality components as a "superstition" (1931/1958, p. 168). According to Adler, we are not mere pawns of innate instinctual urges. We select our fundamental life goals and the methods that we use to achieve them. Even social interest is only a predisposition, and it is all too possible to deny this tendency and choose to be neurotically self-centered.

> *The psychic life of man is determined by his goal.* No human being can think, feel, will, dream, without all these activities being determined, continued, modified, and directed toward an ever-present objective…. A real understanding of the behavior of any human being is impossible without a clear comprehension of the secret goal which he is pursuing…. (Adler, 1927/1957, pp. 29, 49. See also Adler, 1933/1979a, p. 52; 1932/1979i, p. 87.)

Although Adler emphasizes the importance of teleology, he regards infancy and childhood as a time of considerable importance. Our major goals are usually formed during the first few years of life, and they can be deviated from during adulthood only with great difficulty. Therefore, "no one can understand the grown-up who does not learn to understand the child" (Adler, 1931/1958, p. 65; see also Adler, 1927/1957, pp. 18, 31; 1933/1964b, pp. 81–82).

Suppose that a young girl who craves attention from her parents decides to fulfill this goal by becoming ill frequently, so they will spend a great deal of time taking care of her. She is very likely to behave in similar ways as an adult, as by suffering from persistent migraine headaches because they bring welcome concern from her husband. Freud would regard such rewards as only secondary gains, but to Adler they represent fundamental clues for understanding human nature. "We do not suffer from the shock of [traumatic experiences;] we make out of them just what suits our purposes" (Adler, 1931/1958, p. 14).

Life goals need not be realistic, for we often act "as if" certain **fictions** were actually true. A person's behavior will be significantly affected by the belief that virtue is rewarded with an afterlife in heaven, or by neurotic fantasies of exaggerated self-importance, even though these ideas may not correspond very well with reality.

Feelings of Inferiority and the Striving for Superiority.

To Adler, the primary goal of all human behavior is self-perfection. Everyone begins life as a weak and helpless child, and we all possess the innate drive to overcome this inferiority by mastering our formidable environment:

> To be a human being means the possession of a feeling of inferiority that is constantly pressing on towards its own conquest.... The goal of the human soul is conquest, perfection, security, superiority.... Every child is faced with so many obstacles in life that no child ever grows up without striving for some form of significance.... Every voluntary act begins with a feeling of inadequacy. (Adler, 1927/1957, pp. 38, 135; 1933/1964b, pp. 73, 145. See also Adler, 1920/1973, pp. 1–15; 1933/1979g, pp. 32–33.)

Healthy **striving for superiority** (or **perfection**, or **significance**) is guided by social interest, and gives due consideration to the welfare of others. Conversely, the selfish striving for dominance and personal glory is distorted and pathological (Adler, 1931/1958, p. 8).

The feelings of inferiority that underlie the striving for superiority are by no means abnormal or undesirable. If a child faces its weaknesses with optimism and courage, and strives for superiority by making the necessary effort to **compensate** for them, a satisfactory or even superior level of adjustment may be achieved. A famous example is that of Demosthenes, an apparently incurable stutterer, who practiced speaking with pebbles in his mouth and became the greatest orator in ancient Greece (Adler, 1929/1964a, p. 35; Orgler, 1963/1972, p. 67). Or a physically unattractive person may win friends and admirers by becoming genuinely warm and compassionate. The feeling of inferiority "becomes a pathological condition only when the sense of inadequacy overwhelms the individual, and ... makes him depressed and incapable of development." Such a shattering **inferiority complex** can occur as early as the second year of life. (Adler, 1929/1969, pp. 25, 31; 1927/1957, p. 69).

The child who surrenders to an inferiority complex sees only the possibility of evading difficulties, instead of trying to overcome them. "Imagine the goal of the child who is not confident of being able to solve his problems! How dismal the world must appear to such a child! Here we find timidity, introspectiveness, distrust, and all those other characteristics and traits with which the weakling seeks to defend himself" (Adler, 1927/1957, p. 33).

Even an intelligent or capable person can develop an inferiority complex. Adler devotes considerable attention to developmental factors that can turn normal feelings of inferiority (and healthy strivings for self-perfection) into a pathological inferiority complex (and distorted, selfish strivings), as we will see in a subsequent section.

THE STRUCTURE OF PERSONALITY

Since Adler regards personality as an indivisible unity, he makes no assumptions about its structure. He does agree with Freud and Jung that much of personality is beyond our awareness, and that "the hardest thing for human beings to do is to know themselves and to change

CAPSULE SUMMARY
Some Important Adlerian Terminology

Birth order	A child's position in the family (first-born, second born, etc.). To Adler, a major factor in the development of personality.
Community feeling	A synonym for social interest.
Compensation	Overcoming real or imagined inferiority through effort and practice, or by developing abilities in a different area. Physical inferiorities are often compensated for in psychological ways, whereas social interest enables the human race to compensate for its inferiority to the overwhelming forces of nature.
Early recollections	Memories of infancy and childhood. Even if inaccurate, these recollections provide important clues about the style of life because they are strongly influenced by the individual's self-selected goals.
Fictions	Unrealistic life goals that influence behavior because the person acts "as if" they were true.
Individual psychology	The name Adler gave to his theory of personality.
Inferiority complex	Exaggerated and pathological feelings of weakness, including the belief that one cannot overcome one's difficulties through appropriate effort. Usually accompanied by a conscious or unconscious superiority complex.
Inferiority feelings	Normal and inevitable feelings of weakness that result from our helplessness during childhood. May stimulate healthy striving for superiority and compensations.
Masculine protest	Behavior motivated by objections to the belief that society regards men as superior to women. A form of superiority complex that may occur in males or females.
Neglect	Failing to give a child sufficient care and nurturing, which creates the belief that the world is a cold and unfriendly place. One of the three major reasons why a child selects mistaken, pathogenic goals.
Organ inferiority	A significant physiological defect that can cause strong feelings of inferiority. Need not result in pathology if effectively compensated, but often becomes one of the three major reasons why a child selects mistaken and pathogenic goals.
Pampering ("spoiling")	Giving a child excessive attention and protection. Pampering inhibits the development of initiative and independence, and creates the impression that the world owes one a living. One of the three major reasons why a child selects mistaken, pathogenic goals.
Social interest	An innate potential to relate to and cooperate with other people. Everyone possesses the potential for social interest, but it must be developed through appropriate training for personality to become well adjusted.
Striving for superiority (self-perfection, perfection, signifi-cance)	A universal, innate drive to overcome feelings of inferiority by mastering our formidable environment. Healthy strivings for superiority are guided by social interest, whereas pathological strivings ignore the welfare of others.
Style of life	A person's chosen life goals and the methods used to achieve them.
Superiority complex	Pathological feelings of power and arrogance that conceal an underlying inferiority complex.

themselves," but he attributes this lack of self-knowledge to holistic and teleological forces. We deceive ourselves in order to fulfill our chosen goals, and the unconscious is whatever we do not wish to understand:

> There can be no question here of anything like a repressed unconscious; it is rather a question of something not understood, of something withheld from the understanding.... Consciousness and unconsciousness move together in the same direction and are not contradictions, as is so often believed. What is more, there is no definite line of demarcation between them. It is merely a question of discovering the purpose of their joint movement.... Every memory is dominated by the goal idea which directs the personality-as-a-whole.... That which is helpful we are conscious of; whatever can disturb our arguments we push into the unconscious. (Adler, 1927/1957, pp. 21, 50, 90–91; 1933/1964b, p. 16; 1929/1969, p. 15.)

Such socially undesirable traits as vanity, cowardice, and hostility are likely to be deliberately misunderstood (i.e., unconscious) so as to preclude the necessity for changing them. Thus a person who dresses unusually poorly is likely to be concealing powerful (unconscious) arrogance behind a facade of excessive modesty. Socrates is said to have once told a speaker who mounted the podium wearing old and bedraggled clothes, "Young man of Athens, your vanity peeps out through every hole in your robe!" Or hostility may be expressed in a self-deceptive way by forgetting the instructions of a domineering spouse or employer. (See Adler, 1927/1957, p. 158; 1933/1964b, pp. 206–208.)

To Adler, then, conscious and unconscious always work together to achieve those goals (understood or not) that the individual has selected.

THE DEVELOPMENT OF PERSONALITY

Adler shares Freud's belief that personality is formed during the first 5 years of life. But Adler rejects the idea of specific developmental stages, preferring to stress practical guidelines for promoting social interest and avoiding a disastrous inferiority complex. (See Adler, 1931/1958, pp. 12, 34, 200; 1929/1969, pp. 83, 123–130.)

Pathogenic Factors in Personality Development

Ideally, the child's potential for social interest is brought to fruition by the mother. She administers the first lesson in cooperation by nursing the baby at her breast, thereby serving as the child's bridge to social life. "*We probably owe to the maternal sense of contact the largest part of human social feeling, and along with it the essential continuance of human civilization*" (Adler, 1933/1964b, p. 221; see also Adler, 1927/1957, p. 220; 1931/1958, pp. 17–18, 120, 125–126). If the mother is clumsy, uncooperative, or untrustworthy, however, the child will learn to resist social interest instead of striving to develop it.

The father's role is to encourage feelings of self-reliance, and to stress the need for choosing a satisfying and worthwhile occupation. To Adler, all too many parents are poorly prepared for the difficult and challenging task of raising their children:

> The first cooperation among other people which [the child] experiences is [that] of his parents; and if their cooperation is poor, they cannot hope to teach him to be cooperative himself.... Unfortunately, however, parents are neither good psychologists nor good teachers.... Few [of them] are inclined to learn and to avoid mistakes... [and those] who

most need advice are the [ones] who never come for it. (Adler, 1927/1957, p. 219; 1931/1958, pp. 133, 178; 1929/1969, p. 103. See also Adler, 1931/1958, pp. 134–138.)

Pampering.   Perhaps the most serious parental error is to shower the child with excessive attention, protection, and assistance. Such **pampering** (or "spoiling") robs children of their independence and initiative, shatters their self-confidence, and creates the impression that the world owes them a living.

Under the misguided belief that they suffer from a lack of ability, rather than from a lack of training, pampered children develop an intense inferiority complex. Since they have never learned self-reliance, and have been taught to receive but not to give, they try to solve their problems by making unrealistic demands on other people. Pampered children may use enuresis, nightmares, or temper tantrums as manipulative (albeit unconscious) devices for obtaining sympathy and attention. They may expect to be admired and honored without having to put forth any effort, or insist that everyone treat their wishes as laws. They may rebel against parental authority through active opposition or sulking, and act depressed or even suicidal if they do not get everything they want. As adults they approach work and marriage with a selfish orientation, rather than in the spirit of cooperation. Such behavior provokes sharp criticism and rejections, which intensifies the inferiority complex and strengthens the need for more pampering. "Every pampered child becomes a hated child.… There is no greater evil than the pampering of children.… Grown-up pampered children are perhaps the most dangerous class in our community" (Adler, 1931/1958, p. 16; 1933/1964b, p. 154; 1929/1969, p. 10; see also Adler, 1931/1958, pp. 128, 151, 240, 282–283; 1929/1969, p. 33; Orgler, 1963/1972, pp. 72–75).

Pampering may also result in an apparent Oedipus complex, which Adler regards as neither universal nor sexual. "[The] so-called Oedipus complex is not a 'fundamental fact,' but is simply a vicious unnatural result of maternal overindulgence.… The victims of the Oedipus complex are children who were pampered by their mothers… [and whose fathers were] comparatively indifferent or cold" (Adler, 1931/1958, p. 54; 1933/1964b, p. 21).[1] Only a pampered boy wants to eliminate his father and subjugate his mother, and his motive is to preserve the mother's overindulgence. Adler charges psychoanalysis with the error of restricting its study primarily to pampered children, who follow the pleasure principle and become enraged and defensive if their selfish wishes are not fulfilled, and then overgeneralizing its findings to all of humanity. "Psychoanalysis was [preoccupied with] the world of spoiled children… Its transitory success was due to… the immense number of pampered persons who willingly accepted the views of psychoanalysis as universally applicable rules" (Adler, 1933/1964b, p. 36; see also pp. 51, 154, 213–214).

Neglect.   The opposite extreme, failing to provide sufficient care and nurturing (**neglect**), creates the impression that the world is cold and unsympathetic. The neglected child "has never known what love and cooperation can be: he makes up an interpretation of life which does not include these friendly forces.… He will overrate [the difficulties of life] and underrate his own capacity to meet them… [and] will not see that he can *win* affection and esteem by actions which are useful to others" (Adler, 1931/1958, p. 17; see also Orgler, 1963/1972, pp. 76–79). Such children regard life as an enemy, and express their inferiority complex through suspiciousness, stubbornness, and maliciousness. In the words of Shakespeare's *Richard III*, "since I cannot prove a lover… I am determined to prove a villain."

---

[1]Not so coincidentally, this was the situation in Freud's own family.

Other Parental Factors. Establishing unattainable standards or resorting to punishment overemphasizes the child's helplessness, and is therefore likely to bring about an inferiority complex. "Punishment, especially corporal punishment, is always harmful to children. Any teaching which cannot be given in friendship is wrong teaching.... Praise or blame should be given to success or failure in the training and not to the personality of the child" (Adler, 1931/1958, p. 135; 1933/1964b, p. 226). Ridiculing a child is "well-nigh criminal," resulting in the constant dread of being laughed at. Excessive criticism of other people will prejudice the child against sociability and cooperation. So too will a father who adopts the role of family ruler, and who acts superior to the mother because he is the primary breadwinner. (See Adler, 1927/1957, p. 66; 1931/1958, pp. 135, 222.)

Organ Inferiority. In addition to parental errors, a physical deficiency or severe illness may cause strong feelings of helplessness (Adler, 1907/1917b). However, **organ inferiority** need not result in psychopathology. "Imperfect organs offer many handicaps, but these handicaps are by no means an inescapable fate. If the mind... trains hard to overcome the difficulties, the individual may very well succeed in being as successful as those who were originally less burdened" (Adler, 1931/1958, p. 35). One such example is that of Demosthenes, discussed previously. But since organ inferiorities present substantial difficulties, and since the concerned parents are likely to make matters worse by pampering the invalid, the most likely result is a destructive inferiority complex:

> Children who come into the world with organ inferiorities become involved at an early age in a bitter struggle for existence which results only too often in the strangulation of their social feelings. Instead of interesting themselves in an adjustment to their fellows, they are continually preoccupied with themselves, and with the impression which they make on others. (Adler, 1927/1957, p. 65; see also Adler, 1920/1973, p. 81.)

One boy retained his childish soprano and lack of body hair into his late teens. "For eight years he suffered from this failure of development.... During this entire period, he was tortured with the thought that he must always remain a child." By the time he reached his early twenties, his physical development was entirely normal, but these organ inferiorities had shattered his confidence. He tried to gain some relief by acting supremely important, and this lack of social interest destroyed his marriage. "This error, this wrong evaluation of his inferiority, colored his entire life" (Adler, 1927/1957, p. 72).

Birth Order

Adler attributes considerable importance to a child's position in the family. "Above all we must rid ourselves of the superstition that the situation within the family is the same for each individual child" (Adler, 1933/1964b, p. 229; see also Adler, 1927/1957, pp. 123–129; 1931/1958, pp. 144–155; 1929/1964a, pp. 96–120; 1933/1964b, pp. 228–241; 1929/1969, pp. 12–13, 90–94).

The oldest child enjoys a temporary period as the unchallenged center of attention. This pleasurable position is likely to involve considerable pampering, however, and it comes to an abrupt and shocking end with the arrival of a younger sibling. Unless the parents carefully prepare the oldest child to cooperate with the newcomer, and continue to provide sufficient attention after the second child is born, this painful dethronement may well cause an inferiority complex. For this reason, first-born children are the ones most likely to become neurotics, criminals, alcoholics, and perverts (Adler, 1931/1958, pp. 144, 147–148). They also express the fragility of their childhood superiority by having frequent dreams of falling. And they are likely to be politically conservative, and follow in the footsteps of the parent's occupation. "Oldest children... often... have the feeling that those in power should remain in power. It is only an accident that they have lost their power, and they have great admiration for it" (Adler, 1929/1969, p. 91).

The middle child experiences pressure from both sides. "He behaves as if he were in a race, as if someone were a step or two in front and he had to hurry to get ahead of him" (Adler, 1931/1958, p. 148). Second-born children tend to be competitive or even revolutionary, prefer to see power change hands, and have dreams of racing. They are the ones most likely to develop favorably, however, since they never occupy the pathogenic position of pampered only child.

The youngest child, confronted with the presence of several older rivals, tends to be highly ambitious. Such children often follow a unique path, as by becoming the only musician or merchant in a family of scientists (or vice versa). Although they avoid the trauma of being dethroned by a younger sibling, their position as the baby of the family makes them the most likely target of pampering. Therefore "the second largest proportion of problem children comes from among the youngest" (Adler, 1931/1958, p. 151; see also Adler, 1927/1957, pp. 123–125; 1929/1969, pp. 91–92). For example, they may turn away from the challenge of competition and resort to chronic evasions, excuses, and laziness.

Only children are usually pampered, develop unrealistic expectations of always being the center of attention, and form exaggerated opinions of their own importance. They also tend to be timid and dependent, since parents who refuse to have more than one child are typically anxious or neurotic and cannot help communicating their fears to the child. The third of three boys or girls often faces a most unenviable situation, namely parents who longed to have a child of the opposite sex. And a first-born boy who is closely followed by a girl will probably suffer the embarrassment of being overtaken in maturity by his younger sister, since the girl's physiological development proceeds at a faster rate. (See Adler, 1927/1957, p. 127; 1931/1958, pp. 149–154; 1933/1964b, pp. 230, 241; 1929/1969, pp. 92–94.)

Adler emphasizes that the effect of birth order is only a tendency, not a certainty. "Individual psychology is opposed to fixed rules" (Adler, 1933/1964b, p. 233). A bright first-born child may defeat a younger one and not suffer much of a dethronement, a weak oldest child may lose the mantle of leadership to the second-born, or parents may pamper a sickly middle child even more than the youngest or oldest. A child born many years after the older sibling(s) will be treated more like an only child—or, if there are younger siblings as well, an oldest child. Individual psychology advises that the best distance between the births of siblings is approximately three years, by which time the older child has matured sufficiently to accept the parents' preparation for an addition to the family. (See Adler, 1931/1958, pp. 149, 153; 1929/1969, p. 92.)

Character Typology: The Style of Life

The child responds to its feelings of inferiority, birth order, and the parents' behaviors by developing its own **style of life**. (See for example Adler, 1927/1957, pp. 17, 133ff; 1931/1958, pp. 12, 200; 1929/1969, pp. 38–47, 83.) The style of life, which is well formed by age 4 or 5, consists of the child's chosen life goals and the methods used to strive for them. It also includes the perceptions and memories that are shaped by these goals.

A pampered child may select the goal of receiving constant attention, try to achieve this aim through sulking and temper tantrums, and perceive others as potential providers. A neglected child may choose the goal of revenge, become hostile and dominating, and cast others in the role of probable enemies. Or a child given proper care and nurturing may adopt a style of life that ultimately includes a useful and rewarding occupation, a mutually satisfying marriage, and a sincere and sympathetic concern for other people.

Every style of life, and every personality, is at least somewhat unique. Adler concedes that some mention of personality types is probably unavoidable, since our language lacks sufficient precision to describe all of the subtle nuances that distinguish one human being from another. Nevertheless, "we do not consider human beings types, because every human being has an individual style of life. Just as one cannot find two leaves of a tree absolutely identical, so one cannot find two human beings absolutely alike" (Adler, 1929/1969, p. 40; see also Adler, 1933/1964b, pp. 27, 127, 148). According to Adler, there are three valuable sources of information about a person's lifestyle: character traits, physical movements, and early recollections.

Character Traits. Undesirable character traits indicate that the striving for superiority has become selfish and distorted. Some of these characteristics take an aggressive form, as with vain and arrogant individuals who try to appear more important than everyone else. "No other vice is so well designed to stunt the free development of a human being as that personal vanity which forces an individual to approach every event and every fellow with the query: 'What do I get out of this?' " (Adler, 1927/1957, p. 155). Since arrogance clashes so sharply with social interest, it often takes on the more acceptable guise of keen ambition, false modesty, or a pedantic emphasis on accuracy and detail.

Other aggressive character traits include jealousy, avarice, and hostility. Jealousy is often expressed by blaming other people for one's own errors and becoming excessively critical. The avaricious individual rejects social interest and "builds a wall around himself [so as] to be secure in the possession of his wretched treasures." Powerful hostility poisons one's interpersonal relationships, and may well lead to a criminal style of life. These misguided forms of striving for superiority are little more than "cheap tricks by which anyone can imagine whatever he wishes to believe.... [and] whereby the personal evaluation is raised at the cost of another's misfortune" (Adler, 1927/1957, pp. 168, 181, 212; see also pp. 155–184).

Some undesirable character traits are nonaggressive. Shy people seek superiority and safety by turning away from society and excluding close friendships. Some individuals try to gain pity and attention by appearing helpless and anxious, while other lifestyles are characterized by laziness and pessimism. A student who becomes extremely nervous about a forthcoming examination and refuses to prepare for it has a ready-made excuse in case of failure, and avoids the pain and disappointment of trying hard but not succeeding. (See Adler, 1927/1957, pp. 167, 185–198; 1935/1979b, 1935/1979j).

A healthy style of life avoids the "cheap tricks" discussed above. It is typified by such desirable character traits as social interest, cheerfulness, optimism, sympathy, and genuine modesty (Adler, 1927/1957, pp. 199, 216–217).

Physical Movements. The style of life is also revealed by a person's physical movements. For example, constantly leaning on something may reflect dependency and the need for protection. Persistent slouching, remaining a great distance from other people, avoiding eye contact, and sleeping in a fetal position may indicate cowardly tendencies. However, such tentative clues should be checked against other evidence about the individual before firm conclusions are drawn. (See Adler, 1931/1958, pp. 28, 34, 41, 72; 1933/1964b, p. 208; 1929/1969, pp. 35, 58–62.)

Early Recollections. The best way to identify someone's style of life is by obtaining the person's **early recollections** of infancy and childhood. Even inaccurate memories provide vital information, for any distortion in our recollections is deliberately (if unconsciously) designed to serve our chosen life goals (Adler, 1931/1958, p. 74).

The earliest recollection is noteworthy because it reveals the person's fundamental view of life. One man's first memory was that of being held in the arms of his mother, only to be deposited on the ground so she could pick up his younger brother. His adult lifestyle involved persistent fears that others would be preferred to him, including extreme and unwarranted jealousy of his fiancée. Another man, whose style of life was marked by fear and discouragement, recalled falling out of his baby carriage. A woman who developed a lifestyle that emphasized the distrust of others, and the fear of being held back by them, recalled that her parents prevented her from attending school until her younger sister was old enough to accompany her. (See Adler, 1927/1957, pp. 30–31; 1931/1958, pp. 19–22, 71–92; 1929/1964a, pp. 121–127; 1929/1969, pp. 44, 48–57.)

In each of these cases, Adler attributes the sufferer's problems to the faulty goals chosen in childhood and maintained in adulthood, rather than to the childhood incidents themselves. "It is not the child's experiences which dictate his actions; it is the conclusions which he draws from his experiences" (Adler, 1931/1958, p. 123).

FURTHER APPLICATIONS OF INDIVIDUAL PSYCHOLOGY

Dream Interpretation

To Adler, dreams are merely another expression of a person's style of life. Conscious and unconscious are united in the service of our chosen life goals, rather than in opposition (as Freud would have it), so there is no need for a special key to the unconscious. In fact, the information provided by dreams can usually be obtained just as well from early recollections, character traits, and physical movements.

Adler also rejects Freud's contention that virtually all dreams deal with sexuality and wish-fulfillment; this is true only in the case of the pampered individual. However, he does agree with Jung and Freud that dream theory cannot be reduced to a handbook of procedures or symbols. Every dream is at least somewhat unique because every style of life is different, so a firsthand knowledge of the dreamer is essential for accurate interpretation. "One individual's symbols are never the same as another's" (Adler, 1931/1958, p. 108; see also Adler, 1927/1957, pp. 92–100; 1931/1958, pp. 93–119; 1929/1964a, pp. 162–168; 1933/1964b, pp. 242–268; 1929/1969, pp. 69–79; 1931/1979e, pp. 214–216).

To Adler, virtually every dream serves the purpose of self-deception. When a person protects a misguided style of life by relegating undesirable character traits to the unconscious, dreams create an emotional state that remains present upon awakening and helps to achieve those life goals that the dreamer does not want to understand.

Suppose that a student's style of life is highlighted by cowardice and pessimism. On the eve of an important examination, the student may dream of being chased by assailants (or fighting a difficult and losing war, or standing at the edge of a terrifying abyss). This dream enables the student to awaken with feelings of discouragement and fright, emotions that support the secret goal of delaying or avoiding the examination. The student may therefore take an unexcused absence without having to recognize the distasteful personality characteristics that underlie this behavior. (See Adler, 1931/1958, pp. 103–104, 108; 1929/1969, p. 70.)

However, this line of theorizing leads Adler to the dubious conclusion that some people do not dream. Included in this category are healthy people whose lifestyle involves little need for self-deception. "Very courageous people dream rarely, for they deal adequately with their situation in the daytime.... [I myself] stopped dreaming as soon as [I] realized what dreaming meant" (Adler, 1929/1964a, p. 164; 1929/1969, p. 76). Much research has refuted this contention by showing that everyone does dream, and people differ only in the extent to which they forget their dreams. (See, for example, Foulkes, 1966.) Furthermore, Adler seems unable to maintain his conviction that all dreams are unique. He concludes that dreams of falling, "certainly the commonest of all," indicate that the dreamer's delusion of being superior to other people is in imminent danger of being shattered. Dreams of flying reflect a desire to become superior to others, and are often accompanied by warning dreams of falling. And dreams about being improperly clothed express the fear of making an embarrassing mistake (Adler, 1933/1964b, pp. 263–264).

Adler does make a relevant point about the teleological nature of dreams. Since dreams prepare us for the future, it is not at all surprising (or prophetic, or "synchronistic") if they correspond with subsequent reality. For example, the ancient Greek poet Simonides dreamed that the ghost of a dead man warned him against taking an impending sea journey. He therefore remained home and, surely enough, the ship sank in a storm and all hands were lost. Adler argues that Simonides probably did not want to make the trip, since he knew that travel by sea was quite dangerous in those days, and the dream created the emotional state that made it easier for him to follow his true (but unconscious) wishes. The actual disaster was hardly unusual, if somewhat coincidental, and indicated that Simonides's assessment of the situation was an accurate one (Adler, 1927/1957, pp. 98–99; 1929/1969, pp. 73–74).

Psychopathology

The well-adjusted individual fulfills his or her obligations to present and future generations by successfully meeting the three major challenges of life: social interest, work, and love and marriage. (See Adler, 1931/1958, pp. 239–286; 1933/1964b, pp. 13–14, 42–67, 147, 167; 1929/1969, pp. 87, 100.) However, even relatively healthy people possess some undesirable and selfish character traits. Thus Adler agrees with Freud and Jung that psychopathology represents a difference in degree, rather than in kind:

> The psychic anomalies, complexes, [and] mistakes which are found in nervous diseases are fundamentally not different in structure from the activity of normal individuals. The same elements, the same premises, the same movements are under consideration. The sole difference is that in the nervous patient they appear more marked, and are more easily recognized.... [Therefore,] we can learn from the abnormal cases. (Adler, 1927/1957, p. 16.)

Adler's theoretical differences with psychoanalysis and analytical psychology are reflected in his approach to abnormal behavior. Freud and Jung attribute psychopathology to divisive intrapsychic conflicts, but Adler's holistic and unified conception of personality rules out this possibility. Nor can Adler accept Freud's idea of pathogenic fixations and regressions, since he argues that all behavior is designed to serve some future purpose. *"Neurosis is a creative act, and not a reversion to infantile and atavistic forms"* (Adler, 1933/1964b, p. 131; see also pp. 158, 172). Instead, Adler explains psychopathology as the result of a misguided style of life. "I should compare [the pathological individual] to a man who tries to put a horse's collar on from the tail end. It is not a sin, but it is a mistaken method" (Adler, 1931/1958, p. 272).

Origins and Characteristics of Neurosis. Neurosis originates during the first few years of life. Influenced by such factors as pampering, neglect, birth order, and organ inferiorities, the child selects a misguided style of life that clashes with reality. For example, instead of receiving constant attention, pampered children find that they are expected to be cooperative and helpful—behaviors for which they have not been prepared. This unwelcome discovery acts like an "electric shock," intensifying the child's pathology and resulting in the two conditions typical of all neuroses: an inferiority complex and a lack of social interest. (See Adler, 1912/1917a; 1931/1958, pp. 8, 49; 1930/1963; 1933/1964b, pp. 30–31, 106–107, 162–180; 1932/1979i, p. 91.)

Since the neurotic feels unable to cope with the difficulties of everyday life, he or she resorts to various "cheap tricks" for gaining superiority. These include relegating unpleasant character traits to the unconscious, evading responsibilities, attempting only the easiest of tasks, imposing unrealistic demands or expectations on other people, blaming errors or shortcomings on others, avoiding others, anxiety, or any other strategy that appears to turn the apparently inescapable inferiority into an advantage. Such people often become "virtuosos of neurosis, continually extending their repertory, ... [dropping] symptoms with astonishing rapidity and [taking] on new ones without a moment's hesitation" (Adler, 1931/1958, p. 63). Even the suffering caused by their pathology is preferable to the crushing defeat of trying but failing to achieve superiority more legitimately, and having to confront their inferiority complex. "The easy way of escape is neurosis" (Adler, 1931/1958, p. 186; see also Adler, 1927/1957, pp. 133–218; 1933/1964b, pp. 111, 164, 171–174; 1929/1969, pp. 105–106; 1936/1979d, pp. 239–247; 1936/1979f, pp. 102–105).

Inferiority and Superiority Complexes.

One common form of neurotic evasion is to conceal the painful inferiority complex behind a **superiority complex**, which involves the deluded belief of being better than other people. "It is as if a man feared that he was too small, and walked on tiptoe to make himself seem larger" (Adler, 1931/1958, p. 50; see also Adler, 1933/1964b, pp. 40, 120–122, 173; 1929/1969, pp. 27–37, 84, 104). Alternatively, a superiority complex may be hidden by manifestations of weakness.

Whereas healthy striving for superiority is reflected in socially interested abilities and achievements, the superiority complex is another cheap trick. It establishes grandiose and unreachable goals that result in eventual failure, intensifying the underlying inferiority complex and leading to still greater reliance on the pathological sense of superiority. "It is as if [the sufferer] were in a trap: the more he struggles, the worse his position becomes" (Adler, 1931/1958, p. 146; see also p. 51).

Masculine Protest.

Psychopathology is also caused by inequalities in society, notably those concerning men and women. In contrast to Freud, who argues that a woman's place is in the home, Adler emphasizes her right to pursue an occupation. He criticizes men who contend that helping with the housework is beneath their dignity. He regards motherhood as perhaps the highest of all forms of social interest. And he relates many unhappy marriages and personal miseries to the myth of sexual inequality:

> All our institutions, our traditional attitudes, our laws, our morals, our customs, give evidence of the fact that they are determined and maintained by privileged males for the glory of male domination.... Nobody can bear a position of inferiority without anger and disgust.... That woman must be submissive is... [a] superstition.... (Adler, 1927/1957, pp. 104, 202–203; 1931/1958, p. 267. See also Adler, 1927/1957, pp. 111–122; 1931/1958, pp. 122, 241; 1929/1969, pp. 66–68.)

When a girl perceives that men are favored, she may develop the form of superiority complex known as the **masculine protest**. This may include dressing like a boy, insisting on being called by a boy's name, or turning away from heterosexual relationships and marriage. Or a boy may dress and behave like a girl because he doubts his ability to fulfill his supposedly superior role, thus also falling victim to society's irrational stereotype of males. (See Adler, 1931/1958, pp. 191–192, 276; 1929/1964a, pp. 41–45; 1929/1969, p. 68.)

Adler strongly condemns all varieties of social prejudice. He warns that serious inequalities can lead not only to inferiority complexes and psychopathology, but also to such disastrous attempts at compensation as war and revolution.

Varieties of Psychopathology. Although Adler draws some distinctions among the various kinds of psychopathology, he views them all in much the same way: as serious errors in living, designed to achieve an easy and distorted form of superiority.

For example, paranoid behavior helps to preserve a superiority complex by blaming errors and defeats on other people. Depression is an attempt to dominate others by requiring frequent assistance and attention. Suicide is an act of anger and revenge by a pampered individual who expects too much of life, and is therefore easily disappointed. Compulsions may also express hostility, as when an unhappily married woman greatly annoyed her husband by spending entire days washing her home. Phobias may serve to control other people, as with a woman whose fear of leaving home by herself required her errant husband to remain by her side. Alcoholism provides a convenient excuse for not trying to achieve superiority in socially interested ways. Homosexuality represents the masculine protest of a fearful individual who was not properly prepared for heterosexuality during childhood, rather than an innate biological condition. Finally, as we have seen, such psychosomatic symptoms as headaches may support a pampered style of life. (See Adler, 1927/1957, pp. 55, 115–119; 1931/1958, pp. 53, 90, 274–275; 1933/1964b, p. 186; 1929/1969, pp. 47, 117–118; 1920/1973, pp. 51–58, 184–207, 255–260; 1931/1979c.)

Adler is unique among the early personality theorists in devoting considerable attention to the problem of criminality. He regards the criminal as a coward hiding behind a weapon, thereby gaining the only triumph that the underlying inferiority complex will allow. There are no "born criminals," but only individuals who have developed a superiority complex so lacking in social interest that they have little or no concern about the consequences of their behavior. "Crime is [another] one of the easy escapes before the problems of life, and especially before the problem of economics and livelihood.... Crime is a coward's imitation of heroism" (Adler, 1931/1958, pp. 185, 205; see also Adler, 1931/1958, pp. 197–238; 1933/1964b, pp. 136–140; 1929/1969, pp. 8–9, 37, 107). Adler strongly opposes the use of corporal punishment, arguing that this only increases the criminal's feelings of resentment and bravery. Unlike Freud, who preferred not to have criminals as patients, Adler accepted them and achieved some significant successes.

Adler attempts to explain psychosis in much the same way as neurosis. However, his interpretation of psychosis as a more severe expression of inferiority and discouragement is generally regarded as a serious oversimplification. (See for example Arieti, 1974; Fromm-Reichmann, 1950; Searles, 1965; Sullivan, 1962/1974.)

Psychotherapy

Theoretical Foundation. The goal of Adlerian psychotherapy is to promote a new and more socially interested style of life. For this to happen, the painful inferiority complex that underlies the patient's selfish and cowardly mode of striving for superiority must be brought to light. "The important thing is to decrease the patient's feeling of inferiority.... The method of individual psychology—we have no hesitation in confessing it—begins and ends with the problem of inferiority" (Adler, 1929/1969, pp. 45, 131).

The all-important inferiority complex is unearthed by examining the patient's misguided life goals, and the childhood factors that influenced their selection. The patient then makes an important and encouraging discovery: His or her problems result from a deficiency in training and social interest that can be overcome with effort, rather than from an innate lack of ability. The therapist facilitates this reeducation by serving as a model of healthy behavior, and by providing a ready target for the patient's fledgling attempts at cooperation.

Therapeutic Procedures.   A healthy style of life cannot be imposed by coercion, punishment, criticism, or authoritarian displays of omniscience by the therapist, for such tactics are all too likely to reinforce the patient's exaggerated sense of inferiority. Instead, individual psychology attempts to awaken the patient's latent social interest through encouragement and equality. Therapist and patient sit face to face, in chairs of similar size and style. The therapist takes appropriate opportunities to be informal and good-humored, whereas the patient is free to get up and move around the consultation room. Except for the early stages, the patient attends therapy only once or twice per week. And Adlerian therapy rarely lasts more than a single year, with every correctly handled case expected to show at least partial improvement by the third month of treatment. (See Adler, 1929/1964a, pp. 73, 88; 1933/1964b, pp. 286–298; Ellenberger, 1970, p. 620.)

Like Freud and Jung, Adler is not overly fond of hypnosis. (See Adler, 1929/1969, p. 79.) His techniques for unveiling a disordered lifestyle include an analysis of the patient's dreams, early recollections, and body movements, as well as key questions and verbal ploys. Often he would ask a patient: "If you did not have this ailment, what would you do?" The answer usually pointed to the life task that the patient feared, such as getting married (or divorced), making more friends, becoming more aggressive, finding a job, and so forth.

Adlerian therapy consists of three stages. The first task of the therapist is to establish rapport and gain an understanding of the patient's problems and style of life, which may take from 1 day to 2 weeks. Early recollections, dream interpretation, and "The Question" play a prominent role during this period. In the second stage of treatment, the therapist gently and gradually helps the patient become aware of his or her pathogenic lifestyle, secret goals, and inferiority complex. Here the therapist must proceed fairly slowly, for the patient is actually (albeit unconsciously) much more afraid of being proved worthless than of remaining ill. The third and final stage occurs if and when the patient decides to expend considerable effort and adopt a new and more cooperative lifestyle, with the therapist providing both emotional support and appropriate factual information. (See Adler, 1929/1964a, p. 73; 1933/1964b, pp. 165–166; Ellenberger, 1970, pp. 620–621.)

In any of these stages, the therapist may use carefully chosen strategies. Adler might tell a patient, "You can be cured in two weeks if you follow this prescription, but it is difficult and I do not know if you can." At this point he would look doubtfully at the patient, whose curiosity and attention were thereby ensured. Then he would add, "Try to think every day how you can please someone." If the patient objected that this task was impossible, or that others were not worth pleasing, Adler would respond with his "strongest move in the game" by saying: "Then you will need four weeks. . . . Perhaps you had better train yourself a little thus: Do not actually *do* anything to please someone else, but just think out how you *could* do it." If this also proved to be too difficult, Adler would suggest that at least the patient could please him by paying particular attention to dreams or early recollections and reporting them at the next session. (See Adler, 1931/1958, pp. 256–260; 1929/1964a, pp. 8, 25–26.)

Adler developed therapeutic techniques for use with children, including treating them in the natural setting of the home and seeing the parents during part of each session, and he is credited as one of the originators of family and group psychotherapy. However, he stresses that prevention (in the form of proper parenting and training of children) is far easier and less costly than having to cure psychopathology. (See Adler, 1933/1964b, pp. 153, 299–304; Mosak & Dreikurs, 1973, p. 37.)

Resistance and Transference.   Adler rejects Freud's approach to resistance and transference. Patients do resist and frustrate the therapist; but this reflects their inability to cooperate and lack of courage to change, and/or is a protest against the therapist's threatening aura of superiority. Adler regards transference as the result of a therapeutic error that triggers a pampered individual's wishes for excessive love and attention. He even concludes that transference should not occur in properly conducted Adlerian therapy, a contention that appears rather dubious in view of the established tendency to generalize behavior from one authority figure (such as a parent) to another (such as a therapist or teacher). (See Adler, 1931/1958, p. 72; 1933/1964b, pp. 288–290; 1920/1973, pp. 46, 144–152.)

Ideally, the patient in Adlerian therapy learns that he or she is not inferior and has the ability to overcome important problems through appropriate effort. The patient therefore abandons the selfish (and self-defeating) strivings for a cheap and easy superiority, develops a more socially interested style of life, and achieves through courage and cooperation those rewards that the real world can provide.

Work

Adler expressed keen interest in the sociological and psychological aspects of work, and was a strong advocate of humane working conditions and protective labor legislation. He recommends that the choice of vocation should be consistent with one's style of life and early recollections. For example, a patient's first memory was watching through a window while others worked. This man ultimately found satisfaction as an art dealer, a career that enabled him to continue the desired role of onlooker in a socially interested way. Similarly, the earliest recollection of many doctors is a death in the family. (See Adler, 1931/1958, pp. 79, 85–86; 1929/1969, p. 52.)

To Adler, the inability to select a future occupation during childhood and adolescence indicates the existence of an underlying inferiority complex. Therefore, all schoolchildren should be required to write compositions on "what I want to be later in life" to make them confront this important issue (Adler, 1931/1958, pp. 239–251; 1929/1969, pp. 100–101, 121).

Religion

Adler regards "loving thy neighbor" and preferring giving to receiving as desirable expressions of social interest, and he characterizes Freud's cynical rejection of these precepts as the selfishness of the pampered individual. But he stops well short of embracing Jung's belief in an innate religious need, and emphasizes the practical reasons for cooperating with other human beings. The primary purpose of religion is to increase social interest, God symbolizes the goal of self-perfection to which we all aspire, and reincarnation symbolizes the belief that one can change a disordered lifestyle to a healthy one.

Adler does regard the Bible as a wonderful work, but he warns that teaching its contents to children may lead to fanciful and misguided strivings for superiority. For example, a psychotic may misuse religion by developing a superiority complex that involves hearing the voice of God. Or a neurotic may choose to evade the difficulties of present-day living by concentrating on an existence in the hereafter. (See Adler, 1927/1957, pp. 81, 169, 172–174, 187, 207–208; 1931/1958, pp. 60–61, 253; 1933/1979g, p. 33; 1933/1979h.)

Education

Adler devotes considerable attention to the effect of education on personality development. School provides the acid test of a child's readiness for social living, and offers perhaps the only possibility for correcting whatever parental errors may have occurred. "The school is the prolonged arm of the family.... It would be our hope, if all the teachers could be [well] trained, that psychologists would become unnecessary" (Adler, 1931/1958, pp. 156, 180; see also Adler, 1927/1957, p. 222). Unfortunately, few educators know how to help each child's personality develop along proper lines. And classes are often far too large, making it difficult for even a skilled teacher to do much more than merely impart the prescribed curriculum.

Adler sees the educator as facing the difficult and challenging task of preparing the child for cooperation, and inculcating the social ideals that enable civilization to continue. "The true purpose of a school is to build character... [and] the principal aim of education is social adjustment" (Adler, 1929/1969, pp. 82, 103). The role of heredity in personality development must be minimized by the teacher, lest the child evade responsibility (and the educator excuse poor teaching) by blaming failures on genetic factors. "It may ease [the teacher's] position if he can say to a child, 'You have no gift for mathematics,' but it can do nothing but discourage the child" (Adler, 1931/1958, p. 170). The importance of individual ambition and competition must also be downplayed, so as to further the development of social interest.

To Adler, coeducation is an excellent way to prepare the child for cooperation between the sexes. However, special classes for "slow" children should be avoided because they are all too likely to produce discouragement and inferiority complexes. "Where there are brilliant children in a class, the progress of the whole class can be accelerated and heightened; and it is unfair to the other members to deprive them of such a stimulus" (Adler, 1931/1958, p. 171). As always, Adler regards encouragement as far superior to punishment and threats. And teachers must serve as models of social interest, treat their pupils with respect, and genuinely wish to contribute to the welfare of humankind. (See Adler, 1927/1957, pp. 31, 122, 137; 1931/1958, pp. 59, 156–181; 1933/1964, p. 55; 1929/1969, pp. 80–94.)

EVALUATION

Criticisms and Controversies

Oversimplification.   Parsimony is an appealing attribute of any theory, and Adler's practical prescriptions for living offer a refreshing contrast to Jung's abstruse metaphysics. However, it would seem that individual psychology seriously underestimates the complexity of human behavior.

Adler's holistic model rejects the possibility of troublesome intrapsychic conflicts, which many other theorists (including Freud, Jung, and Horney) regard as extremely important. Furthermore, Adler's emphasis on our consciously chosen goals leads to a conception of anxiety that is at best a partial truth and at worst astonishingly naive. Anxiety often involves intense suffering, and it is hardly likely that this emotional turmoil is merely a manipulative attempt to gain the attention of other people. Psychoanalysts would argue that even if a patient consciously selects new life goals and works diligently to achieve them, these efforts may be undermined by powerful opposing unconscious forces that have not been sufficiently analyzed.

Adler frequently implies that the choice of a disordered lifestyle is triggered by one or two key incidents in childhood, such as the birth of a sibling or an organ inferiority. To many psychologists, however, the causes of psychopathology are often more complicated and overdetermined. Adler's claim that transference does not occur in properly conducted psychotherapy is also dubious. And his conclusions that heredity does not influence personality, that healthy people do not dream, and that psychosis is simply a more severe version of neurotic discouragement must be regarded as major errors.

Overemphasis on Social Factors. Adler defines personality wholly in terms of interpersonal relationships. Social psychology is an important discipline, but it represents only one facet of modern psychology. Most current theorists agree that personality exists, and can be studied, in isolation from other human beings.

Overemphasis on Inferiority. Yet another source of controversy concerns Adler's contention that every neurotic, criminal, and psychotic suffers from an inferiority complex. Exaggerated feelings of powerlessness do play an important role in many disorders, but it is questionable whether the myriad varieties of psychopathology can be explained in similar terms. Adler even detects an underlying inferiority complex from such behaviors as sleeping in a curved position and craving strong black coffee, suggesting that "inferiority" is to individual psychology as "sexuality" is to psychoanalysis—a construct so pervasive as to be in danger of losing its explanatory power.

Excessive Optimism. Whereas Freudian theory has been taken to task for being overly pessimistic, individual psychology may well err toward the opposite extreme. If human beings do not have any inherent destructive or illicit traits, and do possess the innate potential for social interest, how can we explain the occurrence of so many wars, murders, crimes, and other human-made disasters? The psychological and sociological influences on growing children would have to be virulent indeed to bring about so much carnage. For this reason, the less sanguine views of Freud or Jung impress some observers as more consistent with the evidence of recorded history.

Other Criticisms. Adler's work (like that of Freud and Jung) reflects a total lack of statistical analysis, with all of his conclusions justified by his own subjective observations. Nor does he establish any quantitative guidelines for distinguishing between substantial but healthy parental love and pampering, or between minimal but sufficient nurturing and neglect. In addition, Adler fails to maintain his professed belief in the uniqueness of every human personality. He makes frequent mention of character traits, types of dreams, and other similarities among human beings, and he implies that pampered (or neglected) children have lifestyles that include many common factors.

Like Freud, Adler is vulnerable to criticism by those theorists who believe that personality continues to develop after the fifth or sixth year of life. Although modern psychologists have often failed to give Adler sufficient credit, he himself seems to overlook his significant agreements with Jung. Self-realization, teleology, pathology as a sick system of social relationships, and the idea that people establish much of the meaning of their own lives are all prominent in analytical psychology as well, yet there is almost no reference to Jung in Adler's writings. Finally, although Adler's literary style is clear and understandable, it is also extremely repetitious. Many of his books consist of unedited lectures, and suffer from an irritating verbosity and lack of organization.

Empirical Research

A considerable amount of research has been devoted to the effects of birth order on various personality and behavioral variables. These variables range from fundamental concerns like success in school and work, peer relationships, dependency, self-confidence, and competitiveness to more singular issues like hypnotizability and handedness. The results suggest that there is a tendency for first-born children to be more successful, more dependent, more fearful, more readily influenced by authority, and less likely to participate in dangerous sports; that later-born children tend to be more readily accepted by their peers; and that, contrary to Adlerian expectations, middle children may well represent the highest proportion of delinquents. (A review of this extensive literature is beyond the scope of the present text. The interested reader is referred to such surveys and listings as American Psychological Association [1984, p. 269], Hetherington & McIntyre [1975, pp. 124–125], and Manaster & Corsini [1982, pp. 81–88, 288–300].)

These research findings are by no means clear-cut, however. Numerous studies indicate that birth order is important, yet other studies do not. Some studies support Adlerian hypotheses, although others do not. One possible reason for the conflicting results is the problem stated previously: A person's nominal birth order need not correspond to the psychological position in the family. For example, consider the second of two children born 6 years apart. This child is likely to be treated differently from the younger of two siblings whose birth is separated by only a single year—namely, more like an only or oldest child. Perhaps the most warranted conclusion is that a child's position in the family probably does have some general influence on personality development (as Adler contended), but that specific predictions about a person's behavior based solely on this one rather unsophisticated variable are unlikely to be very accurate. Nevertheless, interest in the effects of birth order remains high (e.g., Sulloway, 1996).

A substantial amount of research supports Adler's belief concerning the importance of exaggerated feelings of inferiority, albeit using different terminology (e.g., self-esteem, perceived self-efficacy). Since this research is not specifically designed to evaluate Adlerian theory, it will be discussed further in Chapters 9 and 16.

Other research concerning Adlerian theory has dealt with such issues as developing written scales to measure social interest and lifestyles, the relationship of social interest to cooperative behavior and to interpersonal attraction, and the relationship of early recollections to vocational choice and to college achievement. Much of this research has been published in the *Journal of Individual Psychology* and tends to support Adlerian theory, with some exceptions. (See for example Manaster & Corsini, 1982, pp. 288–300.)

With regard to psychotherapy, Fiedler (1950) compared the procedures used by psychoanalytic, nondirective, and Adlerian therapists. He found that skilled therapists tended to use similar methods regardless of their theoretical orientation, and had significantly more in common than did expert and inexpert therapists of the same psychological persuasion. Several studies have proclaimed positive results for Adlerian therapy, including those of Heine (1953) and Shlien, Mosak, and Dreikurs (1962). Also available is a collection of papers dealing with the use of early recollections in psychotherapy (Olson, 1979).

Contributions

The most striking indication of Adler's importance is the extent to which his ideas are reflected in more recent psychological theories. For example:

Adlerian Theory and Practice	Modern Counterparts
Emphasis on the social aspects of personality	Socially oriented theories of Fromm, Horney, and Sullivan
The neurotic tendency to rule, lean on, or avoid others (see Adler, 1935/1979j, p. 68); the misguided quest for personal aggrandizement	Horney's three neurotic solutions, "glory" syndrome

The individual who "guards his wretched treasures"	Fromm's hoarding orientation
The child who determines to prove a villain, or who rejects tenderness	Sullivan's malevolent transformation
Emphasis on the ego	Ego psychology (Erikson and others)
Importance of personal choices and courage in living	"Being-in-the-world," and facing the fear of nothingness, in existential psychology
Importance of self-esteem, of empathy and equality in therapy, and of blaming a child's deeds rather than personality	Rogers' emphasis on self-esteem, empathy, genuineness, and unconditional positive regard
Use of physical movements to reveal a style of life	"Body language"; Allport's study of expressive behavior
Equality of women	Feminist movement
Self-created style of life	Kelly's psychology of personal constructs; Allport's proprium
Social interest	One criterion of mental health in Maslow's theory
Treating children in the company of their parents; establishing child guidance centers in Vienna	Family therapy; group therapy; community psychiatry
Face-to-face interviews in psychotherapy; patient attending only once or twice per week	Many modern forms of psychotherapy

Adler was the first psychologist to stress the social determinants of personality, an important factor that may well have been underestimated by Freud and Jung. He was also unique among the early personality theorists in devoting considerable attention to criminality, education, and child guidance. Unlike Freud, Adler studied children directly, and his practical suggestions for child rearing contain much of value.

Like Jung, Adler emphasized that teleology and self-selected goals play a significant role in personality development. The terms *inferiority complex* and *lifestyle* have become part of our everyday language. The importance of exaggerated feelings of inferiority, and of healthy and distorted attempts at compensation, are also widely accepted by modern psychologists. The relative simplicity of individual psychology offers advantages as well as disadvantages, for some patients may find it easier to understand Adler's teachings than those of Freud or Jung.

Despite these significant contributions, Adler has often been denied his due credit. A noteworthy (and typical) example concerns the Swiss psychoanalyst who once publicly declared that Adler's ideas were nonsense, only to spend the next few moments characterizing a patient as suffering from grievous inferiority feelings compensated for by arrogant manners. Similarly, an obituary in the venerable *New York Times* credited Jung as the discoverer of the inferiority complex. (See Ellenberger, 1970, pp. 641–648.) Although Adler's influence on modern psychological thought has been subtle and unobtrusive, there are those who would argue that it has also been extensive—so much so that despite his significant errors, virtually all current psychologists must be regarded as at least to some extent Adlerians.

Suggested Reading

In view of the repetitiousness of Adler's writings, any one of his more recent works should serve as a sufficient introduction. These include *Understanding Human Nature* (1927/1957), *The Science of Living* (1929/1969), *What Life Should Mean to You* (1931/1958), and *Social*

Interest: A Challenge to Mankind (1933/1964b). Among the useful secondary sources are those by Bottome (1957), Ellenberger (1970), Furtmüller (1946/1979), Manaster and Corsini (1982), and Orgler (1963/1972).

SUMMARY

1. THE BASIC NATURE OF HUMAN BEINGS. *Social Interest*: Every human being has the innate potential to relate to and cooperate with other people. Social interest establishes the guidelines for proper personality development, and enables us to tame the superior forces of nature through cooperation. It is only a tendency, however, and it is all too possible to reject our inherent social interest and become pathologically self-centered. According to Adler, heredity exerts virtually no influence on personality. *Life Goals and Teleology*: We select our own life goals and the means of achieving them, usually by the fifth year of life. It is these future aspirations, rather than prior causes, that determine one's personality. *Feelings of Inferiority and the Striving for Superiority*: The primary goal underlying all human behavior is that of striving for superiority (or self-perfection), which is motivated by the child's feelings of inferiority relative to the formidable environment. Healthy strivings for superiority are guided by social interest, whereas pathological strivings are characterized by selfishness and a lack of concern for others. Everyone grows up with at least some feelings of inferiority, which may stimulate socially interested forms of compensation. If the child is exposed to pathogenic conditions, however, the feelings of helplessness may become overwhelming and result in a shattering inferiority complex.

2. THE STRUCTURE OF PERSONALITY. Adler's holistic theory treats personality as an indivisible unity, and he makes no assumptions about its structure. He does accept the existence of some sort of unconscious, which includes those unpleasant character traits that we do not wish to understand. But he views conscious and unconscious as united in the service of the individual's chosen life goals, rather than as engaged in conflict.

3. THE DEVELOPMENT OF PERSONALITY. The mother serves as the child's bridge to social life, and proper maternal contact is responsible for the child's development of social interest. The father's role is to encourage feelings of self-reliance, and to stress the need for choosing an appropriate occupation. *Pathogenic Developmental Factors*: Personality development is strongly influenced by such potentially pathogenic factors as pampering, neglect, and organ inferiorities. It is not so much the child's experiences that determine personality, however, but rather the conclusions drawn from them. *Birth Order*: The child's position in the family influences personality development. *The Style of Life*: The child responds to the various developmental factors by choosing its life goals and the means of achieving them. These goals and methods, and the corresponding perceptions and memories, are known as the style of life. Every lifestyle is unique and is reflected by a person's character traits, physical movements, and early recollections.

4. FURTHER APPLICATIONS. *Dream Interpretation*: Dreams are merely another expression of an individual's style of life. They create a self-deceptive emotional state that remains present upon awakening and furthers the chosen life goals. *Psychopathology*: Psychopathology always involves an underlying inferiority complex and a lack of social interest. Common symptoms include the superiority complex and masculine protest. Neurosis originates in childhood, when the various pathogenic factors lead to the selection of a misguided style of life. *Psychotherapy*: The goal of Adlerian psychotherapy is to facilitate the development of a new and more socially interested style of life. To this end, the painful inferiority complex that underlies the patient's selfish and distorted mode of striving for superiority must be brought to light. The therapist is encouraging rather than stern or omniscient, and strives to appear as an equal. *Other Applications*: Adler expressed a keen interest in work and education.

   5. EVALUATION. Individual psychology has been criticized for presenting an oversimplified picture of human behavior, placing too much emphasis on social factors and inferiority feelings, expressing an inordinate optimism about human nature, and relying on an unscientific methodology. On the other hand, many of Adler's ideas have been incorporated into the theories of modern psychologists. He is credited with calling attention to the social determinants of personality, originating the well-known terms *inferiority complex* and *lifestyle*, championing the equality of the sexes, emphasizing the role of self-selected goals on personality development, helping to originate group and family therapy, and furthering our understanding of criminality and childrearing.

STUDY QUESTIONS

Part I. Questions

   1. How might Adler's personality and life experiences have influenced his belief that: (a) conscious and unconscious act together to serve a person's chosen goals, and personality is *not* torn by painful inner conflicts? (b) introspectiveness is one of the characteristics with which the "weakling" seeks to defend himself? (c) inherited instincts are a "superstition" and have no effect on personality? (d) unhealthy character traits (such as arrogance and shyness) and anxiety are "cheap tricks" for avoiding life's difficulties, whereas neurosis is also an "easy way of escape?"

   2. Do you agree or disagree with each of Adler's ideas in the preceding question? Why?

   3. Adler argues that social interest should establish the guidelines for proper personality development, rather than a superego. (a) Is this idea likely to be readily accepted in this country? (b) Give a real-life example of a person, or group of people, whose striving for superiority is lacking in social interest and harmful to society.

   4. Give an example from real life, or from a well-known novel, to show how "fictions" can strongly influence behavior.

   5. "Timidity, introspectiveness, [and] distrust [are] characteristics and traits with which the weakling seeks to defend himself." (a) Why does a person become what Adler calls a "weakling?" (b) What positive reasons might Adler have had for using a derogatory term like "weakling?" (c) How do traits such as timidity and distrust enable a person to defend himself or herself, and from what?

   6. Give an example from your own life, from the life of someone you know well, or from fiction to illustrate: (a) how pampering leads to a painful inferiority complex, (b) how neglect leads to a painful inferiority complex, (c) how an inferiority complex may be concealed beneath a superiority complex, (d) how an organ inferiority can lead to a painful inferiority complex, (e) a person who rejects social interest by "[building] a wall around himself [so as] to be secure in the possession of his wretched treasures," (f) a healthy style of life.

   7. What is the difference between praising or blaming a child's success or failure and blaming the personality of the child? Illustrate with an example.

   8. Based on your own life, do you agree with Adler's conclusions regarding birth order? Why or why not?

   9. What unconscious wish of Adler's own might have been fulfilled by his belief that he "stopped dreaming as soon as [I] realized what dreaming meant?"

10. How would Adler interpret the following dreams? (a) The "train" dream described in Chapter 2, study question 12. (b) A young man dreams that he is flying in a jet plane. Suddenly the plane goes into a steep descent and seems about to crash. He is afraid, but wakes up before it hits the ground.

11. Give two examples to illustrate views of Adler that were more equalitarian than the corresponding views of Freud.

12. Adler argues that brilliant children should be placed in regular school classes, and *not* in gifted classes, so they can accelerate the progress of less capable students. (a) What personal reasons might Adler have had for such a belief? (b) Do you agree? Why or why not?

13. A terrorist blows up a building in a hated foreign country. How might Adler explain this behavior?

14. The chief executive officer of a major corporation lies to his coworkers and the public, thereby defrauding them of a great deal of money while making millions for himself. How might Adler explain this behavior?

Part II. Comments and Suggestions

1. Consider Adler's painful parting with Freud and desire to develop his own theory. Recall that Freud emphasized the importance of instinctual drives, the unconscious, and intrapsychic conflicts, and was himself introspective (e.g., his self-analysis). Note that "cheap tricks" and "easy way of escape" imply that unhealthy character traits and neurosis are largely within our conscious control.

2. (a) I disagree. Both my own experience and a substantial amount of clinical evidence indicate that intrapsychic conflicts are extremely important. See section 2 and the last paragraph of section 3 of the case material in the Appendix. (b) I disagree. Freud, Jung, and even Adler himself agree that it is essential and difficult to truly know ourselves, and self-knowledge cannot be obtained without introspection. (c) I disagree. Although the "nature–nurture" controversy is far from easy to resolve, a substantial amount of research indicates that heredity has a significant effect on personality development. (d) I disagree. Severe anxiety is far too painful to be only a conscious "trick" for gaining sympathy and attention, although this may be one of the secondary gains. Nor is there anything "easy" about a severe neurosis. Consider that Freud found his own anxiety and neurosis to be so painful that he was driven to devise appropriate methods of treatment.

3. (a) Which is more common in our society: people who stress charity and caring for others, or people who are individualistic and highly competitive (as with the well-known sentiment, "winning isn't everything, it's the only thing")? (b) Consider the recent Enron scandal.

4. A fictional example of fictions: there are many instances in James Clavell's *Shogun* where a belief in some sort of reincarnation influences the behavior of samurai warriors, notably their willingness to "die gloriously" in this life. A real-life parallel is that of kamikaze pilots during World War II. Of course, social pressures as well as fictions are involved in both examples. Some samurai or kamikaze pilots might well have doubted the desirability (let alone the glory) of dying for their liege lord or country, but feared the reaction of their leaders and peers.

5. (a) Consider the effects of pampering, neglect, and organ inferiorities, and the resulting life goals chosen by the individual. (b) Weakness can be overcome by building up one's strength, as through appropriate training or learning. Conversely, attributing one's problems to inherited influences may make them seem much more difficult or even insuperable. (c) Consider the behaviors that the person avoids because of these traits. How might it be more comforting not to try these behaviors, rather than to try and fail?

6. (a) See section 3 of the case material in the Appendix. (b) and (c) One of my favorite fictional examples, albeit not one that is well known, is that of Clark Fries in Robert Heinlein's *Podkayne of Mars*. Clark is a precocious, unemotional, and highly intelligent 11-year-old who has been neglected by parents busy following their careers. He develops a style of life characterized by a distrust of other people and constant attempts to demonstrate his superiority, which are usually successful. For example, when a woman passenger on a spaceship acts snobbish and sarcastic toward his family, he soaks her washcloth in an undetectable chemical that causes her face to turn bright red for a few days, forcing her to confine herself to her quarters. He grudgingly tolerates his sister, a likable and apparently normal teenager, and takes pleasure in writing critical comments in her diary in invisible ink. Only at the end of the book is there a hint that Clark may some day be able to break through to his feelings and learn to care for other people. (d) See section 4 of the case material in the Appendix. (e) Two fictional examples: Ebenezer Scrooge, for obvious reasons; and Gail Wynand in Ayn Rand's *The Fountainhead*, who detests common people because they are so fallible and keeps a secret cellar containing precious works of art that only he can enjoy. (f) At the risk of sounding cynical, I don't know of many such examples. I hope you do.

7. I once heard a mother (not someone I knew) bawl out a child of about age 5 with words like the following: "What's wrong with you? Nobody good would do something like that! You'll never amount to anything! You're stupid!" Incidents like this are usually not isolated ones; they represent typical patterns of behavior between parent and child. As Adler points out, such attacks on the child's personality can have extremely harmful consequences, including profound resentment and the development of an inferiority complex. Like any parent, I sometimes overreact to my daughter's misbehaviors, but I am careful to criticize her actions and not her personality. I might say: "Don't make so much noise! That's not a good thing to do when mommy is trying to rest."

8. I agree that only children tend to be pampered, expect to be the center of attention, and exaggerate their own importance. But I doubt that accurate predictions about a person's behavior can be made solely from his or her birth order, even though there are some books that claim to be able to do so.

9. Consider Adler's painful parting with Freud, the great emphasis placed by Freud on dreams, and the purpose of the dream of the lawyer who had once been a classmate of Freud's (see the section on dream interpretation in Chapter 2).

10. (a) What emotions might result on awakening from this dream, and how might these emotions influence the dreamer's behavior? (b) What warning might this dream convey about the dreamer's personality?

11. Consider Adler's views about women and his therapeutic procedures.

12. (a) Recall that Adler was not a particularly good student, whereas Freud was. (b) If our society needs more capable people, should we risk slowing the progress of gifted children by placing them in regular classes, where the teacher must proceed in ways that will meet the needs of the majority of students? Or should the needs of slower learners matter just as much as the needs of gifted children?

13. Would Adler attribute the terrorist's behavior to a dark side of personality winning an intrapsychic conflict with more positive components? Why not? Why might the terrorist have developed an inferiority complex and be lacking in social interest? Why might Adler argue that the terrorist was neglected during childhood? Why might Adler regard blowing up buildings as a "cheap trick" for gaining superiority? (Which is more difficult: to blow something up, or to find solutions to important but difficult problems that will benefit everyone?) What fictions might be influencing the terrorist's behavior? How might Adler's warning about the

dangers of social inequalities, and his statement that "nobody can bear a position of inferiority without anger and disgust," apply to the terrorist?

14. Would Adler attribute the executive's behavior to a dark side of personality winning an intrapsychic conflict with more positive components? Why not? Why might the executive have developed an inferiority complex and be lacking in social interest? Why might Adler regard the executive's behavior as a "cheap trick" for gaining superiority? These explanations are the same as in question 13; what might this imply about Adler's theory?

CHAPTER 5

KAREN HORNEY
Neurosis and Human Growth

For Karen Horney, as for Jung and Adler, scientific debate involved some painful moments of professional rejection. Horney's time of trial occurred in 1941, when it became apparent that her approach to psychoanalysis deviated significantly from the traditional Freudian concepts being taught at the New York Psychoanalytic Institute. A vociferous staff meeting ensued, culminating in a vote tantamount to her dismissal. (See Rubins, 1978, pp. 239–240.) In the dead silence of an unforgettably dramatic moment, she arose and slowly walked out with her head held high—and went on to establish her own important theory, one that combines an Adlerian emphasis on social factors and an optimistic view of human nature with the intrapsychic conflict model that Adler specifically rejected.

OBJECTIVES
- *To devise a theory that retains Freud's emphasis on the unconscious but stresses the social determinants of personality, notably the child's relationship with the parents, rather than instincts.*
- *To dispense with Freud's controversial (and unmeasurable) construct of libido.*
- *To correct Freud's pessimistic view of human nature by arguing that our inner potentials are entirely healthy.*
- *To show that Adler was wrong about personality being a unified whole and Freud was right: Personality often becomes a house divided against itself, torn by conflicting wishes and goals.*
- *To explain such intrapsychic conflicts without dividing personality into separate parts like id, ego, and superego.*
- *To show that psychopathology involves the compulsive need to be protected, to dominate others, or to be alone ("neurotic solutions"), severe intrapsychic conflicts, and intense anxiety and self-hate.*
- *To explain why the neurotic isn't satisfied with even significant achievements and compulsively strives for more.*
- *To correct Freud's errors about female sexuality.*

BIOGRAPHICAL SKETCH

Karen Danielsen Horney was born in a small village (Blankenese) near Hamburg, Germany, on September 16, 1885. Her father was a tall, dashing sea captain whose male chauvinistic views frequently clashed with those of her proud, intelligent, and beautiful mother. Her family also included an older brother, several stepsisters and stepbrothers from her father's two other marriages, and a warm and loving stepgrandmother. (See Kelman, 1967; Rubins, 1978.)

Karen was an excellent student throughout her academic career, and received her medical doctorate degree from the University of Berlin in 1915. She underwent psychoanalytic training, joined the Berlin Psychoanalytic Institute in 1918, and began her own private practice one year later. However, she ultimately split with Freudian circles over the issue of female sexuality. Karen married Oskar Horney, a businessman, on October 31, 1909. The union produced three daughters; but a near-fatal bout with meningitis and the runaway postwar inflation in Germany left the formerly successful Oskar bankrupt and withdrawn. The Horneys separated during the 1920s, and were formally divorced in 1939.

Like Freud, Horney has been described as complicated and multifaceted: strong and weak, empathic and aloof, motherly and uncaring, dominating and self-effacing, fair and petty. She was a private person who confided primarily in a diary until her early twenties, kept much of herself hidden from public view, and formed few intimate relationships. Yet she also possessed an evident charisma, capable of captivating individuals and large audiences alike. Interestingly, Horney's own behavior included all three of the neurotic solutions that form the cornerstone of her theory: the need to merge with another person and surrender to a passionate relationship with a man (moving toward people), the need to control such wishes so that she could remain independent and have power over herself and others (moving against people), and occasional desires to resign from the world during difficult periods in her life by becoming listless and aloof (moving away from people). (See McAdams, 1993, pp. 211–221; Quinn, 1988; Rubins, 1978, pp. xii–xiv, 1–4, 239, 302, 338.)

Horney emigrated from Berlin to Chicago in 1932, and joined the New York Psychoanalytic Institute in 1934. However, the differences between her theoretical views and those of orthodox psychoanalysis soon led to acrimonious disputes. Her students' final theses were summarily rejected by the institute because they did not conform sufficiently to standard doctrine, and she suffered the aforementioned fate of being formally disqualified as an instructor and training analyst in 1941. Horney thereupon resigned from the New York Psychoanalytic Society and founded her own American Institute for Psychoanalysis, whose members for a time included Fromm and Sullivan. (They, too, ultimately resigned to pursue their own theoretical predilections.) From then on her writings (in all, six books) were destined to be stubbornly ignored by strict Freudians, while gaining widespread recognition and acclaim elsewhere. Karen Horney died in New York of cancer on December 4, 1952.

THE BASIC NATURE OF HUMAN BEINGS

Horney (pronounced "horn-eye") agrees with Adler that our inherent nature is constructive. We strive to develop our healthy potentialities, and pathological behavior occurs only if this innate force toward positive growth (**self-realization**) is blocked by external, social forces:

> Freud's pessimism as regards neuroses and their treatment arose from the depths of his disbelief in human goodness and human growth. Man, he postulated, is doomed to suffer or to destroy. The instincts which drive him can only be controlled, or at best "sublimated." My own belief is that man has the capacity as well as the desire to develop his potentialities and become a decent human being, and that these deteriorate if his relationship to others and hence to himself is, and continues to be, disturbed. (Horney, 1945, p. 19. See also Horney, 1942, p. 175.)

THE STRUCTURE AND DEVELOPMENT OF PERSONALITY

Horney shares Freud's views about the importance of unconscious processes, including powerful and actively maintained repressions. Thus she emphatically rejects Adler's holistic approach. "[Neurotics are] torn by inner conflicts. . . . Every neurotic . . . is at war with himself" (Horney, 1945, p. 11; 1950, p. 112; see also Horney, 1939, pp. 20–22; 1945, p. 56).

However, Horney has little to say about the structure and development of personality. "I do not consider it feasible to localize neurotic conflicts in a schematic way, as Freud does" (Horney, 1939, p. 191). She prefers to devote the majority of her writings to three major applications: neurosis, psychotherapy, and female sexuality.

FURTHER APPLICATIONS OF HORNEYAN THEORY

Neurosis

Horney agrees with Freud, Jung, and Adler that neurosis differs from more normal behavior in degree, rather than in kind. Life is difficult, and all of us experience conflicts at one time or another. However, there are striking differences between healthy conflicts and neurotic conflicts.

Healthy conflicts may be entirely conscious and can usually be resolved, as when you must choose between going to a party and studying for the next day's exam. Neurotic conflicts are considerably more severe, involve a dilemma that appears to be insoluble, and are always deeply repressed, so that "only slight bubbles of the battle raging within reach the surface" (Horney, 1945, p. 30; see also Horney, 1945, p. 27; 1950, p. 37).

Basic Anxiety.   Horney argues that neurosis results from disturbed interpersonal relationships during childhood, rather than from some instinctual or libidinal drive. The parents may behave in such pathogenic ways as domination, overprotectiveness, overindulgence, humiliation, perfectionism, hypocrisy, inconsistency, partiality to other siblings, blind adoration, or neglect:

> [These errors] all boil down to the fact that the people in the environment are too wrapped up in their own neuroses to be able to love the child, or even to conceive of him as the particular individual he is; their attitudes toward him are determined by their own neurotic needs and responses.... As a result, the child does not develop a feeling of belonging, of "we," but instead a profound insecurity and vague apprehensiveness, for which I use the term *basic anxiety.* (Horney, 1950, p. 18; see also Horney, 1945, p. 41; 1950, pp. 202, 221–222, 275.)

This feeling of being alone in an unfriendly and frightening world (**basic anxiety**) prevents the child from relating to people in a normal way. "His first attempts to relate himself to others are determined not by his real feelings, but by strategic necessities. He cannot simply like or dislike, trust or distrust, express his wishes or protest against those of others, but [must] devise ways to cope with people and to manipulate them with minimum damage to himself" (Horney, 1945, p. 219).

To alleviate the painful feelings of anxiety, the child abandons the healthy drive for self-realization in favor of an all-out quest for safety. The child seeks safety by exaggerating one of the three main characteristics of basic anxiety: helplessness, aggressiveness, or detachment. The neurotic solution of helplessness is denoted by excessive desires for protection (**moving toward people**), the aggressive orientation leads to attempts at domination and mastery (**moving against people**), and the detached solution emphasizes the avoidance of others (**moving away from people**).

Each of these three neurotic solutions is compulsive and inflexible. Unlike the healthy individual, who can move toward, against, or away from people as circumstances dictate, the neurotic rarely deviates from the chosen orientation. At times, however, exceptions do occur. The two orientations that are consciously underemphasized remain powerful in the unconscious, and they occasionally break through to influence overt behavior.

Moving Toward People.   The neurotic who moves toward people tries to reduce anxiety and gain safety by being cared for and protected. The sufferer acts as though others "must love me, protect me, forgive me, not desert me *because* I am so weak and helpless." This feeling of "poor little me" is rather like "Cinderella bereft of her fairy godmother" (Horney, 1945, p. 53; see also Horney, 1945, pp. 48–62; 1950, pp. 214–258).

Such individuals consciously believe that they are sincerely interested in other people and want to be helpful and compliant. They are unaware that they are repressing powerful hostility, selfishness, and healthy self-assertiveness. "Where [this] patient errs is in claiming that all his frantic beating about for affection and approval is genuine, while in reality the genuine portion is heavily overshadowed by his insatiable urge to feel safe. . . . [The patient who moves toward people has strongly repressed a] callous lack of interest in others, attitudes of defiance, ... [the desire] to control and manipulate others, [and] relentless needs to excel or to enjoy vindictive triumphs" (Horney, 1945, pp. 51, 55).

Moving Against People.
The neurotic who moves against people regards life as a Darwinian jungle where only the fittest survive, and tries to reduce anxiety and gain safety through mastery and domination. Like the neglected child in Adlerian theory, the sufferer regards most people as potential enemies. "Any situation or relationship is looked at from the standpoint of 'what can I get out of it?' . . . To [this individual] ruthlessness is strength, [a] lack of consideration for others [is] honesty, and a callous pursuit of one's own ends [is] realism" (Horney, 1945, pp. 65, 68; see also Horney, 1945, pp. 63–72; 1950, pp. 187–213).

Such individuals consciously believe that they are strong and dominating. They are unaware that they are repressing powerful feelings of helplessness and a healthy need for love, and they may behave sadistically toward those who are weak because this serves as an unpleasant reminder of what they most dislike about themselves. Horney (1945, pp. 115–130) refers to this as the **externalization** of unconscious material, a construct that is similar to Freudian and Jungian projection (and one that occurs in all forms of neurosis).

Moving Away From People.
The neurotic who moves away from people tries to reduce anxiety and gain safety by avoiding contact with others. "He is like a person in a hotel room who rarely removes the 'Do Not Disturb' sign from his door" (Horney, 1945, p. 76; see also Horney, 1945, pp. 73–95; 1950, pp. 259–290).

Such individuals consciously believe that they are completely self-sufficient, and that no other person or thing is indispensable. They sustain this belief by unconsciously limiting their needs, numbing their emotions, and overestimating their uniqueness and superiority. They rarely ask for help, even if this means not getting what they want. And they are likely to regard the need to give a birthday gift or be on time for an appointment, the physical pressure of a tight collar or necktie, or the slightest possibility of an emotional attachment to another person as an unwarranted and hostile intrusion from the outside world. They do not realize that no person is an island, and that they are repressing powerful wishes to be dependent and healthy desires for affiliation and love.

The Idealized Image.
The repressed aspects of the neurotic's personality and the painful inner conflicts are further concealed through the development of a glorious **idealized image** (Horney, 1945, pp. 96–114, 139; 1950, pp. 22–23, 86–109). A compliant neurotic may believe that she is so unselfish and attractive as to deserve undying love. An aggressive neurotic may think that he always knows best and never makes a mistake. Or a detached neurotic who actually craves affection may believe that she is so capable and self-sufficient as never to need anything from anyone.

Despite its implausible aspects, the idealized image appears quite realistic to its creator. The result is a vicious circle. The idealized image establishes unattainable standards that either bring about eventual defeat, or cause the sufferer to shrink from the acid test of reality. Such failures increase the hate for and alienation from the fallible true self (**self-contempt**), and this intensifies the inner conflicts and the dependence on the idealized image. (See Figure 5.1.) As this image becomes increasingly unrealistic, the individual feels compelled to bolster it with still greater triumphs (**glory**). (See Horney, 1945, p. 98; 1950, pp. 39, 118, 154–155, 367.)

Like Faust, neurotics "sell their soul to the devil" by abandoning their real desires in favor of the idealized image. And like Frankenstein, their creation arises to destroy them. For the

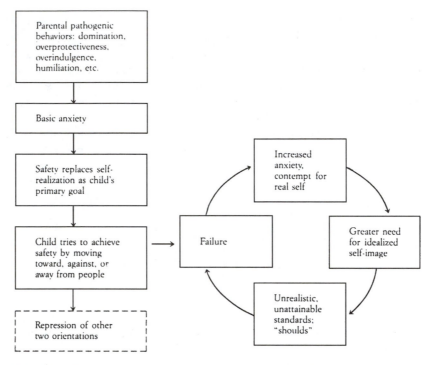

FIG. 5.1. The vicious circle produced by the idealized image, and its antecedents.

battle between the pathological idealized image and the healthy but apparently weak and humiliating real self proves to be the most serious inner conflict of all:

> Roughly speaking, a person builds up an idealized image of himself because he cannot tolerate himself as he actually is. The image apparently counteracts this calamity; but having placed himself on a pedestal, he can tolerate his real self still less and starts to rage against it, to despise himself and to chafe under the yoke of his own unattainable demands upon himself. He wavers then between self-adoration and self-contempt, between his idealized image and his despised image, with no solid middle ground to fall back on.... *The godlike [self] is bound to hate his actual [self].... [and this is] the central inner conflict.* (Horney, 1945, p. 112; 1950, pp. 112, 368.)

The idealized image bears some similarity to the Adlerian superiority complex, since both conceal feelings of weakness from oneself. But the grandiose idealized image is at war with the fallible real self, which differs sharply from Adler's holistic and unified conception of personality. "It was Adler's great contribution to realize the importance for neuroses of drives for power and superiority. Adler, however . . . stayed too much on the surface of the problems involved. . . . [and] is in fact a good example of how even a productive insight into psychological processes can become sterile if pursued onesidedly and without foundation in the basic discoveries of Freud" (Horney, 1950, p. 372; 1937, p. x; see also Horney, 1937, pp. 186–187; 1939, p. 268).

Claims and Shoulds.   The idealized image often converts wishes into unrealistic **claims**, which supposedly entitle the sufferer to triumph and glory. A lonely individual who unconsciously feels unlovable may make no effort to alleviate this painful situation, and

CAPSULE SUMMARY
Some Important Horneyan Terminology

Basic anxiety	The feeling of being alone in an unfriendly and frightening world. The three main characteristics of basic anxiety are helplessness, aggressiveness, and detachment.
Claims	Unrealistic demands and expectations that the neurotic imposes on other people.
Externalization	Experiencing intrapsychic processes as occurring outside oneself; similar to projection.
Glory	Grandiose feelings of triumph because one appears to have fulfilled the demands of the idealized image. However, the neurotic quest for glory is compulsive and insatiable.
Idealized image	A grandiose, glorious self-image that conceals one's weak and hated real self.
Moving against people (mastery)	A neurotic attempt to reduce anxiety and gain safety by dominating and mastering other people, while repressing feelings of helplessness and detachment and healthy needs for love. One of the three neurotic solutions to the problem of basic anxiety.
Moving away from people (detachment)	A neurotic attempt to reduce anxiety and gain safety by avoiding other people and trying to be completely self-sufficient, while repressing feelings of helplessness and aggressiveness and healthy needs for friendship and love. One of the three neurotic solutions to the problem of basic anxiety.
Moving toward people (compliance)	A neurotic attempt to reduce anxiety and gain safety by being cared for and protected, while repressing feelings of aggressiveness and detachment and healthy self-assertiveness. One of the three neurotic solutions to the problem of basic anxiety.
Neurotic conflict (inner conflict)	An unconscious intrapsychic clash between healthy and neurotic drives, or between opposing neurotic drives.
Self-contempt (self-hate)	Hating one's true abilities, feelings, and wishes because they differ from (and seem much worse than) the glorious idealized image.
Self-realization	Developing one's healthy innate potentials and abilities.
Shoulds	Commands to conform to the idealized image that come from one's own personality, but may be externalized and appear (incorrectly) to be imposed by other people.

expect to be invited out by someone else. A neurotic with repressed feelings of professional incompetence may claim to deserve a better job without earning it, or even asking for it. Or patients may expect great gains from psychotherapy without having to work at their problems (Horney, 1950, pp. 40–63).

The neurotic is also driven by self-imposed inner commands that are designed to satisfy the idealized image, which Horney calls "the tyranny of the **should**." This may involve the belief that one should be world famous, totally unselfish, always right, always victorious, a perfect lover or spouse, and so forth. Shoulds may be externalized and appear (incorrectly) to be imposed by other people, such as one's parents or boss. Unlike the Freudian superego, shoulds are always a neurotic force "exactly like political tyranny in a police state" (Horney, 1950, p. 67; see also pp. 64–85, 123).

Other Neurotic Symptoms.   Because the sufferer is pulled in opposite directions by the painful inner conflicts, he or she is likely to behave in ways that are inconsistent and indecisive. A neurotic who moves toward people may occasionally express her healthy self-assertiveness, fear that she will lose the protection of other people, and become even more compliant. Or a detached neurotic may heed dimly sensed desires for love and affection by going to a party, only to leave quickly because the need to move away from people becomes paramount. Such behavior resembles a car that is driven with one foot on the gas pedal and the other foot on the brake, with sufferer lurching first one way and then the other.

Inner conflicts between the neurotic's repressed true desires and the demands of the idealized image may turn relatively minor decisions into major and exhausting crises, such as whether to attend a social function or what to order for dinner in a restaurant. Other common symptoms of neurosis include hopelessness and despair about ever getting well, caused by the impossibility of satisfying the idealized image, and fatigue, which results from wasting substantial energy on the severe inner turmoil. Like Adler, Horney regards the Oedipus complex as a symptom that results from improper childrearing, rather than as a universal phenomenon. (See Horney, 1937, pp. 79–84, 159–161; 1939, pp. 79–87; 1945, pp. 143–190; 1950, p. 143.)

Psychotherapy

Theoretical Foundation.   The goal of Horneyan psychotherapy is to unearth and resolve the patient's deeply repressed inner conflicts, thereby freeing the innate constructive forces to grow and develop. (See Horney, 1939, pp. 276–305; 1945, pp. 217–243; 1950, pp. 333–365.)

Ideally, the patient makes two important discoveries about the supposedly lifesaving neurotic solution: It actually produces increased frustration and self-contempt, and it conceals powerful opposing forces. The neurotic who moves toward people discovers the hostility and selfishness that underlie the excessive desires to please others. The neurotic who moves against people becomes aware of powerful feelings of helplessness. And the neurotic who moves away from people recognizes the strong dependency needs that conflict with the desire to avoid others. The patient must then bring the central inner conflict to light, relinquish the alluring idealized image, and opt for the substantial satisfaction (and challenge) of actualizing the real self. To be effective, however, such insights must be apprehended emotionally as well as intellectually:

> [The patient's] knowledge of himself must not remain an intellectual knowledge, though it may start this way, but must become an *emotional experience*.... The mere intellectual realization is in the strict sense of the word no "realization" at all: it does not become real to him; it does not become his personal property; it does not take roots in him. (Horney, 1950, pp. 342–343.)

Therapeutic Procedures.   Like Freud, Horney makes extensive use of free association and interpretation. However, she is more active than the typical Freudian analyst. Also, like Adler, Horney seeks to change the patient's chosen objectives and expectations. In response to a patient's profound feelings of hopelessness, the therapist may say: "Of course the situation is difficult. But what makes it hopeless is your own attitude toward it. If you would consider changing your claims on life, there would be no need to feel hopeless" (Horney, 1945, p. 186). If a patient suffers from powerful fears of being humiliated by others, the therapist may interpret this as an externalization of intense self-contempt. "It is a long and hard lesson for anybody to learn that others can neither hurt nor establish self-esteem" (Horney, 1950, p. 136).

Unlike Freud, Horney often encourages patients to engage in self-analysis. And she warns that an overemphasis on childhood events may encourage patients to wallow in the memory of past hurts instead of working at the arduous task of therapy. (See Horney, 1942; 1945, pp. 8, 14, 127–129, 177–178; 1950, p. 351.)

Dream Interpretation. Horneyan psychotherapy derives valuable information from a patient's dreams. Unlike Adler, Horney regards dreams as indicative of our true feelings, rather than as an attempt at self-deception.

Dreaming of misplacing one's passport, or of a picture frame that encloses an empty canvas, expresses the loss of the dreamer's real self. As in individual psychology, dreams of falling reveal the insecurity that underlies the patient's conscious conceit; and as in analytical psychology, dreaming of being a tramp or idiot may serve as compensation for conscious arrogance. A nightmare of being trapped in a room with a murderer reflects intense self-contempt, whereas dreaming of tenderly cultivating a growing plant suggests self-concern and sympathy. A dream of making a long-distance telephone call to the therapist indicates the wish to maintain a detached orientation, and dreaming of the analyst as a jailer reveals a desire to blame one's difficulties on others through externalization. (See Horney, 1939, pp. 31–32; 1945, pp. 87, 129; 1950, pp. 31, 152–153, 188, 318, 349–350.)

Resistance and Transference. Horney shares Freud's belief that patients have powerful unconscious resistances to psychotherapy. But Horney argues that patients defend their neurotic solutions and deny the existence of their inner conflicts in order to preserve a sense of personal unity, avoid the frightening prospect of change, and cling to the only apparently successful mode of adjustment that they have ever known. However, resistances are not entirely harmful. They provide clues about important unconscious issues that the patient wishes to avoid, and they afford protection when the therapist offers interpretations that are too threatening. (See Horney, 1942, pp. 267–285; 1945, pp. 187–189; 1950, pp. 201, 334, 340; Singer, 1970, pp. 223–248.)

In marked contrast to Adler, Horney regards transference as Freud's greatest discovery. However, she argues that transference occurs because the therapist becomes a ready target for the patient's habitual attempts to move toward, against, or away from people. The aggressive neurotic tries to dominate the therapist, the detached neurotic waits like a bystander for the therapist to provide miraculous cures, and the compliant neurotic uses pain and suffering to justify expectations of instant help (Horney, 1939, pp. 154–167; 1950, p. 338).

Horney cautions that the goals of therapy are never completely achieved. "It does not lie within the power of the analyst to turn the patient into a flawless human being. He can only help him to become free to strive toward an approximation of these ideals.... The aim of analysis is not to render life devoid of risks and conflicts, but to enable an individual eventually to solve his problems himself" (Horney, 1939, p. 305; 1945, p. 243).

Female Sexuality

Although Horney regards herself as a neo-Freudian, her theory of female sexuality hews more closely to Adler. Her early writings do concede the existence of penis envy; but she emphatically rejects Freud's contention that healthy women crave a boy baby as a disguised penis substitute, and that the lack of a penis produces greater self-contempt and a weaker superego. According to Horney, an organism biologically built for female functions cannot be ruled psychologically by a wish for masculine attributes. She points out that Freudian psychoanalysis is based primarily on studies by male therapists of male patients, which may well have obscured the joys of motherhood and other uniquely feminine superiorities. (See Horney, 1939, pp. 104–105; 1923–1937/1967, pp. 38, 53–55, 60, 63.)

Instead, Horney emphasizes cultural influences on female behavior. If society regards strength, courage, independence, and sexual freedom as masculine characteristics, while depicting frailty and dependence as inherently feminine, women will tend to believe that they deserve a subordinate position. "The view that women are infantile and emotional creatures, and as such, incapable of responsibility and independence is the work of the masculine tendency to lower women's self-respect" (Horney, 1923–1937/1967, p. 146). Horney argues that envy works both ways, with men unconsciously jealous of women's breasts, passivity, and ability to bear children. She also warns that the concept of penis envy may encourage female patients to externalize their problems by blaming them on nature, rather than on their own neurotic behavior. "Every person belonging to a minority group or to a less privileged group tends to use that status as a cover for inferiority feelings of various sources" (Horney, 1939, p. 109).

EVALUATION

Criticisms and Controversies

Horney has been criticized for borrowing too freely from individual psychology and/or Freudian psychoanalysis, and for failing to introduce many new and important constructs. Despite her protestations, externalization is virtually indistinguishable from projection; the idealized image is hardly a radical departure from the superiority complex; shoulds operate much like an overly severe superego; and the idea of intrapsychic conflicts between such opposites as aggressiveness and helplessness closely resembles the defense mechanism of reaction formation. In addition, self-realization is a concept of Jungian origin. Scientific judgment can be unkind to those who merely revise the ideas of others, as Horney herself has observed. "[Many successors] fail to give Freud sufficient credit for pioneering work. It is easy enough to modify, but it takes genius to be the first to visualize the possibilities" (Horney, 1939, p. 154). Nor has her theory stimulated much empirical research.

Perhaps most importantly, Horney's emphasis on neurosis causes her to neglect normal personality development. Since she regards neurosis as a matter of degree, and uses the term *neurotic* only in the sense of "a person to the extent that he is neurotic" (Horney, 1945, p. 27), her theory is applicable to more healthy individuals as well. Yet all too many critics have taken her writings at surface value and characterized her primarily as a clinician, seriously underestimating her importance as a personality theorist.

Contributions

Horney's writings represent the views of a skilled and experienced psychotherapist, and are presented clearly enough to facilitate self-analysis and understanding. Her attempt to modify Freudian psychoanalysis in an Adlerian direction is sufficiently original to be worthy of serious consideration; and it offers a viable alternative for those who accept some of Adler's tenets and reject Freud's libido theory, yet wish to retain the idea of intrapsychic conflict. Her approach to anxiety and transference is considerably more insightful than Adler's, whereas her equalitarian view of women accords well with modern opinion. And Horney provides valuable and well-reasoned insights into the meaning and dynamics of the most common form of psychopathology, neurosis. Although there are those who would regard Horney as outdated, her major works should be required reading for anyone who wishes to acquire a better understanding of the human personality.

Suggested Reading

Horney's most important books are her last two, *Our Inner Conflicts* (1945) and *Neurosis and Human Growth* (1950), which present her theory in its final form. *The Neurotic Personality of Our Time* (1937) is also well regarded, and *Feminine Psychology* (1923–1937/1967) is of interest because it presents her early work on female sexuality, but neither of these captures the true spirit of her ultimate ideas. For a biography of Horney, see Rubins (1978).

SUMMARY

1. **THE BASIC NATURE OF HUMAN BEINGS.** Karen Horney is optimistic about human nature, and concludes that we have the capacity as well as the desire to develop our healthy potentials and become decent individuals. Pathological behavior occurs only if this innate tendency toward self-realization is blocked by external, social forces.

2. **THE STRUCTURE OF PERSONALITY.** Horney stresses the importance of unconscious processes, powerful and actively maintained repressions, and painful intrapsychic conflicts. However, she prefers not to use specific structural constructs.

3. **THE DEVELOPMENT OF PERSONALITY.** Horney has little to say about normal personality development. She attributes neurosis to disturbed relationships with the parents during childhood. Parents who are too wrapped up in their own neuroses to respond to the child's needs engage in such pathogenic behaviors as domination, overprotectiveness, overindulgence, humiliation, neglect, and others. The child therefore develops a sense of being alone in an unfriendly and frightening world (basic anxiety).

4. **FURTHER APPLICATIONS.** *Neurosis*: The child tries to alleviate painful basic anxiety by exaggerating one of its three main characteristics: helplessness, aggressiveness, or detachment. This results in a pathological overemphasis on moving toward, against, or away from people. The sufferer also forms an idealized image that conflicts with the real self, conceals the true wishes and feelings, and establishes unrealistic and unattainable standards. These standards ensure subsequent failure, which increases the hate for the real self (self-contempt) and dependence on the idealized image. Neurosis is also typified by claims, shoulds, the quest for glory, and other symptoms indicative of severe inner conflicts. *Psychotherapy*: Horneyan psychotherapy strives to unearth and resolve the patient's deeply repressed inner conflicts. The patient must learn that the supposedly lifesaving neurotic solution is actually self-defeating, and that it conceals both powerful opposing forces and the sufferer's true desires and feelings. Procedures include free association, interpretation, more active participation by the therapist than in Freudian psychoanalysis, and dream interpretation. *Female sexuality*: Horney rejects Freud's contention that women have greater self-contempt and a weaker superego because they lack the male genital organ. She argues that cultural influences cause women to see themselves as inferior and subordinate, and that men envy certain characteristics of women.

5. **EVALUATION.** Horney has been criticized for adhering too closely to the ideas of Freud and Adler, and for failing to develop a comprehensive theory of her own. But since neurosis represents a difference in degree, rather than in kind, her insights into this disorder contribute significantly to a better understanding of the human personality. In particular, her attempt to modify Freudian psychoanalysis in an Adlerian direction is sufficiently original to be worthy of serious study.

STUDY QUESTIONS

Part I. Questions

1. Give an example from your own life, from the life of someone you know well, or from fiction to illustrate painful inner conflicts and one of the three neurotic "solutions" (moving toward, against, or away from people). Explain how the idealized image in this case produces a vicious circle where matters keep getting worse, and why there is a conflict between the idealized image and this person's real self and wishes. Summarize the key points of this case in a diagram similar to Figure 5.1.

2. Give a real-life example of a person who becomes angry toward someone who is weak because this weakness is a threatening reminder of what the person most dislikes about himself or herself.

3. In Figure 5.1, why do "unrealistic, unattainable standards" lead only to failure? Might they not sometimes lead to success?

4. Give an example from your own life, or from the life of someone you know well, to illustrate: (a) the "tyranny of the should," (b) the neurotic symptoms of inconsistent and indecisive behavior.

5. Give an example from your own life, or from the life of someone you know well, to support Horney's view that "it is a long and hard lesson for anybody to learn that others can neither hurt nor establish self-esteem."

6. How would Horney interpret each of the following dreams? (a) The dreamer looks in a mirror, but doesn't see any reflection. (b) The dreamer sends a long telegram to his or her psychotherapist. (c) The airplane dream described in Chapter 4, study question 10b. (d) The "train" dream described in Chapter 2, study question 12, assuming that the dreamer got to the station too late because the taxi driver insisted on going much too slowly.

7. With regard to women, Horney argues that an organism biologically built for female functions cannot be ruled psychologically by a wish for masculine attributes. Do you agree or disagree? Why?

8. Give a real-life example to support Horney's argument that "Every person belonging to a minority group or to a less privileged group tends to use that status as a cover for inferiority feelings of various sources."

9. What evidence would indicate that Horney's construct of the idealized image is different from (and more useful than) Adler's construct of the superiority complex?

10. A student who works very hard in order to maintain a "straight A" average complains that her parents are pressuring her to be perfect. If in fact her parents aren't pressuring her, how might Horney explain the student's behavior?

11. A professional athlete wins his first world championship. His satisfaction lasts for only a short time, however, and he feels that he "has to" win a second championship in order to be respected. How might Horney explain the athlete's behavior?

12. A terrorist blows up a building in a hated foreign country. How might Horney explain the terrorist's behavior?

Part II. Comments and Suggestions

1. Consider the case history described in the Appendix. The patient suffers from a severe inner conflict between moving toward people and moving away from people, with the latter having been chosen as the neurotic solution. (He is able to describe his conflict because he has made progress in bringing it to consciousness through psychotherapy; otherwise it would be too deeply

repressed.) The idealized image sets unattainable standards, such as never needing other people, which are diametrically opposed to (and thus in conflict with) his needs for love and affection. When he does occasionally try to relate to other people, his efforts are awkward and unsuccessful because he is unpracticed in social skills. These failures are threatening reminders that the idealized image is a fiction, and that the real self is all too capable of error. So the failures (and the real self and wishes) are concealed by emphasizing the idealized image even more, which leads to more unrealistic and unattainable standards, which lead to more failure, and so on.

2. Consider the movie *Patton*, and the well-known scene where the general slaps a soldier who is suffering from battle fatigue. This is rather extreme behavior even for a hardened military leader, and Patton is subsequently disciplined. Might this behavior indicate that Patton unconsciously detested weakness in himself? Is his love for war sufficient evidence to classify him as "moving against people," an orientation where helplessness is repressed because it is incompatible with the desire for mastery? Patton's ill-advised clashes with his superiors did him more harm than good; might this suggest the lack of flexibility that is typical of the neurotic solutions, namely an inability to abandon the "moving against" orientation even when it would have been to his advantage to do so?

3. The standards set by the idealized image are far more demanding than trying to do your best. They are perfectionistic demands that are virtually impossible to satisfy. Even if there is some temporary "success" (e.g., the person writes a novel and becomes world famous or wins an Academy Award), any satisfaction does not last long because the real problem has not been resolved: the person hates his or her real self, and has abandoned his or her true desires in order to satisfy the demands of the idealized image for glorious triumphs. So the person concludes that the fame or award simply isn't enough, and compulsively pursues still greater triumphs—a course that must eventually end in failure.

4. (a) See section 5 of the case material in the Appendix. (b) Using this case history as an illustration: The patient behaves inconsistently by expressing a desire for love and affection (which reflects the dimly sensed healthy needs), while usually avoiding other people (this being the chosen neurotic solution to the problem of basic anxiety). He has great difficulty making such decisions as whether or not to go to a party, which reflects the conflict between his need for love and the usual course of moving away from people. (Since this decision is typically made when he is alone, his anxiety about being with people is not as great, and his true wishes are somewhat more accessible.)

5. When I was younger, I believed that other people could raise or lower my self-esteem. Praise or a favorable book review made me feel like a worthwhile person, whereas criticism or an unfavorable review suggested that there was something wrong with me. However, I now agree with Horney: self-esteem comes from within, and praise or criticism does not determine one's worth as an individual. I still care about the opinions of other people, because I can learn from them, but I am usually able to prevent these opinions from manipulating my self-esteem. It isn't easy to strike a balance between giving proper consideration to the opinions of others and taking these opinions too seriously, and I'm not always successful. But often I am—and it helps to keep Horney's statement in mind.

6. It is difficult to arrive at a valid interpretation from a single dream, let alone dream fragments such as these, especially without knowing anything about the dreamer. But I suspect Horney would argue as follows: (a) The dream reflects the loss of the dreamer's real self. (b) The dreamer wishes to maintain the basic orientation of moving away from people, as expressed by the considerable distance between the dreamer and the therapist. (c) As in Adlerian theory, this dream of falling expresses the insecurity that underlies the dreamer's conscious conceit. (d) The dreamer uses externalization to blame other people, here the taxi driver, for her problems.

7. I would consider this a valid criticism of theories derived primarily by male psychotherapists treating male patients (e.g., Freud's).

8. Consider the complaint of a person who has committed a crime or done something wrong and then says, "You're only against me because I'm ————." (Fill in the name of any minority group.)

9. If neurotics are much more fatigued than more healthy individuals, this would suggest that they are expending considerable amounts of energy on intrapsychic conflicts. If neurotics behave inconsistently much more often than more healthy individuals, as by going to several parties but leaving each one ten minutes after they arrive because they are anxious and uncomfortable, this would suggest that they are being pulled in opposing directions by conflicting wishes. If instead Adler is correct, and personality is always a peaceful and unified whole, the preceding is less likely to be true.

10. What negative feelings might the student have about herself? Why might she want to conceal these feelings from herself? How might an idealized image help her to do so? What "shoulds" might the idealized image demand of her? How might she externalize these shoulds?

11. What might the athlete's idealized image be? Why might he have such an idealized image? Why is it impossible to satisfy the demands of the idealized image?

12. Would Horney attribute the terrorist's behavior to a destructive instinct? Why not? Why might the terrorist have developed basic anxiety during childhood? What neurotic solution has the terrorist chosen? What opposing feelings and wishes might the terrorist be repressing?

CHAPTER 6

ERICH FROMM
The Escape from Freedom

From 1941 to 1943, Karen Horney's American Institute for Psychoanalysis proceeded in an amicable fashion. In April 1943, yet another furor shook the psychiatric community. Her institute withdrew Erich Fromm's privilege to conduct training analyses because he lacked a medical degree, and it was feared that his presence would jeopardize plans to develop a relationship with the New York Medical College (Perry, 1982).

Some colleagues thought it unfair that Fromm should have to suffer the same kind of arbitrary expulsion that Horney herself had encountered previously. In any case, Fromm recovered quite well from this painful professional setback: He went on to become a renowned figure in the realm of personality theory.

OBJECTIVES

- *To devise a theory that retains Freud's emphasis on the unconscious but stresses the social determinants of personality, notably the influence of society and the parents, rather than instincts.*
- *To dispense with Freud's controversial (and unmeasurable) construct of libido.*
- *To correct Freud's pessimistic view of human nature by showing that we have healthy inner potentials.*
- *To warn that being human is a challenging task because, unlike lower species, our behavior is not programmed by instincts and we have to make (often difficult) choices.*
- *To encourage us to make healthy choices, rather than unhealthy ones that seem easier: a loving concern for humanity rather than narcissism and selfishness, a positive and creative influence on our environment rather than destructiveness, identity and independence rather than dependence on and protection by others.*
- *To show that freedom can be threatening, and that we are all too likely to adopt methods for escaping from it that harm ourselves and others.*
- *To correct Freud's belief that mental illness usually has sexual causes by showing that psychopathology is caused by our poorly designed society and pathogenic parenting.*
- *To propose sweeping changes that will make society less pathogenic.*
- *To devise improved methods of dream interpretation.*

BIOGRAPHICAL SKETCH

Erich Fromm was born on March 23, 1900, in Frankfurt, Germany. He was the only child of parents he describes as very neurotic; his father was a wine merchant. Fromm's childhood included a strong Jewish influence, but he rejected organized religion at the age of 26 because "I just didn't want to participate in any division of the human race, whether religious or political" (Fromm, 1962b; see also Fromm, cited by Evans, 1966, p. 56).

Unlike Freud, Jung, Adler, and Horney, Fromm had no medical training. He received his Ph.D. from the University of Heidelberg in 1922, and studied at the internationally renowned Berlin Psychoanalytic Institute. As with Adler, the ravages of World War I came as a profound shock and influenced Fromm toward socialism. Fromm married Frieda Reichmann in 1926, a noted psychoanalyst in her own right and the therapist of Joanne Greenberg ("Hannah Green"), author of the well-known autobiographical novel *I Never Promised You a Rose Garden*. The marriage ultimately ended in divorce. Fromm married Henny Garland in 1944 and, after her death, Annis Freeman in 1953.

Fromm visited the Chicago Psychoanalytic Institute in 1933 as guest lecturer, and emigrated to the United States 1 year later. His first book, the landmark *Escape From Freedom*, appeared in 1941. Because it departed from standard Freudian theory by stressing the effect of social factors on personality, Fromm was dropped as a member of the International Psychoanalytic Association (Roazen, 1973, p. 12). He also suffered the aforementioned split with Horney at about this time.

In 1945, Fromm joined the prestigious William Alanson White Institute of Psychiatry. He also taught at Columbia University, Bennington College, Yale University, Michigan State University, New York University, and the New School for Social Research. Fromm maintained an active interest in social problems and political philosophy, helping to organize SANE (the National Committee for a Sane Nuclear Policy) in 1957. His published works include some 20 volumes, many of which have proved popular with the general public.

Fromm served as professor of psychiatry at the National University in Mexico for 16 years. He died of a heart attack at his home in Muralto, Switzerland, on March 18, 1980.

THE BASIC NATURE OF HUMAN BEINGS

Fromm's theory emphasizes the influence of society on the formation and development of personality. His work strongly reflects the theories of Karl Marx, whom he regards as an even more profound thinker than Freud. (See for example Fromm, 1961; 1962a; 1970/1971a.)

Organic Versus Nonorganic Drives: Isolation and Contradiction

To Fromm (1955/1976b, p. 30), "man [is] an anomaly, . . . the freak of the universe." Our fundamental motive is self-preservation, which we fulfill through our inborn **organic (instinctual) drives:** hunger, thirst, sex, and defense through fight or flight. Yet our superior intellect sets us apart from nature and the animal kingdom. We are unique in many ways, which causes us to feel more isolated and anxious than any other species.

Unlike lower organisms, many crucial human motives consist of learned **nonorganic drives**. Human behavior does not follow a preordained instinctual course, for we possess such unique characteristics as self-awareness and imagination. Instead, we must struggle to ascertain the reasons for our existence and create our own place in the world. We must confront the distinctively human problems of boredom and discontentment. And we must face the threatening realization that death will deprive us of sufficient time to fulfill our potentials, so that "it is the tragic fate of most individuals to die before they are [truly] born" (Fromm, 1955/1976b, p. 32; see also Fromm, 1964/1971b, pp. 147–148; 1968/1974b, p. 62; 1973, pp. 4–8, 72–73, 225–226; 1947/1967a, pp. 48–58, 98).

Nonorganic Drives

Since our nonorganic drives are not instinctual, we have no innate program that ensures their fulfillment. It is all too easy to opt instead for goals that are more alluring, but result in unhappiness—or even in psychopathology.

The Need for Others. Because of our painful and uniquely human feelings of isolation, and because we are woefully weak in comparison with the forces of nature, we must cooperate in order to survive.[1] "Man is *primarily* a social being . . . [and] individual psychology is fundamentally social psychology" (Fromm, 1941/1965, pp. 317–318; see also Fromm, 1976c, pp. 104–105).

---

[1]Fromm originally distinguished between the human needs for "relatedness" to others and "rootedness" in the world, but the distinction between these similar terms is not emphasized in his later works. (See, for example, Fromm, 1973; 1955/1976b, pp. 35–61; 1976c.)

The best way to secure firm roots in the world is **love,** which resembles the Adlerian construct of social interest. The art of loving involves caring for other people, knowing their true feelings and wishes, respecting their right to develop in their own way, and having a sense of responsibility toward humanity:

> Love is not primarily a relationship to a specific person; it is … an *orientation* of *character* which determines the relatedness of a person to the world as a whole.… If I truly love one person I love all persons, I love the world, I love life. (Fromm, 1956/1974a, pp. 38–39. See also Fromm, 1956/1974a, pp. 18–25; 1968/1974b, pp. 81–83; 1947/1967a, pp. 104–107, 134; 1955/1976b, p. 38; 1976c, p. 103.)

Every human being has the capacity for love, but fulfilling this potential is far from easy. We begin life as wholly self-centered infants ("primary **narcissism,**" as in Freudian theory), and pathogenic experiences in later years can cause us to revert to this immature state ("secondary narcissism"). The resulting behavior is like that of an author who meets a friend and talks incessantly about himself, only to conclude with: "Let us now talk about *you*. How did you like my latest book?" (Fromm, 1964/1971b, p. 81. See also Fromm, 1964/1971b, pp. 71–116; 1973, pp. 201–202; 1947/1976a, pp. 132–137; 1955/1976b, pp. 39–41; 1980, pp. 43–54).

Primary narcissism has some value, for we would be unlikely to survive the challenges of life if we regarded ourselves as unimportant. Most of us remain at least somewhat narcissistic throughout our lives (Fromm, cited by Evans, 1966, p. 69). But perhaps the most important of all human goals is to minimize this innate tendency and relate to others with love.

Transcendence.   Unlike other species, human beings are not satisfied with the role of creature. We need to **transcend** the animal state and exert a significant effect on our environment, and Fromm (like Adler and Horney) believes that we have an innate tendency to achieve such superiority in constructive ways. "Strivings for happiness and health … are part of the natural equipment of man.… All organisms have an inherent tendency to actualize their specific potentialities" (Fromm, 1947/1976a, pp. vii, 29; see also Fromm, 1973, pp. 235–237; 1955/1976b, pp. 41–42).

Here again, fulfilling our positive potentials is no easy task. In addition to a genetically determined impulse to preserve ourselves against threat by attacking (**benign aggression**), we also possess the capacity for nonorganically motivated destructiveness that serves no rational defensive purpose (**malignant aggression**). If normal personality development should be blocked, as for example by pathogenic parental behaviors, transcendence may be sought through malignant aggression instead of healthy creativity:

> The more the drive toward life is thwarted, the stronger is the drive toward destruction; the more life is realized, the less is the strength of destructiveness. *Destructiveness is the outcome of unlived life.* (Fromm, 1941/1965, p. 207. See also Fromm, 1964/1971b, pp. 35–69; 1973; 1947/1976a, p. 218.)

Identity.   Lower animals have no sense of **identity,** but humans need to feel: "I am I" (Fromm, 1955/1976b, pp. 62–64). The growing child must learn to surrender its ties with the parents and accept its separateness from other organisms.

As with the other nonorganic drives, identity is not easily achieved. Life has many dangers, and it is tempting to seek safety by acquiring an all-powerful protector. Even the growing child's so-called Oedipal strivings are due solely to this desire for security:

> [The maturing individual is] more aware than the infant of the dangers and risks of life; he knows of the natural and social forces he cannot control, the accidents he cannot

foresee, the sickness and death he cannot elude. What could be more natural, under the circumstances, than man's frantic longing for a power which gives him certainty, protection, and love? ... Thus he is torn between two tendencies since the moment of his birth: one to emerge to the light and the other to regress to the womb; one for adventure and the other for certainty; one for the risk of independence and the other for protection and dependence. (Fromm, 1964/1971b, pp. 120–121. See also Fromm, 1941/1965, pp. 208–230; 1950/1967, pp. 76–80; 1973, pp. 358–362; 1947/1976a, pp. 43–44, 159–161; 1955/1976b, pp. 44–47; 1980, pp. 27–38.)

The desire to be independent conflicts with the wish to escape from the dangers of freedom. Dependence is alluring, since it offers protection from nature and society. But it is also unhealthy, since it precludes the development of a sense of identity. To Fromm, therefore, people are not truly fulfilled as cogs in a machine—even so elegant a one as our modern technological society.

Frames of Orientation.   Like Jung, Fromm concludes that life must have a sense of meaning and purpose. We need a personal philosophy that establishes our values and goals in life, guides our behavior, and delineates our place in the world (a **frame of orientation**). "'Man does not live by bread alone.' . . . [He needs] an answer to the human quest for meaning, and to [the] attempt to make sense of his own existence" (Fromm, 1947/1976a, pp. 55–56; see also Fromm, 1950/1967, pp. 25–26; 1968/1974b, pp. 65–70; 1973, pp. 230–231; 1955/1976b, pp. 64–66; 1976c, pp. 135–139).

Healthy frames of orientation emphasize love, competence, productivity, reason, and the love of life (**biophilia**). But the need for a unifying personal philosophy is so powerful that even an irrational framework, appropriately rationalized, is preferable to none at all. (This is why people can so easily fall under the spell of a warmonger, dictator, or religious zealot.) Unhealthy frames of orientation emphasize the love of death (**necrophilia**), destruction, power, wealth, dependence, and narcissism.

Healthy and unhealthy frames of orientation may blend together in varying degrees. A biophilic and loving person may also be somewhat narcissistic or power-oriented, or a conscious and charitable frame of orientation may conceal one that is unconscious and selfish. Yet regardless of the form, "we do not find any culture in which there does not exist [some] frame of orientation. Or any individual either" (Fromm, 1973, p. 230).

THE STRUCTURE OF PERSONALITY

Fromm devotes relatively little attention to the structure of personality. He concludes that psychology is better off "free from the restrictive influence of the libido theory, and particularly the concepts of *id, ego,* and *superego*" (Fromm, 1973, p. 84; see also Fromm, 1956/1974a, pp. 33–38; 1947/1976a, pp. 145–175; 1955/1976b, pp. 50–51).

Mechanisms of Defense and Escape

Fromm regards unconscious processes as extremely important. He also emphasizes such defense mechanisms as projection, reaction formation, rationalization, regression, fantasy, and repression.

A person, even if he is subjectively sincere, may frequently be driven unconsciously by a motive that is different from the one be believes himself to be driven by.... Freud's revolution was to make us recognize the unconscious aspect of man's mind and the energy which man uses to repress the awareness of undesirable desires. He showed that good intentions mean nothing if they cover up the unconscious intentions; he unmasked "honest" dishonesty by demonstrating that it is not enough to have "meant" well *consciously.…* [Therefore,] only a psychology which utilizes the concept of unconscious forces can penetrate the confusing rationalizations we are confronted with in analyzing either an individual or a culture. (Fromm, 1941/1965, pp. 85, 158; 1973, p. 79. See also Fromm, 1950/1967, pp. 58–59, 74–75; 1947/1976a, pp. 228–230; 1980, pp. 23–26.)

The most likely subjects of repression are such unpleasant emotions and beliefs as destructiveness, necrophilia, hate, envy, hypocrisy, revenge, and the fear of death.

Fromm also describes three other devices that we use to alleviate the painful human condition of isolation, and to escape the threatening freedom from preordained instinctual behaviors. One such **mechanism of escape** is **authoritarianism,** a powerful emotional attachment to another individual that consists of two opposing tendencies: an admiration for authority and desire to submit to powerful others (*masochism*), together with a wish to be the authority and dominate other people (*sadism*). Examples include marriages characterized by excessive submission and domination, often with both partners reflecting both tendencies at different times, and fanatical followers of tyrants such as Hitler. **Malignant aggression** is an escape mechanism that seeks to eliminate external threats. The most common mechanism of escape in our modern society is **automaton conformity,** a chameleonlike immersion in a socially acceptable role. Automaton conformity is undesirable because it conflicts with the need for identity—and because whole societies as well as individuals can be "sick," making the common mode of behavior pathological. (See Fromm, 1941/1965, pp. 163–230; 1964/1971b, pp. 117–134; 1955/1976b, pp. 21–28.)

THE DEVELOPMENT OF PERSONALITY

Unlike Freud, Fromm does not posit specific developmental stages. He also differs from psychoanalysis by arguing that personality can continue to develop during adulthood, although external influences must be intense to affect an older and less impressionable individual (Fromm, 1973, p. 370; 1976c, p. 106). Fromm does share Freud's belief as to the existence of childhood sexuality, however. And he agrees that personality is primarily determined during the early years of life, with the unusually long period of human dependency serving as a powerful lesson about the need to relate to others.

The growing child slowly learns to distinguish between "I" and "not-I" through its contacts with the environment, notably those involving the parents. This increasing sense of identity and separation from the parents is essential to healthy development, but it also intensifies the child's feelings of isolation. The freedom to do what we want is accompanied not only by freedom from the hindrance of authority, but also from the comforts of security and protection. As

---

CAPSULE SUMMARY
Some Important Frommian Terminology

Authoritarianism	A nonproductive frame of orientation that involves powerful desires to dominate others and to submit to others. One of the three mechanisms of escape.
Automaton conformity	Immersion in a socially acceptable role at the cost of one's need for identity. One of the three mechanisms of escape.

Benign aggression	An organic, healthy drive to defend oneself against threat by attacking.
Biophilia	Love of life; a productive frame of orientation.
Exploitative orientation	A nonproductive frame of orientation that seeks to gain rewards by force or cunning.
Frame of orientation	A set of principles or personal philosophy that gives meaning to one's life, establishes one's values and goals, and defines one's place in the world; a nonorganic drive.
Hoarding orientation	A nonproductive frame of orientation that involves miserliness, compulsive orderliness, and stubbornness.
Identity	A sense of oneself as a distinct and separate entity; a nonorganic drive.
Love	A sense of responsibility toward humanity that includes caring for other people, knowing how others feel, and respecting their right to develop in their own way. Similar to Adler's concept of social interest.
Malignant aggression (destructiveness)	Destructive behavior that serves no rational defensive purpose; a nonorganic drive. One of the three mechanisms of escape.
Marketing orientation	A nonproductive frame of orientation wherein one characterizes oneself as a product that will "sell" in the social marketplace, and tries to become what others want.
Mechanism of escape	An undesirable method for resolving threatening feelings of isolation and freedom; similar to nonproductive orientation. Includes authoritarianism, automaton conformity, and malignant aggression.
Narcissism	An innate tendency toward self-centeredness ("primary narcissism"), which may become a nonproductive frame of orientation later in life ("secondary narcissism").
Necrophilia	Love of death; the most pathological and dangerous of the nonproductive frames of orientation. Often occurs in combination with narcissism and malignant aggression.
Nonorganic drive	A noninstinctual, learned motive. Includes relatedness, transcendence, identity, and the need for a frame of orientation.
Nonproductive orientation	A frame of orientation that is undesirable because it involves the surrender of one's innate potentials for healthy growth and self-realization.
Organic drive (instinctual drive)	An instinctual, biological motive. Includes hunger, thirst, sex, and defense through fight (benign aggression) or flight.
Productive orientation	A healthy frame of orientation that involves the fulfillment of one's positive innate potentials. Characterized by love, biophilia, work that benefits oneself and others, and rational thought.
Receptive orientation	A nonproductive frame of orientation that seeks to obtain rewards by being loved and cared for.
Relatedness, rootedness	Terms sometimes used by Fromm to refer to the nonorganic drive for interpersonal relationships, which results from the feelings of isolation and physical weakness of the human species.
Symbolic language	A mode of expression wherein one entity stands for another; found in dreams, fairy tales, and myths.
Transcendence	Rising above the animal state and exerting a significant effect on one's environment; a nonorganic drive. Healthy transcendence is characterized by creativity and love, whereas pathological transcendence includes hate and malignant aggression. Similar to Adler's concept of striving for superiority.

humanity has gained greater independence throughout the course of history, we have become more isolated and anxious. "When one has become an individual, one stands alone and faces the world in all its perilous and overpowering aspects" (Fromm, 1941/1965, p. 45).

If the child's belief in its own ability keeps pace with the increasing feelings of isolation, anxiety is minimal and personality development proceeds normally. Such positive growth is facilitated by parents who are biophilous, affectionate, and nonthreatening. But if the sense of self-reliance is damaged by pathogenic parental behaviors, the child is likely to sacrifice its innate healthy potentials and seek to escape from the threatening human state of isolation in misguided ways. For example, authoritarian parents may use the child to fulfill their frustrated ambition for professional success, or to enjoy a sense of personal power. Such parents may repress their true intentions (and lack of love) by lavishing the child with attention, advice, or gifts—everything but genuine warmth, and the right to be independent:

> The child is put into a golden cage, it can have everything provided it does not want to leave the cage. The result of this is often a profound fear of love on the part of the child when he grows up, as "love" to him implies being caught and blocked in his own quest for freedom. (Fromm, 1941/1965, p. 168. See also Fromm, 1941/1965, pp. 216–217, 268; 1956/1974a, pp. 51–52; 1947/1976a, pp. 136, 157–158.)

Other pathogenic parental behaviors include pessimism, narcissism, necrophilia, and physical abuse. To Fromm, such forms of maltreatment are so prevalent that "one must believe that loving parents are the exception, rather than the rule" (1976c, p. 45).

Character Typology

The healthy personality is typified by biophilia, love, creativity, and reason. These characteristics comprise the **productive** frame of orientation (Fromm, 1964/1971b; 1947/1976a, pp. 89–113).

As we have seen, the undesirable or **nonproductive** frames of orientation include narcissism, necrophilia, dependence, compulsive strivings for power or wealth, and the mechanisms of escape (authoritarianism, automaton conformity, and malignant aggression). In addition, Fromm (1947/1976a, pp. 70–89) has described four other nonproductive orientations. The **receptive** orientation, like Horney's "moving toward people," constantly seeks to be loved and nurtured by others. The person with an **exploitative** orientation strives to obtain rewards through force or cunning, like Horney's "moving against people." The **hoarding** orientation is denoted by miserliness, compulsive orderliness, and obstinacy, and resembles the Freudian anal-retentive character and Horney's "moving away from people." Like Adler's (1927/1957, p. 181) description of people who guard their wretched treasures, "the hoarding character experiences himself like a beleaguered fortress; he must prevent anything from going out and save what is inside" (Fromm, 1973, p. 293). Those who adopt the **marketing** orientation regard themselves as products that will "sell" in the social marketplace. Although some social expertise and polish is desirable, these individuals repress their needs for identity and self-realization in order to become what others want them to be.

FURTHER APPLICATIONS OF FROMMIAN THEORY

Dream Interpretation

Like Freud, Fromm regards dreams as the royal road to the unconscious. He concludes that dream interpretation is probably the most important and revealing technique in psychotherapy, and he recommends that all of us learn to understand the language of dreams. "[As] the Talmud says, 'dreams which are not interpreted are like letters which have not been opened.' ... [Dreams] are important communications from ourselves to ourselves" (Fromm, 1951/1957, p. 10; see also Fromm, cited by Evans, 1966, p. 36).

The Purpose of Dreams. Fromm agrees with Freud that dreams can fulfill our wishes, that they are triggered by day's residues, and that threatening truths may be concealed in various ways. A young lawyer was criticized at work by his boss, but dismissed this incident as trivial. That night, he dreamed of riding a white charger before a cadre of cheering soldiers. Thus he alleviated his fears of failure and restored his self-esteem, which had been shaken by the events of the preceding day. The dream fulfilled these wishes in a disguised manner, similar to military daydreams he sought comfort from as a child when rejected and taunted by his peers (Fromm, 1951/1957, pp. 150–157).

Fromm also shares Jung's belief that dreams can have obvious and undisguised meanings, and that they need not involve childhood conflicts. A dream may express current anxieties and misgivings, provide accurate and important insights about ourselves or other people, or propose solutions to our waking problems. A writer was offered a tempting position that would compromise his integrity for a great deal of money. He resolved this dilemma by dreaming that two opportunists advised him to drive up a peak, whereupon he was killed in a crash and awoke in terror—a clear indication that accepting the job would destroy him psychologically. Similarly, the discoverer of the Benzine ring first visualized the correct chemical structure in a dream of snakes biting each others' tails. "We are not only less reasonable and less decent in our dreams but . . . also more intelligent, wiser, and capable of better judgment when we are asleep than when we are awake" (Fromm, 1951/1957, p. 33; see also Fromm, 1951/1957, pp. 36–45; 1964/1971b, pp. 42, 127–128; 1947/1976a, pp. 168–169; 1980, pp. 100–101).

Regardless of the specific content, every dream is a deliberate creation of the dreamer. "Whatever the role we play in the dream, *we* are the author, it is *our* dream, *we* have invented the plot" (Fromm, 1951/1957, p. 4). Nor is a dream ever unimportant, although its true significance may be concealed by a trivial façade. A young woman once claimed that a dream of hers was meaningless because it consisted only of serving her husband a dish of strawberries, whereupon he pointed out with a laugh: "You seem to forget that strawberries are the one fruit which I do not eat" (Fromm, 1951/1957, p. 149; see also p. 24). Whether this dream expresses a severe marital conflict or only mild annoyance is not clear; but, like all dreams, it deals with important issues.

Dream Symbols. Dreams are expressed in **symbolic language,** an important mode of communication also found in fairy tales and myths. Unlike Freud, Fromm regards many dream symbols as asexual. A person who feels lost and confused may dream of arriving at the outskirts of a city where the streets are empty, the surroundings are unfamiliar, and there is no transportation to where the dreamer wishes to go. Or, since symbolic language has its own syntax and can be quite unrealistic, the dreamer may depict a cowardly human being in the form of a chicken. (See Fromm, 1951/1957, pp. 11–23, 28.)

Some dream symbols have universal meanings because they are intrinsically related to what they represent, such as the power and vitality of fire, the slow and steady quality of moving water, and the security of a valley enclosed by mountains. In contrast to Jungian archetypes, universal symbols result from these intrinsic meanings rather than from racial inheritances (Fromm, 1951/1957, p. 18). Other dream elements possess only an accidental, learned relationship to the concepts that they express. The street or city where one falls in love is likely to symbolize happiness, whereas the identical scene may represent sorrow to an individual who suffered a painful parting there. The meaning of accidental symbols must be supplied by the dreamer, and Fromm (like Freud) uses free association to bring this information to consciousness.

The Dreams of Freud and Jung.   Interpreting one's own dreams is no easy task, and Fromm argues that even Freud and Jung showed a tendency to shy away from threatening truths. Freud once dreamed of having written a botanical monograph, with each copy containing a dried specimen of the plant in question. Based on extensive free associations, Freud interpreted this dream as an expression of pride in his professional achievements. However, Fromm concludes that the dream actually reflects profound self-reproach over Freud's puritanical and lifeless treatment of sexuality. "He has dried the flower, made sex and love the object of scientific inspection and speculation, rather than leave it alive" (Fromm, 1951/1957, p. 93).

Jung once dreamed of killing someone named Siegfried with a rifle, became horror-stricken, and awakened with the thought that he must kill himself unless he could understand the dream. He eventually decided that he had symbolically murdered the hero within himself, thereby expressing a sense of humility. Fromm suggests that Jung was at this time angry with his esteemed mentor Freud, even to the extent of harboring powerful unconscious death wishes (which Freud had commented on, but which Jung indignantly denied). The dream-victim was actually Freud himself, with Jung unable to recognize the truth because he was repressing a necrophilous orientation. "The slight change from *Sigmund* to *Siegfried* was enough to enable a man whose greatest skill was the interpretation of dreams, to hide the real meaning of this dream from himself" (Fromm, 1964/1971b, p. 44; see also Fromm, 1951/1957, pp. 47–108; 1980, pp. 73–89).

Psychopathology

Fromm accepts Freud's definition of mental health as the capacity for love and productive work. He also agrees that psychopathology represents a difference in degree, rather than in kind:

> The phenomena which we observe in the neurotic person are in principle not different from those we find in the normal. They are only more accentuated, clear-cut, and frequently more accessible to the awareness of the neurotic person than they are in the normal.... (Fromm, 1941/1965, p. 159; see also p. 46.)

Causes of Neurosis.   In addition to such pathogenic parental behaviors as authoritarianism, narcissism, pessimism, and physical abuse, neurosis is often caused by the culture in which one lives. Fromm argues that society seeks to make people *wish* to do what they *have* to do, which presents "a difficult problem: *How to break a person's will without his being aware of it?* Yet by a complicated process of indoctrination, rewards, punishments, and fitting ideology, [society] solves this task by and large so well that most people believe they are following their own will and are unaware that their will itself is conditioned and manipulated" (Fromm, 1976c, p. 78; see also p. 133). Ironically, we are pressured into automaton conformity by the society that we have created to serve our ends.

To make matters worse, we are constantly bombarded by pathogenic stimuli. These include the "rationalizing lies" used by modern advertising that play upon our sexual desires, threaten us with social ostracism unless we use the appropriate deodorants, promise revolutionary changes in our love life if we purchase a particular brand of toothpaste, or urge us to buy products simply because they are endorsed by famous or attractive individuals. "All these methods are essentially irrational; they have nothing to do with the qualities of the merchandise, and they smother and kill the critical capacities of the customer like an opiate or outright hypnosis" (Fromm, 1951/1957, p. 35; 1941/1965, p. 149; 1976c, p. 188).

Also adding to our sense of alienation and insignificance are elected politicians whom we hardly ever see in person, and who cunningly hide their true intentions behind jargonistic double-talk; huge bureaucracies that regard the individual as unimportant; repetitive jobs that transform workers into machinelike cogs, and eliminate the pride of producing a complete product; vast and overcrowded cities; conflicting societal prescriptions that advise us to be self-centered winners on the one hand, and charitably selfless on the other; and the ominous threat of nuclear war. And since parents serve as *"the psychological agent[s] of society,"* we are all exposed to these influences (at least indirectly) from the moment of birth. In fact, "the real problem of mental life is not why some people become insane, but rather why most avoid insanity" (Fromm, 1941/1965, p. 315; 1955/1976b, p. 34; see also Fromm, 1947/1976a, p. 132; 1981).

Dynamics of Neurosis.   According to Fromm, neurosis always consists of a conflict between two opposing forces. It occurs when our healthy innate drives toward self-realization and independence are blocked by parental or societal influences. The individual may then opt for narcissism instead of love, malignant aggression instead of transcendence, dependence instead of identity and independence, or any of the other nonproductive frames of orientation. The goal of the psychologist is not to define and treat a set of symptoms, but to understand the neurotic character and the resulting difficulties in living. (See Fromm, 1941/1965, pp. 162, 176, 201; 1950/1967, p. 65; 1947/1967a, p. 222.)

Psychotherapy and Social Reform

Fromm accepts many of the tenets and procedures of Freudian psychoanalysis, including the need to bring unconscious material to consciousness, free association, resistance, transference, countertransference, working through, and the importance of dream interpretation. He also shares Freud's belief that psychoanalysis is not suitable for everyone, nor can it guarantee improvement. Fromm prefers to dispense with transference neurosis, however, and to have the patient perceive the analyst as a genuine human being. He favors the Adlerian technique of early recollections, and he shares Horney's view that insights must be achieved on both an intellectual and emotional level in order to be effective. Analytic therapy strives to help the patient replace the chosen nonproductive frame(s) of orientation with the productive orientation, as by abandoning narcissism in favor of love. (See Fromm, 1950/1967, p. 84; 1973, pp. 205–207; 1947/1976a, p. 225; 1976c, pp. 31, 169–170; Fromm, cited by Evans, 1976, pp. 30–55, 82.)

For the most part, Fromm's psychological prescriptions refer to society rather than to the individual. He warns that the diminishing worldwide supply of food, the environmental deterioration resulting from such influences as the automobile and pesticides, and the proliferation of nuclear weapons have brought us to a crisis that threatens the very survival of our species:

> Some 10–20 million people are starving to death annually now.... [while] population growth increases the probability of a lethal worldwide plague and of a thermonuclear war.... [Thus] for the first time in history, the *physical survival of the human race depends on a radical change of the human heart....* [Yet] we go on plundering the raw materials of the earth, poisoning the earth, and preparing nuclear war. We hesitate not at all leaving our own descendants this plundered earth as their heritage. (Fromm, 1976c, pp. 10, 166, 189.)

To Fromm, the only alternative to disaster is a radical remodeling of society. Unlimited population growth must be checked, and wasting the earth's resources through conspicuous and excessive consumption must be abandoned. The "brainwashing" techniques of modern industrial and political advertising must be prohibited, so that we can wean ourselves from such propaganda and learn to make better use of our powers of reason. Consumer strikes should be used to impress our will on industry, since a boycott by even 20% of the buying public would have a profound impact. The reestablishment of the town meeting would enable people to exert a more meaningful effect on the process of government. Education should enable students to fulfill their innate potentials and experience what they learn, rather than merely memorizing a vast number of unrelated facts. The gap between rich and poor nations must be closed by appropriate foreign aid, so as to decrease the probability of epidemics and nuclear wars instigated by the "have-nots." A guaranteed annual income must be established, ensuring everyone of the right to subsist. Women must be freed from patriarchal domination. Movies should foster pride in the whole human race, rather than one particular national or ethnic group. A Supreme Cultural Council, neither elected by popular vote nor appointed by the government, should be established to advise political leaders and the citizenry. Finally, atomic disarmament is essential (Fromm, 1976c, pp. 173–196; see also Fromm, 1941/1965, p. 273; 1964/1971b, p. 112 n. 14; 1968/1974b, pp. 119–120; 1955/1976b, pp. 291–298; 1981).

Fromm recognizes that many people are too accustomed to our present society to accept such drastic alterations, even at the cost of possible future catastrophes. Nor is he optimistic about the possibility that academic psychology will provide effective answers, concluding that researchers all too often prefer to deal with problems that are insignificant but capable of rigorous measurement. Yet despite the difficulties and limited chances of success, Fromm argues that the attempt to change must be made:

> If a sick person has even the barest chance for survival, no responsible physician will say "Let's give up the effort," or will use only palliatives. On the contrary, everything conceivable is done to save the sick person's life. Certainly, a sick society cannot expect anything less. (Fromm, 1976c, p. 197; see also Fromm, 1976c, p. 11; Fromm, cited by Evans, 1966, p. 74, 84.)

Other Applications

As would be expected from his definition of love, Fromm differs from Freud by regarding "loving thy neighbor as thyself" as our most important standard (Fromm, 1950/1967, p. 84). But Fromm cautions that religions may preach harmful and outdated principles that stifle the healthy growth of individuals and societies. And he dislikes the divisiveness that results from the existence of many religions, so he prefers to emphasize the commonness of all humanity. (See Fromm, 1941/1965, pp. 81–122; 1950/1967; 1947/1976a, pp. 23–24; 1976c, pp. 41–44.)

In addition to dreams, Fromm devotes considerable attention to the symbolic nature of literature and mythology. For example, the story of Little Red Riding Hood symbolically describes a young girl's problems with sexuality and male–female conflicts, with the heroine's red cap representing menstruation and men depicted as dangerous wolves (Fromm, 1951/1957, pp. 235–241).

EVALUATION

Criticisms and Controversies

Not surprisingly, Fromm's sweeping recommendations for social reform have proved to be highly controversial. His socialistic approach is unacceptable to those who believe that capitalism, with its faults, is the best method for meeting the needs of the people. Some of his proposals are vague and lacking in detail, whereas others would be extremely difficult to implement (as he himself concedes). Fromm's writings lack the quantitative analyses commonly expected of a scientist, especially one who proposes such profound social changes. In contrast to Freud, it is even difficult to detect much correspondence between Fromm's conclusions and evidence from his psychoanalytic practice. This absence of hard data gives his books a distinctly sermonic tone, which he justifies with the subjective argument that he finds in psychology that which proves him to be right (Fromm, cited by Evans, 1966, p. 80).

Some noted philosophers have questioned Fromm's interpretation of Marxist socialism as humanistic. Unlike Freud, Fromm often does not clarify the relationships among terms used in his earlier works and those in his later writings. Fromm's theory has generated little empirical research. And he appears to ignore important similarities between the constructs of other theorists and his own.

Contributions

Fromm's warnings about the dangers of abusing our environment, world famine, and nuclear war are timely and important. He has made major contributions to our understanding of dream interpretation and totalitarianism. His inclusion of organic drives is preferable to Adler's rejection of innate determinants of behavior, and his view of feminine equality accords more closely with modern opinion than that of Freud. Fromm's emphasis on narcissism also seems justified when applied to our affluent, "spoiled" society. As a colleague of such noted psychologists as Horney and Sullivan, Fromm has exerted some influence on theories other than his own.

Like Horney, Fromm does not pretend to offer a complete theory of personality. But Horney's insights into neurotic behavior make her writings of considerable value to psychology, whereas Fromm's sweeping yet unsubstantiated social criticisms would seem to belong more in the realm of philosophy. Psychologists and personality theorists are expected to follow a more scientific course, where recommendations are clearly linked to clinical and/or research data. By devoting so much of his attention to apparently unsupported speculations, Fromm himself has limited the impact of his work on modern psychological thought.

Suggested Reading

Among Fromm's many titles, two stand out: *Escape From Freedom* (1941/1965), which has been praised as a landmark in psychological, political, and philosophical thought, and his classic work on dream interpretation, *The Forgotten Language* (1951/1957). *The Art of Loving* (1956/1974a) has also achieved wide popularity, and *The Anatomy of Human Destructiveness* (1973) offers interesting insights into this important area.

SUMMARY

1. THE BASIC NATURE OF HUMAN BEINGS. Fromm emphasizes the conflict between our innate, organic animal side and the uniquely human characteristics of self-awareness, reason, and imagination. He also stresses the importance of such nonorganic drives as the need for others, transcendence, identity, and frames of orientation. Fromm is optimistic about human nature, but he is more pessimistic than Horney about our secondary capacity for learned pathological behavior. Nonorganic drives are difficult to satisfy, since there is no innate program that ensures their fulfillment. Thus love may surrender to narcissism, transcendence to destructiveness, and identity to dependence.

2. THE STRUCTURE OF PERSONALITY. Fromm accepts the importance of unconscious processes, repression, and defense mechanisms. But he rejects the Freudian constructs of id, ego, and superego; nor does he favor any alternative structural model. He does posit three mechanisms that we use to escape the threatening freedom from preordained instinctual behaviors: a sadomasochistic attachment to another person (authoritarianism), eliminating external threats (malignant aggression), and a chameleonlike immersion in a socially accept-able role (automaton conformity).

3. THE DEVELOPMENT OF PERSONALITY. Fromm concludes that personality may continue to develop into adulthood, but he posits no specific developmental stages. He warns against such pathogenic parental behaviors as authoritarianism, narcissism, pessimism, and physical abuse. He also devotes considerable attention to such nonproductive character types or frames of orientation as receptive, exploitative, hoarding, and marketing. In contrast, the healthy productive orientation stresses biophilia, love, and reason.

4. FURTHER APPLICATIONS. Fromm is noted for his major work on dream interpretation, *The Forgotten Language*. He argues that dreams may be relatively obvious as well as disguised, and that we are often wiser in our dreams than when we are awake. Fromm is also a social philoso-pher who offers numerous criticisms of our hypocritical, alienating, and destructive society. He therefore proposes sweeping (and highly controversial) changes in the basic structure of society.

5. EVALUATION. Fromm's radical and sermonistic proposals for social change often seem unscientific and excessive. Yet his works have also been praised as landmarks in psychologi-cal, political, and philosophical thought, and it is by no means clear that his recommendations can be safely ignored.

STUDY QUESTIONS

Part I. Questions

1. Fromm argues that "destructiveness is the outcome of unlived life." Freud contends that destructiveness occurs because we fail to sublimate our illicit instincts. Since both theorists agree that we are destructive, why is this theoretical difference important?

2. According to Adler, it is all too possible to deny our predisposition for social interest and become neurotically self-centered. Fromm argues that we must overcome our innate nar-cissistic tendencies in order to develop healthy and mature love. Does the difference in termi-nology between Adler and Fromm reflect important theoretical differences?

3. Explain how each of the following is related to Fromm's conception of "escape from freedom:" (a) The conflict between the healthy need for identity and the desire for a powerful protector. (b) A growing child gets increasing freedom to do what he or she wants, which involves both freedom from the hindrance of parental authority and freedom from the comforts of security and protection. (c) Unlike lower animals, humans have nonorganic drives. (d) The behavior described in section 5 of the case material in the Appendix.

4. Give a real-life example of a child who grows up with a profound fear of being loved. Why might this happen?

5. Give an example from your own life, from the life of someone you know well, or from fiction to illustrate: (a) the receptive orientation; (b) the exploitative orientation; (c) the hoard-ing orientation; (d) the marketing orientation; (e) the productive orientation.

6. A young woman dreams that she is having breakfast with her husband and hands him the comics section of the newspaper. To her, this dream seems meaningless and unimportant. How would Fromm interpret this dream?

7. Fromm takes a negative view of many aspects of our society, including: (a) advertising by businesses and politicians; (b) politicians; (c) inadequate foreign aid; (d) the lack of a guaranteed annual income; (e) the existence of so many different religions; (f) the threat of nuclear war; (g) plundering our environment and poisoning the earth. Do you agree or disagree? Why?

8. According to Fromm, "one must believe that loving parents are the exception, rather than the rule." Why might he have reached such a pessimistic conclusion?

9. A terrorist blows up a building in a hated foreign country. How might Fromm explain the terrorist's behavior?

Part II. Comments and Suggestions

1. One reason: Fromm devotes considerable emphasis to changing society. Since we do not have any innate illicit tendencies, the causes of psychopathology must be external, namely society (and its agents, the parents). In contrast, Freud devotes considerable emphasis to changing the individual (as through psychoanalytic therapy). Since we have powerful illicit instincts that always remain part of our personality, it is we who must change by sublimating these instincts in order to reduce the inevitable conflicts between ourselves and society.

In my opinion, there is merit in both of these views. We should try to improve our society (which is in need of considerable improvement). We should also strive for self-improvement, and to replace our self-defeating and pathological behaviors with healthy ones. (Recall that we are all at least a little neurotic—some of us more than a little.)

2. I don't think so. Fromm's conception of love is virtually identical to Adler's construct of social interest, since it involves a caring for humanity rather than an infatuation with a specific person, and (secondary) narcissism is the same as exaggerated self-interest. So I regard this as yet another example of Adler's ideas being subsumed into other theories of personality, albeit using a different terminology.

3. (a) and (b) Although everyone needs to feel that "I am I," this is not easy to achieve. Life has many dangers, such as accidents, earthquakes, floods, illness, crime, and death. So it is tempting to abandon our desire for independence and identity, escape from the freedom to make our own choices, and seek out a powerful protector who will provide security by telling us what to do. (c) If we only had organic drives, we would be more like lower organisms whose behavior is determined by innate instincts. Without reason, self-awareness, and imagination, there would be fewer (or perhaps even no) choices for us to make, and little or no freedom from which to escape. (d) Freedom is frightening to this person because he is too weak and conflicted to take advantage of it. He has repressed his real self so well that he usually does not know what he wants, and freedom is a threatening reminder of this painful situation. So he would rather not be free, and he unconsciously creates inner commands for himself that make it seem as though he has no free choice. (Other ways of escaping from freedom that he might have chosen, but did not, include becoming a conformist or someone who blindly follows the orders of a dictator or religious zealot.)

4. See sections 2 and 3 of the case material in the Appendix. Because of such pathogenic parental behaviors as overprotectiveness and destructive criticism, and his own inability to deal with these behaviors, he developed basic anxiety (in Horney's terminology) and surrendered his real self. Yet his parents always said how much they loved him (which, in their way, they did). So he equates love with being overprotected, dominated, criticized, and having to abandon his real wishes. These beliefs are largely unconscious; he is aware only of considerable anxiety concerning the prospect of intimate relationships and love.

5. Possible examples: (a) Horney's description of the patient who resembles "Cinderella bereft of her fairy godmother." (b) Enron executives; a novel popular many years ago, *What*

Makes Sammy Run; the character of Sheldon Grossbart in Philip Roth's short story, "Defender of the Faith." (c) See the comment to Chapter 4, question 6e; the hoarding orientation is much the same as Adler's description of the person who "guards his wretched treasures." (d) A college student wears trendy clothes and drinks alcohol, even though he does not like to do so, in order to be accepted by his peer group. (e) See the comment to Chapter 4, question 6f.

6. Recall that to Fromm, every dream is an important communication from the dreamer to himself or herself. How might Fromm's interpretation vary according to the following additional information? (a) Her husband hates the comics. (b) Her husband loves the comics. (c) At a party on the evening prior to this dream, her husband accused her of being too silly and comical. (d) Her husband likes to talk during breakfast; she prefers to read the paper. (e) She likes to talk during breakfast; her husband prefers to read the paper. (f) On the day prior to this dream, she read a comic strip wherein a presumably happy husband and wife were revealed as having serious marital difficulties. (g) She wants to have cosmetic surgery; her husband argues that it is too expensive. On the day prior to this dream, she read a comic strip wherein a woman had a successful facelift. (Do you see why it is usually necessary to know more about the dreamer, and perhaps obtain the dreamer's free associations, in order to interpret a dream accurately?)

7. (a) Are advertisements illogical? Which is more sensible: to buy a pair of sneakers because a famous athlete wears that brand (and is paid a large amount of money to recommend it), or to buy a brand that is comfortable, durable, and reasonably priced? Do such advertisements impair our ability to use reason and logic? (b) How often do you actually meet those who represent you in government? Do they usually tell the truth in their speeches and statements? (c) and (d) Starvation is a serious problem in "have-not" countries, as is the possibility that they might start a nuclear war. So too is the problem of the homeless in this country. But where is the money to come from? (e) If this is harmful, why is this country respected for allowing freedom of religion? (f) How serious is this threat? Might it get worse in the not too distant future? (g) What are the dangers of following our present course? What changes should be made?

8. Fromm had extremely negative views about our society, and parents act as the agents of society by teaching prevailing standards to their children. However, consider Fromm's opinion of his own parents (biographical sketch). If a child has parents who are very neurotic and don't meet his or her important needs, might it be comforting to believe that this is the norm rather than the exception?

9. Would Fromm attribute the terrorist's behavior to an illicit instinct? Why not? What mechanism of escape is the terrorist using? According to Fromm, what is the cause of human destructiveness? Why, then, might the terrorist have chosen this mechanism of escape instead of the healthy, productive orientation?

CHAPTER 7

HARRY STACK SULLIVAN
The Interpersonal Theory of Psychiatry

For 2 years, Harry Stack Sullivan was an honorary member of Karen Horney's new psychoanalytic institute. However, he was angered by the seemingly arbitrary expulsion of Erich Fromm (Chapter 6). Sullivan therefore resigned from the institute in April 1943, arguing that it is wrong to attack the integrity and judgment of gifted colleagues who prefer the path of innovator and critic.

In the course of defending Fromm, Sullivan also evoked the wrath of the Freudians. He took exception to a scathing review of Fromm's classic *Escape From Freedom* by the psychoanalyst Otto Fenichel, which concluded with the claim that only the true faith—Freudian psychoanalysis—was "pure gold." Sullivan contended that this review was a pro-Freudian diatribe lacking any substantive quality, whose purpose was primarily political. Once again, orthodox psychoanalysis responded to challenge by imposing the penalty of

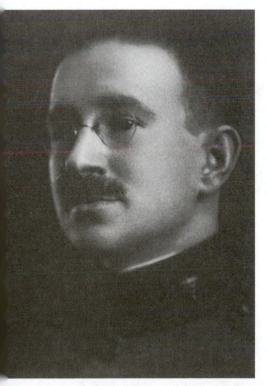

excommunication. Many analysts were asked (in effect) to choose between Freud's beliefs and associating with Sullivan, and those who selected the latter alternative were subjected to various forms of professional intimidation. This political rivalry grew so intense that even today, there are psychoanalysts who have adopted important Sullivanian theories yet who steadfastly refuse to credit him accordingly. (See Perry, 1982, pp. 386–389.) Nevertheless, Sullivan ultimately emerged from these professional difficulties as one of the leading figures in the realm of personality theory.

OBJECTIVES

- *To devise a theory that retains the importance of the unconscious but stresses the social determinants of personality, notably the parents but also schoolmates, friends, and love interests, rather than instincts.*
- *To dispense with virtually all Freudian constructs, including libido, and use his own unique terminology.*
- *To correct Freud's pessimistic view of human nature by showing that we have an inherent drive toward mental health.*
- *To show that personality development proceeds through a series of seven stages from infancy to adulthood, rather than ending at age six as Freud contended.*
- *To show that intense anxiety is an extremely important aspect of psychopathology, and that anxiety in the mother (or whichever adult fulfills this function) is its primary cause.*
- *To emphasize that we need other people, and denying this need is also a major cause of psychopathology.*
- *To explain the causes and dynamics of schizophrenia.*
- *To devise improved methods for treating schizophrenia and other psychological disorders.*

BIOGRAPHICAL SKETCH

Harry Stack Sullivan was born on February 21, 1892, in Norwich, New York. He was the only surviving child of a taciturn father, a farmer and skilled workman, and a mother who "never troubled to notice the characteristics of the child she had brought forth.... 'Her son' was so different from me that I felt she had no use for me, except as a clotheshorse on which to hang an elaborate pattern of illusions" (Sullivan, 1942). Partly because the Sullivans were the only Catholic family in a Protestant community, Harry had a lonely childhood. This helped him develop an unusual empathy for the intense isolation of the schizophrenic, together with a rather withdrawn personality of his own.

Sullivan encountered significant personal problems during his freshman year at Cornell University. He became the cat's-paw for a gang of boys in the dormitory, and shouldered the blame for some illegalities engineered by the group. He is also believed to have undergone a schizophrenic breakdown at about this time. (See Perry, 1982, pp. 3, 143–146, 151.)

Sullivan never returned to Cornell after his one-semester suspension. In 1911 he entered the Chicago College of Medicine and Surgery, the medical branch of Valparaiso University of Indiana. His grades were erratic; but he completed his course work in 1915, and ultimately received the M.D. degree from Valparaiso in 1917 (Perry, 1982, pp. 156–159, 165).

Sullivan demonstrated considerable skill as an internist, but he preferred a career in psychiatry. He therefore entered psychoanalytic therapy as a patient during 1916–1917. After serving in World War I as a first lieutenant in the Medical Corps, Sullivan worked at government and private hospitals in Maryland and Washington, D.C. Here he began his intensive studies of schizophrenia; came under the influence of William Alanson White, who later founded a prestigious psychiatric foundation and named Sullivan its president in 1933; and gradually modified Freudian psychoanalysis to suit his own theoretical predilections.

In 1931, Sullivan moved to New York City and pursued further psychoanalytic training. He suffered financial problems that forced him to file for bankruptcy, but ultimately established a lucrative private practice. During World War II, he served as consultant to the newly formed Selective Service System, and subsequently participated in UNESCO and other world health projects.

Sullivan was a lifelong bachelor. In 1927 he began a close relationship with a young man he describes as a former patient, James Inscoe. "Jimmie" lived with Sullivan for some 20 years as a "beloved foster son … friend and ward," though he was never legally adopted. (See Perry, 1982, pp. 209–210; Sullivan, 1942).

Sullivan's writings fill seven volumes, only one of which he completed himself (1932–1933/1972). Five were published posthumously, and consist of edited lectures. Harry Stack Sullivan died of a cerebral hemorrhage in Paris on January 14, 1949, while returning home from a mental health conference in Amsterdam.

THE BASIC NATURE OF HUMAN BEINGS

Like Horney and Fromm, Sullivan emphasizes the interpersonal nature of personality. But whereas Horney concentrates on neurosis, and Fromm stresses the pathogenic role of society, Sullivan is primarily concerned with two other important areas: the development of personality, and the dynamics and treatment of schizophrenia. "If we go with almost microscopic care over how everybody comes to be what he is at chronologic adulthood, then perhaps we can learn a good deal of what is highly probable about living and difficulties in living" (Sullivan, 1953/1968, p. 4).

The One-Genus Postulate

Like Fromm, Sullivan makes some allowances for the effects of heredity on personality. We are all influenced by such physiological motives as hunger, thirst, respiration, sexuality, and the maintenance of body temperature. This animalistic aspect of personality accounts for individual differences in physical characteristics, sensory abilities, intelligence, and the rate at which we mature.

However, Sullivan also concludes that the similarities among human personalities far exceed the differences (the **One-Genus Postulate**). Even the most retarded individual differs far less from the greatest genius than from any member of any other species. Thus Sullivan (unlike Adler) prefers to minimize the importance of individual differences, and to devote his theoretical attention to those phenomena that humans have in common. (See Sullivan, 1947/1953, p. 16; 1953/1968, pp. 32–33.)

The Need for Others

Sullivan shares Fromm's and Horney's distaste for Freudian libido theory, arguing that it is "completely preposterous" to assume that our behavior is rigidly determined by instincts. Except for such hereditary disasters as congenital idiocy, human nature is extremely pliable and adaptive. "[Even] the most fantastic social rules and regulations [could] be lived up to, if they were properly inculcated in the young, [and] they would seem very natural and proper ways of life" (Sullivan, 1953/1968, pp. 6, 21).

Sullivan concludes that personality is shaped primarily by social forces, with the child's lengthy period of dependence making it particularly vulnerable to influence by others. He posits a powerful human need for interpersonal relationships, so that "it is a rare person who can cut himself off from ... relations with others for long spaces of time without undergoing a deterioration of personality." And he insists that personality exists, and can be studied, only through its interpersonal manifestations:

> *Personality is the relatively enduring pattern of recurrent interpersonal situations which characterize a human life....* A *personality* can never be isolated from the complex of interpersonal relationships in which the person lives ... [Therefore,] psychiatry is the study of the phenomena that occur in interpersonal situations, in configurations made up of two or more people, all but one of whom may be more or less completely illusory. (Sullivan, 1947/1953, p. 10; 1953/1968, pp. 32, 110–111; 1964/1971, p. 33. See also Sullivan, 1953/1968, pp. 18–20, 367–368.)

Since Sullivan's definition of interpersonal relationships includes those that are illusory, even a recluse or psychotic does not lack a personality. Such individuals have memories and/or fantasies of relationships with real or fictitious others, so they are strongly influenced by interpersonal situations.

Tension Reduction

In accordance with Horney and Fromm, Sullivan concludes that human beings have a tendency or drive toward mental health. He also shares Freud's belief that we are motivated by the desire to reduce inner tensions. The ideal human condition is that of total equilibrium (absolute **euphoria**), a state of utter well-being characterized by the absence of any internal deficiencies or noxious external stimuli. The opposite extreme, absolute **tension,** is reciprocally related to euphoria and is similar to a state of terror. Like mathematical limits, however, absolute euphoria and absolute tension can only be approached and do not exist in nature. (See Sullivan, 1947/1953, p. 97; 1953/1968, p. 35; 1954/1970, p. 106; 1956/1973, p. 265.)

According to Sullivan, there are four major causes of tension: the physicochemical needs, the need for sleep, anxiety, and the need to express tenderness.

Physicochemical Needs and Sleep.
A state of inner disequilibrium is created by such important *physicochemical needs* as sexual desire, the necessity of eliminating bodily wastes, and deficiencies in food, water, oxygen, or body heat. This is accompanied by tension that is often (but not always) conscious, thereby motivating us to expend energy and satisfy the need. Tension also arises from the need to sleep, which Sullivan regards as significantly different from the physicochemical needs.

Anxiety.
Perhaps the most important cause of tension is **anxiety.** This unpleasant emotion varies considerably in intensity. At its most extreme, anxiety resembles the **uncanny emotions** of dread, horror, and loathing:

> Uncanny emotions have a sort of shuddery, not-of-this-earth component ... [somewhat like one's] first glimpse into the Grand Canyon.... If you try to analyze the experience, you may talk about your skin crawling ... [and] if there were a great deal more of such emotion, you would be very far from a going concern as long as you had it. That is the nearest I can come to hinting at what I surmise infants undergo when they are severely anxious. (Sullivan, 1953/1968, p. 10; see also pp. 4, 8–11, 41–45, 59.)

Anxiety can be provoked by disturbances in the environment, such as a sudden loud noise or threat. But its major source concerns the child's relationship to its mother, or whichever person fulfills the mothering function. "The basic vulnerabilities to anxiety [are] in interpersonal relations.... The tension of anxiety, when present in the mothering one, induces anxiety in the infant" (Sullivan, 1953/1968, pp. 11, 41; see also pp. 9, 113–117, 144, 204). Anxiety differs from the tension of **fear,** which occurs when the satisfaction of a need is substantially delayed.

The means by which anxiety is communicated from the mothering one to the baby is uncertain, perhaps including some sort of empathy on the part of the latter. In any case, its effects are extremely troublesome. Unlike the physicochemical needs, which are readily satisfied through such actions as eating or drinking, anxiety is best alleviated by safe relationships with nonanxious others (**interpersonal security**). No specific action by the infant is involved, which makes the relief of anxiety significantly different from all other needs—and more difficult to achieve.

To make matters worse, anxiety opposes the satisfaction of other needs. It can interfere with the ability to swallow when hungry or thirsty, or to fall asleep when tired. It can disrupt the capacity for rational thought, much like a severe blow on the head. And it can sabotage potentially gratifying interpersonal relationships, as when the hungry but anxious infant rejects the proffered nipple. For these reasons, we devote much of our lifetimes (and a great deal of energy) to reducing or avoiding the wholly unwanted tension of anxiety—as by ignoring that with which we cannot cope (**selective inattention**), or by unconsciously converting anxiety into the more palatable emotion of anger. "It is anxiety which is responsible for a great part of the inadequate, inefficient, unduly rigid, or otherwise unfortunate performances of people.... [and] for a great deal of what comes to a psychiatrist for attention" (Sullivan, 1953/1968, p. 160; see also Sullivan, 1953/1968, pp. 42, 53, 92–96, 152, 319, 353; 1954/1970, pp. 100, 135; 1956/1973, pp. 38–76).

Tenderness.   Tension also occurs when the mothering one observes activity by the infant that indicates the existence of a need, such as crying. This tension "is experienced as tenderness, and as an impulsion to activities toward the relief of the infant's needs" (Sullivan, 1953/1968, p. 39). Thus the infant's need for the tender cooperation of the mothering one stimulates her need to give it, and produces the baby's first significant interpersonal relationship. If the mothering one should respond to the infant's distress with anxiety, however, her capacity for tenderness will be inhibited. Therefore, "there isn't any right thing to do with infantile anxiety, except for the mother to cease to be anxious" (Sullivan, 1953/1968, p. 54).

Dynamisms

Although Sullivan espouses a tension-reduction model of personality, he rejects the concept of psychic energy. "Energy, when I mention it, is energy as conceived in physics ... There is no need to add adjectives such as 'mental.' ... Physical energy ... is the only kind of energy I know" (Sullivan, 1953/1968, pp. 35–36, 97, 101–102). We transform physical energy, rather than libido, into behaviors designed to satisfy our needs.

To emphasize that personality is a dynamic process, and is constantly in a state of flux, Sullivan refers to such energy transformations as **dynamisms.** A dynamism may take various forms: overt moving or talking, covert reveries and fantasies, or partly or wholly unconscious processes.

For example, the hate dynamism involves the transformation of (physical) energy into behavior that will reduce tension through hostility. The individual may strike or insult someone, have murderous fantasies, and/or form powerful unconscious destructive wishes. The dynamism of lust concerns the use of energy to satisfy sexual needs, as by making love or having erotic daydreams. (See Sullivan, 1953/1968, pp. 102–107; 1964/1971, p. 35 n. 3.)

One particularly important dynamism is the self-system, which serves our need to be free from the tension of anxiety. Since this comes as close as Sullivan ever does to some sort of personality structure, it will be discussed in a subsequent section.

Modes of Experiencing

According to Sullivan, human experience consists entirely of tensions, dynamisms, and need satisfactions. He also argues that this experience occurs in one or more of three modalities: prototaxic, parataxic, and syntaxic.

The Prototaxic Mode. The primitive **prototaxic** mode is the newborn infant's only way of apprehending the environment. This limited form of experience is like a succession of momentary discrete states, and is incapable of such distinctions as before and after or self and others. Prototaxic experience cannot be communicated in any kind of symbols, so it is only an educated guess by Sullivan as to the inner processes of the very young infant. (See Sullivan, 1953/1968, pp. xiv, 28–29, 35–36, 100.)

The Parataxic Mode. As the infant develops, it becomes capable of the **parataxic** mode. This mode is characterized by the use of private or "autistic" symbols (such as nonsense words whose meaning is known only to the user), and by the ability to distinguish differences in time. Parataxic experience is illogical, however, and reflects a lack of understanding about causality. Examples include the superstitious belief that misfortune will result from walking under a ladder, or in front of a black cat; and the psychotic who thinks about rain on a clear day, and concludes that these ruminations caused the downpour that occurred some time thereafter.

The Syntaxic Mode. The most elaborate form of experience is the **syntaxic** mode, which begins to appear as early as the 12th to 18th month of life. Syntaxic experience can be communicated through the use of symbols that are socially accepted and understood, such as "that fantastic evolutionary development, language." It also includes an understanding of conventional concepts of cause and effect (Sullivan, 1953/1968, p. 20).

Teleology

To Sullivan, as to Jung and Adler, human behavior must be understood in terms of both causality and teleology. Our capacity for foresight develops in early infancy, and represents one of the striking characteristics of the human species (Sullivan, 1953/1968, pp. 38–39; see also pp. 51, 64, 82). Unlike Jung, however, Sullivan concludes that psychological phenomena can be translated into physiological events; and his writings include numerous allusions to the anatomical and organic aspects of human functioning.

THE STRUCTURE OF PERSONALITY

Sullivan shares Fromm's and Horney's distaste for the Freudian structural model. According to Sullivan, we organize our experiences by forming mental conceptions of ourselves and others. These **personifications** consist of learned feelings and beliefs, which often do not correspond well with reality.

For example, a mother is likely to misperceive her child to some extent. She may form a personification that is more like the way she wants the child to be, or one that is influenced by her experiences with previous offspring. The infant gradually develops a personification of the good mother from her tender and need-satisfying behaviors, and also forms a personification of the bad mother from her frustrating and anxiety-producing behaviors. These personifications are also somewhat inaccurate, partly because the baby's ability to perceive and interpret the environment is limited. In fact, the infant does not realize at first that the personifications of good and bad mother refer to the same person, although significant portions of each do ultimately fuse into a complicated whole. (See Sullivan, 1953/1968, pp. 110–124, 167, 188–189.)

The irrational aspect of personifications is evident in the case of **stereotypes,** or beliefs that are applied rigidly and equally to a group of people and obscure the true differences among them. Young children commonly form a stereotype of the opposite sex as undesirable, whereas prejudiced individuals incorrectly personify members of a particular group as having certain negative characteristics in common. (See Sullivan, 1953/1968, pp. 236–238, 302–304.) Such irrationality is also apparent in the personification that we form of ourselves.

The Self-System

The growing infant begins to conceive of itself as a separate and distinct entity at about age 6 months, and it organizes this information by forming appropriate personifications. These are so important that Sullivan tends to divide personality into two major categories, the **self-system** (or **self-dynamism**) and everything else. (See Sullivan, 1947/1953, pp. 19–29; 1953/1968, pp. 135–141, 158–171, 198–202; 1954/1970, pp. 101–112, 138.)

The self-system results partly from experiences with the infant's own body. For example, thumb sucking helps the infant differentiate between self and others because it produces unique feelings of both sucking and being sucked. For the most part, however, the self-system originates from the appraisals of significant others (such as the parents). The child must learn to get along with other people, so the unconditional maternal tenderness of early infancy must eventually be replaced by a system of rewards and punishments that will prepare the child for its place in society.

During later infancy and childhood, therefore, tenderness is used as an anxiety-reducing reward for desirable behaviors (such as achieving success at toilet-training, or abandoning the cherished but socially unacceptable activity of thumb sucking). Forbidding gestures, maternal anxiety, punishment, and the absence of tenderness serve as anxiety-inducing responses to the infant's errors and misdeeds. This leads to the development of the two personifications that eventually comprise the self-system: the desirable self or obedient **"good me"** is associated with experiences that are rewarded by a decrease in anxiety, the undesirable self or rebellious **"bad me"** results from experiences that are punished by an increase in anxiety.

As with the infant's conceptions of good and bad mother, the good-me and bad-me personifications ultimately fuse into a single entity. The more intense the early experiences of anxiety, the more rigid and extensive this self-system will be. To Sullivan, therefore, self-centered behavior is a learned response to anxiety, rather than the result of innate narcissism. (See Sullivan, 1947/1953, p. 127 n. 41; 1953/1968, pp. 5, 126–134, 151–202.)

Selective Inattention.   The primary goal of the self-system is the desirable one of reducing anxiety, thereby enabling the child to get along with its parents and satisfy its needs. However, it accomplishes this objective through such dubious "security operations" as **selective inattention.** If the self-system should encounter information that threatens its stability, it simply ignores or rejects the incongruous data and goes on functioning as before.

CAPSULE SUMMARY
Some Important Sullivanian Terminology

Anxiety	A harmful, unpleasant emotion similar to intense nervousness or (at its most extreme) to the uncanny emotions. Caused primarily by anxiety in the mothering one, and the corresponding loss of interpersonal security. To Sullivan, the avoidance or reduction of anxiety is one of the major goals of human behavior.
Dissociation	Unconsciously disowning threatening aspects of one's personality, and associating them with the not-me personification.
Dynamism	The transformation of physical energy into behavior (overt or covert, conscious or unconscious) that will satisfy a need.
Euphoria	A state of well-being characterized by the absence of any internal needs or noxious external stimuli; the converse of tension.
Fear	An unpleasant tension that feels similar to anxiety, but is caused by a delay in the satisfaction of a need.
Interpersonal security	A feeling of safety achieved through relationships with other people; the best way to reduce anxiety.
Malevolent transformation	A distortion in personality development, which results in the belief that other people are enemies and have no tenderness or love to give. Caused by insufficient maternal tenderness and excessive parental hostility, irritability, and anxiety during the childhood stage.
Need	A physiological deficiency that creates a state of discomfort or tension. Includes hunger, thirst, anoxia, sexuality, the maintenance of body temperature, and the necessity of eliminating bodily wastes (the "physicochemical" needs), and sleep.
"Not-me" personification	A normally unconscious component of personality, whose emergence into consciousness produces uncanny emotions and the feeling of not being oneself. Results from extreme anxiety during childhood, too intense even to be dealt with by the "bad me" personification.
One-Genus Postulate	The postulate that the similarities among human personalities far exceed the differences.
Parataxic mode	A mode of experiencing internal and external stimuli that is characterized by the use of private symbols, and an inability to understand conventional concepts of cause and effect.
Personification	An organized perception of another person, which need not (and often does not) correspond well with reality.
Prototaxic mode	The primitive mode of experiencing internal and external stimuli that is prominent in early infancy, consists of a succession of momentary discrete states, is incapable of such distinctions as before and after or self and others, and cannot be communicated.
Selective inattention	Deliberately, albeit unconsciously, not noticing certain (threatening) stimuli in order to reduce anxiety.
Self-system (self, self-dynamism)	The organized perception (personification) of one's own self, including the desirable "good me" and undesirable "bad me."
Stereotype	A personification that is rigidly and equally applied to a group of people, and obscures the true differences among them.
Sublimation	The unconscious substitution of a partially satisfying behavior for one that would be more gratifying, but would arouse greater anxiety.

Syntaxic mode	The most highly developed form of experiencing internal and external stimuli, characterized by the use of socially understood symbols (such as language) and by an understanding of conventional concepts of cause and effect.
Tension	Feelings of discomfort caused by a physicochemical need, the need for sleep, anxiety, or the need to express maternal tenderness; often (but not always) conscious.
Uncanny emotions	Extremely unpleasant feelings, including dread, horror, and loathing, which involve intense anxiety and often indicate the emergence of the "not me" personification.

Selective inattention may occasionally have beneficial aspects, as when you avoid costly distractions by concentrating on the task at hand. But it is primarily disadvantageous, for it impedes our ability to learn from our failures and weaknesses. These sources of information are threatening to the self-system, so it is likely to pay no attention to them. (See Sullivan, 1953/1968, p. 319.) Selective inattention is so pervasive that most of our mental processes occur outside the realm of consciousness.

Because the self-system uses selective inattention to combat anxiety, it differs from other dynamisms by being extraordinarily resistant to change. This rigidity represents the principal stumbling block to constructive growth. "We are being perfectly irrational and simply unpleasant if we expect another person to profit quickly from his experience, as long as his self-system is involved—although this is a very reasonable anticipation in all fields in which the self-system is not involved." The security operations of the self-system also create the impression that we differ more from others than is actually the case (a "delusion of unique individuality"), and may even result in a grandiose self-personification somewhat like the Adlerian superiority complex (Sullivan, 1953/1968, pp. 140, 192; see also Sullivan, 1953/1968, pp. 168–170, 247–248, 319, 346, 374; 1964/1971, pp. 198–226; 1956/1973, pp. 38–76).

The "Not-Me" Personification

Intense anxiety during childhood ("a very poor method of education") leads to the development of the **"not-me" personification,** a shadowy and dreadful aspect of personality that is usually unconscious. The not-me personification involves material so threatening that even the bad-me personification cannot cope with it, so it is unconsciously divorced (**dissociated**) from the self-personification. Dissociation is an extreme form of security operation that resembles "[flinging] something of you into outer darkness, where it reposes for years, quite peacefully," and it must be maintained through constant (if unconscious) vigilance (Sullivan, 1953/1968, pp. 163, 318; see also Sullivan, 1947/1953, p. 71; 1953/1968, pp. 201, 314–328; 1964/1971, pp. 248–249).

For example, a young child or schizophrenic may seek to avoid punishment by arguing and believing, "Oh, I didn't do that, it was my hand." The emergence into consciousness of the not-me personification produces uncanny emotions and the feeling of not being oneself, a terrifying experience that is common in schizophrenia—and in some nightmares and states of shock that befall more healthy individuals.[1]

---

[1]Since the not-me personification represents a more extreme defense against more intense anxiety than does the bad-me personification, some theorists might regard it as a third aspect of the self-system. Thus the continuum would be: good-me (resulting from minimal childhood anxiety, and most desirable), bad-me, not-me (resulting from maximal childhood anxiety, and least desirable). Because of its dissociated nature, however, it seems more a converse than an adjunct to the self-personification.

Other Defensive Behaviors

Sullivan differs from Freud by interpreting sublimation as a device for reducing anxiety, wherein one behavior is unconsciously substituted for another that would be more satisfying but also more threatening. This conception implies that sublimation is not always advantageous, for it may cause us to accept a less satisfying substitute on those occasions when anxiety has mistakenly become associated with acceptable activities. Sullivan also argues that fantasy can help us make useful, realistic plans for the future.

Sullivan is highly (and wryly) skeptical about various other Freudian constructs. He regards introjection as "a great magic verbal gesture, the meaning of which cannot be made explicit." Projection is a "nice [topic] for certain late-evening-alcoholic psychiatric discussions." And regression is something that happens every 24 hours when a child goes to sleep and complicated, recently acquired patterns of behavior collapse, rather than "some great abstruse whatnot" that "psychiatrists often use … to brush aside mysteries which they do not grasp at all" (Sullivan, 1953/1968, pp. 166, 197, 359; see also Sullivan, 1947/1953, p. 54 n. 20; 1953/1968, pp. 113, 191–196, 348–350; 1964/1971, pp. 209–210; 1956/1973, pp. 14–20, 232).

THE DEVELOPMENT OF PERSONALITY

Sullivan regards developmental psychology as the key to understanding human behavior, and he concludes that significant changes in personality often occur during late childhood and adolescence. He posits seven epochs through which personality may develop, each of which represents an optimal time for certain innate capacities to reach fruition.

Infancy

The stage of infancy begins a few minutes after birth and continues until the appearance of speech (however meaningless). (See Sullivan, 1953/1968, pp. 49–187.) Nursing provides the infant's first experience in interpersonal relationships. The infant learns to distinguish among such important external cues as the "good and satisfactory nipple," which is provided by a tender mother and gives milk when the infant is hungry; and the "evil nipple" of the anxious mother, which is so unpleasant that it is rejected even if the infant is hungry. (See Sullivan, 1953/1968, pp. 49–50, 73, 79–81, 88, 122.)

Crying is for some time the infant's most effective method of satisfying needs and reducing anxiety, and varies according to its intent. Crying-when-hungry represents the infant's crude, prototaxic way of expressing the idea "come, nipple, into my mouth," and "has no necessary relatedness, in the infant's experience, with crying-when-cold, crying-when-pained, or crying-under-any-other-circumstances" (Sullivan, 1953/1968, p. 67; see also pp. 52–53, 62, 66–75). When crying does bring the desired relief, such successes help the infant to develop foresight and an understanding of cause and effect. That is, the infant (in some primitive prototaxic fashion) concludes that "I cry when I suffer a certain distress, and that produces something different which is connected with the relief of the distress" (Sullivan, 1953/1968, p. 72).

The self-system begins to develop during mid-infancy. As we have seen, this is due primarily to two factors: bodily explorations such as thumb sucking, and the mothering one's shift from unconditional tenderness to rewards and punishments that cause the "good me" and "bad me" personifications to develop. These rewards and punishments involve such essential tasks as learning to use the toilet and giving up thumb sucking.

During the 12th to 18th month of life, the use of language begins with the imitation of sounds in the environment. This represents the appearance of the parataxic mode (or syntaxic mode, if the infant's utterances happen to correspond to actual words), and ushers in the second stage of personality development.

Childhood

During childhood, parental punishments further the growth of the bad-me aspect of the self-system. (See Sullivan, 1953/1968, pp. 188–226.) So long as the parents also assist the development of the good-me personification by providing sufficient rewards and tenderness, no great harm will result. But if the child's need for tenderness is consistently rebuffed by parental anxiety, irritability, or hostility, the bad-me component will dominate the self-system. As with the neglected child in Adlerian theory, this **malevolent transformation** results in the misguided belief that other people are hostile and unloving:

> [The malevolent transformation] is perhaps the greatest disaster that [could happen] in the childhood phase of personality development.... [Such a child learns] that it is highly disadvantageous to show any need for tender cooperation from the authoritative figures around him. [Instead] he shows ... the basic malevolent attitude, the attitude that one really lives among enemies.... This distortion, this malevolence ... runs something like this: Once upon a time everything was lovely, but that was before I had to deal with people. (Sullivan, 1953/1968, pp. 214, 216.)

The malevolent child may be mischievous, behave like a bully, or express resentment more passively by stubbornly failing to do whatever is required. This transformation also impairs the sufferer's relationships with others, notably authority figures outside the immediate family.

If the parents are too distant and aloof, the child may try to resolve its feelings of loneliness through excessive daydreaming. This will make it difficult for the child to abandon its private, parataxic thoughts and images in favor of the syntaxic mode and effective communication

---

CAPSULE SUMMARY
The Developmental Epochs (Sullivan)

	_____ A few minutes after birth
Infancy _____	
	_____ Appearance of articulate speech, even if meaningless
Childhood _____	
	_____ Appearance of the need for playmates
The Juvenile Era _____	
	_____ Appearance of the need for an intimate relationship with a person of the same sex (chum)
Preadolescence _____	
	_____ Puberty; appearance of the need for an intimate relationship with a person of the opposite sex
Early Adolescence _____	
	_____ Satisfaction of the lust dynamism
Late Adolescence _____	
	_____ Completion of personality development; ability for genuine love
Adulthood _____	

with other people. But the parents must also avoid the opposite extreme of catering to the child's every whim, which will produce a spoiled and self-centered individual (similar to Adler's concept of pampering).

The personifications of good and bad mother begin to fuse into a single entity during childhood. The father now joins the mother as an authority to be reckoned with, leading to the child's formation of a father personification. A knowledge of gender also begins to develop, with the boy or girl wishing to be like the parent of the same sex. To Sullivan, however, such identifications are not due to some sort of Oedipus complex. They occur because most parents are more comfortable with the child of the same sex, and reward behavior typical of that sex with approval and tenderness (Sullivan, 1953/1968, pp. 218–219).

The Juvenile Era

The juvenile era originates with the appearance of the need for playmates, which occurs at about the time of entry into school. (See Sullivan, 1953/1968, pp. 227–244.) Like Adler, Sullivan concludes that the educational system can remedy serious parental errors that occurred during infancy and childhood. Such favorable alterations in personality are possible because the normally rigid self-system is more amenable to change at the inception of each developmental stage, when newly maturing abilities increase the probability of significant changes in behavior.

The juvenile learns to adjust to the demands, rewards, and punishments of such new authority figures as teachers. He or she observes how other juveniles are treated by these authorities (and by each other), learns to deal with peers (including the malevolent bully), and is introduced to the social processes of competition and compromise. School also involves the painful possibility of ostracism by one's peers. The juvenile era is the time when the world begins to be complicated by the presence of other people, and is typified by inexperienced attempts at interpersonal relationships that often reflect a shocking insensitivity to other people's feelings. (See Sullivan, 1947/1953, pp. 38–41; 1953/1968, pp. 227–232.)

The syntaxic mode becomes prominent during the juvenile era. In addition, the parents begin to lose their godlike attributes and take on more human, fallible personifications. "[If one] comes out of the juvenile era with [the feeling that the parents] still have to be sacrosanct, the most perfect people on earth, then one of the most striking and important of the juvenile contributions to socialization has sadly miscarried" (Sullivan, 1953/1968, p. 231). Another potential source of pathology involves parents who constantly disparage other people, which causes the juvenile to feel incapable of knowing what is good:

> If you have to maintain self-esteem by pulling down the standing of others, you are extraordinarily unfortunate…. The doctrine that if you are a molehill then, by God, there shall be no mountains … is probably the most vicious of the inadequate, inappropriate, and ineffectual performances of parents with juveniles…. (Sullivan, 1953/1968, pp. 242–243, 309.)

Preadolescence

The preadolescent stage is highlighted by the need for an intimate relationship with a particular individual of the same sex, or chum. (See Sullivan, 1953/1968, pp. 245–262.) This relatively brief period tends to occur between the ages of $8^1/_2$ and 10, though it may be delayed by as much as a few years if maturation is relatively slow.

The preadolescent chumship is crucial because it represents a sincere interest in the welfare of another person. The influence of this important individual may be sufficient to modify the otherwise rigid self-system, and correct any warps in personality carried over from preceding stages. "Because one draws so close to another, because one is newly capable of seeing oneself through the other's eyes, the preadolescent phase of personality development is especially significant in correcting autistic, fantastic ideas about oneself or others" (Sullivan, 1953/1968, p. 248; see also Sullivan, 1947/1953, pp. 41–44). An effective chumship may alter such misguided views as arrogance, dependence, or the belief that one should be liked by everyone. It may even reverse or cure a malevolent transformation. Conversely, difficulties in dealing with others of the same sex are invariably due (at least in the case of males) to the failure to develop this essential preadolescent relationship, and to the resulting feelings of intense loneliness.

Early Adolescence

The period of early adolescence begins with puberty and the appearance of the powerful lust dynamism, which leads to the desire for a close relationship with a member of the opposite sex. (See Sullivan, 1953/1968, pp. 263–296.) In contrast to the intimacy of the preadolescent stage, which is not necessarily sexual, lust is expressed primarily through sexual behavior and culminates in the experience of orgasm.

Sullivan warns that early adolescence is rife with possibilities for serious maladjustment, because our culture confronts us with singular handicaps in our pursuit of lustful activity. Essential information and guidance may be totally lacking at this important time, and the parents may add to the problem by providing ridicule and sarcasm instead of emotional support. Thus the adolescent's fledgling attempts at heterosexuality may lead to such embarrassing outcomes as impotence, frigidity, or premature ejaculation, causing a sharp decrease in self-esteem; and "customarily low self-esteem makes it difficult indeed for the carrier person ... to manifest good feeling toward another person" (Sullivan, 1953/1968, p. 351; see also Sullivan, 1947/1953, p. 63; 1954/1970, p. 9).

The adolescent who experiences such difficulties may rush into marriage with the first member of the opposite sex who inspires any feelings akin to love, a relationship that is usually far from satisfying. Or the adolescent may develop a fear of the opposite sex, possibly resulting in celibacy, excessive fantasizing, or homosexuality. Or the adolescent may conduct an endless quest for the ideal member of the opposite sex, and blame the inevitable failures on apparent defects in every candidate rather than on the unconscious fear of heterosexuality. An adolescent who has not emotionally outgrown the juvenile era may form numerous superficial sexual liaisons ("Don Juanism"). Whereas occasional masturbation is not harmful (and is virtually universal), an anxious adolescent may rely so heavily on self-stimulation that healthy heterosexuality becomes impossible.

Despite the seriousness of such problems, Sullivan does not regard sexual dysfunction as the most important aspect of psychiatry. He prefers to emphasize the inability to form satisfying interpersonal relationships, which underlies the more manifest sexual difficulties (Sullivan, 1953/1968, pp. 295–296; 1954/1970, p. 13).

Late Adolescence

The latter part of adolescence originates with the achievement of satisfying sexual activity. (See Sullivan, 1953/1968, pp. 287–310). The adolescent must now contend with increasing social responsibilities, such as working and paying income tax. Socioeconomic status also affects this stage of personality development, for those who are able to attend college have several years of extraordinary opportunity for observation and learning that others do not. Faulty personality development may now be evidenced by a pronounced tendency to avoid others, or by such pseudosocial rituals as impersonal card games that provide only the most superficial of contacts.

Adulthood

Sullivan has relatively little to say about the stage of adulthood, which represents maturity and the completion of personality development, because psychiatrists do not get many opportunities to observe well-adjusted behavior. Adulthood is denoted by a mature repertory of interpersonal behaviors and the capacity for genuine love, a state wherein "the other person is as significant, or nearly as significant, as one's self" (Sullivan, 1953/1968, p. 34; see also Sullivan, 1947/1953, p. 42; 1953/1968, pp. 297, 309–310).

This final epoch is somewhat similar to the Freudian genital stage (without the sexual implications) and to Fromm's productive orientation. However, Sullivan is not optimistic about our chances to attain it. "I believe that for a great majority of our people, preadolescence is the nearest that they come to untroubled human life—that from then on, the stresses of life distort them to inferior caricatures of what they might have been" (Sullivan, 1947/1953, p. 56).

FURTHER APPLICATIONS OF
SULLIVANIAN THEORY

Psychopathology

In accordance with all of the theorists discussed thus far, Sullivan regards psychopathology as a difference in degree rather than in kind. Every patient "is *mostly* a person like the psychiatrist," and even the bizarre behavior of the psychotic is related to processes that occur in relatively normal individuals (Sullivan, 1947/1953, p. 96; see also Sullivan, 1953/1968, pp. 208, 223; 1954/1970, pp. 18, 183).

Causes of Psychopathology.   Neurosis and schizophrenia are caused by pathogenic interpersonal relationships. Too much maternal anxiety during infancy, not enough parental tenderness during childhood, the failure to find a satisfactory peer group during the juvenile era or a preadolescent chum, or problems in early adolescence with heterosexual relationships and the lust dynamism damage the child's self-esteem and cause the self-system to become extremely rigid. As a result, the sufferer is unable to develop a repertory of behaviors for dealing effectively with other people.

For example, malevolent individuals cannot apply judicious doses of empathy and compassion because they are constantly preoccupied with the hate dynamism and attempts to dominate others. To Sullivan, then, all mental disorders are to be understood as patterns of inadequate and inappropriate behavior in interpersonal relations. (See Sullivan, 1953/1968, pp. 313–328, 344–363; 1954/1970, pp. 183–208; 1956/1973, pp. 200–202.)

Sullivan shares Fromm's concern about pathogenic societal forces, partly because of the devastation he observed during World War II. "The Western world is a profoundly sick society in which each denizen, each person, is sick to the extent that he is *of it*" (Sullivan, 1964/1971, p. 155; see also pp. 76–84, 100–107).

Varieties of Psychopathology.   Sullivan is critical of the standard psychiatric nomenclature, which he regards as a source of potential confusion. "These trick words, so far as I can discover, merely make one a member of a somewhat esoteric union made up of people who certainly can't talk to anybody outside the union and who only have the illusion that they are talking to one another" (Sullivan, 1953/1968, p. 7). Nevertheless, his major clinical interests concern two of the standard classifications: obsessive-compulsive neurosis and schizophrenia.

Obsessive-compulsive neurosis reflects an extreme vulnerability to anxiety and a profound loss of self-esteem, caused by never having had outstanding success in one's interpersonal relations. Repeated thoughts or actions are (unconsciously) substituted for behaviors that would evoke intense anxiety, as when an adolescent who has suffered sexual embarrassments stays at home and obsesses about romantic triumphs instead of risking going out on a date. Secondary gains also play a significant role in this disorder, as with the patient of Sullivan's who could not leave the second floor of his home because of an obsession about committing suicide by jumping from a flight of stairs. He not only achieved some security against a threatening external world, but also enjoyed the constant sympathy and attention of his wife—at least until she grew weary of his neurotic demands, and divorced him a few years later. (See Sullivan, 1953/1968, pp. 210–211, 318–319; 1964/1971, pp. 231–232; 1956/1973, pp. 229–283.)

Schizophrenia is caused by the occurrence of uncanny emotions early in life, notably extreme anxiety, or by disastrous blows to one's self-esteem during the latter stages of development (particularly adolescence). If a parent has irrational fears about the infant's sexuality and becomes horrified when the baby toys with its genitals, the resulting extreme anxiety is likely to prove as numbing and incomprehensible as a severe blow on the head. Rather than associating the genitals with the bad-me personification, as would be the case with less traumatic punishment, the child may instead dissociate this highly threatening issue from its self-system. Thus sexual impulses and behaviors become associated with the unconscious not-me personification and are attributed to external sources, producing a gap in this area of personality that will create serious difficulties during early adolescence. The schizophrenic's quest for security also involves a regression to parataxic speech that has meaning to the patient, but appears incomprehensible and bizarre to others. To Sullivan, therefore, schizophrenia represents a return to an early form of mental functioning in an attempt to ward off intense anxiety and restore a shattered sense of self-esteem. (See for example Arieti, 1974, pp. 25–29; Sullivan, 1953/1968, pp. 313–328, 360–361; 1956/1973; 1962/1974.)

Psychotherapy

Theoretical Foundation. To Sullivan, psychotherapy is first and foremost a learning process. "There is no *essential* difference between psychotherapeutic achievement and achievements in other forms of education ... [all of which are] in the end reducible to the common denominator of experience incorporated into the self.... [Thus] I am avoiding the term 'cure,' since I do not think it applies in the realm of personality" (Sullivan, 1956/1973, p. 228; 1962/1974, p. 281; see also Sullivan, 1954/1970, p. 238).

Ideally, therapy enables the patient to gain valuable insights into issues that were selectively inattended, reintegrate dissociated aspects of personality, and establish a proper balance between the good-me and bad-me personifications. This expansion of the self-system facilitates the development of a wider, more effective repertory of interpersonal behaviors. Thus therapy may help a patient suffering from dissociated sexual impulses to accept the existence of lustful drives, recognize and eliminate the accompanying shame and guilt, and develop appropriate behaviors for satisfying this need. Or a malevolent patient may learn to reduce an exaggerated bad-me personification, establish some love of self, develop more accurate interpersonal perceptions, and (ultimately) express tenderness and love to others.

Therapeutic Procedures. Sullivanian psychotherapy focuses on the interpersonal relationship between the patient and therapist. The therapist is an active participant as well as an observer, focusing on what the patient is saying "with me and to me" and preventing lengthy forays into inconsequential territory. "The expert [therapist] does not permit people to tell him things so beside the point that only God could guess how they happened to get into the account" (Sullivan, 1954/1970, pp. 34, 58; see also Sullivan, 1953/1968, pp. 13–14; 1954/1970, pp. 3–6, 19–25, 82–85, 113).

Sullivanians eschew the use of a couch and sit at a 90-degree angle to the patient, enabling them to detect sudden changes of posture without being distracted by facial expressions. They also reject the use of free association with schizophrenics as too anxiety-provoking, and limit its use with other disorders to times when the patient is blocked and ready to recognize its value. Sullivan dislikes taking written notes during the therapeutic session, arguing that this method is distracting and cannot register subtle nuances in behavior, but does advocate the use of tape recordings. He also favors relatively brief and simple interpretations, so as to avoid causing excessive anxiety and intensifying the defenses of the patient's self-system. (See Singer, 1970, pp. 196–199; Sullivan, 1953/1968, p. 302; 1954/1970, p. 90; White, 1952, pp. 132–133.)

Psychotherapy begins with the stage of "formal inception," during which the patient first meets the psychiatrist and provides some explanation for entering therapy. Sullivan warns that the therapist's initial behavior is of considerable importance, for even such apparently minor errors as an overly limp handshake, an excessively warm or cool greeting, or somewhat too much arrogance or diffidence can significantly affect the patient's perceptions and distort the subsequent course of treatment. (See Sullivan, 1954.)

The second stage of therapy, or "reconnaissance," occurs when the psychiatrist has formed a fairly good idea as to why the patient is in need of professional assistance. This period generally takes from $7^{1}/_{2}$ to 15 hours and consists of an unstructured inquiry into the patient's life history. The reconnaissance concludes with a summary statement of what the therapist has learned about the patient, whereupon the patient usually agrees that some significant problems have emerged that are worthy of further study.

The third stage, or "detailed inquiry," represents the "long haul" of psychotherapy. No matter how skilled the therapist may be, the preceding brief stages are unlikely to provide a wholly accurate picture. Many patients try to reduce anxiety by making statements designed to please or impress the therapist, by rationalizing or ignoring their failures and embarrassments, or by exaggerating their successes. Or a patient's communications may be deceptively difficult to understand because they include many parataxic symbols. During the detailed inquiry, therefore, the impressions gained from the formal inception and reconnaissance are checked against more substantial data provided by the patient. The therapist probes into important aspects of the patient's developmental history, including such issues as toilet-training, school experiences, the preadolescent chum, sexual relationships, and security operations for avoiding anxiety.

The final stage of therapy ("termination") includes four major steps: a succinct formal statement of what the therapist has learned during the course of treatment, a prescription for actions that the patient should take or avoid, a formal assessment of the patient's probable future course in life, and a clear-cut leave-taking that is neither too indecisive nor too abrupt. Pessimistic prognoses are avoided, however, since they may become self-fulfilling prophecies. "I try never to close all doors to a person; the person should go away with hope and with an improved grasp on what has been the trouble" (Sullivan, 1954/1970, p. 211).

Unlike Freud, Sullivan devoted the majority of his attention to the treatment of schizophrenia. He was sharply critical of the inferior methods and conditions of most mental hospitals, and any ward under his supervision was conducted according to his own unique regulations.

For example, he prohibited female nurses from appearing in all-male wards because the patients were likely to regard them as threatening symbols of authoritarianism. Instead he trained his own (male) assistants, and emphasized on them his belief that the patients' daily life and social contacts on the ward were even more important than the hourly sessions with the psychiatrist. (See Arieti, 1974, p. 541; Sullivan, 1954/1970, pp. xx, 50; 1962/1974, pp. xvi–xix.) Although capable of pronounced sarcasm with colleagues, Sullivan was unfailingly kind and gentle with schizophrenics. Even when an upset patient would slap him in the face, he would strictly prohibit any reprisals and only ask quietly, "Well, do you feel better now?" Nor was he afraid to be somewhat unorthodox, and would compensate for the lack of modern drug therapy by using alcoholic beverages to relax a rigid self-system and make the patient more amenable to change (Sullivan, 1947/1953, p. 219).

Dream Interpretation.   Sullivan does not regard dreams as particularly rich sources of information about personality. He argues that our recall upon awakening is hopelessly distorted by the resurgent self-system, and he criticizes interpretations designed to unearth some sort of latent content as futile efforts to translate the dreamer's private (parataxic) symbology into communicable (syntaxic) experience.

Sullivan limits dream interpretation to reflecting back important aspects, with the goal of stimulating the patient's train of thought. A patient of Sullivan's once dreamed of approaching a highly attractive Dutch windmill, only to find upon entering that it was ruined and inches deep in dust. Sullivan's reply was, "that is, beautiful, active on the outside—utterly dead and decayed within. Does it provoke anything?" Whereupon the patient responded, "my God, my mother," recognizing with astonishment that he actually regarded her as a "sort of zombie … [or] weary phonograph offering cultural platitudes" (Sullivan, 1953/1968, pp. 338–339; see also Sullivan, 1947/1953, pp. 69–72; 1953/1968, pp. 329–337; 1956/1973, pp. 19–20).

Resistance and Transference.   Sullivan concludes that the self-system actively opposes the goals of therapy. But he interprets this as an attempt to reduce anxiety, rather than as an effort to preserve illicit impulses. Sullivan is opposed to the use of transference, which he regards as another erroneous interpersonal perception that the patient must learn to abandon. (See Sullivan, 1953/1968, pp. 237–238; 1954/1970, pp. 104, 139, 219, 231.)

Above all, Sullivan emphasizes the difficulty of doing effective psychotherapy. "There is no fun in psychiatry…. It is work—work the like of which I do not know" (Sullivan, 1954/1970, p. 10).

Psychotherapy and Social Reform.   Like Fromm, Sullivan (1964/1971) discusses such social applications of personality theory as world tensions, national defense, and propaganda and censorship. However, his untimely death prevented him from devoting more than a few articles to this area.

EVALUATION

Criticisms and Controversies

For one who claims to dislike psychiatric jargon, Sullivan is not averse to introducing some formidable terminology of his own. His writings are probably more difficult than any of the theorists discussed thus far except Jung (and perhaps some parts of Freudian theory), and his language poses a considerable barrier to the prospective reader.

Although based on a different premise, Sullivan's tension-reduction model of human motivation is as subject to criticism as Freud's. The concept of dynamism has an all-pervasive quality similar to Freudian sexuality and Adlerian inferiority, and has not enjoyed much popularity among modern psychologists. Also, Sullivan often fails to acknowledge his intellectual debts to his predecessors. He ignores obvious similarities between such concepts as actively maintained dissociations and actively maintained repressions, security operations and defense mechanisms, the malevolent transformation and Adler's theory of the neglected child, personifications and Adler's "fictions," and the self-system and the style of life.

Sullivan has also been criticized for attributing the formation of the self-system primarily to the appraisals of significant others, and for ignoring those distortions introduced by the child's own misperceptions and faulty cognitions. (See Arieti, 1974, p. 78; Ellenberger, 1970, p. 639.) Sullivan's theory has not generated much empirical research. In comparison to Fromm, Sullivan's approach to dreams seems shallow and unconvincing. And Sullivan has been taken to task for overemphasizing the interpersonal aspects of personality.

Contributions

Perhaps Sullivan's greatest contributions concern the understanding and treatment of schizophrenia. He has been credited as the first to offer a convincing psychodynamic interpretation of this disorder (Arieti, 1974, p. 25). As with Horney and Fromm, Sullivan's rejection of libido theory would seem to be a step in the right direction. Sullivan devotes far more attention to the development of personality than either Horney or Fromm, and his emphasis on adolescence appears preferable to Freud's and Adler's relative lack of concern with this stage of life.

Sullivan's conception of anxiety is superior to that of Adler, and reflects a better understanding of the pain and suffering that are involved. As Sullivan puts it, "Under no conceivable circumstances … has anyone sought and valued as desirable the experience of anxiety.… People who ride on roller coasters pay money for being afraid. But no one will ever pay money for anxiety in its own right. No one wants to experience it. Only one other experience—that of loneliness—is in this special class of being totally unwanted" (1954/1970, p. 100).

Sullivan's extensive neologisms are indeed troublesome, so much so that some students of human behavior prefer to avoid his ideas. This is unfortunate, for a careful study of his major writings will yield quite a few pearls of genuine wisdom.

Suggested Reading

The most complete discussion of Sullivanian theory is presented in *The Interpersonal Theory of Psychiatry* (1953/1968). Also well-regarded is his work on psychotherapeutic procedures, *The Psychiatric Interview* (1954/1970). For a biography of Sullivan, see Perry (1982).

SUMMARY

1. THE BASIC NATURE OF HUMAN BEINGS. Sullivan is perhaps less optimistic about human nature than Horney and Fromm, but he does posit an inherent drive toward mental health. *The One-Genus Postulate:* To Sullivan, human personalities more closely resemble each other than anything else in the world. Therefore, unlike Adler, he prefers to emphasize the similarities among human beings rather than the differences. *The Need For Others:* Relationships with other people are essential to proper personality development. In fact, Sullivan defines personality in terms of interpersonal factors. *Tension Reduction:* We are motivated to reduce various tensions, the most notable of which is anxiety. Other tensions arise from the physicochemical needs, the need for sleep, and the arousal of maternal tenderness. *Dynamisms:* Sullivan rejects the construct of psychic energy, concluding instead that behavior can be explained in terms of transformations of physical energy (dynamisms). *Other Factors:* Human experience occurs in one or more of three modalities: prototaxic, parataxic, and syntaxic. Like Jung and Adler, Sullivan concludes that behavior must be understood in terms of both causality and teleology.

2. **THE STRUCTURE OF PERSONALITY.** The growing child organizes its experience by forming mental conceptions (personifications) of other people and, most importantly, of itself. *The Self-System:* Personifications of oneself result from experiences with one's own body, and from the appraisals of significant others (particularly the parents). This self-system consists of the good-me and bad-me personifications, has the goal of reducing anxiety, and is remarkably resistant to change. *The Not-Me Personification:* Aspects of personality that cause intense anxiety are dissociated from the self-system, and comprise the shadowy and dreadful not-me personification. This personification plays a significant role in schizophrenia. *Other Factors:* Sullivan regards much of personality as unconscious, but he attributes this to selective inattention rather than to repression. He interprets sublimation as an attempt to reduce anxiety, rather than as the diversion of illicit impulses.

3. **THE DEVELOPMENT OF PERSONALITY.** Sullivan regards developmental psychology as the key to understanding human behavior. He discusses in detail seven developmental epochs, each of which represents an optimal time for certain innate capacities to reach fruition. Infancy is highlighted by maternal tenderness and anxiety, crying and nursing, and the beginnings of the self-system. Childhood is a time for dealing with parental rewards and punishments, and may give rise to the malevolent transformation or loneliness. The juvenile era originates with the appearance of the need for playmates, and is when the world begins to be complicated by the presence of schoolmates and social groups. Preadolescence is highlighted by the need for an intimate relationship with a particular individual of the same sex, or chum. Early adolescence begins with puberty, and includes the desire for a close relationship with a member of the opposite sex. Late adolescence originates with the achievement of satisfying sexual activity, and involves increasing social responsibilities. Finally, adulthood—a stage of true maturity that is probably not attainable by most people—is denoted by the capacity for genuine love.

4. **FURTHER APPLICATIONS.** *Psychopathology:* Sullivan is particularly concerned with two forms of psychopathology. Obsessive-compulsive neurosis reflects an extreme vulnerability to anxiety and a profound loss of self-esteem, with ritualistic thoughts and actions used to reduce anxiety. Schizophrenia is caused by uncanny emotions that occur early in life, notably extreme anxiety, or by disastrous blows to one's self-esteem during such later stages as adolescence. It involves the dissociation of highly threatening aspects of one's personality. *Psychotherapy:* Sullivan regards psychotherapy primarily as a form of education, rather than as a medically oriented "cure." The goals are to reintegrate dissociated aspects of personality and expand the self-system, thereby leading to a wider and more effective repertory of interpersonal behavior. Sullivan has devoted considerable attention to the technique of psychiatric interviewing, and has published several articles on social change and international problems.

5. **EVALUATION.** Sullivan has been criticized for excessive neologisms, the use of a tension-reduction model of motivation, a shallow approach to dream interpretation, failing to acknowledge similarities between his constructs and those of Freud and Adler, and overemphasizing the importance of the interpersonal aspects of personality. Yet he has also been credited as the first to offer a convincing psychodynamic interpretation of schizophrenia, and he was a pioneer in advocating and using more humane treatment methods with such patients. He has furthered our understanding of personality development (including such stages as adolescence, which Freud ignored), the important phenomenon of anxiety, and psychiatric

interviewing and psychotherapy. And he played a significant role in numerous international projects seeking the elusive goal of world peace.

STUDY QUESTIONS

Part I. Questions

1. Consider the case material in the Appendix. How would Sullivan explain the causes of this man's anxiety, given the following information? (a) His mother suffered from frequent anxiety, and her hand often shook when she held his hand. (b) His mother often referred to relatives and friends in such negative terms as thoughtless, inconsiderate, and likely to hurt one's feelings. (c) He often feared his father's angry criticism and ridicule, but was not afraid of his mother. (d) He could not find a way to alleviate his painful anxiety.

2. Both Sullivan and Jung were particularly interested in schizophrenia. How might Sullivan's concept of the parataxic mode be related to: (a) Jung's construct of synchronicity? (b) the kinds of constructs devised by both theorists?

3. How would Sullivan describe and explain the behavior of schizophrenic teenager Deborah Blau in the well-known autobiographical novel, *I Never Promised You a Rose Garden?*

4. (a) Sullivan rejects Freud's construct of libido on the grounds that "physical energy is the only kind of energy I know." Do you agree with Sullivan or Freud? Why? (b) Describe the purpose of dynamisms in a single sentence. (c) Give examples of behaviors that represent the same dynamism but differ in form and/or intensity.

5. Consider Sullivan's and Freud's definitions of sublimation. (a) How are they similar? (b) How do they differ? Illustrate with an example.

6. Freud contends that personality development is virtually complete by about age 5 or 6. Sullivan argues that personality continues to develop through late childhood and adolescence, influenced by such factors as interactions with one's schoolmates, the preadolescent chum, and the emergence of the lust dynamism. Do you agree with Sullivan or Freud? Why?

7. Sullivan has been criticized for attributing the formation of the self-system primarily to the opinions of other people, and ignoring the distortions caused by the child's own misperceptions and incorrect thoughts. Give a real-life example to illustrate how the child's own errors significantly affect the development of the self-system.

8. Sullivan argues that self-centered behavior is a learned response to anxiety. (a) Who, then, should be the most selfish people in our society? (b) Is this true?

9. Sullivan's theory emphasizes the importance of maternal tenderness and anxiety, and mostly ignores the father. What personal reasons might he have had for this?

10. A terrorist blows up a building in a hated foreign country. How might Sullivan explain the terrorist's behavior?

Part II. Comments and Suggestions

1. (a) "The tension of anxiety, when present in the mothering one, induces anxiety in the infant." One means by which anxiety is communicated is physical. (b) "If you have to maintain self-esteem by pulling down the standing of others, you are extraordinarily unfortunate.... The doctrine that if you are a molehill, then, by God, there shall be no mountains ... is probably the most vicious of the [inappropriate] performances of parents with juveniles." The patient

accepted his mother's views as accurate, which strengthened his resolve to move away from people. He failed to realize that her beliefs were due in large part to her own inability to relate well to others. (c) The child need not be afraid of its mother to become anxious; anxiety in the mothering one is sufficient. Nevertheless, this is more difficult for Sullivan to explain. His theory focuses on the child's relationship with a single "mothering one" (usually the mother), and has virtually nothing to say about the behavior of a second parent (i.e., the father). (d) What does Sullivan regard as the best way to reduce anxiety? Is a person who moves away from people likely to accomplish this?

2. (a) See the comment to Chapter 3, question 12, and recall that the parataxic mode involves a lack of understanding about causality. (b) Consider that the parataxic mode is also characterized by the use of private symbols, and that the theories of Sullivan and Jung contain unusually difficult neologisms.

3. Deborah's private world of Yr, with gods who speak in words that only she can understand, illustrates the parataxic mode. Several childhood incidents are described that caused Deborah intense anxiety. (Recall Sullivan's views concerning the causes of schizophrenia.) In accordance with Sullivan's definition of psychopathology, Deborah's interpersonal behaviors are often inappropriate and inadequate. You may well be able to find other examples.

4. (a) Consider the following arguments: "If libido is *not* the same as physical energy, a person could be physically exhausted yet still have a great deal of sexual energy. That doesn't seem likely." "Physical energy can be measured, but the amount of libido invested in a particular mental event cannot be measured. So the concept of physical energy has scientific value, but the construct of libido does not." (b) To convert physical energy into behavior that will satisfy the person's needs and reduce tension. (c) For the guilt dynamism: Saying "I made a mistake, and I'm sorry" (which involves a small amount of physical energy), agonizing for days over a mistake (which involves considerably more energy), daydreaming about having avoided a mistake by doing the right thing, forming powerful unconscious beliefs that one is a bad person.

5. (a) Both involve substituting a less desirable activity for one that would be more desirable, but would create more anxiety. (b) Freudian sublimation represents ideal behavior; it is helpful to the person, and to society, because it redirects illicit instincts into healthy outlets. In contrast, Sullivanian sublimation can be wholly disadvantageous. Suppose the parents overreact with harsh criticism when the child toys with its genitals. The child responds by becoming anxious, and associates this anxiety with sexuality. As an adult, this person rejects all sexual relationships because they evoke too much anxiety, and substitutes such behaviors as daydreaming about making love. Thus the person is deprived of healthy and socially acceptable gratification.

6. Most modern psychologists would agree with Sullivan, as evidenced by the many college courses in child development and adolescence. The case history discussed in the Appendix doesn't provide much support for this aspect of Sullivan's theory, but Sullivanians (and others) could undoubtedly cite cases that do. Some cases fit one theory better than another, which is why I recommend understanding and using constructs from a variety of theories.

7. See section 6 of the case material in the Appendix.

8. (a) Those who experienced intense anxiety during infancy and childhood, which caused the self-system to become extremely rigid. (b) I think Sullivan is partly correct. Anxiety is extremely painful, so people who suffer from intense anxiety are likely to be too preoccupied with their own problems to care very much about other people. But I suspect that in our affluent society, selfishness is more often due to pampering by the parents or (in such cases as entertainers and professional athletes) by society, as in Adler's theory.

9. Consider Sullivan's description of his mother (biographical sketch).

10. Would Sullivan attribute the terrorist's behavior to an illicit instinct? Why not? Why might the terrorist have undergone a malevolent transformation during childhood? Why might the terrorist have experienced considerable anxiety, and what would this do to the terrorist's self-system? What events might have occurred during other stages of development that influenced the terrorist's behavior? Are there reasons for the terrorist's behavior that don't fit well with Sullivan's theory?

CHAPTER 8

ERIK ERIKSON
Ego Psychology

Being rejected by one's professional colleagues is not among life's more pleasant experiences. Jung, Adler, Horney, Fromm, and Sullivan chose to abandon Freud's psychic energy model, and they all incurred the wrath of the psychoanalytic establishment (as we have seen).

Some seminal thinkers have preferred to retain but modify libido theory. These psychologists readily accept such fundamental Freudian principles as infantile sexuality, unconscious processes and conflicts, and the structural model (id, ego, and superego). But they argue that Freud overemphasized the role of the irrational id and intrapsychic strife, and paid too little attention to more adaptive and peaceful mental functioning. Using some of Freud's later writings as their point of departure (e.g., 1937/1963w; 1940/1969a), these theorists devote considerably more attention to the strengths and abilities of the ego.

Accordingly, this modification of psychoanalysis has become known as **ego psychology**. The primary differences between ego psychology and basic Freudian (or "id") theory are shown in the Capsule Summary on page 169.

Although various theorists have contributed to the development of ego psychology, one has achieved a singular degree of professional and popular acclaim. This unusual and creative man entered the Freudian circle in Vienna as a 25-year-old itinerant artist, with no university degree at all, and emerged as a prominent child psychoanalyst. He contributed the term *identity crisis* to our everyday language, having first faced and resolved this difficult one of his own: Erik Homburger Erikson.

OBJECTIVES

- *To improve psychoanalytic theory by correcting Freud's major errors, and do so in a way that would not alienate the psychoanalytic establishment.*
- *To retain Freud's emphasis on the unconscious but stress the social determinants of personality, notably the influence of the parents and society, rather than instincts.*
- *To retain but deemphasize Freud's controversial (and unmeasurable) construct of libido.*
- *To correct Freud's pessimistic view of human nature by showing that we have both healthy and malignant inner potentials.*
- *To show that identity and mastery are healthy and important human needs.*
- *To show that society can have a positive effect on personality development, rather than always being in conflict with the individual about the need to sublimate illicit instincts as Freud believed.*
- *To retain but modify Freud's structural constructs of id, ego, and superego by showing that the ego is stronger, and the id is weaker, than Freud believed.*
- *To show that personality development proceeds through a series of eight stages from infancy through old age, rather than ending at age 6 as Freud believed.*
- *To show that adolescence and the identity crisis play an important role in personality development.*
- *To devise techniques of play therapy for use with children.*
- *To apply psychoanalytic theory to the lives of such famous people as Gandhi.*

BIOGRAPHICAL SKETCH

Erik Homburger Erikson was born of Danish parents on June 15, 1902, in Frankfurt, Germany. His father, a Protestant, abandoned the family prior to Erik's birth. Some 3 years later his mother married Dr. Theodor Homburger, a pediatrician of the same Jewish faith as herself. Erik experienced considerable identity confusion because of this family upheaval, and because the contrast between his part-Jewish heritage and his Nordic features caused him to be rejected by childhood peers of both groups. Known as Erik Homburger during the first 4 decades of his life, he adopted the surname of Erikson upon becoming a naturalized American citizen in 1939, and he ultimately converted to Christianity. As he was to reflect many years later, "no doubt my best friends will insist that I needed to name [the identity] crisis and to see it in everybody else in order to really come to terms with it in myself" (Erikson, 1975, p. 26; see also Coles, 1970, pp. 180–181; Roazen, 1976a, pp. 93–99).

Erikson was a mediocre student, never earning a university degree of any kind. During his early 1920s he became a wanderer, studied briefly at art schools, painted children's portraits, and struggled with psychological problems bordering between neurosis and psychosis. "I was an artist then, which can be a European euphemism for a young man with some talent, but nowhere to go." In the summer of 1927 he moved to Vienna, accepted a teaching position at a small school established for children of Freud's patients and friends, and enjoyed a "truly astounding adoption by the Freudian circle" (Erikson, 1964, p. 20; 1975, p. 29). Erikson now undertook training in child psychoanalysis, including a personal analysis by Anna Freud at the unusually low rate of 7 dollars per month. He married Joan Serson on April 1, 1930, a successful and enduring union that produced two sons and a daughter.

Erikson foresaw the coming Nazi menace and emigrated via Denmark to Boston in 1933. There he became the city's first practicing child analyst, and joined the staff of Henry Murray's clinic at Harvard. Like Jung, Erikson took a keen interest in cross-cultural studies and engaged in firsthand observation of two native American tribes: the Sioux of South

CAPSULE SUMMARY
Ego Psychology Compared to Freudian Theory

	Freudian (Id) Theory	*Ego Psychology*
The id	The sole component of personality present at birth; entirely unconscious, amoral.	Similar, but less powerful.
The ego	*Origin:* Begins to develop out of the id at age 6–8 months. *Characteristics:* A weak "rider" struggling desperately to control its instinctually energized "horse." Concerned solely with satisfying id impulses in a way that will also please its other two masters, the superego and external world. *Defense Mechanisms:* Used solely to ward off intrapsychic or external threats, primarily illicit id impulses and anxiety.	*Origin:* Begins to develop independently of the id very soon after birth. *Characteristics:* A relatively powerful and autonomous entity, which directs behavior toward such constructive goals as mastery of and adaptation to the environment. These ego functions are unrelated to the satisfaction of id impulses, yet are pleasurable in their own right. *Defense Mechanisms:* Are adaptive as well as defensive.
The superego	Includes introjected ideals and restrictions; may be overly harsh and oppressive.	Essentially similar.
Personality development	Virtually complete by about age 5 years.	Continues throughout the whole life cycle from infancy to old age.
Society	An inevitable source of frustration and conflict, since illicit and irrational id impulses must be sublimated. An external burden imposed on the ego.	Not necessarily a source of frustration and conflict, since the ego functions are constructive and can therefore be expressed directly. Supports the ego by providing social roles and identities.
Libido	The psychic energy that fuels all mental activity.	Essentially similar; but accorded considerably less emphasis, so that greater attention can be devoted to ego and societal forces.
View of human nature	Pessimistic, because of the emphasis on powerful illicit id impulses.	More optimistic, because greater strength is attributed to the rational and adaptive ego.

Dakota in 1938, and the Yurok of northern California 5 years later. His academic affiliations also included Yale University and the University of California at Berkeley, from which he resigned in 1950 rather than sign a loyalty oath. Although eventually declared "politically dependable," he nevertheless objected to the oath on principle: "Why not acquiesce in an empty gesture.... ? My answer is that of a psychologist.... My field includes the study of 'hysteria,' private and public, in 'personality' and 'culture.' It includes the study of the tremendous waste in human energy which proceeds from irrational fear and from the irrational gestures which are part of what we call 'history.' I would find it difficult to ask my subject of investigation (people) and my students to work with me, if I were to participate without protest in a vague, fearful, and somewhat vindictive gesture devised to ban an evil in some magic way—an evil which must be met with much more searching and concerted effort" (Erikson, 1951). During 1950 he also published his first book, *Childhood and Society,* which earned wide acclaim and was reissued in an enlarged edition in 1963. His subsequent study of Gandhi (1969) was honored with both the Pulitzer Prize and National Book Award.

Like Freud, Erikson was a complicated man. The emotional scars left by never knowing his biological father (whose identity was kept secret by his mother), and by a depressed and emotionally depleted mother, may have created a drive for fame that made it easier for him to relate to strangers than to his own daughter. "Despite [my father's] brilliance as an analyst and a writer, and his great charisma, he was an insecure man ... Once, during my adolescence, when Dad and I were alone together, I burst into tears—brokenhearted over the abrupt ending of a teenage romance. I remember the look of terror and grief on his face—terror because in the context of the family he did not feel like an adult with the ability to soothe and comfort.... When a person feels so deeply flawed that he or she cannot imagine ever 'fitting in' in human society, a solution is to imagine rising *above* human society.... Becoming someone special— being charming, talented ... becomes the vehicle for a desperate pursuit of emotional nourishment." (Sue Erikson Bloland, 1999, pp. 52, 56, 58.)

Another indication that Erikson was more comfortable with his work than with family problems: He and Joan had a fourth child, a son who suffered from severe Down's syndrome. This child was institutionalized immediately after birth and lived for 21 years with almost no parental contact, while Erikson preoccupied himself with devising theories about healthy personality development (Friedman, 1999; see also Elms, 2001).

Erikson's writings fill some dozen volumes. The high esteem accorded his work is evidenced by such prominent magazines as *Time* and *Newsweek,* which have referred to him as probably the most influential and outstanding psychoanalyst. Erik Erikson died on May 12, 1994, at a nursing home in Harwich, Massachusetts.

THE BASIC NATURE OF HUMAN BEINGS

Biological Processes: Libido and Sexuality

Erikson remains true to Freudian psychoanalysis by including libido among his theoretical constructs, but not without some significant reservations. On the one hand, he expresses a marked appreciation for the "clear and unifying light ... thrown into [the dark recesses of the mind] by the theory of a libido, of a mobile sexual energy which contributes to the 'highest' as well as to the 'lowest' forms of human endeavor—and often to both at the same time." Yet he also cautions against the literal acceptance of what Freud himself regarded as only a "working hypothesis," and warns that it makes little sense to speak of energies that cannot be demonstrated scientifically (Erikson, 1963, p. 63; see also Erikson, cited by Evans, 1967/1969, pp. 84, 86).

Erikson is similarly reserved about the importance of instinctual drives. He credits Freud for calling attention to the irrational aspects of personality, for discovering that sexuality begins with birth rather than at puberty, and for orienting psychoanalysis in a biological direction. But Erikson also regards our inborn sexual and aggressive instincts as vague drive fragments that are strongly influenced by parental training and cultural factors (such as school), and he argues that psychoanalysis must pay considerably more attention to innate adaptive forces. (See Erikson, 1963, pp. 44–46, 58–71, 95–97.)

Thus Erikson retains, but deemphasizes, the constructs of instinct and libido. He prefers to stress the role played by the ego and societal forces in shaping personality.

Ego Processes: Identity and Mastery

Identity. To Erikson, the ego is far more than a sorely tried mediator among the insistent id, punitive superego, and forbidding environment. The ego not only defends against illicit instincts and anxiety, but serves important healthy functions as well.

One of these constructive ego functions is to preserve a sense of **identity.** This complicated inner state includes four distinct aspects:

1. *Individuality.* A conscious sense of uniqueness and existence as a separate, distinct entity.
2. *Wholeness and synthesis.* A sense of inner wholeness and indivisibility. The growing child forms a variety of fragmentary self-images: more or less lovable, talented, obedient, scholarly, athletic, independent, and so forth. The healthy ego integrates these images into a meaningful whole. (See Erikson, 1968, pp. 160–161, 165; 1974, p. 27.)
3. *Sameness and continuity.* An unconscious striving for a sense of inner sameness and continuity between who you have been in the past, and who you are likely to be in the future. A feeling that your life has consistency, and is headed in a meaningful direction. (See Erikson, 1959, pp. 42, 102, 118; 1963, pp. 261–263; 1964, p. 91; 1968, pp. 19, 87; 1975, pp. 18–19.)
4. *Social solidarity.* Agreement with the ideals and values of some group; feeling that you receive support and recognition from significant others. (See Erikson, 1959, p. 118; 1964, pp. 90–96; 1968, pp. 22, 165.)

Although Erikson's construct of identity is more complicated than Fromm's, he agrees that it represents a vital need of every human being. "In the social jungle of human existence, there is no feeling of being alive without a sense of ego identity. Deprivation of identity, can lead to murder" (Erikson, 1963, p. 240; see also Erikson, 1959, p. 90). The state of **identity confusion** (or **role confusion,** also often referred to as an **identity crisis**) involves feelings of inner fragmentation, little or no sense of where one's life is headed, and an inability to gain the support provided by a social role or vocation. The sufferer may feel like an outcast or wanderer, or not quite somebody—as did Erikson himself during his early twenties.

Every identity includes both positive and negative aspects, which result from parental and societal rewards and punishments. Developing a primarily positive identity is likely to be more difficult for certain segments of a population, such as women in a patriarchal society or members of persecuted minority ethnic and religious groups. Since even a negative identity is likely to seem preferable to the inner turmoil of identity confusion, such individuals may adopt the debased role espoused for them by the majority. (See Erikson, 1958, p. 102; 1963, pp. 243–246; 1974; 1975, pp. 20–21.)

Mastery.   In accordance with Adler and Fromm, Erikson concludes that we have a fundamental need to master our environment. Like identity, **mastery** is an ego function that affords pleasures unrelated to the satisfaction of id impulses, and its frustration also evokes intense rage. (See Erikson, 1963, p. 68; 1964, p. 50; Erikson, cited by Evans, 1967/1969, pp. 27, 68–69.)

As with identity, a sense of mastery depends on the expectations and support of society. A child learns to walk for several reasons: to locate objects that will satisfy its drives, to feel stronger and more effective in its dealings with the external world, and because the status of "one who walks" is approved of by respected elders. "Children cannot be fooled by empty praise and condescending encouragement.... [But] their ego identity [does gain] real strength ... from wholehearted and consistent recognition of real accomplishment— i.e., of achievement that has meaning in the culture" (Erikson, 1963, pp. 235–236; 1968, p. 49).

Society and Culture

Because of his more positive view of human nature, Erikson rejects Freud's conception of society as an inevitable source of conflict:

> The greatest difficulty in the path of psychoanalysis as a general psychology probably consists in the remnants of its first conceptualization of the environment as [a hostile] "outer world." ... Preoccupied with [symptoms and defenses,] ... psychoanalysis had, at first, little to say about the way in which the ego's synthesis grows—or fails to grow— out of the soil of social organization.... [But psychoanalysis today is shifting its emphasis] to the study of the ego's roots in social organization. (Erikson, 1963, pp. 15–16, 282; 1975, p. 105. See also Erikson, cited by Evans, 1967/1969, p. 26.)

A firm sense of identity or mastery requires the support of significant others, as we have seen. Society also helps lighten the burdens of life by holding forth the promise of sanctioned roles, such as laborer, doctor, lawyer, mother, or father, which confirm that an individual has found a workable and effective life plan. In addition, mutually enhancing relationships (**mutuality**) fulfill a major human need. Such recognition provides us with the feeling that we exist in the eyes of others, and the denial of this need arouses intense hatred. (See Erikson, 1959, pp. 20–21; 1963, p. 277; 1968, pp. 87, 219; 1977, p. 88.)

Since Erikson believes that society plays a prominent role in molding the developing ego, he (unlike Freud) has devoted some time to studying the effects of different cultures on personality. Erikson observed firsthand two contrasting Native American tribes: the trusting and generous Sioux, hunters of South Dakota; and the miserly and suspicious Yurok, salmon fishermen of northern California (Erikson, 1963, pp. 111–186). The Sioux allow their children to breast-feed for several years, whereas the Yurok prefer early weaning. The Sioux detest hoarders and insist on sharing with others even when their resources are meager, whereas the Yurok stress the importance of economic security. Thus the different identities of the typical Sioux and Yurok are due primarily to the different values in each society regarding sharing and weaning, including the Sioux "paradise of the practically unlimited privilege of the mother's breast" versus the Yurok "residue of infantile nostalgia for the mother from whom he has been disengaged so forcefully," rather than to some innate instinct (Erikson, 1963, pp. 63, 76).

The influence of society is not always beneficial. It may be difficult to develop a firm sense of identity because we are confronted with contradictory values, as when our society stresses both competition ("winning is the only thing") and cooperation ("do unto others … "). A society may emphasize questionable values, as with the miserly Yurok. Societies create oppressed minorities, whose members may adopt the negative identity imposed by the majority. A seriously pathogenic culture may even inflict this fate on a wide scale, as happened with the youths growing up in Nazi Germany (Erikson, 1963, pp. 326ff; Erikson, cited by Evans, 1967/1969, p. 32).

The Unconscious

To Erikson, the unconscious ranks among Freud's greatest contributions. He concludes that except for the implicit wisdom expressed in the Bible and Shakespeare, we have learned more in the past few decades about human motivation and development than during all of the preceding centuries. Even primitive cultures express an intuitive understanding of the unconscious, as indicated by rituals that attribute unusual dreams to supernatural visitations rather than to an individual's conscious motivation. (See Erikson, 1959, p. 99; 1963, pp. 153, 190, 216; 1964, pp. 78, 147, 243.)

THE STRUCTURE OF PERSONALITY

The Id

Except for the greater emphasis accorded the ego, Erikson's conception of personality structure is similar to Freud's. The **id** is entirely unconscious and amoral. It is the only component that is present at birth, and includes all of our inherited instincts.

The Ego

The **ego** is the logical, self-preservative, problem-solving part of personality. It mediates among the demands of the external world, the id, and the superego, and is largely unconscious. As in Freudian theory, the ego guards against illicit id impulses and an overly severe superego by using various defense mechanisms, including repression, reaction formation, projection, denial of reality, and fantasy. We may attribute to our neighbors those faults of which we are most ashamed (projection), blithely ignore warnings of such impending catastrophes as nuclear war or death (denial of reality), or try to make a negative identity seem like an apparent virtue (reaction formation).

In contrast to Freud, Erikson argues that defense mechanisms may also be used in adaptive ways. For example, fantasies may produce imaginative thoughts that help to solve important problems. The capacities of the ego also include such essential constructive functions as identity and mastery, as we have seen.

The Superego

The **superego** includes introjected ideals and restrictions, which help the ego to control the id. As in Freudian theory, however, the superego can become oppressive and impose overly harsh standards of right and wrong upon the ego. Another drawback of the superego is that it perpetuates internally the relationship of the superior, angry adult and the small, helpless child. If parental training fails to reflect the standards of the society in which one lives, the rift between the ego and superego will deepen and lead to excessive intrapsychic conflict. "Man survives only where traditional child training provides him with a conscience which will guide him without crushing him, and which is firm and flexible enough to fit the vicissitudes of his historical era" (Erikson, 1963, p. 95; see also Erikson, 1963, pp. 60, 122, 192–194, 257, 311–312; 1964, pp. 223–224; 1968, p. 218).

Although Erikson retains Freud's structural model, he cautions against reifying such concepts as id, ego, and superego. He stresses that these are abstract, tentative constructs designed to facilitate the discussion and understanding of personality, rather than concrete and universally established entities located somewhere within the psyche (Erikson, 1963, pp. 414–415; 1964, p. 77; 1975, p. 37).

THE DEVELOPMENT OF PERSONALITY

Although Erikson occasionally devotes some attention to the Freudian concept of fixation (1963, pp. 72–97), his approach to personality development uses different constructs and principles. He also rejects Freud's "originological" efforts to explain personality wholly in terms of the first 4 or 5 years of life. Instead Erikson stresses that personality development continues throughout the whole life cycle, and he posits eight stages that extend from infancy to old age.

The Epigenetic Psychosexual Stages, or "Eight Ages of Man"

The development of our physical organs unfolds according to a predetermined genetic schedule, and Erikson concludes that personality follows a similar course. A predisposition to adapt to each developmental stage is present at birth, and emerges at the appropriate time. Since Erikson accepts the existence of infantile sexuality, he regards these stages as both psychosexual and **epigenetic** (*epi* = upon, *genesis* = emergence).

Every epigenetic psychosexual stage is characterized by a specific problem or **crisis** (in the medical sense of a crucial turning point for better or worse, rather than in the political sense of imminent catastrophe). Each crisis is brought on by the child's increasing physical maturity and by the greater demands made by the parents and society, and must be resolved by the ego for personality development to proceed successfully. However, the outcome of any stage is not necessarily permanent. A severe later crisis may counteract previous successes (or even failures). (See Erikson, 1959, pp. 15, 52; 1963, pp. 248–274; 1964, pp. 138–142; 1968, p. 16; 1982.)

The Oral-Sensory Stage: Basic Trust Versus Mistrust.   As in Freudian theory, the first epigenetic psychosexual stage centers around the oral zone. (See Erikson, 1963, pp. 72–80, 247–251; 1968, pp. 96–107.) Erikson agrees that orality provides libidinal pleasure. Like Sullivan, however, Erikson prefers to stress the interpersonal aspects of the oral-sensory stage—notably maternal nursing and cuddling, which represents the infant's first significant interactions with another person.

If the mother consistently responds to her baby's hunger with appropriate and affectionate feeding, the infant learns to **trust** that its needs will be satisfied. This leads to the infant's first social achievement: "[a] willingness to let the mother out of sight without undue anxiety or rage, because she has become an inner certainty as well as an outer predictability" (Erikson, 1963, p. 247). But if the painful state of hunger is often ignored, or if the mother is anxious

CAPSULE SUMMARY
Some Important Eriksonian Terminology

Crisis (developmental crisis)	A crucial turning point for better or worse that occurs during personality development.
Ego	The logical, self-preservative, problem-solving part of personality that mediates among the demands of the id, the superego, and the external world. In contrast to Freudian theory, the ego possesses important constructive capacities (such as identity and mastery) as well as defenses against illicit id instincts and anxiety.
Ego psychology	A theory of personality that hews more closely to Freudian psychoanalysis than does the work of Jung, Adler, Horney, Fromm, and Sullivan, but stresses the strengths and capacities of the rational ego and deemphasizes the role of instincts and the irrational id.
Id	The irrational, amoral component of personality that is present at birth and includes all innate instincts; similar to Freud's use of the term.
Identity (ego identity)	A complicated inner state that includes feelings of individuality and uniqueness, a sense of wholeness and indivisibility, an unconscious striving for sameness and continuity, and a sense of solidarity with the ideals and values of some group. Identity has both positive and negative aspects, with a preponderance of the former indicative of a healthy personality. But since there is no feeling of being alive without a sense of identity, even a negative one will seem preferable to none at all.
Identity confusion (role confusion)	The inability to achieve a sense of identity. Involves feelings of inner fragmentation, little or no sense of where one's life is headed, and an inability to gain the support provided by a social role.
Identity crisis	(1) A synonym for identity confusion. (2) A crucial turning point in the development of personality that occurs during adolescence, and leads to either a sense of identity or identity confusion.
Id psychology	A synonym for Freudian psychoanalysis.
Libido	The sexual psychic energy that powers mental activity. Similar to Freud's use of the term, but accorded considerably less emphasis by Erikson.
Life cycle	The whole of personality development, from infancy through childhood and adolescence to old age.
Mastery	A sense of competence in dealing with the environment.
Mutuality	The ideal form of human relationship, wherein the partners facilitate the development of each other's healthy potentials.
Play therapy	A form of psychotherapy in which a child creates a scene or story by using toys; the "royal road" to a child's unconscious.
Repression	Unconsciously eliminating threatening material from awareness and being unable to recall it on demand. Similar to Freud's use of the term, as is Erikson's use of the other defense mechanisms.
Ritualizations	Interpersonal rituals that help the ego to adapt to the standards and demands of society.
Role confusion	An often-used synonym for identity confusion.
Superego	The component of personality that includes introjected ideals and prohibitions; similar to Freud's use of the term.

and ineffective, the infant develops a profound sense of impending discomfort and danger (basic **mistrust**):

> The amount of trust derived from earliest infantile experience ... [depends] on the quality of the maternal relationship. Mothers create a sense of trust in their children by ... sensitive care of the baby's individual needs and a firm sense of personal trustworthiness. (Erikson, 1963, p. 249. See also Erikson, 1959, p. 63.)

Not even the best parents behave ideally all of the time, so every personality includes some trust and mistrust. But if there is more mistrust than trust, the ego has been damaged and is less likely to cope with the problems of the following stages. Conversely, if there is significantly more trust than mistrust, the ego learns that its most fervent wishes will be satisfied. The emergence of this healthy ego quality (**hope**) signifies that personality development has proceeded successfully past the crisis of the oral-sensory stage (Erikson, 1964, p. 118).

The Muscular-Anal Stage: Autonomy Versus Shame and Doubt.

Just when the child begins to trust the nurturing mother and external world, its developing musculature makes possible some control over the environment. During the muscular-anal stage, therefore, the child must risk breaching the trustful relationship with the mother in order to exert its **autonomy.** "The strength acquired at any stage is tested by the necessity to ... take chances in the next stage with what was most vulnerably precious in the previous one" (Erikson, 1963, p. 263; see also Erikson, 1963, pp. 80–85, 178, 251–254; 1968, pp. 107–114).

Children in our culture soon learn that cleanliness and toilet-training are serious matters, and that they can now choose between retaining or eliminating bodily wastes. Although Erikson readily accepts such psychoanalytic constructs as anal-retentive, anal-expulsive, and the anal personality (orderly, miserly, stubborn), he continues to emphasize the role of social influences on personality development. If parental control during this stage is supportive and reassuring, the child develops a positive attitude about its displays of autonomy. But if overprotective parents impose rigid and excessive restrictions, if anxious parents respond to the child's incontinence by becoming extremely upset and disgusted, or if overpermissive parents allow the child to take chances that end in shattering failures, the child's wishes to assert itself become associated with feelings of **shame** and **doubt.**

> This whole stage, then ... becomes a battle for autonomy.... The infant must come to feel that his basic trust in himself and in the world (which is the lasting treasure saved from the conflicts of the oral stage) will not be jeopardized by this sudden violent wish to have a choice. (Erikson, 1963, pp. 82, 85. See also Erikson, 1959, p. 68; 1963, pp. 84, 254.)

As with basic trust and mistrust, both autonomy and shame are aspects of every personality. Successful development occurs when there is significantly more autonomy, which results in an "unbroken determination to exercise free choice as well as self-restraint." This ego quality of **will power** also depends on the successful resolution of the preceding oral-sensory stage. "Will cannot be trained until hope is secure ... [and] no person can live, no ego remain intact without hope and will" (Erikson, 1964, pp. 115, 118, 119).

The Locomotor-Genital Stage: Initiative Versus Guilt.

The third epigenetic psychosexual stage is highlighted by the development of such locomotor abilities as walking and running, which help to develop the ego's sense of mastery. (See Erikson, 1963, pp. 85–92, 255–258; 1968, pp. 115–122.) During this stage, the child becomes aware of the differences between the sexes and begins to experience vague genital urges. As in Freudian theory, these desires are at first associated with the nurturing mother; but they ultimately give way to "the boy's assurance that he will marry his mother and make her proud of him, and … the girl's that she will marry her father and take much better care of him" (Erikson, 1963, p. 90; see also Erikson, 1958, p. 73; 1963, pp. 87, 256, 410). The parent of the same sex, to whom the child feels vastly inferior in genital capacity, is cast in the role of rival. However, the child soon realizes that it is too small to satisfy its Oedipal wishes. So the child resorts to sexual and aggressive fantasies, which arouse a deep sense of **guilt** and a fear of punishment in the form of harm to the genitals.

Ideally, the child learns to divert the threatening sexual drive into such acceptable outlets as play. "Play is to the child what thinking, planning, and blueprinting are to the adult, a trial universe … [wherein] past failures can be thought through [and] expectations tested." Erikson finds that the play of boys tends to emphasize the intrusive high–low dimension and the construction of tall objects, whereas girls concentrate on the inclusive dimension of open versus closed and build toy structures that involve containment, and he attributes this difference in part to the physiological differences between the future inseminator and the future child-bearer. (See Figure 8.1.)

Substituting play for Oedipal wishes brings relief from guilt, whereas the parents' approval of the child's accomplishments promotes a sense of **initiative.** A predominance of initiative over guilt enables the ego to develop the quality of **purpose,** or "the courage to envisage and pursue valued goals uninhibited by … the foiling fear of punishment" (Erikson, 1964, pp. 120, 122), which indicates that the crisis of this stage has been passed successfully.

The Latency Stage: Industry Versus Inferiority.

As in Freudian theory, the fourth stage is a time of submerged sexuality and "lull before the storm of puberty" (Erikson, 1963, p. 260; see also Erikson, 1963, pp. 258–261; 1968, pp. 122–128). The latency stage is characterized by an intense curiosity and wish to learn. All cultures assist this effort by providing some sort of systematic instruction, notably school.

The child's successes during this stage contribute to a positive sense of **industry,** whereas failures result in feelings of inadequacy and **inferiority.** Successful personality development occurs when industry predominates over inferiority, and the ego learns that important tasks can be completed and become a source of pride (**competence**).

Adolescence: Identity Versus Role Confusion.

With the development of competence and the advent of puberty, childhood comes to an end. The fifth stage consists of adolescence, a period which Erikson (like Sullivan) regards as one of considerable importance. The adolescent must contend with the reemergence of latent sexual impulses, an inner turmoil that can only be resolved by gaining recognition and support from significant others:

> Like a trapeze artist, the young person in the middle of vigorous motion must let go of his safe hold on childhood and reach out for a firm grasp on adulthood, depending for a breathless interval on a relatedness between the past and the future, and on the reliability of those he must let go of, and those who will "receive" him. Whatever combination of drives and defenses, of sublimations and capacities has emerged from the young individual's childhood must now make sense in view of his concrete opportunities in work and love … [and] he must detect some meaningful resemblance between what he has come to see in himself and what his sharpened awareness tells him others judge and expect him to be. (Erikson, 1964, p. 90; 1958, p. 14. See also Erikson, 1958, p. 43; 1959, p. 161; 1963, pp. 261–263, 306–307; 1968, pp. 128–135.)

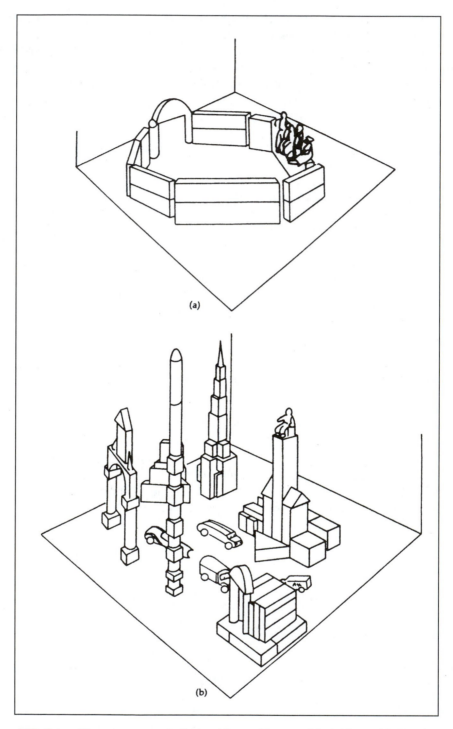

FIG. 8.1. Play structures built by 10- to 12-year-old children. (a) Female inclusiveness. (b) Male intrusiveness.

CAPSULE SUMMARY
The Epigenetic Psychosexual Stages (Erikson)

Stage	Developmental Crisis	Ego Quality That Denotes Successful Development
Oral-sensory	Basic trust versus mistrust	Hope: The enduring belief that one's fervent wishes can be attained
Muscular-anal	Autonomy versus shame and doubt	Will power: The determination to exercise free choice as well as self-control
Locomotor-genital	Initiative versus guilt	Purpose: The courage to visualize and pursue valued goals
Latency	Industry versus inferiority	Competence: The belief that important tasks can be completed, and a source of pride
Adolescence	Identity versus role confusion (identity confusion)	Fidelity: The ability to pledge and maintain loyalty to a cause
Young adulthood	Intimacy versus isolation	Love: The mutuality of devotion that overcomes the conflict between the needs of individuals
Adulthood	Generativity versus stagnation	Care: The increasing concern for others, especially the next generation
Maturity	Ego integrity versus despair	Wisdom: Not fearing death, because one has made the most of life

Notes: (1) *Epigenetic* means "upon emergence," or unfolding according to an innate schedule. (2) Both the positive and negative characteristics of any stage (e.g., basic trust and mistrust) are present to some degree in every personality. A preponderance of the former denotes healthy adjustment, and results in the emergence of the corresponding ego quality. (3) A favorable or unfavorable resolution of each crisis is by no means permanent, but remains subject to future benign and pathogenic conditions. However, a given ego quality is unlikely to appear unless the preceding stages have developed satisfactorily.

The crucial problem of this stage is the **identity crisis,** a fork in the developmental road that leads either to a healthy sense of identity or to the torments of identity confusion (role confusion). As we have seen, identity confusion is a painful state that includes feelings of inner fragmentation and little sense of where one's life is headed. Adolescents are therefore vulnerable to ideologies that offer the prospect of clearly defined roles, whether they be the benevolent principles of organizations that seek to improve society or the vicious doctrines of the Nazi movement in Hitler's Germany. Young criminals may develop a sense of identity by joining a gang and conforming to its roles and standards. Thus the potential dangers of adolescence include not only identity confusion, but also adopting an identity that is primarily negative.

If preceding developmental crises have not been successfully resolved, it may not be possible to achieve either a primarily positive or negative identity. The individual may therefore reject the demands of adulthood and extend the adolescent stage well past the appropriate age. Examples include young adults who fail to complete their studies and adopt a vocation, and

Erikson himself up until the time he joined the Freuds in Vienna at age 25. The successful resolution of the adolescent identity crisis is reflected by a predominance of identity over role confusion and the emergence of the ego quality of **fidelity,** or "the ability to sustain loyalties freely pledged in spite of the inevitable contradictions of value systems" (Erikson, 1964, p. 125).

Young Adulthood: Intimacy Versus Isolation.

The sixth epigenetic psychosexual stage represents the beginning of adulthood, and involves such responsibilities as work and marriage. (See Erikson, 1963, pp. 263–266; 1968, pp. 135–138.) During this stage, the newly acquired sense of identity must be risked in order to achieve close relationships with other people.

If the young adult's sense of identity is very fragile, **isolation** and self-absorption will appear preferable to meaningful contact with others. Conversely, a firm identity can be fused with that of another person without the fear of losing an important part of oneself. Such **intimacy** is an essential aspect of close friendships and a successful marriage, and involves a sincere concern for the welfare of others. To Erikson, therefore, only a person with a strong sense of identity can enjoy intimate personal relationships. A predominance of intimacy over isolation enables the ego to overcome the separate needs of two individuals and enjoy mutual devotion (**love**), which indicates that the crisis of this stage has been passed successfully.

Adulthood: Generativity Versus Stagnation.

The stage of adulthood is a time of **generativity,** which refers primarily to procreation and guiding the next generation. It also includes productivity and creativity. (See Erikson, 1963, pp. 266–268; 1968, pp. 138–139.) The corresponding danger is **stagnation,** an extreme state of self-indulgence similar to behaving as if one were one's own special child.

Merely having children is by no means sufficient evidence that the crisis of adulthood has been resolved. The predominance of generativity over stagnation is reflected by the ego quality of **care**, or "the widening concern for what has been generated by love, necessity, or accident, [which] overcomes the ambivalence adhering to irreversible obligation" (Erikson, 1964, p. 131).

Maturity: Ego Integrity Versus Despair.

Only a person who has successfully resolved the preceding seven developmental crises can achieve **ego integrity,** the feeling that one's life has been valuable and worthwhile. (See Erikson, 1963, pp. 268–269; 1968, pp. 139–141.) The converse of ego integrity is **despair,** the fear that death will intervene before one can find the way to a more meaningful life. Ideally, ego integrity prevails over despair; and this results in the ego quality of **wisdom.** People who are wise do not fear death, because they have made the most of life. Wisdom also exerts a positive influence on subsequent generations, for "healthy children will not fear life if their elders have integrity enough not to fear death" (Erikson, 1963, p. 269; 1964, p. 133).

Ritualizations

Erikson (1966; 1977) has devoted some attention to **ritualizations,** or interpersonal rituals that help the ego to adapt to the standards and demands of society. Among the miserly Yurok Indians, for example, the child is taught at mealtime "to put only a little food on the spoon, to take the spoon up to his mouth slowly, to put the spoon down again while chewing the food—and, above all, to think of becoming rich while he [enjoys and swallows] it" (Erikson, 1963, p. 177; 1977, p. 80). Such a ritual would be inconceivable among the generous and charitable Sioux, indicating once again the powerful influence of societal factors on the development of personality.

FURTHER APPLICATIONS OF ERIKSONIAN THEORY

Dream Interpretation

As with other aspects of ego psychology, Erikson retains but modifies Freudian dream theory. He agrees that dreams provide important information about unconscious feelings and memories, that condensation produces dream symbols with more than one meaning, and that free association and day's residues are valuable aids to interpretation. To Erikson, however, the healthy ego remains relatively powerful even during sleep. It not only makes compromises with illicit id impulses, but also produces dreams of success and achievement that enable us to awaken with a sense of wholeness and competence.

Erikson also rejects Freud's contention that almost every dream fulfills some childhood sexual wish. Instead, dreams may deal with prior epigenetic crises. They may highlight current problems in the dreamer's life, such as an identity crisis, and suggest potential solutions. Or they may even be dreamed for the specific purpose of being interpreted by the dreamer, or the dreamer's psychoanalyst. "Once we set out to study our own dreams ... we may well dream them in order to study them" (Erikson, 1977, p. 134). Erikson also argues that some of Freud's own dreams, if properly reinterpreted, support psychosocial ego theory rather than instinctual id psychoanalysis. (See Erikson, 1954; 1958, p. 142; 1959, p. 154 n. 17; 1964, pp. 57–58, 177–201; 1968, pp. 197–204.)

One young male patient of Erikson's had a dream so traumatic that he feared the loss of his sanity: a horrible huge and empty face surrounded by slimy hair, that might perhaps have been his mother, sitting in a motionless horse and buggy. This patient had serious doubts about his chosen religious vocation, and the empty face symbolized his lack of identity. The Medusa-like hair reflected bisexual confusion, and fears of women and heterosexuality. The horse and buggy called to mind his mother, whose longing for the rural locale of her childhood had intensified his feelings of being unable to progress in a modern and changing world. The face also represented his white-haired grandfather, against whom he had rebelled as a youth in his search for a sense of identity. Finally, the patient was concerned that Erikson (whose own hair is often quite unruly, and who had recently been compelled to interrupt therapy for an emergency operation) would desert him before he could achieve a coherent "face" or identity of his own (Erikson, 1964, pp. 57–76).

Another dream, reported by a young woman patient of Erikson's, is perhaps the shortest on record: the single word S[E]INE lit up against a dark background, with the first "E" in brackets. She suffered from agoraphobia (a fear of open spaces), which had first overcome her in Paris near the river Seine. Her dream reminded her of several German and Latin words, *sehen* (to see), *seine* (his), and *sine* (without). In Paris, she had seen a shocking and frightening picture of Christ, without his loincloth, being circumsized. These thoughts led in turn to a traumatic incident in her childhood, being catheterized by her father (a pediatrician) because of a bladder condition during the locomotor-genital stage. "It will be obvious how traumatic at that stage an event was that both immobilized and exposed the little girl—in an 'oedipal' context." The bracketed first letter of Erikson's name suggested some transference resentment over the analytic requirement that such embarrassing ideas flow freely, like a river or urine, and a wish to turn the tables by exposing him instead. "This interpretation ... led to some ... shared laughter over the tricks of the unconscious, which can condense—and give away—all these meanings in one word" (Erikson, 1977, pp. 130–132).

Psychopathology

Although Erikson defines the course of healthy ego development in greater detail than Freud, he agrees that the well-adjusted individual is one who can do two things well: love and work. He also shares Freud's belief that the study of analytic patients, and their unusually severe intrapsychic conflicts, helps to clarify important aspects of personality that we all experience (such as the defense mechanisms). However, Erikson cautions that healthy ego functions cannot be wholly understood from the behavior of pathological individuals:

> [We psychoanalysts] repeat for our own encouragement (and as an argument against others) that human nature can best be studied in a state of partial breakdown or, at any rate, of marked conflict.... As Freud himself put it, we see a crystal's structure only when it cracks. But a crystal, on the one hand, and an organism or personality, on the other, differ in the fact that one is inanimate and the other an organic whole which cannot be broken up without a withering of the parts.... [Thus] I do not believe that we can entirely reconstruct the ego's normal functions from an understanding of its dysfunctions ... (Erikson, 1968, p. 276. See also Erikson, 1954; 1958, p. 16; 1963, pp. 45, 265, 308; 1968, p. 136.)

Origins of Psychopathology. Psychopathology occurs when the normally competent ego is seriously weakened by social trauma, physical ills, and (most importantly) by the failure to resolve prior epigenetic crises. For example, a young boy suffered from convulsions similar to epilepsy. His ego had been impaired by the failure to develop sufficient autonomy and will power during the muscular-anal stage, primarily because of profound guilt resulting from the (incorrect) belief that his aggressiveness had caused the death of his grandmother. His ego was further weakened by a cerebral disorder predisposing him to such attacks, and by the social difficulties of being the only Jewish family in a gentile town (Erikson, 1963, pp. 23–47).

Some parental behaviors are pathogenic because they prevent effective resolutions of epigenetic crises. These include abrupt weaning or anxious and insensitive nursing during the oral-sensory stage, and overly severe or lenient toilet-training during the muscular-anal stage (as we have seen). However, the child is not without some influence of its own. "This weak and changing little being moves the whole family along. Babies control and bring up their families as much as they are controlled by them" (Erikson, 1963, p. 69; see also Erikson, 1958, p. 70; 1963, pp. 71, 207, 218, 257). For example, the child's negative response to a nervous and ineffective mother is likely to create a vicious circle by making her upset, guilty, and even less affectionate.

Varieties of Psychopathology. Erikson makes some use of the standard psychiatric nomenclature, but he cautions that such labels may become a self-fulfilling prophecy. That is, the sufferer may adopt the pathological classification (such as obsessive-compulsive, criminal, or even just "patient") as a negative identity. Erikson regards Freud's unsuccessful treatment of Dora as a typical example. She was unable to resolve her adolescent identity crisis because of the examples set by her perfidious elders, so she took great pride in being written up in scientific journals as a noted clinical case. "From Freud's early days onward, enlightened people have adapted to his insights by mouthing the names of their neuroses—and keeping the neuroses, too.... To be a famous, if uncured, patient had become for this woman one lasting ... identity element" (Erikson, 1964, p. 173; 1968, p. 28; see also Erikson, 1963, pp. 307–308, 414; 1964, pp. 97, 166–174; 1968, pp. 77, 250–252).

Erikson shares Freud's belief that sexuality and regression often play an important role in psychopathology, and that neurotic symptoms are usually overdetermined. One patient, a 4-year-old boy, was bloated virtually to the bursting point by a steadfast refusal to eliminate his feces. This was due partly to identification with a beloved nurse who had left his family upon becoming pregnant, with the boy concluding that babies were born through the bowels and that he himself was pregnant. It also reflected a desire to become a baby once again so that the nurse would take care of him, expressed through regression to behavior typical of the time when she was present. Fortunately, a simplified and friendly explanation of the facts of life produced a prompt cure. (See Erikson, 1963, pp. 53–58.)

Erikson regards identity confusion as the major problem confronting modern psychotherapy. Patients in Freud's day had a fairly clear idea as to what kind of person they wanted to be, and suffered from inhibitions that prevented them from reaching this goal. In contrast, today's patients often do not know what to believe in and what personal goals to aim for. "The study of identity, then, becomes as strategic in our time as the study of sexuality was in Freud's time" (Erikson, 1963, p. 282; see also pp. 195–208, 279).

Psychotherapy

Theoretical Foundation. Since Erikson regards himself primarily as a psychoanalyst, many of his therapeutic goals are similar to Freud's. The patient strives to bring unconscious material to consciousness, and to achieve important insights on both an emotional and intellectual level. This strengthens the patient's capacity for rational, ego-directed choices. However, Erikson concludes that standard psychoanalytic therapy has serious limitations. He compares the analyst's sitting silently out of sight to "an exquisite deprivation experiment," one that may evoke so much regression and transference as to obscure an understanding of the patient's behavior in more normal situations. He also warns that psychoanalysis is "a cure for which a patient must be relatively healthy in the first place and gifted," and that its use with people for whom it is unsuited may make them even more disturbed (Erikson, 1977, p. 128; see also Erikson, 1958, pp. 17, 151–154; 1964, p. 50; Roazen, 1976a, pp. 67–72).

Therapeutic Procedures. Like Freud, Erikson regards free association as the best way to unravel the meaning of important unconscious material. However, most of his therapeutic procedures are designed to reduce the mystique and potential bias of Freudian psychoanalysis. For example, he adopts the more active Sullivanian role of participant-observer. Like Jung and Adler, Erikson stresses the equality of patient and therapist by often using face-to-face interviews. He also prefers to devote less attention to childhood causes, so that patients will not be encouraged to blame their problems on their parents and refuse to take responsibility for their behavior. (See Erikson, 1963, pp. 16, 33, 195; 1964, p. 58; Erikson, cited by Evans, 1967/1969, pp. 31, 97.)

To Erikson, it is play rather than dreams that represents the "royal road" to a child's unconscious. The aforementioned convulsive young boy was unable to verbalize his fear of being punished by death for his aggression toward his grandmother, but he readily expressed this threatening belief with the aid of **play therapy** by arranging a group of dominoes in the form of a coffin. A young girl revealed the Oedipal nature of her repressed anger by creating a play scene wherein a girl doll shuts the mother doll in the bathroom, and gives the father doll three shiny new cars:

> Children are apt to express in spatial configurations what they cannot or dare not say.... A child can be counted upon to bring into the solitary play arranged for him whatever aspect of his ego has been ruffled most ... for to "play it out" is the most natural self-healing measure childhood affords.... As William Blake puts it: "The child's toys and the

old man's reasons are the fruits of the two seasons." (Erikson, 1963, pp. 29, 222; see also pp. 98–99, 107–108, 186, 209.)

Resistance, Transference, and Countertransference.   Erikson accepts the existence of unconscious resistances to therapy, such as long silences and avoiding important but unpleasant issues. But he attributes them to the patient's fears that a weak identity will be shattered by the analyst's stronger will, rather than to a desire to preserve illicit impulses.

Insofar as transference is concerned, Erikson takes a somewhat ambivalent position. He shares Freud's belief that it represents an essential source of information and emotional attachment, and Jung's concern that intensive levels (e.g., transference neurosis) will provoke excessive regressions and infantile wishes to depend on an omnipotent provider. Erikson does agree that analysts are capable of such damaging countertransferences as the desire to dominate or love the patient, and that a personal analysis is therefore an indispensable part of psychoanalytic training. In addition, no therapeutic approach (Freudian, Eriksonian, Jungian, or whatever) can be effective unless it is compatible with the therapist's own identity (Erikson, 1963, pp. 190–191, 223; 1964, pp. 36–37, 43, 236; 1975, pp. 34, 105–106, 115–116; Erikson, cited by Evans, 1967/1969, p. 95).

Psychotherapy and Social Reform.   Since society plays an integral role in the development of a firm sense of identity, the treatment of specific individuals can accomplish only so much. Our technological culture is a common source of discontent, for it turns all too many workers into mere extensions of complicated machines. Racial and other forms of prejudice contribute to identity confusion, negative identities, and psychopathology. And the danger of nuclear war creates the pressing need to recognize our allegiance to the human species as a whole. "The only alternative to armed competition seems to be the effort to activate ... what will strengthen [another] in his historical development even as it strengthens the actor in his own development." That is, mutuality may well be the only way to ward off total atomic destruction (Erikson, 1964, p. 242; see also Erikson, 1963, pp. 155, 237, 241–246, 323; Erikson, cited by Evans, 1967/1969, pp. 108–110).

Like Fromm and Horney, Erikson is highly critical of the psychoanalytic approach to female sexuality. He shares Horney's belief that penis envy is symbolic of women's jealousy over the favored role of men in a patriarchal society, and agrees that men (consciously or unconsciously) envy women's capacity for motherhood. He also expresses the hope that emancipated women will help our nuclear age to replace a masculine proclivity for war with new directions for peace and survival. (See Erikson, 1963, pp. 88, 411; 1964, pp. 113, 235; 1968, pp. 261–294; 1975, pp. 225–247; Erikson, cited by Evans, 1967/1969, pp. 43–47.)

Work

Like Adler, Erikson regards the inability to choose a vocation during adolescence as indicative of psychopathology. Conversely, as we have seen, the support afforded the ego by a satisfying career helps to prevent identity confusion. Although Erikson (1958, p. 17) regards work as probably the most neglected problem in psychoanalysis, his theory (like those of his predecessors) has relatively little to say about this area of human endeavor.

Religion

Unlike Freud, Erikson does not dismiss religion as a collective neurosis. He does agree that some forms of religious thought resemble psychopathology, and seek to exploit our infantile wishes for safety by offering illusory promises that cannot be fulfilled. Erikson also shares Freud's belief that religion is not an innate need, and that many people prefer to derive faith from productive work and artistic creation. However, religion does provide valuable support for such essential ego qualities as trust and hope. There are millions who cannot afford to be without it, and whose apparent pride in not being religious is merely whistling in the dark. (See Erikson, 1958, p. 265; 1959, pp. 64–65; 1963, pp. 250–251, 277–278; 1964, pp. 153–155.)

Erikson restates the "golden rule" in terms of mutuality. Doing unto others as we wish they would do unto us may be unwise, for their needs and tastes may differ from ours. Instead, ideal behavior is that which enhances both another's development and one's own. "Understood this way, the Rule would say that it is best to do to another what will strengthen you even as it will strengthen him—that is, what will develop his best potentials even as it develops your own" (Erikson, 1964, p. 233; see also Erikson, 1964, pp. 219–243; Erikson, cited by Evans, 1967/1969, pp. 72–73, 101–102). Erikson (1969) regards Mohandas Gandhi as a particularly good example, for his famous philosophy of nonviolent resistance ("Satyagraha") stresses the need for solutions that benefit both parties to a dispute.

Literature

To Erikson, the frequent allusions of some Black writers to namelessness and facelessness reflect the identity confusion that typically befalls an exploited minority. The character Biff in *Death of a Salesman* suffers from a similar problem, complaining that he can't get any sort of hold on life. However, Erikson cautions against always inferring pathology from such examples. He once discussed *Tom Sawyer* with a group of social workers, calling attention to Ben Rogers's playful imitation of a steamboat and its captain. Some members of the audience promptly decided that Ben was escaping from a tyrannical father with fantasies of being an official, and others concluded that he was symbolically reliving some previous bedwetting or toilet trauma by imitating a boat displacing substantial quantities of water. Erikson regards Ben as a healthy growing boy whose play symbolically makes a well-functioning whole out of such physiological processes as the brain (captain), the nerves and muscles (signal system and engine), and the body (boat). Tom does prove to be the better psychologist by inducing Ben to take over the tiresome job of whitewashing a fence, however, "which shows that psychology is at least the second-best thing to, and under some adverse circumstances may even prove superior to ordinary adjustment" (Erikson, 1963, p. 210; see also Erikson, 1963, pp. 211, 307; 1968, pp. 25, 131).

Psychohistory

Erikson has devoted considerable attention to the writings and lives of noted historical figures, including Luther (1958), Hitler (1963, pp. 326–358), Gorky (1963, pp. 359–402), Gandhi (1969; 1975, pp. 113–189), and Jefferson (1974). Although he warns that autobiographies cannot be interpreted in the same way as free associations, and that the psychohistorian cannot avoid all countertransferential biases, Erikson seeks to illuminate the intrapsychic world of such personages with the aid of his theoretical principles. He has also used this technique in a conversation with Black Panther leader Huey Newton (Erikson, 1973).

EVALUATION

Criticisms and Controversies

Pro-Freudianism and Political Expediency. To some critics, Erikson's writings reflect a pronounced and disturbing schism. On the one hand, he professes a strong allegiance to Freudian theory, characterizes himself as a psychoanalyst, and retains the controversial construct of libido. Erikson goes so far as to attribute his own original construct of identity to his illustrious predecessor, repeatedly citing a single obscure speech in which Freud merely mentioned this term in passing. Yet despite these protestations, Erikson's theory often seems more like a radical departure from id psychology. His emphasis on positive ego and societal processes differs significantly from Freud's theoretical pessimism; and his actual references to libido are minimal and ambivalent, varying from a casual acceptance of this construct to virtual rejection because it cannot be measured. In fact, there are critics who consider Erikson to be something of a creative genius as a personality theorist. (See, for example, McAdams, 1997.)

Erikson may simply be demonstrating an understandable loyalty to the group that took him in as a 25-year-old wanderer, and helped him to resolve his painful identity crisis. However, the gap between his self-proclaimed Freudianism and his revisionist constructs is so substantial as to give some critics (e.g., Roazen, 1976a) the impression of political expediency. That is, Erikson may well have feared the excommunication from psychoanalytic circles that befell those theorists who forthrightly rejected libido theory—a dire fate that even involved the total exclusion of their works from the reading lists given psychoanalytic trainees. Whatever the cause, Erikson's ambivalence has at least to some extent confused the nature and direction of his own theoretical contributions.

Social Conservatism and Optimism.

Although Erikson explicitly denies any desire to advocate conformity, his theory is regarded by some as antipathetic to social change. He argues that healthy ego development requires the support of existing social roles, which has been interpreted as an endorsement of the status quo. Erikson's revised "golden rule" of mutuality has been criticized as overly optimistic, since many problems may not have solutions that benefit all of the opposing parties.

Other Criticisms.

Erikson's findings are based entirely on clinical observation, and his work lacks any quantification or statistical analyses. Some critics contend that no set of developmental stages can apply to everyone (or nearly everyone) because human personalities are too different, and Erikson's claim that we all proceed through the same eight epigenetic stages (and in the same order) is incorrect. Erikson fails to specify the influences that contribute to favorable or unfavorable ego development in some of the later stages, such as industry versus inferiority. To those who regard anxiety as a construct of considerable importance, his superficial treatment suffers by comparison to the work of Horney and Sullivan. As we have seen, the construct of libido has been rejected by many modern psychologists. Finally, although he is overly appreciative of Freud's influence, Erikson fails to give sufficient acknowledgment to such predecessors as Adler, Fromm, and Sullivan.

Empirical Research

Although the universality of Erikson's epigenetic stages is open to question, the evidence is more positive concerning certain aspects of his theory. Research results strongly support his belief that basic trust in and attachment to one's mother, mistrust, hope, and autonomy play an important role in personality development. There is also some indication that a firm sense of identity increases the likelihood of developing intimate relationships, and is related to the successful resolution of previous developmental crises. However, a review of this voluminous research is beyond the scope of the present text. (See for example Ainsworth, 1985; Bowlby, 1969; 1988; Karen, 1990; Marcia, 1966; 1980; 1993; McAdams, 1993; Rutter, 1995; Schiedel & Marcia, 1985; Waterman, 1982; Waterman et al., 1970.)

Contributions

Perhaps Erikson's most notable contribution has been to broaden the scope of psychoanalytic theory. By rejecting Freud's contention that society must be a source of frustration and conflict, and by stressing the effects of social and cultural influences on personality development, he has helped to integrate psychoanalysis and sociology. His psychohistories represent an attempt to combine psychoanalysis and history. Because of his emphasis on healthy and adaptive ego processes, psychoanalysis is no longer limited to the study of those characteristics that clinical cases and more healthy individuals have in common.

For these reasons, some critics regard ego psychology as the most significant new direction to be taken by psychoanalytic theory since its inception. These psychologists emphatically reject the stereotype of the rigid and dogmatic psychoanalyst, who cannot accept even the slightest deviation from the verbatim writings of Freud. They argue that psychoanalytic thinking is a continuing evolution of new ideas, as evidenced by ego psychology and by such relatively recent modifications as object relations theory.

The term *identity crisis* has become part of our everyday language. Erikson was one of the first analysts to treat children, and to devise valuable techniques of play therapy. His emphasis on adolescence appears preferable to Freud's exclusive concern with childhood. Many modern psychologists accept the importance of basic trust, mistrust, autonomy, and identity. Erikson's stage theory has achieved greater popularity than Sullivan's or Freud's, as shown by college textbooks on developmental psychology that use his epigenetic stages as their organizational framework (e.g., Newman & Newman, 1999).

Erikson's study of Gandhi has been widely acclaimed as a major contribution. Erikson was one of the early defenders of the rights of minority groups, and his view of female sexuality is more equalitarian than Freud's. Finally, despite his pro-Freudianism, Erikson has called attention to some of the potential biases in psychoanalytic therapy that Freud preferred to overlook.

There remains some question as to whether Erikson deserves a far more illustrious reputation than theorists like Horney and Sullivan, who also stressed the importance of social forces but forthrightly rejected the currently unpopular construct of libido. To many psychologists, however, Erikson's psychosocially oriented ego theory retains the considerable strengths of Freudian psychoanalysis and rectifies its most serious errors.

Suggested Reading

The best place to begin a firsthand study of Erikson's works is with his first book, *Childhood and Society* (1963). This eminently readable and comprehensive work includes most of his theoretical constructs, presents several interesting case histories, and describes his study of the Sioux and Yurok. Also notable is his prizewinning biography, *Gandhi's Truth* (1969). Some important ideas are restated and expanded, albeit in a more dry and academic fashion, in *Insight and Responsibility* (1964) and *Identity: Youth and Crisis* (1968). Among the useful secondary sources are a laudatory biography by Coles (1970), a much more critical effort by Roazen (1976a), an even-handed biography by Friedman (1999), and an article by Erikson's daughter (Bloland, 1999).

SUMMARY

Using some of Freud's later writings as their point of departure, some theorists have sought to broaden psychoanalytic theory by deemphasizing the role of the irrational id and stressing the capacities of the rational ego. This approach has become known as ego psychology, and one of its leading exponents is Erik Homburger Erikson.

1. THE BASIC NATURE OF HUMAN BEINGS. *Biological Processes:* Erikson retains, but deemphasizes, the Freudian constructs of libido and instinct. He prefers to stress the role played by the ego, and by societal forces, in shaping the human personality. *Ego Processes:* The ego not only defends against illicit instincts and anxiety, but serves important healthy functions as well. These constructive and adaptive ego functions are relatively independent of id instincts. Two of the most important are identity, a complicated inner state that includes feelings of individuality and uniqueness, wholeness and synthesis, sameness and continuity, and social solidarity; and a sense of mastery over the environment. Other essential ego qualities, such as hope and will power, are related to the various developmental stages. *Societal Processes:* Erikson regards society as a valuable source of support to the ego. A firm sense of identity or mastery is impossible without the approval of significant others, and society holds forth the promise of sanctioned roles. Erikson regards the social affirmation provided by mutually enhancing relationships (mutuality) as another human need, and concludes that different cultures exert differing effects on the development of the ego. *The Unconscious:* Erikson regards the unconscious as of considerable importance.

2. THE STRUCTURE OF PERSONALITY. Erikson retains Freud's structural model of id, ego, and superego. He agrees that the id is the sole component of personality present at birth and includes all of our inherited instincts, and that the superego consists of introjected ideals and restrictions and is capable of becoming overly moral. But Erikson accords much greater emphasis to the capacities and strengths of the ego.

3. THE DEVELOPMENT OF PERSONALITY. *The Epigenetic Psychosexual Stages:* Erikson posits eight developmental stages that extend from infancy to old age. A predisposition to adapt to each stage is present at birth and emerges at the appropriate time. Each stage is characterized by a specific developmental crisis brought on by increasing physiological maturity and external demands, which must be resolved by the ego during that stage for personality development to proceed successfully. The outcome of any stage is by no means permanent, however, and future benign or pathogenic conditions may counteract prior deficiencies or accomplishments. The various stages, associated crises, and ego qualities or strengths indicative of healthy development have been delineated in a preceding Capsule Summary. *Ritualizations:* Repeated interpersonal rituals during childhood help the ego to adapt to the standards and demands of society.

4. FURTHER APPLICATIONS. *Dream Interpretation:* Erikson's approach to dream interpretation is similar in many respects to that of Freud. But he regards the ego as relatively powerful even during sleep, so that dreams are more likely to be constructive and teleological. *Psychopathology:* Neurosis and psychosis occur when the ego cannot maintain its usual adaptive and integrative functions because it has been seriously weakened by unresolved epigenetic crises, social trauma, and physical ills. Erikson shares Freud's view of psychopathology as a difference in degree rather than in kind, but concludes that the ego's normal functions cannot be entirely understood from the study of clinical cases. According to Erikson, identity confusion is the major problem confronting modern psychotherapists. *Psychotherapy:* Erikson regards himself primarily as a psychoanalyst, but cautions that this method is suitable only in some cases. He seeks to avoid some of the potential biases in Freudian therapy by using face-to-face interviews, rejecting transference neurosis, and avoiding a preoccupation with the patient's past. Erikson uses play therapy as the royal road to a child's unconscious. *Other Applications:* Unlike Freud, Erikson regards religion as a potentially valuable support for such essential ego qualities as trust and hope. He has also engaged in psychohistorical analyses of such noted figures as Luther, Gandhi, Hitler, Gorky, and Jefferson.

5. EVALUATION. Erikson has been criticized for professing a strong allegiance to Freud but espousing different theoretical constructs, a schism that may reflect excessive loyalty or a politically expedient attempt to avoid expulsion by the psychoanalytic establishment. He retains the currently unpopular construct of libido, gives some critics the impression of being overly conformist and optimistic, and eschews any quantification or statistical analyses. Nevertheless, Erikson has significantly broadened the scope of psychoanalytic theory by stressing the role of healthy and adaptive ego processes, and by integrating psychoanalysis with such disciplines as sociology and history. The identity crisis, play therapy, the study of social influences on personality development and its continuation through adolescence and adulthood, and his prize-winning study of Gandhi are widely regarded as important contributions.

STUDY QUESTIONS

Part I. Questions

1. Using the case material in the Appendix, give an example to illustrate each of the following Eriksonian ideas: (a) The cause of basic mistrust, and the failure to satisfy the crisis of the oral-sensory stage. (b) The failure to satisfy the crises of the muscular-anal and locomotor-genital stages. (c) The failure to satisfy the crisis of young adulthood. (d) Parents who harm the child by using training that does not reflect the standards of the society in which they live. (e) How might certain aspects of this case history be interpreted as *not* supporting Eriksonian theory?

2. Give an example from real life or from fiction to illustrate identity confusion.

3. Give an example from real life or from fiction of a person who adopts a negative identity, rather than suffer the inner turmoil of identity confusion.

4. Erikson argues that a child enjoys mastery of the environment for its own sake, and not just as a means to the end of satisfying instinctual drives. Do you agree or disagree? Why?

5. (a) Give a real-life example to support Erikson's belief that our society creates difficulties for us by stressing contradictory values. (b) Give an example to illustrate the positive support provided by a socially sanctioned role.

6. Erikson regards mutuality as the ideal form of interpersonal relationship. What societal influences make it more difficult for us to develop mutuality?

7. Are there important theoretical differences between Erikson's construct of a negative identity and such related ideas as the Adlerian neglected child, Horney's concept of moving against people, and the Sullivanian malevolent transformation? Or are they all much the same?

8. Give examples from two different stages to illustrate the following statement by Erikson: "The strength acquired at any stage is tested by the necessity to … take chances in the next stage with what was most vulnerably precious in the previous one."

9. Does a healthy personality have no basic mistrust at all? Why or why not?

10. What important Freudian principles are supported by the "S[E]INE" dream?

11. A terrorist blows up a building in a hated foreign country. How might Erikson explain the terrorist's behavior?

Part II. Comments and Suggestions

1. (a) His mother was anxious and ineffective. (See Chapter 7, question 1a.) He mistrusts other people, and his ego did not develop the quality of hope. (See sections 1, 2, and 4 of the Appendix.) (b) He has severe doubts about his ability and lacks will power and purpose. The

episode described in section 3 of the Appendix occurred during one of these stages. (c) This is clearly shown by his preference for isolation. (d) Our society stresses initiative and independence, especially (albeit unfairly) with regard to men. Yet his parents consistently approved of submissiveness, and they reacted harshly to many of his attempts at independence. (e) Some of these events did not occur at the ages, or in the order, predicted by Erikson. The tendency toward isolation was well established long before young adulthood, whereas signs of an identity crisis were visible before adolescence.

2. Consider Erikson's own young adulthood (biographical sketch).

3. Possible fictional examples: Shakespeare's Richard III, Darth Vader. Possible real-life examples: young criminals who become gang members, Adolf Hitler.

4. I agree. My daughter has often seemed to enjoy her accomplishments for their own sake, such as sitting up for the first time in her crib during infancy, learning to walk, and operating the VCR by herself. As Erikson points out, parental expectations play a part; I'm sure she knows that her parents value achievement. But we take a fairly relaxed approach to her performance, and her enjoyment doesn't depend on words of approval from us. What I have seen is contrary to Freud's view that a child must always be "kicked upstairs" to the next stage of development, and supports Erikson's contention that mastery affords pleasure over and apart from the satisfaction of instinctual impulses.

5. (a) Consider the contradiction between "winning isn't everything, it's the only thing" and "do unto others as you wish they would do unto you." How does one reconcile the desire for personal success, which may well involve defeating other people, with the need to be caring and considerate? Who should be our role model: the collegiate coach who follows every rule about recruiting high school athletes and loses the important game (and perhaps the job as well), or the coach who defeated him or her by bending or breaking the regulations in order to acquire some first-class talent? (b) Consider anyone who derives pride and satisfaction from being a mother, father, husband, wife, doctor, mechanic, teacher, member of a particular religion or political group, and so forth.

6. Consider the tremendous emphasis that our society devotes to sports. We receive frequent and powerful messages that the only way to be a winner is by making someone else a loser. Might such beliefs make it difficult for us to act in ways that benefit others as well as ourselves?

7. There are numerous similarities, including feelings of self-hate and hostility toward others. One possible difference is that society often contributes to the development of a negative identity, whereas the other constructs result primarily from parental pathogenic behaviors. Unfortunately, these theorists did not clarify matters by comparing the various constructs.

8. Is it possible to exert your autonomy, yet always do what your parents approve of? (See also the comment to Chapter 6, questions 3a and 3b.) Is it possible to have an intimate relationship without making any changes in your identity?

9. How would parents have to behave for this to happen? What would happen to a person who trusted everyone?

10. Some possibilities: repressed memories, condensation, displacement and/or transference, childhood sexuality and Oedipality, the importance of childhood causes of psychopathology, and perhaps others. And all this in a dream consisting of a single word! What better example could there be of how deceptively complicated our personalities are?

11. Would Erikson explain the terrorist's behavior in the same way as Freud (Chapter 2, question 15)? How might Erikson use such constructs as identity (or the lack thereof), mastery (or the lack thereof), and mutuality (or the lack thereof) to explain the terrorist's behavior? To what social trauma might Erikson attribute the terrorist's behavior?

Comparing Psychodynamic Theorists On Various Issues

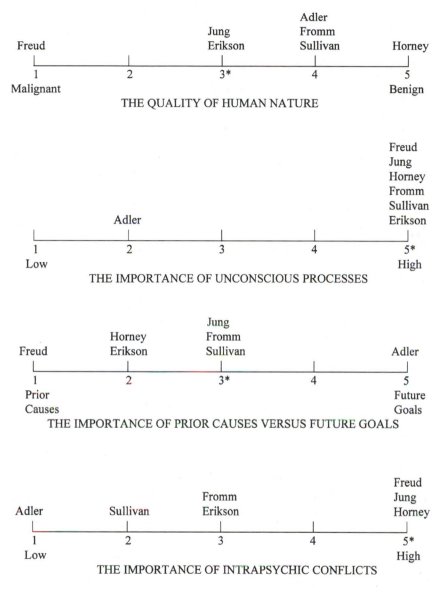

```
                                      Adler
                         Jung         Fromm
Freud                    Erikson      Sullivan           Horney
  |_____|_____|_____|_____|_____|
  1        2        3*       4        5
Malignant                                       Benign
```

THE QUALITY OF HUMAN NATURE

```
                                                     Freud
                                                     Jung
                                                     Horney
                                                     Fromm
                                                     Sullivan
                 Adler                               Erikson
  |_____|_____|_____|_____|_____|
  1        2        3        4        5*
Low                                             High
```

THE IMPORTANCE OF UNCONSCIOUS PROCESSES

```
                            Jung
              Horney        Fromm
Freud         Erikson       Sullivan                  Adler
  |_____|_____|_____|_____|_____|
  1        2        3*       4        5
Prior                                           Future
Causes                                          Goals
```

THE IMPORTANCE OF PRIOR CAUSES VERSUS FUTURE GOALS

```
                              Fromm                  Freud
                                                     Jung
Adler          Sullivan       Erikson                Horney
  |_____|_____|_____|_____|_____|
  1        2        3        4        5*
Low                                             High
```

THE IMPORTANCE OF INTRAPSYCHIC CONFLICTS

```
                                                     Freud
               Jung                                  Horney
Adler          Erikson                    Fromm      Sullivan
  |_____|_____|_____|_____|_____|
  1        2        3        4        5*
Low                                             High
```

THE IMPORTANCE OF ANXIETY

Note: These scales are intended as approximations, designed to facilitate comparisons among the theorists, and not as mathematically precise measures. They reflect my opinions; others might disagree with the ratings in some instances. For those who may be interested, my position on each issue is shown by an asterisk.

continued

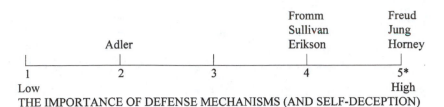

THE IMPORTANCE OF DEFENSE MECHANISMS (AND SELF-DECEPTION)

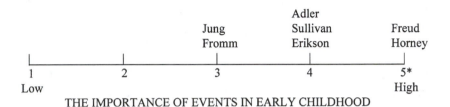

THE IMPORTANCE OF EVENTS IN EARLY CHILDHOOD

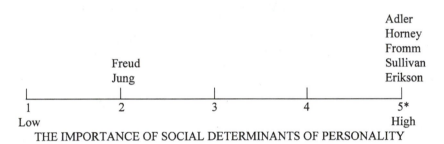

THE IMPORTANCE OF SOCIAL DETERMINANTS OF PERSONALITY

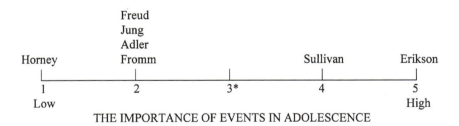

THE IMPORTANCE OF EVENTS IN ADOLESCENCE

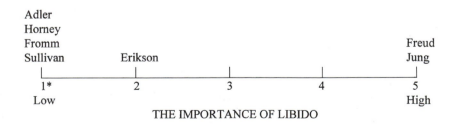

THE IMPORTANCE OF LIBIDO

PART II

The Humanistic Perspective

Overview	Humanistic theories emphasize our inborn potential for healthy growth and development. Psychopathology occurs when our healthy potentials are blocked by pathogenic parenting or other harmful environmental forces. Common symptoms include an inability to know what one really wants and to enjoy a meaningful life.
Carl Rogers	Rejected Freud's pessimistic view of human nature and argued that our inner potentials are entirely positive. We have an innate tendency to develop these healthy capacities (actualization), and we are born with the ability to value positively (or negatively) that which will actualize (or not actualize) these potentials. However, we also have a powerful need for our parents' love (positive regard). Psychopathology occurs when parents make their affection and nurturing conditional on the child's personality meeting their standards, which causes the child to give up the healthy drive for actualization in order to keep the parents' positive regard. The child therefore introjects the parents' standards, and tries to satisfy these conditions of worth instead of actualizing his or her true potentials. The psychotherapist uses genuineness, empathy, and unconditional positive regard to establish a constructive personal relationship with clients, who learn to abandon their conditions of worth and replace them with their real needs and wishes.
Abraham Maslow	Argued that our inner potentials are entirely positive, but are weak and can easily be overwhelmed by pathogenic learning. Sought to integrate the best aspects of various theories of personality (eclecticism). Human needs form a hierarchy, where we do not try to satisfy (and do not even become aware of) higher-level needs until lower-level needs have at least to some extent been satisfied. The highest-level need (self-actualization) involves fulfilling our healthy innate potentials, leads to different kinds of behavior, and is very difficult to achieve.
Rollo May	Devised an existential theory of personality that emphasizes the science of being (ontology): what it means to exist as a distinctively human organism for one fleeting and random moment in an eternity of time, in one small and random corner of an infinitely vast universe. Personality is a unified whole, the unconscious is very important, and we must have the courage to assert our existence and make our own choices despite our anxiety about nonbeing and death.

CHAPTER 9

CARL R. ROGERS
Self-Actualization Theory (I)

As the 20th century progressed toward the halfway point, some psychoanalysts and psychotherapists encountered a puzzling phenomenon. Social standards had become far more permissive than in Freud's day, especially with regard to sexuality. In theory, this greater liberalism should have helped to alleviate troublesome id-superego conflicts and reduce the number of neuroses. Yet while hysterical neurosis and repression did seem to be less common than in Victorian times, more people than ever before were entering psychotherapy. And they suffered from such new and unusual problems as an inability to enjoy the new freedom of self-expression (or, for that matter, to feel much of anything), and

an inner emptiness and self-estrangement. Rather than hoping to cure some symptom, these patients needed an answer to a more philosophical question: how to remedy the apparent meaninglessness of their lives.

As we have seen, some theorists tried to resolve this pressing issue within a more or less psychoanalytic framework (e.g., the Eriksonian identity crisis, Fromm's conception of escape from freedom). However, other noted psychologists called into question the basic rationale underlying analytic therapy. They pointed out that Freud's insights may have applied brilliantly to the Victorian era, when an aura of repulsiveness surrounded the topic of sexuality and people suffered from the misconception that personality was wholly rational and conscious. But they argued that constructs like psychic determinism and the structural model, and Freud's pessimism about human nature, were now aggravating the modern patient's apathy by depicting personality as mechanical, fragmented, malignant, and totally preordained by prior causes.

One major critic of Freudian pessimism was Carl Rogers. Like Adler and some of the neo-Freudians, Rogers was no stranger to the rancorous side of scientific inquiry. In 1939, some 10 years after receiving his doctorate degree in psychology, Rogers's position as director of a child guidance clinic was strongly challenged by orthodox psychiatrists—not because of any question as to the quality of his work, but on the grounds that no nonmedical practitioner could be sufficiently qualified to head up a mental health operation.

"It was a lonely battle, … a life-and-death struggle for me because it was the thing I was doing well, and the work I very much wanted to continue" (Rogers, 1974/1975, p. 129; see also Rogers, 1967, pp. 360, 364; 1977, pp. 144–145). A few years later he established a counseling center at the University of Chicago, and he again met with charges from psychiatrists that its members were practicing medicine without a license. Fortunately, Rogers won both of these confrontations; and his work has helped gain recognition and respect for the field of clinical psychology.

OBJECTIVES

- *To correct Freud's pessimistic view of human nature by showing that our inborn potentials are entirely positive.*
- *To show that each of us has an innate tendency to develop our healthy potentials (actualization), and an innate ability to know what is actualizing for us and what is not.*
- *To show that psychopathology occurs when pathogenic parenting causes the child to abandon the healthy quest for actualization in order to keep the parents' love and respect (positive regard), resulting in such symptoms as "I wonder who I really am" and "I don't know what I want."*
- *To emphasize the conscious aspects of personality because they are easier to study using empirical research, and recognize that the unconscious aspects of experience can be useful and important.*
- *To define the construct of self (self-concept) and show that it is important for understanding personality.*
- *To stress the importance of equality in human relationships, including parent and child.*
- *To show that effective psychotherapy requires only a constructive relationship between therapist and client, wherein the therapist demonstrates genuineness, empathy, and unconditional positive regard, and that Freudian procedures are not necessary.*
- *To obtain information about personality from both psychotherapy and empirical research, and to make the former more accurate by using tape recordings and verbatim transcripts (with the client's permission).*

BIOGRAPHICAL SKETCH

Carl R. Rogers was born on January 8, 1902, in Oak Park, Illinois, a suburb of Chicago. His father was a successful civil engineer. His close-knit family, which included four brothers and one sister (three of them older), was committed to conservative Protestantism and the value of hard work. When Carl was 12, the Rogerses decided to escape the evils and temptations of suburban life by moving to a farm west of Chicago. There he read extensively about scientific approaches to soils and feeds, reared lambs and calves, bred moths, and often rose before the crack of dawn to help with such chores as milking the cows. (See Rogers, 1961, pp. 4–15; 1967.)

Carl's study of farming generated a marked respect for the scientific method and led him to pursue an undergraduate degree in agriculture at the University of Wisconsin, but he soon became more interested in the helping professions. At first he considered joining the clergy and attended the Union Theological Seminary in New York, but his experiences at this liberal institution introduced him to a more enticing profession: psychotherapy. He therefore transferred to Columbia University Teachers College, where he received his Ph.D. in 1928. Carl married Helen Elliott on August 28, 1924. The union proved to be a happy and successful one, and the Rogerses were to have one son and one daughter.

Rogers's first professional position was at a child guidance clinic in Rochester, New York, where he had the aforementioned confrontation with orthodox psychiatry. Educated in Freudian theory among others, Rogers found that analytic insight often did not seem to benefit his clients and began to formulate his own approach to psychotherapy. In 1940 he accepted a full professorship at Ohio State University, about which he was later to observe: "I heartily recommend starting in the academic world at this level. I have often been grateful that I have never had to live through the frequently degrading competitive process of step-by-step promotion in university faculties, where individuals so frequently learn only one lesson—not to stick their necks out" (Rogers, 1961, p. 13; see also Rogers, 1967, p. 361).

Rogers moved to the University of Chicago in 1945, where he established a counseling center. In accordance with his theory, he gave up control of the center in 1947 and allowed everyone an equal voice in running it—including student interns, secretaries, and faculty. This equalitarian approach produced so much enthusiasm and involvement that when the center lost its grant, everyone pooled their pay and worked for very little until new funding could be obtained (Gendlin, 1988).

In 1957, Rogers joined the University of Wisconsin to conduct research on psychotherapy and personality. The return to his alma mater proved to be a trying one, however. The doctoral program emphasized the memorization of trivial facts and rigid formal examinations, and many of his most able and creative graduate students either failed or left in disgust. Rogers resigned in 1963 and joined the Western Behavioral Sciences Institute in La Jolla, California, where he pursued the humanistic study of interpersonal relationships and founded the Center for Studies of the Person.

Personally, Rogers has been described as compassionate, patient, and even-tempered. He cared deeply about people but not about institutions, appearances, credentials, or social class, and he doubted every authority including his own (Gendlin, 1988).

Throughout his career, Rogers devoted an average of some 15 to 20 hours per week to the practice of client-centered therapy. He has authored some 10 books and numerous articles, and his honors include receiving the Distinguished Scientific Contribution Award of the American Psychological Association in 1956. Rogers was keenly interested in promoting world peace, organized the Vienna Peace Project that brought together leaders from 13 nations in 1985, and conducted peace workshops in Moscow during 1986. Carl Rogers died on February 4, 1987, from cardiac arrest following surgery for a broken hip sustained in a fall.

THE BASIC NATURE OF HUMAN BEINGS

Rogers rejects the concept of a superior, prescient psychotherapist, on whom the "patient" passively depends for shrewd interpretations. Instead he emphasizes that only we can know, and choose, our proper directions in life. In accordance with this belief, Rogers originally named his approach "client-centered therapy." Having subsequently expanded his ideas to include such nonclinical areas as parenting, education, and interracial relations, he now prefers the broader designation of **person-centered theory.** (See Rogers, 1951, p. 7 n. 1; 1977, p. 5.)

Actualization

According to Rogers, we are motivated by a single positive force: an innate tendency to develop our constructive, healthy potentials. This **actualizing tendency** includes both drive-reducing and drive-increasing behavior. On the one hand, we seek to reduce the drives of hunger, thirst, sex, and oxygen deprivation. Yet we also demonstrate such tension-increasing behavior as curiosity, creativity, and the willingness to undergo painful learning experiences in order to become more effective and independent:

> Persons have a basically positive direction... [It is the urge] to expand, extend, become autonomous, develop, mature.... The first steps [of a child learning to walk] involve struggle, and usually pain. Often it is true that the immediate reward involved in taking a few steps is in no way commensurate with the pain of falls and bumps.... Yet, in the overwhelming majority of individuals, the forward direction of growth is more powerful than the satisfactions of remaining infantile. The child will actualize himself, in spite of the painful experiences in so doing. (Rogers, 1951, p. 490; 1961, pp. 26, 35. See also Rogers, 1951, pp. 487–491; 1959, p. 196; 1961, pp. 90–92, 105–106; 1977, pp. 7–8.)

Rogers's theoretical optimism does not blind him to our capacity for cruel and destructive behavior, but he attributes this to external forces. There are many potential pitfalls along the path to actualization, and a pathogenic environment may cause us to behave in ways that belie our benign inner nature.

The Need for Positive Regard

All of us need warmth, respect, and acceptance from other people, particularly such "significant others" as our parents. This need for **positive regard** is innate, and remains active throughout our lives. But it also becomes partly independent of specific contacts with other people, leading to a secondary, learned need for **positive self-regard.** That is, what significant others think of us strongly influences how we come to regard ourselves. (See Rogers, 1951, p. 524; 1959, pp. 207–209, 223–224.) The quest to satisfy the powerful need for positive regard represents the single most serious impediment to the actualizing tendency, as we will see in a subsequent section.

Teleology

Rogers agrees that childhood events play a prominent role in forming the adult personality. But he prefers to emphasize currently active needs and our striving toward the goal of actualization. "Behavior is not 'caused' by something which occurred in the past. Present tensions and present needs are the only ones which the organism endeavors to reduce or satisfy" (Rogers, 1951, p. 492; see also Rogers, 1942, p. 29; 1959, pp. 198–199; Rogers, cited by Evans, 1975, pp. 8, 75–76).

THE STRUCTURE OF PERSONALITY

Since actualization involves the total organism, Rogers sees little need to posit specific structural constructs. Yet his theory is not truly holistic, for he shares Horney's belief that we often suffer from painful intrapsychic conflicts. "The great puzzle that faces anyone who delves at all into the dynamics of human behavior … [is] that persons are often at war within themselves, estranged from their own organisms" (Rogers, 1977, p. 243).

Experience and the Organismic Valuing Process

Experience.   Each of us exists at the center of our own private, ever-changing world of inner **experience (experiential field, phenomenal field)**, one that can never be perfectly understood by anyone else. (See Rogers, 1951, pp. 483–484, 494–497; 1959, pp. 191, 197–198, 210.) Experience includes everything that is available to your awareness at any given moment: thoughts; emotions; perceptions, including those that are temporarily ignored (such as the pressure of the chair seat on which you are sitting); and needs, some of which may also be momentarily overlooked (as when you are engrossed in work or play). However, only a small portion of experience is conscious. The greatest part consists of stimuli and events that we perceive below the level of awareness ("subceptions," similar to subliminal perceptions in Jungian theory[1]):

> The individual's functioning [is like] a large pyramidal fountain. The very tip of the fountain is intermittently illuminated with the flickering light of consciousness, but the constant flow of life goes on in the darkness as well, in nonconscious as well as conscious ways. (Rogers, 1977, p. 244.)

Like George Kelly, Rogers concludes that we evaluate our experiences by forming and testing appropriate hypotheses. If you perceive a white powder in a small dish as salt, taste it, and find it to be sweet, the experience will promptly shift to that of sugar. Also, as in Kelly's theory, how we interpret events is more important than objective reality. An infant who is picked up by a friendly adult, but who perceives this situation as strange and frightening, will respond with cries of distress. Or a daughter who initially perceived her father as domineering, but who has learned through psychotherapy to regard him as a rather pathetic person trying desperately to retain a shred of dignity, will experience him quite differently even though he himself has not changed. (See Rogers, 1951, pp. 484–486; 1959, pp. 199, 222–223.)

The Organismic Valuing Process.   According to Rogers, there is no need for us to learn what is or is not actualizing. Included among the primarily unconscious aspects of experience is an innate ability to value positively whatever we perceive as actualizing, and to value negatively that which we perceive as nonactualizing (the **organismic valuing process**). Thus the infant values food when hungry but promptly becomes disgusted with it when satiated, and enjoys the life-sustaining physical contact of being cuddled.

These nonconscious aspects of experience are an invaluable addition to our conscious thoughts and plans. It is at this deepest level of personality that we know what is good for us (actualizing) and what is not. This implies that only we ourselves, rather than a parent or a

---

[1]Although Rogers (1959, p. 199) attributes the concept of subception to an article published by two psychologists in 1949, his usage of this term parallels Jung's discussion of some twenty years earlier (1927/1971b, p. 38).

CAPSULE SUMMARY
Some Important Rogerian Terminology

Actualizing tendency	An innate tendency to develop our constructive, healthy potentials. The fundamental motive underlying all human behavior.
Conditional positive regard	Accepting and respecting another person only if that person's self-concept and feelings meet with one's approval. The typical way in which parents behave toward the child.
Conditional positive self-regard	Accepting and respecting oneself only if one satisfies the introjected standards of significant others (conditions of worth), even though these run counter to the actualizing tendency.
Condition of worth	A standard that must be satisfied to receive conditional positive regard from a significant other, which is introjected into the self-concept. Supersedes the organismic valuing process, and leads to behaviors that are not actualizing.
Congruence	A healthy state of unison between the organismic valuing process and the self-concept, and therefore between the actualizing and self-actualizing tendencies.
Defense	Responding to experiences that threaten the self-concept and evoke anxiety by distorting them, or (less frequently) by screening them out from awareness.
Empathy	A reasonably accurate understanding of someone else's experience; putting oneself in another person's shoes. One of the three essential characteristics of the successful therapeutic relationship.
Encounter group (T group)	A group of relatively well-adjusted individuals who meet with a facilitator to pursue further personal growth.
Experience (experiential field, phenomenal field)	Everything that is presently within or potentially available to awareness, including thoughts, needs, perceptions, and feelings. A relatively small part of experience is conscious, whereas the greatest portion is unconscious.
Fully functioning person	An optimally psychologically healthy individual.
Genuineness	Having an accurate knowledge of one's inner experience and a willingness to share it when appropriate. One of the three essential characteristics of the successful therapeutic relationship.
Incongruence	A split between the organismic valuing process and a self-concept burdened by conditions of worth (and, therefore, between the actualizing and self-actualizing tendencies), which results in feelings of tension and confusion. The converse of congruence.
Introjection	Unconsciously incorporating the standards of another person into one's own personality; similar to Freud's use of the term.
Openness to experience	A willingness to accept any experience into awareness without distorting it. The converse of defense.
Organismic valuing process	An innate ability to value positively those experiences that are perceived as actualizing, and to value negatively those that are perceived as nonactualizing.
Person-centered theory (client-centered therapy)	The name given by Rogers to his theory of personality.
Positive regard	Warmth, respect, and acceptance from another person; a universal, innate human need.

Positive self-regard	Accepting and respecting oneself. A learned human need, derived from the need for positive regard.
Self-actualization	The tendency to satisfy the demands of the self-concept. If the learned self-actualizing tendency remains unified with the inborn actualizing tendency, the individual is psychologically well adjusted.
Self-concept (self)	A learned, conscious sense of being separate and distinct from other people and things.
Significant other	An important source of positive regard, such as a parent.
Unconditional positive regard	Accepting and respecting another person's feelings and self-concept; a nonjudgmental and nonpossessive caring for another person. (Does *not* apply to specific behaviors, which may be valued negatively.) One of the three essential characteristics of the successful therapeutic relationship.
Unconditional positive self-regard	An ideal state of total self-acceptance, or absence of any conditions of worth. Theoretically due to receiving unconditional positive regard from significant others, but probably never occurs in reality.

psychotherapist, can identify our true organismic values and know how best to actualize our own potentials:

> *Experience is, for me, the highest authority....* When an activity *feels* as though it is valuable or worth doing, it *is* worth doing.... [Thus I trust] the totality of my experience, which I have learned to suspect is wiser than my intellect. It is fallible I am sure, but I believe it to be less fallible than my conscious mind alone. (Rogers, 1961, pp. 22–23. See also Rogers, 1951, pp. 498–499; 1959, pp. 210, 222; 1977, pp. 243–246.)

The Self-Concept (Self) and Self-Actualization

Definitions.   Guided by the actualizing tendency, the growing infant expands its experiential field and learns to perceive itself as a separate and distinct entity. This **self-concept (self)** is entirely conscious, and represents part of the tip of the constantly flowing fountain of subjective experience.[2]

Some of the actualizing tendency now becomes directed toward an attempt to satisfy the demands of the self-concept. This is referred to as **self-actualization,** after a term first popularized by Kurt Goldstein. (See Goldstein, 1939; 1940; Rogers, 1951, pp. 497–498; 1959, pp. 196–206, 223; Rogers, cited by Evans, 1975, pp. 6–7.)

How Conflict Develops Between the Actualizing and Self-Actualizing Tendencies.   To actualize our true potentials, we must follow the inner guidelines provided by the organismic valuing process. However, self-actualization is achieved in a different way: the self-concept must be supported by positive regard from significant others, such as the parents. Therefore, the child must pay close attention to parental requests and demands.

In the best of all possible worlds, parents would never do anything that interfered with the child's organismic valuing process. They would show **unconditional positive regard** for the child's self-concept and feelings, and limit their criticisms to specific undesirable behaviors.

---

[2]Rogers defines the self-concept as wholly conscious on practical rather than theoretical grounds. He argues that a theory of personality must be tested through empirical research, and the concept of a partially unconscious self would cause great difficulties in this regard because it cannot be operationally defined (Rogers, 1959, p. 202).

For example, if a little girl expresses hostility toward her brother, her mother might ideally respond: "I can understand how satisfying it feels to you to hit your baby brother … and I love you and am quite willing for you to have those feelings. But I am quite willing for me to have my feelings, too, and I feel very distressed when your brother is hurt … and so I do not let you hit him. Both your feelings and my feelings are important, and each of us can freely have [our] own" (Rogers, 1959, p. 225; see also Rogers, 1951, pp. 498–503; 1959, pp. 208–210, 224). The girl's positive self-regard is not threatened by this response, since she was not accused of having shameful feelings or being a "bad girl." So she will accept her aggressiveness as one aspect of her self-concept, and this view of herself will be consistent (**congruent**) with her experience and organismic valuing process (that hitting her brother is pleasant). And she will remain psychologically well-adjusted.

Unfortunately, this favorable sequence of events is an unlikely one. Instead, parents typically respond to the child with **conditional positive regard.** That is, they provide affection and respect only if the child's self-concept and feelings meet with their approval. They may indicate in direct or subtle ways that wishing to hit her brother will result in the loss of their love, or that this urge "should" cause feelings of guilt and unhappiness instead of satisfaction. This presents the child with a difficult and painful choice: to accept her true inner experience (i.e., that hitting her brother is pleasurable), which risks the shattering possibility of becoming unloved; or to succumb to temptation, disown her real feelings, and distort her experience in ways that will please others (as by concluding that hitting her brother is distasteful).

Because the need for positive regard is so powerful, the child ultimately elects to disown her true feelings at least to some extent (as in Horney's theory). She incorporates the parental standards into her self-concept, a process for which Rogers borrows the Freudian term **introjection.** Her positive self-regard now depends on satisfying these introjected **conditions of worth,** which replace the organismic valuing process as an inner guide to behavior. Instead of being guided by her true feelings ("hitting my brother is pleasant"), she concludes that hitting her brother is unpleasant, and that she must feel this way in order to think well of herself (have **conditional positive self-regard**). Thus her actualizing and self-actualizing tendencies become divided (**incongruent**) and work at cross purposes, leading to a state of confusion and anxiety:

> The accurate symbolization [of the child's experience] would be: "I perceive my parents as experiencing this behavior as unsatisfying to them." The [actual but] distorted symbolization, distorted to preserve the threatened concept of self, is: "*I* perceive this behavior as unsatisfying." … In this way the values which the infant attaches to experience become divorced from his own organismic functioning, and experience is valued in terms of the attitudes held by his [significant others].… It is here, it seems, that the individual begins on a pathway which he later describes as "I don't really know myself." (Rogers, 1951, pp. 500–501. See also Rogers, 1959, pp. 203–205, 209–210, 224–226.)

At a later age, the journey away from self-knowledge is encouraged by various social institutions and groups. Many of us introject these external standards and believe them to be our own ("Making lots of money is the most important goal of all;" "I should be extremely thin, just like that famous model;" "I need to wear the same brand of sneakers that this great athlete wears"), even though they may well run counter to our true organismic needs and values. (See Rogers, 1977, p. 247; Rogers & Stevens, 1967/1971, pp. 10–11.)

Defense

Experiences that serve as a threatening reminder of the incongruence between the self-concept and organismic experience are likely to be **defended** against by distorting them, or (less frequently) by blocking them from consciousness. When the aforementioned little girl next sees her brother, she has a problem: her true (organismic) experience is that hitting him is pleasurable, yet she must believe that hitting him is unpleasant in order to protect her self-concept and preserve some positive self-regard. To defend against this threatening incongruence, she may decide that she feels nothing but love and would not dream of hurting him.

Even such positive feelings as love or success may be defended against if they fail to agree with the self-concept. A college undergraduate who thinks he is a poor student may attribute a high grade to luck or an error by the professor, whereas a woman with a negative self-concept may refuse to believe that others regard her as intelligent or likable. (See Rogers, 1951, pp. 503–520; 1959, pp. 202–205, 227–228; Rogers & Wood, 1974, p. 218.)

THE DEVELOPMENT OF PERSONALITY

Rogers posits no specific developmental stages. Instead, he emphasizes the desirability of responding to the child with unconditional positive regard. This should begin as soon as the infant leaves the womb, with soft lights, stroking, and immersion in warm water preferable to the usual method of loud noises, harsh lights, and slaps. The growing child should be allowed to evaluate experience in his or her own way, and to make the choices indicated by the organismic valuing process. The parents are also entitled to respect, and to have rights that cannot be overridden by the child.

In the all too common authoritarian family, the parents make every decision and issue various orders ("You must be neat! Clean up your room at once!"). The children resort to devious strategies for gaining some power of their own, such as sulking, pleading, setting one parent against the other, and complaining ("You're mean! Johnny's parents let *him* be sloppy!"). In contrast, the person-centered family emphasizes the sharing of nonjudgmental feelings. The mother may say, "I feel badly when the house is messy, and would like some help resolving this"—and find to her amazement that her children devise ingenious and effective ways of keeping the house neat, now that this is clearly and honestly defined as her problem rather than theirs. (See Rogers, 1977, pp. 29–41.)

Establishing a person-centered family is not an easy task, but Rogers argues that it is well worth the effort. It permits children to grow up with a minimum of pathogenic conditions of worth, and enables them to pursue their own path toward actualization.

The Fully Functioning Person

Rogers has formulated a list of criteria that define mental health. The **fully functioning person** is characterized by the *absence of any conditions of worth*. Since this person does not have to satisfy the introjected standards of other people, he or she is guided entirely by the organismic valuing process and enjoys total self-acceptance (**unconditional positive self-regard**). There is no incongruence, and no need for defense. Because of this **openness to experience,** any choices that work out poorly are soon corrected, since these errors are perceived openly and accurately. So the actualizing and self-actualizing tendencies work in unison toward the fulfillment of the person's healthy innate potentials.

For example, such creative individuals as El Greco, Hemingway, and Einstein knew that their work and thought were idiosyncratic. Rather than misguidedly accepting the prevailing standards, and hiding their true feelings behind a socially acceptable façade, they trusted their inner experience and persisted in the difficult but essential task of being themselves. "It was as though [El Greco] could say, good artists do not paint like this, but *I* paint like this" (Rogers, 1961, p. 175).

Fully functioning persons feel that they are worthy of being liked by other people and that they can care deeply for others, and they satisfy their need for positive regard by *forming successful interpersonal relationships.* They demonstrate unconditional positive regard for others, as well as toward themselves. Finally, such individuals *live wholly and freely in each moment.* They respond spontaneously to their experiences, and they regard happiness not as some fixed utopia but as an ever-changing journey. "The good life is a *process*, not a state of being. It is a direction, not a destination" (Rogers, 1961, p. 186; see also Rogers, 1959, pp. 234–235; 1961, pp. 163–196).

FURTHER APPLICATIONS OF ROGERIAN THEORY

Psychopathology

The fully functioning person represents an ideal that is rarely if ever achieved. No parent is perfect, so every child encounters at least some conditional positive regard and develops some conditions of worth. Thus there is no sharp dividing line between normality and psychopathology, but rather a difference in degree.

The self-concept of the more pathological individual is burdened by powerful conditions of worth. Instead of being guided by the organismic valuing process, the sufferer tries to achieve positive self-regard by satisfying these introjected parental standards. This brings the self-actualizing tendency into conflict with the actualizing tendency. To conceal this painful incongruence, the sufferer resorts to various forms of defense. But this only increases the inner confusion, and leads to such complaints as "I feel I'm not being my real self," "I wonder who I really am," "I don't know what I want," and "I can't decide on anything." (See Rogers, 1951, pp. 509–511; 1959, p. 201; compare also with the similar views of Horney.)

Rogers prefers to avoid formal diagnostic categories. He argues that such labels depict the client as a dependent object, rather than as the only person who can identify his or her proper direction in life. "[If] the client perceives the locus of judgment and responsibility as clearly resting in the hands of the clinician, he is ... further from therapeutic progress than when he came in" (Rogers, 1951, p. 223; see also Rogers, 1951, pp. 219–225; 1959, pp. 228–230; Rogers, cited by Evans, 1975, pp. 92–101). Even the so-called psychotic is simply an individual who has been badly hurt by life, and who desperately needs the corrective influence of an understanding and caring interpersonal relationship—the hallmark of Rogerian psychotherapy.

Psychotherapy

Theoretical Foundation.   The goal of Rogerian psychotherapy is to help clients abandon the introjected conditions of worth that seem so necessary for positive self-regard, and replace them with their own true needs and wishes. In the safety of the therapeutic situation, clients are able to tear down the defenses that protect the incongruent self-concept, cope with the resulting anxiety, and recognize that this false view of themselves is responsible for their painful problems. They revise their self-concept appropriately, as by concluding: "I don't have to think and feel the way other people want me to in order to be loved, and to love myself. I can open myself to experience, and be who I really am." This enables them to end the estrangement between the self-actualizing and actualizing tendencies, reclaim the ability to heed the organismic valuing process, and become more fully functioning persons.

For example, a client who has steadfastly claimed to have only positive feelings for her parents may conclude: "I have thought that I must feel only love for my parents in order to regard myself as a good person, but I find that I experience both love and resentment. Perhaps I can be that person who freely experiences both of these feelings." Or a client whose self-concept has been primarily negative, and who has therefore blocked feelings of self-acceptance from awareness, may learn: "I have thought that in some deep way I was bad, that the most basic elements in me must be dire and awful. I don't experience that badness, but rather a positive desire to live and let live. Perhaps I can be that person who is, at heart, positive" (Rogers, 1961, p. 104).[3] Since the deepest levels of personality are entirely positive, the client finds true self-knowledge to be far more satisfying than painful. The resulting inner harmony is evidenced by feelings like "I've never been quite so close to myself," and by increased positive self-regard that is expressed through a quiet pleasure in being oneself (Rogers, 1961, p. 78; see also Rogers, 1951, pp. 72–83; 1959, pp. 212–221, 226–227; 1961, pp. 36, 63–64, 85–87, 125–159, 185).

Therapeutic Procedures.   Except for the use of tape recordings and verbatim transcripts, aids to research that Rogers helped to pioneer, person-centered therapy excludes virtually all formal procedures. There is no couch, no use of interpretation by the therapist, no discussion of the client's childhood, no dream analysis, no analysis of resistances and transferences. According to Rogers, positive therapeutic change can be accomplished in only one way: by providing a healthy and constructive relationship with another person, which the client uses to recover the actualizing tendency. For this to occur, the client must perceive the therapist as having three characteristics that Rogers regards as essential to any successful human relationship: genuineness, empathy, and unconditional positive regard.

A therapist who is **genuine** is in touch with his or her own inner experience, and is able to share it when appropriate. This does not mean that therapists should burden their clients with their own personal problems, or impulsively blurt out whatever comes to mind. It does imply that the therapist should reject defensive façades and professional jargon, maintain an openness to experience, and achieve congruence. This encourages a similar trusting genuineness on the part of the client, thereby reducing the barriers to open and honest communication:

> To withhold one's self as a person and to deal with the [client] as an object does not have a high probability of being helpful.... It does not help to act calm and pleasant when actually I am angry and critical. It does not help to act as though I know the answers when I do not. It does not help ... to try to maintain [any] façade, to act in one way on the surface when I am experiencing something quite different underneath.... [Instead,] I have found that the more that I can be genuine in the relationship, the more helpful it will be. This means that I need to be aware of my own feelings, in so far as possible ... [and willing to express them]. (Rogers, 1961, pp. 16–17, 33, 47. See also Rogers, 1965; 1977, pp. 9–10; Rogers & Wood, 1974, pp. 226–229.)

In addition to genuineness, the therapist must be perceived as **empathic** to the client's feelings and beliefs. The therapist remains closely attuned to the client's verbal and non-verbal messages, including tones of voice and bodily movements, and reflects back the perceived meaning. If a client observes that "for the first time in months I am not thinking about my problems, not actually working on them," the therapist might respond: "I get the impression that you don't sort of sit down to work on 'my problems.' It isn't that feeling at all." If the therapist's view is accurate, the client is likely to reply: "Perhaps that *is* what I've been trying to say. I haven't realized it, but yes, that's how I *do* feel!" (Rogers, 1961, p. 78; 1977, p. 11). Conversely, disagreement by the client indicates a flaw in the therapist's understanding, rather than some form of resistance. Empathy serves as a powerful

---

[3]This bears some similarity to the Kellyan formulation of relaxing rigid personal constructs and adopting a more flexible view of oneself and others, as Rogers himself has noted (1961, pp. 132ff).

aid to healthy growth because it gives the client the feeling of being understood by a significant other:

> In the emotional warmth of the relationship with the therapist, the client begins to experience a feeling of safety as he finds that whatever attitude he expresses is understood in almost the same way that he perceives it, and is accepted.... It is only as I *understand* the feelings and thoughts which seem so horrible to [the client,] or so weak, or so sentimental, or so bizarre ... that [the client feels] really free to explore all the hidden nooks and frightening crannies of [his] inner and often buried experience. (Rogers, 1951, p. 41; 1961, p. 34. See also Rogers, 1959, pp. 210–211; 1961, pp. 18–19; 1965; 1980, pp. 137–163; Rogers & Wood, 1974, pp. 232–236.)

The therapist must also be perceived as demonstrating a nonjudgmental, nonpossessive respect and caring for the client's self-concept and feelings (the aforementioned quality of **unconditional positive regard**). "[This] is a caring enough about the person that you do not wish to interfere with his development, nor to use him for any self-aggrandizing goals of your own. Your satisfaction comes in having set him free to grow in his own fashion" (Rogers, 1961, p. 84). Such unqualified acceptance enables the client to explore feelings and beliefs that were too threatening to admit to awareness, safe in the knowledge that they will not evoke criticism—or any form of judgment. "[Even] a positive evaluation is as threatening in the long run as a negative one, since to inform someone that he is good implies that you also have the right to tell him he is bad" (Rogers, 1961, p. 55). In one notable instance, Rogers sat quietly with a silent, schizophrenic client for long periods of time, indicating support and understanding through his physical presence yet not imposing any pressure to speak:

> To discover that it is *not* devastating to accept the positive feeling from another, that it does not necessarily end in hurt, that it actually "feels good" to have another person with you in your struggles to meet life—this may be one of the most profound learnings encountered by the individual, whether in therapy or not. (Rogers, 1961, p. 85. See also Rogers, Gendlin, Kiesler, & Truax, 1967, pp. 401–406; Rogers & Wood, 1974, pp. 229–232.)

Achieving unconditional positive regard, empathy, and genuineness is by no means an easy task, and the therapist is not expected to do so all of the time. But the frequent expression of these three qualities, duly perceived by the patient, is to Rogers necessary—and sufficient—for therapeutic progress to occur.

Encounter Groups.   Becoming a fully functioning person is a lifelong quest. Therefore, even people who are relatively well adjusted are likely to seek ways of achieving further personal growth.

One method for meeting this need is the **encounter group** (or **T group**—for "training"), devised by Kurt Lewin and further developed by Rogers (1970/1973a). Perhaps a dozen people meet with one or two facilitators for a relatively brief period of time, often a single weekend but sometimes a few weeks. The facilitator uses genuineness, empathy, and unconditional positive regard to establish a psychological climate of safety and trust. There are no rules or formal procedures, hence the title "facilitator" rather than "leader." Ideally, group members gradually reduce their defensive distortions, bring out their true feelings toward each other and themselves, learn about their real impact on others, share deep emotional relationships with one another, and devise new goals and directions for themselves. To Rogers, encounter groups fill a major void in our impersonal and technological society:

The psychological need that draws people into encounter groups … is a hunger for something the person does not find in his work environment, in his church, certainly not in his school or college, and sadly enough, not even in modern family life. It is a hunger for relationships which are close and real; in which feelings and emotions can be spontaneously expressed without first being carefully censored or bottled up; where deep experiences—disappointments and joys—can be shared; where new ways of behaving can be risked and tried out; where, in a word, he approaches the state where all is known and all accepted, and thus further growth becomes possible. (Rogers, 1970/1973a, p. 11. See also M. H. Hall, 1967c, p. 20; Rogers, 1977, pp. 143–185.)

Although Rogers has found encounter groups to be generally successful in promoting personal growth, a cautionary note must be sounded regarding their use with relatively unskilled facilitators. Emotional sessions of such short duration may prove to be more than some members can handle, especially if there is little prior screening and more maladjusted persons are permitted to participate, resulting in psychological "casualties" of various kinds (Yalom & Lieberman, 1971).

Psychotherapy and Social Reform.   As with several of the theorists discussed thus far, Rogers regards our society as very sick indeed. For example, he characterizes Watergate as blatant official contempt for the rights of the individual. The vast discrepancy in wealth between the "haves" and "have-nots" of the world sows the seeds of hatred, evidenced in part by terrorist groups who wreak their violence on innocent people. The resulting specter of nuclear war leaves humanity in mortal danger, teetering on the knife edge between survival and destruction. (See Rogers, 1961, pp. ix, 61; 1973b, p. 379; 1977, pp. 115–116, 255–260; Rogers, cited by Evans, 1975, p. 65.)

Rogers does conclude that we have achieved some significant social advances in just a few decades, such as improved civil rights and increased efforts toward population control. He also argues that the person-centered approach offers us the means for living together in harmony: rather than trying to seize and hold power, the peoples of the world can treat one another with genuineness, empathy, and unconditional positive regard, and work together toward the common goal of helping to actualize humankind's benign potentials. (See Rogers, 1951, p. 224; 1972, pp. 71–72; 1977, pp. 115–140; 1982.)

Education

Rogers is highly critical of the authoritarian and coercive philosophy that pervades our educational system. All too often, the teacher assumes the mantle of power and directs the activities of passive, subservient students. Grades are based primarily on examinations, which require students to parrot back specific facts that the teacher considers important. Pronounced distrust is evidenced by the teacher constantly checking up on the students' progress, and by students remaining on guard against trick questions and unfair grading practices. And there is a total emphasis on thinking, with the emotional aspects of experience regarded as irrelevant and nonscholarly. The unfortunate result is that many potentially outstanding students develop negative attitudes toward further learning, which they perceive as an unpleasant obligation rather than a golden opportunity. "Our schools are more damaging than helpful to personality development, and are a negative influence on creative thinking. They are primarily institutions for incarcerating or taking care of the young, to keep them out of the adult world" (Rogers, 1977, p. 256; see also Rogers, 1951, pp. 384–428; 1961, pp. 37, 273–313; 1969; 1977, pp. 69–89; 1980, pp. 263–335; Rogers, cited by Evans, 1975, pp. 38–48).

The person-centered teacher seeks to create a psychological climate that facilitates the students' capacity to think and learn for themselves. The teacher demonstrates empathy and unconditional positive regard for the students' feelings and interests, and genuineness concerning his or her own inner experience. Decision making is a shared process, with students helping to devise their own program of learning. Class periods are unstructured, with no lectures or formal procedures, so that students may form and express their own opinions. The teacher serves as an optional resource, and provides comments or suggested readings only when asked to do so. And grades are mutually agreed upon, with the student providing evidence as to the amount of personal and educational growth that has been achieved during the course. This primarily self-directed approach enables students to enjoy the process of learning, and to discover and develop directions that are truly rewarding. (See Rogers, 1969; 1983.)

The person-centered approach to education often arouses initial resistance and hostility, since students expect to be told what to do. "Students who have been clamoring for freedom are definitely frightened when they realize that it also means responsibility." However, Rogers concludes that this approach typically leads to more rapid and thorough learning at all educational levels—and to such positive student evaluations as "I was surprised to find out how well I can study and learn when I'm not forced to do it," "It was like I was an adult—not supervised and guided all the time," and "I've never read so much in my life" (Rogers, 1977, pp. 76–78).

Rogerian Theory and Empirical Research

Rogers has a strong interest in empirical research, which he attributes to his need to make sense and order out of psychological phenomena. Rogers cautions that psychologists are too fearful and defensive about appearing unscientific, so they concentrate on methodologically precise but trivial research topics. He argues that a truly human science must deal with subjective experience and pursue innovative directions—especially a fledgling discipline like psychology, where it is difficult to achieve the precise measurements that are found in more mature sciences.

Like Kelly, therefore, Rogers concludes that any theory must be regarded as expendable in the light of new discoveries. "If a theory could be seen for what it is—a fallible, changing attempt to construct a network of gossamer threads which will contain the solid facts—then a theory would serve as it should, as a stimulus to further creative thinking" (Rogers, 1959, p. 191; see also M. H. Hall, 1967c, pp. 20–21; Rogers, 1959, pp. 188–190; Rogers, cited by Evans, 1975, pp. 88–90; Rogers & Skinner, 1956).

EVALUATION

Criticisms and Controversies

Like Adler, Rogers has been criticized for an overly optimistic and simplified view of human nature. Actualizing all of our innermost potentials is desirable only if the deepest levels of personality are healthy and constructive. Yet it seems doubtful that an inherently peaceful and cooperative species would so frequently engage in war, crime, and other destructive behaviors solely because of parental pathogenic behaviors and introjected conditions of worth.

Psychotherapists of different theoretical persuasions do not agree that positive change can be achieved by relying entirely on genuineness, empathy, and unconditional positive regard. It now appears that Rogers may well have gone too far in this respect, and that at least some interpretation, discussion of childhood causes, and other standard procedures are also necessary. Except for a few brief references, Rogers ignores important similarities between his theory and those of Horney, Sullivan, and Jung. In spite of Rogers's contention that theories are readily expendable in the light of new discoveries, his own approach changed relatively little during the last 20 years of his life—except perhaps for a greater acceptance of unconscious processes, which raises doubts as to the validity of defining the self-concept as entirely available to awareness and measuring it through the client's self-reports.

Empirical Research

Rogerian Psychotherapy.   A substantial amount of research has dealt with the characteristics of genuineness, empathy, and unconditional positive regard. These studies have used rating scales of and by psychotherapists, and analyses of transcripts of tape-recorded therapy sessions (of course, with the client's permission). As is common in the challenging field of psychotherapy research, the results have been equivocal: Numerous studies have found these variables to be significantly related to constructive change, whereas other findings have been negative.

For example, some studies suggest that unconditional positive regard is *not* sufficient for clients to improve; more active interventions, such as interpretations and/or training in the desired new behaviors, are also necessary. Other researchers caution that genuineness may be damaging in some instances, as by telling a narcissistic but vulnerable client that such constant self-preoccupation is causing the therapist to feel bored and angry. Still others prefer to replace the construct of genuineness with a broader concept, such as the "working alliance" or "therapeutic relationship." (See for example Bachelor & Horvath, 1999; Boy & Pine, 1999; Cain & Seeman, 2002; Epstein, 1980, pp. 122–127; Kahn, 1985, p. 901; Rogers, 1961, pp. 41–50; Rogers & Dymond, 1954; Rogers et al., 1967.)

The Self-Concept.   Another popular research topic is the self-concept, which can readily be investigated through direct inquiry since it is defined as entirely conscious. One common procedure is the *Q-sort* (Stephenson, 1950; 1953), which uses a number of cards that contain a single descriptive phrase ("I set high standards for myself," "I make friends easily," "I often seek reassurance from other people"). The client sorts the cards into a 9-point scale with an approximately normal distribution, ranging from those items that are most self-descriptive to those that are least self-descriptive. A specific number of cards must be placed in each of the nine categories, with the smallest number at the extremes (1, or least descriptive; 9, or most descriptive) and the greatest number at the center (5).

An alternative method is to present self-descriptive phrases in the form of a written questionnaire, with clients asked whether they strongly agree, agree, are undecided, disagree, or strongly disagree with each item. Or the questionnaire may contain a series of adjectives ("friendly," "honest," "suspicious"), with clients asked to check the ones that are applicable to them. Various well-regarded measures of the self-concept have been devised by different researchers (e.g., Coopersmith, 1984; Harter, 1982; Hattie, 1992; Marsh, 1990; Piers, 1984; Rold & Fitts, 1988; Wylie, 1989).

One finding of interest is that improvement during psychotherapy is usually related to increased self-acceptance, which leads to a greater acceptance of other people. It also appears that the self-concept is a more complicated construct than might be imagined. Some self-descriptions may apply only under certain circumstances (e.g., "I'm a patient father except when I have a headache"). The social self-concept, or how we think others perceive us, may differ from the personal self-concept, or how we see ourselves. Different social self-concepts may be used when dealing with different individuals or groups. And there are also ideal personal and social self-concepts, or what we want to be like and how we would like to be perceived by others. (See for example Rogers, 1961, pp. 199–270; Wylie, 1974; 1979; 1989.)

Self-Esteem.   Do you think of yourself as attractive or unattractive? A superior or an average student? A worthy friend or someone few people would like? In general, do you approve or disapprove of yourself? Such an evaluation of your self-concept is referred to as *self-esteem*. As with most aspects of personality, self-esteem is a continuous variable; a person's score may fall anywhere from low through average to high.

Although self-esteem is perhaps the most widely studied aspect of the self-concept, research in this area has been hindered by methodological problems. Most investigators have focused on the conscious aspects of self-esteem, in accordance with Rogers's definition of the self-concept, and have ignored the role played by unconscious processes and intrapsychic conflicts. Furthermore, various psychologists have devised their own constructs to define feelings of self-worth, for example:

> *Self-Esteem:* How you evaluate yourself; your sense of personal worth.
> *Positive Self-Regard (Rogers):* Accepting and respecting yourself, even in the absence of receiving positive regard from other people.
> *Perceived Self-Efficacy (Bandura):* The extent to which you believe that you can cope with the demands of a given situation. (See Chapter 16.)
> *An Inferiority Complex (Adler):* The belief that you cannot overcome your problems through appropriate effort. (See Chapter 4.)
> *Self-Contempt (Horney):* Hatred for your true abilities and personal qualities, because they fall far short of the unrealistic idealized image. (See Chapter 5.)

A common theme underlies all of these definitions: Having a low opinion of yourself is pathological, and prevents personality development from proceeding to a successful conclusion. They appear to be very similar, if not identical. Yet each theorist has focused on his or her own constructs, without relating them to those of other theorists. As a result, much of the data that have been obtained in this area are disorganized, fragmented, and often inconsistent. (See Hattie, 1992; Marsh, 1992.)

One finding of interest which has emerged is that self-esteem influences our response to failure. Those with low self-esteem lack confidence in their ability, pay little attention to any successes that they may achieve, and regard their failures as confirmation that they are incapable ("I knew I couldn't do that"). Those who are high in self-esteem expect to do well, and take their failures more or less in stride because they view them as rare exceptions ("I usually succeed, so I know I'll get it right next time"). Therefore, failure is more discouraging to those who suffer from low self-esteem. (See, for example, Brown & Gallagher, 1992; Brown & Smart, 1991; Kernis et al., 1989; Leary, 1999; Tafarodi & Vu, 1997.)

According to Rogers, we all need to receive positive regard from significant others. However, those who are low in self-esteem are less likely to behave in ways that will earn admiration and respect. They are motivated primarily by the desire to protect their fragile self-concept against criticism and embarrassment. Rather than risking failure, they often prefer to do nothing, attempt only the easiest of tasks, or refuse to try very hard so that they will have a ready-made excuse in case of failure. People with high self-esteem expect to succeed, so they are willing to undertake difficult projects and risk criticism in order to obtain positive regard. (See, for example, Baumeister et al., 1989; Baumeister & Tice, 1990; Tice, 1991.)

Whereas Rogers focuses primarily on overall feelings of self-worth, research has shown that self-esteem is multidimensional. That is, how you feel about yourself is likely to vary in different situations (e.g., academic, social, athletic). Both of these views have merit: Some patients suffer from intense feelings of inadequacy and self-contempt that pervade most aspects of their lives, whereas some individuals lack confidence in certain areas but are more self-assured in others.

The Real Versus Ideal Self.

One procedure devised by Rogers to measure self-esteem is to compare an individual's self-concept with what he or she would like to be. Suppose that a college student describes herself as shy, not very likable, rather disorganized, and intelligent. When asked how she would like to regard herself, her answer is outgoing, likable, organized, and intelligent. Her actual self-concept differs from her *ideal self* in three respects: shy versus outgoing, not very likable versus likable, and disorganized versus organized. This suggests that she has not yet become the person whom she would like to be, and that her self-esteem is in need of improvement. In Rogerian terminology, there is substantial incongruence between her real and ideal selves.

The ideal self may be measured by using the Q-sort procedure, with the client asked to sort the cards into a scale ranging from "least like my ideal self" to "most like my ideal self." The results are then compared to the Q-sort used to measure the client's real self. Or the client may be asked to respond twice to a series of 7-point scales, such as good–bad, friendly–unfriendly, and conscientious–lazy, with one trial describing "myself" and the second trial describing "my ideal self." A greater discrepancy between scores on the two trials is assumed to reflect lower self-esteem.

Rogers's approach suffers from an important conceptual problem: It is desirable to be aware of our weaknesses. Most personality theorists, including Freud, Jung, Adler, Allport, and Maslow, regard accurate self-knowledge as an important criterion of mental health. A very close correspondence between the real and ideal selves may mean that the person is using defenses to conceal painful weaknesses, whereas a moderate discrepancy may indicate a more self-perceptive and mature individual. Therefore, greater agreement between the real and ideal selves may *not* indicate a higher level of self-esteem. Studies have found that people who were high in maturity and competence had *less* congruence between their real and ideal selves than did participants who were less mature and competent, as would be expected from the preceding argument. (See for example Leahy, 1981; Leahy & Huard, 1976.) These results suggest that the relationship between self-esteem and the discrepancy between one's real and ideal selves is more complicated (and more curvilinear) than Rogers believed.

Contributions

Rogers was a sensitive and effective psychotherapist, and he has called attention to important aspects of the client–therapist relationship. He was among the first to unveil the mysteries of the therapy session by using tape recordings and publishing verbatim transcripts, which has stimulated a substantial amount of empirical research. Rogers has added to our understanding of parental pathogenic behaviors and how they lead to psychopathology. The self has proved to be an important, widely studied construct. To some psychologists, Rogers's emphasis on healthy inner potentials represents an important alternative (or "third force") to psychoanalysis (with its emphasis on the illicit aspects of personality) and behaviorism (which concentrates on observable behaviors, as we will see in Chapter 14).

Rogers has offered a challenging and provocative extension of the democratic principles on which our society is based. Rather than being directed by an expert who presumes to know what is best for us (such as a teacher, parent, or psychotherapist), Rogers advises us to treat one another as equals and derive our satisfactions from freeing others to pursue their own path toward actualization. Not surprisingly, this approach has proved more than a little threatening to those accustomed to striving for higher positions in the social pecking order and passing judgment on others. The expert authority is an idea that is widely accepted, and has advantages as well as disadvantages. And it may be possible to carry the principle of equality too far, as when children need the security of dependency and inequality to their parents in order to explore and learn. Although Rogers would seem to have taken too favorable a view of human nature, his humanistic approach makes an important point: To be psychologically healthy, each of us must heed those positive inner potentials that are uniquely our own.

Suggested Reading

Rogerian theory is clearly described in *On Becoming a Person* (1961) and *Carl Rogers on Personal Power* (1977). A rather tedious but thorough discussion of person-centered definitions and theory may be found in an article (Rogers, 1959). Rogers's views on education are presented in *Freedom to Learn* (1969), and his thoughts on encounter groups appear in *Carl Rogers on Encounter Groups* (1970/1973a).

SUMMARY

1. **THE BASIC NATURE OF HUMAN BEINGS.** *Actualization:* The primary motive underlying all human behavior is an innate tendency to develop our constructive, healthy capacities (actualization). Among the aspects of the actualizing tendency are creativity, curiosity, and the willingness to undergo even painful learning experiences in order to become more effective and independent. *The Need for Positive Regard:* Pathogenic parental behaviors may cause us to behave in ways that belie our benign inner nature. This is likely to happen because we have a powerful need for positive regard, especially from such significant others as our parents. *Teleology:* We are oriented toward future goals, rather than driven by prior causes.

2. **THE STRUCTURE OF PERSONALITY.** *Experience and the Organismic Valuing Process:* Each of us exists at the center of our own private, ever-changing world of inner experience. Experience is largely nonconscious, though it is potentially available to awareness. It includes an innate ability to value positively (or negatively) that which we perceive as actualizing (or nonactualizing), which is called the organismic valuing process. The nonconscious aspects of experience are trustworthy and invaluable additions to our conscious thoughts and plans, and only we can know what is good for us (actualizing) and what is not. *The Self-Concept (Self) and Self-Actualization:* Personality also includes a conscious conception of oneself as a separate and distinct entity. Some of the actualizing tendency is directed toward an effort to reach the goals represented by this self-concept. If significant others make their positive regard conditional on meeting their standards, the child will try to preserve their love by introjecting these standards into the self-concept and behaving accordingly. Such introjected conditions of worth supersede the innate organismic valuing process as an inner guide to behavior. This results in a painful inner schism, since the attempts to satisfy the conditions of worth fail to actualize the individual's true needs and potentials. *Defense:* This incongruence leads to defensive attempts to protect the self-concept by distorting or denying the real needs and feelings, furthering the schism between the actualizing and self-actualizing tendencies.

3. **THE DEVELOPMENT OF PERSONALITY.** Rogers posits no specific developmental stages, criteria, or types. He emphasizes the desirability of treating children with unconditional

positive regard, and enumerates various characteristics that define the optimally adjusted ("fully functioning") person.

4. FURTHER APPLICATIONS. *Psychopathology:* The self-concept of the more pathological person includes powerful conditions of worth. The sufferer therefore abandons the healthy quest for actualization in order to satisfy these introjected standards and keep the (conditional) positive regard of significant others. This makes it impossible to satisfy his or her true needs, and leads to such feelings of profound confusion as "I don't know who I am or what I really want." *Psychotherapy:* Positive therapeutic change is accomplished solely by establishing a constructive interpersonal relationship between therapist and client. A climate conducive to personal growth is created through the use of genuineness, empathy, and unconditional positive regard. Genuineness encourages a similar trusting genuineness on the part of the client, empathy provides the client with a deep sense of being understood, and unconditional positive regard provides an unqualified acceptance that enables the client to explore those feelings and beliefs that were too threatening to admit to awareness. *Education:* Genuineness, empathy, and unconditional positive regard are also advisable in the educational setting, as by devising unstructured classes that involve shared decision making.

5. EVALUATION. Rogers has been criticized for an overly optimistic and simplified view of human nature, ignoring important similarities between his theoretical constructs and those of such predecessors as Horney and Sullivan, failing to update and revise his theory, relying solely on genuineness and empathy and unconditional positive regard to produce positive therapeutic change, and devoting insufficient attention to the unconscious aspects of the self-concept. Yet he is also credited with calling attention to significant aspects of the client–therapist relationship, emphasizing the importance of the self-concept, stimulating a substantial amount of empirical research, helping to establish a major theoretical alternative to psychoanalysis and behaviorism, and stressing that each of us must heed our own unique positive potentials in order to be psychologically healthy.

STUDY QUESTIONS

Part I. Questions

1. Use the case material in the Appendix to illustrate each of the following Rogerian constructs: (a) the need for positive regard; (b) introjected conditions of worth; (c) incongruence between the actualizing and self-actualizing tendencies; (d) confusion and anxiety resulting from such feelings as "I wonder who I really am" and "I don't know what I want."

2. Rogers argues that we are motivated to develop our innate healthy tendencies. "The child will actualize himself [as by learning to walk], in spite of the painful experiences in so doing." Do you agree or disagree? Why?

3. What is the difference between criticizing a child's undesirable behaviors (which Rogers considers acceptable), and using conditional positive regard (which is harmful)? Illustrate with an example.

4. Rogers argues that creative individuals trust their inner experience in spite of public criticism. "It was as though [El Greco] could say, 'good artists do not paint like this, but *I* paint like this.'" How can one distinguish between healthy self-confidence and an unhealthy, stubborn refusal to accept justified criticism?

5. Give an example to illustrate each of the following: (a) genuineness; (b) empathy; (c) unconditional positive regard.

6. According to Rogers, genuineness, empathy, and unconditional positive regard are essential to any successful human relationship. How would you evaluate each of the following on these characteristics? (a) Your best friend. (b) Freud, during a therapy session.

7. Rogers believes that "[Even] a positive evaluation is as threatening in the long run as a negative one, since to inform someone that he is good implies that you also have the right to tell him he is bad." Do you agree or disagree? Why?

8. According to Rogers, "The good life is a *process*, not a state of being. It is a direction, not a destination." (a) Do you agree or disagree? Why? (b) How does our society try to persuade us that this statement is untrue?

9. The popularity of encounter groups has waned since their heyday in the 1970s. Why might such groups not be as effective as Rogers believes?

10. A terrorist blows up a building in a hated foreign country. How might Rogers explain the terrorist's behavior?

Part II. Comments and Suggestions

1. (a) He very much wants his parents' approval, and is devastated when they disapprove of his behavior (as in section 3). (b) He introjected his parents' standard that the most important thing in life is to be safe. See section 3. (c) Actualization involves satisfying his real needs and wishes, including those for love and affection. But because of his introjected conditions of worth, his self-concept is supported by being safe, remaining totally independent, and not needing other people. (d) See sections 1, 2, and 5.

2. See the comment to Chapter 8, question 4.

3. See the comment to Chapter 4, question 7.

4. It isn't easy. Some years ago, my writing style had certain idiosyncrasies that I strongly defended ("*I* write like this"). Now I no longer agree with some of them, and have changed them so my writing will be more clear. Every time I revise this textbook, I find ways to improve sections that seemed to be beyond reproach. However, I still trust my inner experience insofar as my writing is concerned.

5. From the noted autobiographical novel *I Never Promised You a Rose Garden:* (a) Deborah, the young girl suffering from schizophrenia, recalls how much she hated being lied to as a child by her doctors. They promised her that she would feel nothing when they treated her vaginal ailment ("this won't hurt a bit"), yet she experienced searing pain ("the hardest, longest burning of that secret place she could imagine"). Her therapist replied: "Those damn fools! When will they learn not to lie to children! Pah!" This genuine expression and sharing of justified anger did much to encourage Deborah's trust. (b) The therapist understood, intellectually and emotionally, how traumatic it was for Deborah to be lied to. (c) When Deborah had a serious relapse and deliberately scarred herself, the therapist criticized only this behavior and continued to express caring and respect for Deborah's self-concept and feelings.

6. (a) Based on my experiences with friends, I'm inclined to agree with Rogers. But I have never met anyone who is very high on all three characteristics. (b) Did Freud express his true beliefs and feelings during therapy? Can a therapist of any theoretical persuasion be effective without at least some openness to experience and empathy? Was Freud empathic in the case of Dora? Could a person as opinionated as Freud practice unconditional positive regard?

7. If this is true, how can we justify the use of constructive criticism, as with a teacher to a student or a parent to a child?

8. (a) I'm inclined to agree. Often we get what we want, enjoy it for awhile, and then find that it is no longer satisfying. In the movie *Chariots of Fire*, an athlete who wins an Olympic

gold medal after years of arduous preparation experiences moments of depression when he realizes that his quest is finally over. Though I may look forward to completing the writing of a difficult textbook and enjoying the rewards, I usually find that the real pleasure is in the process of writing, revising, and seeing my words take shape on the page. (b) Consider advertisements that proclaim that we will be happy if we purchase various luxury items, and the emphasis on receiving an award or winning a championship.

9. Even if the encounter group enables participants to discover and express their true feelings, is one weekend long enough to produce significant personal change? What is likely to happen when the participants return to their usual work and social environments? Rogers emphasizes that facilitators should *not* direct the group toward their own goals, try to turn the members into worshipful followers by being forceful and charismatic, or act like an authority who knows more about human behavior than anyone else. Are many leaders likely to be comfortable with such equalitarian standards?

10. Would Rogers attribute the terrorist's behavior to an illicit instinct? Why not? Why might the terrorist have developed powerful conditions of worth? What might these conditions of worth be? Why might the terrorist lack empathy and unconditional positive regard for people in the other country? What differences between the terrorist's country and the other country might have influenced the terrorist's behavior? Should the terrorist's behavior be attributed entirely to environmental influences, as Rogers would argue?

CHAPTER 10

ABRAHAM H. MASLOW
Self-Actualization Theory (II)

One day shortly after the bombing of Pearl Harbor, at age 33, Abe Maslow witnessed a pathetic and beggarly civilian parade—one that seemed to emphasize the futility and tragic waste of war. With tears streaming down his face, he made a firm vow: to prove that the human race is capable of something grander than hate and destructiveness, and to do so by studying the psychologically healthiest people that he could find (M. H. Hall, 1968a, pp. 54–55).

OBJECTIVES
- *To integrate the best aspects of various theories of personality (eclecticism), including Freudian psychoanalysis and the importance of the unconscious.*
- *To correct Freud's pessimistic view of human nature by showing that our inner potentials are entirely healthy, but that they are weak and can easily be overwhelmed by pathogenic environmental forces.*
- *To distinguish between two kinds of motives: deficiency motives, which involve drive reduction and filling an internal lack, and growth motives, which represent a higher level of functioning and include pleasurable tension increases and fulfilling one's unique potentials.*
- *To show that fundamental human needs form a hierarchy, wherein higher level needs do not become motivating (or even recognizable) until lower level needs have at least to some extent been satisfied.*
- *To learn about the highest level need, self-actualization, by studying the psychologically healthiest people.*
- *To describe the behaviors that differentiate self-actualizers from those who have not achieved this level of behavior.*
- *To show that psychopathology is caused by the failure to satisfy our fundamental needs, and that the failure to self-actualize leads to markedly different symptoms.*
- *To advocate an eclectic approach to psychotherapy, wherein different procedures (including Freudian psychoanalysis, briefer forms of psychotherapy, and behavior therapy) may be used depending on the nature and severity of the patient's problems.*

BIOGRAPHICAL SKETCH

Abraham H. Maslow was born on April 1, 1908, in Brooklyn, New York. His parents were un-educated Jewish immigrants from Russia; his father owned a barrel manufacturing company. Maslow's childhood was economically and socially deprived, and he was later to compare his position in a non-Jewish neighborhood to that of the first Black in an all-White school (M. H. Hall, 1968a, p. 37). Isolated and unhappy, he grew up in the company of libraries and books rather than friends.

Maslow originally enrolled at Cornell University but soon transferred to the University of Wisconsin, primarily because its catalog advertised the presence of various prominent scientists. To his considerable disappointment, he found that these notables were only visiting professors who had long since departed. Yet he stayed to earn not only his bachelor's degree, but also his Ph.D. in psychology in 1934. Maslow's doctoral dissertation dealt with the sexual behavior of monkeys, under the supervision of Harry Harlow. His professors at Wisconsin also provided him with instruction in the social amenities that he had neglected, such as the fine art of buying a suit (M. H. Hall, 1968a, p. 37). Maslow married Bertha Goodman, his high school sweetheart, while a 20-year-old undergraduate. The marriage proved to be very happy and successful, and the Maslows were to have two daughters.

At first an ardent behaviorist, Maslow's firsthand experience with his children convinced him to abandon this approach as inadequate. In 1937 he accepted a position at Brooklyn College, where he was to remain for some 15 years. During this time he furthered his knowledge by obtaining personal interviews with such noted theorists as Adler, Fromm, and Horney, underwent psychoanalysis, and experienced the aforementioned profound reaction to World War II. In 1951 Maslow moved to Brandeis University, and became perhaps the foremost exponent of humanistic personality theory. In addition to his academic endeavors, he also spent more than 10 years practicing brief, nonanalytic psychotherapy.

Maslow's writings consist of some six books and numerous articles in psychological journals, and his honors include election to the presidency of the American Psychological Association in 1967. Long troubled by heart problems, Abe Maslow died of a heart attack on June 8, 1970.

THE BASIC NATURE OF HUMAN BEINGS

For the most part, Maslow shares Rogers's optimistic view of human nature. Our innate (**instinctoid**) tendencies are predominantly healthy, and they include the capacity for constructive growth, kindness, generosity, and love. Yet Maslow also agrees with Erikson that these "instinct–remnants" are very weak, and are easily overwhelmed by the far more powerful forces of learning and culture. "The human needs ... are weak and feeble rather than unequivocal and unmistakable; they whisper rather than shout. And the whisper is easily drowned out" (Maslow, 1970b, p. 276; see also Maslow, 1965; 1968, pp. 164, 171, 191; 1970b, pp. ix, xvii–xix, 27–28, 77–95, 103).

A pathogenic environment can easily inhibit our positive potentials and evoke hatred, destructiveness, and self-defeating behavior. Thus Maslow prefers an eclectic approach to personality, and he advises psychologists to guard against excessive theoretical optimism by acquiring a thorough knowledge of Freudian psychoanalysis:

> [My goal is] to integrate into a single theoretical structure the partial truths I [see] in Freud, Adler, Jung, ... Fromm, Horney, [and others].... Freud is still required reading for the humanistic psychologist ... [yet] it is as if [he] supplied to us the sick half of psychology, and we must now fill it out with the healthy half.... [Thus] it is already possible to reject firmly the despairing belief that human nature is ultimately and basically depraved and evil, ... [and to conclude that the striving toward health] must by now be accepted beyond question as a widespread and perhaps universal human tendency. (Maslow, 1968, p. 5; 1970b, pp. xi–xiii. See also Maslow, 1968, pp. vii, 3–8, 48; 1966/1969; 1970b, pp. ix–xxvii, 117–129; 1971, pp. 4, 32.)

Deficiency and Growth Motives

Maslow espouses a dualistic theory of motivation.

Deficiency Motives. Some of our instinctoid impulses aim toward the reduction of such drives as hunger, thirst, safety, and obtaining love and esteem from others. These **deficiency motives** (**deficit motives, D-motives**) are possessed by everyone, and involve important lacks within us that must be satisfied by appropriate objects or people.

Growth Motives.   In contrast to the deficiency motives, **growth motives** (**being motives, B-motives**) are relatively independent of the environment and are unique to the individual. These needs include pleasurable drive increases (e.g., curiosity), the unselfish and nonpossessive giving of love to others, and the development of one's healthy potentials:

> Growth is, *in itself,* a rewarding and exciting process. [Examples include] the fulfilling of yearnings and ambitions, like that of being a good doctor; the acquisition of admired skills, like playing the violin or being a good carpenter; the steady increase of understanding about people or about the universe, or about oneself; the development of creativeness in whatever field; or, most important, simply the ambition to be a good human being.... It is simply inaccurate to speak in such instances of tension-reduction, implying thereby the getting rid of an annoying state. For these states are not annoying. (Maslow, 1968, pp. 29–31. See also Maslow, 1968, pp. 21–43.)

Although deficiency motives serve such necessary goals as self-preservation, growth motives represent a more pleasurable, higher, and healthier level of functioning. "Satisfying deficiencies avoids illness; growth satisfactions produce positive health ... [like the] difference between fending off threat or attack, and positive triumph and achievement" (Maslow, 1968, p. 32). Maslow argues that Freud emphasized drive reduction because he studied only sick people, who have good reason to fear (and repress) their impulses because they cope with them so poorly. In contrast, healthy individuals welcome drive increases because they signal potential satisfaction. They may well protest that "the trouble with eating is that it kills my appetite" (Maslow, 1968, p. 28).

The Complexity of Human Motives.   Maslow prefers not to list specific human needs. Our motives are so complicated and interrelated, and our behavior is so overdetermined, that it is usually impossible to explain personality in terms of separate and distinct drives.

For example, making love may be due to needs for sex, power, and to reaffirm one's masculinity or femininity. A hysterically paralyzed arm may fulfill simultaneous wishes for revenge, pity, and attention. Or eating may satisfy the hunger need and offer solace for an unrequited love. (See Maslow, 1970b, pp. 22–26, 35–58.) Maslow also argues that the various human needs differ considerably in their level of importance, with some remaining virtually unnoticed until others have at least to some extent been satisfied. He therefore favors a general, **hierarchical** model of human motivation. (See Figure 10.1.)

The Hierarchy of Human Needs

The Physiological Needs.   The lowest level of the hierarchy involves the **physiological needs,** including hunger, thirst, sex, oxygen, sleep, and elimination. A starving person cares very little about writing majestic poetry, buying an impressive-looking car, finding a sweetheart, or avoiding injury—or anything other than the overriding goal of obtaining food. Many of the physiological needs are deficiencies, but not all; among the exceptions are sexual arousal, elimination, and sleep. (See Maslow, 1968, p. 27; 1970b, pp. 35–38.)

The Safety Needs.   As the physiological needs become increasingly satisfied, the next level in the hierarchy gradually emerges as a motivator. These **safety needs** involve the quest for an environment that is stable, predictable, and free from anxiety and chaos.

For example, a young child may seek reassurance and protection after being frightened by a sudden loud noise or injury. Or an adult in the grip of safety needs may pursue a tenured professorship, amass a substantial savings account, or constantly prefer the familiar and routine

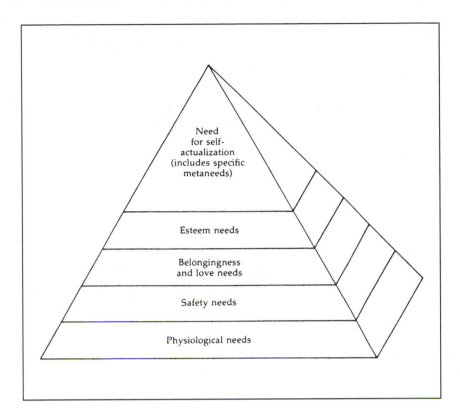

FIG. 10.1. The Hierarchy of Human Needs.

to the unknown. Although the safety needs help us to avoid severe pain and injury, they can become so powerful as to interfere with personality development—as when people willingly yield some of their rights during periods of rampant crime or war in order to gain a measure of security. "In the choice between giving up safety or giving up growth, safety will ordinarily win out" (Maslow, 1968, p. 49; see also Maslow, 1968, pp. 46–47, 54; 1970b, pp. 39–43).

The Belongingness and Love Needs.   Once the physiological and safety needs have been more or less satisfied, the **belongingness and love needs** come to the forefront as motivators. The individual now hungers for affectionate relationships with friends, a sweetheart or spouse, and/or offspring.

To Maslow, love consists of feelings of affection and elation, yearnings for the loved one, and (often) intense sexual arousal. Our hunger to receive such love from others is a relatively selfish deficiency need (**D-love**), one that often involves anxious and manipulative efforts to win the loved one's affection. Yet this need must be satisfied in order for us to develop growth-oriented or "being" love (**B-love**), which is nonpossessive, unselfish, and more enjoyable than D-love. B-love is also denoted by honesty, including a willingness to reveal one's weaknesses as well as strengths, and by respect for the loved one's needs and individuality. (See Maslow, 1968, pp. 41–43; 1970b, pp. 43–45, 182–183, 250, 275–276.)

The Esteem Needs.   In accordance with Adler, Rogers, Fromm, and Erikson, Maslow attributes considerable importance to our need for superiority and respect. We strive to achieve self-confidence and mastery of the environment, and to obtain recognition and appreciation from others. However, these **esteem needs** usually act as motivators only if the three lower types have been satisfied to some degree. Maslow cautions that true self-esteem is based on real competence and significant achievement, rather than external fame and unwarranted adulation (a theme well illustrated by Ayn Rand's classic novel *The Fountainhead*).

The Need for Self-Actualization.

The highest form of need is **self-actualization,** which consists of discovering and fulfilling one's own innate potentials:

> Self-actualization is idiosyncratic, since every person is different.... The individual [must do] what *he*, individually, is fitted for. A musician must make music, an artist must paint, a poet must write, if he is to be ultimately at peace with himself. What a man *can* be, he *must* be. (Maslow, 1968, p. 33; 1970b, p. 46. See also Maslow, 1968, pp. 7, 25; 1970b, pp. 47, 150.)

Self-actualization is similar to actualization in Rogerian theory, except that it does not become important (or even noticeable) until the physiological, safety, love, and esteem needs have been at least partially satisfied. Therefore, self-actualization is found only among older people. The young are more concerned with such issues as obtaining an education, developing an identity, seeking love, and finding work, which Maslow regards as only "preparing to live."

The specific needs of those rare individuals who achieve this highest level differ considerably from the lower needs. Among their **metaneeds** are a love of beauty, truth, goodness, and justice. "It seems probable that we must construct a profoundly different psychology of motivation for self-actualizing people" (Maslow, 1970b, p. 159; see also Maslow, 1964/1970a, pp. 91–96; 1970b, pp. xx, 134; 1971, pp. 43–44, 192–195, 299–340). Maslow devotes considerable attention to the characteristics of self-actualizing individuals, as we will see in a subsequent section.

Characteristics of Higher and Lower Needs.

Maslow views the higher needs as distinctively human. "We share the need for food with all living things, the need for love with (perhaps) the higher apes, [and] the need for self-actualization with [no other species]" (Maslow, 1970b, p. 98; see also Maslow, 1968, p. 31; 1970b, pp. 67, 97–104).

The emergence of a higher need reflects a greater degree of psychological health, somewhat like reaching a more advanced developmental stage in Eriksonian or Freudian theory, and its satisfaction is valued far more highly by the individual than fulfilling a lower need. Yet the higher needs are also less urgent and tangible, they are not necessary for survival, and they are more easily blocked by a pathogenic environment. For these reasons, even recognizing the existence of these needs represents a considerable achievement. Maslow estimates that the average American citizen has satisfied perhaps 85 percent of the physiological needs and 70 percent of the safety needs, but only 50 percent of the love needs, 40 percent of the esteem needs, and 10 percent of the need for self-actualization (1970b, p. 54). Thus to Maslow, as to most personality theorists, achieving true self-knowledge is a difficult—albeit essential—undertaking.

The hierarchy of needs is presumed to apply to most people, though the specific form of satisfaction often varies in different cultures. Members of a primitive tribe may gain esteem by becoming great hunters, whereas people in a technological society are more likely to gratify such needs by advancing to an executive position. However, Maslow does allow for various exceptions. Some people regard esteem as more important than love, whereas others accord the highest status to creativity. Or the higher needs may sometimes emerge after the lower ones have been severely frustrated, as with the displacement of unsatisfied sexual needs onto artistic endeavors. Nevertheless, the easiest way to release us from the dominance of our lower

---

CAPSULE SUMMARY
Some Important Maslowian Terminology

B-cognition	A special form of thinking that is common during peak experiences. B-cognition is nonjudgmental, does not aim toward the fulfillment of some motive, and emphasizes the unity of oneself and the cosmos.
B-love	An unselfish and nonpossessive giving of love and affection to another person. A growth motive that is more enjoyable than D-love.
D-cognition	A common, self-preservative form of thinking that aims toward the satisfaction of deficiency motives. D-cognition is judgmental, and emphasizes the separateness of oneself and the environment.
D-love	The selfish need to receive love and affection from others. A deficiency motive, prerequisite to the emergence of B-love.
Deficiency motive (D-motive)	The need to reduce a drive such as hunger, thirst, or D-love by filling some lack within oneself. Deficiency motives are common to all human beings.
Eupsychian	As psychologically healthy as possible.
Growth motive (being motive, B-motive)	The need to develop one's inner potentials, including the enjoyment of pleasurable drive increases and the giving of B-love to others. Growth motives are relatively independent of the environment and are unique to the individual.
Hierarchy of needs	A model of motivation wherein certain needs usually do not become important, or even noticeable, until other lower level needs have to some extent been satisfied. Includes five levels of needs: physiological (lowest), safety, love, esteem, and self-actualization (highest).
Instinctoid need	An inborn, healthy, but weak instinctual impulse that is easily overwhelmed by the far more powerful forces of learning and culture.
Metaneeds (metamotives)	The atypical, nonhierarchical needs of those rare individuals who have achieved self-actualization. Metaneeds include the love of beauty, truth, goodness, and justice.
Metapathology	Occurs when an individual has largely gratified the four lowest need levels, but cannot satisfy his or her metamotives and achieve self-actualization. The highest form of psychopathology.
Peak experience	A mystical and awesome experience that represents the highest and healthiest form of human functioning. Somewhat similar to numinosum in Jungian theory.
Self-actualization	Fulfilling one's own innate potentials; the highest and most pleasurable need, but also the most difficult to recognize and satisfy. A growth motive, similar to actualization in Rogerian theory.

---

and more selfish needs (and to promote healthy psychological development) is by satisfying them. (See Maslow, 1970b, pp. 51–53, 59–60.)

The Unconscious and Teleology

Since our weak instinctoid needs are so easily obscured by environmental influences, they readily assume the status of unconscious processes. "[There is a] tremendous mass of evidence that indicates the crucial importance of unconscious motivation.... The basic needs are often largely unconscious.... [Thus a sound] theory cannot possibly afford to neglect the unconscious life" (Maslow, 1970b, pp. 22, 54; see also Maslow, 1968, pp. 5, 196; 1970b, pp. 27, 270, 273; 1971, pp. 114, 173). The unconscious also includes memories of our more shameful actions, and such important positive potentials as love, creativity, and humor.

In contrast to Freud's emphasis on causality, Maslow stresses the teleological goals toward which we strive. "No theory of psychology will ever be complete which does not centrally incorporate the concept that man has his future within him, dynamically active at the present moment" (Maslow, 1968, p. 15).

THE STRUCTURE OF PERSONALITY

Maslow differs from Freud by rejecting specific structural constructs. But he does accept the existence of such defense mechanisms as repression, projection, reaction formation, and rationalization:

> Freud's greatest discovery is that *the* great cause of much psychological illness is the fear of knowledge of oneself—of one's emotions, impulses, memories, capacities, potentialities, of one's destiny.... If the psychoanalytic literature has taught us nothing else, it has taught us that repression is not a good way of solving problems. (Maslow, 1968, p. 60; 1971, p. 49. See also Maslow, 1968, pp. 66–67, 191; 1964/1970a, p. 41; 1970b, pp. 211, 220; 1971, pp. 29, 37.)

Maslow also concludes that we have both a humanistic and an introjected conscience. Like the Rogerian organismic valuing process, the inborn humanistic conscience troubles us whenever we behave in ways that are contrary to our inner nature:

> The only way we can ever know what is right for us is that it feels better subjectively than any alternative.... The born painter who sells stockings instead, the intelligent man who lives a stupid life, the man who sees the truth and keeps his mouth shut, the coward who gives up his manliness, all these people perceive in a deep way that they have done wrong to themselves and despise themselves for it. (Maslow, 1968, pp. 7, 45. See also Maslow, 1968, pp. 121, 194–195; 1971, pp. 46–47, 184, 338–339.)

The second, learned form of conscience represents introjected parental standards, which may well clash with our true organismic needs and values. Like Horney and Rogers, Maslow concludes that every growing child faces a crucial fork in the developmental road: the healthy choice of heeding its own inner guidelines, or the pathological (yet probably inevitable) alternative of sacrificing its true potentials in order to conform to the standards of the all-important parents (Maslow, 1968, pp. 51–52).

THE DEVELOPMENT OF PERSONALITY

Whereas Freud contends that the child must be forced against its will toward maturity, Maslow argues that healthy children actively seek to gain new skills and satisfy their growth motives. Once they have received enough need satisfaction appropriate to a given developmental level, they become bored with these old delights and eagerly proceed to higher and more complicated ones. "Given sufficient gratification, free choice, and lack of threat, [the child] 'grows' out of the oral stage and renounces it himself. He doesn't have to be 'kicked upstairs'"

(Maslow, 1968, p. 56 n. 4; see also pp. 23–24, 46, 49–50, 55). For example, the infant ready to be weaned willingly and enthusiastically prefers solid to liquid food. Personality development will proceed normally so long as children are given the opportunity to heed their own inner guidelines, rather than having their judgment and self-trust undermined by excessive external pressures:

> A priori plans for the child, ambitions for it, prepared roles, even hopes that it will become this or that ... represent demands upon the child that it become what the parent has already decided it *should* become. Such a baby is born into an invisible straitjacket. (Maslow, 1970b, pp. xxiv–xxv. See also Maslow, 1970b, pp. 276–277.)

However, Maslow cautions that overpermissiveness also has undesirable consequences. Some rules and training are necessary to help the child avoid costly errors, provide a welcome sense of safety and structure in an otherwise confusing world, and prevent the development of a pampered style of life. Furthermore, a certain amount of frustration serves to strengthen the growing personality. "The person who hasn't conquered, withstood, and overcome continues to feel doubtful that he *could....* [Thus] grief and pain are sometimes necessary for the growth of the person" (Maslow, 1968, pp. 4, 8; see also Maslow, 1968, p. 119; 1970b, pp. 40–41, 71, 87, 121–122). For the most part, however, satisfying the child's needs is the best way to promote healthy personality development.

The Self-Actualizing (Fully Human) Person

Maslow shares Allport's and Rogers's interest in defining optimal psychological adjustment. He has studied those rare individuals whom he regards as having achieved the highest level of need gratification, self-actualization (or "full humanness"). This relatively small sample includes living persons and such historical personages as Thomas Jefferson, Albert Einstein, Eleanor Roosevelt, Jane Addams, William James, Albert Schweitzer, and Baruch Spinoza. (See Maslow, 1968, pp. 26, 71–114, 135–145, 153–160; 1970b, pp. 149–180; 1971, pp. 28–30, 41–53, 183–184, 280, 299–340.)

Although self-actualizers are unique in many ways, they tend to share the following characteristics:

More Accurate Perception of Reality.   Self-actualizing people are more free of unwarranted optimism, pessimism, and other defensive distortions of reality. They are able to evaluate people and events with considerable accuracy.

Greater Acceptance of Self and Others.   Self-actualizers are more tolerant of human weaknesses. They avoid judging other people or themselves, although they may experience some guilt about any personal deficiencies that they have been unable to overcome.

Greater Spontaneity and Self-Knowledge.   Self-actualizing individuals behave more spontaneously because they better understand their true motives, emotions, and abilities. They are guided primarily by their own code of ethics, which often makes them feel like aliens in a foreign land—and makes them difficult for other people to understand.

Greater Problem Centering.   Self-actualizers tend to have a consuming mission in life that occupies much of their time and energy. They are keenly interested in external problems and do not care much about introspection. They have a devotion to excellence, combined with a lack of worry about minor details that makes life easier for themselves and their associates.

Greater Need for Privacy.   Self-actualizers prefer a greater amount of privacy and solitude. This healthy detachment is due in part to their tendency to rely on their own feelings and values. Yet it is often resented by those who mistake it for snobbishness, unfriendliness, or hostility.

Greater Autonomy and Resistance to Enculturation.   Self-actualizers are motivated by the need to fulfill their own inner potentials, rather than by a desire for external rewards or possessions. Since their needs for love and esteem are largely satisfied, they are less likely to manipulate others for selfish purposes. Self-actualizers are less indoctrinated by the prevailing standards of the imperfect society in which they live, and they avoid popular styles of dress or forms of entertainment that run counter to their personal criteria:

> [Self-actualizing individuals] taught me to see as profoundly sick, abnormal, or weak what I had always taken for granted as humanly normal: namely that too many people do not make up their own minds, but have their minds made up for them by salesmen, advertisers, parents, propagandists, TV, newspapers, and so on. (Maslow, 1970b, p. 161. See also Maslow, 1968, pp. 11–12, 34–37; 1970b, pp. 172, 177.)

Greater Freshness of Appreciation and Richness of Emotional Response.   Any goal that we may achieve, such as job success, marriage, or a new car, is all too easily taken for granted once the novelty has worn off. Self-actualizers live richer and more fulfilling lives because they cherish those blessings that they have received:

> [There is a] widespread tendency to undervalue one's already achieved need-gratifications, or even to devalue them and throw them away. Self-actualizing persons are relatively exempted from this profound source of human unhappiness.... For such a person, any sunset may be as beautiful as the first one, any flower may be of breath-taking loveliness.... The thousandth baby he sees is just as miraculous a product as the first one he saw. He remains as convinced of his luck in marriage thirty years after [it], and is as surprised by his wife's beauty when she is sixty as he was forty years before. (Maslow, 1970b, pp. xxi, 163. See also Maslow, 1970b, pp. xv–xvi, xxi, 60–61, 72, 164.)

Greater Frequency of Peak Experiences.   Most self-actualizing individuals have had mystical moments of absolute perfection, during which the self is lost in feelings of sublime ecstasy, wonder, and awe. Like numinosum in Jungian theory, these **peak experiences** are difficult to describe to those who have not had them. They may ensue from love, sex, appreciating a great symphony or work of art, bursts of creativity, moments of profound insight or scientific discovery, or the full use of one's abilities and potentials. But whatever the form, their heavenly delight is the major reason why life is worth living.

Greater Frequency of B-cognition.   Self-actualizing persons more often engage in a type of thinking called "being cognition" (**B-cognition**), which always accompanies a peak experience and may occur at other times as well. B-cognition is a unique form of thought that is nonjudgmental, does not aim toward the fulfillment of some motive, and emphasizes the unity of oneself and the cosmos. In contrast, the more common "deficiency cognition" (**D-cognition**) is judgmental, concerns our need to satisfy the deficiency motives, and stresses the separateness of oneself and the environment. (See Maslow, 1968, pp. 71–102; 1971, pp. 251–266.)

Greater Social Interest.   Like Adler, Maslow regards *Gemeinschaftsgefühl* as typical of the mature individual. Self-actualizers strongly identify with the human species, and have a genuine sympathy for and desire to help others. If they do express hostility or anger, it is usually both well deserved and for the good of some third party.

Deeper, More Loving Interpersonal Relationships.   Self-actualizing people prefer intimate relationships with a few close friends. rather than superficial contacts with many people. Their love is nonpossessive (B-love), and they are proud of rather than threatened by a loved one's achievements. Self-actualizers regard sex as meaningless without love, and may temporarily opt for chastity rather than accept opportunities that are devoid of genuine affection. And they are more attracted by such qualities as decency and considerateness than by physical characteristics.

More Democratic Character Structure.   Self-actualizers befriend people of all classes, races, and ethnic groups, and often seem virtually unaware of such differences. They strongly and effectively oppose injustice, cruelty, and the exploitation of others.

Greater Discrimination Between Good and Evil.   Self-actualizing individuals have strong moral and ethical standards, and rarely vacillate as to the course of action they consider right or wrong. They accept the responsibility for their actions, rather than rationalizing or trying to blame their errors on other people.

More Unusual Sense of Humor.   Most self-actualizers prefer humor that is philosophical and instructive. They dislike humor based on hostility or superiority, such as ethnic or "insult" jokes.

Greater Creativity.   Every self-actualizing person demonstrates a fresh and creative approach to life, a virtue by no means limited to the artist or genius. A self-actualizing homemaker may devise novel ways of preparing and serving the family meals, thereby turning the dinner table into a visual and culinary delight. Or a creative psychotherapist may develop unorthodox but successful methods geared to the individual patient, rather than attempting to apply textbook methods indiscriminately.

Maslow cautions that self-actualization is a matter of degree, rather than an all-or-nothing affair. At times self-actualizing persons may display such weaknesses as ruthlessness, discourtesy, outbursts of temper, silliness, irritation, or boredom. *"There are no perfect human beings!"* (Maslow, 1970b, p. 176; see also Maslow, 1968, pp. 97, 163; 1964/1970a, p. 37; 1971, p. 50). Conversely, the less healthy individual may on rare occasions achieve moments that approach peak experiences. The self-actualizer is characterized by a much more frequent display of maturity, helpful behavior, creativity, happiness, and wisdom—so much so as to afford distinct hope for the prospects of our strife-torn species.

FURTHER APPLICATIONS
OF MASLOWIAN THEORY

Psychopathology

Causes of Psychopathology.   According to Maslow, the primary cause of psychopathology is the failure to gratify our fundamental needs: physiological, safety, love, esteem, and self-actualization. "[These needs] *must* be satisfied, or else we get sick" (Maslow,

1970b, p. 92; see also Maslow, 1968, pp. 4, 21; 1970b, pp. 62, 67, 102, 268–269, 279; 1971, p. 316).

The lower the level at which such need frustration occurs, the more severe the pathology. An individual who has satisfied only the physiological needs and is preoccupied with safety (as in Horneyan theory) is more disturbed than one who has gratified the physiological, safety, and love needs, but cannot gain much esteem and respect. A person who has satisfied all but the need for self-actualization is healthier than either of the preceding two individuals. Thus, like most theorists, Maslow regards psychopathology as a difference in degree rather than kind.

Since self-actualization cannot be achieved without first satisfying lower needs that involve other people (safety, belongingness and love, respect), interpersonal behaviors play an important role in causing (or preventing) psychopathology:

> Let people realize clearly that every time they threaten someone, or humiliate or hurt [someone] unnecessarily, or dominate or reject another human being, they become forces for the creation of psychopathology, even if these be small forces. Let them recognize also that every man who is kind, helpful, decent, psychologically democratic, affectionate, and warm is a psychotherapeutic force, even though a small one. (Maslow, 1970b, p. 254. See also Maslow, 1964/1970a, pp. xiii–xiv; 1970b, pp. 252–253.)

Characteristics of Psychopathology.   Like Erikson and Kelly, Maslow objects to the use of formal diagnostic labels. "I hate all these words, and I hate the medical model that they imply because [it] suggests that the person who comes to the counselor is a sick person, beset by disease and illness, seeking a cure. Actually, of course, we hope that the counselor will ... [help] foster the self-actualization of people" (Maslow, 1971, p. 51; see also pp. 30–36). He even prefers to substitute the term *human diminution* for *neurosis,* so as to emphasize that psychopathology involves the failure to fulfill one's true potentials.

Pathological needs do not reflect the sufferer's true desires and potentials, and are therefore insatiable and unfulfilling. For example, a person with a vast hunger for power is unlikely ever to satisfy this drive because it is actually an unconscious substitute for some more fundamental need, such as love, esteem, or self-actualization. "A statement by Erich Fromm that has always impressed me very much [is:] 'Sickness consists essentially in wanting what is not good for us.' ... Healthy people are better choosers than unhealthy people" (Maslow, 1968, p. 169; 1971, p. 211; see also Maslow, 1968, pp. 48, 150–152, 198–201; 1964/1970a, pp. 99–101; 1970b, pp. 78, 276–277).

Other pathological symptoms include: (1) guilt, shame, and/or anxiety, at least one of which is present in every neurosis; (2) apathy and hopelessness, as in Horneyan theory; (3) a faulty conception of oneself and the environment, as in Kellyan theory: "The neurotic is not [only] emotionally sick—he is cognitively *wrong!*" (Maslow, 1970b, p. 153; see also Maslow, 1968, pp. 7–8; 1970b, pp. xxii, 143–144, 155, 268, 274); (4) an excessive dependency on other people for need satisfaction; (5) a fear of knowledge of oneself and others, resulting in the use of various defense mechanisms; (6) a steadfast adherence to the familiar and routine, especially in obsessive-compulsive neurosis: "The healthy taste for the novel and unknown is missing, or at a minimum, in the average neurotic" (Maslow, 1970b, p. 43; see also Maslow, 1968, pp. 60–67; 1970b, pp. 42, 68, 218–219, 232).

The person who has satisfied all but the need for self-actualization experiences symptoms of a higher form, albeit ones that are quite painful. Such **metapathology** involves the repression or denial of one's metaneeds, and is all too common in a society that elevates material rewards above idealistic standards like truth and justice. It is typically denoted by such feelings as alienation, boredom, cynicism, joylessness, uselessness, and an inability to arrive at a satisfactory system of personal values. (See Maslow, 1970b, p. 71; 1971, pp. 316–322.)

Psychotherapy

Theoretical Foundation. Like Rogers, Maslow's therapeutic goal is to help patients regain the path toward self-actualization and fulfill their own unique potentials. But since he attributes psychopathology to the frustration of our fundamental needs, he concludes that the most important function of psychotherapy is to bring about their gratification.[1] "For a child who hasn't been loved enough, obviously the treatment of first choice is to love him to death, to just slop it all over him" (Maslow, 1971, p. 34; see also Maslow, 1970b, pp. 68–69, 93–95, 241–264, 270). The needs for safety, belongingness and love, and esteem can only be satisfied by other people. So the patient must learn to establish and maintain good human relationships, and ultimately replace formal psychotherapy with such sources of satisfaction as friends and marriage.

The preceding model does not apply to those patients who are lacking only in self-actualization, since they have fulfilled their interpersonal needs and are concerned solely with inner growth and self-direction. These individuals must be helped to overcome the social forces that have caused them to repress their metaneeds, and to discover those values toward which they truly wish to strive.

Therapeutic Procedures. Unlike Rogers, Maslow adopts an eclectic approach to psychotherapy. He does agree that the therapist should often be accepting, genuine, kind, and concerned, since these behaviors help to satisfy the patient's needs for safety and belongingness. However, he cautions that there are too many patients who do not thrive in a warm and friendly atmosphere for this to become a universal procedure. People with authoritarian personalities are likely to interpret kindness as weakness, whereas distrustful individuals may regard friendliness as a dangerous trap. With such patients, Maslow recommends that the therapist assume the role of authority.

Maslow also differs from Rogers by favoring the use of Freudian psychoanalysis with seriously disturbed patients, notably those who are too afraid or suspicious to accept nurturance, love, respect, and other need satisfactions. In less severe cases, however, briefer forms of psychotherapy may well suffice. This includes behavior therapy (see Chapter 14), so long as it does not uproot defenses and symptoms too quickly. "Change in *behavior* can produce personality change" (Maslow, 1970b, p. 311; see also pp. 44, 142, 257–264). In addition, Maslow advocates the use of Rogerian encounter groups to further the personal development of relatively healthy people.

Whatever the form, Maslow strongly recommends psychotherapy as the best way to understand and treat psychopathology. "[Therapy] is the best technique we have ever had for laying bare men's deepest nature, as contrasted with their surface personalities.… The good professional psychotherapist has left the intuitive helper far behind" (Maslow, 1970b, pp. 241, 260).

Resistance, Transference, and Countertransference. Like Freud and Jung, Maslow argues that the psychotherapist must be sufficiently self-aware to avoid harmful countertransferences. Ideally, the therapist should be warm, sympathetic, emotionally secure,

---

[1]Not including the physiological needs, however; psychotherapy is hardly suitable for alleviating hunger and thirst (Maslow, 1970b, p. 100).

self-confident, financially successful, and supported by a happy marriage and satisfying friendships.

Maslow also accepts the existence of resistance and transference. But he agrees with Horney and Kelly that resistance may well represent a healthy and justified objection to therapeutic blunders, such as being arbitrarily assigned to a diagnostic category (e.g., "anal," "Oedipal") that neglects the patient's personal uniqueness and identity. (See Maslow, 1968, pp. 126–130; 1970b, pp. 250–253, 260, 309.)

Work

Maslow is one of the few personality theorists who takes an active interest in the area of work. "If you are unhappy with your work, you have lost one of the most important means of self-fulfillment" (Maslow, 1971, p. 185; see also Maslow, 1965; 1966/1969; 1970b, pp. 277–278; 1971, pp. 208, 237–248, 306, 313).

At work, as elsewhere, those whose lower needs are satisfied will seek higher level gratifications. Organizations should therefore be designed so that employees can satisfy their needs for belongingness, dignity, respect, and self-actualization (an approach Maslow refers to as **Eupsychian** management). Maslow also contends that the ability of any organization to satisfy its workers' needs must be ascertained by studying the specific nature of employee complaints, rather than merely tabulating their frequency. If many workers object to the physical conditions as unsafe, wet, and cold ("low grumbles"), even the lowest need levels are not being gratified. If numerous employees express dissatisfaction with their opportunities for belongingness or respect ("high grumbles"), the lower needs are reasonably well satisfied but the intermediate levels are not. And if most complaints involve the inability to self-actualize ("metagrumbles"), the emergence of this highest level need indicates that the four lowest levels have at least to some extent been satisfied.

Religion

In accordance with his theoretical optimism, Maslow emphatically denies the existence of innate evil or original sin. He also shares Jung's opposition to unthinking faith, and Freud's contention that the dogma of religion must fall before the onslaught of science and truth:

> [Faith] in the hands of an anti-intellectual church [tends] to degenerate into blind belief ... [which] tends to produce sheep rather than men ... [When religion] was cut away from science, from knowledge, from further discovery, from the possibility of skeptical investigation, from confirming and disconfirming, and therefore from the possibility of purifying and improving, such a ... religion was doomed. (Maslow, 1964/1970a, pp. 13–14. See also Maslow, 1964/1970a, pp. 9–10; 1970b, pp. 83, 94, 122, 266.)

Maslow argues that the supposedly supernatural revelations claimed by prophets and seers are nothing more nor less than peak experiences, the potential for which is inherent in every human personality. It is these private, personal, unscheduled, and profoundly meaningful occurrences that constitute true religious experience, rather than rituals arbitrarily assigned to a particular building and day of the week. Thus most self-actualizers have enjoyed deep religious experiences, even though they often are not religious in any formal sense, whereas many people who regularly practice their religion have not. And only those who have had peak experiences can become effective religious leaders, for only they will be able to communicate the nature of such experiences to those who have not had them. (See Maslow, 1964/1970a, pp. viii, xi, 4, 11, 20, 24, 26, 29, 33; 1971, pp. 195, 339–340.)

Education

Like Rogers, Maslow advocates a nondirective and person-centered approach to education. He takes strong exception to the rigid formalities found in higher education: Courses must all span precisely the same number of weeks, even though some subjects are more difficult and comprehensive than others. Academic departments are totally independent, as though human knowledge could be neatly divided into separate and distinct categories. The emphasis is on learning many specific facts, rather than on personal growth. And motivation is provided by such external rewards as grades, which often leads students to do only the work that is specifically required by the teacher. "The present school system is an extremely effective instrument for crushing peak experiences and forbidding their possibility" (Maslow, 1971, p. 188; see also Maslow, 1964/1970a, pp. 16–17, 48–58; 1970b, pp. 94, 177–178, 223; 1971, pp. 48, 168–195).

The ideal university would have no formal credits, required courses, or degrees. It would serve as an educational retreat where people could explore various subjects, discover their true interests, and appreciate the joys of learning and the preciousness of life. The teacher would show students how to hear the beauty of a great symphony, rather than merely having them repeat back the date of the composer's birth on an examination. He or she would be a self-actualizer, thereby serving as a model for the students' inevitable identifications. Thus education would achieve its proper goal: to help people become fully human and actualize their highest potentials.

Maslowian Theory and Empirical Research

Like Rogers, Maslow regards empirical research as a vital source of knowledge about the human personality. But he also agrees that all too many psychologists try to imitate the precision of the physical sciences by concentrating on trivial issues that can be measured accurately:

> The besetting sin of the academicians [is] that they prefer to do what they are easily able rather than what they ought, like the not-so-bright kitchen helper I knew who opened every can in the hotel one day because he was so *very* good at opening cans.... The journals of science are full of instances that illustrate [this] point, that what is not worth doing, is not worth doing well. (Maslow, 1970b, pp. 18, 181. See also Maslow, 1968, pp. viii, 216; 1970b, pp. 1–17, 224; 1971, pp. 170–171.)

The creative scientist avoids a rigid commitment to specific techniques or content areas. He or she dares to search for the truth in innovative and unusual ways, and to tackle important but difficult research issues.

EVALUATION

Criticisms and Controversies

Maslow has been criticized for an overly optimistic view of human nature, although his acceptance of Freudian principles renders him less vulnerable to this charge than Rogers. However, Maslow's eclecticism does not seem sufficiently well thought out. He fails to reconcile his holistic approach with his acceptance of Freudian defense mechanisms and Horney's idealized image (1971, p. 113), which imply the existence of intrapsychic conflicts. Eclecticism requires more than merely accepting under one theoretical roof all those constructs of other theorists that one likes. The various ideas must also be integrated into a meaningful and noncontradictory whole, and this Maslow has not done.

Maslow's study of self-actualizing individuals defines such people subjectively, using his own personal criteria. It has been suggested that the behaviors he characterizes as ideal (and even the hierarchy of needs itself) represent not some fundamental truth, but his own idiosyncratic conception of what human values should be like. The sample is quite a small one on which to base such far-reaching findings, and Maslow's report lacks any statistical analyses and excludes such important biographical data as the intelligence, educational level, socioeconomic level, and ages of his participants.

Maslow repeatedly refers to his theoretical ideas as empirically testable, yet many modern psychologists emphatically disagree. They criticize his constructs as vague and imprecise, and they raise the issue of how to measure the amount of satisfaction that must be achieved at a given level for the next higher need to become prominent. Maslow allows for so many theoretical exceptions (e.g., the possible emergence of a higher need after the *frustration* of a lower one) that his theory appears equivocal. In contrast to such theorists as Freud, Adler, and Erikson, Maslow's discussion of personality development seems vague and ill defined. And his idiosyncratic writing style includes numerous extensive and rather dull lists, offhand and unexplained references to the work of other psychologists, and assertions that seem more philosophical than scientific and psychological.

Empirical Research

Maslow's theory has not generated a great deal of empirical research. There exists a validated instrument (the Personal Orientation Inventory) which measures the degree of self-actualization that one has achieved (Shostrom, 1963; 1965). There is some evidence in favor of the need hierarchy (e.g., Graham & Balloun, 1973), as well as a survey that fails to support it (Wahba & Bridwell, 1976). And some of the research on self-esteem is related to Maslow's ideas. (See Chapter 9.) On the whole, however, major research support for Maslow's theoretical contentions is still lacking.

Contributions

Maslow's emphasis on the study of healthy people offers a welcome contrast to those personality theories based solely on clinical data, and his model of deficiency and growth motives is preferred by many psychologists to Freud's preoccupation with drive reduction. Unlike many theorists, Maslow accords due credit to such predecessors as Freud, Jung, Adler, Horney, and Fromm. His ideas about religion are interesting and provocative, as is the general idea of a hierarchical model of human needs. Maslow is widely regarded as perhaps the foremost exponent of humanistic psychology, and his writings have proved popular with the general public. Although Maslow's theory seems too flawed to stand on its own as a viable alternative to its competitors, he has nevertheless made significant contributions toward a goal shared by Rogers and succinctly stated by Sören Kierkegaard: to help a person be that self that one truly is.

Suggested Reading

Of Maslow's various titles, there are two that represent the cornerstones of his theory: *Motivation and Personality* (1970b) and *Toward a Psychology of Being* (1968). Also of interest are Maslow's memoirs and personal introspections (Lowry, 1979). For a biography of Maslow, see Hoffman (1988).

SUMMARY

1. THE BASIC NATURE OF HUMAN BEINGS. We are born with healthy but very weak instinctoid needs, which are all too easily overwhelmed by the far more powerful forces of learning and culture. Maslow therefore advises psychologists to guard against excessive theoretical optimism by acquiring a thorough knowledge of Freudian psychoanalysis. *Deficiency and Growth Motives:* Our instinctoid needs include both deficiency motives and growth motives. The former involve drive reduction and filling crucial lacks within us through some external source, whereas the latter include pleasurable increases in tension and the development of one's own unique potentials. Although deficiency motives serve essential purposes (such as self-preservation), growth motives represent a higher, healthier, and more pleasurable level of functioning. *The Hierarchy of Human Needs:* Some needs do not become important, or even noticeable, until others have at least to some extent been satisfied. The hierarchy of human needs consists of five levels: physiological (lowest), safety, belongingness and love, esteem, and self-actualization (highest). The higher needs are less tangible, not necessary for survival, and more easily blocked by a pathogenic environment, so even recognizing their existence is a considerable achievement.

2. THE STRUCTURE OF PERSONALITY. Maslow's approach to personality is holistic, and he posits no specific structural constructs. He does accept the existence of Freudian defense mechanisms and two forms of conscience, one resembling the Rogerian organismic valuing process and one introjected from important others.

3. THE DEVELOPMENT OF PERSONALITY. Maslow has little to say about personality development. He argues that the child should be given sufficient opportunities to heed its own inner guidelines, and have its fundamental needs satisfied. *The Self-Actualizing (Fully Human) Person:* Maslow devotes considerable attention to those people he regards as extremely psychologically healthy, and describes some 15 characteristics typical of such self-actualizers.

4. FURTHER APPLICATIONS. *Psychopathology:* Psychopathology is caused primarily by the failure to satisfy our fundamental needs. The lower the level at which such dissatisfaction occurs, the more pathological the individual. Psychopathology involves wanting what is not good for oneself, anxiety, hopelessness, being cognitively wrong, and other symptoms. Those who have satisfied all but the need for self-actualization experience symptoms of a higher and different form. *Psychotherapy:* Maslow finds merit in various types of psychotherapy, depending on the severity of the patient's problems. Except for self-actualization (and the physiological needs), the patient's unfulfilled needs can only be satisfied by other people, so he or she must learn to establish and maintain effective interpersonal relationships. *Other Areas:* Maslow has also applied his theory to work, religion, and education.

5. EVALUATION. Maslow's eclecticism renders him less vulnerable to the criticism of excessive optimism than Rogers, but seems insufficiently thought out and includes too many confusions and contradictions. His study of self-actualizers has been criticized on methodological grounds, and his theoretical constructs have been characterized as vague, equivocal, and untestable. Yet Maslow is widely regarded as perhaps the most prominent exponent of humanistic psychology, his writings have gained widespread popularity, and his study of healthy people represents a welcome contrast to theories based solely on clinical observation.

STUDY QUESTIONS

Part I. Questions

1. Use the case material in the Appendix to illustrate each of the following statements by Maslow: (a) "People [who] perceive in a deep way that they have done wrong to themselves … despise themselves for it." (b) "[Excessive external pressures, and] demands upon the child that it become what the parent has already decided it *should* become, [are like being] born into an invisible straitjacket." (c) "The neurotic is not [only] emotionally sick—he is cognitively *wrong!*" (d) "The healthy taste for the novel and unknown is missing, or at a minimum, in the average neurotic."

2. Give an example to support each of the following arguments by Maslow: (a) It is very difficult to recognize and satisfy our highest-level needs (metaneeds), such as the love of truth and justice, because society teaches us that material rewards are more important. (b) True self-esteem is based on real competence and significant achievement, rather than on external fame and unwarranted adulation.

3. The following statements by Maslow express significant disagreements with Freud: (a) "Growth is, *in itself*, a rewarding and exciting process … Given sufficient gratification, free choice, and lack of threat, [the child] renounces … [the oral stage] himself. He doesn't have to be 'kicked upstairs.'" (b) "Healthy people welcome drive *increases,* and may well complain that the trouble with eating is that it kills my appetite." (c) "For the child who hasn't been loved enough, obviously the treatment of first choice [during psychotherapy] is to love him to death, to just slop it all over him." In each case, do you agree with Maslow or Freud? Why?

4. Maslow states that "every time [people] threaten someone, or humiliate or hurt [someone] unnecessarily, or dominate or reject another human being, they become forces for the creation of psychopathology." What does this imply about: (a) Athletes who use "trash talk" to put down their opponents? (b) Politicians who use negative and derogatory commercials to win an election?

5. Where would each of the following be classified according to the hierarchy of human needs? (a) The young man whose case history is discussed in the Appendix. (b) You.

6. (a) According to Maslow, a vast hunger for power is unlikely ever to be satisfied because it is actually an unconscious substitute for such fundamental needs as love or esteem. Do you agree or disagree? Why? (b) By classifying self-actualization as the highest need (and thus the last to emerge), Maslow takes the position that discovering and fulfilling your true potentials is extremely difficult. Do you agree or disagree? Why?

7. Consider the fifteen characteristics of self-actualizing (or "fully human") persons. (a) Would Maslow consider Freud to be a self-actualizer? (b) Does the young man whose case history is described in the Appendix fit any of these characteristics, or is he deficient in all of them?

8. According to Maslow, self-actualizing people taught him to see that too many people are "profoundly sick … [because they] have their minds made up for them by salesmen, advertisers, parents, propagandists, TV, newspapers, and so on." Do you agree or disagree? Why?

9. Maslow argues that there is a widespread tendency to undervalue need gratifications that one has already achieved, and that this is a profound source of human unhappiness. Do you agree or disagree? Why?

10. Is it possible for a job to be self-actualizing, yet have poor working conditions and not be esteemed by others? What would this imply about Maslow's theory?

11. A terrorist blows up a building in a hated foreign country. How might Maslow explain the terrorist's behavior?

Part II. Comments and Suggestions

1. (a) See section 8 of the case material in the Appendix. He has considerable self-hate because he knows that he has sacrificed his true desires (e.g., for love and adventure) in order to please his parents (as by seeking safety), although he rarely allows this knowledge to become conscious. (b) See sections 3 and 9. (c) He is wrong about safety always being the best choice, and to expect that his father will be affectionate and nurturing in spite of ample evidence to the contrary. (d) This is evident in his constant quest for safety.

2. (a) Consider our legal system. Does it encourage a quest for truth and justice? Or is the primary emphasis on winning by hiring the best counsel and confusing the issues to one's own advantage, even if one is guilty? (b) See Chapter 5, question 5, and the corresponding comment.

3. (a) I agree with Maslow. See the comment to Chapter 8, question 4. (b) I agree with Maslow. Some years ago, I was hospitalized with severe pneumonia. I love to eat; I even go into a mild depression when what I order in a restaurant proves to be dissatisfying, because this means that there will be one less meal that I will enjoy in my lifetime. Because of this illness, I lost my appetite (and about 15 pounds, which I could not afford; I'm slightly underweight even when healthy). Food tasted like cardboard, and chewing and swallowing it was a miserable experience. I only ate because I was threatened with the alternative of intravenous feeding, and I'm not fond of needles. Needless to say, I was delighted when I eventually regained my appetite. (c) Freud would undoubtedly regard this procedure as all too likely to reinforce the patient's secondary gains, and I'm inclined to agree. This goes far beyond the therapist being empathic and caring—much too far, in my opinion.

4. Can behavior that is so common be harmful to us, or is Maslow being overly sensitive? What might such actions reveal about the people who use them? (See Chapter 15, question 6, and the corresponding comment.)

5. (a) He is clearly preoccupied with the safety needs, which overwhelm his needs for belongingness and love. But he is at least somewhat aware of his belongingness needs and also recognizes some esteem needs, which does not accord well with Maslow's hierarchy. (b) I seem to be working on some of these levels simultaneously, rather than in succession as Maslow would argue.

6. (a) Consider some of the well-known people who have a great deal of power. Do they quit when they have enough, or are they always striving for more? (b) I agree. See the comment to Chapter 3, question 7.

7. (a) Consider the following characteristics of self-actualizers: They are relatively unconcerned with introspection, more tolerant of human weaknesses, less judgmental of themselves and others, guided by strong moral and ethical standards, able to evaluate people more accurately, consumed by some mission in life that occupies much of their energy, and creative. (b) He is clearly lacking in many of these characteristics. He does not perceive reality very accurately, does not accept himself and others, worries over minor details, lacks much emotional response, lacks social interest, and does not have deep and loving interpersonal relationships. But he is autonomous (albeit excessively so), has strong moral and ethical standards, and is creative. This is yet another illustration that pathology often differs from healthy behavior in degree, rather than in kind.

8. I'm inclined to agree with the statement, but I don't agree that this belief can only be ascertained from the study of healthy individuals; Fromm and Rogers reached the same

conclusion from their clinical work. See Chapter 6, question 7a, and Rogers's discussion of how the journey away from self-knowledge is encouraged by certain social institutions.

9. Consider the professional athlete who is receiving an extremely large salary but becomes so unhappy about not earning more that he (or, less often in our society, she) sits out part of the season, sulks, and perhaps even damages his career.

10. Consider an artist who loves to paint and values his or her own work, but who is not appreciated by the public and lives in squalor. Does this suggest that it is possible to complain about physical conditions, or not satisfy the need for esteem from others, yet still be able to self-actualize?

11. Would Maslow attribute the terrorist's behavior to an illicit instinct? Why not? Can the terrorist's behavior be attributed to the failure to satisfy one or more of the needs in Maslow's hierarchy? To being threatened, humiliated, or hurt? (See the quote in question 4, this chapter.) To the terrorist being more easily manipulated by propagandists because he or she has not achieved self-actualization? (See the quote in question 8, this chapter.)

CHAPTER 11
ROLLO MAY
Existential Psychology

One psychoanalyst contracted tuberculosis during his late 30s, and his fight against this formidable illness proved to be a turning point in his life. At that time, effective medication had not yet been developed. So Rollo May waited hour by hour and day by day in an upstate New York sanitarium for the verdict that would spell either a return to health, lifelong invalidism, or death. May spent much of this suspenseful time reading, and he made a surprising discovery: his own profound anxiety had far more to do with the dread of nonbeing, as described by such existentialists as Kierkegaard, than with the mechanical and metaphysical construct of libido.

Fortunately, May recovered from his illness. But his psychoanalytic orientation did not, and his subsequent professional life has been devoted to an existential approach to personality.

OBJECTIVES

- *To devise a theory of personality based on existentialism, a philosophy of human nature that emphasizes the science of being (ontology).*
- *To show that anxiety about death and non-being has a powerful (albeit often unconscious) influence on our behavior.*
- *To emphasize the importance of courageously asserting our existence in the world and choosing a course in life that fulfills our own unique potentials, despite the ultimate nothingness that awaits us all.*
- *To argue that we have both benign and malignant innate potentials, and we must accept and learn to control our dark side.*
- *To adopt a holistic approach that does not divide personality into separate parts and does not regard intrapsychic conflicts as important.*
- *To retain Freud's emphasis on unconscious processes, but to do so in a holistic way: when we hide important truths about ourselves from ourselves, it is because we lack courage.*
- *To show that psychopathology involves symptoms of an existential nature: losing one's sense of purpose in life (intentionality), and failing to fulfill one or more of the essential aspects of being (physiological, psychological, and social).*
- *To devise a method of psychotherapy that helps patients regain their courage to exist in the world, recapture their lost intentionality, and make choices that fulfill their unique potentials.*

BIOGRAPHICAL SKETCH

Rollo Reese May was born on April 21, 1909, in Ada, Ohio, but spent most of his childhood in Marine City, Michigan. May received his bachelor of arts degree from Oberlin College in 1930, after which he pursued an Eriksonian course by touring Europe as an itinerant artist and teacher. During this time he attended the summer school of Alfred Adler, whose work he admired but regarded as somewhat oversimplified. (See May, 1975, p. 37; Reeves, 1977, pp. 251–263.)

May returned to the United States to earn a divinity degree from the Union Theological Seminary in New York in 1938, where he first encountered existential thought, and later served in a parish in Montclair, New Jersey. But he became more interested in psychology and underwent training in psychoanalysis at the William Alanson White Institute, where he met and was influenced by Fromm and Sullivan. May opened his own private practice in 1946, and received the first Ph.D. in clinical psychology ever awarded by Columbia University in 1949. At about this time he underwent the aforementioned traumatic bout with tuberculosis, which did considerably more to influence him toward existentialism than his formal education. May married Florence deFrees in 1938, a union that was to produce one son and two daughters, and was married to Georgia Johnson at the time of his death.

May's published works include some dozen books, notably the bestselling *Love and Will* (1969c), and numerous articles. In addition to his work as a practicing psychotherapist, he lectured at such institutions as Harvard, Yale, Princeton, Columbia, Dartmouth, Vassar, Oberlin, New York University, and the New School for Social Research. Rollo May died of congestive heart failure at his home in Tiburon, California, on October 22, 1994.

THE BASIC NATURE OF HUMAN BEINGS

Being-in-the-World (Dasein)

Each of us has an inherent need to exist in the world into which we are born, and to achieve a conscious and unconscious sense of ourselves as an autonomous and distinct entity. The stronger this **being-in-the-world**[1] or *Dasein* (*sein* = to exist, or be alive; *da* = there), the healthier the personality.

To fulfill one's own innate potentials (that is, to develop *Dasein*) requires constant effort and courage. The only way to enjoy a meaningful life is by affirming and asserting our being-in-the-world—even (if need be) in the face of social pressures to conform, misguided parental standards, and the threat of death itself:

> The hallmark of courage in our age of conformity is the capacity to stand on one's own convictions—not obstinately or defiantly (these are expressions of defensiveness, not courage) nor as a gesture of retaliation, but simply because these are what one believes. It is as though one were saying through one's actions, "This is my self, my being." … [Thus it is through self-assertion and] will that the human being experiences his identity. "I" is the "I" of "I can." (May, 1969c, p. 243; 1953/1973, p. 236. See also May, 1958/1967b, pp. 37, 41–47, 55–61; 1958/1967c, pp. 31–32; 1969a, pp. 13, 19, 45; 1972, pp. 40–41; 1977b, pp. 303–304.)

No one else can tell an individual how or what to be-in-the-world. Each of us must discover our own potentials and values, and the best way to do so is by experiencing each moment actively and spontaneously. Even such basic human drives as sexuality and aggression are of secondary importance to *Dasein*. Drives are an abstraction, and perceiving ourselves as "having" them is dehumanizing. We *are* our hunger, thirst, sexuality, feelings, and ideas, and it is this experiencing that is truly and distinctively human. (See May, 1958/1967b, pp. 42–44; 1969a, p. 14; 1969b, pp. 73, 78.)

Modes of Being-In-The-World. Our being-in-the-world comprises three simultaneous and interrelated modes (or "regions"): the world of internal and external objects, which forms our physiological and physical environment (***Umwelt;*** literally, "world around"); the social world of other people (***Mitwelt;*** literally, "with-world"); and the psychological world of one's self, potentials, and values (***Eigenwelt;*** literally, "own-world"). Whereas some personality theorists prefer to concentrate on only one of these modes, existential psychology holds that all three must be accorded equal emphasis in order to achieve a true understanding of the human personality. (See May, 1958/1967b, pp. 61–65.)

The *Umwelt* is the mode that so concerned Freud. In addition to our physical surroundings, it includes the state of need into which every person is cast by birth: hunger, thirst, sleep, and so forth. The conditions into which we are born, such as having instinctual needs, a genetically

---

[1]Difficulties in translation have beset existential psychology. Here, a compound word easily formed in German must be expressed through hyphenation in English, an awkward method that does not quite convey the unity implied by the construct.

predetermined height, and a culture with certain expectations, represent the few aspects of existence that we cannot control through our own choices. This circumstance is sometimes referred to as **thrownness,** or **facticity.**

The *Mitwelt* involves our inherent need to form personal relationships for their own sake, rather than to sublimate some instinctual drive. No one can achieve a meaningful existence in isolation, as stressed by such theorists as Adler, Fromm, Horney, and Sullivan.

The *Eigenwelt* is the uniquely human world of self-awareness (as in Rogerian theory), or knowing that we are the center of our existence and recognizing our own particular potentials. This mode is evident when we judge accurately what we do or do not like or need, or personally evaluate an experience. Conversely, feelings of emptiness and self-estrangement reflect some distortion of *Eigenwelt.* (See May, 1958/1967b, p. 63; 1967d; 1981.)

In contrast to Erikson's construct of identity, Eigenwelt and Dasein do *not* depend on the opinions and expectations of other people. "If your self-esteem must rest in the long run on social validation, you have, not self-esteem, but a more sophisticated form of social conformity" (May, 1958/1967b, p. 45; see also pp. 46–47, 79).

Nonbeing and Anxiety

Although the subjective and objective aspects of personality are inextricably intertwined, there is one absolute fact about being-in-the-world: death, which none of us ever escapes. Our tenuous existence may be terminated at any moment by such vagaries of fate as an automobile accident, criminal's bullet, earthquake, or heart attack. The awareness of an eventual end to our being, and the impending psychological destruction posed by rejections and insults, evoke the painful emotion of **anxiety:**[2]

> Anxiety is the apprehension cued off by a threat to some value that the individual holds essential to his existence as a personality.... [It] is the subjective state of the individual's becoming aware that his existence can become destroyed, that he can lose himself and his world, that he can become "nothing." (May, 1958/1967b, p. 50; 1977a, p. 205. See also May, 1953/1973, pp. 34–80; 1977a, pp. 204–239; Reeves, 1977, pp. 66–99, 176.)

Anxiety differs from fear in that it is **ontological,** or related to human existence. For example, suppose that a professor whom you know and respect passes by on the street without speaking. This snub may strike at the core of your self-esteem ("Am I not worth noticing? Am I nobody—nothing?"), thereby evoking anxiety that haunts you long after the event. Or if you conclude that survival is impossible without the love of a certain person (or a particular job, or some status symbol), the prospective loss of that love (or job, or symbol) will occasion considerable anxiety. In contrast, the fear caused by sitting in a dentist's chair does not attack Dasein—and is therefore soon forgotten once the incident is over. "Anxiety is ontological, fear is not.... Anxiety can be understood only as a threat to Dasein" (May, 1958/1967b, p. 51; 1977a, p. 205). Thus May attributes anxiety not to some divisive intrapsychic conflict or external danger, but to the fundamental clash between being and the threat of nonbeing. A certain amount of anxiety is therefore a normal, and inevitable, aspect of every personality.

Ontological anxiety confronts each of us with a major challenge. This unpleasant emotion intensifies whenever we choose to assert our *Dasein* and strive to fulfill our innate potentials, for emphatically affirming that we exist also brings a reminder that someday we will not. It is all too tempting to repress or intellectualize our understanding of death, deny our *Dasein,* and

---

[2]Another difficulty in translation: *anxiety* is a fairly weak rendition of the German word *Angst,* which has no English equivalent, wherefore some theorists prefer *dread* or *anguish.*

opt for the apparent safety of social conformity and apathy. That is, we may try to deprive nonbeing of its sting by (consciously or unconsciously) treating our being-in-the-world as meaningless. "The awareness of death is widely repressed in our day.... [In fact,] the ways we repress death and its symbolism are amazingly like the ways the Victorians repressed sex" (May, 1969c, p. 106). Nevertheless, the healthy course is to accept nonbeing as an inseparable part of being. This will enable us to live what life we have to the fullest:

> To grasp what it means to exist, one needs to grasp the fact that he might not exist, that he treads at every moment on the sharp edge of possible annihilation and can never escape the fact that death will arrive at some unknown moment in the future.... Without this awareness of nonbeing ... existence is vapid [and] unreal.... But with the confrontation of nonbeing, existence takes on vitality and immediacy, and the individual experiences a heightened consciousness of himself, his world, and others around him.... [Thus] the confronting of death gives the most positive reality to life itself. (May, 1958/1967b, pp. 47–49. See also Becker, 1973; May, 1969a, p. 30.)

Fallibility and Guilt

No one ever deals perfectly with the three modes of being-in-the-world. Try as we may, our choices fail to fulfill at least some of our innate potentials (a denial of *Eigenwelt*). Perfect empathy is impossible, so even the best intentioned person sometimes relates to others in ways that are biased and dissatisfying (a denial of *Mitwelt*). And it is easy to overlook our communion with nature and the environment, and misperceive ourselves as separate and distinct from *Umwelt*.

Such inevitable failures evoke ontological **guilt,** another normal and necessary aspect of every personality. As with anxiety, the ideal course is to accept and use our guilt for constructive purposes—as by developing a healthy humility concerning the possibility of our own errors, and a readiness to forgive others their mistakes. (See May, 1958/1967b, pp. 52–55.)

Intentionality and Significance

In contrast to Freud, May attributes considerable importance to both psychic determinism and teleology. We are all to some extent impelled by forces from infancy and childhood, especially those of us who are more neurotic. Yet we also have the freedom, and the responsibility, to strive toward those goals that we select. Psychologically healthy people can readily imagine some desirable future state and then prepare to move in this direction, a capacity May refers to as **will** or **intentionality.**[3] (See May, 1939/1967a, pp. 45–53; 1958/1967b, pp. 41, 65–71; 1969c, pp. 92–94, 223–272; Reeves, 1977, pp. 147–221.)

According to May, a conscious and unconscious sense of purpose pervades all aspects of our existence—perceptions, memories, and so forth. For example, suppose that an individual perceives a house in the mountains. A prospective renter will look to see if it is well constructed and gets enough sun, a real-estate speculator will regard it primarily in terms of probable profit or loss, and a person who encounters unpleasant hosts will more readily observe its flaws. In each case the house is the same, but the experience depends on the viewer's intentions. Also, as in Adlerian theory, our goals and plans for the future affect our memories of childhood. (See May, 1958/1967b, p. 69; 1969c, p. 232.)

---

[3]In *Love and Will* (1969c), May uses both *intentionality* and *intention* to describe the way in which we anticipate the future. However, he now regards this as an error. Intentionality concerns the basic human capacity to behave teleologically, and is evident in the specific intentions that a person has (May, 1977b, p. 306). Also, intentionality cuts across both conscious and unconscious and thus represents a deeper sense of purpose than will, which is conscious.

To May, the loss of intentionality represents the major psychopathology of our time. "The central core of modern man's 'neurosis' ... is the undermining of his experience of himself as responsible, the sapping of his will and ability to make decisions" (May, 1969c, p. 184). May also concludes that the related feelings of intense powerlessness are likely to result in violence, a last-ditch attempt to prove that the sufferer can still affect someone significantly. Whereas Freud stressed psychic determinism in order to shatter the Victorian misconception that personality is wholly free of childhood influences and irrationalities, May argues that we now must emphasize intentionality in order to remedy our current self-estrangement and apathy:

> Everyone has a need for ... significance; and if we can't make that possible, or even probable, in our society, then it will be obtained in destructive ways. The challenge before us is to find [healthy] ways that people can achieve significance and recognition ... For no human being can stand the perpetually numbing experience of his own powerlessness. (May, 1969c, p. 14; 1972, p. 179. See also May, 1939/1967a, p. 216; 1969c, pp. 16, 31, 162, 182–183; 1972, pp. 21–23, 243.)

Love

One constructive way of affirming *Dasein* is through **love,** another important ontological characteristic. "[Love is] a delight in the presence of the other person, and an affirming of his value and development as much as one's own" (May, 1953/1973, p. 241; see also May, 1953/1973, pp. 227, 238–246; 1958/1967b, pp. 64–65, 75; 1969c, pp. 37–38, 72–79, 289–293, 302, 317–319; Reeves, 1977, pp. 100–146).

Love always involves a blending of four components, albeit in varying proportions. As in Freudian theory, our need for **sex** is satisfied through drive reduction and physical release. Another particularly important aspect of love is **eros,** a striving for fulfillment through union with significant others. In contrast to sex, eros includes such pleasurable tension increases as thinking of and yearning for the loved one. One noted example is the passion and vitality of Romeo, who compares his Juliet to rare jewels and the stars in heaven. The other two characteristics of love (to which May devotes considerably less attention) are friendship and liking (**philia**), as with the Sullivanian chum, and a nonpossessive devotion to the welfare of the other person (**agapé**), like Maslow's construct of B-love. Thus love is a rich experience that encompasses all three modes of being-in-the-world: biological drives (*Umwelt*), relationship to others (*Mitwelt*), and the affirmation of one's self and values (*Eigenwelt*).

Not all aspects of love are pleasant. Love may also lead to increased anxiety, since it can bring disaster as well as joy—as one may well discover on becoming a parent for the first time, and realizing that the beloved child is all too vulnerable to potential nonbeing and the whims of fate. Therefore, the ability to love requires a strong being-in-the-world. Conversely, the widespread loss of *Dasein* and intentionality in our society has resulted in an inability to experience and express genuine love. We have repressed eros, and replaced it with an emphasis on the mechanical and depersonalized aspects of sex:

> There is nothing *less* sexy than sheer nakedness, as a random hour at any nudist camp will prove. It requires the infusion of the imagination (which I ... call intentionality) to transmute physiology and anatomy into [passion and eros].... [Yet today,] elaborate accounting-and ledger-book lists—how often this week have we made love? did he (or she) pay the right amount of attention to me during the evening? was the foreplay long enough?—[hover] ... in the stage wings of the drama of love-making the way Freud said one's parents used to ... [and result in] alienation, feelings of loneliness, and depersonalization.... [In fact, whereas] the Victorian nice man or woman was guilty if he or she

CAPSULE SUMMARY
Some Important Existential Terminology

Anxiety	Apprehension caused by a threat to the existence of one's personality (i.e., a threat to *Dasein*); the awareness that one can be destroyed, physically or psychologically, and become nothing. Since death is the one inevitable aspect of existence, a certain amount of anxiety is a natural characteristic of being human (i.e., ontological).
Being-in-the-world (*Dasein*)	A conscious and unconscious sense of oneself as a distinct and autonomous entity who exists in the world of physiological and physical surroundings (*Umwelt*), other people (*Mitwelt*), and one's own self (*Eigenwelt*). A strong *Dasein* is essential to the healthy personality.
Daimonic	Innate benign and illicit forces that are capable of dominating one's personality, such as sex, passion and eros, procreation, rage, hostility, and the quest for power. Psychological health requires that the daimonic be accepted and integrated into consciousness.
Eigenwelt	The world of one's self, potentials, and values ("own-world"). One of the three simultaneous and interrelated modes of being-in-the-world.
Eros	A passionate striving for self-fulfillment through union with a significant other, including such pleasurable tension increases as thinking of and yearning for the loved one. One of the four components of love, and the one all too often denied or repressed in our society.
Existential psychology	A philosophy of human nature that stresses the ontological characteristics, and the necessity of asserting our *Dasein* despite the inevitable death that awaits us all.
Guilt	Regret resulting from the impossibility of fulfilling all of one's innate potentials (a denial of *Eigenwelt*), of relating perfectly to others (a denial of *Mitwelt*), and of always recognizing our communion with nature (a denial of *Umwelt*); an ontological characteristic.
Intentionality	The capacity of human beings to have a conscious and unconscious sense of purpose; an ontological characteristic.
Love	A delight in the presence of another person, and a readiness to affirm that person's values and development as much as one's own; an ontological characteristic. Love always involves a blending of four components, albeit in varying proportions: sex, eros, philia (friendship and liking), and agapé (nonpossessive devotion).
Mitwelt	The world of relationship to other people ("with-world"). One of the three simultaneous and interrelated modes of being-in-the-world.
Ontological characteristics	Those qualities that are distinctively human, including *Dasein,* anxiety, guilt, intentionality, and love.
Ontology	The science of existence or being, notably of being human.
Repression	Excluding any of the ontological characteristics from consciousness.
Throwness (facticity)	A term referring to those few aspects of existence into which we are cast by birth and cannot control through our own choices, such as having instinctual needs and a culture with certain expectations.
Umwelt	The world of internal and external objects, which forms our physiological and physical environment ("around-world"). One of the three simultaneous and interrelated modes of being-in-the-world.
Will	The conscious capacity to move toward one's self-selected goals.

did experience sex, now we are guilty if we *don't*. (May, 1969c, pp. 40, 43–44; see also pp. 13–15, 30–33, 37–72, 102, 107, 111.)

The solution to our inability to love is to rediscover our *Dasein* and will, and reunite sex with eros and passion.

The Daimonic

According to May, our motives include innate urges that are both benign and illicit. Among the former are sex, passion and eros, and procreation; whereas the latter include hostility, rage, cruelty, and the quest for power. Any of these aspects has the potential to dominate one's personality. May refers to them as the **daimonic,** after an ancient Greek word for both the divine and diabolical. (See M. H. Hall, 1967b, p. 29; May, 1969c, pp. 122–177; 1977b, pp. 304–306.)

To achieve psychological health, we must consciously accept and attempt to control the daimonic. Yet this is no easy task, for it is all too tempting to deal only with our virtues and repress the dark side of our personality. Such a denial of the daimonic produces a naive innocence that often has disastrous consequences, like the failure to understand and check a Hitler until it is too late or the misguided belief that one can walk safely through an armed confrontation like Kent State; to be unaware of evil is to be readily destroyed by it. Or a daimonic that is allowed to remain unconscious may be projected onto members of other countries or ethnic groups, resulting in violence, assassination, and war.

THE STRUCTURE OF PERSONALITY

Since we are our Dasein, anxiety, guilt, and love, it would be misleading—and depersonalizing—to attribute these ontological characteristics to abstract structural constructs. Therefore, existential psychology adopts a holistic approach to personality. May does accept the importance of unconscious processes, however, and of such defense mechanisms as repression, intellectualization, projection, and reaction formation:

> The great contribution of Freud was his carrying of the Socratic injunction "know thyself" into new depths that comprise, in effect, a new continent, the continent of repressed, unconscious motives.… He uncovered the vast areas in which motives and behavior—whether in bringing up children, or making love, or running a business, or planning a war—are determined by unconscious urges [and] anxieties.… (May, 1969c, pp. 51, 182. See also May, 1958/1967c, pp. 22–23, 28; 1958/1967b, pp. 68, 79, 88–91; 1969a, p. 19; 1969c, pp. 132–133, 158, 174, 199, 205–206, 241, 260; 1953/1973, p. 52.)

When we repress anxiety, eros, or the daimonic (as we all too often do), it is not because one part of a fragmented personality is at war with some other part. It is the whole individual who lacks courage, chooses not to experience such threatening human characteristics, and (as in Fromm's theory) escapes from the freedom to know and be oneself—a misguided decision that inevitably results in the loss of *Dasein*.

THE DEVELOPMENT OF PERSONALITY

The development of a healthy personality may be impeded by various pathogenic parental behaviors. Rejection causes the child to deny *Mitwelt* and shy away from other people, especially when it is hypocritically disguised as loving concern. Stifling the child's natural expressions of will tends to result in a neurotic quest for safety, wherein *Dasein* is sacrificed in an attempt to become obedient and angelic. Catering to children's every whim prevents them from establishing their individuality by rebelling against parental authority, with such pampering particularly likely in the case of the only child (as in Adlerian theory):

> There is great temptation to overprotect the [only child]. When he calls, the parents run; when he whimpers, they are abashed; when he is sick, they are guilty; when he doesn't sleep, they look as though *they* are going to have nervous breakdowns. The infant becomes a little dictator by virtue of the situation he is born into.... [Yet] all this attention actually amounts to a considerable *curtailing* of the child's freedom, and he must, like a prince born into a royal family, carry a weight for which children were never made. (May, 1969c, p. 120. See also May, 1969a, pp. 17–18; 1969c, pp. 119, 140, 278; 1972, pp. 113–114, 123–126, 144, 159, 176; 1953/1973, pp. 195–196; 1975, pp. 56–58.)

For the most part, however, existential psychology devotes relatively little attention to personality development.

FURTHER APPLICATIONS OF EXISTENTIAL PSYCHOLOGY

Dream Interpretation

Since intentionality and *Dasein* involve unconscious as well as conscious aspects, May often turns to dreams for information about an individual's being-in-the-world. Every dreamer uses personal symbols in order to express particular ideas, so free association may be needed to unravel the meaning of this private language. But since May views personality as a unified whole, he rejects the idea of a Freudian dream-censoring component. Therefore, May's approach to dream interpretation tends to be more straightforward than Freud's.

An impotent patient dreamed of having a metal pipe inserted in his head by his therapist, the end of which emerged below as an erect penis. This passive solution reflected his loss of *Dasein* and pathological dependence on other people, together with his misguided view of himself as a brainy but heartless sex machine. A college student who participated in violent protest movements proved to be compensating for unconscious feelings of intense powerlessness, as shown by recurrent nightmares wherein his parents and cousins did not know him and he disappeared, unmourned, into the Pacific Ocean. Another young man, who was just beginning to discover and accept his strength and *Dasein,* revealed this improvement through various dreams. In one of these he was a rabbit, chased by wolves, who turned on and attacked his pursuers. In another, he climbed a ladder with weak rungs by holding the sides together.

Some dreams cannot occur until the individual has made an appropriate decision in waking life. A dream that reveals the domineering nature of an employer (or a parent) may be possible only after the dreamer has decided to quit the job in question (or to leave home). Thus dreams, like perceptions and memories, are a function of intentionality. (See May, 1958/1967b, pp. 77, 88; 1960; 1969b, p. 80; 1969c, pp. 56–57; 1972, pp. 36, 50, 133, 139; 1975, pp. 125ff; May & Caligor, 1968.)

Psychopathology

Like Erikson and Maslow, May cautions that a complete theory of personality cannot be derived solely from the study of psychopathology. Yet clinical data are invaluable because they transcend our everyday defenses, and reveal vital aspects of human nature:

> It is one thing to discuss the hypothesis of aggression as resulting from frustration, but quite another to see the tenseness of a patient, his eyes flashing in anger or hatred, his

posture clenched into paralysis, and to hear his half-stifled gasps of pain from reliving the time a score of years ago when his father whipped him because, through no fault of his own, his bicycle was stolen.... Such data are empirical in the deepest meaning of the term. (May, 1969c, p. 19.)

Psychopathology as Constricted Dasein.

The healthy individual enjoys a strong *Dasein,* and lives actively and purposefully in *Umwelt, Mitwelt,* and *Eigenwelt.* In contrast, psychopathology involves a loss of will and the subjugation of one mode of being-in-the-world to another.

For example, the sufferer may reject interpersonal relationships (*Mitwelt*) as irreconcilable with his or her own needs and values *(Eigenwelt).* Or Eigenwelt may be sacrificed to *Mitwelt,* with the individual becoming a social chameleon and constantly trying to adapt to the wishes of others. Or the sufferer may deny *Umwelt,* and an important drive like sexuality, in order to conform to parental demands. Whatever the form, such a constriction or loss of *Dasein* results in self-estrangement, apathy, and an inability to experience one's existence as real. "The fundamental neurotic process in our day is the repression of the ontological sense, the loss of [one's] sense of being" (May, 1958/1967b, p. 86; see also May, 1969b, p. 75; 1969c, pp. 111, 212–218, 244).

Causes of Psychopathology.

To May, as to Freud, psychopathology may be caused by trauma that occur early in life. For example, the child's love, trust, and will may be shattered by such pathogenic parental behaviors as overprotectiveness, overpermissiveness, domination, rejection, and hypocrisy. Yet since May's goal is to free personality theory from the shackles of psychic determinism, he prefers to stress the teleological aspects of psychopathology.

According to May, the sufferer's inability to accept ontological anxiety and guilt leads to an extremely poor choice: namely, to neutralize the dread of nonbeing by sacrificing *Dasein.* But abandoning one's true innate potentials by attempting to be what others want, by denying *Mitwelt* and living as a recluse, or by rejecting one's own biological drives is always to be on the verge of loneliness or frustration. Paradoxically, therefore, the sufferer's all-out quest for safety results in an existence so limited as to be all the more easily destroyed, and causes even greater anxiety and guilt. (Conversely, the healthy person who asserts *Dasein* and readily accepts all three modes of being-in-the-world is far less vulnerable to threats in any one of them). Thus May, like most theorists, regards psychopathology as a difference in degree rather than in kind. (See May, 1969c, pp. 16, 20–21, 25–26; Reeves, 1977, pp. 69–71, 87, 119.)

Varieties of Psychopathology.

Existential psychologists look with disfavor on the standard psychiatric nomenclature, which they regard as yet another depersonalizing abstraction. May himself is not totally opposed to the use of diagnostic terminology, so long as it does not become dogma and preclude a true understanding of the patient. He characterizes the majority of modern patients as suffering from obsessive-compulsive neurosis, and concludes that this typically represents a misguided effort to achieve some measure of personal significance.

One young man suffered through a highly pathogenic childhood that included a pampering and seductive mother, a rejecting father who would hold grudges for weeks over trivial incidents, and belittlement by his peers. To survive in this virulent emotional climate, he denied his power to choose and became totally submissive. As a result, his assertive potentials emerged in an indirect and tortuous form: a daily compulsive ritual wherein he had to lift the bedsheets exactly the proper distance before arising, put his clothes on in precisely the right order, eat breakfast in a rigid and predetermined manner, and so on, or else something terrible would happen to a member of his family. "What strikes us immediately in this complex system is the *tremendous power* it gives him. Any chance deed of his could decide whether someone lived or died" (May, 1972, p. 130; see also May, 1969a, pp. 22–23; 1969c, pp. 27, 196; 1972, pp. 126–137).

Psychotherapy

Theoretical Foundation.   The goal of existential psychotherapy is to help patients recover their repressed *Dasein,* integrate their daimonic into consciousness, recapture their lost will, take responsibility for their lives, and make choices that lead to the fulfillment of their own innate potentials. "The aim of therapy is that the patient *experience his existence as real* … which includes becoming aware of his potentialities, and becoming able to act on the basis of them" (May, 1958/1967b, p. 85; see also pp. 37, 80, 86).

Although May retains the Freudian term *patient,* he shares Kelly's belief that it is misleadingly passive; changing one's personality requires considerable effort and courage. May also agrees that the therapist must be sufficiently flexible to understand and use each patient's constructs and language, rather than seeking to impose a single theoretical framework on all humanity. "The existential analysis movement is a protest against the tendency to see the patient in forms tailored to [the therapist's] own preconceptions" (May, 1958/1967c, p. 8; see also May, 1969a, pp. 22–23; 1969c, pp. 196–197).

Therapeutic Procedures.   The existential psychotherapist strives to develop a genuine and empathic relationship with the patient, as in Rogerian psychotherapy. A variety of therapeutic procedures may be used, including face-to-face interviews and Rogerian unconditional positive regard, deducing vital information from the patient's bodily movements (as in Adlerian theory), and/or the Freudian couch and free association. Regardless of the specific methods, the therapist's primary goal is to engage the patient's will and capacity to choose. "[If] the intentionality of the patient is not reached, he … never fully commits himself, is never fully *in* the analysis" (May, 1969c, p. 248; see also May, 1958/1967b, pp. 45, 78, 84, 87; 1958/1967c, pp. 5, 27; 1969a, p. 21; 1969b, p. 76; 1969c, pp. 91, 231–232, 235, 241, 246–272).

According to May, the main purpose of free association is to reveal the patient's conscious and unconscious intentions. Other ways to raise the issue of intentionality include direct questions, such as "What do you wish from me today?" or "Why did you come today?" And any fledgling expressions of will by the patient, such as "perhaps I can try to do thus-and-so," are always focused upon by the therapist.

Resistance and Transference.   To a person who has surrendered *Dasein* and intentionality, the prospect of assuming responsibility and choosing a course in life is highly threatening. It is these fears, rather than some illicit instinct, that evoke the resistances described by Freud. However, May does accept Freud's contention that paying for one's therapy helps to overcome such difficulties. "The whole meaning of resistance and repression testifies to the anxiety and pain accompanying [the] disclosures about one's self. That is one reason why it is good that the patient pay for his sessions; if he won't take too much when he pays for it, he will take scarcely a thing given him gratis!" (May, 1969c, p. 165; see also May, 1958/1967b, p. 79).

May regards transference as one of Freud's great contributions, and agrees that patients often unconsciously displace feelings and behaviors from previous significant others (such as the parents) to the therapist. But here again, he cautions that an excessive emphasis on the past can only erode the patient's sense of responsibility. Transference involves forces from the present as well, for the typical patient is so emotionally immature as to seek a beloved and omnipotent savior, and the therapist becomes a natural target for these current wishes and feelings. (See May, 1958/1967b, pp. 83–85, 89; 1969a, pp. 16–17.)

Psychotherapy and Social Reform.   Like Fromm, May argues that our society is in many ways pathogenic. He contends that technology and technique have overwhelmed eros and passion, so that we are more concerned with functioning like well-oiled machines than with caring and loving. May is very critical of such inhuman behaviors as the Vietnam War, interracial strife, the cacophonous din and faceless hordes of the rush-hour subway, the assembly-line impersonality of giant corporations and universities, professors who write point-less books because they are more concerned with augmenting their list of publications than with pursuing exciting truths, television advertising that uses subtle lies to sell various products, and government officials who show their contempt for us by "explaining" national policy in evasions and double-talk. Finally, looming above us all is the hideous prospect of nuclear war. (See May, 1969c, pp. 31, 96, 185; 1972, pp. 29–31, 53–54, 68–71, 243.)

May does not share Fromm's inclination to propose a radical remodeling of society. How-ever, he does emphasize that we must achieve a more equitable distribution of authority and responsibility.

Literature and Art

The relatively small number of people who enter psychotherapy are, for the most part, unusually sensitive and gifted. They suffer from conflicts that the average person has managed to repress or rationalize, but that typically become major social issues in subsequent years. Literature and art also represent communications from the unconscious of a person living on the psychological frontier of society, and illuminate vital human conflicts that have not as yet gained widespread recognition.

For example, novels like Camus's *The Stranger* and Kafka's *The Castle* offer a compelling picture of a man's estrangement from the world and from those he pretends to love. Play-wrights such as Beckett, Pinter, Genêt, and Ionesco have dramatized our profound alienation and inability to communicate with one another on a truly human level. Melville's *Billy Budd* depicts the dangers of innocence, with the title character ultimately destroyed because of his blindness to the evil nature of a shipmate. Innocence is also a theme of the popular movie *The Last Picture Show,* wherein women deprived of any economic or political power resort to a guise of purity and devious sexual machinations in an effort to achieve some measure of per-sonal significance. The cruelty of the daimonic is vividly portrayed by the mutual emotional butchery of the leading characters in *Who's Afraid of Virginia Woolf.* And artists like Cézanne, Picasso, and van Gogh express our depersonalization visually, as by painting people who are literally in fragments. (See May, 1958/1967b, p. 57; 1958/1967c, pp. 16–17; 1969c, pp. 21–24, 110–111, 128, 148–149; 1972, pp. 49–50, 68, 116, 205–211, 253; 1953/1973, pp. 17–18, 58–59; 1985.)

EVALUATION

Criticisms and Controversies

Confusions and Contradictions.   All too often, May fails to define and/or interrelate his constructs with sufficient clarity. For example, *intentionality* is used in four different ways. The opposite of *apathy* is sometimes defined as love, and sometimes as care. And neurosis is variously equated with the repression of one's ontological sense, and with a conflict between two different ways of not fulfilling oneself (May, 1969c, pp. 29, 89, 247; Reeves, 1977, pp. 57–60, 63, 135–136, 209–210).

Major constructs disappear completely from one of May's books to the next, leaving considerable doubt as to those that are essential to his theory. Even a fundamental concept like *Dasein* is virtually ignored in two of his major works, *Love and Will* (1969c) and *Power and Innocence* (1972). May's discussion of the causes and dynamics of neurosis appears vague in comparison with the theories of other humanistically oriented psychologists, such as Horney and Rogers.

Lack of Originality. May has been criticized for presenting intentionality as a radically new addition to psychological thought in 1969, some 10 to 50 years after the teleologically oriented theories of Adler, Jung, and Allport. May's treatment of power and innocence bears a marked similarity to the Adlerian concepts of striving for superiority and inferiority complex. Sacrificing *Mitwelt* to *Eigenwelt* (or vice versa), and the resulting increase in anxiety, is similar to Horney's conception of moving away from (or toward) people and the resulting vicious circle (Figure 5.1).

Lack of Scientific Rigor. The existential approach to science tends to rule out quantification and statistical analysis, a viewpoint most modern psychologists would reject. May makes sweeping statements (e.g., most Americans lack mercy) without any supporting data (1972, p. 53), giving his writing a distinctly sermonic, Frommian tone.

Empirical Research

Some existential psychologists have chosen to devise objective personality measures, and there exist inventories designed to measure such constructs as meaninglessness or "existential vacuum" (Crumbaugh, 1968) and existential morale and identity (Thorne & Pishkin, 1973). Other researchers have tried to determine whether we are motivated by powerful unconscious fears of death, as the existentialists claim. Unfortunately, this area is beset by methodological difficulties. It is not easy to study unobservable, unconscious processes in the research laboratory. Furthermore, the fear of death is a complicated and multidimensional variable: It is partly conscious and partly unconscious, and the fear of nonbeing is only one of several reasons for fearing death. (Others include the fear of physical suffering, fears about the psychological and economic impact that death will have on loved ones, and being unable to achieve important goals.) Thus the results have been too equivocal for any definitive conclusions to be drawn. (See Schulz & Ewen, 1993, pp. 390–397.) In general, however, existential psychology has not generated much empirical research.

Contributions

To some psychologists, concepts such as being-in-the-world offer a useful new way of conceptualizing the human personality. The work of May and others led some clinicians to add a new category to the diagnostic list, "existential neurosis," which refers to chronic feelings of alienation and the belief that life is meaningless. May has made interesting and significant points about our repressed fear of death, and the difficulty of asserting our true values and *Dasein* in a dangerous and unpredictable world. *Love and Will* (1969c) focused on such important issues as intentionality and personal responsibility, and became a national bestseller. And May's writings represent the thoughts of a compassionate and insightful psychotherapist.

As a commentary on our time, May's books include ideas of interest and importance. But as a theory of personality, his approach appears too flawed to stand on its own as a viable entity. Given these deficiencies, and the conceptual abstruseness of the major alternative approaches (Binswanger, Boss), existential psychology seems destined to occupy a secondary position to the similarly humanistic theories discussed in the preceding chapters.

Suggested Reading

May's existentialist constructs are most comprehensively presented in four articles (1958/1967b, 1958/1967c, 1969a, 1969b), and his readable and provocative books include *Man's Search for Himself* (1953/1973), *Love and Will* (1969c), *Power and Innocence* (1972), and *The Meaning of Anxiety* (1977a). Also useful is a comprehensive, if at times difficult, analysis of May's theory by Reeves (1977).

SUMMARY

Existential psychology is a philosophy of human nature that seeks to explain such modern forms of psychopathology as apathy and depersonalization. A leading exponent of this approach is Rollo May.

   1. THE BASIC NATURE OF HUMAN BEINGS. *Being-in-the-world (Dasein):* Each of us has an inherent need to exist in the world into which we are born, and to achieve a conscious and unconscious sense of ourselves as an autonomous and distinct entity. This being-in-the-world (*Dasein*) comprises three simultaneous and interrelated modes: our physical and physiological surroundings (*Umwelt*), the social world of other people (*Mitwelt*), and the psychological world of one's self, values, and potentials (*Eigenwelt*). Asserting Dasein is a task that requires constant effort, courage, and a willingness to accept the freedom and responsibility to choose one's own course in life. *Nonbeing and Anxiety:* Death is one aspect of being-in-the-world that none of us ever escapes, and it may terminate our existence at any moment. The prospect of eventual nonbeing evokes anxiety, a certain amount of which is a normal and inevitable aspect of every personality. *Guilt:* No one ever fulfills all of his or her innate potentials, or deals perfectly with the three modes of being-in-the-world. These failures evoke guilt, a certain amount of which is also a normal and inevitable aspect of every personality. *Intentionality:* We are our choices, and our plans for the future pervade all aspects of our personality—perceptions, memories, dreams, and so forth. To May, the main symptom of modern neurosis is the loss of will and personal responsibility. *Love:* Love always involves a blending of four components, albeit in varying proportions: sex, eros, philia, and agapé. Modern neurosis typically involves the repression of eros and passion, resulting in a mechanical and unsatisfactory sexuality. *The Daimonic:* Although human destructiveness is due in large part to the powerlessness resulting from the loss of *Dasein,* we also have potentially powerful innate urges that are both benign and illicit. To achieve psychological health, we must consciously accept and attempt to control the daimonic.

   2. THE STRUCTURE OF PERSONALITY. May adopts a holistic approach to personality and rejects the use of specific structural constructs. He does accept the importance of the unconscious, however, and of repression and other Freudian defense mechanisms.

   3. THE DEVELOPMENT OF PERSONALITY. May warns that such damaging parental errors as overprotection, overpermissiveness, domination, rejection, and hypocrisy are likely to shatter the child's independence and *Dasein.* For the most part, however, he devotes little attention to personality development.

   4. FURTHER APPLICATIONS. *Dream Interpretation:* Since intentionality and *Dasein* involve unconscious as well as conscious aspects, May often turns to dreams for information about a person's being-in-the-world. Since he regards personality as a unified whole, he

rejects the idea of a dream-censoring component in favor of a more commonsense approach to dream interpretation. *Psychopathology:* Neurosis is typified by an inability to accept ontological anxiety and guilt, which causes the sufferer to try and neutralize the dread of non-being by sacrificing *Dasein.* One mode of being-in-the-world may be subjugated to another, as by rejecting interpersonal relationships in an attempt to preserve one's own needs and values (sacrificing *Mitwelt* to *Eigenwelt*). This abandonment of one's true needs and potentials results in a loss of intentionality and *Dasein,* increased anxiety, and an inability to experience one's existence as real. *Psychotherapy:* The goal of existential psychotherapy is to help patients recover their repressed *Dasein,* integrate their daimonic into consciousness, recapture their lost will, take responsibility for their own lives, and make choices that lead to the fulfillment of their own innate potentials. The therapist is procedurally eclectic, and may use various techniques (e.g., Freudian, Rogerian). *Literature and Art:* May finds many important examples of existential thought in literature and art, and refers to these sources frequently in his writings.

5. Evaluation. May has been criticized for theoretical confusions and contradictions, failing to adhere to a consistent set of constructs, an inadequate explanation of the causes and dynamics of neurosis, a lack of originality, and a lack of scientific rigor. His contributions include an emphasis on such important issues as intentionality, personal responsibility, anxiety, and our repressed fear of death, useful criticisms and insights concerning our present society, and books that have achieved widespread popularity.

STUDY QUESTIONS

Part I. Questions

1. Consider the case history discussed in the Appendix. (a) According to May, a person who has surrendered *Dasein* and intentionality is threatened by the need to choose his or her own course in life. "The central core of modern man's 'neurosis' ... [is] the sapping of his will and ability to make decisions." Does the case of this young man support May's belief? (b) If this young man was an only child, is the behavior of his parents what May would expect?

2. May's theory has been criticized as lacking in originality. Compare each of the following ideas to the related views of the theorist named in parentheses. Do these comparisons support the criticism? Why or why not? (a) Feelings of intense powerlessness may be concealed behind violent attempts to act powerful. (Adler) (b) Repression is *not* caused by one part of personality banishing material to another part, since personality is unified and holistic. The whole individual lacks courage and chooses not to experience threatening material, such as anxiety or the daimonic. (Adler) (c) Neurosis may take the form of rejecting interpersonal relationships (*Mitwelt*) in order to protect one's own needs and values (*Eigenwelt*), or sacrificing *Eigenwelt* to *Mitwelt* and trying to adapt to the wishes of others. (Horney) (d) One way to gain relief from the fear of nonbeing is through the apparent safety of social conformity. (Fromm) (e) No one else can tell a person how or what to be-in-the-world; each of us must discover our own potentials and needs. (Rogers)

3. May argues that *Eigenwelt* must be independent of the opinions and expectations of other people, because adopting external standards will eventually result in a loss of *Dasein* and greater feelings of alienation. Erikson contends that identity requires social solidarity, or validation in the eyes of significant others. Do you agree with May or Erikson? Why?

4. (a) May contends that the primary cause of anxiety is the fear of nonbeing. Horney argues that anxiety results from repressing one's real self and wishes. How might these views be interpreted as supporting each other, rather than as contradictory? (b) Horney attributes

anxiety to intrapsychic conflict, whereas May's conception of personality as a unified whole rules out the possibility of inner conflict. Which view do you prefer? Why?

5. Give an example from real life or from fiction to support May's argument that emphatically affirming our Dasein takes considerable courage.

6. A critic of existential theory argues that if we were overwhelmingly afraid of death, we would not spend so much time watching the extreme acts of violence that are common in movies and television programs. Explain two reasons why this argument is not necessarily correct.

7. Give an example to show that several people viewing exactly the same object can see it quite differently because their intentions are different.

8. May concludes that obsessive-compulsive behavior can provide the sufferer with "tremendous" feelings of power. (See the section on varieties of psychopathology.) Consider section 10 of the case material in the Appendix. What other (possibly unconscious) reasons might underlie this behavior?

9. According to May, the neurotic's attempt to reduce anxiety and feel safe by constricting *Dasein* has a paradoxical effect: It results in an existence so limited as to be all the more easily destroyed. (a) Is this true of the case history discussed in the Appendix? (b) If I become a workaholic and ignore my family in order to spend most of my time writing textbooks, how will this affect my ontological anxiety and guilt? (c) Is becoming an altruist who cares only about other people, and not about oneself, a good way to avoid the dangers of a limited existence?

10. A terrorist blows up a building in a hated foreign country. How might May explain the terrorist's behavior?

Part II. Comments and Suggestions

1. (a) I think so. See the comment to Chapter 5, question 4b, and section 5 of the case material in the Appendix. (b) Yes. The quote in the section on the development of personality accurately describes the relationship between this man and his parents.

2. (a) See the discussion of inferiority and superiority complexes in the section on psychopathology in Chapter 4. (b) See the discussion of the structure of personality in Chapter 4. (c) See the discussion of moving away from and toward people in Chapter 5. (d) See the discussion of mechanisms of escape and defense in Chapter 6. (e) See the discussion of experience and the organismic valuing process in Chapter 9. May does devote more emphasis to gaining superiority through explicit violence than does Adler; he is somewhat more specific about the parental behaviors that cause neurosis than is Horney; and he differs from Fromm by stressing our dread of nonbeing, rather than our need to escape from the frightening choices that we must make because our behavior is not preordained by innate instincts. But I don't regard these as major differences.

3. I find merit in both of these views, even though they are contradictory. I agree with May that it is highly inadvisable to base *Eigenwelt* on the opinions of other people. (See Chapter 5, question 5.) But I also think that social solidarity can support one's identity without overwhelming it. (See Chapter 8, question 5b.) What harm might befall the individual from carrying either of these views to an extreme—that is, depending heavily on social solidarity or never paying any attention to the opinions of others?

4. (a) Is death the only form of nonbeing? Is there a great difference between "nonbeing" and the loss of one's real self, or between physical destruction and psychological destruction? (b) I prefer Horney's. See section 2 of the case material in the Appendix and the comment to Chapter 5, question 1.

5. Ayn Rand's novel *Atlas Shrugged* contrasts a small group of people who love life and are willing to take considerable risks to affirm their *Dasein* (e.g., John Galt) with the large majority who are afraid to affirm their being-in-the-world and merely go through the motions of living. Her characters are rather one-dimensional and unrealistic, but her argument is a cogent one. The man whose case history is discussed in the Appendix is afraid to affirm his *Dasein*. And there have been times in my own life when I preferred to back down and not be noticed, rather than assert my beliefs and/or existence and risk physical or psychological destruction.

6. Consider the Freudian defense mechanism of reaction formation. Also consider May's argument that confronting death is what makes life meaningful, and that life in our large, technological, and impersonal society may have lost meaning for many people.

7. Three people are watching a college basketball player during an important game. A pro scout who is considering drafting this player looks to see if his skills match up well with those required in the NBA, a coed evaluates his desirability as a romantic interest, and a professor whose course he is flunking sees him as a symbol of what is wrong with the priorities in higher education.

8. Might a person sometimes express in physical actions what he or she is unable or unwilling to put into words, such as: "I am inept. I feel so ineffectual that I can't even trust an inert object like an alarm clock to stay set after I pull the lever. This is what my parents wanted, and what I must be to keep their love"? Might these repeated actions keep him too busy to focus on highly threatening feelings, such as his sadness over his inability to obtain love and affection? Might reaction formation be taking place (as if he is concealing strong feelings of depression, so much so that he might be considering never waking up again)?

9. (a) I think so. He has sacrificed his need for people (*Mitwelt*) in order to satisfy his need for safety (*Eigenwelt*), which makes him more vulnerable because he has no good interpersonal relationships to fall back on when things go wrong. (b) Both will increase. For example, a bad review will be extremely traumatic because I am unwisely placing far too much emphasis on *Eigenwelt*. (c) No. Ignoring *Eigenwelt* is also pathological.

10. Would May attribute the terrorist's behavior to an illicit instinct? How might the denial of the daimonic influence the terrorist's behavior? How might a lack of significance and feelings of powerlessness influence the terrorist's behavior? (See the quote at the end of the section on intentionality and significance.)

Comparing Humanistic Theorists and Freud on Various Issues

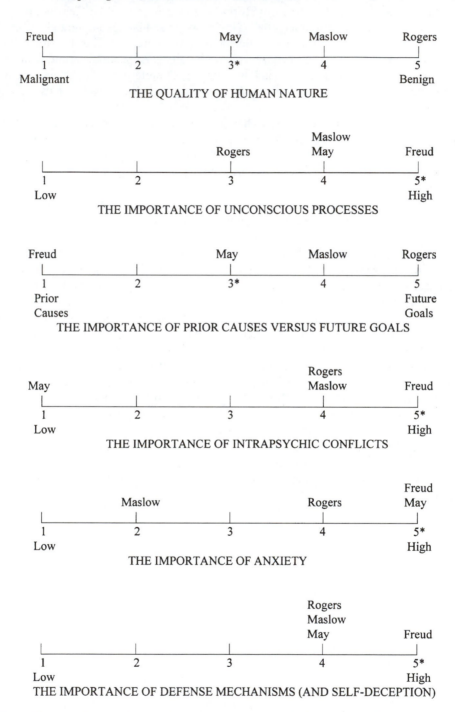

THE QUALITY OF HUMAN NATURE

THE IMPORTANCE OF UNCONSCIOUS PROCESSES

THE IMPORTANCE OF PRIOR CAUSES VERSUS FUTURE GOALS

THE IMPORTANCE OF INTRAPSYCHIC CONFLICTS

THE IMPORTANCE OF ANXIETY

THE IMPORTANCE OF DEFENSE MECHANISMS (AND SELF-DECEPTION)

Note: These scales are intended as approximations, designed to facilitate comparisons among the theorists, and not as mathematically precise measures. They reflect my opinions; others might disagree with the ratings in some instances. For those who may be interested, my position on each issue is shown by an asterisk.

THE IMPORTANCE OF EVENTS IN EARLY CHILDHOOD

THE IMPORTANCE OF SOCIAL DETERMINANTS OF PERSONALITY

PART III

The Trait Perspective

Overview

Trait theories emphasize a surface-oriented approach to personality. They describe the conscious and concrete aspects of personality in straightforward terms (e.g., "friendliness," "ambitiousness"), while deemphasizing the unconscious and abstract explanations of human behavior. They are based on empirical research, rather than on clinical observation.

Gordon W. Allport

Originated trait theory in response to what he regarded as Freud's excessive emphasis on hidden motives and meanings. Personality is an organizing force within the individual that determines characteristic patterns of behavior. These patterns of behavior take the form of traits, such as friendliness and ambitiousness, although every personality is unique and cannot be accurately described with single words. We are motivated both by the desire to reduce drives and to seek out drive increases. The unconscious and defense mechanisms are important only in unhealthy personalities. Allport draws some of the most unique and controversial conclusions in all of personality theory: infancy is not particularly important for personality development; adult motives differ in kind from childhood motives; psychopathology differs in kind from healthy behavior (rather than in degree); description is sufficient for psychology, and there is no need to probe for deeper explanations. "A man likes blue because he likes blue."

Raymond B. Cattell

Used the statistical technique of factor analysis to determine which of the thousands of traits are most important. There are sixteen major personality traits, some of which support Freudian constructs and the unconscious. Cattell's theory is based on a vast amount of research; but because of his unusual and difficult terminology, the impact of his theory has been limited.

Hans J. Eysenck

Three traits consistently emerge from his factor-analytic research as the most important: introversion—extraversion, neuroticism—stability, and psychoticism. Sought to make trait theory more explanatory by relating traits to physiological and social causes.

"Big Five" Theory   Five traits consistently emerge from factor-analytic research as the most important: introversion—extraversion (reserved vs. outgoing), neuroticism (calm and secure vs. nervous and insecure), conscientiousness (lazy and unreliable vs. hard-working and reliable), agreeableness (suspicious and uncooperative vs. trusting and helpful), and openness (conventional vs. creative).

In 1920, one year after receiving his bachelor's degree from Harvard, Gordon Allport met Sigmund Freud for the only time—an event he was later to describe as "a traumatic developmental episode." Having written for and received an appointment "with a callow forwardness characteristic of age 22," Allport was unprepared for the expectant silence with which Freud opened their meeting. Thinking to lighten the tension, he recounted an incident that had occurred on the tram car on the way to Freud's office: a 4-year-old boy had displayed a pronounced phobia toward dirt, the cause of which clearly appeared to be the dominating and "well-starched" mother sitting beside him. Freud then fixed the rather prim and proper young Allport with a kindly therapeutic stare and asked, "And was that little boy you?"

Although this question was by no means inappropriate, Allport reacted negatively. "Flabbergasted and feeling a bit guilty, I contrived to change the subject.... This experience taught me that depth psychology, for all its merits, may plunge too deep, and that psychologists would do well to give full recognition to manifest motives before probing the unconscious" (Allport, 1968, pp. 383–384).

OBJECTIVES

- *To correct what he regarded as Freud's excessive emphasis on hidden motives and meanings by devising a surface-oriented theory that focuses on the conscious and concrete aspects of personality.*
- *To base his theory on empirical research, rather than on clinical observation.*
- *To show that we are motivated by both drive reduction and the desire to seek out drive increases.*
- *To show that adult motives differ in kind (are functionally autonomous) from childhood motives.*
- *To argue that every personality is unique, and that psychology must therefore devote special attention to studying the single case.*
- *To define six values that we use as a unifying philosophy to give meaning to our lives, and to develop a questionnaire that measures these values.*
- *To describe personality in terms of consistent patterns of behavior (traits), and to reject deeper and more abstract explanations of human behavior.*
- *To deemphasize personality development because adult motives are functionally autonomous of their childhood counterparts.*
- *To show that the unconscious and defense mechanisms are important only in unhealthy personalities.*
- *To discuss the nature and causes of prejudice.*

BIOGRAPHICAL SKETCH

Gordon W. Allport was born on November 11, 1897, in Montezuma, Indiana. His father was a country doctor, his mother a schoolteacher; and his home life was "marked by plain Protestant piety and hard work." Gordon's family included three older brothers, one of whom (Floyd) also was to become an academic psychologist. Most of his childhood and adolescence was spent in Cleveland, Ohio, where the Allports moved when he was 6 years old. Gordon was somewhat of a misfit as a child, quick with words but poor at games, and a schoolmate once observed sarcastically that "that guy swallowed a dictionary." Yet he "contrived to be the 'star' for a small cluster of friends" (Allport, 1968, pp. 378–379).

Allport was an excellent and dedicated student, earning his B.A. from Harvard in 1919. During the following year he taught in Istanbul, traveled in Europe, and had his fateful meeting with Freud. He received his Ph.D. in psychology from Harvard in 1922. Except for two years of study in Europe immediately thereafter and a teaching position at Dartmouth College from 1926 to 1930, he was to spend the rest of his life at this renowned institution. Allport's personality course at Harvard is believed to be the first on this subject ever offered at an American college, and his textbook soon became a standard (*Personality: A Psychological Interpretation*, 1937, later wholly revised as *Pattern and Growth in Personality*, 1961). Gordon married Ada Gould on June 30, 1925, a union that produced one son.

Allport's publications include some dozen books, numerous articles in psychological journals, and two personality inventories. Among his honors are being named president of the American Psychological Association in 1937 and receiving its Distinguished Scientific Contribution Award in 1964. But his most prized memento was a gift from 55 of his former psychology students: two handsomely bound volumes of their scientific publications, with the dedication: "From his students—in appreciation of his respect for their individuality" (Allport, 1968, p. 407). Gordon Allport died on October 9, 1967.

THE BASIC NATURE OF HUMAN BEINGS

In contrast to the interpersonal theories of Adler and Sullivan, Allport regards personality as something within the individual. "Of course the impression we make on others, and their response to us are important factors in the development of our personalities.... [But] what about the solitary hermit ... or Robinson Crusoe before the advent of his man Friday? Do these isolates lack personality because they have no effect on others? [My] view is that such exceptional creatures have personal qualities that are no less fascinating than those of men living in human society ... [and that] we must have something inside our skins that constitutes our 'true' nature" (Allport, 1961, p. 24).

After reviewing some fifty definitions proposed by other theorists, Allport also reaches the following conclusions about personality: It is dynamic, growing and changing throughout one's life. It forms an organized pattern in the healthy person. It involves an inseparable union of mental and physical functions. It consists of complicated systems of interacting elements. And it motivates or determines everything we do:

> There is, of course, no such thing as a correct or incorrect definition. Terms can only be defined in ways that are useful for a given purpose. For [our] purposes ... *personality is the dynamic organization within the individual of those psychophysical systems that determine his characteristic behavior and thought.* (Allport, 1961, p. 28. See also Allport, 1937.)

Instinctual Drives

Everyone strives to reduce such innate drives as hunger, thirst, sex, elimination, the need for oxygen, and the need for sleep. "All human beings in all the world do have drives.... If someone is very hungry, very much in need of oxygen, water, or rest, all other motives fade away until the drive is satisfied" (Allport, 1961, p. 205).

Instinctual drives are active to some degree throughout our lives and completely dominate the motivational scene of the very young child, whom Allport regards as an "unsocialized horror"—excessively demanding, pleasure seeking, impatient, destructive, and conscienceless. Like Freud and Fromm, therefore, Allport concludes that we must learn to overcome our inherent narcissism. "Self-love, it is obvious, remains always positive and active in our natures. [My] theory holds only that it need not remain dominant" (Allport, 1955, pp. 28, 30; 1961, p. 196; see also Allport, 1961, pp. xi–xii, 84–91, 197–257).

Unlike Freud, Allport argues that we possess the positive innate potential to outgrow our self-centered beginnings. Furthermore, Allport does not consider drive reduction to be an important cause of *adult* behavior. He is the only major personality theorist who contends that the motives of children and adults differ significantly in kind, rather than merely in degree.

The Functional Autonomy of Adult Motives

According to Allport, adult motives differ from those of childhood in four significant ways.

Drive Increases.   Instincts continue to operate during adulthood, and we remain concerned with such pleasurable drive-reducing activities as eating, drinking, sleeping, and sexuality. But most adult motives are relatively independent of biological drives, differ from individual to individual, and often maintain or even increase levels of tension in order to achieve relatively distant goals.

For example, the Norwegian explorer Roald Amundsen pursued his chosen calling even though it involved severe hardships—and, ultimately, the loss of his life. Some college students avoid enjoyable activities and spend countless hours preparing for a medical career. Kamikaze pilots during World War II sacrificed their lives for their country. Examples like these lead Allport to conclude that much of adult behavior cannot be explained in terms of drive reduction, or a Freudian pleasure principle:

> [Drive reduction is] only half the problem. While we certainly learn habitual modes of reducing tension, we also come to regard many of our past satisfactions to be as worthless as yesterday's ice cream soda. Though we want stability, we also want variety, ... [and so] many things we are motivated to do merely increase our tensions, diminish our chances of pleasure, and commit us to a strenuous and risky course of life. (Allport, 1955, p. 66; 1961, p. 200. See also Allport, 1955, pp. 49, 57, 67; 1961, pp. 83, 90, 203.)

Variety and Uniqueness.   The preceding examples also indicate to Allport that adult motives vary considerably from one person to another. Therefore, it is impossible to explain personality in terms of a few universal drives. "[There is an] extraordinary diversity of adult motives, unique in each particular personality" (Allport, 1961, p. 203; see also pp. 221, 226).

For this reason, Allport argues that personality theory must concern itself with the single case. Psychological research typically deals with groups of people (samples), and attempts to unearth general principles about human behavior (the **nomothetic** approach). Allport does not wholly reject the nomothetic approach, but he prefers to study those idiosyncrasies that distinguish a particular individual from all others (the **idiographic** approach):

> Suppose you wish to select a roommate or a wife or a husband, or simply to pick out a suitable birthday gift for your mother. Your knowledge of mankind in general will not help you very much.... [Any given individual] is a unique creation of the forces of nature. There was never a person just like him, and there never will be again.... To develop a science of personality we must accept this fact. (Allport, 1961, pp. 4, 19, 21. See also Allport, 1955, pp. 19–28; 1961, pp. 11–16, 358, 1965, p. 159; 1968, pp. 81–102.)

Teleology.   Like Jung and Adler, Allport concludes that much of human behavior is not determined by prior causes. Instead, we are often guided by our **intentions**. This teleological form of motivation involves both an emotional want and a plan to satisfy it that is directed toward some future goal, such as exploring new lands or becoming a doctor. "To understand what a person is, it is necessary always to refer to what he may be in the future, for every state of the person is pointed in the direction of future possibilities" (Allport, 1955, p. 12; see also Allport, 1955, pp. 51, 76, 89, 92; 1961, pp. 85, 206, 221–225).

Functional Autonomy.   Most theorists regard childhood and adult behavior as varying expressions of the same basic motives (such as sexuality and aggression in Freudian psychoanalysis, or striving for superiority in Adlerian theory). In contrast, Allport argues that adult motives often become independent in purpose (**functionally autonomous**) of their childhood or adolescent origins.

A man who long ago earned his living as a sailor may feel a powerful urge to return to the sea, even though he has become financially independent and the original motive has disappeared. A

CAPSULE SUMMARY

Some Important Allportian Terminology

Common trait	A structural and motivational aspect of personality that initiates and guides consistent forms of behavior, such as friendliness, ambitiousness, and so forth. Common traits facilitate nomothetic comparisons among people, but are only a rough approximation as to any individual's unique personality.
Functional autonomy	The independence in purpose of adult motives from their childhood counterparts. A means to an end becoming an end in itself, and continuing to influence behavior after the original motive has disappeared.
Idiographic approach	Studying the single case in order to discover those factors that make a given individual unique.
Intention	The fusion of an emotional want and a plan to satisfy it that is directed toward some future goal.
Nomothetic approach	Studying (usually) groups of people in order to discover general principles concerning human behavior.
Personal disposition (personal trait)	Similar in definition to common trait, but unique to a given individual. A single cardinal personal disposition may influence virtually all of one's behavior. Usually, however, behavior is guided by some 5 to 10 central personal dispositions. Personality also includes numerous, less influential secondary personal dispositions.
Proprium	The unifying core of personality. Somewhat similar to "self" or "ego" but more comprehensive, including the sense of bodily self, the sense of continuing self-identity, self-esteem, self-extension, the self-image, the self as rational coper, propriate striving, and the self as knower.
Value (value orientation)	A unifying philosophy that gives meaning to one's life. Important values include theoretical, economic, esthetic, social, political, and religious.

---

college student who chose a medical career because of parental pressures may now pursue these studies because they have become interesting and enjoyable. Or a miser who learned thrift because of an impoverished childhood may come to love the feel of gold or the size of a large bank account, and remain stingy despite having accumulated great wealth. In all of these examples, what was originally a means to an end becomes a functionally autonomous end in itself. (See Allport, 1961, pp. 277, 299, 364.)

Because most adult motives are functionally autonomous (the reduction of instinctual drives being one of the few exceptions), Allport sees no need to investigate the childhood causes of behavior. "A functionally autonomous motive *is* the personality ... [and we] need not, and cannot, look 'deeper'" (Allport, 1961, pp. 244; see also pp. 238–243).

Values

To Allport, as to Jung and Fromm, we need a unifying philosophy that gives meaning to our lives and affords some answers to such tragic problems as suffering and death. (See Allport, 1961, pp. 252, 294–304, 453–457.) Basing his ideas on the work of a German philosopher, Eduard Spranger, Allport concludes that there are six important **values** (**value orientations**):

Theoretical: An intellectual desire to discover truth and organize one's knowledge, as by becoming a scientist or philosopher.

Economic: A businesslike concern with the useful and practical.

Esthetic: An emphasis on the enjoyment of form, beauty, and the artistic.

Social: A concern for and love of other people.

Political: A love of power, not necessarily related to the field of politics.

Religious: A mystical desire for unity with some higher reality.

This classification is partly nomothetic, since it applies to people in general. Yet it is also idiographic, since any system of values consists of a unique combination of the six possibilities. One person may be interested in the theoretical and esthetic, but not in the political or religious. Another individual may reflect the reverse emphasis. Or a person may care about most or even all of the six values, with one or two slightly more important than the others. There are also those who lack any values or commitments, however depressed this may make them (Allport, 1955, pp. 76–77). Allport is the first theorist discussed thus far who has devised a written questionnaire to measure such constructs as values, as we will see in a subsequent section.

Consciousness and Concreteness

Allport's approach to the unconscious is somewhat ambivalent. On the one hand, he shares the psychoanalytic belief that "most of what goes on in our personalities belongs in some way to a nonconscious stratum.... [Much motivation] is unconscious, infantile, and hidden from oneself." Yet he also concludes that the healthy individual is motivated primarily by conscious impulses and conflicts, and he attributes the Freudian emphasis on unconscious processes to an excessive concern with psychopathology. "Freud was a clinician who worked year in and year out with disordered personalities. His insights are more applicable to these cases than to personalities marked by healthy functioning ... [who] have a far more autonomous ego than [he] allows ... [and whose motivation is] largely conscious" (Allport, 1961, pp. 140, 150, 152, 155, 217; see also Allport, 1961, pp. 139–164, 221–224; Allport, cited by Evans, 1970, pp. 11–12).

In addition, Allport prefers to stress the concrete aspects of human motivation. We do not and cannot aim directly at the achievement of pleasure; we focus instead on such concrete goals as marrying a particular person, obtaining a college degree, or earning a good living. Similarly, Allport would consider a woman's love of entertaining to be her true and complete motive, rather than interpreting this behavior as the sublimation of some illicit wish or a desire for superiority or mastery. "There are surely a million kinds of competence in life which do not interest [her] at all. Her motive is highly concrete. Entertaining, not abstract competence, is the bread of life to her; and any abstract scheme misses that point completely, and therefore sheds little or no light on her personality as it actually functions" (Allport, 1961, p. 226).

Because Allport regards healthy adult motives as primarily conscious and concrete, he argues that important aspects of personality can be ascertained by direct inquiry. His counterpart to Adler's "Question" would be to ask about what the individual expects to be doing in a few years, thereby tapping conscious intentions rather than seeking to unearth unconscious motives. "If you want to know something about a person, why not first ask him?" (Allport, 1942; see also Allport, 1961, pp. 224–225.)

THE STRUCTURE OF PERSONALITY

Unlike Freud and Jung, Allport does not draw a clear distinction between the motivational and structural aspects of personality. Although the constructs to be discussed in this section are essentially structural, they also play a significant role in determining our behavior.

Common Traits and Personal Dispositions

In accordance with his belief in the concreteness of human motives, Allport describes personality in terms of straightforward **traits** like friendliness, ambitiousness, cleanliness, enthusiasm, punctuality, shyness, talkativeness, dominance, submissiveness, generosity, and so forth (with emphasis on the "and so forth," since he estimates that there are some 4,000 to 5,000 traits and 18,000 trait names!).

Definition of Traits.   Allport does not claim that a shy or talkative person acts this way on every occasion. Behavior may become atypical because of changes in the environment, pressures from other people, and internal conflicts, so that *"no trait theory can be sound unless it allows for, and accounts for, the variability of a person's conduct."* Yet traits are extremely important, since they guide the many constant aspects of one's personality:

> A trait is … a neuropsychic structure having the capacity to render many stimuli functionally equivalent, and to initiate and guide equivalent (meaningfully consistent) forms of adaptive and expressive behavior. (Allport, 1961, pp. 333, 347; see also Allport, 1960, pp. 131–135; 1961, pp. 332–375; 1968, pp. 43–66.)

A person who is guided by the trait of shyness will often behave in such consistent ways as preferring to be alone, not having much to say to other people, and not looking at people when she does talk to them. She may be more outgoing in a favorable environment, as when she is with a close friend or at her own birthday party. She may converse with a distant relative because her parents have urged her to be polite. Or she may risk talking to an attractive stranger because, at least for the moment, her shyness has been overcome by her need for love. But these are exceptions (which trait theory must be able to explain); her typical behavior will be shyness.

A trait (such as shyness) is more general than a habit (like regularly avoiding eye contact when talking to someone). Traits are often interrelated, as when friendly individuals also tend to be talkative. Allport refers to traits as "neuropsychic" because, like Freud and Sullivan, he believes that it will ultimately be possible to relate the elements of personality to specific physiological processes.

Types of Traits.   Although every personality is unique, a particular culture tends to evoke similar modes of adjustment. **Common traits** refer to "those aspects of personality in respect to which most people within a given culture can be profitably compared … [and are] indispensable whenever we undertake to study personality by scales, tests, ratings, or any other comparative method." But since common traits are nomothetic, they provide only a rough approximation of any particular personality. Many individuals are predominantly outgoing or shy, yet "there are endless varieties of dominators, leaders, aggressors, followers, yielders, and timid souls.… When we designate Tom and Ted both as aggressive, we do not mean that their aggressiveness is identical in kind. Common speech is a poor guide to psychological subtleties" (Allport, 1961, pp. 339–340, 355–356; compare also with the identical views of Adler, 1933/1964b, pp. 27, 148).

The true personality consists of **personal traits (personal dispositions)**, which determine each person's unique style of behavior (Allport, 1961, p. 373). Since personal dispositions reflect the subtle shadings that distinguish a particular individual from all others, they usually cannot be described with a single word. We might say that "little Susan has a peculiar anxious helpfulness all her own," or a young man "will do anything for you if it doesn't cost him any effort" (Allport, 1961, p. 359).

A personality can be dominated by a single *cardinal personal disposition* that influences most behavior. Examples include Scrooge's miserliness, Don Juan's seductiveness, and Machiavelli's cleverness. But most personalities contain from 5 to 10 *central personal dispositions,* as might be included in a carefully written letter of recommendation. There are also numerous, less influential *secondary personal dispositions.* A professor who leaves the departmental library in total chaos may have an office or home that is neat and orderly, because these contradictory secondary personal dispositions are governed by a more central one of selfishness. (See Allport, 1961, pp. 363, 365; Allport, cited by Evans, 1970, pp. 27–28.)

Problems in Identifying Traits.   Since personal dispositions cannot be measured physiologically, their existence must be inferred from a person's behavior. Allport concedes that this can be a difficult task.

No act is ever the result of a single trait. Writing a letter to a relative may be due in part to the traits of responsibility and friendliness, as well as to various intentions (e.g., to receive a reply) and external pressures (as from one's parents). Furthermore, apparently obvious inferences may prove to be incorrect. The giving of a gift may suggest the trait of generosity, yet actually represent a self-seeking bribe. Or a student who is late to class may be a punctual person who met with an unexpected emergency. (See Allport, 1961, pp. 334, 337, 361–364.)

A personal disposition leads to behaviors that occur frequently and intensely. For example, rejecting one invitation to a party may merely indicate a temporary mood (or a prior engagement). But a person who consistently refuses to attend parties, and who often insists on being alone, would be described as shy or aloof. However, it is not clear how frequent and intense behaviors must be before the existence of a personal disposition can safely be inferred.

The Proprium

Although the healthy adult personality is complicated by the presence of numerous dispositions, intentions, and instincts, it is organized around those matters that are most personal and important. Since terms like *self* and *ego* have been used by other theorists in a variety of ways, Allport refers to this unifying core of personality as the **proprium**. (See Allport, 1955, pp. 36–65; 1961, pp. 111–138). The proprium includes eight personal characteristics that develop at different times of life.

The Sense of Bodily Self.   The newborn infant cannot distinguish between self and others, and only gradually learns to separate internal from external events. Although Allport (like Sullivan) cautions that we do not really know what the infant experiences, he shares Freud's belief that the first aspect of selfhood to emerge is related to the body. The sense of bodily self develops from organic sensations and external frustrations, for "a child who cannot eat when he wants to, who bumps his head, soon learns the limitations of his too, too solid flesh" (Allport, 1961, p. 113). Throughout our lives, bodily movements and sensations constantly remind us that "I am I."

The Sense of Continuing Self-Identity.   Like Erikson, Allport regards a feeling of inner sameness and continuity as an important aspect of personality. "Today I remember some of my thoughts of yesterday, and tomorrow I shall remember some of my thoughts of both yesterday and today; and I am certain that they are the thoughts of the same person—of myself." The sense of self-identity beings in early infancy, aided by having and hearing a name of one's own (Allport, 1961, pp. 114–117).

Self-Esteem (Ego-Enhancement).   The need to express autonomy becomes important at about age 2 years (as in Erikson's theory), and the child's successes and failures strongly affect his or her self-esteem. "[The] child wants to push his stroller, wants to control his world, wants to make things *do* things.... Within a few minutes, the curious two-year-old can wreck the house.... [But] when the exploratory bent is [too severely] frustrated, the child feels it [as] a blow to his self-esteem" (Allport, 1961, p. 118).

Self-Extension (Ego-Extension).   At about age 4 to 6 years, the sense of self gradually extends to important external objects. This developing concept of "mine" includes the child's parents, siblings, and toys, and it establishes the foundation for such important later self-extensions as the love of one's country, religion, and career.

The Self-Image.   The capacity for self-evaluation also originates at about age 4 to 6. As in Sullivanian theory, the self-image includes a sense of "good-me" and "bad-me" that develops in response to parental rewards and punishments. Ideally, this aspect of the proprium serves as an accurate guide to one's strengths and weaknesses. But it may become a grossly exaggerated idealized image that establishes unrealistic and unattainable standards, as in Horney's theory (Allport, 1955, p. 47).

The Self as Rational Coper (and Sometime User of Defense Mechanisms). Like the Freudian ego, the proprium must relate inner needs to outer reality. Starting at about age 6 years, the proprium forms rational plans for coping with instinctual drives, environmental demands, and the prohibitions of one's conscience.

Even a healthy adult will sometimes choose to evade such difficulties rather than face them, behavior "brilliantly" explained by the various Freudian defense mechanisms. A mother who unconsciously hates her offspring may be consciously solicitous and overly protest her love (reaction formation). A child who resents the birth of a sibling may keep repeating "no baby, no baby" (denial of reality). Or people given an uncomplimentary evaluation may argue that their critics don't really know them (rationalization). However, a personality dominated by defense mechanisms is abnormal. "Ego-defense mechanisms are present in all personalities. [But] when they have the upper hand we are dealing with a badly disordered life." The healthy individual usually confronts reality, and is able to achieve satisfying solutions rather than having to settle for sublimations (Allport, 1961, p. 164; 1968, p. 72; see also Allport, 1955, pp. 23, 46; 1961, pp. 155–163, 224).

Propriate Striving.   One particularly important function of the proprium is to form the intentions and goals that give purpose to one's life. This distinctively human characteristic first begins to develop in adolescence. "Mature [propriate] striving is linked to long-range goals ... [which] are, strictly speaking, unattainable.... The devoted parent never loses concern for his child ... [and the scientist] creates more and more questions, never fewer. Indeed, [one] measure of our intellectual maturity ... is our capacity to feel less and less satisfied with our answers to better and better problems" (Allport, 1955, pp. 29, 67).

The Self as Knower.   The proprium also observes its other seven functions and the conscious aspects of personality. Thus we know that it is ourselves who have bodily sensations, self-identity, self-extension, and so forth.

Allport cautions that there is no sharp dividing line between the proprium and the rest of personality, nor is the proprium an entity or "little man" in the psyche ("homunculus") that manipulates whatever we do. "If we ask why this hospital patient is depressed, it is not helpful to say that 'the self has a wrong self-image.' To say that the self does this or that, wants this or that, [or] wills this or that, is to beg a series of difficult questions" (Allport, 1961, pp. 129–130; see also Allport, 1955, pp. 36–38, 54–56, 61).

Conscience

Allport shares Freud's belief that a moral sense is not innate, and that the child introjects parental standards of right and wrong. But Allport argues that the adult conscience differs in kind from that of childhood. That is, the child's fearful sense of what "must" and "must not" be done eventually develops into a more mature "ought" and "ought not" that is based on one's own standards. "Conscience in maturity is rarely tied to the fear of punishment, whether external or self-administered. It is rather a feeling of obligation … [the obligation] to continue one's chosen lines of propriate striving" (Allport, 1961, p. 136; see also Allport, 1955, pp. 68–74; 1961, pp. 134–137).

THE DEVELOPMENT OF PERSONALITY

Since Allport regards most adult motives as functionally autonomous of their childhood and adolescent origins, he sees little need to study personality development. Allport even concludes that "in a sense the first year is the least important year for personality, assuming that serious injuries to health do not occur" (1961, p. 78; see also Allport, 1961, p. 238; Allport, cited by Evans, 1970, p. 79).

To Allport, as to Horney, the unsocialized infant becomes a socially adjusted adult primarily because of innate healthy potentials. Unless the parents behave in highly pathogenic ways, such as erratic and inconsistent rewards and punishments, anxiety-provoking threats of castration, or failing to provide the needed security and love, personality development is free to pursue a course of positive growth. (See Allport, 1955, pp. 26–35; 1961, pp. 102, 122–126, 288).

Criteria of Maturity

Allport (1960, pp. 155–168; 1961, pp. 275–307) has formulated criteria of mental health that are more extensive than Freud's "love and work." Mature adults possess a *unifying philosophy* or set of values that gives purpose to their lives. They apply propriate *self-extension* to such meaningful areas as their spouse, family, work, friends, hobbies, and political party. The healthy personality is also characterized by a capacity for *compassionate and loving relationships* that are free of crippling possessiveness and jealousy. Compassion also involves an appreciation of the considerable difficulties in living faced by all human beings:

> No one knows for sure the meaning of life; everyone … sails to an unknown destination. All lives are pressed between two oblivions. No wonder the poet cries, "Praise the Lord for every globule of human compassion" … [In] contrast, the immature person feels [that] … he and his kind matter, no one else. His church, his family, and his nation make a safe unit, but all else is alien, dangerous, [and] to be excluded from his petty formula for survival. (Allport, 1961, pp. 285–286.)

Other criteria of maturity include *emotional security and self-acceptance*, or the ability to endure the inevitable frustrations of life without surrendering to childish rages or self-pity.

Mature adults have a *realistic orientation* toward themselves and others, and can meet the difficult task of economic survival without fear or defensiveness. And they have developed *accurate self-insight* regarding their desirable and disagreeable qualities. Like Freud and Jung, Allport cautions that true self-insight is deceptively difficult to achieve. "Since we think about ourselves so much of the time, it is comforting to assume … that we really know the score.… [But] this is not an easy assignment. [As] Santayana wrote, 'Nothing requires a rarer intellectual heroism than willingness to see one's equation written out'" (Allport, 1961, pp. 290–291).

The Style of Life

Because Allport regards every personality as unique, he rejects the use of typologies in favor of Adler's concept of the style of life. He argues that there are so many respects by which a person could be categorized, (e.g., liberal, narcissistic, introverted, authoritarian, anal, and so forth) that any individual would have to be located in hundreds of types, and that typologies cannot reflect the unique pattering of any specific personality. "Typologies are convenient and seductive, but none has ever been invented to account for the total individual.… [Instead,] Adler's position … is essentially the same as the one [I advocate]" (Allport, 1955, p. 55; 1961, p. 17; see also Allport, 1955, pp. 39, 81–82; 1961, pp. 16–18, 349–353; Allport, cited by Evans, 1970, pp. 7–9, 52–53).

FURTHER APPLICATIONS OF
ALLPORTIAN THEORY

Psychopathology, Psychotherapy, Social Reform

Unlike most theorists, Allport posits a difference in kind between mental health and psychopathology. The healthy individual usually confronts the various difficulties of life, and is guided by motives that are primarily conscious and functionally autonomous. But the neurotic or psychotic, whose innate predisposition for normal development has been blocked by pathogenic childhood influences, escapes important problems through self-deceiving defense mechanisms and is dominated by unconscious motives that are not functionally autonomous of their childhood origins. This childishness and lack of self-insight makes it impossible for the sufferer to achieve the balanced give and take required for meaningful interpersonal relationships. (See Allport, 1961, pp. 150–152.)

Not himself a practicing clinician, Allport finds some merit in various kinds of psychotherapy. However, he warns that delving into a patient's childhood can only resolve those self-defeating behaviors that have not become functionally autonomous. Whatever the form, the goal of psychotherapy should be to help the patient grow toward the six criteria of maturity (Allport, 1961, pp. 239–240, 304–305; Allport, cited by Evans, 1970, pp. 34–36).

Like Fromm and Sullivan, Allport has taken some interest in social reform and international relations. He argues that even an infant discipline like psychology can and should offer properly cautious opinions concerning important world issues, notably that of facilitating peace. He also concludes that psychology and sociology are far more difficult sciences than physics and chemistry, and merit considerably greater governmental research support. "It required years of labor and billions of dollars to gain the secret of the atom. It will take a still greater investment to gain the secrets of man's irrational nature" (Allport, 1954/1958, p. xi; see also Allport, 1960, pp. 169–180, 327–362; Allport, cited by Evans, 1970, pp. 105–111).

Religion

According to Allport, religion becomes important during the third decade of life and fortifies us against anxiety and despair. He is therefore critical of personality theories that devote little attention to this area, although he cautions that a science such as psychology can neither prove nor disprove religious concepts.

Allport's view of religion is by no means entirely positive. He concludes that some 2,000 years of religion have not had much success in improving human morality. He also argues that using religion as the means to an end, such as making business contacts or becoming socially prominent, is undesirable and is related to such abuses as prejudice. Allport has therefore devised a questionnaire to distinguish between the extrinsic uses of religion and sincere, intrinsic religious belief. Those who take a more extrinsic approach to religion are likely to endorse such statements as "One reason for being a church member is that such membership helps to establish a person in the community" and "The church is most important as a place to formulate good social relationships." Those whose beliefs are more intrinsic tend to agree with statements like "Quite often I have been keenly aware of the presence of God or the Divine Being" and "It is important to me to spend periods of time in private religious thought and meditation."

As always, Allport's approach is one of direct inquiry. He is not concerned with the possibility that an individual who feels guilty about being extrinsic might claim to be intrinsic, or that people who are embarrassed about feeling religious in a scientific society might hide their intrinsic beliefs from themselves and claim that they are extrinsic. (See Allport, 1950; 1955, pp. 72–73, 93–98; 1961, pp. 299–303; 1968, pp. 55–59, 218–268; Allport, cited by Evans, 1970, pp. 67–74, 106.)

The Nature of Prejudice

Allport has taken a keen interest in the psychology of *prejudice*, which he defines as an irrational hostility toward other people solely because of their presumed membership in a particular group. Because prejudice involves erroneous negative views about people or groups, "a wit defined [it] as 'being down on something you're not up on'" (Allport, 1954/1958, p. 8). Unlike most factual errors, prejudice is rigid and unyielding: A prejudiced individual who believes that members of a minority group have various undesirable characteristics will not be swayed by evidence to the contrary.

Allport regards prejudice as a complicated phenomenon with multiple causes. As an illustration, consider prejudice against Blacks in America. Such prejudice is due partly to the lingering effects of slavery, and the failure of reconstruction in the South following the Civil War (historical factors). Sociocultural factors also play a part, as when Blacks are underrepresented in higher level jobs. Prejudice is more readily learned in areas where it is widely practiced and observed (situational factors). Some people who suffer major disappointments, such as losing a job, look for a scapegoat to blame (psychodynamic factors). And dark skin (a physical factor) may evoke irrational fears and hostility. (See Allport, 1954/1958, pp. 28–67, 184–212, 271–322, 327; 1960, pp. 219–267; 1968; pp. 187–268.)

Prejudice may be taught by parents who indicate (covertly or overtly) that groups to which the family belongs are superior and desirable, whereas other groups are inferior and hateful. Or prejudice may result from pressures to conform to national norms, as in Nazi Germany. Interestingly, those who are prejudiced against one minority are very often prejudiced against most others.

Like Adler, Allport regards prejudice as a cause of psychopathology. The effects of prejudice include the increased use of defense mechanisms, such as denial of reality and a hatred for other people that may be a projection of intense self-hate. Prejudice may also lead to severe intergroup conflicts, or even to war. Thus, like Fromm and Sullivan, Allport concludes that we must pursue the difficult course of striving to reduce prejudice by developing a primary allegiance to humanity as a whole. "It seems today that the clash between the idea of race and of One World … is shaping into an issue that may well be the most decisive in human history. The important question is, Can a loyalty to mankind be fashioned before interracial warfare breaks out? Theoretically it can" (Allport, 1954/1958, pp. 42–43).

Personality Measurement

A Study of Values. Allport and his associates have devised and validated two personality inventories, the A-S Reaction Study of ascendance–submission (Allport & Allport, 1928/1949) and the better-known A Study of Values (Allport, Vernon, & Lindzey, 1931/1960; see also Allport, 1961, pp. 453–457; 1968; pp. 51–54). The latter instrument measures the extent to which an individual prefers the six values (theoretical, economic, esthetic, social, political, religious), as follows: In part 1 the respondent scores pairs of statements 3–0 or 2–1, depending on the degree to which one is favored over the other. In part 2, four choices must be ranked from 4 (most preferred) through 1. (See Figure 12.1.)

If you give a high score to one alternative (which represents one of the six values), you must give lower scores to other values. So if you obtain a high total score on (say) the religious value, this means only that religion is more important to you than some of the other values. It does *not* reveal *how much* you like religion. All of the values may be very important to you, with religion the top priority in your life. Or you may not care much for religion, but like the other values even less. A Study of Values indicates only the *relative* importance of the six values. The use of such self-oriented or "ipsative" scales remains a matter of some controversy, although Allport's questionnaire is generally regarded as a viable instrument. (See, for example, Anastasi, 1976, pp. 539–540, 552–554.)

Allport regards *A Study of Values* primarily as an aid to self-insight. If you understand your personal hierarchy of values, you are more likely to select the right job or spouse.

Letters From Jenny. Allport (1965) has conducted a purely idiographic study into the writings of one neurotic elderly woman, Jenny Masterson (a pseudonym), using some 301 letters she wrote to a young married couple over a 12-year period (1926–1937, from age 58 to 70). After suggesting how her personality might be viewed by Freudians, Jungians, Adlerians, ego psychologists, and existential psychologists, Allport characterizes her in terms of eight central personal dispositions: paranoid suspiciousness, self-centeredness, independence, dramatic intensity, artistic appreciation, aggressiveness, cynical morbidity, and sentimentality. Although it proved impossible to delve deeply into Jenny's motives, Allport concludes that this procedure shows how quantitative psychological research can be conducted with the single case.

Other Research. Like Adler, Allport has taken considerable interest in overt expressive behavior (or "body language"). He concludes that important inferences about an individual's personality can be drawn from gestures, facial expressions, vocal intonation, and posture (including one's bodily position while asleep). Even handwriting analysis predicts certain information at better than a chance level, although it is not nearly as flawless as some

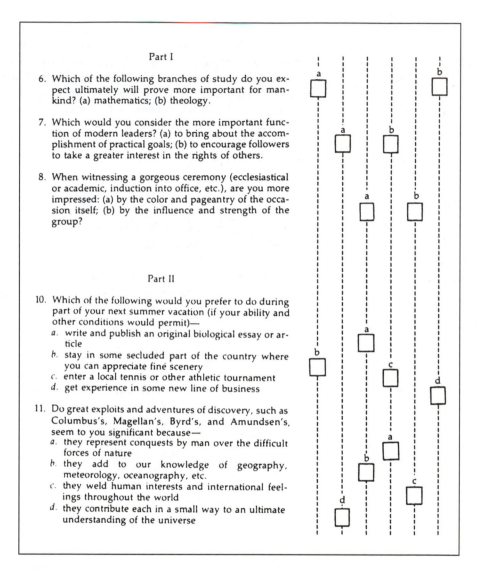

Part I

6. Which of the following branches of study do you expect ultimately will prove more important for mankind? (a) mathematics; (b) theology.

7. Which would you consider the more important function of modern leaders? (a) to bring about the accomplishment of practical goals; (b) to encourage followers
to take a greater interest in the rights of others.

8. When witnessing a gorgeous ceremony (ecclesiastical
or academic, induction into office, etc.), are you more
impressed: (a) by the color and pageantry of the occasion itself; (b) by the influence and strength of the
group?

Part II

10. Which of the following would you prefer to do during
part of your next summer vacation (if your ability and
other conditions would permit)—
a. write and publish an original biological essay or article
b. stay in some secluded part of the country where
you can appreciate fine scenery
c. enter a local tennis or other athletic tournament
d. get experience in some new line of business

11. Do great exploits and adventures of discovery, such as
Columbus's, Magellan's, Byrd's, and Amundsen's,
seem to you significant because—
a. they represent conquests by man over the difficult
forces of nature
b. they add to our knowledge of geography,
meteorology, oceanography, etc.
c. they weld human interests and international feelings throughout the world
d. they contribute each in a small way to an ultimate
understanding of the universe

FIG. 12.1. Sample items from "A Study of Values."

overenthusiastic graphologists would suggest and is best studied in combination with the
other types of expressive behavior (Allport, 1961, pp. 460–494; Allport, cited by Evans,
1970, pp. 111–112; Allport & Vernon, 1933). Allport has also investigated the psychology of
rumor and the psychology of radio (Allport, 1960, pp. 311–326; Allport & Postman, 1947;
Cantril & Allport, 1935).

Insofar as the general philosophy of research is concerned, Allport concludes that psychological journals contain all too many studies that are elegantly designed but have little bearing
on truly important problems. He also warns research psychologists against an excessive commitment to any one method or theory. "Narrow systems, dogmatically held, tend to trivialize the
mentality of the investigator.... No single brand of modern psychology is wholly adequate to the
problem of man's individuality and growth.... [especially those] based largely upon the behavior of sick and anxious people or upon the antics of captive and desperate rats" (Allport, 1955,
pp. 5, 17–18; see also Allport, cited by Evans, 1970, pp. 86–97).

EVALUATION

Criticisms and Controversies

Iconoclasms and Oversimplifications. Some of Allport's conclusions set him apart from virtually all other personality theorists. He denies the importance of the first few years of life to a degree that most modern psychologists would regard as excessive. His contention that all forms of psychopathology differ in kind from healthy behavior, rather than in degree, is also highly unusual and extremely questionable. The same is true of one of the cornerstones of Allport's theory, functional autonomy. He argues that adult motives differ radically in kind from those of childhood, yet his supporting anecdotal evidence does not rule out alternative explanations. For example, Amundsen might have been driven to become famous by an overly severe superego that resulted from the introjection of harsh parental standards. The retired sailor may have gone to sea as a way of mastering the environment and sublimating illicit instincts, as well as to earn a living, and these motives may still influence his behavior. Or the miser may continue to hoard his wealth because he developed an anal personality during his childhood.

In comparison to the meticulously detailed psychoanalytic theories, the explanatory power of trait theory appears at best somewhat incomplete when it leads to such statements as: A man likes blue because he likes blue (Allport, cited by Evans, 1970, p. 37). Therefore, Allport's emphasis on the conscious, concrete, and present aspects of personality has been criticized as a serious oversimplification.

Science and the Idiographic Approach. Valuable information can be obtained by studying the single case, but investigating millions of individuals is an impossible task. Psychologists must be able to rely on at least some general principles, which permit information gleaned from patients or research subjects to be generalized to wider groups of people. Despite Allport's protestations that psychology not only must but can become more idiographic, his emphasis on the uniqueness of every human personality seems to imply that psychology can never become a true science. In fact, most of Allport's own research was primarily nomothetic.

Circularity. Trait theory depends too heavily on circular reasoning, where the existence of a trait is inferred from certain behavior and then used to explain that behavior. If we deduce that John is aggressive because he hit Mary, we cannot then turn the same definition around and say that John did so *because* he is aggressive. Such circular reasoning would explain nothing at all about the causes of aggressiveness. (How do we know that John is aggressive? Because he hit Mary. Why did he hit Mary? Because he is aggressive.)

A theory that attributes aggressiveness to unconscious intrapsychic conflicts may be right or wrong, but at least it tries to explain the causes of this behavior. Traits explain nothing. They do not tell us why we do what we do; they only describe our behavior by giving it a name (aggressiveness, shyness). Yet it is all too easy to overlook the problem of circularity, and to conclude that traits actually explain the phenomena that they describe.

The Person–Situation Controversy. The extent to which human behavior depends on where we are, and whom we are with, poses considerable difficulties for trait theory. Some critics contend that our behavior is not consistent enough to be described in terms of traits. They argue that we behave differently in different situations, and that trait theory cannot explain these common exceptions. Even Allport himself indicated a similar concern (1968, p. 63; see also Mischel, 1973; 1984; 1990.)

For example, a shy young woman may be more outgoing at her own birthday party. A student may be conscientious about keeping social appointments, but not about doing homework. A parent may be agreeable when his child is submissive, but become irritated when the child acts assertively. In one early study, researchers studied the honesty of more than 8,000 elementary school children (Hartshorne & May, 1928). They found that a child who was honest in one situation (such as not cheating on a test) was not necessarily honest in other situations (such as telling the truth about breaking the parent's favorite piece of pottery).

Furthermore, human behavior is often conditional. A young woman may be agreeable only when she is trying to get someone to do her a favor. Or a man may be submissive with his boss but not with his wife, and even the extent of his submissiveness with his boss may vary with changes in the boss's behavior or whether other people are present. Traits do not deal with such conditional relationships; they only describe how agreeable or submissive a person is in general.

One possible way to improve the predictive power of traits is by identifying whether or not a trait is a central personal disposition. If so, such behavior is more likely to occur in different situations. Another possibility is to obtain information about both traits and situations. For example, a shy person may be most likely to behave this way when she is with a large group of people who are all strangers. Nevertheless, the consistency of traits across different situations remains a controversial issue.

Focusing Only on the Surface of Personality.

Some critics agree that traits provide useful information, but argue that they represent only one aspect of personality. To truly understand human behavior, we must consider other levels as well:

> [Traits represent] a very important level of personality, partly because it is at this level that the most impressive evidence for personality consistency can be garnered.... Things do not change too much at the level of such general traits as extraversion [and] conscientiousness, especially in the adult years.... [But traits] cannot justify a life. They cannot tell a person who he or she is. They cannot provide a life with unity, purpose, direction, and coherence.... One does not need to be a psychoanalyst or depth psychologist of any sort to endorse the view that the human personality should be understood in terms of multiple, identifiable levels. (McAdams, 1994, pp. 299–300, 307; see also McAdams, 1992.)

Misunderstanding Freud's Pleasure Principle.

Henry Murray, a personality theorist and colleague of Allport's who prefers to emphasize the importance of the unconscious, argues that the pleasure principle applies far more widely to human behavior than Allport believes. Even apparently distasteful activity is guided by the pleasure principle, a position that Allport fails to understand because he does not look deeply enough:

> Most people do a great many things every day that they do not enjoy doing. "I don't do this for pleasure," a man will affirm, thinking that he has refuted the principle of hedonism. But in such cases, I believe ... that the man is determined (consciously or unconsciously) by thoughts of something unpleasant (pain, criticism, blame, self-depreciation) that might occur if he does not do what he is doing. He goes to the dentist to avoid future pain or disfigurement, he answers his mail in order not to lose social

status, and so forth. If it is not the thought of expected unpleasantness that prompts him, it is the thought of expected pleasure, possibly in the very distant future. Visions of heaven after death, for example, have often encouraged men to endure great suffering on earth. (Murray et al., 1938, p. 92.)

Empirical Research

Trait theory has stimulated a vast amount of empirical research. Numerous research studies have dealt with such traits as introversion–extraversion and shyness (see Chapter 3), locus of control (the extent to which you believe that your rewards and punishments depend primarily on your own behavior, as opposed to mere chance and the actions of other people; see Chapter 16), cautiousness, rigidity, and many others. These studies seek to relate a particular trait to other important aspects of behavior, and have led to such findings as: Extraverts tend to be more satisfied with life in general than introverts. People who believe that they control their rewards and punishments tend to be higher in mental and physical health. Those who are shy expect to be rejected because they lack social skills, and try to avoid this unpleasant fate by talking less and agreeing more with other people.

Although these studies have yielded useful information, they are not designed to evaluate Allport's theory. Therefore, a review of this voluminous literature is beyond the scope of the present text.

Other researchers have adopted a different approach. They assume that a few fundamental traits underlie every human personality, and that these core traits can be identified by using a complicated mathematical procedure known as factor analysis. These findings will be discussed in the following chapter.

Contributions

Allport's most important contribution is his construct of traits, which has proved to be of major importance and has stimulated a great deal of research. We can all relate to traits like shyness and aggressiveness, which seem refreshingly clear in comparison to such arcane issues as the Oedipus complex and the collective unconscious, and even critics of trait theory concede that it has valuable aspects (as we have seen).

Allport's inclusion of drive-increasing and teleological motives has helped to correct Freud's excessive emphasis on drive reduction and causality. Those who take a more positive approach to religion prefer Allport's approach to Freud's profound cynicism. Allport sought empirical support for his ideas through research and statistical analyses, and "A Study of Values" is a respected personality inventory. His work on prejudice has furthered our understanding of this important area. Before Allport, there were no college courses devoted specifically to personality; and his 1937 textbook is credited as the one that first made this area an integral part of academic psychology, by showing that personality is amenable to scientific conceptualization and investigation (Pettigrew, 1990). Allport was also a gifted teacher, and his respect for each student's individuality and unique professional interests inspired many of them to become successful psychologists.

Gordon Allport's theory of personality does not seem sufficient to stand as a viable alternative to those discussed in preceding chapters, and few current psychologists would characterize themselves as pure Allportians. Nevertheless, his ideas have been credited as exerting a considerable influence on the development of modern psychological thought.

Suggested Reading

The most comprehensive presentation of Allport's views is his textbook, *Pattern and Growth in Personality* (1961). A brief introduction to his theory is provided in *Becoming: Basic Considerations for a Psychology of Personality* (1955).

SUMMARY

1. THE BASIC NATURE OF HUMAN BEINGS. *Instinctual Drives:* Everyone strives to reduce such innate drives as hunger and thirst. Instincts dominate the child's motivation. *The Functional Autonomy of Adult Motives:* Allport differs from virtually all personality theorists by concluding that the motives of children and adults differ in kind, rather than merely in degree. The healthy adult is influenced primarily by motives that are independent in purpose (functionally autonomous) from their childhood counterparts. Adult motives are relatively independent of instincts, are often teleological, and may involve seeking out drive increases in order to reach one's goals. Adult motives are also unique to each individual, hence Allport recommends a more idiographic approach to the study of personality. *Values:* We need a unifying philosophy that gives meaning to our lives, and Allport posits six such value orientations. *Consciousness and Concreteness:* We cannot aim directly at achieving pleasure. We must focus instead on concrete goals, such as obtaining a particular job or spouse. If a woman loves to entertain, this is her true and complete motive, rather than some underlying need for superiority.

2. THE STRUCTURE OF PERSONALITY. *Common Traits and Personal Dispositions:* Allport does not clearly distinguish between motivational and structural constructs. Traits initiate and guide consistent forms of behavior. Common traits refer to those aspects of personality on which people can be meaningfully compared, but provide only a rough approximation as to any individual's personality. Personal dispositions (personal traits) reflect an individual's true and unique personality, and determine that person's behavior. A personality can be dominated by a single cardinal personal disposition; but most personalities contain from 5 to 10 central personal dispositions that strongly influence behavior, and numerous less influential secondary personal dispositions. It is not easy to identify traits, since they cannot be measured physiologically and must be inferred from a person's behavior. *The Proprium:* The proprium is the unifying core of personality, which organizes the various dispositions (traits), instincts, and intentions. The proprium includes eight characteristics that develop at different times. *Conscience:* Whereas the child's conscience is based on the fear of punishment, the adult conscience is based on feelings of personal obligation.

3. THE DEVELOPMENT OF PERSONALITY. Since Allport regards most adult motives as functionally autonomous of their childhood origins, he sees little need to study personality development. He even concludes that the first year of life is the least important for personality development. *Criteria of Maturity:* Allport posits six criteria of mental health or maturity. *The Style of Life:* Allport prefers the Adlerian construct of the style of life to the use of character typologies.

4. FURTHER APPLICATIONS. *Psychopathology, Psychotherapy, and Social Reform:* Allport differs from most personality theorists by regarding psychopathology as different in kind from healthy behavior, rather than in degree. Not himself a practicing psychotherapist, he finds some merit in various forms of psychotherapy. Allport cautions that we must develop an allegiance to humanity as a whole in order to survive such threats as nuclear war. *Religion:* Allport concludes that religion can fortify us against anxiety and despair. But he warns that using religion as the means to an end, rather than having a sincere interest in religion, is undesirable and is related to such abuses as prejudice. *The Nature of Prejudice:* Allport takes a keen interest in the psychology of prejudice, which he regards as a complicated phenomenon with multiple causes. *Personality Measurement:* Allport has devised a personality inventory to measure an individual's preference for the six value orientations. He has also conducted a purely idiographic study of personality and many primarily nomothetic studies.

5. EVALUATION. Allport's theory has been criticized for a lack of explanatory power, circular reasoning, not being able to explain why we behave differently in different situations, focusing only on the surface of personality, denying the importance of early childhood, the idiosyncratic and questionable concept of functional autonomy, advocating an idiographic approach that seems unscientific, overemphasizing the conscious and concrete aspects of personality, and misunderstanding Freud's pleasure principle. His contributions include the highly popular construct of traits, showing that motivation involves both drive reduction and drive increases, seeking support for his ideas through empirical research, enabling personality to become an integral part of academic psychology by writing the first textbook in this area, and an important work on prejudice.

STUDY QUESTIONS

Part I. Questions

1. (a) Why might Allport's reaction to Freud's question during their meeting in 1920 ("And was that little boy you?") be regarded as excessive? What might this imply about Allport's personality? About his theory? (b) Allport regards the very young child as an "unsocialized horror." What might this imply about his personality? About his theory?

2. An explorer spends months in frozen wastelands, which involves severe hardships. A Kamikaze pilot sacrifices his life during World War II. Allport argues that these behaviors cannot be explained by a Freudian pleasure principle, since they are painful and unpleasant. How might Freud defend the pleasure principle in each case?

3. A man who long ago earned his living as a sailor yearns to return to the sea, even though he is now financially independent. Allport regards this as an example of the functional autonomy of adult motives. How might Freud or Erikson reply?

4. (a) Allport stresses the conscious and concrete aspects of personality, whereas Freud prefers to probe deeply into the unconscious. Which approach do you prefer? Why? (b) Traits have proved much more popular among psychological researchers during the past few decades than psychoanalytic constructs. How can this be explained?

5. Suppose that you took Allport's personality inventory, "A Study of Values." How would the results depict you with regard to the six values?

6. Allport argues that the healthy adult shows compassion for the considerable difficulties in living faced by all human beings, and he is highly critical of the person who feels that "he and his kind matter, no one else. His church, his family, and his nation make a safe unit, but all else is alien, dangerous, [and] to be excluded from his petty formula for survival." Do you agree or disagree? Why?

7. Consider this statement by Allport: "Since we think about ourselves so much of the time, it is comforting to assume … that we really know the score.… [But] this is not an easy assignment. [As] Santayana wrote, 'Nothing requires a rarer intellectual heroism than willingness to see one's equation written out.'" Do you agree or disagree? Why?

8. (a) Consider the criticism of circularity regarding Allport's theory, and his statement that "a man likes blue because he likes blue." What does this imply about the ability of

Allport's theory to *explain* human behavior? (b) Why might the idiographic approach favored by Allport imply that psychology can never become a true science?

9. What traits are illustrated by the case material in the Appendix?

10. A terrorist blows up a building in a hated foreign country. How might Allport explain the terrorist's behavior?

Part II: Comments and Suggestions

1. (a) Why didn't Allport reply calmly (and perhaps with a friendly smile), "No, it was a boy I saw on the tram car on the way to your office"? What does defensive behavior suggest about that individual's personality? How might these personality characteristics have influenced Allport to devise a theory that stresses the conscious and concrete aspects of personality? (b) Although young children can behave in highly unsocialized ways (and provoke considerable parental irritation), it would never occur to me to describe my daughter in this way. What might Allport's statement imply concerning his feelings about children in general? How might these feelings have influenced him to devise a theory of personality that rejects the importance of events in infancy and early childhood?

2. The explorer may anticipate the pleasure of making great discoveries and achieving world fame. Even if Kamikaze pilots did not believe that their actions would be rewarded in a hereafter, they knew that cowardice would have highly unpleasant consequences.

3. Consider that behavior is often overdetermined, and other motives might also have caused him to seek the sea as a youth.

4. (a) I prefer Freud's. I am convinced (from my own experience, and from Chapters 2–8) that we often hide important but unpleasant truths about ourselves from ourselves. I also believe that abstract constructs like "striving for superiority" help us to better understand such diverse behaviors as a woman who wants to be the world's best entertainer, a person who seeks to become president of the United States, and a pathological individual who enjoys denigrating other people. However, I agree with those who argue that both of these approaches can provide useful information about personality. (b) Which is easier for researchers to investigate: constructs that are primarily unconscious (such as the id, ego, and superego), or conscious traits that can be measured by asking direct questions? What problems arise if psychological researchers conduct too many studies dealing with conscious processes and too few dealing with unconscious processes?

5. Remember that "A Study of Values" indicates only the relative standings of each of the six values, and not how much you like each one. What job or career is consistent with your system of values? Would you prefer a spouse who had similar or different values?

6. I agree, but I suspect that many people do not. Consider such all too common behaviors as war, religious and ethnic prejudice, and fans of one football team who insult and abuse fans of the opposing team. Are there societal influences that make it more difficult for us to develop compassion for humanity by strengthening our ties to specific groups?

7. See Chapter 3, question 7.

8. (a) What is the difference between describing behavior and explaining that behavior? What is the best way to prevent reasoning from becoming circular? (Hint: If a theorist concludes that extraverts seek external stimulation because they have low levels of cortical brain arousal that need to be increased, whereas introverts avoid crowds and noise because they have high levels of cortical arousal that will become painful if increased, why is this reasoning *not* circular?) (b) Why does psychological research rely on such techniques as drawing samples from populations and using inferential statistics?

9. Keep in mind that common traits, such as "shyness" and "seclusiveness," provide only a rough description of one's personality. Try to use more descriptive personal dispositions that

may take one or two sentences, such as: "seeks out relatively impersonal contacts with a very small number of trusted friends, but is highly anxious with strangers and avoids large groups."

10. He can't. (At least not by using trait theory.) Traits such as "hostile" and "vengeful" describe behavior, but do not explain it. (See the discussion of circular reasoning in the evaluation section.) Allport does argue that the effects of prejudice include the increased use of defense mechanisms, and that hating people who belong to a different group or country may be an unconscious projection of intense self-hate. (See the section on prejudice.) Does this suggest that he might use Freudian constructs to explain the terrorist's behavior? (Recall that Allport's primary objection to Freudian theory is that it doesn't apply well to healthy behavior.)

CHAPTER 13

RAYMOND B. CATTELL AND OTHERS
Factor-Analytic Trait Theory

Even the most dedicated trait theorist would undoubtedly agree that Allport's list of 4,000 to 5,000 traits is unmanageable. It would seem reasonable to conclude that human nature cannot be this diverse, and that there must be a much smaller number of traits that energize and guide most of our behavior.

Raymond B. Cattell argues that psychology must become far more objective and mathematical if it is to be a mature science, and he bases his extensive research into the dimensions of personality on a complicated statistical technique known as **factor analysis**. The results do point toward a smaller number of fundamental human traits. But Allport might well be disconcerted to learn that some of Cattell's findings lead in the direction of Freudian theory and depth psychology.

OBJECTIVES

Cattell's Objectives

- *To determine which of the thousands of traits are most important by using the statistical technique of factor analysis, which he regards as the only way to identify the basic components of personality.*
- *To make psychology more scientific by making it more mathematical.*
- *To obtain information about personality by conducting a vast amount of empirical research.*
- *To derive mathematical equations that can be used to predict human behavior from trait scores, and to quantify the amount of intrapsychic conflict that an individual experiences.*
- *To identify which traits are more influenced by heredity.*
- *To define psychopathology operationally, by obtaining trait scores of neurotic and psychotic individuals and comparing them to trait scores of more healthy people.*

Eysenck's Objectives

- *To determine which of the thousands of traits are most important by using the statistical technique of factor analysis.*
- *To make trait theory more explanatory by relating traits to physiological and social causes.*
- *To devise a theory that is superior to Freudian psychoanalysis, which he regards as unscientific and ineffective.*

Objectives of "Big Five" Theory

- *To determine which of the thousands of traits are most important by using the statistical technique of factor analysis.*
- *To show that these traits represent the core of personality by relating them to important issues, such as their stability across the adult life span.*

BIOGRAPHICAL SKETCH

Raymond Bernard Cattell was born in Hilltop, a village on the outskirts of Birmingham, England, on March 20, 1905. He was the second of three sons, and his father was a mechanical engineer who helped develop innovations for World War I military equipment and the new internal combustion engine. Cattell's family moved to Torquay, a resort town in the south of England, when he was 6 years old. Cattell was an excellent student who won a scholarship to the University of London, and he earned his bachelor of science degree with first-class honors in chemistry from Kings College in 1924. (See Horn, 2001.) But his interests soon shifted to more social concerns, and he shocked his friends and advisers by switching to psychology (then a field of rather dubious repute) upon graduating in 1924. "My laboratory bench began to seem small, and the world's problems vast. I concluded that to get beyond human irrationalities, I had to study the workings of the mind itself" (Cattell, 1974, p. 64).

Cattell earned his Ph.D. from the University of London in 1929, with his graduate studies directed by the inventor of factor analysis, Charles Spearman. Cattell was married three times: to Monica Campbell, an artist, from 1930 to 1938; to Alberta Schuettler, a mathematician with whom he published several articles and tests, from 1946 to 1980; and to Heather Birkett, a clinical psychologist. Cattell had one son from the first marriage, and three daughters and a son from the second.

Cattell worked at various fringe jobs in psychology until 1937, including one in England's first child guidance clinic, when he came to the United States to accept a position at Columbia University. Shortly thereafter he moved on to Clark University in Massachusetts, and then to Harvard. He ultimately accepted a research professorship at the University of Illinois in 1945. There he founded and directed the Laboratory of Personality Assessment, and remained for 27 years. When university policy mandated his retirement in 1973, Cattell moved to Colorado, where he supervised the construction of a house shaped like a sailboat in the mountains overlooking Denver. In 1978, he left the high altitude of Colorado for health reasons and relocated to Hawaii, where he taught at the University of Hawaii. (See Horn, 2001.)

Cattell was one of the most prolific of all personality theorists, and his writings include some 56 books and hundreds of journal articles. Cattell's honors include the Wenner–Gren Prize from the New York Academy of Sciences and the American Psychological Foundation Gold Medal Award for Life Achievement in Psychological Science. Raymond Cattell died in his home in Honolulu, Hawaii, on February 2, 1998.

THE GENERAL LOGIC OF FACTOR ANALYSIS

A rough idea as to the conceptual difficulties presented by Cattell's theory may be gleaned from the following simplified example, which illustrates the general logic of one kind of factor analysis.

Illustrative Example

Step 1: The Correlation Matrix. Suppose that we wish to determine the dimensions that underlie human intellectual ability, which is somewhat easier than investigating the more abstract aspects of personality. We obtain a sample of 100 sixth-grade students and administer six tests: vocabulary, spelling, verbal analogies, addition, subtraction, and multiplication. The first step in this factor analysis is to compute the correlation coefficient[1] between each pair of variables. Let us assume that the results (listed for convenience in matrix form) are:

	Voc.	*Sp.*	*V.A.*	*Add.*	*Sub.*	*Mult.*
Vocabulary	—	.52	.46	.16	.18	.12
Spelling		—	.44	.15	.11	.13
Verbal Analogies			—	.10	.19	.15
Addition				—	.62	.57
Subtraction					—	.59
Multiplication						—

---

[1]For an introduction to the correlation coefficient and related statistics, see Welkowitz, Ewen, and Cohen (2000), Chapter 12.

Thus the correlation between vocabulary and spelling is .52, that between vocabulary and verbal analogies is .46, and so on. (The correlation between spelling and vocabulary is of course also .52, since the same two variables are involved. So there is no need to list the values to the left of the diagonal, as these would merely duplicate the corresponding ones on the right.)

Step 2: Factor Analysis.   The correlation matrix in this simplified example is small enough to be analyzed by inspection. The typical research study includes many variables, however, and hundreds of correlation coefficients. Some method is needed to bring order out of chaos and make the data more comprehensible, and this is accomplished by subjecting the correlation matrix to the process of factor analysis. There are various ways to do so, and some thorny statistical issues to contend with (as we will see). But for now, let us suppose that the results are as follows:

Variable (Test)	Factor 1	Factor 2
Vocabulary	.14	.67
Spelling	.16	.58
Verbal Analogies	.11	.61
Addition	.73	.12
Subtraction	.68	.09
Multiplication	.61	.15

Each of the numerical "factor loadings" shown above represents the correlation of one test with one **factor**, a hypothetical construct that is designed to simplify our understanding of the area being studied. Addition, subtraction, and multiplication all correlate highly with one another, but not with the other three variables; so they all have high loadings on Factor 1, whereas the loadings of the remaining variables on this factor are much lower. Vocabulary, spelling, and verbal analogies form a cluster that defines Factor 2. Thus there are two factors underlying these six tests, and it does not require great perspicacity to identify them as "mathematical ability" and "verbal ability," respectively. In this example, we have simplified our understanding of human intellectual functioning by explaining six variables (tests) in terms of only two dimensions (factors).

It is also possible to factor analyze the results of a factor analysis and determine the underlying, "second-order" factors. If this were done in our example, we might find that "general intelligence" is a second-order factor fundamental to both mathematical ability and verbal ability. Or correlation coefficients might be computed between pairs of participants or occasions (Cattell, 1952b).

Methodological Controversies

Factor analysis would seem to add a much-needed quantitative aspect to the study of personality. Appearances are often deceiving, however, and this technique is more controversial and less objective than its mathematical nature might imply.

Input Problems.   The results of any factor analysis depend on the variables that a researcher chooses to include in the correlation matrix. Our example could not have yielded a factor of spatial relations, even though this is widely regarded as one component of intellectual ability, because no such tests were administered to the students. If only the addition, subtraction, and multiplication tests had been used, no verbal factor would have emerged. Factor analysis is nothing more than a mathematical device for clarifying the dimensions that underlie a particular correlation matrix, and a researcher who omits important variables (or includes the wrong variables) will emerge with a limited and misleading set of factors.

Mathematical Issues.   There is more than one way to factor analyze a correlation matrix, and it is often unclear how many factors to extract in any given study. (The maximum possible number of factors is equal to the total number of variables, a highly undesirable outcome that would produce no simplification at all.) Even when appropriate variables are included in the correlation matrix, factor analysis will not necessarily yield the one best set of underlying dimensions. When Overall (1964) factor analyzed data based on the sizes of various books, he did not obtain the expected three factors of length, width, and height. Instead, the results indicated that books vary in terms of "general size" (a composite of the three physical dimensions), "obesity" (thickness relative to page size), and "departure from squareness."

Factor Naming.   Although it was easy to identify the two factors in our illustrative example, matters would have been considerably more complicated if one factor had consisted of spelling and multiplication. Such ambiguity is far from unusual in personality research, and factor naming can be a subjective and controversial issue.

For these reasons, the results of any factor-analytic study must be viewed with caution. The mathematical nature of this method does *not* mean that it is free from bias, or that it automatically yields the "truth" about the human personality.

THE BASIC NATURE OF HUMAN BEINGS

To Cattell (1946, p. 566; 1950, p. 2), personality enables us to predict what a person will do in a given situation. Cattell shares Allport's preference for describing these relatively stable and predictable characteristics in terms of **traits**, but his approach differs in four significant respects. He concludes that the basic elements of personality (**source traits**) can be identified only by using factor analysis. He regards only some traits as unique, with many genuine common traits shared to varying degrees by different individuals. He is more favorably disposed toward psychoanalytic theory. And he distinguishes more clearly between the motivational and structural aspects of personality.

Dynamic Traits

Ergs, Sentiments, and Attitudes.   Human behavior is energized and directed toward specific goals by **dynamic traits**. Some of these motivational traits are inborn, whereas others are learned through contact with the environment.

Since the term *instinct* has been used in various ways by prior theorists, Cattell refers to our hereditary motives as **ergs** (after the Greek word *ergon* for work or energy). Learned dynamic traits include general patterns of behavior (**sentiments**) and specific tendencies and actions (**attitudes**), the ultimate goal of these being to reduce ergic tensions.

Cattell's list of innate traits is considerably longer than Freud's sexuality and aggressiveness. His extensive factor analyses of attitudes (the basic unit of motivation) have identified ten well-substantiated and six more tentative human ergs, which are part of every personality but vary in strength from one person to the next:

Well-Substantiated Ergs		More Tentative Ergs
Food	Security	Appeal
Mating	Self-assertion	Rest
Gregariousness	Narcissistic sex	Constructiveness
Parental protectiveness	Pugnacity	Self-abasement
Exploration	Acquisitiveness	Disgust
		Laughter

For example, the security erg is characterized by such attitudes as "I want my country to have a stronger system of national defense" and "I want to see the danger of death by accident and disease reduced." Each attitude is subsidiary to one or more sentiments:

Attitude (Learned)	Possible Sentiments (Learned)	Erg (Innate)
Want stronger system of national defense	Patriotism and love of country Preference for one political party	Security
Want danger of death reduced	Favor funding medical research Support Mothers Against Drunk Driving	Security

Similarly, attitudes of "I want to fall in love with a beautiful woman," "I want to satisfy my sexual needs," "I like sexual attractiveness in a woman," "I like to enjoy smoking and drinking," and "I want to listen to music" denote the sex erg.[2] Each of these attitudes is also subsidiary to one or more sentiments, such as faithfulness to one's spouse.

Sentiments are also identified by factor analyzing sets of attitudes. For example, the religious sentiment is defined by attitudes like "I want to feel that I am in touch with God, or some principle in the universe that gives meaning and help in my struggles" and "I want to see the standards of organized religion maintained or increased throughout our lives." The sentiment for sports and games is characterized by such attitudes as "I like to watch and talk about athletic events" and "I like to take an active part in sports and athletics." Other important sentiments include one's profession, home, spouse, country, school, pets, and interests (including scientific, economic, theoretical, philosophical, mechanical, outdoor, and travel).

Like ergs, sentiments vary in strength among different individuals. But sentiments are neither innate nor permanent, so it is quite possible to change them. We cannot abandon the mating and narcissistic sex ergs, since they are inborn and permanent; but we can seek more ergic satisfaction by divorcing our spouse and marrying someone else. Or we may try to increase our ergic satisfaction by changing professions, switching to a different church or synagogue, moving to a new home, transferring from one school to another, or abandoning a former interest that has become boring and trying a new avocation.

---

[2]Cattell regards the last two attitudes as sexual on psychoanalytic grounds: smoking and drinking are forms of orality, while listening to music is a sublimation. A psychologist hostile to Freud's ideas might instead view these two items as asexual, consider their inclusion on this factor as indicative of some imperfection in the analysis, and object to Cattell's interpretation as an overly imaginative effort to identify the factor in a way consistent with his theory.

Subsidation Chains and the Dynamic Lattice. Cattell refers to the relationship between an attitude, sentiment, and erg as a **subsidation chain**, a term borrowed from Henry Murray. The aforementioned relationship between the national defense attitude, patriotism sentiment, and security erg may be depicted like this:

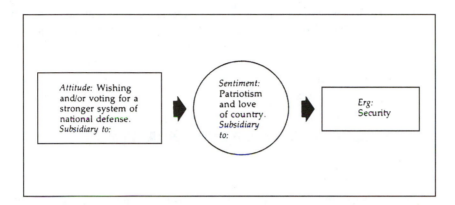

Each individual's motivational structure (**dynamic lattice**) consists of an involved criss-cross of many such subsidation chains, some of which may "go underground" at some point and involve aspects that are unconscious. In Figure 13.1, for example, taxes are disliked (attitude)

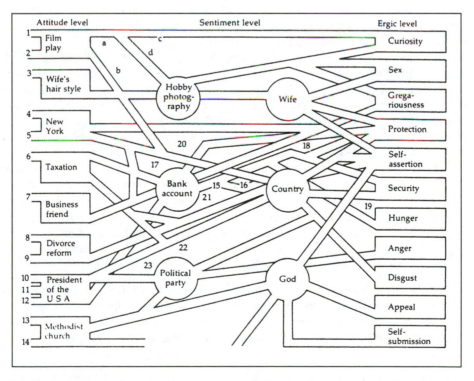

FIG. 13.1. A portion of one individual's dynamic lattice, illustrating subsidation chains and their component attitudes, sentiments, and ergs (Cattell, 1965; Cattell & Child, 1975, p. 24; Cattell & Kline, 1976, p. 177).

because they make it difficult to maintain a suitably large bank account (sentiment) and satisfy the ergs of hunger and security, but they are also somewhat desirable since they strengthen the sentiment for country and the security that it provides. Thus Cattell shares Freud's view of human motivation as highly complicated, and behavior as frequently overdetermined.

How Attitudes Are Measured.   Attitudes must be measured before they can be subjected to factor analysis. Cattell (1973, p. 3) uses three methods: self-reports and questionnaires, where participants are asked to describe themselves (**Q data**); written and other tests (**T data**); and examining life records, such as academic report cards and employer's ratings (**L data**). Although the results obtained from these methods are often consistent, different methods do at times lead to different sets of factors (as we will see).

THE STRUCTURE OF PERSONALITY

Temperament and Ability Traits

Whereas dynamic traits determine *why* we do what we do, **temperament traits** and **ability traits** are concerned with the style and success of our actions—*how* we do what we do, and *how well*. Cattell has subjected Allport's list of some 4,000 to 5,000 traits to factor analysis and identified a far smaller number of structural source traits, which he defines with his own particular brand of neologisms. These are shown in the accompanying Capsule Summary, where the traits are listed in descending order of importance; Factor B is an ability trait, whereas the others are temperament traits. Each factor or trait is continuous, so an individual's score may fall anywhere from low through average to high. "Q" factors appear only in factor analyses of Q data, whereas the others are derived from both L and Q data.

Cattell has devised a written personality inventory to measure these source traits (the **Sixteen Personality Factor Questionnaire**, or **16 P.F.**), and has administered it to members of various work and diagnostic groups. To help clarify the meaning of each factor, some of these results are included in the following discussion.[3] (See Cattell, 1973; Cattell & Child, 1975; Cattell, Eber, & Tatsuoka, 1970; Cattell & Kline, 1976.)

Factor A: Affectia–Sizia.   The most important factor among the temperament and ability traits is related to Jungian extraversion–introversion. Affectics are outgoing, warmhearted, and easygoing. They enjoy dealing with people, as in the case of salespersons, social workers, successful psychotherapists, Shakespeare's Falstaff, and F. D. Roosevelt.[4] Sizics are reserved, detached, critical, and aloof. They are more comfortable with the world of ideas, as with scientists, writers, artists, musicians, creative people in general, and Calvin Coolidge. Attempted suicides, criminals, and paranoids tend to be sizic, whereas affectia is high in sociopaths. (See, for example, Cattell, 1965; 1973; Cattell & Kline, 1976.)

Factor B: Intelligence.   An ability trait, intelligence is related to the capacity for abstract thinking, sound judgment, and perseverance. Its position as the second-largest structural factor attests to its importance, and accords well with the substantial attention that psychologists have devoted to this human characteristic. (See also Cattell, 1971.)

---

[3]These are not meant to imply that (say) every scientist is aloof, but rather that scientists as a group tend to be more aloof than the average. Undoubtedly, there are exceptions in all of the professional and clinical categories.

[4]In addition to those groups indicated by his research findings, Cattell includes well-known historical and fictitious personages as further illustrations of the structural traits.

Factor C: Ego Strength.   This (temperament) trait concerns the ability to control one's impulses, remain calm, and deal realistically with one's problems. As posited by Freudian theory, low ego strength is characteristic of virtually all forms of psychopathology. It is also common among accountants, clerks, artists, professors, and Shakespeare's Hamlet. High ego strength is more typical of airline pilots, administrators, nurses, and George Washington.

Factor E: Dominance–Submissiveness.   Dominant people are assertive, aggressive, competitive, and stubborn, whereas submissive individuals are humble, docile, and accommodating. Dominance is more common among males, competitive athletes, engineers, psychologists (notably Freud), and writers. Submissiveness is exemplified by females, priests, farmers, clerks, Gandhi, and Buddha. Sociopaths are high in dominance, whereas neurotics and most psychotics are submissive.

Factor F: Surgency–Desurgency.   Although this trait bears some similarity to Factor A, Cattell regards it as a different form of behavior. Surgency is denoted by a happy-go-lucky, enthusiastic, and impulsive manner, including an ability to forget punishment easily. Desurgency is reflected by a sober, taciturn, and serious demeanor. Surgency is common among athletes, military personnel, airline pilots, and delinquents. Desurgency is more typical of accountants, administrators, artists, professors, writers, neurotics, and alcoholics.

Factor G: Superego Strength.   This trait resembles Freud's construct of the superego, and is low in criminals and sociopaths. Among those high in superego strength are airline pilots, priests, musicians, and Abraham Lincoln.

Factor H: Parmia–Threctia.   Parmia, or venturesome boldness, is typified by brash salespersons, competitive athletes, musicians, and practicing psychologists. It is also very high in sociopaths. The converse, shy timidity (threctia), is characteristic of priests, farmers, obsessive-compulsive neurotics, and attempted suicides.

Factor I: Premsia–Harria.   This factor was posited some 100 years ago by William James. Premsia, which stands for "protected emotional sensitivity," refers to tenderminded-ness and dependency. It is high in artists, professors, administrators, social workers, neurotics, attempted suicides, criminals, and Eleanor Roosevelt. Harria, or "hard realism," involves tough-mindedness and self-reliance. It is typical of physical scientists, airline pilots, police officers, and Napoleon.

Factor L: Protension–Alaxia.   Protension resembles the Freudian concept of projected anger and introverted, paranoid suspiciousness. It is common among artists, criminals, homosexuals, attempted suicides, and Charles de Gaulle. The converse, a trusting and accepting approach to other people (alaxia), is more characteristic of accountants, administrators, airline pilots, musicians, and Dwight D. Eisenhower.

Factor M: Autia–Praxernia.   Autia (derived from "autistic") involves disdain for the external world, absent-mindedness, unconventional behavior, and imaginativeness. It is exemplified by bohemians, artists, drug addicts, criminals, homosexuals, Lewis Carroll, and Picasso. In contrast, praxernia (derived from "practical concern") reflects a practical, down-to-earth approach to life. It is common among police officers, airline pilots, and those with psychosomatic illnesses.

CAPSULE SUMMARY
The Structure of Personality (Cattell)

Factor	Characteristics of Individual With Low Score on Factor	Characteristics of Individual With High Score on Factor
A	*Sizia:* Reserved, detached, critical, aloof	*Affectia:* Outgoing, warmhearted, easygoing
B	*Low Intelligence:* Dull	*High Intelligence:* Bright
C	*Low Ego Strength:* Emotionally unstable, easily upset	*High Ego Strength:* Emotionally stable, calm, realistic
E	*Submissiveness:* Humble, docile, accommodating	*Dominance:* Assertive, competitive, stubborn
F	*Desurgency:* Sober, taciturn, serious	*Surgency:* Happy-go-lucky, enthusiastic
G	*Weak Superego:* Expedient, disregards rules	*Strong Superego:* Conscientious, moralistic
H	*Threctia:* Shy, timid	*Parmia:* Venturesome, bold
I	*Harria:* Tough-minded, self-reliant	*Premsia:* Tender-minded, sensitive, clinging
L	*Alaxia:* Trusting, accepting	*Protension:* Suspicious, projects anger
M	*Praxernia:* Practical, down-to-earth	*Autia:* Imaginative, absent-minded
N	*Artlessness:* Forthright and genuine, but socially clumsy	*Shrewdness:* Astute, socially aware
O	*Untroubled Adequacy:* Secure, self-assured, serene	*Guilt Proneness:* Apprehensive, self-reproaching
Q_1	*Conservatism of Temperament:* Conservative, traditional	*Radicalism:* Experimenting, liberal, free-thinking
Q_2	*Group Adherence:* Joins and obeys a group	*Self-Sufficiency:* Resourceful, self-reliant
Q_3	*Low Self-Sentiment Integration:* Lax, impulsive	*High Strength of Self-Sentiment:* Controlled, compulsive
Q_4	*Low Ergic Tension:* Relaxed, tranquil, composed	*High Ergic Tension:* Tense, frustrated, driven

Factor N: Shrewdness–Artlessness.   Shrewdness, astuteness, and social awareness are more often found among business executives, psychologists, salespersons, and such worldly individuals as Casanova. Behavior that is forthright and genuine, but socially clumsy is common among artists, priests, manic depressives, and Joan of Arc.

Factor O: Guilt Proneness–Untroubled Adequacy.   Self-reproach, apprehensiveness and guilt are common in most instances of psychopathology, and among religious leaders (Christ, Buddha), artists, farmers, and Winston Churchill. A secure, self-assured sense of untroubled adequacy is characteristic of competitive athletes, administrators, physicists, psychologists, and ruthless leaders like Stalin.

Factor Q_1: Radicalism–Conservatism.   This is the first of four factors that appear only in analyses of Q data. Radical, free-thinking behavior is typical of artists, writers, professors, Karl Marx, George Bernard Shaw, Leonardo DaVinci, and Napoleon. Conservative, traditional behavior is more common among athletes, priests, farmers, police officers, obsessive-compulsive neurotics, Winston Churchill, and most popes.

Factor Q₂: Self-Sufficiency–Group Adherence. Self-reliant, resourceful behavior is exemplified by research scientists, creative writers, professors, and artists. Football players, nuns, social workers, domestic help, and those with psychosomatic illnesses tend to join and obey the standards of some group.

Factor Q₃: Self–Sentiment Strength. The self-sentiment is concerned primarily with integrating personality and maintaining a sense of identity. Self-sentiment strength is typically high among university administrators, airline pilots, scientists, and paranoids. Low self-sentiment strength, reflected by laxity and impulsiveness, is common among artists, priests, delinquents, neurotics, and attempted suicides.

Factor Q₄: Ergic Tension. This trait bears some relationship to the concept of undischarged instinctual (id) energy in Freudian theory, but has not been found by Cattell to be related to any clinical disorders. Those high in ergic tension are tense, frustrated, and driven; whereas people low in ergic tension are relaxed, tranquil, and composed. Ergic tension tends to be high among farmers, writers, Shakespeare's Macbeth, neurotics, homosexuals, and alcoholics. Low ergic tension is more common among airline pilots, physical scientists, and social workers.

Other Temperament Traits. Cattell (1973) also reports seven more recently discovered and less well-defined temperament traits. These include "insecure excitability" (Factor D), which is high in school dropouts but low in neurotics; introverted reflectiveness (as with Hamlet) versus zestful and extraverted sociality ("coasthenia"–"zeppia," Factor J); polite behavior ("mature socialization") versus "boorishness" (Factor K); and casual self-assurance and a lack of ambition ("sanguine casualness," Factor P). In addition, Cattell has identified 21 primarily different structural traits that emerge from analyses of T data (Cattell & Kline, 1976). It would seem that even his extensive research has not yet arrived at the final word concerning the structure of personality.

The Specification Equation

Having defined personality in terms of traits, Cattell proceeds to predict human behavior by means of **specification equations**:

$$P_j = b_1T_1 + b_2T_2 + \cdots + b_NT_N$$

where P_j is the performance j, the response predicted in a given situation; $T_1, T_2, \ldots, T_N$ are the traits of the individual for whom the prediction is being made (including dynamic, temperament, and/or ability traits); and $b_1, b_2, \ldots, b_N$ are the weights determined by factor analysis, reflecting the relevance of each trait to the predicted response.

For example, suppose that a young man considers asking out a sexually attractive woman who is rather uncongenial and disliked by his parents. Assuming for simplicity that the only traits involved in this behavior are the narcissistic sex erg (T_1), the gregariousness erg (T_2), and the parental sentiment (T_3), the specification equation for predicting whether or not he will do so (P_1) might prove to be

$$P_1 = 0.5T_1 - 0.4T_2 - 0.1T_3$$

The negative signs preceding the weights for T_2 and T_3 indicate that parental disapproval and the woman's lack of congeniality count against asking her out, whereas the positive weight for T_1 shows that the sex erg operates in favor of this decision. The largest weight is b_1, so the sex

CAPSULE SUMMARY
Some Important Cattellian Terminology

Ability trait	A trait that determines how well one succeeds in reaching a particular goal.
Attitude	An overt or covert interest in pursuing a specific course of action. A learned dynamic trait that represents the basic unit of motivation, and is subsidiary to the sentiments and ergs.
Common trait	A trait shared to varying degrees by different individuals.
Dynamic lattice	An individual's complete motivational structure, composed of a complicated network of interrelated subsidation chains and their component attitudes, sentiments, and ergs.
Dynamic trait	A trait that energizes behavior and directs it toward a particular goal; includes innate ergs, and learned sentiments and attitudes.
Erg	An innate dynamic source trait; similar to "instinct," but defined by factor analysis. There are some 16 ergs, which differ in strength from one person to the next.
Factor (dimension)	A hypothetical construct designed to simplify our understanding of a larger set of variables, persons, or occasions.
Factor analysis	A mathematical technique for explaining a set of variables, persons, or occasions in terms of a smaller number of factors.
L data	Personality data obtained by examining life records, such as academic report cards or employer's ratings.
Q data	Personality data obtained through self-reports or questionnaires wherein participants describe themselves.
Sentiment	A learned dynamic source trait that is more general than an attitude, and is subsidiary to one or more ergs.
Sixteen Personality Factor Questionnaire (16 P.F.)	A measure of 15 temperament source traits, and one ability source trait (intelligence).
Source trait	A basic element of personality, identifiable only through factor analysis. The converse of surface trait.
Specification equation	A weighted sum of an individual's traits, used to predict what that person will do in a given situation.
Subsidation chain	The relationship between an attitude, a sentiment, and the erg they are intended to satisfy. The basic unit of a dynamic lattice.
Surface trait	A manifest personality characteristic resulting from the combination of two or more source traits; *not* a basic element of personality, no matter how fundamental it may appear.
T data	Personality data obtained through written or other tests.
Temperament trait	A trait that determines the style with which one strives to reach a particular goal.
Traits	Psychological structures that are relatively stable and predictable, and characterize an individual's personality. Traits vary in function (dynamic traits, temperament traits, ability traits), origin (innate traits, learned traits), centrality (source traits, surface traits), and uniqueness (common traits, unique traits).
Unique trait	A trait characteristic of a particular individual, but not others.

erg (T_1) is the most important factor in this decision. If this trait is a powerful one, the young man is likely to pursue a date with this woman; but if it is relatively weak, and the gregariousness erg and parental sentiment are quite strong, he will seek romantic gratification elsewhere. Measures of the strength of each trait are obtained from appropriate personality inventories and inserted into the specification equation, yielding a single numerical estimate as to the strength of response P_1.

Suppose that the young man's trait scores are 80 on T_1 (strong sex erg), 10 on T_2 (weak gregariousness erg), and 20 on T_3 (weak parental sentiment). We then have

$$P_1 = (0.5)(80) - (0.4)(10) - (0.1)(20)$$
$$= 40 - 4 - 2$$
$$= 34$$

If instead the young man obtained trait scores of 40 on T_1 (moderate sex erg), 10 on T_2 (weak gregariousness erg), and 80 on T_3 (strong parental sentiment), we would have

$$P_1 = (0.5)(40) - (0.4)(10) - (0.1)(80)$$
$$= 20 - 4 - 8$$
$$= 8$$

As the higher total score indicates, the young man is more likely to ask the woman out if his personality is characterized by the pattern of trait scores in the first example.

Measures of Conflict.   The procedure described above also permits Cattell to quantify the degree of intrapsychic conflict experienced over this decision. One (simplified) method for doing so is the Conflict Index:

$$\text{Conflict Index} = \sqrt{\frac{\text{Sum of squared negative } b \text{ weights}}{\text{Sum of squared positive } b \text{ weights}}}$$

$$= \sqrt{\frac{(-0.4)^2 + (-0.1)^2}{+0.5^2}}$$

$$= 0.8$$

The nearness of this ratio to 1.0 indicates a high degree of internal conflict, with the positive and negative influences on this decision being fairly equal. If instead the ratio were close to zero or infinity, the decision would be relatively clear-cut, and there would be little or no conflict. Thus Cattell claims not only to predict human behavior with mathematical precision, but to measure quantitatively the strength of inner conflicts described so vaguely and prescientifically by Freud, Horney, and others. (See, for example, Cattell & Child, 1975, pp. 88–89, 235, 247; Cattell & Kline, 1976, pp. 160, 194.)

THE DEVELOPMENT OF PERSONALITY

In contrast to some personality theorists, who draw their conclusions about childhood solely from the retrospections of adult patients or subjects, Cattell has factor analyzed large quantities of data obtained from children and adolescents. Measuring the same trait(s) at different age levels is not an easy task, since the surface behaviors may be considerably different. But Cattell has devised various statistical techniques to resolve such problems, and he has drawn a variety of conclusions regarding the development of personality.

Influences on Personality Development

Heredity Versus Environment.   Cattell has attempted to measure the extent to which the structural source traits are determined by heredity, as opposed to learning and the environment. These *heritability* studies involve analyses of data obtained from pairs of twins and siblings, some reared in the same home and others brought up in different homes due to adoption. If identical twins reared apart are very similar on a particular trait, this would suggest a strong hereditary influence for that trait. (See, for example, Cattell, 1960; 1973, pp. 144–148; 1982.)

Not surprisingly, Cattell finds intelligence to be the structural trait most influenced by heredity. Such aspects of personality as a happy-go-lucky nature (surgency), introverted reflectiveness (coasthenia, one of the more recently discovered factors), outgoingness (affectia), tendermindedness (premsia), and suspiciousness (protension) are determined to a moderate extent by heredity. Lowest in heritability, and most due to environmental influences, are radicalism–conservatism and ergic tension. This is a highly controversial area, however, and it is by no means generally accepted that Cattell's statistical procedures are sufficient to resolve the age-old issue of heredity versus environment.

Learning.   Although some traits are more heritable than others, environmental influences and learning also strongly affect personality development. Emotional responses (such as attachments to other people and phobias) become associated with environmental stimuli through the well-known process of classical conditioning. (For a definition and discussion of conditioning, see Chapter 14.) The dynamic lattice results largely from operant conditioning, and it is through such reward learning that we discover the behaviors that will satisfy our innate ergs. (See, for example, Cattell, 1965.)

Parental Behaviors.   Cattell agrees that parents exert a significant influence on the child's personality, but prefers to discuss this in terms of the structural source traits. He relates affectia to a warm home background where the father is cheerful, the mother is calm, and reasoning is used to control the child rather than punishment. Ego strength also tends to be higher among children whose parents prefer reasoning to punishment. Dominance is more common among children whose parents are authoritarian and enforce strict discipline. Superego strength is higher among children whose parents are warm, prefer reasoning to punishment, and do not criticize their choice of friends. Guilt proneness tends to be higher in children disciplined by physical punishment. High self-sufficiency is more common among children whose parents are happily married. The formation of other structural source traits is also related to various parental behaviors (Cattell, 1973, pp. 158–178).

Birth Order.   Cattell has examined other potential influences on personality development, one of which is the Adlerian issue of birth order. He finds that oldest children tend to be high in ego strength, dominance, and (as Adler would expect) conservatism, but low in self-sentiment strength. Only children tend to be more conservative and high in self-sentiment strength, whereas those who are not only children are more likely to be surgent. (See Cattell, 1973.)

Development of the Structural Source Traits

Cattell has also studied the ways in which the structural source traits develop over time. Many of these patterns appear to have logical and relatively straightforward explanations.

For example, people typically become higher in shrewdness as they grow older. This reflects their greater practice in, and skill at, human relationships. Ego strength shows a decrease in males during adolescence, a period that can occasion considerable inner turmoil (as Erikson and Sullivan have stressed). Afterward there is an increase in ego strength, as the individual discovers more successful outlets for ergic expression. Superego strength also drops more sharply in males during adolescence, presumably because they rebel more strongly against authority at this time than do females.

Males and females become increasingly dominant up to about age 20, indicating that children are permitted a greater degree of assertiveness as they grow older. Young children become less affectic and surgent upon entering school, a turning inward that Cattell attributes to the difficulties of leaving the safe and warm home environment and having to contend with the impersonal and competitive classroom. These traits increase in strength thereafter, indicating a return of socially outgoing behavior as the child adjusts to the new situation. For the same reasons, ergic tension shows a sharp increase at the time of entering school and then declines. Radicalism–conservatism is the only trait that shows virtually no change in strength from childhood through adulthood and thereafter. (See, for example, Cattell, 1973, pp. 148–156.)

FURTHER APPLICATIONS OF CATTELLIAN THEORY

Psychopathology and Psychotherapy

Neurosis.   Yet another way in which Cattell differs from most personality theorists is by defining psychopathology operationally. He argues that the meaning of neurosis must be determined by obtaining actual trait scores of neurotic individuals and comparing them to the typical pattern obtained from more healthy people. Thus he defines neurotics as people who seek (or are sent to) treatment because their feelings and behaviors are a burden to themselves or to others, and who are diagnosed accordingly. A more detailed description is drawn from his research findings: low ego strength (as Freud would predict), submissiveness, desurgency, low superego strength,[5] threctia, premsia, guilt proneness, high ergic tension, and high anxiety. (The different types of neuroses differ from each other in some respects, but not a great deal.)

With these data-based observations at hand, it is possible to investigate such issues as the causes of neurosis. For example, a high degree of premsia is fostered by parents who are overprotective and overindulgent. (See for example Cattell & Kline, 1976, pp. 241–272; Cattell & Scheier, 1961.)

Psychosis.   Neurosis and mental health differ primarily in degree, so the structural source traits are to a large extent descriptive of both. Cattell concludes that psychosis is quite a different matter—more a difference in kind than in degree—as evidenced by such extreme symptoms as thought disorders and a lack of contact with reality. Since he prefers an operational definition here also, he has found it necessary to expand upon the list of traits by factor analyzing data obtained from various clinical groups. He has thereby unearthed twelve *pathological primaries* on which psychotics (and neurotics) differ from more healthy people.

---

[5]Although this is contrary to the psychoanalytic conception of an overly developed and tyrannical superego, Cattell notes that the characteristics of guilt proneness and high ergic tension do resemble the syndrome that Freud described.

For example, high "hypochondriasis" is evidenced by an excessive concern with bodily functions and the possibility of becoming ill, while a low (more healthy) score on this trait is denoted by not finding ill health frightening. "Suicidal disgust" is reflected by disgust with life and thoughts of (or actual attempts at) suicide, as contrasted with those who are content with life and harbor no death wishes ("zestfulness"). "High anxious depression" involves frequent disturbing dreams and becoming easily upset, whereas "low anxious depression" is denoted by calmness, poise, and confidence. "Low energy" consists of feelings of weariness and worry, whereas "high energy" involves enthusiasm for one's work and the ability to sleep soundly. "High guilt and resentment" is characterized by blaming oneself for everything that goes wrong, whereas those with "low guilt" are not troubled by such feelings. As with any Cattelian trait, the pathological primaries are continuous: An individual may score anywhere from low through moderate to high on any of them. (See, for example, Cattell, 1973, pp. 180–182; Cattell & Kline, 1976, pp. 53–57.)

CAPSULE SUMMARY
Some Applications of Cattell's Traits

Trait	Definition	Research Findings
Affectia	Extraverted, easygoing	Moderately heritable Parents were warm, calm, cheerful Likely to marry early in life, make social contacts easily Common among effective psychotherapists, good teachers, officially chosen leaders
Alaxia	Trusting, accepting	Moderately heritable
Artlessness	Genuine, but socially clumsy	Decreases with increasing age
Autia	Imaginative, absent-minded	Common among good teachers
Conservatism	Traditional, conservative	Mostly learned, rarely changes Common among oldest and only children
Desurgency	Sober, taciturn, serious	Increases when child first enters school Common among neurotics
Dominance	Assertive, competitive, stubborn	Parents were strict, authoritarian Common among oldest children Likely to make social contacts easily Unlikely to be an officially chosen leader, have a better marriage
Ego Strength	Low: Unstable, easily upset	Found in most forms of psychopathology Common among adolescent males, those frequently unemployed
	High: Stable, calm, realistic	Parents preferred reasoning to punishment Typical of oldest children More common after adolescence Likely to have a better marriage, be an unofficial but effective leader
Ergic tension	Low: Relaxed, composed	Mostly learned Common among officially chosen leaders, unofficial but effective leaders

| | | High: Tense, frustrated, driven | Likely to be socially unpopular
Common among neurotics, children first entering school |

Group adherence	Joins and obeys a group	Unlikely to have a better marriage
Guilt proneness	Self-reproaching, apprehensive	Found in most forms of psychopathology Parents used physical punishment Less likely to enjoy sex in marriage, be an officially chosen leader
Harria	Tough-minded, self-reliant	Common among good teachers, good mathematics students
Parmia	Bold, venturesome	Likely to have a better marriage, make social contacts easily Common among effective psychotherapists, good teachers, officially chosen leaders, unofficial but effective leaders
Praxernia	Practical, down-to-earth	Common among officially chosen leaders
Premsia	Tender-minded, sensitive, clinging	Moderately heritable Parents were overprotective, overindulgent Likely to marry early in life Common among neurotics
Protension	Suspicious, projects anger	Moderately heritable Unlikely to marry early in life Likely to be socially unpopular
Radicalism	Liberal, free-thinking	Mostly learned, rarely changes
Self-sentiment strength	Low: Lax, impulsive	Common among oldest children, college dropouts
	High: Controlled, compulsive	Common among only children, good teachers, officially chosen leaders, unofficial but effective leaders
Self-sufficiency	Self-reliant, resourceful	Parents were happily married Likely to have a better marriage
Shrewdness	Astute, socially aware	Increases with increasing age Common among effective psychotherapists
Sizia	Introverted, critical	Increases when child first enters school
Submissiveness	Humble, docile	Common among neurotics
Superego strength	Weak: Disregards rules	Common among neurotics, sociopaths, adolescent males, corporation presidents
	Strong: Conscientious, moralistic	Common among effective psychotherapists, good students
Surgency	Happy-go-lucky, enthusiastic	Moderately heritable Likely to marry early in life, make social contacts easily, be an officially chosen leader, *not* be an only child
Threctia	Shy, timid	Common among neurotics
Untroubled adequacy	Self-assured, serene	Common among unofficial but effective leaders

Note: These findings represent general trends and should *not* be assumed to apply to every child, adolescent, and so forth. Traits are continuous, and an individual may score anywhere from one extreme through moderate to the other extreme.

Psychotherapy.   Cattell sees merit in various kinds of psychotherapy. His research findings indicate that effective psychotherapists are high in affectia, superego strength, parmia, and shrewdness. Cattell recommends that patients' traits be measured frequently during therapy, to determine the nature and extent of any changes in personality that result from the various interventions by the therapist. He concedes that this suggestion is unlikely to meet with widespread approval, however, since few therapists can afford the substantial amount of time needed to administer and interpret numerous written tests. (See Cattell & Kline, 1976, pp. 243, 269.)

Work

Some relationships between the structural source traits and various occupational groups were presented in a previous section. (For a more detailed discussion, see Cattell, Eber, & Tatsuoka, 1970; Cattell & Kline, 1976, pp. 293–312.) Also of interest are Cattell's findings that low ego strength is characteristic of people who are frequently unemployed, and that presidents of corporations tend to be low in superego strength (which supports the stereotype of the ruthless and conscienceless top executive).

Cattell recommends that measures of the structural traits be used in vocational guidance and selection, since a more thorough and accurate personality profile will make it easier to match a given individual's abilities and temperament with the demands of the job. He cautions that T-data are preferable to Q-data for purposes of selection, because applicants may falsify self-reports in order to have a better chance of being chosen by the organization. In vocational guidance, where the sole purpose is to assist the job seeker, it is reasonable to expect honest self-descriptions and to use Q-data. (See also Cattell, 1957; 1973; Cattell & Child, 1975.)

Education

The structural trait most highly related to success in school is intelligence, as would be expected. Next in importance is high superego strength. Some traits appear to be helpful in certain areas of study, but not others: premsia is positively correlated with performance in language courses, but negatively correlated with grades in mathematics. Low ego strength is characteristic of truants, whereas low self-sentiment strength is typical of college dropouts. Traits commonly found among good teachers include affectia, parmia, autia, high self-sentiment strength, and harria. (See Cattell, 1973; Cattell & Kline, 1976, pp. 273–291.)

Social Psychology

Leadership.   People who are officially chosen to lead a group tend to demonstrate affectia, surgency, parmia, high superego strength, high self-sentiment strength, praxernia, and low ergic tension. Conversely, dominant and guilt prone individuals are unlikely to be selected as leaders. Those who function as unofficial but effective group leaders are typically high in ego strength, self-sentiment strength, and parmia, and low in guilt proneness and ergic tension.

Marriage.   Those who are affectic, surgent, and premsic are more likely to marry early in life (during their 20s), although those high in protension are less likely to do so. Better, more stable marriages are characterized by spouses who demonstrate ego strength, parmia, and self-sufficiency, but not dominance. An individual who is high in guilt proneness is less likely to enjoy sexual satisfaction in marriage.

Group and Religious Behavior. People who are characterized by affectia, dominance, surgency, and parmia make social contacts easily and more often. Those who are high in ergic tension and protension are likely to be socially unpopular, with the latter also acting as a detriment to group effectiveness. Frequent activity in church affairs is related to affectia and self-sufficiency, but is less common among those high in dominance and radicalism. (See for example Cattell, 1973; Cattell & Child, 1975; Cattell & Kline, 1976.) Cattell has also conducted research dealing with the personality of groups (*syntality*), and the prediction of group behavior through appropriate specification equations (e.g., 1948; 1964).

EVALUATION

Criticisms and Controversies

Although factor analysis is a valuable tool for simplifying large correlation matrices, its capacity for testing hypotheses and arriving at fundamental truths is far more debatable. In view of the limitations and controversies that beset this technique, some critics reject Cattell's contention that he has discovered the basic elements of personality and view his findings as no more than tentative (e.g., Anastasi, 1976, p. 509). Other theorists (such as Carl Rogers and Robert Oppenheimer) warn that quantification is no panacea and argue that psychologists should devise methods more appropriate to their own unique subject matter, rather than trying to emulate the numerical precision of physics and chemistry. Unfortunately, those who wish to investigate the debate firsthand will find that Cattell's writings offer considerable difficulty because of their mathematical, neologistic nature.

Cattell's motivational model of ergic tension is essentially similar to drive or instinct reduction, and is subject to the same criticisms. Most psychologists prefer to define neurosis and psychosis on theoretical grounds, rather than operationally. Nor have Cattell's constructs and nomenclature been widely accepted: It is doubtful whether many psychologists would recognize such terms as praxernia and threctia, let alone be able to define them. If the worthiness of a theory is to be assessed by its impact on the field of psychology, rather than by critical reviews that politely praise the theorist's tireless research efforts and impressively complicated network of ideas, it would seem that Cattell's success has been at best minimal.

Contributions

Cattell has been commended for grounding his theory in empirical research, rather than subjective speculation. His extensive investigations have encompassed a wide variety of measurement techniques, areas of psychological inquiry, and cultures and nationalities, a breadth and diligence of effort that represents a staggering accomplishment. Quantifying such abstruse issues as inner conflicts and trait strength might well make psychology a more scientific discipline. And Cattellian factors offer a potentially useful and well-researched set of dimensions for describing and studying the human personality. Thus it is difficult to ignore Cattell's contributions to personality theory, even though his ideas remain well outside of the mainstream of psychological thought.

Suggested Reading

A more extensive discussion of Cattell's theory may be found in *Personality and Mood by Questionnaire* (Cattell, 1973), *Motivation and Dynamic Structure* (Cattell & Child, 1975), *The Scientific Analysis of Personality and Motivation* (Cattell & Kline, 1976), and the two-volume opus *Personality and Learning Theory* (Cattell, 1979; 1980).

OTHER FACTOR-ANALYTIC TRAIT THEORIES

Eysenck's Three-Factor Theory

Hans J. Eysenck, a German-born theorist who spent most of his professional life in England, has also tried to ascertain the basic elements of personality by using factor analysis. Unlike Cattell, Eysenck is extremely critical of psychoanalytic theory, which he regards as unscientific and ineffective. And in marked contrast to Cattell's plethora of traits, Eysenck concludes that the core of personality consists of three **supertraits:** introversion–extraversion, neuroticism–stability, and psychoticism. (See Eysenck, 1952; 1965; 1966; 1967; 1975; 1982; Eysenck & Eysenck, 1968; 1975.)

Introversion–Extraversion.   The supertrait of **introversion–extraversion** is similar to to Jung's construct, except that Eysenck defines it in terms of various traits rather than libido. The more extraverted person is outgoing, sociable, and impulsive, whereas the more introverted person is reserved, aloof, and introspective:

> [The extraverted individual is] outgoing, impulsive, and uninhibited, having many social contacts and frequently taking part in group activities. [He] is sociable, likes parties, has many friends, needs to have people to talk to, and does not like reading or studying by himself. [Conversely, the introverted individual] is a quiet, retiring sort of person, introspective, fond of books rather than people; he is reserved and distant except to intimate friends. (Eysenck & Eysenck, 1968, p. 6.)

As with any trait, introversion–extraversion is continuous. That is, a person may score anywhere along the scale from highly introverted to highly extraverted.

Eysenck concludes that about two thirds of the variation among people in introversion–extraversion is due to heredity. Therefore, much of his research has dealt with the biological correlates of personality. According to Eysenck, more extraverted individuals seek external stimulation because they have low levels of cerebral cortex arousal that they want to increase, whereas more introverted individuals avoid crowds and noise because they have high levels of cortical arousal that will become painful if increased further.

Although Eysenck's cortical hypothesis has not received strong research support, physiology may be important in a different way. Those who are more introverted may be more sensitive to external stimulation, more easily aroused and overwhelmed by social events and noise, and better able to perceive subtle cues in the environment. Therefore, they are more comfortable with lower levels of stimulation (as by being alone). Those who are more extraverted may require greater stimulation in order to become aroused, making them more likely to prefer noisy crowds and loud music.

Neuroticism.   Those with high scores on the supertrait of **neuroticism** tend to be emotionally unstable. They are likely to agree with such statements as "When trouble occurs, I often become too emotional" and "I have difficulty returning to an even keel after an emotional experience." Conversely, those who have low neuroticism scores (are more **stable**) are more calm and even-tempered. They are less likely to experience large swings in emotion, or to overreact to frustration and disappointment.

Psychoticism.   Individuals with high scores on the supertrait of **psychoticism** are egocentric and think that the world revolves around them. They also tend to be aggressive, impersonal, and lacking in concern for the rights and feelings of other people.

***The Relationship Between Introversion–Extraversion and Neuroticism–
Stability.*** Neurotic and healthy behavior takes different forms for extraverts and introverts.
Those who are more extraverted and more neurotic are likely to be touchy, restless, aggressive,
and excitable, whereas those who are more introverted and more neurotic tend to be anxious,
moody, rigid, and pessimistic. Among those who are more stable, extraverts are typically care-
free, easygoing, and lively, whereas introverts are calm, even-tempered, and reliable. (See Figure 13.2.)

Like Cattell, Eysenck bases his theory on extensive empirical research. Some areas of
agreement between Eysenck and other theorists suggest that he may well be focusing on
fundamental traits: Jung's construct of introversion–extraversion has proved to be extremely
important and useful, whereas neuroticism is part of the "Big Five" theory (discussed below)
and is related to such Cattellian traits as ego strength and ergic tension.

As we observed at the beginning of this chapter, however, (and as is evident from the vastly
different results obtained by Eysenck and Cattell), factor analysis does not automatically yield
the "truth" about the human personality. It is not easy to decide which variables to include in

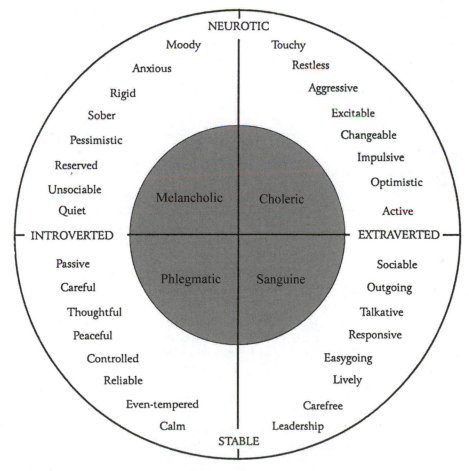

FIG. 13.2. Eysenck's supertraits: The relationship of introversion–extraversion
and neuroticism to each other and to the four temperaments identified by
ancient Greek physicians (Eysenck, 1975).

a correlation matrix that is to be factor analyzed, or to decide how many factors to extract in any given study, and the decisions that the researcher makes can have a profound effect on the factors that are obtained. Perhaps for these reasons, it now appears that Eysenck's three supertraits are not quite enough.

"Big Five" (Five-factor) Theory

One group of researchers has found that five traits consistently emerge from factor-analytic studies. These "Big Five" traits are:

Introversion–extraversion: Aloof and retiring versus sociable and talkative (as in Jung's and Eysenck's theories).
Neuroticism: Calm and secure versus nervous and insecure (as in Eysenck's theory).
Agreeableness: Suspicious and uncooperative versus trusting and helpful.
Conscientiousness: Lazy and unreliable versus hardworking and reliable.
Openness to experience: Conventional and down-to-earth versus nonconformist and creative.

Although not all Big Five research has produced the same results, advocates of this model cite a substantial amount of evidence to support their contention that these traits represent the core of personality. The Big Five traits describe aspects of personality that are remarkably consistent, especially among adults. "In the course of thirty years, most adults will have undergone radical changes in their life situations. They may have married, divorced, remarried. They have probably moved their residence several times.... And yet, most will not have

---

CAPSULE SUMMARY
Other Factor-Analytic Trait Theories

Agreeableness	The extent to which one is trusting and helpful (more agreeable) or suspicious and uncooperative (less agreeable). One of the Big Five personality traits.
Big Five personality traits	Five traits that consistently emerge from numerous researchers' factor-analytic studies as the most important: introversion–extraversion, neuroticism, agreeableness, conscientiousness, and openness to experience.
Conscientiousness	The extent to which one is hardworking and reliable (more conscientious) or lazy, unreliable, and careless (less conscientious). One of the Big Five personality traits.
Introversion–extraversion	The extent to which one is more social and outgoing (extraverted) or more aloof, retiring, reserved, and introspective (introverted). Similar to Jung's definition. One of the Big Five personality traits, and one of Eysenck's three supertraits.
Neuroticism	The extent to which one is nervous and insecure (emotionally unstable), as opposed to calm and secure (emotionally stable). One of the Big Five personality traits, and one of Eysenck's three supertraits.
Openness to experience (openness)	The extent to which one is creative and nonconformist (more open) or conventional and down-to-earth (less open). One of the Big Five personality traits.
Supertraits	Three traits that consistently emerge from Eysenck's factor-analytic studies as the most important: introversion–extraversion, neuroticism, and psychoticism.

changed appreciably in their standing on any of the five dimensions" (McCrae & Costa, 1990, p. 87). Currently, the Big Five model dominates the landscape of psychological research. (See, for example, Costa & McCrae, 1988; 1992a; 1992b; 1994; Digman, 1990; Endler & Speer, 1998; Goldberg, 1990; 1993; John, 1990; McCrae, 1992; McCrae & Costa, 1987; 1990; McCrae et al., 1998; 1999.)

Big Five theory has various practical applications. A few examples: an individual who is high in openness may well be advised to seek out a career that involves originality and curiosity, such as the arts or scientific research. A person who is low in agreeableness may be too suspicious to be helped by certain forms of psychotherapy. Various patterns of scores on the five factors may suggest specific forms of psychopathology (e.g., high scores on neuroticism and conscientiousness may indicate an obsessive–compulsive personality). And introversion–extraversion can be useful in vocational and academic guidance, as we observed in Chapter 3.

Evaluation

It is not difficult to understand the popularity of Big Five theory. It includes two of Eysenck's three supertraits and is more comprehensive, and it is far less overwhelming (and bewildering) than Cattell's abstruse terminology. However, it must be emphasized once again that traits provide information only about the surface levels of personality, and they do not explain human behavior. (See the evaluation section in Chapter 12.) To truly understand personality, therefore, we must also consider other levels—and other theories of personality.

SUMMARY

Raymond B. Cattell argues that psychology must become far more objective and mathematical if it is to be a mature science. He bases his extensive research into the dimensions of personality on the complicated statistical technique of factor analysis.

1. **THE BASIC NATURE OF HUMAN BEINGS.** Human behavior is energized and directed toward specific goals by dynamic traits, which include some 16 innate ergs and numerous learned sentiments and attitudes. As with drives or instincts, our goal is to reduce the tension created by an activated innate need (erg). Attitudes and sentiments serve the objectives of the ergs, with human motivation involving a complicated dynamic lattice of interconnected erg–sentiment–attitude chains.

2. **THE STRUCTURE OF PERSONALITY.** Cattell defines personality structure in terms of temperament and ability traits, which determine the style and effectiveness of our actions. Sixteen of these structural traits have emerged from his factor analytic studies, as well as numerous additional and more tentative ones. Once numerical measures of each structural trait have been obtained for a given individual, appropriate specification equations are then used to predict that person's behavior.

3. **THE DEVELOPMENT OF PERSONALITY.** Cattell has factor analyzed large quantities of data obtained from children and adolescents, as well as from adults. He has attempted to measure the extent to which each structural trait is determined by heredity, as opposed to the environment. Much human learning takes the form of conditioning, with erg–sentiment–attitude chains and the dynamic lattice resulting primarily from operant conditioning. Parental behaviors also play a significant role in shaping the child's personality. The various structural traits follow different developmental patterns from childhood through adulthood.

4. FURTHER APPLICATIONS. Cattell defines neurosis and psychosis operationally, rather than theoretically. He has factor analyzed data from various clinical populations, and has discovered additional traits (pathological primaries) on which psychotics and neurotics differ from more healthy individuals. Cattell is procedurally eclectic with regard to psychotherapy, and recommends the frequent measurement of patients' traits so as to best understand their progress. He has also devoted considerable attention to the areas of work, education, and social psychology.

5. EVALUATION. Cattell's claims to have unearthed the basic elements of personality, and to measure and predict human behavior with mathematical precision, are doubtful in view of the controversies and limitations that beset the technique of factor analysis. His model of ergic tension is subject to the same criticisms as drive reduction, and his constructs and nomenclature have not had much impact on the field of psychology. Yet the scope of his research represents a staggering accomplishment, and his factors represent a potentially valuable set of dimensions for describing and studying the human personality.

6. OTHER FACTOR-ANALYTIC TRAIT THEORIES. Hans Eysenck concludes that the core of personality consists of three supertraits: introversion–extraversion, neuroticism–(emotional) stability, and psychoticism. He has sought to relate introversion–extraversion to such biological factors as cerebral cortex arousal. "Big Five" theory emphasizes five traits that consistently emerge from factor-analytic studies, albeit with some exceptions: introversion–extraversion, neuroticism, agreeableness, conscientiousness, and openness to experience. These traits remain remarkably consistent during adulthood and have various practical applications.

STUDY QUESTIONS

Part I. Questions

1. (a) How might Cattell's personality and life experiences have influenced his decision to devise so many neologisms? (b) Should a theorist be faulted if his or her ideas are unusually difficult to understand?

2. Discuss three important errors to watch out for when reading a factor-analytic study.

3. Compare Cattell's list of ergs to Freud's "list" instincts. Which do you prefer? Why?

4. Give an example of a subsidation chain that involves several attitudes, sentiments, and ergs.

5. Based on Cattell's research findings, are you likely to be: (a) An effective psychotherapist? (b) A good teacher? (c) Officially chosen as a group leader?

6. Cattell finds that low ego strength is characteristic of people who are frequently unemployed. Does this mean that low ego strength causes unemployment?

7. Consider the case material in the Appendix. (a) How would this man score on each of the structural traits measured by the 16 P.F.? (b) Does this profile agree with Cattell's findings regarding the pattern of traits typically found among neurotics? (c) Cattell relates affectia to a warm home background where the father is cheerful and the mother is calm, and premsia to parents who are overprotective. Are these ideas supported by this case history?

8. Would Cattell be surprised by the scandals involving corporation presidents, such as Enron?

9. (a) How would the man whose case is described in the Appendix score on Eysenck's supertraits? (b) How would he score on the Big Five traits? (c) How would you score on Eysenck's traits and the Big Five traits? (Remember that all traits are continuous.)

10. A terrorist blows up a building in a hated foreign country. Would any of the theories discussed in the chapter be able to explain the terrorist's behavior?

Part II. Comments and Suggestions

1. (a) Consider that the use of private symbols is one way to gain power over people, since the user understands things that others do not. See Chapter 7, questions 2b and 3. (b) I think so. Some theorists might argue that their ideas are too complicated to be explained in simple terms. But after some 30 years of teaching such subjects as Jungian theory and inferential statistics, I believe that complicated ideas can usually be explained in relatively clear language if one is willing to make the necessary effort.

2. (1) Using samples that are too small (say, fewer than 30 subjects), which makes it very likely that the correlation coefficients and factors obtained from the study will not accurately depict what is happening in the corresponding populations. (2) Failing to include a sufficiently broad range of variables in the study. Factor analysis reduces those variables chosen by the researcher to a smaller set of dimensions, and an incomplete or misleading set of variables will yield a misleading set of factors. (3) Naming a factor in a way that supports the researcher's theory, when other names are as or more reasonable. See footnote 2 in this chapter.

3. Are such human characteristics as security, gregariousness, and exploration separate and distinct from sexuality and aggression (and from each other)? Do any of Cattell's 16 ergs seem considerably less important than the others?

4. A man's wife (sentiment) helps him to satisfy the ergs of mating, gregariousness, and narcissistic sex. But she also spends too much money and insists on doing things her way, making it difficult for him to satisfy the ergs of acquisitiveness and self-assertion. Among his attitudes are "I like sexual attractiveness in a woman," "A wife should adhere to the family budget," and "I don't like it when a woman tells me what to do."

5. (a) I meet only one of the four criteria (high affectia, superego strength, parmia, and shrewdness), and I don't believe that I would be an effective psychotherapist. (b) I meet two or three of the five criteria (high affectia, parmia, autia, harria, and self-sentiment strength), but objective evidence indicates that I'm a good teacher. (c) I meet only two of the seven criteria (high affectia, surgency, parmia, superego strength, self-sentiment strength, and praxernia, and low ergic tension), and I'm usually not chosen as a leader. One case doesn't prove anything, of course, but I find it interesting that two of the three areas are in accordance with Cattell's findings.

6. When there is a sizable correlation between two variables (here, ego strength and employment), there are three possible reasons: low ego strength causes unemployment, unemployment causes low ego strength, or both low ego strength and unemployment are caused by some third variable. Might each of these possibilities be true in this case?

7. (a) My answers: Very sizic, very intelligent, very low in ego strength, neither dominant nor submissive (he is stubborn but not assertive), very desurgent, very high in superego strength, very threctic, neither premsic nor harric (he is self-reliant but also sensitive), very high in protension, high in autia, artless (especially with regard to social clumsiness), very high in guilt proneness, somewhat conservative, very self-sufficient, very high in self-sentiment strength and very high in ergic tension. (No doubt you had to consult the definition of most of these terms in order to understand this. So did I. This is a good indication as to why Cattell's theory has not had much of an impact on modern psychology.) (b) Yes, with regard to low ego strength, desurgency, threctia, guilt proneness, ergic tension, and anxiety. No, with regard to submissiveness, low superego strength, and premsia. (c) Yes, in that his mother was anxious (rather than calm), his father was demanding and critical (and not overly cheerful), and he became sizic (rather than affectic). No, in that his parents were overprotective yet he did not become clinging and dependent.

8. I don't think so. Recall that his research found that corporation presidents tend to be low in superego strength.

9. (a) Highly introverted, since he is uncomfortable with most people and often prefers to be alone. High on neuroticism, since he often suffers from intense anxiety. Moderately high on psychoticism, since his painful problems keep him focused on himself and make it difficult for him to care about other people. (b) Highly introverted, high on neuroticism, low on agreeableness (he is very wary of other people, and is usually too preoccupied with his own problems to care about helping them), highly conscientious, and fairly low on openness (although he is sometimes creative, he often tries to reduce anxiety by conforming and being what others want). As Big Five theory would expect from his high scores on neuroticism and conscientiousness, he is obsessive-compulsive. (See section 10 in the Appendix.) (c) Are you likely to answer accurately? Or might you try to fool yourself and/or other people into thinking that you are psychologically healthier than you really are?

10. I don't think so. See the comment to Chapter 12, question 10.

Comparing Trait Theorists and Freud on Various Issues

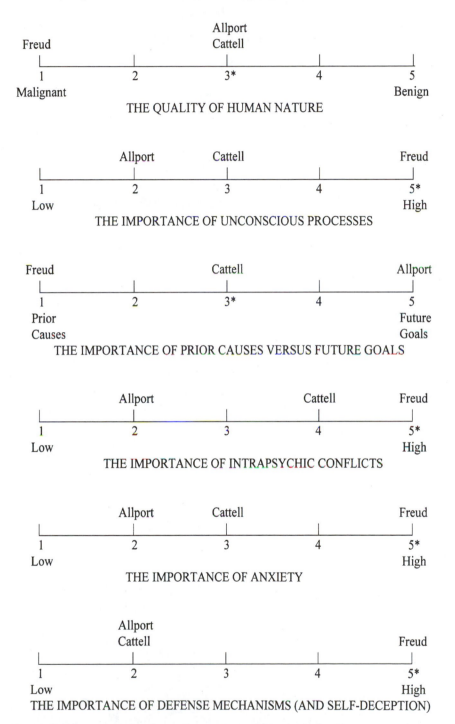

THE QUALITY OF HUMAN NATURE

THE IMPORTANCE OF UNCONSCIOUS PROCESSES

THE IMPORTANCE OF PRIOR CAUSES VERSUS FUTURE GOALS

THE IMPORTANCE OF INTRAPSYCHIC CONFLICTS

THE IMPORTANCE OF ANXIETY

THE IMPORTANCE OF DEFENSE MECHANISMS (AND SELF-DECEPTION)

Note: These scales are intended as approximations, designed to facilitate comparisons among the theorists, and not as mathematically precise measures. They reflect my opinions; others might disagree with the ratings in some instances. For those who may be interested, my position on each issue is shown by an asterisk.

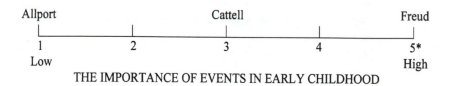

THE IMPORTANCE OF EVENTS IN EARLY CHILDHOOD

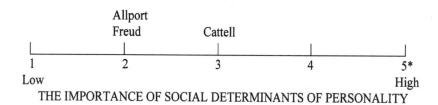

THE IMPORTANCE OF SOCIAL DETERMINANTS OF PERSONALITY

PART IV

The Behaviorist Perspective

Overview

Behaviorism seeks to make psychology more scientific by studying only what can be observed. It therefore redefines psychology as the study of overt behavior. Behaviorism eliminates from consideration virtually all of what personality theorists consider to be important: inner causes of behavior, wishes, needs, thoughts, emotions, memories, beliefs, expectations, preferences, self-perceptions, unconscious processes, intrapsychic conflicts, dreams. Thus behaviorism is not another approach to personality theory, but rather an alternative to personality theory.

Ivan Pavlov

First demonstrated the simple form of learning called classical conditioning in his famous experiment with dogs, food, a tone, and salivation. In classical conditioning, the organism learns that one stimulus will be followed by another stimulus because the two stimuli repeatedly occur closely together in time.

John B. Watson

Also an advocate of classical conditioning, he demonstrated that fear to a previously neutral stimulus can easily be conditioned in his famous experiment with "little Albert."

B. F. Skinner

Argued that most behavior is learned through operant conditioning, wherein the organism must make the correct response to be reinforced (receive a reward or avoid punishment). A response operates on the environment to produce consequences that either strengthen or weaken that behavior. If the response is reinforced, it is more likely to occur again; if it is not reinforced, it is less likely to recur. All of our behavior is determined by prior causes and by our environment; we have no free will. Therefore, the only way to change (and improve) our behavior is to design the environment appropriately, so that it will reinforce desired responses and not reinforce undesired responses. How reinforcement is administered (schedules of reinforcement) strongly influences learning and behavior. Even the most complicated behaviors consist of sequences of specific responses that have been learned through operant conditioning. Psychotherapy should be based on behaviorist principles, rather than seeking to change unobservable and abstract inner processes.

CHAPTER 14

B. F. SKINNER
Radical Behaviorism

Personality theorists seek to explain human behavior in terms of inner causes: instincts, archetypes, feelings of inferiority, traits, needs, conditions of worth, intentions, conflicts between various components, and so forth. However, some psychologists have tried to dispense with all such intrapsychic motives.

At about the time Freud was introducing the death instinct and structural model, the noted American psychologist John B. Watson sought to discredit such theories by proving that a phobia could be induced solely through external forces. Watson had been favorably impressed by the work of Ivan Pavlov (1906; 1927; 1928), who first demonstrated the simple form of learning called *classical conditioning.* Pavlov placed a dog in restraint in a soundproof room, presented a neutral stimulus (such as a musical tone), and immediately followed it with food, which caused the dog to salivate. After numerous repetitions of this procedure, the dog salivated to the tone alone. Because the tone was repeatedly paired with an *unconditioned stimulus* (food), which automatically elicited salivation (the *unconditioned response*), the tone became a *conditioned stimulus* that could by itself evoke salivation (a response learned through conditioning, or *conditioned response*).

In accordance with Pavlov's procedure, Watson obtained an 11-month-old infant (Albert) who feared nothing but loud noises. Watson presented Albert with a tame (and readily accepted) white rat, and then crashed a hammer against a steel bar held just behind Albert's head. After only seven repetitions of this traumatic sequence, Albert was conditioned: He now showed a strong fear of the rat alone, some of which not only lasted for a full month but also generalized to such other furry animals as rabbits. (See, for example, Harris, 1979; 1980; Samelson, 1980; Watson, 1913; 1919; 1924; Watson & Rayner, 1920; Watson & Watson, 1921.)

Watson therefore concluded that it was patently foolish (and dangerously misleading) to relate psychopathology to any inner cause. Instead he argued that psychology should be redefined as the study of overt behavior.

311

B. F. Skinner is also an outspoken critic of any theory that attributes behavior to unobservable inner causes. Skinner does *not* claim that inner states (such as emotions, thoughts, and unconscious processes) do not exist. He argues that psychology can be scientific only if it restricts its attention to observable behaviors, and to visible external operations that are performed on the organism. Skinner therefore discards such concepts as human nature, structural and developmental aspects of personality, and even personality itself. His radical behaviorism is not a theory of personality, but rather an alternative to personality theory. (Thus he is the only psychologist discussed in this book whose work cannot be organized according to our usual framework.)

Unlike Watson and Pavlov, however, Skinner argues that most behavior is learned through *operant conditioning*. Skinner also contends that human beings do not and cannot plan for the future, and that we have no free will. Because of such ideas, Skinner's writings have caused a furor similar to that evoked by Freudian psychoanalysis.

Like many of the theorists discussed in this book, Skinner experienced some painful moments of professional rejection. In Skinner's case, however, these problems involved a field other than psychology.

Skinner's initial goal was to become a novelist. He majored in English at Hamilton College and sent several of his short stories to the noted poet Robert Frost, who responded so favorably that Skinner spent some time after his graduation trying to write fiction. Yet one year later he abandoned his dream, having reached the unhappy conclusion that he had nothing literary to say and was only frittering away his time. Skinner also lacked the support of any peer or religious group, making this trying period much like an Eriksonian identity crisis (Elms, 1981; see also Mindess, 1988).

Interestingly, Skinner did not attribute his failure as a writer to some deficiency within himself. Instead, he regarded this failure as the inevitable result of the circumstances in which he found himself. When he later pursued a career in psychology, he followed a similar course: He concluded that human behavior is determined not by any inner causes, but solely by the effects of the external environment.

OBJECTIVES

- *To make psychology more scientific by studying only observable behaviors and external operations performed on the organism, and eliminating from consideration all inner causes and unobservable behaviors.*
- *To emphasize the importance of operant conditioning, wherein the organism must make the correct response to be reinforced (receive a reward or avoid punishment).*
- *To show that we have no free will: all of our behavior is determined by conditioning, mostly operant conditioning.*
- *To show that learning and behavior are strongly influenced by the ways in which reinforcement is administered, and to define and explain such schedules of reinforcement.*
- *To explain concepts used by personality theorists, including psychoanalytic theory and trait theory, in behaviorist terms.*
- *To replace psychotherapy that seeks to change abstract and unobservable inner processes with procedures based on behaviorist principles.*
- *To apply behaviorist principles and procedures to such areas as education and work.*
- *To improve our society and the world by creating the correct contingencies of reinforcement.*

BIOGRAPHICAL SKETCH

Burrhus Frederic Skinner was born on March 20, 1904, in Susquehanna, Pennsylvania. He remembers his father as a lawyer who gave the impression of conceit, yet hungered for praise. His mother was attractive and socially successful, but frigid and puritanical about sexual matters. The family also included a younger brother.

Skinner recalls growing up in a bountiful environment: enjoying a variety of fruits that grew in the back yard of his ramshackle home, driving to the country in the fall to gather hickory nuts, and catching turtles, mice, and chipmunks. He also built numerous toys and gadgets, one of which attached to a hook in his bedroom closet and confronted him with a sign whenever he failed to hang up his pajamas—a pet peeve of his mother's. (See Skinner, 1967; 1976/1977.)

Skinner received his A.B. from Hamilton College in 1926, where he was Phi Beta Kappa. After his failure to succeed as a novelist (previously described), Skinner opted to pursue his interest in animal and human behavior through graduate work in psychology at Harvard University. Here he followed a rigorous daily schedule: rising at 6 in the morning to study, going to classes, studying again until 9 in the evening, and then going to bed, with virtually no time for movies or dates. (See Skinner, 1967, p. 398; 1976/1977, pp. 248–249, 263–265, 291–292.) Skinner became interested in the ideas of Pavlov and Watson, and received his Ph.D. in 1931. Save for the years 1936–1948, when he was at the University of Minnesota and University of Indiana, Skinner spent his entire professional career at Harvard. He married Yvonne Blue on November 1, 1936, a union that produced two daughters.

Skinner's invention of the laboratory apparatus that bears his name was an interesting, and often amusing, process. Years later he recalled that having the animal's responses reinforce themselves was done primarily to make the experimenter's task easier, that intermittent reinforcement was originally a desperation measure when faced with a dwindling supply of food on a Saturday afternoon, and that the effects of extinction were first discovered when the food-delivering mechanism happened to jam (Skinner, 1972b, pp. 101–124). Skinner also devised a mechanical baby tender (or air crib), which he used with his second child. This spacious, temperature-controlled, soundproof, and germ-free enclosure is intended to provide an optimal environment for the growing baby. And it helps the parents as well, since it requires far less effort than changing bedding or clothing. However, his invention has not been widely accepted. (See M. H. Hall, 1967a, pp. 21–22; Skinner, 1972b, pp. 567–573; 1979.)

Skinner is the author of many journal articles and some dozen books, including a novel about an ideal behaviorist community (*Walden Two,* 1948)—one that has by now sold very well, although it was strongly attacked by critics and virtually ignored by the public for a dozen years following its publication. (See Skinner, 1969, pp. 29–30; 1978, p. 57.) His honors include the Distinguished Scientific Contribution Award of the American Psychological Association and various scientific medals.

Skinner's last public appearance was on August 10, 1990, when he gave the keynote address at the opening ceremony of the American Psychological Association's annual convention. He also received a special citation for his lifetime contributions to psychology. Skinner died 8 days later of complications arising from leukemia.

CLASSICAL VERSUS OPERANT CONDITIONING

Causality and Science

Skinner agrees that the goal of scientific psychology is to predict and control behavior. (See Chapter 1.) However, he warns that this objective cannot be achieved by any theory that attributes our actions to inner causes.

Skinner likens all such approaches to the prescientific fallacies of the ancient physicists, who believed that a falling rock accelerates because it becomes happier when it is closer to the earth. To Skinner, the so-called inner causes of human behavior are useless redundancies: To say that an organism eats *because* it is hungry, attacks *because* it feels angry, or looks into a mirror *because* it is narcissistic explains nothing whatsoever, for we are still left with the task of discovering why the organism happened to feel hungry, angry, or narcissistic. Even heredity does no more than set certain limits on the behaviors that a person can execute. "The doctrine of 'being born that way' has little to do with demonstrated facts. It is usually an appeal to ignorance" (Skinner, 1953/1965, p. 26). Psychology can only escape its own dark age by rejecting the unscientific constructs that pervade personality theory, and studying how observable behavior is influenced by the external environment:

> A causal chain [consists] of three links: (1) an operation performed upon the organism from without—for example, water deprivation; (2) an inner condition—for example, physiological or psychic thirst; and (3) a kind of behavior—for example, drinking.... [Therefore,] we may avoid many tiresome and exhausting digressions by examining the third link as a function of the first. Valid information about the second link may throw light upon this relationship, but can in no way alter it.... [Thus my] objection to inner states is not that they do not exist, but that they are not relevant in a functional [i.e., causal] analysis. (Skinner, 1953/1965, pp. 34–35. See also Skinner, 1953/1965,

pp. 6, 23–42, 143–144, 202–203, 257–282; 1969, pp. 242–243; 1971/1972a, pp. 5–13, 68; 1974–1976, pp. 39–40, 54–57, 174–183.)

Types of Conditioning

Skinner agrees with Pavlov and Watson that some behaviors are learned through classical conditioning. For example, the dentist's chair may become a source of anxiety because it has been repeatedly paired with the painful drill. In Pavlovian conditioning, however, the conditioned stimulus (e.g., tone) precedes and elicits the conditioned response (salivation). In contrast, Skinner argues that the vast majority of learning is due to what happens *after* the behavior occurs. "It is now clear that we must take into account what the environment does to an organism not only before but after it responds. Behavior is shaped and maintained by its consequences" (Skinner, 1971/1972a, p. 16; see also Skinner, 1953/1965, pp. 52–58, 66).

According to Skinner, behaviors that operate on the environment to produce effects that strengthen them (are **reinforced**) are more likely to occur in the future. He refers to such behaviors as **operants,** and to the process by which they are learned as **operant conditioning.**[1] Any stimulus that increases the probability of a response when presented (**positive reinforcer**), or when removed (**negative reinforcer**), is by definition a reinforcer. Thus Skinner makes no assumptions at all about inner satisfactions or drive reduction.

As an illustration, consider a person who has not consumed any liquids for several hours. This individual may well be positively reinforced by going to the kitchen and drinking a glass of water. If so, he or she will more frequently emit this response under similar conditions. If not, some other response is likely to prevail on a subsequent occasion (such as drinking some juice or soda). We cannot assume that water is a reinforcer; we must determine this by studying its effects on the organism. Nor is there any need to deal with unobservable inner states, such as a thirst drive. Similarly, if taking off a tight shoe provides a reduction in pressure that proves to be negatively reinforcing, the probability of this behavior will be greater the next time a shoe pinches. Unlike Pavlovian conditioning, the organism receives the reward or avoids punishment only if it emits the correct response—going to the kitchen and turning on the water tap, or taking off the shoe. (See Skinner, 1953/1965, pp. 72–75, 171–174, 185; 1969, pp. 5–7, 109; 1974/1976, pp. 44, 51.)

Beyond Freedom and Dignity

Perhaps Skinner's most controversial assertion is that we have no capacity to plan for the future, no purpose, no will. *All* behavior is determined by prior conditioning, usually operant. We drink water or remove a troublesome shoe not as the result of some carefully formulated plan, but only because responses like these have previously been reinforced:

> Instead of saying that a man behaves because of the consequences which *are* to follow his behavior, [I] simply say that he behaves because of the consequences which *have* followed similar behavior in the past.... [Thus] no behavior is free. (Skinner, 1953/1965, pp. 87, 111. See also Skinner, 1971/1972a.)

Many of us prefer to believe that we are free to choose our own course in life. To be sure, we may blame our failures and transgressions on external causes and "extenuating circumstances."

---

[1]Some psychologists use the term *instrumental conditioning* as a synonym for operant conditioning, but Skinner does not. (See Skinner, 1969, p. 109.)

Yet we cling to the myth of human freedom and dignity by refusing to surrender the credit for our achievements, even though they also are solely the result of conditioning—subtle and complicated though it may be. Just as Freud did with psychoanalysis, Skinner compares behaviorism to the two great historical shocks to our self-esteem: the Copernican theory of the solar system, which displaced us from our preeminent position at the center of the universe; and the Darwinian theory of evolution, which challenged our presumed distinction from the animal kingdom (Skinner, 1953/1965, p. 7; 1971/1972a, p. 202).

Nevertheless, Skinner contends that the behaviorist rejection of free will has important advantages. The only way to resolve the potential catastrophes that we face today, such as world famine and nuclear holocaust, is by developing a true technology of behavior. This will enable us to understand the external forces that control our actions, and design our environment in ways that will ensure the survival and betterment of humankind:

> It is hard to imagine a world in which people live together without quarreling, maintain themselves by producing the food, shelter, and clothing they need, enjoy themselves and contribute to the enjoyment of others in art, music, literature, and games, consume only a reasonable part of the resources of the world and add as little as possible to its pollution, bear no more children than can be raised decently ... and come to know themselves accurately and, therefore, manage themselves effectively. Yet all this is possible ... [The behavioristic] view of man offers exciting possibilities. We have not yet seen what man can make of man. (Skinner, 1971/1972a, pp. 204–206. See also Skinner, 1978, pp. 29–30.)

PRINCIPLES OF OPERANT CONDITIONING

The Skinner Box

Although Skinner is keenly interested in the prediction and control of human behavior, his extensive research deals mostly with animals (which are more easily investigated under laboratory conditions). His primary method for studying operant conditioning is the well-known piece of apparatus that he invented, which is referred to by others as the **Skinner box.** (He himself prefers the term *operant conditioning apparatus*.)

One version of Skinner's apparatus consists of a soundproof box, approximately 1 foot square, in which a pigeon is placed. A lighted plastic key (disk) at one end permits access to food when pecked. (See Figure 14.1a.) This is not a difficult operant for a pigeon to learn, especially since it is deprived of food for some time prior to the experimental session. The key is connected to an electronic recording system that produces a graph of the pigeon's response rate (see Figure 14.1b), and the apparatus can be programmed so that reinforcement is available after every peck of the disk or only intermittently. (See M. H. Hall, 1967a, p. 22; Skinner, 1953/1965, pp. 37–38, 63–67; 1969, pp. 7, 109–113; 1972b, pp. 104–113, 259.)

Skinner has created somewhat different versions of the box for use with animals that are not capable of pecking disks. For example, rats are positively reinforced by receiving food for pressing a bar. The Skinner box may also be used to study the effects of negative reinforcement, as by having a peck of the disk or press of the bar turn off or prevent an electric shock. Or complicated sequences of behavior may be conditioned, as when a pigeon is reinforced for pecking a series of disks (with the correct order depending on their positions or colors). Skinner's apparatus permits him to study the **contingencies of reinforcement** that he believes to control all behavior, namely the interrelationships among environmental stimuli (e.g., the disk), the organism's response, and the reinforcing consequences.

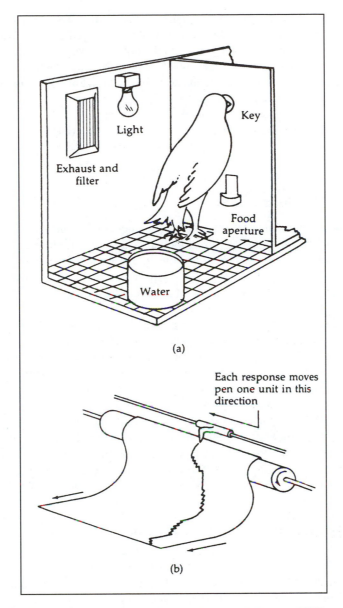

(a)

(b)

FIG. 14.1.   Skinner box used with pigeons (Ferster & Skinner, 1957, pp. 14, 24). (a) The experimental chamber (enclosed on all sides). (b) Diagram of the automatic cumulative recorder connected to the key.

Shaping

No pigeon or rat placed in a Skinner box is acute enough to rush over and peck the disk, or press the bar; it wanders about, hesitates, and so forth. Rather than waiting until the first correct response is emitted and reinforced, the experimenter typically speeds up the learning process by **shaping** behavior in the desired direction.

When the pigeon turns toward the disk, the experimenter presses a button that operates the reinforcement mechanism. (The pigeon has previously been acclimated to the Skinner box and food aperture, so it readily eats when given the opportunity.) This increases the probability that the pigeon will face the disk, and this behavior is reinforced until it is well learned. The experimenter then withholds reinforcement until the pigeon makes a slight movement toward the disk, then reinforces it only for moving still closer, and then only for touching the disk with its beak, thereby leading it step by step to the desired response. Such shaping usually takes no more than a few minutes. (See Skinner, 1953/1965, pp. 91–93.)

Shaping plays an important role in the learning of virtually every operant. The growing child learns to walk and talk through a series of successive approximations, which are reinforced by success (e.g., becoming more nearly able to stand or speak) and by the approval of others.

Schedules of Reinforcement

Although the Skinner box can be programmed to provide reinforcement after every correct response (**continuous reinforcement**), this is not the most common form of learning. The avid golfer does not sink every putt, and the gambling addict frequently fails to collect, yet both continue to pursue their respective avocations. Skinner has conducted extensive studies of the ways in which behavior is affected by such **intermittent** (or **partial**) **reinforcement.**

Interval Schedules. In a **fixed-interval schedule** of (say) 1 minute ("FI 1"), reinforcement is given only for the first correct response that occurs at least 1 minute after the preceding reinforcement. This makes it impossible to obtain more than one feeding per minute, so the pigeon eventually ceases pecking the disk after each reinforcement and gradually accelerates its responses to a high rate as the critical moment approaches.

Such pauses can be eliminated by varying the time interval randomly from trial to trial. A 1-minute **variable-interval schedule** ("VI 1") includes some intervals of a few minutes and some of only a few seconds, with the average of all intervals being 1 minute. Variable-interval schedules produce learning that is extremely long lasting, with some pigeons continuing to respond as many as 10,000 times after all reinforcement has ceased. (See Ferster & Skinner, 1957; Skinner, 1953/1965, pp. 70, 99–106; 1974/1976, pp. 64–67; 1978, p. 21.)

Ratio Schedules. Reinforcement may instead be given for every *n*th correct response (**fixed-ratio schedule**), or for an average of every *n*th correct response (**variable-ratio schedule**). A fixed-ratio schedule of 50 ("FR 50") reinforces the fiftieth correct response following the preceding reinforcement, whereas a variable-ratio schedule of 50 ("VR 50") sometimes reinforces the fortieth subsequent response, sometimes the 60th, and so on.

Ratio schedules typically lead to very high response rates, since this produces more reinforcements. Fixed-ratio schedules as high as 5,000 can be conditioned through shaping, as by giving reinforcement at first for every 5th response, then for every 10th response, and so on, but requiring so much effort may ultimately prove damaging to the organism.

Combined Schedules. Skinner has also devised and studied many complicated reinforcement schedules. Reinforcement may be given according to either a fixed-ratio or fixed-interval schedule, whichever is satisfied first. Both a fixed-ratio and a fixed-interval schedule may have to be satisfied in order to gain reinforcement. Or reinforcement may depend on two or more schedules that alternate at random. Whatever the form, Skinner regards the schedule of reinforcement as a far more important determinant of behavior than the amount or type. (See Ferster & Skinner, 1957; Skinner, 1953/1965, p. 101; 1968, p. 20; 1971/1972a, p. 32; 1978, p. 61.)

Conditioned Reinforcement (Secondary Reinforcement)

If a neutral stimulus is repeatedly paired with a reinforcer, it acquires the power to act as a reinforcer in its own right. Such **conditioned** (or **secondary**) **reinforcers** differ from the Pavlovian model in that they occur after a response, and serve to strengthen rather than elicit it.

Suppose that a pigeon in a Skinner box always receives its food together with a brief flash of light. It will learn to peck a different key in order to produce the light alone, because the light has become a conditioned positive reinforcer. If instead the light is repeatedly paired with an electric shock, a pigeon will learn to peck a disk in order to turn off the light (which has become a conditioned negative reinforcer). Among humans, money (which is worthless in itself) serves as a conditioned positive reinforcer because we have learned that it can be exchanged for food, clothing, and other desirable items. (See Skinner, 1953/1965, pp. 76–81, 173–176; 1971/1972a, pp. 115–117; 1978, pp. 22–23.)

Deprivation and Satiation

Reinforcement is not the only factor that affects the probability of an operant. A pigeon that has undergone food **deprivation** for some time will peck the disk more frequently than does a satiated bird. Similarly, a child who refuses to drink its milk may have the probability of this response increased by restricting its water intake. "It is decidedly not true that a horse may be led to water but cannot be made to drink. By arranging a history of severe deprivation, we could be 'absolutely sure' that drinking would occur" (Skinner, 1953/1965, p. 32).

In accordance with his rejection of inner causes, Skinner defines such drives as hunger, thirst, sex, and sleep in terms of an external and precisely measurable set of operations: either the amount of time one has been without food or water ("hours of deprivation"), or the reduction in weight resulting from such deprivation (measured as the percent of the weight achieved when allowed to eat freely):

> The net result of reinforcement is not simply to strengthen behavior, but to strengthen it *in a given state of deprivation*.... We [use] a *hungry* pigeon in our experiment[s], and we could not ... [demonstrate] operant conditioning otherwise. (Skinner, 1953/1965, pp. 82, 149; see also pp. 68, 141–159.)

Whereas deprivation increases the probability of an operant, **satiation** may be used to decrease it. For example, a restaurant that charges a fixed price for dinner and wishes to get by with small portions may serve a large supply of good bread at the outset of the meal. Or bread lines and welfare programs may reduce the likelihood of aggressive behavior by the poorer members of society. (See Skinner, 1953/1965, p. 147.)

Stimulus and Response Generalization

An operant tends to generalize to stimuli that resemble the conditioned stimulus, without any further conditioning. A pigeon that has been reinforced for pecking a red key will also peck a key that is orange or yellow, albeit not as frequently. Such **stimulus generalization** is also common among humans, as when one is expecting an important telephone call and rushes to the phone when the doorbell rings. Stimulus generalization is necessary for learning to occur, since no two situations are ever identical in every respect.

Conditioning also strengthens other responses that are similar to the operant (**response generalization**). Training in one behavior may improve performance in another, as when learning Latin facilitates one's proficiency in English. (See Skinner, 1953/1965, pp. 93–95, 132–134, 218.)

Discrimination

If an organism can perceive a difference between two stimuli, or between the presence and absence of a stimulus, it can learn to respond to them in different ways (behavior known as **discrimination**). A rat will learn to press the bar only when a light is on if reinforcement is withheld when the light is off. A pigeon that is presented with a red key and a green key will learn to peck only the one that produces food. And a child is taught to discriminate between right and wrong by being reinforced with approval for correct behaviors ("That's right!"), but not for incorrect behaviors ("That's wrong!").

Discrimination is also essential to learning, as otherwise we would respond to every situation in much the same way. It plays a particularly important role in the learning of skilled behaviors: The expert pianist or golfer becomes able to recognize and correct subtle physical errors that the novice cannot identify, and is reinforced for doing so with better performances. (See Skinner, 1953/1965, pp. 107–110, 134–136, 258–261; 1974/1976, p. 116.)

CAPSULE SUMMARY
Some Important Behaviorist Terminology (I)

Behaviorism	An approach to psychology that focuses on observable behavior.
Classical conditioning	A simple form of learning first demonstrated by Pavlov, wherein a conditioned stimulus (e.g., tone) becomes capable of eliciting a conditioned response (salivation) by being repeatedly paired with an unconditioned stimulus (food) which automatically elicits that response.
Conditioned reinforcement (secondary reinforcement)	Reinforcement that is provided by a conditioned stimulus.
Conditioned response	A response to a conditioned stimulus that has been learned through conditioning.
Conditioned stimulus	A previously neutral stimulus that acquires positive or aversive properties through conditioning.
Contingencies of reinforcement	The relationships among environmental stimuli, the organism's responses, and the reinforcement that follows those responses.
Continuous reinforcement	Reinforcement given after every correct response. The converse of intermittent reinforcement.
Deprivation	Withholding a primary reinforcer (such as food or water) for some time, so that it may be used to reinforce and condition an operant.
Discrimination	(1) Reinforcing an organism for responding to some difference between two or more stimuli. (2) The resulting increase in the probability of responding to the reinforced stimulus.
Extinction	(1) Consistently following an operant with no reinforcement, thereby decreasing or eliminating its probability of occurrence. (2) The resulting decrease in frequency or cessation of an operant.
Fixed-interval schedule (FI)	Reinforcing the first correct response that occurs after a specified interval of time, measured from the preceding reinforcement. A schedule of intermittent reinforcement.
Fixed-ratio schedule (FR)	Reinforcing the last of a specified number of correct responses, counted from the preceding reinforcement. A schedule of intermittent reinforcement.

Intermittent reinforcement (partial reinforcement)	Reinforcement given after some correct responses, but not all. The converse of continuous reinforcement.
Negative reinforcer (aversive stimulus)	A stimulus that increases the probability of a response when removed following that response, such as an electric shock or disapproval.
Operant	A type of behavior on which reinforcement is contingent, such as pecking the key in a Skinner box.
Operant conditioning	A form of learning wherein a response operates on the environment to produce a positive reinforcer or to remove a negative reinforcer, and is therefore more likely to recur.
Positive reinforcer	A stimulus that increases the probability of a response when presented following that response, such as food or approval.
Probability of a response	The likelihood that a response will be emitted in the future.
Punishment	A procedure designed to reduce the probability of an operant, wherein the operant is followed by the presentation of a negative reinforcer or the removal of a positive reinforcer. The converse of reinforcement.
Reinforcement	(1) In operant conditioning: following a response with the presentation of a positive reinforcer (positive reinforcement), or with the removal of a negative reinforcer (negative reinforcement), thereby increasing its probability of occurrence. (2) In classical conditioning: presenting a conditioned stimulus followed by an unconditioned stimulus.
Response	(1) A single instance of an operant, such as one peck of the disk in a Skinner box. (2) A synonym for operant.
Response generalization	A change in the probability of a response that has not been conditioned, because it is similar to one that has.
Satiation	(1) Decreasing the probability of an operant by providing reinforcement without requiring the correct response to be made. (2) The resulting decrease in the probability of an operant.
Schedules of reinforcement	Programs of (usually) intermittent reinforcement, including interval schedules, ratio schedules, and various combinations thereof.
Shaping (response shaping)	Facilitating learning by reinforcing increasingly more accurate approximations of the desired response.
Spontaneous recovery	A temporary increase in the probability of an operant that is undergoing extinction, which occurs without any additional reinforcement.
Stimulus generalization	The occurrence of a conditioned response to a stimulus that resembles the conditioned stimulus, without any further conditioning.
Unconditioned response	An automatic, unlearned response elicited by an unconditioned stimulus.
Unconditioned stimulus	A stimulus that automatically elicits a particular (unconditioned) response, without any learning or conditioning being necessary.
Variable-interval schedule (VI)	Reinforcing the first correct response that occurs after a varying interval of time, measured from the preceding reinforcement, with the series of intervals having a specified mean. A schedule of intermittent reinforcement.
Variable-ratio schedule (VR)	Reinforcing the last of a varying number of correct responses, counted from the preceding reinforcement, with the series of ratios having a specified mean. A schedule of intermittent reinforcement.

Extinction

If a pigeon that has learned to peck the key should subsequently receive no food for doing so, and this lack of reinforcement is repeated numerous times, the frequency of disk-pecking will decrease—and ultimately cease. Eliminating or diminishing a response by removing the reinforcement is called **extinction**.

To Skinner, organisms stop doing something not because they become bored or discouraged, but because that behavior is no longer reinforced by the environment. "One who readily engages in a given activity is not showing an interest, he is showing the effect of reinforcement.... [Conversely,] to become discouraged is simply to fail to respond because reinforcement has not been forthcoming" (Skinner, 1953/1965, p. 72; see also pp. 69–71, 98).

Extinction takes longer when learning has occurred under intermittent reinforcement. Gamblers who become addicted to slot machines continue to insert their coins even though they usually lose. Slot machines pay off only infrequently, and this intermittent reinforcement leads to behavior that is highly resistant to extinction. But if you put your money into a vending machine that you have learned "pays off" on every trial (continuous reinforcement), and no candy emerges, this response is likely to extinguish very quickly.

As these examples indicate, schedules of reinforcement have a strong influence on learning and behavior. Behavior is learned more quickly under continuous reinforcement, but it also extinguishes more quickly. Behavior is learned more slowly under intermittent reinforcement, but is longer lasting (more resistant to extinction).

A response that is undergoing extinction sometimes increases in frequency at the beginning of a new experimental session, without any additional reinforcement. This phenomenon is known as **spontaneous recovery,** and is attributed by Skinner to the fact that extinction is not yet complete (Ferster & Skinner, 1957, p. 733).

Complicated Sequences of Behavior

According to Skinner, even the most complicated sequence of behavior—driving a car, building a home, talking—can be explained in terms of operant conditioning. As a laboratory illustration, he has conditioned rats to pull a string that produces a marble from a rack, pick up the marble with the forepaws, carry it to a tube, and drop it inside. Such learning is accomplished by beginning with the lattermost response (here, dropping the marble into the tube), which is reinforced by food. When this behavior has been well learned, the next prior response (carrying the marble) is conditioned by using the tube as a secondary reinforcer, and so forth.

Skinner has used this approach to teach pigeons to peck out a few tunes on the piano and to play a sort of Ping-Pong, although this latter experiment caused more notoriety than he would have liked. He even argued that properly reinforced pigeons could accurately guide surface-to-air missiles, but his plan was never adopted by the government. (See Hall, 1967a, pp. 22, 72; Hilgard & Bower, 1975, pp. 206, 231; Skinner, 1953/1965, p. 224; 1972b, pp. 533–535, 574–591.)

THE OPERANT EXPLANATION OF CONCEPTS RELATED TO PERSONALITY THEORY

Emotion

Skinner readily accepts the *existence* of private as well as overt behaviors, such as emotions and thoughts; it is their purported *causal* function to which he objects. He defines emotion as a predisposition to behave in certain ways, which is due to some external event (Skinner,

1953/1965, p. 166; see also Skinner, 1953/1965, pp. 69–70, 160–170, 178–181, 259, 361; 1974/1976, pp. 25–28, 35, 52–54, 241–243).

For example, an "angry" individual is more likely to turn red and act aggressively. This is due to a specific event, such as a stuck desk drawer that stubbornly refuses to budge. A "frightened" person has a greater probability of running away because of some aversive stimulus, such as a mugger wielding a knife. And an "anxious" individual is more likely to behave in distressed and inefficient ways because of a conditioned aversive stimulus, such as a parent's contorted facial expression that typically precedes a spanking or ridicule. In each case, the emotion is real (and internal), but is caused by clearly identifiable external stimuli.

It is possible to ask people how they feel, and to gain some useful information from these self-reports, because humans can sense such internal stimuli. But Skinner warns that the language of emotion is far from scientifically precise: We learn to label our feelings by using words taught to us by other people, yet no one else can truly know one's own inner world. Therefore, emotion is best studied behavioristically. "Men do not work to maximize pleasure and minimize pain, as the hedonists have insisted; they work to produce pleasant things and to avoid painful things" (Skinner, 1971/1972a, p. 102; see also Skinner, 1971/1972a, pp. 100–101; 1974/1976, p. 242).

Thinking

Making decisions, recalling something that has been forgotten, and solving problems are also primarily private behaviors that Skinner explains in behaviorist terms. "Thinking is behaving. The mistake is in allocating the behavior to the mind" (Skinner, 1974/1976, p. 115; see also Skinner, 1953/1965, pp. 213–216, 242–256; 1957; 1969, pp. 133–171; 1971/1972a, pp. 184–186; 1974/1976b, pp. 113–131, 245–246).

Decision Making. Indecision occurs when a response cannot be emitted because it is interfered with by another response of equal strength, and is aversive because it prevents the individual from gaining reinforcement. Conversely, making a decision occurs when the strength of one response increases sufficiently for it to prevail over the other(s), and is negatively reinforcing.

Suppose that a person who wishes to take a vacation finds that the responses of going to the seashore and to the mountains are equally powerful. No decision is made, and no reinforcement is obtained. The prospective vacationer therefore pores through various travel magazines until one response gains considerably in strength, emits the words "I am going to the seashore," and escapes from the aversive state of indecision. Skinner regards decision making as a deficient form of behavior that has been unwisely reinforced by other people (e.g., "Look before you leap!"), for conditioning that produced a more immediate response would yield reinforcement more quickly (1953/1965, p. 244).

Recall. Some behaviors help us to emit other behaviors, thereby allowing recall to take place. Suppose that you see an acquaintance whose name you have forgotten. You may ask yourself whether the name begins with the letter *a*, *b*, and so on, with this "self-probe" increasing the probability that you will recall and emit the name. Similarly, a student preparing for an examination may use mnemonic codes to prompt the recall of important facts during the test.

Problem Solving. A problem occurs when a response with a high probability cannot be emitted because of some external impediment, making reinforcement impossible. Conversely, solving the problem involves behavior that alters the external situation so that the appropriate response can be made.

Suppose that a person who wants to drive home from work cannot start the car. The immobilized driver uses self-probes to review such possible solutions as looking under the hood and checking the gas, decides on the latter, finds that the gauge reads "empty," and has gas put in the tank. The problem is now solved, and the response of driving home is promptly emitted. To Skinner, the operant approach to thinking and problem solving offers considerable advantages:

> So long as originality is identified with spontaneity, or [with] an absence of lawfulness in behavior, it appears to be a hopeless task to teach a man to be original or to influence his process of thinking in any important way.... [But if my] account of thinking is essentially correct, there is no reason why we cannot teach a man how to think. (Skinner, 1953/1965, p. 256. See also Skinner, 1968, pp. 115–144.)

Punishment

Punishment is a procedure designed to reduce the probability of an operant, and is therefore the opposite of reinforcement. In punishment, behavior is followed by *presenting* a negative reinforcer (such as a spanking) or by *removing* a positive reinforcer (as by taking candy from a baby). Conditioned reinforcers may also be used for purposes of punishment, as when one issues a verbal reprimand or cuts off a dependent without a cent. (See Skinner, 1938; 1953/1965, pp. 71, 73, 182–193, 318–319, 342–344; 1971/1972a, pp. 56–95; 1974/1976, pp. 68–71.)

Punishment tends to produce an immediate decrease in the behavior that it follows, a consequence that is reinforcing to the punisher. Nevertheless, Skinner regards punishment as an inherently defective technique. "Punishment does not permanently reduce a tendency to respond, [which] is in agreement with Freud's discovery of the surviving activity of what he called repressed wishes" (Skinner, 1953/1965, p. 184; see also p. 361). Furthermore, the effects of punishment may interfere with later healthy behaviors. If adolescents are severely punished for a sexual act, they may subsequently have difficulty engaging in marital sex because their own preliminary actions generate sights and sensations that have become conditioned aversive stimuli—ones that make doing virtually anything else reinforcing.

A better way to reduce the probability of an operant is by reinforcing acceptable behaviors that are incompatible with the undesirable ones. A parent may pay no attention to a child's temper tantrums, and respond only to more quiet and orderly behavior. Since the child gets what it wants only after being calm, such behavior is more likely to be emitted in the future. Unfortunately, "we are still a long way from exploiting the alternatives [to punishment]" (Skinner, 1953/1965, p. 192; see also Skinner, cited by Evans, 1968, p. 35).

Freudian Concepts

Since Skinner attributes all behavior to prior conditioning, his approach is as deterministic as Freudian psychoanalysis. "[Freud's great achievement] was to apply the principle of cause and effect to human behavior. Aspects of behavior which had hitherto been regarded as whimsical, aimless, or accidental, Freud traced to relevant variables" (Skinner, 1953/1965, p. 375; see also Skinner, 1972b, p. 239). Skinner has found that the effects of conditioning can last as long as half the life of a pigeon, which supports Freud's contention that childhood events influence adult behavior. "If, because of early childhood experiences, a man marries a woman who resembles his mother, the effect of certain reinforcements must have survived for a long time" (Skinner, 1953/1965, p. 71).

Skinner accepts the existence of parapraxes, but refuses to attribute them to unconscious inner causes. For example, a young woman was once asked to speak in favor of the repeal of Prohibition. She became extremely ill at ease about appearing before a large audience, and sought to gain sympathy by saying: "This is the first time I have ever faced a speakeasy." Skinner attributes this "Freudian slip" to the subject of her talk (which concerned the evils of the speakeasy), the presence of the microphone before her (a device which helps one to speak more easily), and her thoughts about whether or not she could in fact speak easily, all of which greatly increased the probability of emitting the word *speakeasy* (Skinner, 1953/1965, p. 212; see also pp. 209–216, 238–239, 366–367).

For the most part, however, Skinner regards Freudian theory as an elaborate set of explanatory fictions. Repression occurs because it is reinforcing to avoid an aversive stimulus, such as the thought of behavior that has previously led to punishment. Other processes that seem to be unconscious actually represent a lack of discrimination, for we will not distinguish among and identify our own behaviors unless we have been reinforced for doing so. A person who seems to be influenced by an id impulse, such as a child who grabs a toy from another child, has previously been reinforced for such behavior. And since the same individual has undoubtedly also been reinforced for other behaviors that benefit people, any contingencies that produce these cooperative actions give the appearance that a superego has taken control. "We do not need to say that [the id, ego, and superego] are the actors in an internal drama. The actor is the organism, which has become a person with different, possibly conflicting repertoires [of behavior] as the result of different, possibly conflicting contingencies [of reinforcement]" (Skinner, 1974/1976, p. 167; see also Skinner, 1953/1965, pp. 189, 216–217, 222–223, 284–294, 375–378; 1971/1972a, pp. 58–59; 1974/1976, pp. 166, 169–174).

Traits

Skinner agrees that traits such as "wise," "ignorant," "enthusiastic," "discouraged," "intelligent," and "narcissistic" convey useful information about a person. However, he argues that such concepts do not in any way explain the behavior that they describe. "[The trait theorist begins] by observing a preoccupation with a mirror which recalls the legend of Narcissus, [invents] the adjective 'narcissistic' and then the noun 'narcissism,' and finally [asserts] that the thing presumably referred to by the noun is the cause of [this] behavior.... But at no point in such a series [does he] make contact with any event outside the behavior itself which justifies the claim of a causal connection" (Skinner, 1953/1965, p. 202; see also pp. 194–203).

As always, Skinner stresses that a causal analysis must be based on contingencies of reinforcement. The "wise" individual has been reinforced for acquiring knowledge that the "ignorant" person has not, the "enthusiastic" person has been reinforced more effectively than the "discouraged" individual, and an "intelligent" individual becomes conditioned more quickly than someone who is "unintelligent."

Intentions and Teleology

As we have seen, Skinner argues that human beings have no purpose or will. What we mistakenly believe to be intentions are actually responses to internal stimuli.

For example, saying that you plan to go home is the equivalent of saying, "I observe events in myself which characteristically precede or accompany my going home." Similarly, "I feel like playing cards" may be translated as "I feel as I often feel when I have begun to play cards." "A person disposed to act because he has been reinforced for acting may feel the condition of his body at such a time and call it 'felt purpose,' but what behaviorism rejects is the causal efficacy of that feeling" (Skinner, 1974/1976, p. 246; see also Skinner, 1953/1965, p. 262; 1969, pp. 105–109; 1971/1972a, p. 112; 1974/1976, pp. 31–32, 61–63, 180; 1978, pp. 38, 103).

FURTHER APPLICATIONS OF SKINNERIAN PSYCHOLOGY

Psychopathology

Skinner dismisses neurosis as another explanatory fiction that suggests the existence of mythical inner causes. Instead, he defines psychopathology as behavior that is disadvantageous or dangerous to the individual and/or to other people. Such behavior can result from poorly designed contingencies of reinforcement, but is more often due to punishment. The more frequent the punishment, the greater the number of behaviors that generate conditioned aversive stimuli, and the more inhibited the individual.

Alternatively, a child may engage in temper tantrums because the parents have reinforced such behavior with attention and concern. Or a busy parent may fail to respond to the child's polite requests and answer only louder calls, thereby shaping the child in the direction of becoming noisy. "[Such] differential reinforcement supplied by a preoccupied or negligent parent is very close to the procedure we should adopt if we were given the task of conditioning a child to be annoying" (Skinner, 1953/1965, p. 98; see also Skinner, 1953/1965, pp. 166–167, 361–366, 372–374, 381; 1972b, pp. 565–566).

Compulsions are likely to be caused by particularly inept schedules of reinforcement. Suppose that a hungry pigeon is given a small amount of food every 15 seconds. Whatever the pigeon may be doing at that moment is reinforced, even though this behavior does not operate to produce food. Eventually, some wholly irrelevant (*superstitious*) behavior becomes conditioned, such as hopping from one foot to another or bowing and scraping. Such "noncontingent reinforcement" is generally harmful, as when a person given unconditional welfare payments demonstrates a reduced probability of engaging in constructive work. (See Hall, 1967a, pp. 68–69; Skinner, 1953/1965, pp. 55, 84–87, 350–351; 1972b, pp. 524–532; 1978, pp. 12–13.)

Psychotherapy

Rationale.   The goal of Skinnerian **behavior modification** (or **behavior therapy**[2]) is to change the client's pathological behaviors by establishing more effective contingencies of reinforcement. These new contingencies may extinguish the disadvantageous behaviors, or they may reinforce incompatible and more acceptable responses. "It is not an inner cause of behavior but the behavior itself which [must be changed] … [and behavior is] changed by changing the conditions of which it is a function" (Skinner, 1953/1965, p. 373; 1971/1972a, p. 143; see also Skinner, 1953/1965, pp. 367–383).

Modern behavior therapists use a variety of techniques. Some of these are based on Skinner's ideas, whereas others involve somewhat different concepts and procedures. Behavior

---

[2]Skinner uses *behavior modification* to refer to the change of behavior through changes in the relevant contingencies of reinforcement, notably positive reinforcement (1978, pp. 10, 40–41). But probably the majority of psychologists use this term synonymously with *behavior therapy,* a general term that includes both operant and nonoperant techniques.

therapy differs from the forms of psychotherapy devised by personality theorists in the following ways:

— The goal of behavior therapy is to change clearly specified behaviors and/or symptoms, rather than unobservable inner states.
— Active control is exercised by the therapist, who selects and imposes specific procedures designed to bring about the desired changes in behavior.
— Behavior therapy emphasizes the present aspects of the client's difficulties, and is less concerned with childhood causes.
— Behavior therapists use different techniques to treat different types of problems, rather than imposing the same form of therapy on every client.
— Behavior therapy is typically of shorter duration than psychotherapy, and may last as little as a few months.
— Behavior therapy is not concerned with resistances and transferences.
— The techniques of behavior therapy are based on empirical research, rather than on a psychotherapist's theoretical speculations and subjective judgments.

Skinnerian Procedures.   Skinner has not written extensively about therapeutic applications, primarily because he sees little conceptual difference between psychotherapy and other areas of behavior modification. For example, *positive reinforcement* and *shaping* may be used to help an autistic child or psychotic adult speak in coherent sentences. The client is first reinforced for sounds that approximate real words, then for simple words, then for basic phrases, and so on, and reinforcement is withheld following bizarre utterances or silence. Typical reinforcers include candy, praise, smiles, or an opportunity to play freely. As always, whether or not any of these is reinforcing for a particular client must be determined by actual test.

Conditioned positive reinforcers play an important role in the **token economy,** a complicated procedure that has many applications (e.g., with hospitalized psychotics, juvenile delinquents, and mentally retarded and normal schoolchildren). The first step is to specify desirable behaviors, such as spelling a word correctly, keeping one's room clean, or proceeding in an orderly fashion to the dining room at mealtime. These behaviors are then reinforced with plastic tokens or points, a sufficient number of which can later be exchanged for some special treat chosen by the client (such as candy, watching television, or a private room). Although a token economy by no means cures psychosis, it is capable of producing marked improvements in behavior. (See, for example, Ayllon & Azrin, 1968; Kazdin, 1977.)

The *extinction* of undesirable behaviors may be facilitated by placing an unruly child in a comfortable but uninteresting area until more quiet behavior is emitted, which is then reinforced by allowing the child to leave and pursue other activities. (Modern parents refer to this procedure as "time out.") Or an alcoholic may be shown pictures of liquor together with graphic illustrations of kidney disease (**aversion therapy**), so that avoiding alcoholic beverages will become negatively reinforcing. Some behavior therapists have sought to extend this procedure by following pictures of alcohol with a mild electric shock, but Skinner regards such punishment as inferior to reinforcement because its effects are only temporary. (See Skinner, 1953/1965, pp. 56–57, 174–175.)

Related Procedures.   **Reciprocal inhibition** is an essentially Pavlovian approach originated by Mary Cover Jones (1924a; 1924b) and Joseph Wolpe (1958). In this procedure, the behavior therapist uses a positive stimulus to elicit responses that will inhibit the client's anxiety.

For example, suppose that little Albert were known to be fond of gumdrops. His animal phobia could be treated by presenting the feared tame rat at a considerable distance, while allowing him to eat a piece of this candy. Since the rat is far away, the anxiety that it elicits is very weak and is overwhelmed by the more powerful positive responses evoked by the candy. The process is then repeated with the rat somewhat closer, with eating again inhibiting the anxiety. The distance between Albert and the rat is gradually reduced until he can eat the candy with one hand and pet the rat with the other, whereupon his anxiety is gone and the phobia is cured. (This illustration is only hypothetical, for Albert never was deconditioned by Watson. See Harris, 1979.)

A second technique devised by Joseph Wolpe (1973; Wolpe & Lazarus, 1966), **systematic desensitization,** differs from reciprocal inhibition in two respects. The client merely imagines the feared stimuli (in most cases), and inhibits the resulting anxiety by relaxation.

As an illustration, consider a capable college student who frequently fails examinations because of intense anxiety. This student would be a poor candidate for reciprocal inhibition, since there is no way to present a genuine testing situation during a therapy session. Instead, the student is first taught techniques of deep muscular relaxation, which consist of successively tensing and relaxing various muscles of the body in a sequence determined by the therapist. The client then constructs an *anxiety hierarchy,* which lists the fearful stimuli in order of the amount of anxiety evoked. For example, the student may specify the most anxiety-provoking item (Number 1) as going to the university on the day of the exam, the next most feared item (Number 2) as beginning to answer the exam questions, Number 3 as the moment just before the doors to the exam room open, and so on down to a 14th and least anxiety-provoking stimulus, having an exam a month away (Wolpe, 1973, p. 116). As this actual example illustrates, anxiety hierarchies must be constructed by the client because they are an individual matter: Many students might find item Number 2 to be the most anxiety provoking, but this particular client does not. The client is then asked to imagine the lowest-ranking item in the hierarchy (Number 14) while relaxing deeply. After this has been well learned, the client practices relaxing while imagining item Number 13, and gradually proceeds up the hierarchy until item Number 1 no longer elicits any anxiety. This usually requires some 30 therapy sessions and suffices to resolve the client's difficulties, although *in vivo* desensitization may be necessary for those who cannot imagine themselves in the relevant situations vividly enough to feel anxious.

Aversion therapy, reciprocal inhibition, and systematic desensitization are examples of **counterconditioning**. In counterconditioning, the behavior therapist tries to condition a desirable response (e.g., relaxation, fear of alcoholic beverages) that is incompatible with an undesirable response (anxiety, drinking alcohol) and therefore replaces it.

Behavior Modification and Social Reform.

In a rare moment of agreement with certain personality theorists, Skinner warns that our present existence on earth is precarious. Haphazard contingencies of reinforcement are strengthening behaviors that jeopardize our survival, notably overpopulation and pollution. "Unless something is done, and soon, there will be too many people in the world, and they will ever more rapidly exhaust its resources and pollute its air, land, and water, until in one last violent struggle for what is left, some madman will release a stockpile of nuclear missiles" (Skinner, 1978, p. 17; see also Skinner, 1969, pp. 37, 40, 46, 98; 1978, pp. 6–7, 21, 46, 112; 1986; 1987).

To avoid such a catastrophe, Skinner advocates the design of contingencies that will strengthen appropriate behaviors without wasting essential reinforcers (as by using more intermittent schedules). This concern for the future will require us to undergo certain deprivations, the *sine qua non* of operant conditioning. But since schedules of reinforcement are a more important determinant of behavior than the amount, it is possible that skillfully designed survival-oriented contingencies will make us happier even while receiving less (Skinner, 1978, pp. 41, 61).

Work

Skinnerian principles have also been applied to the area of work. For example, one group of employees created a serious hazard by crowding into a narrow passageway at quitting time. They were induced to substitute safer incompatible responses, such as stopping to adjust their clothing, by the simple expedient of installing mirrors on the walls (Skinner, 1953/1965, p. 316).

Pay is a conditioned positive reinforcer that has no value in and of itself, but can be exchanged for many primary reinforcers. Piecework pay is a form of fixed-ratio schedule, since the employee receives a specified amount of money for producing or selling a given number of items. Such schedules are likely to be effective so long as the ratio is not too high, and the workers do not have to produce a large number of units just to gain a minimal wage. However, Skinner is highly critical of the usual contingencies of reinforcement found in the workplace. He argues that these contingencies do not induce many people to work hard or carefully, or enjoy what they are doing. (See Skinner, 1953/1965, pp. 384–391; 1978, pp. 25, 27.)

Religion

According to Skinner, religion is merely another example of behavior control through conditioning. Religious belief is due primarily to an accident of birth, namely the conditioning

---

CAPSULE SUMMARY
Some Important Behaviorist Terminology (II)

Aversion therapy	Using an aversive stimulus to reduce the probability of undesirable behavior.
Behavior modification	(1) A synonym for behavior therapy. (2) Skinnerian methods for changing behavior, including areas other than psychopathology.
Behavior therapy	An approach to psychotherapy that seeks to change particular behaviors and/or symptoms, rather than trying to alter some unobservable or unconscious inner state.
Counterconditioning	Conditioning a desirable response (e.g., relaxation) that is incompatible with an undesirable response (anxiety) and therefore replaces it.
Programmed instruction	A Skinnerian approach to education wherein specific correct responses are promptly reinforced, often by a teaching machine, in a sequence designed to produce optimal learning.
Reciprocal inhibition	Using a positive stimulus to inhibit the anxiety caused by an aversive stimulus, with the latter first presented at a considerable distance and gradually brought closer until it can be handled without anxiety. A form of behavior therapy devised by Mary Cover Jones and Joseph Wolpe.
Systematic desensitization	A form of behavior therapy, devised by Joseph Wolpe, wherein the client imagines a hierarchical sequence of feared stimuli and inhibits the resulting anxiety by practicing previously taught techniques of muscular relaxation. Alternatively, *in vivo* desensitization may be used with clients who are unable to imagine the feared situations vividly enough to feel anxious.
Token economy	A form of behavior therapy, based on Skinnerian operant conditioning, wherein desirable behaviors are followed with conditioned positive reinforcers (such as plastic tokens) that can later be exchanged for reinforcers chosen by the client.

imposed by the parents (or by the religious school to which they send the child). Some religions try to discourage behavior that they define as immoral by using aversive stimuli and negative reinforcement, as with the threat of Hell, and promise that moral behavior will earn the rewards of Heaven. Other religions reinforce with approval and recognition those behaviors that they deem to be virtuous, such as the "Golden Rule" and large financial donations. "A person does not support a religion because he is devout; he supports it because of the contingencies [of reinforcement] arranged by the religious agency" (Skinner, 1971/1972a, p. 111; see also Hall, 1967a, p. 23; Skinner, 1953/1965, pp. 9, 310, 345, 350–358; 1971/1972a, pp. 60, 108–110).

Education

Skinner strongly disagrees with the contingencies of reinforcement used by most educators. Some teachers excuse students from additional homework as a form of reward, a procedure that is exactly the opposite of proper behavior modification (which would make extra schoolwork positively reinforcing). Crowded classrooms make it impossible for even the most dedicated teacher to meet every student's needs, with lectures and other group methods proceeding too quickly for some students and too slowly for others. Although the birch rod has generally been abandoned, teachers still use such forms of punishment as sharp criticism and failing grades. Positive reinforcements typically occur minutes or even hours after a correct response, which destroys most of their effectiveness. So it is hardly surprising that more and more young people fail to learn, resort to vandalism, or drop out of school. They have not "lost their love of learning," but have been victimized by educational contingencies of reinforcement that are not very compelling. (See Skinner, 1953/1965, pp. 402–412; 1968; 1972b, pp. 171–235; 1978, pp. 129–159; 1984; Skinner, cited by Evans, 1968, p. 70.)

The solution advocated by Skinner is **programmed instruction,** wherein specific correct responses are promptly reinforced in a carefully prepared sequence designed to produce optimal learning. This is typically accomplished by using a "teaching machine" (originally an idea of Sidney Pressey), one simple form of which works as follows: certain information and a question based on this information appear in an opening on the front of the machine. The student writes down an answer and advances the program, revealing the correct answer and the next question. (See Figure 14.2.) In some versions, the program cannot be advanced until the correct response has been made. Alternatively, programmed instruction may be presented using the printed page or personal computer. The latter method makes it possible to provide helpful hints following an incorrect response, or even to switch automatically to a program of remedial instruction after a predetermined number of errors.

To Skinner, programmed instruction has numerous advantages. Students gain immediate (and thus more powerful) reinforcement for correct answers, can proceed at their own pace, and are presented with material in a maximally effective order. The teacher is freed from many tedious chores, such as grading vast numbers of test papers, and has more time to give individual assistance to those who most need it. And since the behaviors in question are to be of later advantage to the student, natural reinforcers will eventually take over and make the teaching machine no longer necessary.

Literature

Skinner is one of the few psychologists to author a novel, which depicts a society designed in accordance with operant principles. Contrary to what some skeptics might expect, *Walden Two* (Skinner, 1948) does *not* consist of a group of people frantically pressing bars in Skinner-type

Sentence To Be Completed	Word To Be Supplied
1. The important parts of a flashlight are the battery and the bulb. When we "turn on" a flashlight, we close a switch which connects the battery with the _____.	bulb
2. When we turn on a flashlight, an electric current flows through the fine wire in the _____ and causes it to grow hot.	bulb
3. When the hot wire glows brightly, we say that it gives off or sends out heat and _____.	light
4. The fine wire in the bulb is called a filament. The bulb "lights up" when the filament is heated by the passage of a(n) _____ current.	electric
5. When a weak battery produces little current, the fine wire, or _____, does not get very hot.	filament
6. A filament which is *less* hot sends out or gives off _____ light.	less
7. "Emit" means "send out." The amount of light sent out, or "emitted," by a filament depends on how _____ the filament is.	hot
8. The higher the temperature of the filament, the _____ the light emitted by it.	brighter, stronger

FIG. 14.2   The first 8 items of a 35-item sentence completion program in high school physics (Skinner, 1968, p. 45). The machine presents one item at a time, and the student completes the item and then uncovers the corresponding word shown at the right. Or such a program might be printed in a textbook, with the student instructed to cover the answers with a sheet of paper.

boxes. It is a satisfied and largely self-sufficient community, characterized by such psychological and organizational innovations as: a pleasant rural setting that is free from such modern "advances" as rush-hour traffic and long lines, skillfully designed work schedules that require only 4 hours per person per day, education that stresses positive reinforcement and is a source of enjoyment rather than anxiety, comfortable clothing that is designed to accentuate the more attractive physical attributes of each person, lawns kept trim by grazing sheep (which also serve as a source of food) rather than by lawnmowers (which waste fuel), and excellent sanitation and medical care.

Interestingly, the least satisfied individual in *Walden Two* is its designer. He has found that his goal of creating the ideal society can be achieved only by assuring other people of positive reinforcement, so he does not have (or seek) any power or prestige. Nevertheless, the idea of a planned community such as *Walden Two* has evoked considerable criticism from those who regard it as a grave threat to fundamental and essential human freedoms. (See Skinner, 1948; 1969, pp. 29–30; 1972b, p. 123; Skinner, cited by Evans, 1968, p. 49.)

Social Psychology

According to Skinner, the operant principles that explain an individual's responses are equally applicable to group behavior. As we have seen, pigeons can be conditioned to "compete" at a sort of Ping-Pong. Or operant techniques can be used to facilitate cooperation, as by requiring two hungry pigeons to peck two different disks simultaneously in order to receive food.

Human interactions are considerably more complicated, and involve such *social reinforcers* as attention, approval, smiles, and hugs. Yet these behaviors are also due solely to conditioning. For example, suppose that a loquacious individual keeps talking much too long. It may well be that the listener is unwittingly providing such reinforcements as attention, eye contact, and polite smiles—and that the removal of these reinforcers will help to extinguish this unwanted behavior. (See Skinner, 1953/1965, pp. 297–349; 1971/1972a, pp. 102–111; 1972b, pp. 533–537.)

Verbal Behavior

Skinner has devoted considerable attention to an operant explanation of speech, which he regards as similar in principle to other forms of behavior. For example, a *mand* is a verbal operant that makes some demand on the hearer. It is reinforced by a characteristic consequence, as when "Stop that!" is applied to an external action and is strengthened by its cessation. *Tacts* refer to the discrimination and naming of different stimuli, as illustrated by a child who correctly refers to objects of a particular color as red and is reinforced by parental approval. This aspect of Skinner's work is controversial, however, with some psychologists regarding it as a major contribution and others dismissing it as largely fallacious. (See, for example, Chomsky, 1959; 1971; Bower & Hilgard, 1981, pp. 192–194, 206–209; MacCorquodale, 1969; 1970; Skinner, 1957; 1969, pp. 10–13; 1972b, pp. 359–417; 1974/1976, pp. 98–112.)

Aging and Memory

Old age tends to bring lapses in memory, as Skinner himself found on reaching age 80. As could be expected, he proposes various behavioristic techniques for overcoming such problems.

Suppose that a half hour before an elderly person is to leave the house, the television weather report predicts rain. The obvious response is to take an umbrella. But this behavior cannot yet be emitted, and it may well be forgotten when the time comes to leave. The solution is to hang the umbrella on the doorknob at that moment, so that the individual cannot leave without seeing it. Similarly, when Skinner got a useful scientific idea in the middle of the night, he immediately recorded it on a notepad or tape recorder kept by the side of his bed. By appropriate manipulation of the environment, it is possible to guard against forgetting. "In place of memories, memoranda" (Skinner, 1983, p. 240; see also Skinner & Vaughan, 1983).

EVALUATION

Criticisms and Controversies

Skinner's writings have provoked an uproar rivaling that caused by Freudian psychoanalysis. Some critics have misinterpreted his ideas, as by claiming that he denies the existence of thoughts, emotions, and self-knowledge. However, some of the attacks on Skinner's behaviorism merit serious consideration.

Is Behavior Control Benevolent?   Significant abuses can occur when behavior is controlled by external forces. To some critics, behaviorism resembles a totalitarian state run by a dictator who believes that the goal of efficiency justifies any means whatsoever.

Skinner agrees that behavior change can be induced destructively as well as constructively, as in the case of punishment. But he argues that dictatorial forms of behavior control are far *less* likely if we become aware of the contingencies of reinforcement that regulate our actions, design these contingencies more effectively, and arrange for appropriate methods of countercontrolling the controllers. He also stresses that the most effective form of behavior control is a benign one, namely positive reinforcement. However, this argument overlooks an important fact: operant conditioning is impossible without deprivation, a state that many would consider aversive. To condition a pigeon to peck a disk, or to control certain behaviors of a child with candy, the pigeon and child must be made hungry and prevented from eating at other times. (See Skinner, 1953/1965, pp. 32, 82, 149, 319, 443–445; 1971/1972a, p. 163; 1972b, pp. 122–123; 1974/1976, pp. 267–268.)

Comparing behavior modification to a dictatorship may seem rather silly in light of the many clients helped by this form of therapy. Nevertheless, it is by no means clear that effective behavior control is as benevolent as Skinner would have us believe.

People and Pigeons.   Skinner has also been accused of basing his conclusions too heavily on studies of pigeons and rats, and denying the unique qualities of human beings. His defense is that human behavior is perhaps the most difficult of all subjects to study scientifically, so the best course is to begin with the simplest and most easily revealed principles (a procedure followed by virtually all other sciences). Skinner believes that humans and animals do not differ very much with regard to basic aspects of behavior. So he sees little reason not to use animal subjects, which are far more easily studied under laboratory conditions. And he argues that even if human beings are unique in some respects, a full understanding of these characteristics may not be necessary to achieve important results—as indicated by the various successful applications of operant principles to human life. (See Skinner, 1953/1965, pp. 12, 38, 41, 204; 1969, pp. 109–113; 1971/1972a, pp. 150–152; 1972b, pp. 101, 120–122.)

Nevertheless, it would seem that psychology does need to understand certain human qualities that are not found in lower organisms. For example, cognitions may have causal aspects that are beyond the capacity of rats and pigeons. To some critics, ruling inner and unconscious causes out of psychology because they cannot be measured scientifically resembles the ludicrous "solution" offered by some cynics during the Vietnam War: Define your way out of the problem by declaring a victory and withdrawing, even though you actually have achieved no victory at all.

People as Puppets.   Since Skinner's conception of behavior is as deterministic as that of Freud, he is open to similar criticisms by those who attribute considerable importance to intentions and teleology. Skinner contends that it is the Pavlovian model that conceptualizes people as puppets, since it posits that responses are *elicited* by external stimuli, whereas operant conditioning holds that we *emit* behaviors whose strength is contingent on their consequences. However, some modern learning theorists have concluded that there is much less of a distinction between classical and operant conditioning than Skinner believes (e.g., Bower & Hilgard, 1981, pp. 199–203).

Despite Skinner's various references to emitted behaviors and countercontrol, environmental rule is clearly his reigning principle. This raises the paradox of how supposedly controlled organisms can ever be sufficiently free to change the prevailing contingencies of reinforcement. (See Bandura, 1978, p. 344.)

Other Criticisms.   Skinner is not overly concerned with the issue of why a reinforcer is reinforcing, which gives his definitions a distinctly circular quality: A reinforcer is whatever strengthens a response, and this increased frequency of responding is what proves that the item in question is a reinforcer. He does suggest that reinforcers facilitate survival, and that their existence is due to a Darwinian evolutionary process. (See Skinner, 1953/1965, p. 55; 1969, p. 46; 1971/1972a, p. 99; 1974/1976, pp. 41, 51; 1978, p. 19.)

Punishment is regarded by some modern psychologists as a valuable technique when properly used, as by administering the punishment immediately after the undesirable response and providing a more desirable way to obtain reinforcement. (See Bower & Hilgard, 1981, pp. 187–188.) Other theorists question whether complicated behaviors, such as writing a book or human speech, can be explained by a series of conditioned operants.

Contributions

Behavior modification has proved to be of considerable value in many areas, and these innovative forms of psychotherapy have gained widespread acceptance during the past 4 decades. Programmed learning and other varieties of personalized instruction have been used by numerous educational institutions. Behaviorism is based on a vast amount of empirical research, rather than on the subjective and frequently untestable speculations that pervade personality theory.

Skinner's status as a major learning theorist is unquestioned. One need not be a behaviorist to appreciate his concepts, or to agree that there are some very poorly designed contingencies of reinforcement in our present society. The Skinner box is widely used by psychologists studying animal behavior, his work on schedules of reinforcement has called attention to an important determinant of behavior, and some of the internally oriented "explanations" of which he is so critical do seem to be redundant.

The behaviorist redefinition of psychology has been rejected by modern psychologists. Virtually all current textbooks define psychology as the science of behavior *and mental processes* (e.g., Myers, 2001, p. 4), and regard inner causes and unobservable behaviors as extremely important. Nevertheless, Skinner's work has added considerably to our knowledge. Whether one attributes his remarkable performance to particularly effective conditioning (as he would), or to an unusually brilliant and inventive mind (as would a personality theorist), there is no denying his profound contributions to psychology—or the desirability of acquiring a firsthand knowledge of his writings.

Suggested Reading

The most comprehensive statement of Skinner's position is provided in *Science and Human Behavior* (1953/1965). *Beyond Freedom and Dignity* (1971/1972a) is both readable and provocative, as is his novel *Walden Two* (1948), and *About Behaviorism* (1974/1976) represents an attempt to answer some 20 common criticisms of his position. Papers concerning his invention of the Skinner box and the air crib, and his studies of Ping-Pong-playing pigeons, are included in *Cumulative Record* (1972b), and his views on education are presented in *The Technology of Teaching* (1968).

SUMMARY

Whereas personality theorists seek to explain behavior in terms of hypothesized inner causes, behaviorists redefine psychology as the study of observable behavior. A leading exponent of this approach is B. F. Skinner, who strongly opposes the idea of intrapsychic causes of behavior.

1. CLASSICAL VERSUS OPERANT CONDITIONING. Skinner agrees with Pavlov and Watson that some behaviors are learned through classical conditioning. However, Skinner contends that the vast majority of learning is due to the consequences of our actions (operant conditioning): Those responses that operate on the environment to produce effects that strengthen them (are reinforced) are more likely to occur in the future, whereas those that do not are less likely to recur. A positive reinforcer increases the probability of a response when presented, whereas a negative reinforcer does so when removed. According to Skinner, human beings have no capacity to plan for the future; all behavior is determined by prior conditioning.

2. **PRINCIPLES OF OPERANT CONDITIONING.** Skinner uses a laboratory apparatus of his own invention (commonly referred to as the Skinner box), and pigeons and rats, to study principles of operant conditioning. These include learning, shaping, schedules of reinforcement (which he regards as extremely important determinants of behavior), conditioned reinforcers, deprivation (a *sine qua non* of operant conditioning, since a satiated organism will not learn), satiation, generalization, discrimination, extinction (which shows that reinforcement is necessary for the maintenance of behavior, as well as for learning), and complicated sequences of behavior.

3. **THE OPERANT EXPLANATION OF CONCEPTS RELATED TO PERSONALITY THEORY.** Skinner accepts the existence of such internal stimuli as emotions and thinking; it is their causal status to which he objects. He has attempted to explain these phenomena, and various concepts proposed by Freud and other personality theorists, in terms of operant conditioning. Skinner is opposed to the use of punishment, which he regards as far less effective than the positive reinforcement of alternative acceptable behaviors.

4. **FURTHER APPLICATIONS.** Skinner defines psychopathology as behavior that is disadvantageous or dangerous to the individual, and results from punishment or faulty reinforcement procedures. The goal of psychotherapy is to remove or replace the client's pathological behaviors and symptoms. Skinner has not written extensively about behavior therapy, since he sees little conceptual difference between this area and other applications of behavior modification. But many other behaviorists have devoted considerable attention to such forms of therapy, including the token economy, reciprocal inhibition, and systematic desensitization. Skinner also advocates the use of programmed instruction, and has related operant conditioning principles to work, religion, social psychology, verbal behavior, and aging and memory.

5. **EVALUATION.** Skinner has been severely criticized for contending that the environment wholly controls our behavior, and for denying the importance of cognitive and other inner causes. He is also accused of overstating the benign nature of behavior control, basing his conclusions too heavily on research with animal subjects, failing to resolve the paradox of how totally controlled organisms can make the changes in their environment that he recommends, exaggerating the differences between classical and operant conditioning, circular definitions, an overly negative view of punishment, and failing to provide a satisfactory explanation of the more complicated forms of human behavior. Yet his status as a major learning theorist is unquestioned, he has devised many valuable concepts and the Skinner box, and his work is grounded in empirical research rather than subjective speculation.

STUDY QUESTIONS

Part I. Questions

1. Disappointment is an inevitable aspect of life, and many people learn to take it more or less in stride. Why, then, do some critics argue that Skinner's psychological ideas were unduly influenced by his failure as a writer?

2. Skinner argues that operant conditioning is an unselfish and benign form of behavior control, because others must be assured of reinforcement. Yet some critics contend that his ideas represent a serious threat to individual freedom. Which view do you prefer? Why?

3. Give an example from real life or from fiction to illustrate each of the following Skinnerian concepts: (a) response shaping, (b) partial reinforcement, (c) stimulus generalization, (d) discrimination, (e) extinction.

4. I wish to decide whether to include more or fewer study questions in this chapter. I decide that I feel like adding a few questions, and I do. I then claim that this shows I have free will, since I could just as easily have chosen to delete a few questions. (a) How would Skinner reply? (b) Do you agree or disagree with Skinner? Why?

5. Rats in a Skinner box learn by what is called "trial and error": They try out various responses (e.g., rearing up on their hind paws, crouching, moving to the rear of the box) until they hit on the one that produces reinforcement (pressing the bar). Why do some critics regard Skinner's approach as *not* applicable to many areas of human endeavor?

6. According to Skinner, emotion is a predisposition to behave in certain ways that is caused by some external event (such as anger over a drawer that is stuck). Can an emotion such as anger be caused by an event within the individual?

7. Give some examples of poorly designed contingencies of reinforcement that are common in our society.

8. Give an example from real life or from fiction to support the following statement by Skinner: A good way to reduce the probability of undesirable behavior is by reinforcing incompatible, desirable behavior.

9. Skinner argues that apparently unconscious processes actually reflect a lack of discrimination. (a) How does this idea compare to the quote by Kelly at the end of the section on the structure of personality in Chapter 15? (b) Do you agree or disagree with Skinner? Why?

10. Skinner is highly critical of current educational practices, and argues that they do *not* produce a lasting love of learning. "Suppose we wish to teach a student to read 'good books'—books which do not reinforce the reader sentence by sentence or even paragraph by paragraph, but only when hundreds of pages have prepared him for a convincing denouement. The student must be exposed to a program of materials that builds up a tendency to read in the absence of reinforcement. [But] schools are likely to arrange just the wrong conditions, [as by forcing] books on students before they have had adequate preparation. It is therefore not surprising that few students even in good universities learn to read books of this sort and do so for the rest of their lives" (1968, p. 79). What is your evaluation of Skinner's criticism?

11. (a) Explain the difference between classical conditioning and operant conditioning. (b) Explain the difference between negative reinforcement and punishment. (c) Explain the difference between Freud's concept of repression and Skinner's view of repression.

12. A terrorist blows up a building in a hated foreign country. How might Skinner explain the terrorist's behavior?

Part II. Comments and Suggestions

1. How might the belief that there are no inner causes, and that there is no free will, have helped Skinner to rationalize his failure as a writer? Do extreme theoretical positions suggest that the theorist has been overly influenced by personal issues? (See also Chapter 2, questions 1 and 2, and Chapter 3, question 1.) Is 1 year a long time to try without success, especially where one's heartfelt dream is concerned?

2. Who is more subject to external control: A person using a programmed instruction machine, or an individual who browses through various books in the library? A behaviorist who prepares complicated schedules of reinforcement that a hungry animal must satisfy to obtain a food reward, or the animal that causes food to appear by making the correct responses? An individual who is deprived, or one who is satiated? (Recall that deprivation must exist for

operant conditioning to be possible.) If Skinnerian ideas are a threat to individual freedom, how has behavior therapy been able to help so many clients?

3. (a) A disturbed child who must wear eyeglasses to see properly keeps taking them off and throwing them on the ground. An acceptable reinforcer is found (say, the child likes a particular kind of candy). When hungry, the child is given a piece of this candy for touching the eyeglasses gently while they are on a table. When this response has been well learned, the child is reinforced for picking up the eyeglasses carefully, then for bringing them nearer to his face, then for trying them on, and so on until he routinely wears the eyeglasses without incident. The reinforcement provided by his improved vision eventually replaces that provided by the candy. (b) A gambler continues to play a slot machine, even though it only pays off once in a great many trials. (c) I go to the supermarket to buy a loaf of my favorite bread. The loaf I see on the shelf is not exactly the same as the bread I bought yesterday; no two loaves are identical. But it is very similar, so I am able to emit the behavior of placing it in my shopping cart. (d) During a bridge tournament, I make a play that works out badly and fails to provide any reinforcement. On another occasion, the same play succeeds brilliantly. So I decide that the first situation is different from the second one and requires a different strategy. When I next encounter the former situation, I use my new strategy. My plan succeeds, and this reinforcement increases the probability that I will continue to behave differently in these two situations. (e) After 20 years of playing tournament bridge, I give up this avocation permanently. Skinner would argue that I did not lose interest in bridge, but rather that external contingencies of reinforcement were too poorly designed for me to continue to emit the behavior of playing.

4. (a) Skinner would say that I detected certain feelings within myself, which resemble those that I experienced on prior occasions when I was about to add more questions. However, these feelings didn't cause anything. (Recall that Skinner does not deny the existence of inner thoughts and feelings; it is their causal status to which he objects.) What I might have done instead is irrelevant. (b) I disagree. Psychologists and philosophers have debated the issue of free will at great length, and I'm not about to resolve it in a few sentences. But I believe that being human means the freedom to choose, and that who we are is defined to a great extent by the choices that we make.

5. Consider what would happen to a person who knows nothing at all about each of the following tasks, and tries to learn them by trial and error: brain surgery, driving a bus, flying an airplane, acupuncture, defusing a bomb, being a parent. (On second thought, perhaps that last example does support Skinner . . .)

6. I am alone in my room. My thoughts wander to a person who treated me badly in the past. As I think about this incident, I become increasingly angry. Does such an example contradict Skinner's ideas, or would he be able to explain it in terms of operant conditioning?

7. Do people who make the most money contribute the most to improving our society? Are the best employees the ones who avoid downsizing and are given the largest raises? Are procedures for changing the behaviors of criminals generally effective? Does your best schoolwork always earn the highest grades? What changes would you recommend?

8. A young child is making noise at a time when the parent would prefer quiet. The parent encourages the child to undertake a different activity that is incompatible with making noise, such as drawing a picture that requires a great deal of concentration or watching a television program with the volume turned down low.

9. (a) Both theorists argue that supposedly unconscious processes actually reflect a failure to identify or construe the behaviors in question. (b) I disagree. See Chapter 8, question 10, and Chapter 15, question 8.

10. My few experiences with programmed learning were negative: I quickly supplied the missing word in each frame, moved rapidly through the program, and forgot everything I had

"learned" soon after I finished. But I agree with Skinner about my college education, which did little to promote a love of learning on my part. And I fear that this textbook may prove difficult for those who have not been prepared to deal with technical material, which cannot provide the frequent reinforcement so common in our newspapers and magazines.

11. (a) In classical conditioning, the organism associates one stimulus with another stimulus because the two stimuli occur closely together in time. In operant conditioning, the organism associates a response with its consequences. A response that is reinforced is strengthened (more likely to recur), whereas a response that is not reinforced is weakened (less likely to recur). In operant conditioning, the organism must make the correct response to receive reinforcement. (b) Negative reinforcement strengthens a response by removing something undesirable. If you have a headache and take Tylenol, and your headache goes away, this desirable consequence will make you more likely to take Tylenol the next time you have a headache. (If instead Tylenol does not cure your headache, the lack of reinforcement will weaken this response and make you more likely to select a different medication in the future.) Punishment is the opposite: it weakens a response by presenting something undesirable (or by removing something desirable), as when a child does something wrong and the parents respond with disapproval or a spanking. (c) Freud argues that the ego prevents undesirable id impulses from reaching consciousness. Skinner contends that removing unpleasant (aversive) thoughts is negatively reinforcing.

12. Would Skinner attribute the terrorist's behavior to an illicit instinct? Why not? What contingencies of reinforcement might explain the terrorist's behavior? Is it possible to change the terrorist's behavior by changing these contingencies?

Comparing Skinner and Freud on Various Issues

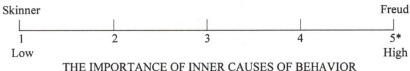

THE IMPORTANCE OF INNER CAUSES OF BEHAVIOR
(Including the unconscious, intrapsychic conflicts, and defense mechanisms)

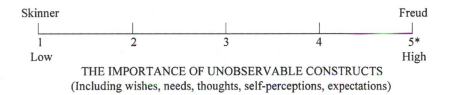

THE IMPORTANCE OF UNOBSERVABLE CONSTRUCTS
(Including wishes, needs, thoughts, self-perceptions, expectations)

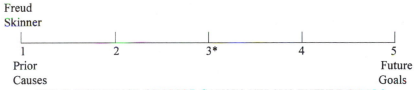

THE IMPORTANCE OF PRIOR CAUSES VERSUS FUTURE GOALS
(Including events in early childhood)

Comparing Behaviorists' Views of Conditioning

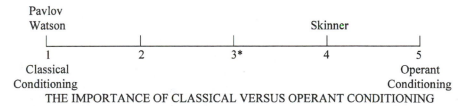

THE IMPORTANCE OF CLASSICAL VERSUS OPERANT CONDITIONING

Note: These scales are intended as approximations, designed to facilitate comparisons among the theorists, and not as mathematically precise measures. They reflect my opinions; others might disagree with the ratings in some instances. For those who may be interested, my position on each issue is shown by an asterisk.

PART V

The Cognitive Perspective

Overview	Cognitive theories emphasize the importance of thinking. Behavior is determined by how we interpret (construe), predict, and evaluate events, rather than by innate instincts or reality. As Hamlet observed, "There is nothing either good or bad but thinking makes it so."
George Kelly	Argued that we behave much like the research scientist: Each of us creates our own hypotheses and experimental tests for dealing with the world. We strive for a sense of order and control over our environment by anticipating the future accurately. There are many ways to interpret events, each of us creates our own constructs for doing so, and it is these personal constructs that psychologists must seek to understand. Psychopathology involves acting like an incompetent scientist who clings to hypotheses that don't work, and whose predictions are often incorrect. The goal of psychotherapy is to help clients devise and test out better ways of anticipating the future.
Albert Bandura	Emphasized the importance of inner causes of behavior, including thoughts, expectations, self-perceptions, and beliefs. We exert a reciprocal influence on our environment, rather than being controlled by it. Much of what we learn takes place through observation and does not necessarily involve reinforcement. Aggression and destructiveness are due primarily to observational learning (social learning, modeling), rather than to innate instincts or conditioning. Believing that we can perform the behaviors required by a particular situation (high perceived self-efficacy) is likely to lead to more persistent and more effective behavior. Self-reinforced behavior tends to be maintained more effectively than behavior that has been externally reinforced. Psychopathology can be caused by pathogenic thoughts as well as by faulty learning, and psychotherapy should help patients believe that they can achieve their desired goals through their own efforts.

CHAPTER 15

GEORGE A. KELLY
The Psychology of Personal Constructs

To most people, the scientist is a breed apart: a trained professional preoccupied with abstruse thoughts, esoteric procedures, and the mysteries of the unknown. In contrast, George Kelly argues that we all behave much like the scientist. Each of us creates our own "hypotheses" and "experimental tests" for dealing with the world in which we live; and it is these unique personal constructs that psychologists must seek to understand, rather than trying to impose their own set of constructs on all humanity.

OBJECTIVES

- *To reject all theories of personality that impose the same set of constructs on everyone.*
- *To argue that we are naturally active, so the only assumption that must be made about motivation is that we seek a sense of order and control over our environment by anticipating the future accurately.*
- *To emphasize that there are many ways of interpreting (construing) the world from which we can choose.*
- *To show that each of us creates and tests out own constructs for predicting and interpreting the world, and it is these personal constructs that determine our behavior.*
- *To devise empirical measures of a client's personal constructs and psychological problems.*
- *To define psychopathology as acting like an incompetent scientist who clings to hypotheses that don't work, and whose predictions are often incorrect.*
- *To devise methods of psychotherapy that help clients discover more accurate ways of anticipating the future.*
- *To argue that any theory, even his own, is only tentative and must be considered an eventual candidate for the trash can.*

BIOGRAPHICAL SKETCH

George A. Kelly was born on April 28, 1905, on a farm in Kansas. He was the only child of devoutly religious parents, a doting mother and father trained as a Presbyterian minister. Kelly's undergraduate degree was in physics and mathematics. Only after trying jobs as an aeronautical engineer and teacher of speech and drama, and winning an exchange scholarship to the University of Edinburgh in Scotland, did he decide on a career in psychology. Kelly received his Ph.D. in 1931 from Iowa State University, with his dissertation dealing with speech and reading disabilities. He married Gladys Thompson shortly thereafter, and the Kellys were to have one daughter and one son.

Kelly's first postdoctoral position was at Fort Hays Kansas State College, and included the establishment of traveling psychological clinics in the state of Kansas. At first he used Freudian theory with some success, then gradually evolved his own approach and abandoned psychoanalysis. Kelly served with the Navy during World War II as an aviation psychologist, had a brief postwar stint at the University of Maryland, and spent the next 20 years as professor of psychology and director of clinical psychology at Ohio State University.

Personally, Kelly has been described as modest and self-critical. When he published his psychology of personal constructs in 1955, he told his students that he would "try it on for size" for 10 years. If it failed to prove its worth by that time, he would chuck the whole thing. Kelly could be tough with his graduate students in clinical psychology, however, some of whom complained that he cared more for the profession than for themselves. He would challenge them by playing the role of a person suddenly shifting from one pole of a construct to its opposite, without warning them, to see if they truly understood his theory and could be equally flexible. Those who answered with challenges of their own had much less trouble relating to him than those who responded more passively. Yet he was also supportive, sensitive, and caring with students who were having difficulties. (See Fransella, 1995; Rychlak, 1997.)

Kelly's magnum opus is a two-volume work, *The Psychology of Personal Constructs* (1955), and his honors include the presidency of the clinical and counseling divisions of the American Psychological Association. George Kelly died in March 1966, shortly after accepting a position at Brandeis University.

THE BASIC NATURE OF HUMAN BEINGS

Kelly's theory of personality has many unusual aspects. He prefers to leave virtually all familiar landmarks behind, including even the fundamental concept of motivation:

> [In our theory,] the term *learning* … scarcely appears at all. That is wholly intentional; we are for throwing it overboard altogether. There is no *ego*, no *emotion*, no *motivation*, no *reinforcement*, no *drive*, no *unconscious*, no *need*.… [Thus] the reader who takes us seriously will be an adventuresome soul who is not one bit afraid of thinking unorthodox thoughts about people.… (Kelly, 1955, pp. x–xi.)

Kelly defends these radical ideas by pointing out that psychology is a young science, so we should not expect any theory of personality to explain a wide variety of behavior. To be useful, a theory must be limited to those aspects of behavior for which it is especially well suited (its **focus** and **range of convenience**). Kelly's **psychology of personal constructs** is designed for the realm of clinical psychology, and its primary goal is to help people overcome problems with their interpersonal relationships. "If the theory we construct works well within this limited range of convenience, we shall consider our efforts successful, and we shall not be too much disturbed if it proves to be less useful elsewhere" (Kelly, 1955, p. 23; see also pp. 9–11, 17–18).

Activity and Anticipation

Kelly's rationale for avoiding the thorny issue of motivation (and constructs like instincts and psychic energy) is simple and idiosyncratic: he defines human nature as naturally active.

> By assuming that matter is composed basically of static units, it became immediately necessary to account for the obvious fact that what was observed was not always static, but often thoroughly active.… To [my] way of thinking … movement is the essence of human life itself … [and a person] is himself a form of motion.… Thus the whole controversy as to what prods an inert organism into action becomes a dead issue. (Kelly, 1955, pp. 35, 37, 48, 68. See also Kelly, 1955, p. 52; 1969, p. 77; 1970a, p. 8.)

The only assumption that Kelly makes about why we do what we do is that we seek a sense of order and predictability in our dealings with the external world. "Confirmation and disconfirmation of one's predictions [have] greater psychological significance than rewards, punishments, or … drive reduction" (Kelly, 1970a, p. 11). Thus human nature is teleological, and the sole purpose of our behavior is to anticipate the future.

THE STRUCTURE OF PERSONALITY

Personal Constructs

According to Kelly, we achieve our goal of anticipating the future by behaving much like a research scientist. We make up theories about the environment in which we live, test these hypotheses against reality, and (if we are relatively healthy) retain or revise them depending on their predictive accuracy:

> *The scientist's ultimate aim is to predict and control.* This is a summary statement that psychologists frequently like to quote in characterizing their own aspirations. Yet, curiously enough, psychologists rarely credit the human subjects in their experiments with having similar aspirations.... [In contrast, I] propose that every man is, in his own particular way, a scientist. (Kelly, 1955, p. 5. See also Kelly, 1955, pp. 6–12, 49; 1970a, pp. 7–8; 1970b, p. 259.)

Each of us devises and "tries on for size" our own **personal constructs** for interpreting, predicting, and thereby controlling the environment. Whether we construe (interpret) the external world accurately or inaccurately, it is our creative interpretation of reality that gives events their meaning and determines our behavior.

By "creative interpretation of reality," Kelly means that there are a great many alternative constructs from which we can choose. If Demosthenes had construed his childhood stuttering as an insurmountable obstacle, he undoubtedly would have succumbed to despair. But he interpreted it as a challenge to be overcome with effort and courage, and became a great orator. Similarly, a student who construes Kellyan (or any other) theory as an exciting new mode of thought is likely to approach it more successfully than one who interprets it as hopelessly confused jargon. "The events we face today are subject to as great a variety of constructions as our wits will enable us to contrive.... Even the most obvious occurrences of everyday life might appear utterly transformed if we were inventive enough to construe them differently." Such **constructive alternativism** is an excellent way to overcome unpleasant present circumstances or unhappy childhood events (Kelly, 1970a, p. 1; see also Kelly, 1955, pp. 8–16; 1970a, pp. 11–13).

Characteristics of Personal Constructs: I. Postulates and Corollaries. Kelly describes our "scientific" personality in highly technical terms. He posits one **fundamental postulate,** or assumption so crucial that it underlies everything that follows, and 11 **corollaries** that clarify and elaborate upon the nature of personal constructs.

Fundamental Postulate: A person's processes are psychologically channelized by the ways in which he anticipates events (Kelly, 1955, p. 46). Our naturally active psychological processes are shaped into customary patterns ("channelized") by the ways in which we anticipate the future. We make these predictions by creating and using personal constructs, as explained in the following corollaries.

1. Construction Corollary: A person anticipates events by construing their replications (Kelly, 1955, p. 50). In order to predict the future, we interpret what has happened in the past.

Suppose that you must deal with two classmates or coworkers. To anticipate what will happen in these relationships, you use personal constructs that have previously been helpful. You may recall that Fred has often been friendly (as opposed to unfriendly), whereas Joan is frequently lazy (as opposed to conscientious). You therefore anticipate that Fred will greet you warmly when you see him tomorrow, but Joan still will not have done the homework assignment that was due last Thursday. If these predictions prove to be accurate, you will continue to use the constructs of friendly–unfriendly and conscientious–lazy to anticipate the behavior of these people.

CAPSULE SUMMARY
Some Important Kellyan Terminology (I)

Fundamental Postulate	The psychological processes that make up our personality are naturally active, and are molded into patterns by the ways in which we anticipate the future.
Construction Corollary	Our anticipations of the future are based on our constructions (interpretations) of previous events.
Individuality Corollary	Different people construe events differently.
Organization Corollary	To make it easier to anticipate the future, we organize our personal constructs into a hierarchical system. Such hierarchies also differ among different individuals.
Dichotomy Corollary	Every personal construct is dichotomous (bipolar).
Choice Corollary	We value more highly the pole of a dichotomous personal construct that enables us to predict the future more accurately.
Range Corollary	A personal construct is useful for anticipating only some types of events, and this *range of convenience* may be narrow or wide.
Experience Corollary	We frequently revise our system of personal constructs in order to improve its ability to anticipate the future.
Modulation Corollary	Some personal constructs less readily admit new elements to their range of convenience, which limits the extent to which the system can be revised.
Fragmentation Corollary	The same person may use contradictory personal constructs at different times.
Commonality Corollary	We are psychologically more similar to those people whose personal constructs have more in common with our own.
Sociality Corollary	To relate effectively to another person, we must understand how that person construes the world (but we do *not* have to use the identical constructs).

Notice that you are doing much more than merely remembering prior events. You are creating and using your own constructs to interpret what has happened and to predict what will happen. Since constructs are a personal matter, someone else might interpret these situations differently—as we will see in the next corollary.

2. Individuality Corollary: Persons differ from each other in their construction of events (Kelly, 1955, p. 55). Different people construe events differently.

In the preceding example, someone else might construe Fred as an opportunistic charmer who is only interested in what he can get from you (as opposed to sincere), or Joan as easily distracted and perhaps suffering from attention deficit disorder (as opposed to well focused). Kelly does not go to Adler's and Allport's extreme of regarding every personality as unique, for we can and do use constructs like "friendly versus unfriendly" in similar ways. (See Kelly, 1955, pp. 41–42, 113, 197, 455; 1969, p. 117; 1970a, p. 12; and the Commonality Corollary, following.) But the personal constructs of any two people are never identical and often differ considerably, so it is essential to determine how each of us construes the world.

3. Organization Corollary: Each person characteristically evolves, for his convenience in anticipating events, a construction system embracing ordinal relationships between constructs (Kelly, 1955, p. 56). Anticipating the future will be easier if our personal constructs are organized in some way. Therefore, we accord some constructs greater importance than others. The resulting hierarchical system may consist of several levels, is usually flexible enough so that different constructs may become prominent at different times, and is even more personal and distinctive than the specific constructs that one uses.

Suppose that a man forms a major (**superordinate**) personal construct of "good versus bad" and includes two less influential (**subordinate**) constructs, "intelligent versus stupid" and "neat versus sloppy," in this hierarchy. For this man, predicting whether something is good or bad is very important. So he behaves in highly judgmental ways, as by often evaluating the intelligence and neatness of other people:

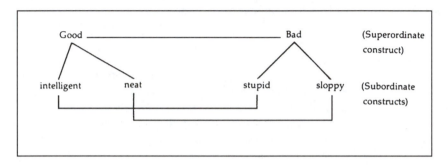

Now suppose that a woman gives superordinate status to the construct of "safe versus dangerous," and places "good versus bad" and "friends versus strangers" on a subordinate level. For this woman, predicting whether something is safe or dangerous is very important. Since she believes that it is good to be safe, she consistently strives for security and prefers the company of familiar faces:

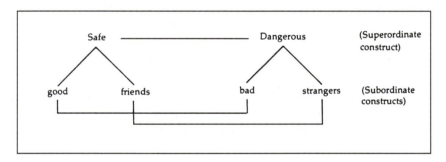

Both of these individuals use the personal construct of "good versus bad." But their behaviors are different because their hierarchies are different.

Since we create all of our personal constructs, superordinate and subordinate, we determine our own guidelines for living (Kelly, 1955, p. 78). However, some of our self-imposed rules are much harder to change than others. Suppose that the woman eventually decides that seeking security is rather boring. It will be necessary to reconstruct the hierarchy in order to change this behavior, as by making "safe versus dangerous" subordinate to the construct of "interesting versus boring." (That is, predicting whether an activity is interesting must become more important than predicting whether it is safe.) This will not be too difficult if "safe versus dangerous" is already subordinate to other constructs in the hierarchy. (Hierarchies usually have more than two levels.) But if "safe versus dangerous" is at the highest level (a **core** construct), it will dominate her behavior, and she will probably refuse to abandon her all-out quest for safety by making other constructs more important. When this happens, change is likely to be impossible without the aid of psychotherapy.

4. Dichotomy Corollary: A person's construction system is composed of a finite number of dichotomous constructs (Kelly, 1955, p. 59). Every personal construct is dichotomous (bipolar).

A personal construct is defined by two **poles**, and we cannot understand what is meant by one pole without knowing its opposite. Consider three people who wish to predict the behavior of a stranger. A woman who would like to make new acquaintances uses the construct of "friendly versus unfriendly." A man who was victimized by sarcastic and abusive parents during childhood, and who remains wary of such treatment, devises the construct of "friendly versus humiliating." A paranoid individual creates the construct of "friendly versus out to get me." None of these people construe the world in the same way, even though they all use the pole of "friendly." (See Kelly, 1955, p. 71.)

Because all personal constructs are dichotomous, it may seem as though Kelly is making the mistake of advocating "either–or" thinking ("people are either considerate or inconsiderate, honest or dishonest, good or bad, and there is no middle ground"). But Kelly is well aware that our world consists of shades of grey, and he argues that we can (and should) use our personal constructs to predict such subtle differences. Suppose that being considerate involves caring (as opposed to selfishness), helpfulness (as opposed to indifference), and politeness (as opposed to rudeness). The more of these characteristics that a person demonstrates, the more considerate we should expect this person to be. Or a construct such as "honest versus dishonest" (or "good versus bad") may be applied successively to several politicians, with X construed as honest compared to Y and W as honest compared to X. This establishes the scale of W (most honest), X, and Y (least honest). So we may predict that X will act honestly more often than Y, but not as often as W. Only the tools that we use to interpret events in the world are dichotomous, *not* the events themselves. (See Kelly, 1955, pp. 66, 142–143; 1970a, pp. 12–14.)

5. Choice Corollary: A person chooses for himself that alternative in a dichotomized construct through which he anticipates the greater possibility for extension and definition [elaboration] of his system (Kelly, 1955, p. 64; 1970a, p. 15). We value more highly the pole of a dichotomous personal construct that enables us to predict the future more accurately.

Since personal constructs are our only means of anticipating the future, we constantly strive to improve their usefulness. There are two quite different ways to do this. We may choose the more secure course of further clarifying those constructs that we already use, and "trying to become more and more certain about fewer and fewer things." But a wider understanding of the world in which we live can only be achieved by sailing for a time in uncharted waters, testing out new constructs, and risking some incorrect predictions. We may therefore select the more adventurous path of exploring new aspects of life, extending the applicability of our system of constructs, and "trying to become vaguely aware of more and more things on the misty horizon" (Kelly, 1955, p. 67).

Having chosen either security or adventure (a decision that may well vary at different times), we choose the pole of a personal construct that will enable us to achieve this goal. Suppose that a person who regards the world as hostile, and who usually opts for security by construing every stranger as "unfriendly," decides to seek out new experiences by taking the risk of positing a newcomer as "friendly." Because this pole is so unfamiliar, this individual is likely to make some erroneous predictions and encounter some disappointments before becoming able to predict friendly behaviors accurately. "There is no such thing as adventure with safety guaranteed in advance" (Kelly, 1970a, p. 7).

6. Range Corollary: A construct is convenient for the anticipation of a finite range of events only (Kelly, 1955, p. 68). Any personal construct is useful for anticipating only some types of events.

Like a good theory of personality, a personal construct has a limited range of convenience: It helps to anticipate some events, but is useless for others. For example, people and buildings are often construed as "tall" or "short." But we do not refer to "tall weather" or "short fear," for weather and fear lie outside the range of convenience of this construct and are therefore perceived as irrelevant. Some personal constructs have a wider range of convenience than others; you can probably apply the construct of "good versus bad" to many more items than the construct of "vulgar versus polite."

7. Experience Corollary: A person's construction system varies as he successively construes the replications of events (Kelly, 1955, p. 72). We often revise our system of personal constructs so that it will anticipate the future more accurately.

Even the best personal construct system is imperfect, and must be frequently revised in order to cope with an ever changing world. However, this is not an easy task. Some individuals are so afraid that new information will "catch them with their constructs down," and shatter their guidelines for living, that they refuse to make any changes in their personal constructs. Thus parents may stubbornly insist that their spoiled and undisciplined child is virtuous (as opposed to selfish), despite substantial evidence to the contrary. Alternatively, as in any science, it is possible to maintain a faulty construct system by designing flawed experiments. An individual who construes a neighbor's behavior as unfriendly may "test" this belief by building a fence that encroaches on the other's property, receive an angry rebuke, and conclude that the personal construct has been confirmed.

Well-adjusted individuals proceed differently. They test their personal constructs against reality in logical ways, confirm or disconfirm the predictive accuracy of these constructs, and revise them appropriately. Consider once again our illustration of the Construction Corollary: If Fred behaves in an unfriendly way when you next see him, you may conclude that he is "having a bad day" and continue to regard him as friendly. But if he is unfriendly on several occasions, you will change your anticipation of his behavior by following the Choice Corollary and switching to the opposite pole. Or if Fred consistently acts as though his mind is somewhere else, you may decide to predict his behavior by replacing the construct of "friendly versus unfriendly" with one like "preoccupied versus attentive." In either case, you will not continue to use a pole or construct that anticipates the future incorrectly.

Suppose that a college student does poorly on an exam. She may consider several different interpretations of this event: She may be incompetent (as opposed to competent); the professor may have been unfair (as opposed to fair); her answers to the essay questions may have been shallow (as opposed to comprehensive). The next step is to select the most relevant construct, which we will assume is "shallow versus comprehensive." She therefore decides to give this construct a more superordinate place in her hierarchy, as by writing longer and more technical answers to the essay questions. She anticipates a high grade on the next exam, receives it, and concludes from this confirming evidence that the revision of her construct system has achieved greater predictive accuracy—at least insofar as this particular professor is concerned. (See Kelly, 1955, pp. 515–526; 1970a, p. 18.)

8. Modulation Corollary: The variation in a person's construction system is limited by the permeability of the constructs within whose range of convenience the variants lie (Kelly, 1955, p. 77). Some personal constructs less readily admit new items to their range of convenience (are less **permeable**). This limits the extent to which the system of personal constructs can be revised, so it is usually desirable for constructs to be relatively permeable.

A cynical woman who concludes that "all men are unfaithful" has made the construct of "faithful versus unfaithful" impermeable to men, since no man will ever be classified as faithful. Whenever she encounters a man who is faithful, her anticipations will be incorrect. Because this construct is impermeable, she cannot make the needed revisions in her construct system, so she will continue to make erroneous predictions. (See Kelly, 1955, pp. 81, 486–487.)

9. Fragmentation Corollary: A person may successively employ a variety of construction subsystems which are inferentially incompatible with each other (Kelly, 1955, p. 83). The same person may use contradictory personal constructs at different times.

Kelly recognizes that human behavior can be inconsistent. "A man may move from an act of love to an act of jealousy, and from there to an act of hate, even though hate is not something that would be inferred from love." Most often, however, our anticipations form a consistent pattern. "One can tolerate some incompatibility [in one's system of personal constructs], but not too much" (Kelly, 1970a, p. 20; 1955, p. 496).

10. Commonality Corollary: To the extent that one person employs a construction of experience which is similar to that employed by another, his processes are psychologically similar to those of the other person (Kelly, 1970a, p. 20; see also Kelly, 1955, p. 90). We are psychologically more similar to those people whose personal constructs resemble our own.

Suppose that you are a student in my course in theories of personality. If I characterize this course by using such personal constructs as fascinating (as opposed to boring) and mind-expanding (as opposed to tedious), and you use the same constructs, our personalities are much alike. Even if we disagree about whether the course is mind-expanding or tedious, we interpret the world in similar ways. But if you use different personal constructs, such as convenient (versus inconvenient, referring to the time at which the course is scheduled) and prerequisite (as opposed to unnecessary), your personality differs considerably from mine. I expect students to take this course because they want to discover fascinating new ways to understand the human personality, whereas you took it because it meets at a convenient hour and you must pass it to take the course in clinical psychology.

11. Sociality Corollary: To the extent that one person construes the construction processes of another, he may play a role in a social process involving the other person (Kelly, 1955, p. 96). To relate effectively to another person, we must understand how that person construes the world. But we do *not* have to use the identical constructs ourselves.

In the preceding example, our relationship is not necessarily doomed to failure even though I do not use the constructs of "convenient versus inconvenient" and "prerequisite versus unnecessary." So long as I understand that this is how you construe the course, I can anticipate your behavior and respond accordingly. For example, I may predict that you will be reluctant to study a complicated theory like Kelly's because your reasons for taking the course had little to do with the specific content. If this prediction is confirmed, we may engage in some useful discussions about whether it is desirable for you to drop this course and substitute one in which you are more interested. But if I do not understand your personal constructs, we will probably be unable to communicate. I will keep trying to persuade you that Kelly's theory has many interesting aspects, but you will wonder why I don't realize that this isn't at all important to you.

To help us understand each other's personal constructs, Kelly recommends that we play various **roles.** "When one plays a *role,* he behaves according to what he believes another person thinks … [and puts] himself tentatively in the other person's shoes" (Kelly, 1955, pp. 177–178; 1970a, p. 26). Roles are determined by construing the constructs of other people, rather than by the standards of society. A person who can play such roles as spouse, parent, friend, leader, or subordinate is more easily anticipated by other people, and is therefore more likely to develop effective interpersonal relationships.

Characteristics of Personal Constructs: II. Basic Requirements.

Every personal construct must specify a way in which at least two of the things that it describes (its **elements**) are alike, but different from a third.

CAPSULE SUMMARY
Some Important Kellyan Terminology (II)

Anxiety	The awareness that important events fall mostly outside the range of convenience of every personal construct in one's system, making it impossible to anticipate the future.
Constellatory construct	A construct that limits the ways in which other constructs are used, as with prejudiced beliefs: "A person who is 'Jewish' must also be 'miserly' and 'ruthless.'" A converse of propositional construct.
Construct system (construction system)	The hierarchically organized collection of personal constructs that an individual uses to anticipate the future.
Constructive alternativism	The principle that there are always alternative constructs that we can use to interpret the world, so no one need be a victim of childhood events or current circumstances.
Core construct	A construct so superordinate that it dominates one's behavior. The converse of peripheral construct.
Core role	Subordinating the "self" pole of the self-construct to constructs that involve important people in one's life, as when a woman adopts the core role of nourishing mother and construes herself and her family accordingly.
Elements	The things described by a personal construct; may be people, inanimate objects, events, or one or both poles of another construct.
Fixed-role therapy	A form of psychotherapy wherein the client tries to enact in everyday life a role designed by a panel of therapists, with the goal of discovering and using more effective personal constructs.
Focus and range of convenience	The particular aspects of behavior for which a personal construct, or a scientific theory, is maximally (focus) and generally (range) suited.
Guilt	The awareness that "self" has been dislodged from the core role, as when a woman who adopted the core role of nourishing mother can no longer construe herself in this way because her children have grown up and left home.
Impermeable construct	A construct that is closed to new elements. The converse of permeable construct.
Loose construct	A construct that leads to varying, contradictory predictions. The converse of tight construct.
Peripheral construct	A construct that can be revised without greatly altering any core constructs because it is relatively subordinate. The converse of core construct.
Permeable construct	A construct that readily admits new elements to its range of convenience, and is therefore easily revised in the light of experience. The converse of impermeable construct.
Personal construct	A dichotomous concept that we create in order to interpret and predict, and thereby control, our environment.
Poles	The two opposites that define a personal construct.
Preemptive construct	A construct that prohibits any other constructs from applying to its elements; e.g., "'psychoanalysis' is nothing but 'biased thinking.'" A converse of propositional construct.
Preverbal construct	A construct that is not associated with a verbal label, usually because it was learned prior to the development of language skills, and is therefore difficult to identify and communicate.

Propositional construct	A construct that does not limit other constructs from applying to its elements; e.g., "'psychoanalysis' may be 'biased' or 'scientific,' 'good' or 'bad,' 'interesting' or 'boring,' and so forth." The converse of preemptive construct and constellatory construct.
Psychology of personal constructs	The name given by Kelly to his theory of personality.
Role	A specific pattern of behavior that is determined by construing the personal constructs of other people.
Role Construct Repertory Test (Rep Test)	A measure designed to provide preliminary information about a client's personal constructs and psychological problems. The client forms triads of significant people (mother, father, a favorite teacher, someone intelligent, and so forth), and devises constructs to describe how two members of each triad are alike yet different from the third.
Self-construct	The personal construct that distinguishes those elements that relate to oneself from those that involve other people.
Submergence	Difficulty in becoming aware of one pole of a personal construct, usually because it has intolerable implications.
Superordinate construct	A personal construct that includes another construct (called a *subordinate* construct) among its elements. The more constructs that it includes, the more superordinate it is.
Threat	The awareness of imminent, widespread changes in one's core constructs.
Tight construct	A construct that leads to unvarying, clear-cut predictions. The converse of loose construct.

To Kelly, it would be meaningless to say that Mary is the only gentle person in the world. If we cannot compare her to anyone else on this characteristic, the term *gentle* does not tell us anything different than the name "Mary." Nor can we understand what is meant by "gentle" without knowing its opposite (the Dichotomy Corollary). For a personal construct to be useful, we must be able to make a statement like: "Mary and Alice are gentle, but Jane is aggressive." (See Kelly, 1955, pp. 59–61.)

Characteristics of Personal Constructs: III. Preemptive, Constellatory, and Propositional Constructs.

Some personal constructs are inflexible, and prevent the system from undergoing needed revisions. This can lead to such undesirable characteristics as closed-mindedness and prejudice.

Consider a critic who contends that psychoanalytic theory is *nothing but* Freud's biased opinion. This critic refuses to concede the possibility that psychoanalysis may have other characteristics, such as some potentially valuable ideas. The critic is using the construct of "biased versus scientific" **preemptively** with regard to "psychoanalysis," and is not allowing this element to belong to any other constructs (such as "valuable versus useless"). This will make it impossible ever to revise the system and construe psychoanalysis in a more favorable light. (See Kelly, 1955, pp. 154–157.)

Almost as rigid is the **constellatory** construct, which limits the ways in which other constructs can be used. For example, a prejudiced individual may conclude that a person who is construed as Jewish *must also* be "miserly" and "ruthless." Once an element is classified according to the constellatory construct of "Jewish versus non-Jewish," its membership in the ranges of other constructs ("miserly versus generous," "ruthless versus benevolent") is immediately determined.

A more open-minded approach is represented by the **propositional** construct, which does not limit other constructs from applying to its elements. A person who uses the construct of "Jewish versus non-Jewish" propositionally leaves open the possibility that an element construed as Jewish might be miserly or generous, ruthless or benevolent, friendly or unfriendly, and so forth, rather than regarding such issues as arbitrarily decided by the single attribute of Jewishness. "The propositional construct, therefore, represents one end of a continuum, the other end of which is represented by the preemptive and constellatory constructs" (Kelly, 1955, p. 155).

Characteristics of Personal Constructs: IV. The Self-Construct.

One personal construct is found in virtually everyone's system: "self versus others." However, this **self-construct** is likely to be subordinated in different ways. A person who includes "self" under "friendly" and "considerate" will act accordingly, whereas another person who subordinates "self" to "intelligent" and "others" to "stupid" will expect to be considerably more clever than everyone else. (Since we do not necessarily construe ourselves as others do, someone else might argue that the latter individual would be better described as "conceited.") One woman may include "self" under "nourishing mother" and devote herself to her family, whereas another may subordinate "self" to "professional" and become annoyed at any suggestion that her place is in the home.

Because personal constructs are our own creation, any term that you apply to other people must have some personal implications as well. Therefore, how you construe others provides valuable clues about your self-concept. "One cannot call another person a bastard without making bastardy a dimension of his own life also" (Kelly, 1955, p. 133; see also pp. 114, 131–135, 151).

Characteristics of Personal Constructs: V. Threat, Anxiety, and Guilt.

Threat is caused by the awareness of imminent, widespread changes in one's most important personal constructs. Clients who enter psychotherapy are likely to be threatened by the prospect of making sweeping changes in their construct system, whereas someone whose behavior is dominated by the construct of "safe versus dangerous" is too threatened to construe the world in more adventurous ways. Threat impedes our ability to revise our personal constructs so that they will predict the future more accurately.

Anxiety occurs when an individual is unable to construe important events and anticipate the future. "The deeply anxious person has ... [a] construction system [that] fails him.... He is confronted with a changing scene, but he has no guide to carry him through the transition" (Kelly, 1955, p. 496; see also pp. 166–167, 489–508). Consider once again the college student who does poorly on an examination. If she can identify several possible constructions of this event (she is "incompetent" as opposed to "competent," the professor is "unfair" as opposed to "fair," her answers to the essay questions were "shallow" as opposed to "comprehensive"), she may be threatened by the need to revise her construct system, but she will not be anxious. Her failure will evoke anxiety only if it falls mostly outside the range of convenience of every personal construct in her system, leaving her too confused to interpret this event and anticipate some sort of corrective action.[1]

The woman who subordinates "self" to "nourishing mother" regards motherhood as an extremely important role (her **core role**). **Guilt** occurs when "self" is dislodged from the core role, as when her children get married and leave home and she can no longer mother them.

---

[1]Events that fell entirely outside the range of every construct in the system would not be perceived at all, since the individual would lack any means of understanding them, and would therefore not create any anxiety.

Characteristics of Personal Constructs: VI. Preverbal and Submerged Constructs. Some personal constructs are not readily accessible to awareness. **Preverbal** constructs are learned at a very early age, before the child can use language correctly, and are difficult to identify because they lack a convenient verbal label. Or a person may **submerge** one pole of a construct because it has intolerable implications, as with the woman who refuses to construe men as "faithful" and always predicts that they will be "unfaithful."

However, Kelly rejects the idea of a Freudian unconscious. When apparently unconscious processes occur, this is because we are using the wrong constructs to interpret what is happening. A child who has been dominated and ridiculed by his parents, yet steadfastly proclaims that he feels nothing but love for them, is not repressing intense anger and concealing it by using reaction formation. His construction of his behavior is mistaken, and he needs to replace it with the correct interpretation:

> If a client does not construe things in the way we [therapists] do, we assume that he construes them in some other way, not that he really must construe them the way we do but is unaware of it. If later he comes to construe them the way we do, that is a new construction for him, not a revelation of a subconscious construction which we have helped him bring to the fore.... If a client is today able to see hostility in his behavior whereas yesterday he could not see hostility, that does not necessarily mean that he ... was unconsciously hostile all the time.... [Rather, he] came to construe [his behavior] as hostile. (Kelly, 1955, p. 467; see also p. 235, 483–485.)

THE DEVELOPMENT OF PERSONALITY

Parents can impair the child's ability to anticipate the future by behaving in various pathogenic ways. Overindulgence teaches the child to predict that other people will satisfy its every need. Intense pressure or punishment leads the child to cling rigidly to a few familiar constructs, rather than seeking new ways to interpret the environment. Erratic and inconsistent behavior makes it impossible for the child to predict the parents accurately. Characterizing the child in such negative ways as "you're a liar!" may cause the child to form these constructs, subordinate "self" to "liar," and behave in the very ways that the parents are trying to prevent.

Except for such maladaptive influences, personality development unfolds in a healthy way. The growing child gradually makes its constructs more permeable, less preemptive, and more propositional, as by abandoning its conception of the parents as only perfect and all-powerful and construing them as people who can be strong or weak, helpful or harmful, loving or inconsiderate, and so forth. (See Kelly, 1955, pp. 7, 170, 365, 668–671, 710–711, 753, 841.)

FURTHER APPLICATIONS OF KELLYAN THEORY

Dream Interpretation

Kelly regards dreams as potential clues to the less obvious aspects of personality, including submerged and preverbal constructs. However, he stresses that dream interpretation is primarily a technique for weaning a client from constructs that have become overly rigid.

A dream may depict a parent or friend in such contradictory, **loose** ways as friendly and unfriendly or comforting and threatening, thereby allowing the dreamer to explore various ways of classifying this person. A client who always predicts that other people will be unfriendly may awaken one morning with vague memories of a satisfying dream-romance, and report this to the therapist. This serves to loosen the construct of "friendly versus unfriendly" and bring the submerged former pole to light, after which the dreamer can firm up (**tighten**) this construct by predicting that another person will be friendly. A client who needs to loosen certain constructs, but who has difficulty recalling any dreams, may be asked to keep a pad and pencil beside the bed and write them down immediately upon awakening. (See Kelly, 1955, pp. 133, 465, 470–472, 484–485, 1030–1031, 1037–1048.)

Kelly takes a skeptical view of "gift dreams," which are designed to please the therapist by fitting his or her theoretical orientation (Oedipal, archetypal, or whatever). Such dreams indicate that the therapist's constructs have been imposed upon the client, at least to some extent, and that little progress is being made toward understanding the client's own system (Kelly, 1955, pp. 1040–1042).

Psychopathology

Definition of Psychopathology. Psychologically healthy people design appropriate tests to evaluate the predictive accuracy of their personal constructs, and make whatever revisions are necessary. In contrast, the pathological individual resembles an incompetent scientist who clings to hypotheses that have been disconfirmed. The sufferer expects to enjoy success, make friends, or find romance, but never does; and these consistently inaccurate predictions make daily life intolerable. "From the standpoint of the psychology of personal constructs, we may define a disorder as any personal construction which is used repeatedly in spite of consistent invalidation" (Kelly, 1955, p. 831).

Causes of Psychopathology. Since there are always alternative constructs that we can use to interpret the world, no one need be a victim of prior events (the principle of constructive alternativism). Rather than focusing on childhood, therefore, Kelly attributes psychopathology to a construct system that is currently defective in some way.

For example, a woman may never confirm her prediction that she will fall in love because she makes the construct of "faithful versus unfaithful" impermeable to men. A paranoid individual's self-construct may be too permeable, leading to erroneous predictions that people plan to harm him. A compulsive person may use constructs that are too tight and specific, as by predicting that he will be successful if he wears a red tie every day. Or a person who is engaged in an all-out quest for safety may make the construct of "safe versus dangerous" too superordinate in her hierarchy. Whatever the form, psychopathology is caused by personal constructs that are too faulty to accomplish their primary objective of anticipating the future, which typically evokes "that most common of all clinic commodities, anxiety" (Kelly, 1955, p. 58; see also pp. 62, 111–119, 468–469, 497).

Varieties of Psychopathology. Like Erikson, Kelly prefers to avoid the usual diagnostic categories because they may become a self-fulfilling prophecy. That is, the client may subordinate "self" to such labels as "compulsive" or "paranoid" and behave accordingly. Kelly even opposes the common trichotomous classification of normal, neurotic, and psychotic, preferring once again to establish a dichotomy (e.g., "normal versus pathological") rather than to exclude the possibility that a client might behave in ways that are typical of both neurosis and psychosis. (See Kelly, 1955, pp. 193, 198–200, 366, 453, 764, 775, 866.)

Psychotherapy

Theoretical Foundation. The goal of Kellyan psychotherapy is to provide a setting in which the client can safely experiment with new core constructs, discard those that are faulty, and revise the system in ways that lead to more accurate predictions. To make such sweeping (and threatening) changes requires a great deal of effort, which is why Kelly prefers the designation of "client" to the more passive-sounding one of "patient." "Submitting *patiently* and unquestioningly to the manipulations of a clinician ... is a badly misleading view of how a psychologically disturbed person recovers" (Kelly, 1955, p. 186; see also pp. 161–170).

The personal constructs of different individuals vary in many respects: hierarchical organization, poles, ranges of convenience, permeability, tightness and looseness, preemptiveness, and so forth. Therefore, the therapist must devise and test tentative hypotheses about a client's particular way of viewing the world. One good way to do this is by adopting a *credulous attitude,* which involves accepting and discussing whatever statements the client may make. The therapist should also use propositional constructs that allow for various possibilities, rather than the preemptive and constellatory constructs that are all too common in other theories (e.g., "this disorder must also involve Oepidal childhood conflicts"). As with any role, the therapist must construe the constructs used by each client. "[Therapy] is a matter of *construing* the [client's] experience, and not merely a matter of having him hand it to [the therapist] intact across the desk" (Kelly, 1955, p. 200; see also pp. 173–174, 196–198, 321, 595–596).

Therapeutic Procedures. Kellyan psychotherapy is conducted in 45-minute sessions, with the number of weekly appointments depending on the nature and severity of the client's problems. Kelly shares Sullivan's preference for having the client seated at right angles to the therapist, so either party can look at or away from the other. He also accepts the Freudian contention that most clients should avoid major life changes (such as marriage or quitting a job) until therapy has been concluded, but he differs by taking written notes or (preferably) using tape recordings as an aid to the therapist's memory (Kelly, 1955, pp. 627–638, 646).

To provide some preliminary indications as to a client's personal constructs and psychological problems, Kelly (1955, pp. 219–318) has devised the **Role Construct Repertory Test (Rep Test).** The client gives the names of some 15 people who play significant roles in his or her life, is presented with three of these "role titles," and must specify one important way in which two of these people are alike and are different from the third person. (As we have seen, this is the basic requirement that any personal construct must meet.) For example, consider the first triad in the accompanying Capsule Summary. The person whom the client would like to know better and the person whom the client most wants to help are both "sympathetic," whereas the close associate who dislikes the client is not. The client is then asked to designate the opposite of "sympathetic," which we will assume is "sarcastic." Therefore, "sympathetic versus sarcastic" is a personal construct that this client uses to interpret the behavior of other people.

The Rep Test may be administered on a one-to-one basis, with each role title on a separate card that is sorted by the client, or as a written questionnaire suitable for use with groups. A complete analysis of the results is rather complicated, involving grid layouts of role titles versus constructs and the mathematical procedure of factor analysis. A construct that is used to describe numerous role titles is likely to be superordinate and/or permeable, whereas a client who uses very few constructs, or constructs that are superficial and impersonal (mother and sister "have blue eyes," father and employer "are both men"), will probably have difficulty construing other people and forming effective relationships.

CAPSULE SUMMARY

The Role Construct Repertory Test (Rep Test), Group Form

PART A: ROLE TITLE LIST.   The client is asked to provide the name of each of the 15 persons listed below. No name may be used more than once. If the client does not have a brother or sister or cannot remember a particular person, the most similar individual that can be recalled is substituted.

1. Mother
2. Father
3. Brother nearest client's age
4. Sister nearest client's age
5. Teacher client liked
6. Teacher client disliked
7. Most recent boy or girl friend
8. Wife or husband, or present boy or girl friend
9. Employer or supervisor
10. Close associate who dislikes client
11. Someone client would like to know better
12. Person client most wants to help
13. Most intelligent person client knows
14. Most successful person client knows
15. Most interesting person client knows

PART B. CONSTRUCT SORTS.   For 3 of the 15 persons in the role title list, the client is asked to specify one important way in which two of these people are alike and different from the third. The client then states the opposite of this construct.

Triad	Client's Thoughts	Construct	Opposite
10 ("Sam") 11 ("Joan") 12 ("Dan")	"Joan and Dan are sympathetic, but Sam is not."	Sympathetic	Sarcastic
6 ("Mrs. Green") 13 ("Jeff") 14 ("Barry")	"Jeff and Barry are very sure of themselves, but Mrs. Green is not."	Self-confident	Insecure
6 ("Mrs. Green") 9 ("Jennifer") 12 ("Dan")	"Mrs. Green and Jennifer often make me feel inferior, but Dan does not."	Condescending	Supportive

The same procedure is followed for twelve additional triads: (3, 14, 15), (4, 11, 13), (2, 9, 10), (5, 7, 8), (9, 11, 15), (1, 4, 7), (3, 5, 13), (8, 12, 14), (4, 5, 15), (1, 2, 8), (2, 3, 7), (1, 6, 10). The same construct may be used in more than one triad, or with a different opposite in different triads.

In addition to the Rep Test, Kelly shares Allport's preference for direct self-reports. "The most useful clinical tool of the physician is the four-word question uttered audibly in the presence of the patient: 'How do you feel?' There is a similar golden rule for clinical psychologists. If you don't know what's wrong with a client, ask him; he may tell you!" (Kelly, 1955, p. 201). Each client is asked to provide a personal character sketch, which is phrased in the third person as though it were written by an intimate and sympathetic friend.

The information gleaned from this method sometimes suggests the desirability of **fixed-role therapy,** wherein a panel of clinicians devises a contrasting role for the client to enact in everyday life. For example, one client's self-characterization revealed a marked inability to construe other people accurately. The client was therefore asked to spend two weeks acting and living in the manner of "Kenneth Norton," a fictitious individual described in four carefully written paragraphs as having a knack for perceiving the viewpoints and subtle feelings of others:

Kenneth Norton is the kind of man who, after a few minutes of conversation, somehow makes you feel that he must have known you intimately for a long time. This comes about, not by any particular questions that he asks, but by the understanding way in which he listens. It is as if he had a knack of seeing the world through your eyes....

Kenneth Norton's complete absorption in the thoughts of the people with whom he holds conversations appears to leave no place for any feelings of self-consciousness regarding himself.... He is too much involved with the fascinating worlds of other people with whom he is surrounded to give more than a passing thought to soul-searching criticisms of himself.... This is the kind of fellow Kenneth Norton is, and this behavior represents the Norton brand of sincerity.

For the next two weeks I want you to do something unusual.... Try to forget that you are [who you are] or that you ever were. You *are* Kenneth Norton! You *act* like him! You *think* like him! You *talk* to your friends the way you think he would talk! You *do* the things you think he would do! You even *have his interests* and enjoy the things he would enjoy! ... You might say that we are going to send [you] on a two weeks' vacation.... In the meantime, Kenneth will take over.... Of course you will have to let people keep on calling you [by your own name], but you will think of yourself as Kenneth. After two weeks, we will let [you] come back and then see what we can do to help [you]. (Kelly, 1955, pp. 374–375, 384–385. See also Kelly, 1955, pp. 319–451; 1970b, pp. 265–267.)

Fixed-role therapy allows the client to experiment with radically new constructions and behaviors by pretending to be someone else, somewhat like trying on a new suit of clothes that can easily be removed if it does not fit very well. But this procedure involves considerable work for both therapist and client, and is suitable for only about 1 in 15 cases.

More often, the Kellyan psychotherapist helps reconstruct the client's system in other ways. These include playing the roles of people to whom the client has difficulty relating, and telling stories to introduce children to new constructs. Kelly even recommends that the therapist study the ways in which environmental influences validate a client's predictions, and he presents detailed guidelines for making firsthand inspections of schools and evaluating their effects on a child's construct system. (See Kelly, 1955, pp. 134–135, 162, 619, 687–731, 1029–1092, 1141–1155.)

Resistance and Transference.

Since the client relies on the faulty construct system to anticipate the future, the prospect of changing it is likely to evoke anxiety and resistance. A client may balk at the idea of revising core constructs, argue that a prescribed fixed role is silly or impossible to enact, or retain faulty constructs in order to "show what a mess my parents made out of me" (Kelly, 1955, p. 572; see also pp. 58–59, 406, 492, 679). Like Horney, however, Kelly concludes that resistance can also protect the client from a therapist who tries to induce change too quickly.

Every client anticipates the therapist's behavior by using personal constructs that are derived from prior experiences with other people (the Construction Corollary). Therefore, transference is an inevitable aspect of psychotherapy. Some transferences are helpful because they enable the therapist to gain a firsthand knowledge of the client's construct system. However, other transferences impede therapeutic progress. The client may construe the therapist as a savior who will provide solutions on a silver platter, just as the parents did during childhood, and refuse to work at the difficult task of therapy. Or the client may become preoccupied with learning the therapist's theoretical terminology and fail to devise new *personal* constructs, possibly because the therapist is imposing the same constructs on every client instead of trying to understand how the client construes the world. (See Kelly, 1955, pp. 575–581, 662–686, 1100.)

Kelly takes strong exception to the belief, so commonly espoused by psychoanalysts, that high fees benefit the client by motivating change or regular attendance. "Because some of the necessities and conveniences of life are bound up with our economic system, it is necessary that a reasonable proportion of the clinician's services be financially rewarded. [But] fees assessed under this necessity are for the welfare of the clinician, not the client. Let us make no mistake about that!" (Kelly, 1955, p. 611; see also pp. 608–610, 671–674.)

Constructive Alternativism and Psychological Research

To Kelly, a good theory must meet several important criteria. It should provide a framework that enables us to organize a multitude of data, generate hypotheses and predictions about human behavior that can be tested experimentally, be supported by research results, and lead to applications that help us to resolve important social problems. (Compare with the criteria discussed in Chapter 1.)

Kelly emphasizes that it is far from an easy task to test out personality theories in the research laboratory. Among the many challenging problems are those of obtaining a representative sample of participants, controlling for extraneous and biasing influences, and quantifying important abstract constructs (such as unconscious processes, or "mental health"). The results of any research study are likely to be open to question, or admit to more than one interpretation. Even sound hypotheses are never substantiated with absolute finality, and a psychologist whose ideas appear to have been discredited can often find ways to dispute the findings and resurrect the theory in question. "Rarely does a scientific theory wholly stand or fall on the outcome of a single crucial experiment.... [Instead,] I have noted privately over the years that mostly they sort of lean, at about the .08 level of confidence ... [and that] it is almost impossible to give any comprehensive theory the final coup de grâce" (Kelly, 1955, pp. 24–25; 1970b, p. 259; see also Kelly, 1955, pp. 22–43, 102–103; 1970a, p. 4).

Since there are many ways to construe a personal or scientific event, any theory of personality can only be of temporary value. Even Kelly's psychology of personal constructs will be expendable when enough new discoveries are made:

> A [scientist] who spends a great deal of his time hoarding facts is not likely to be happy at the prospect of seeing them converted into rubbish. He is more likely to want them bound and preserved, a memorial to his personal achievement.... [Thus our assumption that all facts] are wholly subject to alternative constructions looms up as culpably subjective and dangerously subversive to the scientific establishment.... [Nevertheless, we must] consider any scientific theory as an eventual candidate for the trash can. (Kelly, 1955, p. 31; 1970a, p. 2.)

EVALUATION

Criticisms and Controversies

All too often, Kelly's invitation to adventure seems more like a dull exercise in neologisms. His dryly scientific theory omits most of the characteristics that seem vitally and distinctively human: love and hate, passion and despair, achievement and failure, inferiority and arrogance, sexuality and aggression. Kelly's exclusion of virtually all familiar constructs, and his extreme emphasis on cognition, also pose problems for his theory. In view of the significance that he accords to experience and replications, his refusal to accept the construct of learning appears particularly arbitrary and unconvincing. If emotion is unimportant, it is unclear why the prospect of revising major constructs should be anxiety provoking or threatening.

Kelly devotes little attention to infancy and childhood, which most psychologists regard as a time of considerable importance for personality development. Psychoanalytically oriented theorists view Kelly's contention that there is no latent or repressed hostility, but only a failure to construe one's behavior accordingly, as a gross oversimplification. Patients who steadfastly refuse to interpret themselves as angry may nevertheless be angry, as shown by their behavior (e.g., becoming physically tense and using a harsh tone of voice when talking about their parents). For these reasons, it has been argued that personal construct theory fails to convey a convincing picture of the human personality.

Empirical Research

Personal construct theory has attracted a fairly small number of devoted followers, who have conducted a substantial amount of empirical research. Some of these investigators have tried to redress Kelly's emphasis on cognition by devoting more attention to the emotional aspects of personality. Others have attempted to relate personal construct theory to established clinical concepts, such as schizophrenia and depression, and to focus more on a theory of persons than on abstract and technical construct systems. (See, for example, Bannister, 1985; Neimeyer & Neimeyer, 1990; 1992; Winter, 1992.) However, whether it is possible to reconcile so idiosyncratic a theory as Kelly's with the mainstream of modern psychology remains open to question.

Contributions

Kelly has called attention to important ways in which cognitions, and an empathy for the personal constructs of other people, affect our interpersonal relationships. In contrast to the pompous claims of some psychoanalysts, who seek to enshrine untestable ideas as monuments to their unique insight and scathingly reject any attempts at innovation, Kelly's conception of a theory as a limited and ultimately expendable tool is particularly refreshing. His theory allows for a considerable degree of personal uniqueness and provides logical guidelines for the nomothetic, scientific study of personality. To some psychologists (e.g., Fiske, 1978, p. 39), Kelly's approach provides the key to understanding all theories of personality: they represent the personal constructs of their creators, albeit ones that are more systematic and explicit than those of most people.

Kelly himself (1955, p. 130) once expressed the concern that his theory might be nothing more than the fulminations of his own unique construct system, and not readily usable by most psychologists. Although it would not be surprising if his reservations ultimately proved to be correct, his general approach and emphasis on personal cognitions represents an unusual and significant contribution to the field of personality theory.

Suggested Reading

Kelly's ideas are concentrated primarily in one two-volume work (1955). Also of interest are Kelly's articles (1969; 1970a, 1970b). For a biography of Kelly, see Fransella (1995).

SUMMARY

1. **THE BASIC NATURE OF HUMAN BEINGS.** Among the most idiosyncratic of personality theorists, Kelly rejects the use of explicit motivational constructs. He assumes only that human beings are naturally active, and that our behavior is directed toward the goal of anticipating the future.

2. The structure of personality. Each of us forms our own personal constructs for interpreting and predicting the environment. The psychologist must seek to understand the ways in which a particular individual views the world, rather than trying to impose a single set of scientific constructs on all humanity. *Postulates and Corollaries:* Kelly's description of our "scientific" personality is couched in terms of 1 fundamental postulate, and 11 corollaries. The former states that our psychological processes are channelized by the ways in which we anticipate the future, whereas the latter clarify and elaborate on the nature of personal constructs (as delineated in a preceding Capsule Summary). *Other Characteristics of Personal Constructs:* Personal constructs must specify a way in which at least two elements are alike and different from a third. They may be preemptive, constellatory, or propositional. Every construct system includes that of "self versus others." This self-construct is typically subordinated to certain constructs that concern important people in one's life, a subsystem referred to as the core role. Imminent changes in the core aspects of a person's construction system produce guilt or threat, whereas the inability to construe important events and anticipate the future results in anxiety. Some constructs are not readily accessible to one's awareness, but this is due to limitations in the construction system rather than to supposedly unconscious processes.

3. The development of personality. Pathogenic parental behaviors may impair the child's ability to anticipate the future. Except for such maladaptive influences, personality development unfolds in a healthy way.

4. Further applications. *Dream Interpretation:* Dreams offer potential clues to the less obvious aspects of personality, but are useful primarily for weaning a client from constructs that have become overly rigid and tight. *Psychopathology:* The pathological individual resembles an incompetent scientist who clings rigidly to outmoded hypotheses, and whose predictions are frequently incorrect. Thus the causes of psychopathology are in the present, and concern a personal construct system that is in some way defective. *Psychotherapy:* The goal of Kellyan psychotherapy is to enable the client to devise and safely experiment with new core constructs, discard those that are faulty, and reconstruct the system in ways that lead to more accurate predictions. Procedures include interviews, the Rep Test, self-reports, and fixed-role therapy.

5. Evaluation. Kelly has been criticized for excessive and complicated neologisms, omitting most of the vital characteristics that make us distinctively human, arbitrarily rejecting such established constructs as learning, and an oversimplified view of personality and human nature. Yet his conception of a theory as a limited and ultimately expendable tool offers a refreshing contrast to the pompous claims of certain psychologists, he has called attention to the importance of cognitions and empathy as aspects of personality and interpersonal relations, his theory allows for personal uniqueness while providing logical guidelines for nomothetic research, and his approach may represent the key to understanding the myriad of personality theories.

STUDY QUESTIONS

Part I. Questions

1. (a) How might Kelly's personality and life experiences have influenced his decision to devise so many neologisms? (b) Should a theorist be faulted if his or her ideas are unusually difficult to understand?

2. Using the case material in the Appendix, give an example to illustrate each of the following Kellyan concepts: (a) A core construct that can be changed only with the aid of psychotherapy. (b) The conflict over whether to choose the safer course of further clarifying the constructs that one already uses, or the more adventurous path of trying to use unfamiliar

constructs. (c) A poorly designed "test" of a personal construct that yields an erroneous conclusion. (d) How anxiety results from the inability to construe important events and anticipate the future. (e) A preverbal construct.

3. Give an example to illustrate each of the following: (a) Construing an event based on prior experiences. (b) A permeable construct. (c) An impermeable construct. (d) A preemptive or constellatory construct.

4. Two people use the personal construct of "preoccupied" to describe my behavior when I am working on a book. Their opposite poles are different: one uses "available," whereas the other uses "friendly." What behavior should I expect from each person?

5. Give an example to illustrate each of the following: (a) Two people have a serious disagreement because they use different personal constructs to interpret the same event. (b) Two people have a serious disagreement because they are unable to construe each other's constructs. (c) The amount of time that you spend studying this chapter is influenced by how you construe the material.

6. According to Kelly, "One cannot call another person a bastard without making bastardy a dimension of his own life also." What does this imply about: (a) Athletes who use "trash talk" to put down their opponents? (b) Politicians who use negative and derogatory commercials to win an election? (c) Anyone who insults someone else?

7. Kelly contends that we always have the ability to construe events in alternative ways. Is this true of such tragic events as the death of a loved one or the events of September 11, 2001?

8. Freud contends that we are capable of repressing intense anger, which remains powerful but unconscious. Kelly argues that there is no such thing as latent or repressed hostility, but only the failure to construe our behavior correctly. Which view do you prefer? Why?

9. Why does Kelly conclude that "it is almost impossible to give any comprehensive theory the final coup de grâce?"

10. (a) How would Kelly interpret the "S[E]INE" dream discussed in Chapter 8? (b) Who did Kelly have in mind when he wrote about the therapist who tries to impose his construct system on every client, and the theorist who "is more likely to want [his theoretical constructs] bound and preserved, a memorial to his personal achievement.... [even though we must] consider any scientific theory as an eventual candidate for the trash can"?

11. In each of the following cases, how might it be helpful to use Kelly's principle of constructive alternativism? (a) A driver who is prone to "road rage" is cut off by a driver in a hurry. (b) You must take a course that you don't expect to like because it is a prerequisite for a course that you want to take. (c) An athlete who has played well all season makes a critical error that is primarily responsible for the team's loss in the championship game.

12. A terrorist blows up a building in a hated foreign country. How might Kelly explain the terrorist's behavior?

Part II. Comments and Suggestions

1. See Chapter 13, question 1.

2. (a) Consider the construct of "safe versus dangerous." (b) He consistently predicts that other people will be "intimidating" (as opposed to "nurturing"), and does not risk using the opposite pole even though he wants love and affection. (c) He meets someone at a party and decides to test the possibility that this person is "friendly" (as opposed to "unfriendly"). But his social skills suffer from a lack of practice, his opening remarks are awkward, his hands perspire, and he is more concerned with his own anxiety than learning about his new acquaintance. The other person is somewhat disconcerted by all this and responds cautiously, whereupon the patient concludes that this person is "unfriendly." (d) Note that his predictions are often

incorrect: he is fearful but no real danger appears, he expects someone else to be friendly but they act distant and unfriendly, and so on. (e) See section 7 of the case material in the Appendix.

3. (a) You decide whether a forthcoming examination is likely to be "difficult" (as opposed to "easy") by construing previous examinations in that course as "difficult" or "easy." (b) On reaching this point in the book, you decide that the remaining material may be interesting or uninteresting. (c) On reaching this point in the book, you decide that none of the remaining material can possibly be interesting. (d) All too many authors seem to assume that a textbook must only be "scholarly," and not also "entertaining."

4. Which person is more likely to understand that I have a busy schedule? Which person is more likely to blame me for not being cordial?

5. (a) At a family picnic, I see a six-year-old child hanging on to the top of a jungle gym. I construe his behavior as "adventurous" (as opposed to "timid"), because the drop is only a few feet and the ground is soft. But his mother construes the situation as "dangerous" (as opposed to "safe"), and is angry because I make no effort to help him. (b) One individual regards abortion as "murder" (as opposed to "life-saving"), while another construes it as "freedom" (as opposed to "fascism"). (c) Consider such constructs as "interesting versus boring," "useful versus useless," and "thought-provoking versus incomprehensible."

6. Remember that we create all of our personal constructs. What might such behaviors reveal about how these people construe themselves? Can you call someone a loser without ever thinking that you are a loser?

7. Consider such personal constructs as "despair" ("my life is over") versus "fortitude" ("I'll be strong so my loved one would be proud of me, or because my children need me"). Can an event be so catastrophic that it represents an exception to the principle of constructive alternativism?

8. I prefer Freud's. See the quote in Chapter 11 at the beginning of the section on psychopathology.

9. Psychological researchers can never study all of the cases in which they are interested, such as all adults or all obsessive-compulsives, because these populations are much too large. They must use relatively small samples drawn from the specified populations. One or two studies never disprove (or prove) a theory, because studies using different samples might have yielded different results. A substantial number of studies that disconfirm a theory would be another story, but it is not easy to obtain such consistency in psychological research.

10. (a) He would probably conclude that the client has become preoccupied with learning Erikson's theoretical constructs (such as repression, condensation, and Oedipality), is offering this dream as a gift to show how well she is doing, and is not devising the new personal constructs that she needs to solve her problems. (b) Surely, Freud. (Recall that Kelly used psychoanalytic theory at one time.) These comments could also be applied to other theorists whose work we have discussed, however.

11. (a) Instead of construing the other driver as "selfish" (as opposed to "caring") or "out to annoy me" (as opposed to "considerate"), the cut-off driver construes the other driver as "desperately worried" and in a hurry to see his wife who is in the hospital (as opposed to "rude"). This could be true, and believing it is a good way to prevent road rage. (b) In what favorable ways might you construe the prerequisite course? How might this help you? (c) Rather than construing this situation as a "hopeless disaster," how might the athlete construe it in a way that is honest but also more positive?

12. Would Kelly attribute the terrorist's behavior to an illicit instinct? Why not? How might the terrorist be construing people in the other country and the political situation faced by his or her country? Why might these *personal* constructs be difficult to change? Is there a practical and effective way to change them?

CHAPTER 16

ALBERT BANDURA
Social-Cognitive Theory

Are such behaviorist concepts as reinforcement incompatible with the inner causes favored by personality theorists? Is our behavior entirely determined by external forces, as Skinner contends? Albert Bandura does not think so. His **social-cognitive theory** (also called **social learning theory**) stresses the mutual interrelationships among behavior, internal causes, and environmental factors.

OBJECTIVES

- *To correct behaviorism's limited approach to psychology by emphasizing the importance of inner causes of behavior, including thoughts, expectations, self-perceptions, and beliefs.*
- *To correct Skinner's overemphasis on external influences by showing that we exert a reciprocal influence on our environment.*
- *To correct Skinner's overemphasis on external influences by showing that we set standards for ourselves and reinforce ourselves for doing well, and that self-reinforced behavior tends to be maintained more effectively than behavior that has been externally reinforced.*
- *To correct Skinner's overemphasis on operant conditioning (and trial-and-error learning) by showing that the majority of human learning takes place through observation, and does not necessarily involve reinforcement.*
- *To argue that aggression and destructiveness are due primarily to observational learning (social learning, modeling), with emphasis on violence in the media.*
- *To show that the extent to which we believe that we can perform the behaviors required by a particular situation (perceived self-efficacy) has a significant effect on our behavior.*
- *To show that psychopathology can be caused by dysfunctional thoughts as well as by faulty learning.*
- *To advocate methods of psychotherapy that help patients increase their perceived self-efficacy and believe that they can achieve their goals through their own efforts.*

BIOGRAPHICAL SKETCH

Albert Bandura was born on December 4, 1925, in Mundare, a small town in Alberta, Canada. His family included five older sisters. There was only one school in Mundare, which was so understaffed that two teachers handled the entire high school curriculum and students had to take charge of their own education. Bandura actually profited from this difficult situation: He developed a grasp of the material that was often better than that of the two overworked teachers, as well as a sense of self-directedness that was to serve him well throughout his life.

Bandura's choice of a career in psychology was due partly to chance. He took a carpool to school that arrived very early in the morning, he needed a course that would complete his schedule by filling the earliest time slot, and a psychology course happened to be available. He liked his serendipitous choice so much that he devoted the rest of his professional life to psychology. He received his B.A. from the University of British Columbia in 1949 and his Ph.D. in psychology from the University of Iowa in 1952, which he recalls as an intellectually lively and demanding place where major theoretical issues were pursued with a passion. He then joined Stanford University, where he began the researches into social learning theory that were to occupy him for the next 5 decades. He became a full professor in 1964, and was honored with an endowed chair in 1974.

Bandura married Virginia Varns while a graduate student at the University of Iowa; they have two daughters. Personally, he has been described as exuding a cheerful self-confidence in his ideas and an infectious optimism for what individuals and societies are capable of accomplishing (Maddux, 1998). Bandura is the author of seven books and many journal articles, and his honors include several distinguished scientist awards and election to the presidency of the American Psychological Association in 1974.

THE BASIC NATURE OF HUMAN BEINGS

Reciprocal Determinism

Bandura is highly critical of Skinner's emphasis on a totally controlling environment, and the apparent paradoxes to which this conception leads:

> [To contend] that people are [wholly] controlled by external forces, and then to advocate that they redesign society by applying psychotechnology, undermines the basic premise of the argument. If humans were in fact incapable of influencing their own actions, they might describe and predict environmental events but they could hardly exercise any intentional control over them. When it comes to advocacy of social change, however, [Skinnerians nevertheless] become ardent advocates of people's power to transform environments in pursuit of a better life. (Bandura, 1977, pp. 205–206. See also Bandura, 1978, p. 344; 1986.)

Bandura argues that behavior, environmental influences, and internal personal factors (including beliefs, thoughts, preferences, expectations, and self-perceptions) all cause and can be caused by each other (**reciprocal determinism**). For example, the behavior of watching a particular television program is dictated in part by your personal preferences. Both of these factors exert an effect on the environment, since producers cancel shows that do not attract enough viewers. And external forces also help to shape preferences and behaviors, for you cannot like or select a program that is not televised:

> In the social learning view, people are neither driven [solely] by inner forces nor buffeted by environmental stimuli. Rather, psychological functioning is explained in terms of a continuous reciprocal interaction of personal and environmental determinants.... [Therefore,] to the oft-repeated [Skinnerian] dictum "change contingencies and you change behavior," should be added the reciprocal side "change behavior and you change the contingencies." In the regress of prior causes, for every chicken discovered by a unidirectional environmentalist, a social learning theorist can identify a prior egg. (Bandura, 1977, pp. 11–12, 203. See also Bandura, 1973, p. 43; 1977, pp. vii, 108–109, 194–213; 1978, pp. 345–346.)

As a second example, consider how reciprocal determinism applies to your college courses:

The environment influences behavior: There is a course that you very much want to take, but it isn't being offered this semester (or quarter), so you have to make an alternate selection. A course that you want to take has a prerequisite that doesn't appeal to you, but you sign up for the latter in order to satisfy the requirement.

Behavior influences the environment: Too few students sign up for a course, so the college cancels it rather than lose money. So many students sign up for a course that the college decides to offer it more often. Students sign a petition objecting to what they think is an unnecessary prerequisite, and the college eliminates this requirement.

Personal factors influence behavior: You're more likely to sign up for a course that you expect to be interesting, or that you believe will be useful in your future profession. You're less likely to sign up for a course that you don't think you'll do well in.

Behavior influences personal factors: You are taking a (required) course that you don't think you'll do well in, so you study harder and get help from a friend. Your efforts seem to be fruitful, so your thoughts become more positive and you expect to do well on the first exam.

Personal factors influence the environment: A course has to be canceled because students expect it to be boring and believe that it will involve a great deal of work. Extra sections of a course have to be scheduled because students expect it to be very interesting and believe that the workload will be reasonable.

The environment influences personal factors: A course that is boring causes you to think negatively about that subject and believe that you won't like other courses in that area. Being at a top-rated college causes you to expect more difficult assignments and believe that you will have to work hard.

Here again, two aspects of reciprocal determinism may both influence the third. Students who expect a course to be boring (personal factor) don't sign up for it (behavior), which causes the college to cancel it (environmental effect).

Reciprocal determinism implies that we enjoy some freedom to act. But the number of options open to us is limited by external constraints (as when the college doesn't offer the course that you want to take), and by our inability or unwillingness to behave in certain ways. (See Figure 16.1.)

Cognitive Causes

Bandura agrees with Skinner that some so-called inner causes of behavior are merely redundant descriptions. But unlike Skinner, Bandura readily accepts the existence of causal cognitions.

If you are walking down a deserted street in a crime-ridden city late at night, thoughts about a mugger who might be headed your way can cause you to become highly anxious. People can make themselves angry by thinking about previous insults or injustices (such as a sarcastic boss who used unfair and destructive criticism), or sexually aroused by conjuring up erotic fantasies. And some innovators or unpublished authors think so much about being right that they labor for years to achieve their goals, with these cognitive self-inducements substituting for the lack of any reinforcing recognition. "Because some of the inner causes invoked by theorists over the years have been ill-founded does not justify excluding all internal determinants from scientific inquiry.... [There is] growing evidence that cognition has causal influence on behavior ... [and that any theory which] denies that thoughts can regulate actions does not lend itself readily to the explanation of complex human behavior" (Bandura, 1977, p. 10; see also Bandura, 1969, pp. 49, 364; 1973, pp. 39–53; 1977, pp. 2–3, 61, 68, 207–208).

Reinforcement

Pavlov and Skinner conclude that reinforcement operates without our awareness. Bandura disagrees, and argues that we must be aware of reinforcement in order for it to be effective. In particular, reinforcement involves a change in our conscious anticipations: we are more likely to act in ways that we *expect* to produce rewards, and/or to avoid punishment:

> The notion of "response strengthening" is, at best, a metaphor.... Outcomes change behavior in humans largely through the intervening influence of thought ... [while]

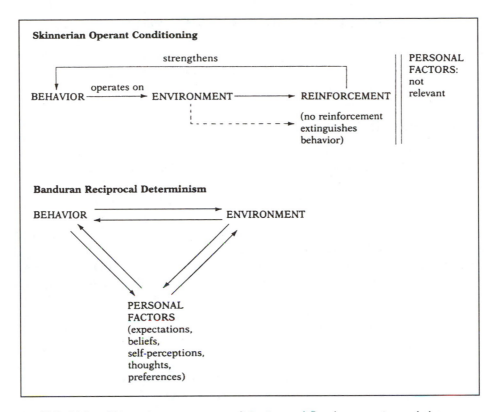

FIG. 16.1.   Skinnerian operant conditioning and Banduran reciprocal determinism compared.

consequences generally produce little change in complex behavior when there is no awareness of what is being reinforced. Even if certain responses have been positively reinforced, they will not increase [in probability] if individuals believe, from other information, that the same actions will not be rewarded on future occasions. (Bandura, 1977, pp. 18, 21; see also pp. 17–22, 67, 96–97, 109.)

Suppose that you would like to improve your grade in one of your college courses, and the teacher offers you extra credit if you do an additional project well. You work hard on the project, even though you haven't as yet received any (external) reinforcement at all, because you expect to gain a reward when you are finished. After completing the project and receiving extra credit that you feel is adequate, you ask the teacher if you can improve your grade still further by doing more work. However, the teacher replies that extra credit can only be earned once in that course. You will not do another project, even though you were reinforced for the previous one, because you don't expect that a second project will be reinforced.

Partial reinforcement produces greater resistance to extinction because we expect that our efforts will eventually be successful, as with the slot machine player who continues to invest quarters despite frequent losses. Secondary reinforcers, such as money, approval, or criticism, are previously neutral stimuli that we expect to be associated with primary reinforcers. And irrational fears are difficult to eliminate because we keep away from whatever causes them, which confirms our expectation of avoiding harm and prevents us from learning that there is no real danger. "Humans do not simply respond to stimuli; they interpret them" (Bandura, 1977, p. 59; see also pp. 58–62, 102, 116).

THE STRUCTURE OF PERSONALITY

Bandura sees little value in abstract structural constructs. But he does devote substantial attention to the ways in which we regulate and reinforce our own behavior, and to the effects of an individual's perceived self-effectiveness.

Self-Reinforced Behavior

According to Bandura, our behavior is also influenced by learned criteria that we establish for ourselves (**self-reinforcement**). "If actions were determined solely by external rewards and punishments, people would behave like weathervanes, constantly shifting in different directions to conform to the momentary influences impinging upon them.... [In actuality, people also] set certain standards of behavior for themselves, and respond to their own actions in self-rewarding or self-punishing ways" (Bandura, 1977, pp. 128–129; see also Bandura, 1973, pp. 48–49; 1977, pp. 130–158; 1978).

Authors do not need someone hovering over their shoulder and reinforcing each well-phrased sentence with praise (or a piece of candy). They are guided by an inner standard of what constitutes acceptable work. They rewrite each page numerous times until this criterion is met, and then reinforce themselves with satisfaction. The more exacting the author's standards, the more effort spent in revision—perhaps even to the extent of doing more editing than is necessary, or becoming so self-critical as to be unable to complete the manuscript.

Consider once again the example of earning extra credit in one of your college courses. You don't receive any *external* reinforcement while you are working on the project, since the teacher will not give you any extra credit (or opinions) until it is completed. But you are likely to reinforce yourself with thoughts like: "I did a really good job on that section. I think my teacher will be pleased." "This page isn't good enough. I'd better fix it." "I like what I'm doing, and I believe it will earn the extra credit when I turn it in."

Some individuals appear to be totally guided by self-standards, as when Thomas More was beheaded rather than renounce his beliefs. Most often, however, self-standards are related to external standards. "Individuals who regard their behavior so highly that the reactions of their associates have no effect are rare indeed" (Bandura, 1977, p. 149; see also pp. 153–155). Nevertheless, self-standards and self-reinforcement play an important role in determining human behavior. "Self-rewarded behavior tends to be maintained more effectively than if it has been externally reinforced.... Including self-reinforcement processes in learning theory thus greatly increases the explanatory power of reinforcement principles as applied to human functioning" (Bandura, 1977, pp. 129, 144).

Perceived Self-Efficacy

We tend to undertake tasks that we judge ourselves to be capable of, but avoid activities that we regard as beyond our abilities. That is, our behavior is influenced by the extent to which we believe that we can perform the actions required by a particular situation (our **perceived self-efficacy**).

Perceived self-efficacy is closely related to self-esteem and the Rogerian self-concept. (See Chapter 9.) Whereas self-esteem deals with how you evaluate your self-concept, perceived self-efficacy involves your belief that you can achieve a personal goal through your own efforts. If you believe that you can earn an A on a test based on the material in this chapter, you are high in perceived self-efficacy with regard to this task.

CAPSULE SUMMARY

Some Important Banduran Terminology

Modeling	(1) A synonym for observational learning. (2) A form of behavior therapy wherein the client observes one or more people demonstrating desirable or effective behavior.
Observational learning (modeling, social learning)	Learning by watching other people's behavior and its consequences for them. Reinforcement is *not* necessary for observational learning to occur; but it may facilitate paying attention to the model and remembering the relevant information, or it may be essential to make the subject perform what has been learned.
Perceived self-efficacy	The extent to which a person believes that he or she can perform the behaviors required by a particular situation.
Reciprocal determinism	The continuous interrelationship of behavior, internal personal factors (e.g., thoughts, beliefs, expectations), and environmental influences, any one of which may cause any of the others.
Reinforcement	An increase in the frequency of certain behaviors because of expectations that they will gain rewards or avoid punishment.
Self-reinforcement	Establishing standards of behavior for ourselves, and praising or criticizing ourselves accordingly.
Social-cognitive theory (Social learning theory)	The name Bandura gave to his psychological theory.
Vicarious punishment	A decrease in the frequency of certain behaviors, which occurs as the result of seeing others punished for the same actions (i.e., through observational learning).
Vicarious reinforcement	An increase in the frequency of certain behaviors, which occurs as the result of seeing others rewarded for the same actions (i.e., through observational learning).

Perceived self-efficacy is *not* simply a matter of "talking a good game;" it involves fundamental beliefs about yourself. "Simply saying that one is capable is not necessarily self-convincing. Self-efficacy beliefs are the product of a complex process of self-persuasion that relies on [the] cognitive processing of diverse sources of efficacy information" (Bandura, 1995, p. 11). As in Kelly's theory, perceived self-efficacy is determined to a great extent by your interpretation of prior events. If you believe that you have been successful on a task, you are likely to conclude that you can do so again. After a series of failures, you may well decide that the task is beyond your abilities.

People with high perceived self-efficacy tend to set higher goals for themselves and persist when they encounter obstacles or setbacks. For example, children who are high in perceived self-efficacy with regard to academic achievement are more likely to try difficult projects, take notes in class, and complete their homework assignments (Bandura et al., 1996). Those with low perceived self-efficacy tend to view their problems as more formidable than they actually are, and try less hard or quit altogether in the face of adversity, because they attribute their failure to a basic lack of ability.

Like self-esteem, perceived self-efficacy is multidimensional: You may perceive yourself as likely to do well in some areas (such as your work in this course, or your academic work in general), but not as well in other areas (a course in nuclear physics, a social or athletic activity). Thus Bandura differs from Rogers by concluding that a single global self-concept is *not* sufficient to explain human behavior. How we evaluate ourselves varies from one area to another, which is one reason why we may well behave differently in different situations. (See Bandura, 1977; 1977b; 1981; 1982a; 1982b; 1986; 1995; 1997.)

As would be expected from the principle of reciprocal determinism, the influence exerted on behavior by personal factors (such as perceived self-efficacy) may be altered by the environment. A repressive and authoritarian leader may discourage even those who are high in perceived self-efficacy from trying, as when a dictatorial teacher truns off capable students by imposing many trivial and irritating requirements that have little educational value.

THE DEVELOPMENT OF PERSONALITY

Observational Learning (Modeling)

In contrast to Skinner, Bandura argues that behavior need not be performed and reinforced for learning to occur. **Modeling** (or **observational learning,** or **social learning**) involves learning by observing other people's behavior and its consequences for them, and is responsible for the vast majority of human learning.

The novice does *not* learn to drive an automobile or perform brain surgery by emitting various random behaviors, and having the unsuccessful ones negatively reinforced by the resulting carnage. He or she learns through instruction, and by watching others perform these tasks correctly. Bandura argues that if the pigeons and rats in Skinner's operant conditioning experiments had faced such dangers as drowning or electrocution, the limitations of this form of learning would have been revealed. "Observational learning is vital for both development and survival. Because mistakes can produce costly or even fatal consequences, the prospects for survival would be slim indeed if one could learn only by suffering the consequences of trial and error" (Bandura, 1977, p. 12; see also Bandura, 1969; 1971, pp. 2–3; 1977, pp. 58, 91).

In a famous early experiment, preschool children watched an adult spend ten minutes hitting, kicking, and throwing a large inflatable Bobo doll around the room. The adult also shouted, "Sock him in the nose. Hit him. Kick him." Afterward, the children were given some enticing toys to play with for a few minutes. They were then frustrated by being separated from the appealing toys and taken to another room, which contained a few mediocre toys and a Bobo doll. Children who observed the aggressive adult were much more likely to behave aggressively toward the Bobo doll than children who were frustrated but had not watched the aggressive behavior (Bandura, 1969; Bandura et al., 1961).

In another experiment, observers learned to fear a buzzer by watching a model who supposedly received intensely painful electric shocks immediately after hearing it. (This was only a simulation, with the model a convincing—and unshocked—actor.) Similarly, a child learns as much or more about the expression of anger from watching the parents' behavior when they are angry as from their verbal explanations. Thus Bandura shares the belief of certain theorists (e.g., Fromm, Rogers) that human destructiveness is typically due to learning, notably observational learning, rather than to some innate instinct.

Socially acceptable behavior is often learned by observing conformist models get along well with others—as with the dictum "When in Rome, do as the Romans do" (Bandura, 1977, pp. 87–88). Those who watch others being courageous, compassionate, or charitable are more likely to behave in similar ways. And observing the parent of the same gender facilitates personality development by helping a child learn the behavior that is expected of a male or female. Observational learning (of both desirable and undesirable behavior) is more likely to occur if the model is liked and respected by the observer, and is perceived as similar to the observer. (See Bandura, 1971, pp. 16–26; 1973; 1977, pp. 22–29, 55–67, 117–128, 151; Bandura & Walters, 1963.)

Observational learning also influences perceived self-efficacy. Children who watch their peers succeed at a task are more likely to believe that they can also succeed and to try that task. Conversely, children who see others fail are more likely to conclude that they can't do it and refuse to try. That is, watching similar people succeed or fail can raise or lower the observer's perceived self-efficacy with regard to that task.

Processes in Observational Learning. How does observational learning occur? Bandura concludes that cognitions play a vital role: We imagine ourselves in the same situation and incurring similar consequences. Observational learning can therefore change the effectiveness of certain reinforcers, as when a modest amount of money (or praise) produces little behavior change because an underpaid employee has seen other workers getting much more for the same responses.

As the preceding example implies, observational learning involves significantly more than imitation; it is *not* simply a matter of "monkey see, monkey do." We formulate rules, concepts, and conclusions based on what we observe, and we may apply these inferences in ways that lead to behavior that is related but not identical. For example, people who watch the hero(ine) in a movie or television show destroy the "bad guys" with acts of violence are unlikely to copy this behavior by going out and shooting someone. But they may well conclude that aggression is a good way to solve problems, and be more likely to insult or even hit someone when faced with such frustrations as being cut off by another car on the expressway. (See Bandura, 1991.)

Reinforcement may also play a role in observational learning. Rewarding a model tends to increase the probability that the observer will behave this way (**vicarious reinforcement**), whereas punishing the model makes imitating the model less likely (**vicarious punishment**). In a variation of the Bobo doll study, preschool children observed an adult's aggression toward the doll on film. In this version, the adult even hit the Bobo doll with a hammer, and the film had three different endings. One group of children saw the adult rewarded for aggressive behavior, a second group saw the adult punished, and a third group saw an ending where the adult was neither rewarded or punished. When the children were then allowed to play with a Bobo doll, those who had seen the adult model being rewarded were most likely to attack the doll, while those who observed the model being punished were least likely to be aggressive. Similarly, the probability of illicit or criminal behavior is increased by seeing others perform such actions without incurring any punishment. We learn not only by watching what a model does, but also by observing the consequences of the model's behavior.

Observational learning often occurs without either the model or the participant being reinforced, as in the first Bobo doll study. But reinforcement may facilitate behavior change by motivating the participant to pay attention and remember, or it may be necessary to make the participant perform the learned responses. (See Bandura, 1971, pp. 16–26; 1977, pp. 22–29, 38, 88–90.)

FURTHER APPLICATIONS OF BANDURAN THEORY

Psychopathology

Bandura attributes psychopathology to faulty learning, and to the resulting incorrect anticipations. Children may develop pathological behaviors because these actions are reinforced, as when a well-meaning but misguided teacher pays attention to a shy student only when she separates herself from her classmates and sulks. The student thus learns to expect that isolation and sulking will be rewarded with the teacher's concern. Or parents may inadvertently teach their children to be annoying by responding only to their loudest requests, as Skinner has also pointed out. Perhaps the most painful of all problems is an overly severe set of self-standards, and the resulting attempts to avoid guilt or external punishments through excessive self-criticism. "There is no more devastating punishment than self-contempt.... Linus, the security-blanketed member of the 'Peanuts' clan, also alluded to this phenomenon when he observed, 'There is no heavier burden than a great potential' " (Bandura, 1977, pp. 141, 154).

As the last example indicates, Bandura differs from Skinner by attributing considerable importance to inner, cognititve causes of psychopathology. "Many human dysfunctions and ensuing torments stem from problems of thought. This is because, in their thoughts, people often dwell on painful pasts and on perturbing futures of their own invention.... They drive themselves to despondency by harsh self-evaluation ... And they often act on misconceptions that get them into trouble." (Bandura, 1986, p. 515.)

For example, phobias are related to perceived self-efficacy and expectations. Consider people who have a phobia for heights that are more than two stories high. They will show little anxiety and physiological arousal to threats that they believe they can control, such as the balcony of a private home that is only a few feet above the ground. But when they face threats for which they don't believe they can cope (have low perceived self-efficacy), such as walking to a seat in the highest row of a football stadium, their anxiety and arousal level increase markedly. This leads to avoidance of the feared situation (as by never going to another foot-ball game), which confirms their expectation of avoiding harm and prevents them from learning that the situation is not dangerous. (See Bandura, 1995.)

Low perceived self-efficacy is also related to depression. If you believe that you do not have the ability to achieve the standards that you have set for yourself, this may well lead to bouts of depression. Depression may also result from an inability to control the related negative thoughts ("I'm not measuring up to my potential, and I probably never will"). A person who is lacking in social perceived self-efficacy, and does not believe that he or she can develop the relationships and support from others that are necessary for a satisfying life, is also prone to depression (and physical illness). "Social support is not a self-forming entity waiting around to buffer harried people against stressors. Rather, people have to go out and find or create supportive relationships for themselves. This requires a strong sense of social efficacy" (Bandura, 1995, pp. 9–10).

Psychotherapy

Theoretical Foundation.   Pathological individuals suffer from a troublesome problem: They cannot behave in ways that they expect to gain rewards or avoid punishments. The psychotherapist's primary goal is therefore to help clients learn to believe that they can achieve their desired goals through their own efforts. This increased perceived self-efficacy makes it more likely that the client will confront irrational fears, instead of avoiding them. Bandura is critical of both the Freudian "talking cure" and behavior therapy procedures that aim solely at the removal of painful symptoms, rather than dealing with the client's cognitions:

> The greatest benefit that psychological treatments can bestow are not specific remedies for particular problems, but the sociocognitive tools needed to deal effectively with whatever situations might arise. To the extent that treatment equips people to exercise influence over events in their lives, it initiates an ongoing process of self-regulative change. (Bandura, 1997, p. 319.)

Bandura therefore advocates methods of psychotherapy that involve the actual perform-ance of feared or discouraging tasks (*guided mastery*). "Conversation is not an especially effective way of altering human behavior. In order to change, people need corrective learning experiences.... [Clients] who persist in performing activities that are [frightening but safe] will gain corrective experiences that further reinforce their sense of efficacy, thereby eventually eliminating their fears and defensive behavior. [But] those who give up prematurely will retain their self-debilitating expectations and fears for a long time" (Bandura, 1977, pp. 78, 80; see also Bandura, 1969; 1977, pp. 5, 79–85). Bandura is also critical of insight therapies because, like Kelly, he believes that clients' thoughts are all too often molded in the direction of the therapist's theory of personality.

Therapeutic Procedures. A client who is too anxious or unskilled to behave in desirable ways may be shown one or more people demonstrating these behaviors, either live or on film, and then imitate them (the technique of **modeling**). A child who is afraid of dogs may see and then imitate a peer who first observes a dog from a distance, then moves somewhat closer, then still closer, and then pets the dog (a form of shaping called "graduated modeling"). Or a group of unruly children may watch a film of children playing together cooperatively, and perhaps receive reinforcement for behaving in similar ways.

According to Bandura, therapy that combines modeling with guided participation is particularly effective in eliminating irrational fears and inhibitions. "Through this form of treatment, incapacitated clients lose their fears, become able to engage in activities they formerly inhibited, and develop more favorable attitudes toward the things they abhorred" (Bandura, 1977, p. 84).

It is by no means undesirable for clients to emerge from psychotherapy with perceived self-efficacy that is somewhat too high, so that they tend to overestimate their abilities. "This is a benefit rather than a character flaw to be eliminated. If efficacy beliefs always reflected only what people could do, they would remain steadfastly wedded to an overly conservative judgment of their capabilities" (Bandura, 1995, p. 12).

Psychotherapy and Social Reform. In accordance with some personality theorists, Bandura strongly recommends certain social reforms. He is highly critical of the extent to which television and other media portray violent behaviors, which are all too likely to serve as models (especially in the case of children). He favors such controls as a privately funded board that would try to sway public opinion against media violence, and in favor of programs that are nonviolent and informative (such as the well-known *Sesame Street*). (See Bandura, 1973.) Bandura has also related perceived self-efficacy to such areas as group and family behavior, educational methods and intellectual development, physical health and illness, stress, political beliefs, and social change (1995; 1997).

EVALUATION

Criticisms and Controversies

Bandura has been criticized for ignoring such important and complicated aspects of human behavior as conflicts, both conscious and unconscious, and for an excessive bias against psychoanalysis. He all too readily accepts the negative findings of outdated and outmoded laboratory studies of the defense mechanisms, and he rejects the value of clinical data without considering the other side of the story (Bandura, 1986, pp. 3–4). In addition, there would seem to be some pronounced (yet largely ignored) similarities between Bandura's ideas and those of other theorists: Kelly's emphasis on the importance of interpreting (construing) our environment, and of our expectations and predictions; the stress of Adler, Erikson, Fromm, and May on a sense of mastery, and the debilitating effects of intense feelings of powerlessness and inferiority; Freud's concept of an overly severe superego; and Horney's emphasis on self-contempt. Thus it would appear that Bandura has achieved more of a rapprochement with personality theory than his writings indicate.

Empirical Research

Observational Learning and Violence in the Media.   Incidents such as the Columbine High School shootings have raised questions about the effects of violent television programs, movies, and video games on human behavior. It is difficult to prove that observing a violent act caused subsequent aggressive behavior. Perhaps the Columbine killers were disturbed individuals who would have behaved this way sooner or later; few people who watch violent movies and television programs go out and perform the identical actions themselves. Nevertheless, more than 20 years of laboratory and other experiments has confirmed Bandura's belief as to the importance of observational learning: Televised violence has powerful negative effects on children's behavior, beliefs, and values. (See, for example, Myers, 2001, pp. 670–673; Newman & Newman, 1999, pp. 241–242; Sternberg, 2001, pp. 471–472.)

As was discussed earlier in this chapter, observational learning involves significantly more than imitation; we formulate rules, concepts, and conclusions based on what we observe. Children who are exposed to frequent episodes of televised violence are more likely to believe that aggressive behavior is an acceptable way to resolve conflicts, and to use or accept such behavior in peer relationships. Because acts of aggression in the media greatly outnumber acts of love and affection, children who watch a great deal of television worry more about being victims of aggression and view the world as a more dangerous place. During their first 18 years, most children in the United States spend more time watching television than they spend in school. When the hero(ine) is rewarded or seen as successful because of his or her violent actions, children's tendencies to behave aggressively increase still further. Watching televised violence also increases emotional arousal, which is particularly likely to affect children who inherited a more aggressive temperament.

Teenagers who spend many hours playing violent video games tend to be more physically aggressive. And exposure to media violence desensitizes adults as well as children; we become more indifferent to actual acts of violence and tend to take them for granted. ("Another home invasion murder? Yawn. I wonder if the Yankees won.") Watching cruelty fosters indifference (Myers, 2001, p. 673).

The influence of the media is by no means entirely negative. Here again, positive models have positive effects. Television shows and movies have modeled such desirable social behavior as the values of family life, the need to work hard and sacrifice to achieve important goals, and achievements by minorities that help observers overcome social stereotypes and prejudices. Although it is all too easy for critics to question psychological research (which is far from infallible), the harmful effects of media violence are clear and incontrovertible—as Bandura has argued for the last three decades.

Other Research.   In addition to Bandura's own extensive research, various researchers have investigated issues that are related to his ideas. Some of this research will be discussed at the conclusion of this chapter in the section dealing with concepts in cognitive psychology.

Contributions

Social learning theory has been praised for its grounding in empirical research, for emphasizing studies with human rather than animal subjects, for promulgating such significant new forms of psychotherapy as modeling, and for providing behaviorism with a more convincing rationale than Skinner. The importance of observational learning is unquestionable, and Bandura's warnings about the dangers of violence in the media have been supported by a large amount of research. Perceived self-efficacy has significant effects on human behavior, and has also been the subject of a great deal of psychological research.

Bandura has made major contributions to our knowledge. In a recent survey of eminent psychologists of the 20th century, Bandura ranked fourth–behind only Skinner, Freud, and Jean Piaget.

Suggested Reading

A more detailed discussion of Bandura's views may be found in *Social Learning Theory* (1977) and the rather dry and technical *Social Foundations of Thought and Action* (1986), whereas a comparison of various alternative explanations of modeling is presented in *Psychological Modeling: Conflicting Theories* (1971). In addition, he has authored a social learning analysis of aggression (Bandura, 1973). For Bandura's views on perceived self-efficacy, see *Self-Efficacy: The Exercise of Control* (1997).

OTHER CONCEPTS IN COGNITIVE PSYCHOLOGY

Cognitive psychology is extremely popular. There is a vast amount of research dealing with congitions, as well as college courses and textbooks devoted solely to cognitive psychology (e.g., Manktelow, 1999; Sternberg, 1999; Sternberg & Ben-Zeev, 2001). Much of this research deals with areas other than personality, and the demarcation between cognitive psychology and other perspectives (e.g., trait theory, humanistic theory) is not always exact. Nevertheless, let us try to bridge the gap between theory and research by briefly examining some important constructs that involve thinking, beliefs, and expectations.

Constructs Dealing With Self-Evaluation and Performance

Self-Esteem.   As we observed in Chapter 9, self-esteem refers to how you evaluate your self-concept. It is similar to perceived self-efficacy with regard to both definition and research findings: Those who are high in self-esteem, and those who are high in perceived self-efficacy, set more challenging goals for themselves and are more persistent when faced with obstacles or setbacks. Those who are low in self-esteem, and those who are low in perceived self-efficacy, try less hard or quit in the face of adversity because they attribute their failures to a basic lack of ability (similar to the Adlerian inferiority complex). Also, both self-esteem and perceived self-efficacy are multidimensional. Such self-evaluations may be high with regard to a particular course or academic work in general, but low with regard to playing tackle football or social relationships (or vice versa). Self-esteem and perceived self-efficacy are based on cognitions and beliefs: It is not how good (or bad) you really are, but how good (or bad) you *think* you are that determines your behavior.

Learned Helplessness.   **Learned helplessness** involves the belief that one's behavior will have no effect on the environment. This perceived lack of control may not correspond with reality, and is typically learned from repeated punishments that one cannot avoid.

In a famous experiment, dogs were restrained in a harness and given a series of painful electric shocks. When the dogs were then placed in a situation where they could escape from the shocks simply by leaping a hurdle, they cowered hopelessly in a corner of the chamber and refused to move. Because they had not been able to escape from the previous shocks, they "learned" that they were helpless. (See Seligman, 1975; 1991.)

In the second part of the experiment, the dogs were *not* helpless; they were fully capable of jumping the hurdle. But they *believed* that they were helpless, and these cognitions are what determined their behavior. Similarly, children who are pampered by their parents (and who may be quite capable) learn to believe that they cannot solve their problems through their own efforts, which has a powerful negative effect on their behavior. (See Chapter 4.)

Locus of Control.   Locus of control is a trait that is based on cognitions. Some people believe that obtaining rewards and avoiding punishment is primarily within their control and depends on their own behavior (**internal locus of control**). Others expect their good and bad experiences to be caused largely by chance, fate, and the actions of other people (**external locus of control**).

If you are primarily internal, you are likely to agree with such statements as "People's misfortunes are due to their own mistakes" and "There is a direct connection between how hard I study and the grades I receive." If instead you are primarily external, you are likely to endorse such statements as "Many of the good and bad things in life are due largely to luck" and "The grading system in my school is often unfair, but there's nothing I can do about it." As with any trait, locus of control is a continuous variable; a person's score may fall anywhere along the scale from strongly internal to strongly external. Like self-esteem and perceived self-efficacy, locus of control is multidimensional: You may perceive yourself as having more control in your academic work and less in your social life (or vice versa), or having more control over your grades and your social life but less over our system of government. (See Rotter, 1966; Paulhus, 1983.)

Locus of control has important behavioral consequences. Although the relationship between locus of control and mental health is far from perfect, those who are more internal tend to be psychologically healthier, cope better with personal crises, are more satisfied with their lives, and have higher self-esteem, whereas those who are more depressed and anxious tend to be more external. Here again, it is cognitions—namely, the extent to which you *think/believe* that you control the rewards and punishments you receive—that determines your behavior.

Happiness With Life.   A relatively new area, *positive psychology,* deals with the study of optimal human functioning. Like Maslow's work, and in contrast to the Freudian emphasis on psychopathology, positive psychology studies the best that humans have to offer in order to learn about and promote conditions where people (and communities) will thrive.

Positive psychology is not the same as humanistic psychology. Humanistic psychology sought to improve the treatment of clients suffering from psychological disorders by devising methods that differed radically from Freudian psychoanalysis, whereas positive psychology focuses on the study of healthy people (and institutions). Humanistic psychology deals with the abstract and unmeasurable construct of human nature, which is assumed to be entirely benign, whereas positive psychology investigates specific areas that can be measured and studied through psychological research.

Some of the findings of positive psychology involve cognitions and personality. Kelly and Bandura argue that our overall happiness with life depends to a great extent on how we construe and evaluate what happens to us, rather than on the events themselves. In fact, most people are about as happy as they make up their minds to be (Lyubomirsky, 2001).

Constructs Dealing With Learning and Perception

Schemas.   A **schema** is a mental framework for organizing and interpreting information. This construct was devised by Swiss psychologist Jean Piaget to help explain how children's cognitive processes develop as they grow older. For example, a young child may have a schema of "people in uniforms." When the child sees police officers and firefighters, she may mistakenly conclude that they do the same things because they both fit into (are assimilated by) this schema. As she grows older, she learns to change her cognitions by forming two new schemas: "people in uniforms who put out fires," and "people in uniforms who arrest criminals." And her schemas will continue to undergo change (accommodation), as by expanding the schema of "people who arrest criminals" to include "people who issue traffic tickets."

Some schemas are related to personality. Suppose that a woman who is greatly concerned about being overweight meets some new acquaintances at a party. She immediately notices how thin most of them are, feels unattractive by comparison, mutters a word or two, and makes an early exit. A minister who is seeking to increase the size of his congregation views the same acquaintances as potential new members, pays no attention to their weight, and engages them in a lively conversation about their interest in religion. The woman is unsociable and defensive, and the minister is sociable and outgoing, because they are using different frameworks to process information: One schema focuses on weight, the other on membership. As Kelly observed, knowing how a person construes events helps us to understand and predict his or her behavior.

CAPSULE SUMMARY
Other Concepts In Cognitive Psychology

Availability heuristic	Making a decision, albeit not necessarily the correct one, by thinking about a relevant example that easily comes to mind.
External locus of control	The extent to which one believes that obtaining rewards and avoiding punishment is due to chance, fate, and the actions of other people.
Functional fixedness	Perceiving an object as having only one purpose; being unable to perceive an object in new ways that will solve a problem.
Internal locus of control	The extent to which one believes that obtaining rewards and avoiding punishment is within one's control and depends on one's own behavior.
Learned helplessness	The belief that one's behavior will have no effect on the environment; a perceived lack of control that may not correspond with reality, and often results from repeated punishments that one cannot avoid.
Mental set	A tendency to approach a problem in only one way, and not necessarily the best way, because this method has been successful in the past.
Perceptual set	A predisposition to perceive events in one way rather than another.
Schema	A mental framework for organizing and interpreting information.

Perceptual Set.   **Perceptual set** is a predisposition to perceive events in one way rather than another. Suppose that there are some oval white objects in the sky that appear to have ridges and compartments. A science-fiction fanatic who has a schema for interpreting events as "otherworldly" may be convinced that these objects are flying saucers. A cynic who doesn't believe in life on other planets, and whose schemas interpret events more conservatively, may be equally certain that they are only clouds. What we think influences what we perceive—and such personality traits as stubbornness and conservatism.

Constructs Dealing With Problem Solving and Decision Making

Mental Set.   **Mental set** refers to a tendency to approach a problem in only one way, and not necessarily the best way, because this method has been successful in the past.

Suppose that a driver's daily route to work involves an annoying left turn. There is no left turn arrow, only one or two cars can make the turn when the light changes from green to yellow, and the light rarely changes. So it may take as much as 10 or 15 minutes for the driver to negotiate this one turn. Day after day, he waits behind a long line of cars in the left turn lane, grousing about the inept traffic flow in his city. A better plan could be to stay in the right-hand lane, go past the street where he wants to turn, and make three right turns, which might well have him headed in the desired direction in just a minute or two. But he fails to consider this possibility because his mental set is that the only way to make a left turn is from the left turn lane, and he is eventually successful in getting to work by doing so. Such mental sets are a matter of cognitions (how one thinks about or interprets a situation), and are related to such personality traits as stubbornness and creativity (or the lack thereof).

Functional Fixedness.   **Functional fixedness** involves perceiving an object as having only one purpose. Like mental sets, functional fixedness can prevent us from solving a problem in the best way (or at all).

Suppose that on a fishing trip, you realize that you have made a serious error: instead of bringing your tackle box, you packed the sewing box. If you perceive a needle as a device only for sewing clothes, this functional fixedness will cause you to give up and go home. But if you are creative enough to realize that the needle can be used as a hook, you will bend it, use a length of thread as a fishing line, fashion a lure out of some brightly colored threads, and see if your handmade fishing gear can snag a fish or two.

The Availability Heuristic.   One way to make a decision, albeit by no means the best way, is by thinking about a relevant example that easily comes to mind (the **availability heuristic**). Suppose that a few days ago, a commercial jet plane crashed and many lives were lost. You are well aware of this tragedy because it was reported on television, and the wreckage and flames are clearly etched in your mind. Two weeks from now, you have to make a trip of a thousand miles, and you want to choose the safest method of travel. Because your memory of the plane crash is so vivid, you incorrectly decide that driving is safer than flying, and you put yourself at greater risk by taking your car instead of making an airline reservation.

Mental sets, functional fixedness, and the availability heuristic all involve cognitions. The driver *thinks/believes* that the only way to make a left turn is from the left-hand lane, the fisherman *thinks/believes* that only a rod and reel can catch fish, the potential traveler *thinks/believes* that flying is unsafe because of the easily remembered accident. All of these are the converse of Kelly's principle of constructive alternativism. That is, they prevent us from construing events in different ways. And they illustrate Bandura's contention that we do not experience life situations or events passively; we interpret and evaluate what happens to us, and it is these thoughts, expectations, and beliefs that determine our behavior.

Evaluation

Cognitive psychology has many important applications. However, it deals with only one aspect of human functioning. There is considerably more to behavior than thinking and interpreting. To obtain a true understanding of personality, it is essential also to consider the perspectives that we have discussed in the preceding pages.

SUMMARY

1. THE BASIC NATURE OF HUMAN BEINGS. Bandura is highly critical of Skinnerian behaviorism. He argues that psychological functioning involves a continuous reciprocal interrelationship among behavior, environmental influences, and internal personal factors (including expectations, beliefs, thoughts, preferences, and self-perceptions). He accepts the existence of cognitive causes, and explains reinforcement in terms of our expectation that certain behaviors will gain rewards or avoid punishments.

2. THE STRUCTURE OF PERSONALITY. Bandura concludes that we can and do set standards of behavior for ourselves, and praise or criticize ourselves accordingly. Self-reinforced behavior tends to be maintained more effectively than if it had been externally reinforced. Our behavior is also affected by the way in which we perceive our potential effectiveness in coping with the demands of a particular situation (perceived self-efficacy). The higher our perceived self-efficacy, the more likely we are to try that task and persist when we encounter obstacles.

3. THE DEVELOPMENT OF PERSONALITY. The majority of human learning occurs through observational learning (social learning, modeling), rather than performing a response and being reinforced. Observational learning involves much more than imitation; we formulate rules, concepts, and conclusions based on what we observe, and we may apply these inferences in ways that lead to behavior that is related but not identical. Bandura regards aggression and destructiveness as due primarily to observational learning, rather than to some innate instinct, and he is strongly opposed to violence in the media.

4. FURTHER APPLICATIONS. Bandura attributes psychopathology to faulty learning, and to the resulting cognitions and anticipations. Defensive behaviors serve to confirm one's prediction of avoiding harm, and prevent self-defeating fearful expectations from being unlearned. He therefore advocates the use of procedures wherein the client increases perceived self-efficacy by performing the feared tasks.

5. EVALUATION. Bandura has been criticized for ignoring such important issues as conscious and unconscious conflicts, ignoring similarities between his constructs and those of personality theorists, and for an excessive bias against psychoanalysis. He has been credited with grounding his work in empirical research, emphasizing studies with humans rather than animals, calling attention to the importance of observational learning and perceived self-efficacy, and providing behaviorism with a more convincing rationale than his predecessors. In a recent survey, Bandura was ranked among the five most eminent psychologists of the 20th century.

6. OTHER CONCEPTS IN COGNITIVE PSYCHOLOGY. There is a great deal of research dealing with cognitive psychology. Some constructs and issues with relevance to personality include learned helplessness, internal and external locus of control, the causes of happiness, schemas, perceptual set, mental set, functional fixedness, and the availability heuristic.

STUDY QUESTIONS

Part I. Questions

1. You have to take an exam on the material in this chapter. Use this example to illustrate each of the following aspects of reciprocal determinism: (a) The environment influences behavior. (b) Behavior influences the environment. (c) Personal factors influence behavior. (d) Behavior influences personal factors. (e) Personal factors influence the environment. (f) The environment influences personal factors.

2. Unlike Skinner, Bandura argues that cognitions are valid causes of behavior. Give an example to illustrate each of the following: (a) Thinking about an event in different ways can cause different behaviors. (b) Thoughts alone can cause a person to become angry or depressed.

3. Give an example to support the following arguments by Bandura: (a) The effectiveness of a reinforcer depends on our conscious expectations. (b) Observational learning can change the effectiveness of a reinforcer.

4. (a) Give an example to support Bandura's argument that self-reinforcement has a strong influence on behavior. (b) According to Bandura, self-standards are usually related to external standards. Is this wise, or should a person's self-standards be entirely independent of environmental influences?

5. Consider the case material in the Appendix. Is this man high or low in perceived self-efficacy? How does this affect his behavior?

6. Give an example to illustrate each of the following: (a) Observational learning is necessary because Skinnerian trial-and-error learning would be too dangerous. (b) Observational learning in the classroom. (c) Observational learning in sports. (d) How observational learning in our society leads to more violent behavior.

7. (a) Bandura argues that low perceived self-efficacy can lead to anxiety and depression. Is this supported by the case described in the Appendix? (b) What kind of psychotherapy might Bandura recommend for this man?

8. How would you rate the man whose case is described in the Appendix on each of the following? (a) Learned helplessness. (b) Locus of control.

9. Use the case material in the Appendix to illustrate each of the following: (a) A schema this man would use at a party. (b) His perceptual set when meeting people. (c) His mental set when dealing with his social problems. (d) The availability heuristic when he decides whether to call a girl for a date.

10. A terrorist blows up a building in a hated foreign country. How might Bandura explain the terrorist's behavior?

Part II. Comments and Suggestions

1. (a) You show up for the exam because the teacher required you to take it. (b) Because many students do poorly on the exam, the teacher schedules extra lectures on this material and an additional exam. (c) You think that the exam will be difficult, so you study harder. (d) After a great deal of studying, you become more confident and believe that you will do well on the exam. (e) Many students mistakenly believed that the exam would be easy (and didn't study hard), which is why they did so poorly that the teacher scheduled extra lectures. (f) The extra lectures are so well designed that the students now believe that they understand the material, and they like it more.

2. (a) See Chapter 15, question 5a. A second example: believing that a forthcoming exam will be difficult is likely to lead to more studying than thinking about it as very easy. (b) See

Chapter 14, question 6. Consider also a patient in psychotherapy who enters the day's session in a quiet mood, thinks about important but distressing material, and becomes emotional and tearful (which may well be necessary for therapy to succeed).

3. (a) A man tells two young boys that he will "pay them well" for shoveling the snow off his walk. Unwisely, they do not negotiate a specific amount. The first boy expects to be paid $5, but the second boy expects $20. When they are finished, the man gives each boy $10. The amount of the reinforcer is identical, but its effects on each boy are quite different because of their expectations. (b) A professional athlete is quite happy making $2 million per year until he discovers that two teammates, whose performance he regards as inferior to his own, are making $5 million per year. He becomes extremely unhappy, sulks, and holds out for half the season. The reinforcer (his salary) has not changed, but its effect has because of observational learning.

4. (a) It takes me 6 months to prepare the revised sixth edition of this textbook. During that time, I receive no external reinforcement. I motivate myself by telling myself when I have done well and when I need to make additional changes. (b) See Chapter 5, question 5, and Chapter 9, question 4.

5. Remember that perceived self-efficacy is multidimensional, and be careful to avoid oversimplified answers. He is a good student and has high perceived self-efficacy with regard to academics, but his perceived self-efficacy is very low with regard to social situations and personal relationships. He tries hard in school because he expects to do well (and does), but he gives up very easily in social situations because he expects to fail (and does).

6. (a) Consider becoming a brain surgeon or learning to fly an airplane. (b) A quiet student who wants to earn a higher grade notices that the teacher seems to like students who participate, so the student raises her hand and asks questions more often. In another class, the student observes that the teacher does not like to be interrupted, so she remains quiet in that situation. (c) A freshman on the football team sees a teammate being yelled at by the coach for not trying hard enough. Although he is tired, he plays harder in order to avoid similar criticism. (d) Consider the discussion in this chapter of violence in the media.

7. (a) Yes. He is highly anxious in social situations because of his inability to cope with them, and depressed because he can't get love and affection. (b) Therapy in which he improves his perceived self-efficacy by actually practicing the social behaviors that he believes he can't do well.

8. Here again, it depends on the situation. He is high in learned helplessness in social situations, but not in the classroom. He is highly external in social situations because he knows that he is too incapable to succeed unless someone else takes pity on him, but highly internal in the classroom.

9. (a) He expects people to dislike him because he is nervous and uncertain, so he immediately notices how calm and poised others are. This makes him even more anxious, and prevents him from taking an interest in others. (b) Because he expects people to dislike him, he is predisposed to perceive their facial expressions as negative. (c) He consistently approaches his social problems in only one way, by avoiding most people, because he has reduced anxiety by doing so in the past and is convinced that this is the only way he can gain a measure of peace. (d) He has vivid memories of embarrassing himself during a recent call that went very badly, so he decides not to call someone else. He fails to realize that the next girl he calls may help him to behave more appropriately by being more sympathetic or compatible.

10. Would Bandura attribute the terrorist's behavior to an illicit instinct? Why not? How might observational learning have influenced the terrorist's behavior? How might perceived self-efficacy have influenced the terrorist's behavior? Can the terrorist's behavior be changed through observational learning, or by altering his or her perceived self-efficacy in some area(s)?

Comparing Cognitive Theorists, Freud, and Skinner on Various Issues

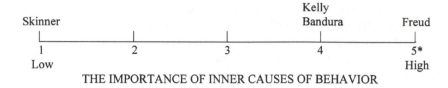

THE IMPORTANCE OF INNER CAUSES OF BEHAVIOR

THE IMPORTANCE OF UNCONSCIOUS PROCESSES

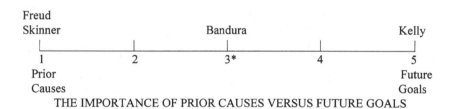

THE IMPORTANCE OF PRIOR CAUSES VERSUS FUTURE GOALS

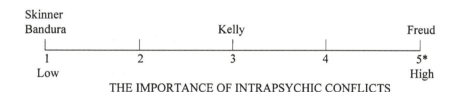

THE IMPORTANCE OF INTRAPSYCHIC CONFLICTS

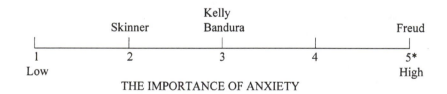

THE IMPORTANCE OF ANXIETY

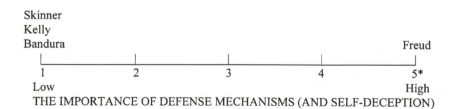

THE IMPORTANCE OF DEFENSE MECHANISMS (AND SELF-DECEPTION)

Note: These scales are intended as approximations, designed to facilitate comparisons among the theorists, and not as mathematically precise measures. They reflect my opinions; others might disagree with the ratings in some instances. For those who may be interested, my position on each issue is shown by an asterisk.

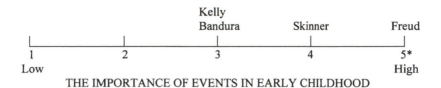

THE IMPORTANCE OF EVENTS IN EARLY CHILDHOOD

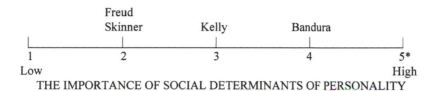

THE IMPORTANCE OF SOCIAL DETERMINANTS OF PERSONALITY

Comparing Skinner's and Bandura's Views of Learning

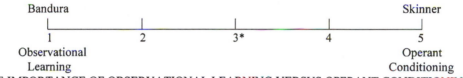

THE IMPORTANCE OF OBSERVATIONAL LEARNING VERSUS OPERANT CONDITIONING

CHAPTER 17

CONCLUSION
Perspectives and Postscript

Our journey into the realm of personality theory has featured a formidable array of constructs and principles, many contradictory ideas and heated disputes, and some islands of general agreement. In this concluding chapter, we will briefly consider two additional perspectives. Then we will return to our organizing framework for one last time, and try to determine the conclusions most justified by the wealth of information that we have surveyed.

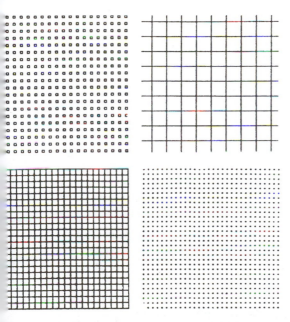

Quotes to Ponder

- *"The news that reaches your consciousness is incomplete and often not to be relied on.... Turn your eyes inward, look into your own depths, learn first to know yourself!"*

  —Sigmund Freud

- *"Loneliness does not come from having no people about one, but from being unable to communicate the things that seem important to oneself, or from holding certain views which others find inadmissible."*

  —Carl Jung

- *"Every pampered child becomes a hated child.... There is no greater evil than the pampering of children."*

  —Alfred Adler

- *"[Neurotics are] torn by inner conflicts ... Every neurotic ... is at war with himself."*

  —Karen Horney

- *"Dreams which are not interpreted are like letters which have not been opened.... Dreams are important communications from ourselves to ourselves."*

  —Erich Fromm

- *"If you have to maintain self-esteem by pulling down the standing of others, you are extraordinarily unfortunate."*

  —Harry Stack Sullivan

- *"Like a trapeze artist, the [adolescent] in the middle of vigorous motion must let go of his safe hold on childhood and reach out for a firm grip on adulthood, depending for a breathless interval ... on the reliability of those he must let go of and those who will 'receive' him."*

  —Erik Erikson

- *"The good life is a process, not a state of being. It is a direction, not a destination."*

  —Carl Rogers

- *"Growth is, in itself, a rewarding and exciting process."*

  —Abraham Maslow

- *"Everyone has a need for significance; and if we can't make that possible, or even probable, in our society, then it will be obtained in destructive ways."*

  —Rollo May

- *"Since we think about ourselves so much of the time, it is comforting to assume ... that we really know the score.... [But] this is not an easy assignment. [As] Santayana wrote, 'Nothing requires a rarer intellectual heroism than willingness to see one's equation written out.'"*

  —Gordon Allport

- *"[The trait theorist begins] by observing a preoccupation with a mirror which recalls the legend of Narcissus, [invents] the adjective 'narcissistic' and then the noun 'narcissism,' and finally [asserts] that the thing presumably referred to by the noun is the cause of [this] behavior.... But at no point in such a series [does he] make contact with any event outside the behavior itself which justifies the claim of a causal connection."*

  —B. F. Skinner

- *"Because some of the inner causes invoked by theorists over the years have been ill-founded does not justify excluding all inner determinants from scientific inquiry.... [There is] growing evidence that cognition has causal influence on behavior."*

—Albert Bandura

OTHER PERSPECTIVES ON PERSONALITY

The Biological Perspective

Overview.   Virtually all of our behaviors are influenced by both psychology and physiology. The biological perspective emphasizes the physiological and hereditary aspects of our thoughts and actions, including the brain and its neurons, the nervous system, hormones and the endocrine system, genetics, and evolutionary influences.

Introversion–Extraversion.   As we observed in Chapter 13, whether you are more introverted or extraverted may well be related to physiological functioning. Eysenck theorizes that those who are more extraverted seek external stimulation because they have low levels of cerebral cortex arousal that they want to increase, whereas those who are more introverted avoid external stimulation because they have high levels of cortical arousal that will become painful if increased further. Alternatively, introversion–extraversion may be related to one's sensitivity to external stimulation. Introverts may seek lower levels of stimulation because they are more sensitive, whereas extraverts may prefer higher levels of stimulation because they are less sensitive.

Introversion–extraversion also appears to be significantly influenced by heredity. Although it is far from easy to resolve the nature–nurture issue, twins who come from the same fertilized egg (identical twins, monozygotic twins) and who therefore have identical genes have been found to be more similar on this trait than are twins who come from different eggs (fraternal twins, dizygotic twins) and are no more alike genetically than two siblings who were born at different times. These findings support Jung's belief that each of us has an innate tendency to be more introverted or extraverted, and that it is an error to force a child in the opposite direction.

Temperament.   Some infants seem to be relaxed, cheerful, and easygoing from the moment of birth; they sleep through the night and are easy to feed. Others are irritable, intense, excitable, colicky, and frequently arouse their parents during the night with cries of distress. This personality trait, called *temperament,* appears to be inherited. Various studies that have compared identical and fraternal twins have found the former to be significantly more similar in activity level, irritability, and sociability. Also, infants who are more irritable and intense have higher heart rates and a more reactive nervous system than those with a calm temperament. (See Glassman, 2000, pp. 301–302; Myers, 2001, pp. 97–98.)

Other Traits.   Other traits appear to be influenced to varying degrees by heredity. Cattell concludes from his factor-analytic research that intelligence, surgency (a happy-go-lucky nature), affectia (outgoingness, similar to extraversion), premsia (tendermindedness), and protension (suspiciousness) are moderately heritable. The "Big Five" personality traits also appear to be determined to a moderate extent by heredity (Loehlin et al., 1998).

Evaluation.   You can (and should) improve your understanding of human behavior by learning about biological processes. But while it is reasonable to consider a biological perspective with regard to psychology in general, this is not true insofar as personality is concerned. There is no outstanding physiological theorist who has focused on personality to the same extent as the psychologists whose work we have examined, or who has devised an important and comprehensive set of constructs about personality.

Throughout this book, we have seen that psychological constructs are extremely important. To focus primarily on the biological aspects of behavior because they are "more scientific," as some critics recommend, is to risk losing the hard-won insights gleaned by Freud, Jung, Adler, Horney, Fromm, Sullivan, Erikson, Rogers, Maslow, May, Allport, Cattell, Kelly, Skinner, and Bandura—insights that have greatly increased our understanding of human behavior, and have helped many people improve their lives and resolve painful problems. As Bandura observes:

> Although psychological principles cannot violate the neurophysiological capabilities of the systems that subserve them, the psychological principles need to be pursued in their own right. Were one to embark on the road to reductionism, the journey would traverse biology and chemistry and would eventually end in atomic particles, with neither the intermediate locales nor the final stop supplying the psychological laws of human behavior. (Bandura, 1997, p. 4.)

The Cross-Cultural Perspective

Overview.   Some psychological theories, such as the "Big Five" personality traits, appear to apply reasonably well to a variety of cultures. (See, for example, McCrae et al., 1998.) However, many cultures throughout the world interpret concepts like achievement, identity, responsibility, and morality differently from Western Europeans and North Americans, who developed the theories that we have examined. Therefore, some psychologists argue that personality theory must necessarily include a cross-cultural perspective.

Self-Esteem and Achievement.   Countries that emphasize a collective orientation, such as Japan, value self-esteem and personal achievement less highly than do North Americans. In the United States, a professional athlete who scores a touchdown or hits a home run is likely to call attention to himself by doing a victory dance in the end zone or celebrating on his way around the bases. This would be considered to be in very poor taste in the Orient, where one is expected to credit one's teammates and family rather than oneself. Similarly, when asked to complete a sentence beginning with the words "I am," students in Japan and China are much less likely than Americans to describe personal traits ("I am an excellent student"), and much more likely to relate themselves to others ("I am the third son in my family"). (See, for example, Myers, 2001, pp. 517–519; Triandis, 1989a; 1989b; 1994a; 1994b.)

Evaluation.   A personality theorist's culture may influence, and limit, the constructs and principles of that theorist. You should therefore be aware that the theories presented in this book may not apply very well in some (or many) respects to Oriental, third-world, and other non-Occidental peoples. It has even been argued that a theory may hold true only for those people whose background resembles that of the theorist. (Recall Adler's contention that children become Oedipal only if they have been as pampered as Freud himself.) Thus the cultural issue may be regarded as an extension—albeit an important one—of this type of criticism.

A theory need not be universal in scope to be useful. Our goal in this book has been to keep the workload within reasonable bounds by discussing the most important theories of personality. Those who wish to acquire an understanding of different cultures should now have a sufficiently strong background to do so.

OVERVIEW AND CONCLUSIONS

The Basic Nature of Human Beings

The Quality of Human Nature. Many personality theorists have been concerned with the quality of human nature: Are our inborn motives malignant or benign?

At the most negative extreme is Freudian psychoanalysis, with its emphasis on innate incestuous and destructive drives. This implies that we must sublimate our true wishes into less satisfying but more socially acceptable outlets, and that conflict must occur with society and within one's own psyche. At the other extreme are such theorists as Horney and Rogers, who assume that our innate potentials and desires are wholly positive (and need not be compromised through sublimation). And some theorists take a more moderate position by concluding that our innate drives are both malignant and benign.

All personality theorists are well aware that we behave in both good and evil ways; it is our innate nature that is at issue. Pessimistic Freudian theory has little trouble explaining healthy behavior: Proper parenting urges the reluctant child along the path to effective sublimations and socially acceptable satisfactions. Conversely, those who posit a partly or wholly optimistic view of human nature can readily explain psychopathology: misguided parental (and societal) behaviors cause the child to surrender its healthy desires and potentials, and to replace them with the quest to be safe or to satisfy the standards of other people. To these theorists, destructiveness and self-hate are not innate but learned—"the outcome of unlived life."

This theoretical adroitness, plus the virtual impossibility of measuring the quality of human nature empirically, might lead you to question the importance of this issue. However, such assumptions significantly affect other aspects of a theory. For example, Freud recommends not allowing the child too much (or too little) gratification at any stage of development, so as to prevent innate illicit wishes from becoming dominant. He also regards psychotherapy as a long and difficult struggle against the patient's efforts to retain forbidden wishes (resistances), which the therapist must be careful not to encourage. But Maslow stresses that the child's needs must be fully satisfied, recommends a similar course for patients in therapy, and interprets resistance more positively (e.g., as protection against a therapist who is moving too quickly). Important conclusions and practical recommendations depend to a considerable extent on the theorist's view of human nature.

Although it is valuable to know where a given theorist stands on this issue, it appears impossible to draw any definitive conclusions about our innate predisposition for good or evil. We may reasonably speculate that Freud's pessimistic position is overly negative, and that human beings seem to have at least some innate capacity for (and enjoyment of) constructive growth. But the extreme optimism of a Horney or Rogers also seems unwarranted when we consider the frequency of war, crime, and other human evils. Perhaps, then, those theorists who have opted for the middle ground on this issue have come closest to an appropriate characterization of human nature.

Drive Reduction. Freud, Sullivan, and Cattell conclude that our sole motivation is to reduce various drives, eliminate the accompanying unpleasant tensions, and achieve a state of inner equilibrium. Other theorists, such as Maslow and Allport, take exception to this exclusive emphasis on drive reduction. They argue that our behavior must also be explained in terms of pleasurable tension-maintaining and tension-increasing activities, including curious exploration, acquiring an admired skill or level of competence, and increasing our understanding of the world or of ourselves.

Here the available evidence supports the latter view. That is, human beings are motivated both by drive reduction and by pleasurable drive increases.

Causality Versus Teleology.

Freud also posits, as does Skinner, that all mental and physical behavior is determined by prior causes. But many theorists conclude that our behavior must also be understood in terms of its purposes or goals, although some attribute virtually all motivation to teleology.

Even such theorists as Adler and Rogers, who emphasize the importance of teleology, concede that our goals and plans for the future are significantly influenced by childhood events. We may therefore conclude that human beings are motivated by both causality and teleology. One interesting possibility is that relatively healthier individuals may be more influenced by teleology, and less limited by the effects of earlier experiences. However, the past can never be entirely circumvented: Allport's idiosyncratic concept of functional autonomy leads to statements that lack any explanatory power whatsoever ("a man likes blue because he likes blue"), and is best rejected in favor of the majority view that traces adult motives back to childhood and adolescent origins.

Unconscious Motivation.

Most personality theorists agree about the substantial importance of unconscious motivation, and regard true self-knowledge as a difficult goal to achieve. We may conclude that significant, influential aspects of every personality are concealed from awareness in some way. Conceivably, relatively healthier people may be less influenced by unconscious processes; but no personality is ever entirely (or even mostly) conscious.

What material is most likely to become unconscious? Likely candidates include threats to major aspects of one's personality (Freud, Adler, Horney, and others), events that would otherwise evoke strong anxiety (Freud, Horney, Sullivan, May), subliminal perceptions (Jung, Rogers), and that which occurs at too early an age to be labeled properly (Kelly). Whatever the exact processes and dynamics may be, anyone who wishes to understand his or her own personality—or to devise a satisfactory theory of human behavior—must devote considerable attention to unconscious motivation.

The Catalog of Human Motives.

Another controversy concerns the number and specific nature of human motives. Some theorists prefer to emphasize one or two overriding drives or goals: sexuality and destructiveness (Freud), striving for superiority and social interest (Adler), developing our healthy innate potentials (Horney, Rogers), existing in the world into which we are born (May), and anticipating the future (Kelly). Other theorists espouse a list of motives that is significantly longer. And Allport contends that human motives are so unique to the individual that no list of drives or needs, however lengthy, will suffice.

We can discern a few motives on which some theorists agree: identity (Fromm, Erikson), mastering our environment (Adler, Erikson, Fromm, Cattell's self-assertion erg), fulfilling our true potentials (Jungian individuation, Horneyan self-realization, Rogerian actualization, Maslowian self-actualization), the need for other people (Adler, Erikson, Fromm, Sullivan, Maslow, Cattell's gregariousness erg), and an organizing framework that gives meaning to one's life (Jung, Fromm, Allport). But personality theorists mostly disagree with regard to specific human motives, so we can only conclude that this issue is as yet unresolved.

The Structure of Personality

Structural Constructs: Pro and Con.   Some theorists have sought to depict the complicated, often contradictory aspects of personality by devising appropriate structural constructs. Others regard such constructs as unnecessary, or even misleading.

In one camp are those theorists who regard personality as a house that is often divided against itself, and believe that structural constructs are the best way to describe and explain such intrapsychic conflicts. Typical of this approach is Freud's tripartite classification of id, ego, and superego.

Other theorists attribute great importance to intrapsychic conflicts, but do *not* regard structural constructs as necessary or desirable. Perhaps the leading exponent of this approach is Horney. These theorists warn that structural constructs are all too likely to become reified: continuous use of such terms may result in the belief that there is an id, ego, and superego lurking somewhere within every personality. In actuality, such constructs are not undeniable truths. Nor are they concrete entities that exist somewhere within the psyche. They are concepts that have been created (or adopted) by a personality theorist in order to better describe and explain human behavior. To these critics, discussions of "the ego doing this" and "the id doing that" create a misleading impression. It is people who do things; ids and egos are only metaphors.

Still other theorists make use of structural constructs, but devote little attention to intrapsychic conflicts. Examples include Allport's proprium and Kelly's personal constructs.

Finally, some theorists argue that structural constructs are unnecessary because personality is a unified, indivisible whole that is never in conflict with itself. Adler is the main advocate of this position.

Once again we have an area that is marked more by controversy than agreement. However, the evidence discussed throughout this book supports the existence and importance of intrapsychic conflicts. Our unconscious motives may differ considerably from our conscious beliefs, and we may be tormented by contradictory needs and wishes that we do not understand. Therefore, those theorists who ignore intrapsychic conflicts must be charged with neglecting a vital aspect of human behavior.

If structural constructs were necessary in order to describe and explain intrapsychic conflicts, that alone would justify their existence. But this is not the case, as Horney and others have shown. Although structural constructs have helped to increase our understanding of the human personality, they also have their weaknesses, and those theorists who prefer to reject them are well within their rights to do so.

Anxiety and the Defense Mechanisms.   One major contribution of personality theory has been to improve our understanding of (and concern about) anxiety. The discovery that psychological pain is real despite the lack of observable wounds, and that anxiety can be a problem that is even more serious than physical pain, is an important addition to our knowledge.

Whether or not one accepts Freud's theory of anxiety and defense, the importance of such behaviors as reaction formation, projection, displacement, denial of reality, rationalization, identification, and fantasy has been firmly established. These concepts have been incorporated into virtually every theory of personality, if at times with changes in terminology and underlying rationale. Although more healthy people probably rely less on such defense mechanisms, all of us have undoubtedly used them at some time in our lives. Thus we may consider this as another major contribution that has been provided by personality theory.

The Development of Personality

Stages of Development. Only a few theorists posit specific developmental stages, and they do not agree with one another. There are five psychosexual stages in Freudian theory, with personality development assumed to be virtually complete by about age 5 years. Sullivan argues that there are seven developmental epochs, ranging from infancy to adulthood. And Erikson discusses eight epigenetic psychosexual stages, which extend into middle and old age.

Although some of these theorists' ideas about the development of personality have been generally accepted, no one set of stages is universally regarded as correct. Most modern psychologists prefer Sullivan's and Erikson's view that personality development continues through late childhood and adolescence. But it now appears that many aspects of personality tend to remain relatively stable during adulthood, barring such special efforts to change as formal psychotherapy. (See, for example, Schulz & Ewen, 1993, Chapter 7.)

The Importance of Early Childhood. Virtually all theorists agree that events during infancy and childhood are extremely important for personality development. (The sole exception is Allport.) Another major contribution of personality theory has been to identify the ways in which parents cause their children to become neurotic: pampering, neglect, overpermissiveness, overprotectiveness, frequent anxiety, perfectionism, domination, rejection, ridicule, hypocrisy, inconsistent standards, a lack of tenderness and warm affection, conditional positive regard, and others. This provides useful guidelines for those who seek to become better parents, and is a source of reassurance to anyone who does suffer from neurosis. Since these self-defeating behaviors and beliefs were learned during childhood, they have a logical cause. And this implies that there is also a logical remedy, in that relief can be gained by unlearning them (as through psychotherapy).

The Importance of Adolescence. Sullivan and Erikson deserve credit for emphasizing the importance of adolescence. This is indeed a time of turmoil and potential change—one that can have a corrective effect on a troubled personality, or exert a pathogenic influence of its own. However, events during infancy and childhood play a greater role in shaping one's personality. A person who emerges from childhood with a faulty view of self and others is more likely to behave in misguided and self-defeating ways during adolescence, bringing on disapproval and rejection from others and intensifying the sufferer's problems. Conversely, a psychologically healthier child is more likely to handle the rigors of adolescence successfully.

Character Typologies. Several theorists, including Freud, Jung, and Fromm, have devoted some attention to personality types. In contrast, Adler and Allport strongly oppose the use of character typologies. They argue that each of us develops our own unique style of life, making it impossible for any typology to describe the human personality.

The importance of certain typological constructs has been supported by research evidence: the oral personality, the anal personality, introversion, extraversion. But here again, no one theory is currently regarded as correct in all (or even most) aspects.

Criteria of Mental Health. Freud's well-known definition of mental health consists of two characteristics, the ability to love and to work. Allport, Rogers, and Maslow prefer to expand on the ideal personality. These theorists tend to agree that mental health is denoted by greater emotional security and self-acceptance; more loving and nonpossessive interpersonal relationships; greater spontaneity; greater self-knowledge (self-insight); and a greater reliance on one's own needs and values, rather than on external standards. Yet they disagree in various other respects, indicating that it is not yet possible to define the criteria of mental health in universally acceptable terms.

Further Applications of Personality Theory

As we have seen throughout this book, personality theory has made important contributions to our understanding of various areas: dreams, psychopathology, psychotherapy, work, religion, education, literature. Here again, however, the controversies that have beset personality theory have taken their toll. Dream interpretation is used far less widely today than Freud (and Fromm) would have hoped, although there is some indication that it may be regaining the popularity that it deserves (Lippmann, 2000). No one method of psychotherapy (Freudian, Rogerian, behaviorist) is clearly best, nor is there widespread agreement as to which type of therapy should be used with which disorders. Therefore, we can only conclude that the value of the various applications of personality theory is likely to be a matter of some debate.

Evaluation

Personality theory has had a distinguished past. However, its future is more uncertain.

Theory and Research. As we observed in Chapter 1, theories help us to bring order out of chaos by organizing substantial amounts of information. They focus attention on those matters that are of greater importance. And they offer explanations for the phenomena being studied. Research allows us to test predictions derived from a theory, so that it may be evaluated and improved (or discarded). In the absence of research, theory remains subjective, and we have only the theorists' beliefs to support their ideas. In the absence of theory, research produces myriad fragments of unrelated and often unimportant information.

Freud, Jung, and Adler focused entirely on comprehensive personality theories and clinical insight. Today, the emphasis has shifted to the opposite extreme. Most modern psychologists do not ally themselves with any theory of personality. They are concerned with empirical research that deals with limited aspects of human behavior. They identify their professional interests in terms of specific content areas, such as social psychology, developmental psychology, clinical psychology, or more narrowly defined issues (e.g., the interaction of traits and situations; the relationship between self-esteem and other behaviors). Of the 40-odd divisions of the American Psychological Association that are organized by subject matter, not one is devoted solely (or even primarily) to personality theory. It may not be entirely coincidental that no current psychologist comes close to enjoying the popular esteem accorded to Freud, Jung, Adler, and Erikson.

Rather than leading to a renaissance of knowledge, the shift from clinical insight to academic research has produced a great deal of trivial information occasionally enlivened by some useful findings. Some might argue that this is the inevitable course for any science, and that the development of improved research techniques will eventually resolve the difficulties that pervade this area. But there is another, more troublesome possibility: it may be beyond our abilities to study personality scientifically. The scientific method may not work very well with human beings, who have the disconcerting ability to conceal the truth not only from the outside world but also from themselves.

To many psychologists, science represents our best defense against ignorance and superstition. Even in our modern era, there are many beliefs that remain popular even though they are wholly incorrect. (See, for example, Sagan, 1996.) If we wish to live in an enlightened society, these psychologists argue, science must show the way. It will be interesting to observe whether personality research is able to meet this challenge in the years to come.

Personality Theories.   Some personality theories have continued to evolve during the past few decades. For example, there are psychoanalysts who deemphasize libido theory and focus more on parent–child interactions, meet with patients twice a week and use face-to-face interviews, and take a more equalitarian view toward women. You should therefore be aware that modern approaches to certain theories may differ in some important respects from the original versions.

One problem with such innovations is that they tend to occur solely within the framework of a particular theory. If psychoanalytic theory is to become more socially oriented, it would seem appropriate to make use of the valuable ideas and constructs devised by the neo-Freudians. But psychoanalysts who emphasize parent–child relationships have *not* incorporated the seminal work of Horney and Sullivan. They have retained and modified Freudian constructs with which they are familiar, as by developing what is known as "object relations theory."

All of the theorists whose work we have examined have made at least some valuable contributions. Therefore, it would seem that the course most likely to benefit the discipline of psychology is to integrate the best ideas from several theories. Given the reluctance of most theorists to do this, and the current emphasis on specific and limited research areas, it is unlikely that any new and important theory of personality will emerge in the foreseeable future.

POSTSCRIPT: SOME PERSONAL PERSPECTIVES

Now that we have reached the end of our journey into the realm of personality theory, let me relinquish the scholarly form of narrative and close with some personal perspectives and comments.

On the one hand, I am impressed by the many profound insights which personality theorists have gained into the mysteries of human behavior (notably those derived from clinical observation). Yet I am also disappointed by their inability to resolve the most fundamental of issues, indicating that psychology is still far from a mature science. And I fear that the capacity of humans to think, to lie to others, and to deceive themselves will prevent psychology from ever achieving the precision of physics and chemistry.

I am also troubled by the failed expectations that pervade personality theory. Freud and the neo-Freudians believed that their discoveries would revolutionize our approach to human behavior. Yet few laypersons today take much interest in unconscious processes, or in the difficult but essential task of achieving greater self-understanding. Instead the emphasis is on external rewards, and on such gimmicks as "personal power" infomercials. Rogers and Skinner believed that their educational innovations would produce radical improvements, but this has not happened. Instead, our educational system struggles along using more or less traditional methods. Such major disappointments raise troublesome questions concerning the general usefulness of personality theory.

Since the unconscious aspects of behavior are so difficult to measure, it is understandable that many psychologists prefer to turn their attention elsewhere. Yet since virtually every theory discussed in this book accepts the existence of some sort of unconscious processes (even Skinner's), those who claim that psychology can study only overt or conscious forces and still be comprehensive (and/or who pursue safely objective but trivial research topics) strike me as substituting expediency for scientific integrity.

I can empathize with the frustrations of my readers, who have had to learn a new language in every chapter. Personality theorists have been far too free with neologisms, and have often duplicated one another's efforts without any apparent knowledge of having done so. Perhaps these theorists genuinely believed that their own ideas were different. Perhaps they were not aware of, or did not understand, the ideas of other theorists. Or they may have been influenced by an academic system that penalizes agreement while rewarding controversy, since the latter is far more likely to generate large quantities of scholarly publications (a view shared by Fiske, 1978, p. 63). The issue here is *not* necessarily to arrive at one "right" theory, which could all too easily prove to be stultifying; lively debate is healthy for a science. But too many theorists have created too many supposedly new constructs, instead of relating their work to that of other psychologists.

In my opinion, however, there is another more positive reason for the great diversity of personality theories: People think differently, and some of these individuals are psychologists who have formulated their personal construct systems in more detail than most. (See also Fiske, 1978, p. 39.) Although my respect for a genius like Freud remains profound, I am less impressed by any approach that regards a single construct system as applicable to all humanity. No doubt Oedipal complexes do exist; yet I wonder how much time has been lost in psychoanalytic therapy because some "resistant" patients conceptualized their childhood problems differently, in terms that the therapist could not understand psychoanalytically, and would not adopt the analyst's construct system. (In fairness to Freud, a similar criticism could be made of almost every personality theory.) Psychologists have made substantial efforts to eliminate prejudice in many areas, yet all too many still advocate a form of constructual tyranny: Any way but their own of conceptualizing behavior (and/or the philosophy of psychology) is wrong, or "prescientific."

For this reason, I believe that the study of personality theory offers considerable benefits. If you truly understand the various theories, you will have a more versatile and openminded approach to psychology, and a much better understanding of human behavior.

SUMMARY

1. OTHER PERSPECTIVES ON PERSONALITY. Virtually all of our behaviors are influenced by both psychology and physiology. Although it is important to understand physiological processes, a biological perspective is better suited to psychology in general than to personality. Many cultures throughout the world interpret personality concepts differently than do Western Europeans and North Americans, who developed the theories that we have examined. However, the cross-cultural perspective is best considered as an adjunct to the study of personality theory.

2. OVERVIEW AND CONCLUSIONS. *The Basic Nature of Human Beings:* Freudian psychoanalysis concludes that human nature is entirely malignant. At the opposite extreme are such theorists as Horney and Rogers, who assume that our innate desires and potentials are wholly positive. Still other theorists adopt a more moderate (and perhaps more justifiable) position by attributing to us both malignant and benign instincts. We are motivated by both drive reduction and pleasurable drive increases, and by both causality and teleology. Nearly all personality theorists agree that unconscious motivation is important. However, there is little agreement regarding the number and nature of human motives. *The Structure of Personality:* Some theorists have sought to depict the complicated and often contradictory aspects of personality by devising appropriate structural constructs. Others regard such constructs as unnecessary, or even misleading. The evidence does support the existence and importance of conscious and unconscious intrapsychic conflicts. The discovery that psychological pain (anxiety) can be as or more serious than physical pain is an important contribution to our knowledge. The same is true of the Freudian defense mechanisms, which have been accepted and incorporated into virtually every theory of personality (if at times with changes in terminology and underlying rationale). *The Development of Personality:* Only a few theorists posit specific developmental stages, and they do not agree with one another. Events in infancy and childhood are extremely important for personality development. Most modern psychologists also agree that personality development continues through late childhood and adolescence. Some theorists have also posited various personality types and criteria of mental health. *Further Applications:* Personality theory has made important contributions to our understanding of dreams, psychopathology, psychotherapy, work, religion, education, and literature. *Evaluation:* Although personality theory has a distinguished past, its future is uncertain. Because most psychologists specialize in particular research areas, it is unlikely that any new and important theory of personality will emerge in the foreseeable future.

3. POSTSCRIPT: SOME PERSONAL PERSPECTIVES. The present writer is impressed by the many profound insights that personality theorists have gained into the mysteries of human behavior, disappointed by their inability to resolve the most fundamental of issues, concerned that psychology may never achieve scientific precision, and troubled by the failed expectations that pervade personality theory. Since virtually every theory accepts the existence of some sort of unconscious processes, those who claim that psychology can study only overt or conscious forces and still be comprehensive (and/or who pursue safely objective but trivial research topics) would seem to be substituting expediency for scientific integrity. If you truly understand the various theories of personality, you will have a more versatile and open-minded approach to psychology, and an excellent background for further work in this field.

APPENDIX

Case Material for Use with the Study Questions

Note: The case material in this Appendix refers to a young man who gained valuable insights from formal psychotherapy, and who is reflecting on previous experiences in his life.

SECTION I

It is fairly late at night, and I am walking in a large city on the way home from a friend's house. I am only a few blocks away from my apartment, and the area is not especially dangerous. Yet I feel that something very bad is about to happen. I'm afraid! So I start to walk faster. Soon I'm running. I reach my apartment building and safety, and I turn to look back. The street is almost empty, except for a few harmless-looking individuals who are strolling casually and enjoying the night air. The area is well lit.

There is no danger. It's all been in my imagination.

It isn't only city streets that I fear. When I am with other people, especially those I don't know well, I often get the same reaction: sweaty palms, butterflies, and a desire to escape as soon as possible. So I shy away from other people and spend lots of time alone in my room. I don't know why I feel this way, which only makes matters worse. I'm confused and guilty about feeling afraid for no apparent reason, so I hide my true feelings from everyone else. I keep my thoughts, emotions, and perceptions in a narrow shell around me, like a cocoon, because I don't see any hope for me in the outside world and I just want to avoid hurting any more than I do now. I feel as though my interactions with other people and the outside world are like a game I'm playing and observing with a small part of my mind, while most of my attention is tied up by the emotional pain and turmoil going on inside me. I suspect that something is desperately wrong with me, but that something seems so strange and frightening that I don't dare look for it.

I'm so tired of being afraid.

SECTION 2

Anxiety and inner conflict: that's the story of my life. I want friendship, affection, and love. But when I'm in a room with several people I don't know, my hands sweat so much that I'm ashamed to shake hands with anyone. I keep mostly to myself, and when I do talk to someone I stumble over my words and embarrass myself. I feel the pain and confusion of being pulled in two different directions at the same time: wanting close relationships, yet also constantly trying to avoid other people.

SECTION 3

My parents were always nervous about the possibility of something happening to me. When I was very young, they told me never to walk through the kitchen. The quickest way to get from the dining room to my room was through the kitchen, and I saw every day that nothing bad ever happened there. So one day I broke the rule while they were watching, to show them what I thought. I was proud of myself for a minute, but then my parents said how disappointed they were in me and turned their backs on me in disgust. I was shattered; I felt all alone, like I'd been kicked out of my own family. [The patient had previously suffered an extremely painful separation from one parent for nearly a year, which may well have left him particularly sensitive to rejection.] Recently, when I asked my parents about this, they explained that they had read a newspaper story about a kitchen stove blowing up in an apartment down the street. "What else could we do? It was our responsibility to protect you."

Thinking back over my life, I found many other instances when my parents were pampering and overprotective. It often seemed like they were trying to satisfy my needs even before I expressed them (or even knew I had them). So I learned never to show any initiative, and that the most important thing in life is to be safe. I decided that I had no right to take any chances at all, even if I really wanted to. And avoiding risk wasn't easy, what with unexplained danger lurking in my own kitchen.

I was too young to put these rules of life that I had learned into words. So they became unconscious, and have been directing my behavior ever since. Only recently have I become aware that my conflict between wanting to try new things and needing to be safe represents a conflict between my true desires and a need to keep my parents' love—love that I felt was taken away when I walked through the kitchen.

SECTION 4

I look many years younger than my actual age, which has caused all too many people to treat me like a child. As a teenager, a girl I asked to dance rejected me with contempt because she thought she was much older. In my early 20s, people would refer to me as a "nice boy" and ask me what high school I was attending. When I told a new acquaintance that I was a graduate student, she thought I was lying and walked away in disgust.

Even though there were friends and women who seemed to like me, the effects of my youthful appearance were extremely painful. I came to dread talking to strangers. I decided that I had no chance of impressing people, so I tried to get what I wanted by being the passive child that I thought they expected. And I felt that there must be something radically wrong with me because others would not treat me like an adult. Even today, when I meet men who look their age, I feel that they are superior to me—more mature, more dominant, more masculine.

SECTION 5

Because I learned during childhood to fear any attempts at showing initiative and to dread the possibility of making mistakes, I approached my college work with extreme anxiety. I never took any courses just for the fun of it, even though I had room in my schedule for electives; I limited myself to those courses that I needed for my future profession. When I realized after the first week of a course in advanced chemistry that I was in way over my head, I felt that I had no choice but to stick it out, even though dropping a course was clearly permitted by college regulations. So I suffered a great deal, learned nothing, and wound up with a D. It was like that all the time; there were always commands that I had to follow.

I never realized that these orders came from my own mind, and that they served to conceal some very threatening aspects of reality. I had been ignoring my own wishes and seeking safety for so long that I no longer had any idea what I really wanted. By always having things that I "should" do, I was able to avoid facing up to the fact that I was free—but too weak and helpless to take advantage of it.

SECTION 6

I still think about the time when I walked through my kitchen and my parents said how disappointed they were in me. Maybe this wasn't such a terrible rejection. I vaguely recall my parents saying something about my behavior being "cute," and perhaps even trying to hide a chuckle or two. Maybe my conclusion that they were very angry because there was great danger in my own kitchen (and in the world), and that I should seek safety at all costs, was based on a faulty interpretation of what happened.

I never discussed my feelings about this incident with my parents for two reasons: I was very young and had trouble putting my feelings into words, and I was afraid. If I criticized my parents, as by arguing that they were wrong or had overreacted, I thought my father would have one of his angry outbursts. But that may also have been a misperception on my part. I was hurt and confused; I should have let them know.

SECTION 7

One of the most traumatic incidents in my life was when my father was drafted into the army. I was only 3 at the time, and we were very close. [The patient did not experience severe difficulties with his father until some time later, when independence became an issue.] My parents tried to explain what was happening, but the concept of the draft was incomprehensible to me. So when my father said goodbye to me at the door, I only sensed dimly that this was very different from other occasions. Maybe because I wanted to believe it, I decided that he was just going shopping at a nearby store and would be back soon. So I didn't run to him for a goodbye hug, and I didn't tell him that I loved him very much and was sorry that he was going. (Even now, I can feel how much I wanted that hug!) But it was many months—a period that seemed like an eternity—before I saw him again.

My failure to realize that he would be gone for a long time, and that this was my last chance to get a hug, made me feel stupid. Not showing my emotions made me feel like a coward. But words like "stupid" and "coward" were beyond me at that age, so I felt only a strong and long-lasting self-hate that I never really understood.

SECTION 8

I developed some self-destructive habits in late childhood that remained with me as a young adult. I would pick at my fingers until they became chafed and sore, or chew on the inside of my cheek, and stop only when I went too far and felt a sharp stab of pain. I wasn't trying to hurt or injure myself, at least consciously. But it somehow felt right to treat myself this way, so I kept doing it.

SECTION 9

My father was very perfectionistic, and he regarded scholarly pursuits as extremely important. One day I gave him a paper that I had written for a high school geography class, hoping for a few helpful comments. Later that day, he handed it back to me without a word. I took one look, and I wanted to cry. Every line of every page was covered with corrections in glaring red pencil. I felt so crushed, so stupid … Once my father bawled me out so intensely for "not amounting to anything" that I became physically ill. Yet I was an honor student, with grades that put me in the top 10% of my class.

My parents had my intelligence tested when I was 8 years old, and my score was very high. After that, I guess the only thing that might have satisfied my father would have been a Nobel Prize. Or maybe even that wouldn't have been enough.

SECTION 10

Every night before going to bed, I feel compelled to check the alarm clock to be sure that it is set to go off the following morning. I do this not just once, but 10 or 15 times. I feel as though I want to stop this ritual; it's annoying and even embarrassing. But if I do stop, I worry about whether or not the clock is really set. Eventually I get so nervous that I have to examine the clock once again to be sure it's set properly—which, of course, it is.

Glossary of Terms

Note: Numbers after each definition indicate the page on which the term is first discussed. To help students who may wish to use this Glossary for further study, some terms have been included that do not appear or are not formally defined in the text, and these terms are not followed by a page number.

Ability trait (Cattell)   A trait that determines how well one succeeds in reaching a particular goal. (p. 288)

Actualization (Rogers)   A synonym for actualizing tendency.

Actualizing tendency (Rogers)   An innate tendency to develop our constructive, healthy potentials. Similar to self-actualization in Maslow's theory. (p. 198)

Affectia (Cattell)   Being more outgoing, warmhearted, and easygoing; the converse of sizia. A temperament trait, similar to extraversion. (p. 288)

Agape (May)   A nonpossessive devotion to the welfare of another person; similar to Maslow's construct of B-love. One of the four components of love. (p. 242)

Aggression   *See* Benign aggression; Malignant aggression.

Aggressiveness (Freud)   A synonym for destructiveness.

Aggressiveness (Horney)   A synonym for moving against people.

Agreeableness   The extent to which one is trusting and helpful (more agreeable) or suspicious and uncooperative (less agreeable). One of the "Big Five" personality traits. (p. 302)

Alaxia (Cattell)   Being more trusting and accepting; the converse of protension. A temperament trait. (p. 289)

Ambivalence (Freud)   Simultaneously holding opposite feelings toward someone or something, such as love and hate.

Anal-expulsive (Freud)   A personality that is excessively generous, yielding, and sloppy. (p. 30)

Anal fixation (anal personality) (Freud)   *See* Anal-expulsive; Anal-retentive.

Anal-retentive (Freud)   A personality that is excessively miserly, stubborn, and orderly. (p. 30)

Anal stage (Freud)   The second stage of personality development. Duration is from about age 1 to 3 years, and the primary source of pleasure is the anus. (p. 27)

Analyst   *See* Psychoanalyst.

Analytical psychology (Jung)   The name Jung gave to his theory of personality. (p. 60)

Anima (Jung)   The female archetype in man. Predisposes man to understand the nature of woman, is sentimental, and compensates for the powerful male persona. (p. 66)

Animus (Jung)   The male archetype in woman. Predisposes woman to understand the nature of man, is powerful, and compensates for the sentimental female persona. (p. 66)

Anticathexis (Freud)   Psychic energy that is used by the ego to oppose a dangerous or immoral cathexis. Also called countercathexis. (p. 20)

Anxiety (Freud)   A highly unpleasant emotion similar to intense nervousness. Realistic anxiety (also called objective anxiety) is related to threats in the external world, neurotic anxiety is related to powerful id impulses, and moral anxiety is related to the superego's standards of right and wrong. (p. 20)

Anxiety (Sullivan)   A highly unpleasant emotion similar to intense nervousness. Caused primarily by anxiety in the mother (or whichever adult fulfills this function); becomes an uncanny emotion when very intense. (p. 148)

Anxiety (Rogers)   A state of uneasiness and tension, which results from experiences that are incongruent with the self-concept.

Anxiety (May)   Apprehension caused by a threat to the existence of one's personality (a threat to *Dasein*); the awareness that one can be destroyed, physically or psychologically, and become nothing. (p. 240)

Anxiety (Skinner)   A reduction in the rate of an operant that is caused by a conditioned aversive stimulus.

Anxiety (Kelly)   The awareness that important events fall mostly outside the range of convenience of every personal construct in one's system, making it impossible to anticipate the future. (p. 354)

Anxiety hierarchy   A sequence of feared stimuli, from most frightening to least frightening, that is used in systematic desensitization. (p. 328)

Apathy (Sullivan)   A "safety" dynamism that serves the desirable purpose of preventing psychological tension from becoming too intense. However, too much apathy can be harmful.

Archetype (Jung)   A predisposition to perceive the world in certain ways that is inherited from past generations; *not* a specific idea or belief. Is much the same across different cultures (a "universal thought form") and is in the collective unconscious. (p. 66)

Artlessness (Cattell)   Being more forthright and genuine but socially clumsy; the converse of shrewdness. A temperament trait. (p. 290)

Attitude (Jung)   Introversion or extraversion. (p. 71)

Attitude (Cattell)   An overt or covert interest in pursuing a specific course of action. A learned dynamic trait that represents the basic unit of motivation, and is subsidiary to the sentiments and ergs. (p. 285)

Authoritarianism (Fromm)   A nonproductive frame of orientation that involves powerful desires to dominate others and to submit to others. One of the three mechanisms of escape. (p. 134)

Autia (Cattell)   Being more imaginative and absent-minded; the converse of praxernia. A temperament trait. (p. 289)

Automaton conformity (Fromm)   Immersion in a socially acceptable role at the cost of one's need for identity. One of the three mechanisms of escape. (p. 134)

Autonomy (Erikson)   The willingness and ability to behave independently and do things on one's own. (p. 176)

Availability heuristic   Making a decision, albeit not necessarily correct one, by thinking about a relevant example that easily comes to mind. (p. 380)

Aversion therapy   Using an aversive stimulus (e.g., a mild electric shock) to reduce the probability of undesirable behavior (e.g., drinking alcohol). (p. 327)

Aversive control   A synonym for aversion therapy.

Aversive stimulus (Skinner)   A synonym for negative reinforcer.

Awareness   A synonym for consciousness.

"Bad-me" personification (Sullivan)   How an individual perceives his or her undesirable aspects, notably ones that have been punished by the parents. Part of the self-system. (p. 151)

Basic anxiety (Horney)   The feeling of being alone in an unfriendly and frightening world. (p. 118)

Basic trust (Erikson)   The belief that the environment is predictable and capable of satisfying one's needs. (p. 174)

B-cognition (being cognition) (Maslow)   A special form of thinking that is common during peak experiences, is nonjudgmental, does not aim toward the fulfillment of some motive, and emphasizes the unity of oneself and the cosmos. (p. 226)

Behaviorist perspective (behaviorism)   An approach that seeks to make psychology more scientific by studying only what can be observed, and redefines psychology as the study of overt behavior. An alternative to, rather than a type of, personality theory. (p. 309)

Behavior modification (1)   A synonym for behavior therapy. (2) Skinnerian methods for changing behavior, including areas other than psychopathology. (p. 326)

Behavior therapy   An approach to psychotherapy that seeks to change particular behaviors and/or symptoms, rather than trying to alter some unobservable or unconscious inner state. (p. 326)

Being-in-the-world (*Dasein*) (May)   A conscious and unconscious sense of oneself as a distinct and autonomous entity who exists in the world of physiological and physical surroundings (*Umwelt*), other people (*Mitwelt*), and one's own self (*Eigenwelt*). (p. 239)

Being orientation (Fromm)   Emphasizing the development of one's positive innate potentials rather than amassing a large number of possessions (the having orientation). Similar to productive orientation.

Benign aggression (Fromm)   An organic, healthy drive to defend oneself against threat by attacking. (p. 132)

"Big Five" personality traits   Five traits that consistently emerge from factor-analytic studies as the most important: introversion–extraversion, neuroticism, agreeableness, conscientiousness, and openness to experience. (p. 302)

Biological perspective   Theories that emphasize the physiological and hereditary aspects of behavior. (p. 389)

Biophilia (Fromm)   Love of life; a productive frame of orientation. (p. 133)

Birth order (Adler)   A child's position in the family (e.g., firstborn, secondborn, only child). (p. 97)

B-love (being love) (Maslow)   An unselfish and nonpossessive giving of love and affection to another person. A growth motive that is more enjoyable than D-love. (p. 221)

B-motive (being motive) (Maslow)   A synonym for growth motive.

Bureaucratic orientation (Fromm)   A nonproductive frame of orientation wherein a person is controlled from above in a power structure and has authority over one or more subordinates, and is likely to use rigid rules and red tape to express power and hostility.

B-values (Maslow)   A synonym for metaneeds.

Cardinal personal disposition (cardinal personal trait) (Allport)   A single personal disposition that influences nearly all of one's behavior, as with Scrooge's miserliness. (p. 266)

Care (Erikson)   The increasing concern for others, especially the next generation. The emergence of this ego quality indicates that the crisis of the seventh epigenetic stage has been successfully resolved. (p. 180)

Care (May)   The feeling that something in life does matter; an ontological characteristic.

Castration anxiety (Freud)   The boy's fears that his sexual organ will be removed as punishment for his Oedipal wishes. (p. 27)

Cathexis (Freud)   Psychic energy that is invested in a mental representation of an object. The stronger the cathexis, the greater the amount of psychic energy and the more the object is desired. (p. 16)

Causality   The belief that personality is shaped by events that happened in the past. (p. 63)

Central personal dispositions (central personal traits) (Allport)   Five to ten personal dispositions that influence most of a person's behavior, as might be included in a carefully written letter of recommendation. (p. 266)

Channelize (Kelly)   To shape into customary patterns. (p. 346)

Character-rooted passion (Fromm)   A synonym for nonorganic drive.

Choice corollary (Kelly)   Posits that we value more highly the pole of a dichotomous personal construct that enables us to predict the future more accurately. (p. 349)

Claims (Horney)   Unrealistic demands and expectations that the neurotic imposes on other people. (p. 120)

Classical conditioning (Pavlov, Watson)   A simple form of learning wherein a conditioned stimulus (e.g., tone) becomes capable of eliciting a conditioned response (e.g., salivation) by being repeatedly paired with an unconditioned stimulus (e.g., food) which automatically elicits that response. (p. 311)

Client-centered therapy (Rogers)   The name Rogers originally gave to his theory of personality, which he later changed to person-centered theory. (p. 198)

Cognition(s)   Thinking; thought(s). May also include knowing and remembering. (p. 368)

Cognitive perspective   Theories of personality that emphasize the influence of thinking on behavior and how we predict, interpret (construe), and evaluate events. (p. 341)

Collective unconscious (Jung)   A storehouse of inherited predispositions to perceive the world in certain ways (archetypes). The deepest and most inaccessible part of personality. (p. 66)

Commonality corollary (Kelly)   Posits that we are psychologically more similar to those people whose personal constructs have more in common with our own. (p. 351)

Common trait (Allport)   A structural and motivational aspect of personality that initiates and guides consistent forms of behavior (e.g., friendliness, ambitiousness). Common traits facilitate nomothetic comparisons among people, but are only a rough approximation as to any individual's unique personality. (p. 265)

Common trait (Cattell)   A trait shared to varying degrees by different individuals. In contrast to Allport's theory, common traits represent aspects of one's true personality. (p. 285)

Community feeling (Adler)   A synonym for social interest. (p. 92)

Compensation (Jung)   The tendency of one part of personality to balance or adjust for another part, as when the unconscious emphasizes an aspect of personality that has been undervalued by consciousness. (p. 62)

Compensation (Adler)   Overcoming real or imagined inferiority through effort and practice, or by developing one's abilities in a different area. (p. 93)

Competence (Erikson)   The belief that important tasks can be completed and a source of pride. The emergence of this ego quality indicates that the crisis of the fourth epigenetic stage has been successfully resolved. (p. 177)

Complex (Freud)   *See* Oedipus complex.

Complex (Jung)   A constellation of related and emotionally charged thoughts, feelings, or ideas. Varies in strength according to the amount of psychic energy at its disposal (its value), and may be conscious or unconscious. (p. 61)

Complex (Adler)   *See* Inferiority complex.

Compliance (Horney)   A synonym for moving toward people.

Compulsion to repeat   *See* Repetition compulsion.

Condensation (Freud)   The unconscious combination of various symbols or words into a single entity with several meanings. (p. 19)

Conditional positive regard (Rogers)   Accepting and respecting another person only if that person's self-concept and feelings meet with one's approval. (p. 202)

Conditional positive self-regard (Rogers)   Accepting and respecting oneself only if one satisfies the introjected standards of significant others (conditions of worth), even though these run counter to the actualizing tendency. (p. 202)

Conditioned reinforcement (Skinner)   Reinforcement that is provided by a conditioned stimulus. Also called secondary reinforcement. (p. 319)

Conditioned response   A response to a previously neutral (conditioned) stimulus that has been learned through conditioning. (p. 311)

Conditioned stimulus   (1) In classical conditioning, a previously neutral stimulus that now elicits the conditioned response because of conditioning. (2) In operant conditioning, a previously neutral stimulus that acquires positive or aversive properties through conditioning. (p. 311)

Conditioned suppression (Skinner)   A synonym for anxiety.

Condition of worth (Rogers)   A standard that must be satisfied to receive conditional positive regard from a significant other, which is introjected into the self-concept. Supersedes the organismic valuing process, and leads to behaviors that are not satisfying. (p. 202)

Conflict   *See* Intrapsychic conflict.

Conflict Index (Cattell)   A mathematical formula for quantifying the amount of intrapsychic conflict that an individual experiences. (p. 293)

Congruence (Rogers)   A healthy state of unison between the organismic valuing process and the self-concept, and therefore between the actualizing and self-actualizing tendencies. (p. 202)

Conscience (Freud)   The part of the superego that punishes undesirable actions, thoughts, and wishes by making the ego feel guilty and anxious. (p. 25)

Conscientiousness   The extent to which one is hardworking and reliable (more conscientious) or lazy, unreliable, and careless (less conscientious). One of the "Big Five" personality traits. (p. 302)

Conscious (consciousness)   The part of personality that includes material of which one is aware. (p. 21)

Conservatism of temperament (Cattell)   Being more traditional and conservative; the converse of radicalism. A temperament trait. (p. 290)

Conservative nature of instincts (Freud)   The tendency of instincts to try to restore a previous state of existence. (p. 46)

Constellatory construct (Kelly)   A construct that limits the ways in which other constructs are used. A converse of propositional construct. (p. 353)

Construct   A term or principle that is created (or adopted) by a theorist. A theory consists of a set of constructs that are related to each other in a logical and consistent way. (p. 4)

Construct (Kelly)   *See* Personal construct.

Construction corollary (Kelly)   Posits that our anticipations of the future are based on our constructions (interpretations) of previous events. (p. 346)

Constructive alternativism (Kelly)   The principle that there are always alternative constructs that we can use to interpret the world, so no one need be a victim of childhood events or current circumstances. (p. 346)

Construct system (construction system) (Kelly)   The hierarchically organized collection of personal constructs that an individual uses to anticipate the future. (p. 352)

Contingencies of reinforcement (Skinner)   The relationships among environmental stimuli, the organism's responses, and the reinforcement that follows those responses. (p. 316)

Continuous reinforcement (Skinner)   Reinforcement given after every correct response. The converse of intermittent (partial) reinforcement. (p. 318)

Core construct (Kelly)   A construct so superordinate that it dominates one's behavior. The converse of peripheral construct. (p. 348)

Core role (Kelly)   Subordinating the "self" pole of the self-construct to constructs that involve important people in one's life. (p. 354)

Countercathexis (Freud)   A synonym for anticathexis.

Counterconditioning   Conditioning a desirable response (e.g., relaxation) that is incompatible with an undesirable response (e.g., anxiety) and therefore replaces it. (p. 328)

Countertransference (Freud)   An unconscious displacement of emotion or behavior, by the psychoanalyst, from some other person to the patient. (p. 41)

C-P-C Cycle (Kelly)   Making a decision by first construing (interpreting) a situation in various ways (circumspection), then focusing on one personal construct to the exclusion of all others (preemption), and then choosing the pole of this construct that appears more likely to predict the future accurately (control, choice).

Credulous attitude (Kelly)   Accepting and discussing whatever statements a client may make. The goal is to encourage clients in psychotherapy to recant their misstatements on their own, rather than making them more rigid by challenging statements that appear to be false. (p. 357)

Crisis (Erikson)   A crucial turning point for better or worse that occurs during personality development. (p. 174)

Cross-cultural perspective   Theories that compare the ways in which different cultures behave. (p. 390)

Daimonic (May)   Innate benign and illicit forces that are capable of dominating one's personality. Psychological health requires that the daimonic be integrated into consciousness. (p. 244)

Dasein (May)   A synonym for being-in-the-world.

Daydreaming   A synonym for fantasy.

Day's residues (Freud)   Memories of the preceding day that trigger a dream because they are related to important unconscious issues. (p. 32)

D-cognition (deficiency cognition) (Maslow)   A common and self-preservative form of thinking that aims toward the satisfaction of deficiency motives, is judgmental, and emphasizes the separateness of oneself and the environment. (p. 226)

Death instinct (Freud)   An instinct that aims at returning us to our prior state of nonexistence. (p. 15)

Defense (Rogers)   Responding to experiences that threaten the self-concept and evoke anxiety by distorting them, or (less frequently) by screening them out from awareness. (p. 202)

Defense mechanism (Freud)   A method used by the ego to ward off threats from the id, superego, or external world, and to reduce the corresponding anxiety. Most defense mechanisms operate unconsciously, which makes possible the goal of self-deception. (p. 20)

Deficiency motive (D-motive) (Maslow)   The need to reduce a drive such as hunger, thirst, or D-love by filling some lack within oneself. Also called deficit motive. (p. 219)

Denial of reality (Freud)   Refusing to believe, or even to perceive, some threat in the external world; a defense mechanism. (p. 22)

Dependency constructs (Kelly)   Personal constructs that interpret other people as essential to one's survival.

Deprivation (Skinner)   Withholding a primary reinforcer (such as food or water) for some time, so that it may be used to reinforce and condition an operant. (p. 319)

Despair (Erikson)   Feeling that one's life is meaningless and has been lived the wrong way, and that death will intervene before these mistakes can be corrected. The converse of ego integrity. (p. 180)

Destructiveness (Freud)   *See* Instinct (Freud).

Destructiveness (Fromm)   A synonym for malignant aggression.

Desurgency (Cattell)   Being more sober, taciturn, and serious; the converse of surgency. A temperament trait. (p. 289)

Detachment (Horney)   A synonym for moving away from people.

Developmental crisis (Erikson)   *See* Crisis.

Dichotomy corollary (Kelly)   Posits that every personal construct is dichotomous (bipolar). (p. 349)

Differentiation (Jung)   The development of separate and distinct parts of personality out of the original, undifferentiated whole.

Dimensional approach (Allport)   A synonym for nomothetic approach.

Discrimination (Skinner)   (1) Reinforcing an organism for responding to some difference between two or more stimuli. (2) The resulting increase in the probability of responding to the reinforced stimulus. (p. 320)

Displacement (Freud)   (1) Transferring behaviors or feelings, often unconsciously, from one object to another that is less threatening; a defense mechanism. (p. 22) (2) A shift of psychic energy to a substitute object-cathexis, as when the infant sucks its thumb because the bottle is not available.

Dissociation (Sullivan)   Unconsciously disowning threatening aspects of one's personality, and associating them with the "not-me" personification. (p. 153)

D-love (deficiency love) (Maslow)   The selfish need to receive love and affection from others. A deficiency motive, prerequisite to the emergence of B-love. (p. 221)

D-motive (Maslow)   *See* Deficiency motive.

Dominance (Cattell)   Being more assertive, competitive, and stubborn; the converse of submissiveness. A temperament trait. (p. 289)

Doubt (Erikson)   *See* Shame and doubt.

Dream interpretation   Identifying the true meaning of a dream and what it reveals about the unconscious. (p. 32)

Dream-work (Freud)   The unconscious process that converts latent dream-thoughts into manifest content. (p. 32)

Drive   (1) A psychological state of tension and discomfort that is caused by a physiological need. (p. 15) (2) Sometimes used as a synonym for instinct.

Drive reduction   Eliminating or decreasing the discomfort and tension of a drive, which satisfies the underlying physiological need. (p. 15)

Dynamic lattice (Cattell)   An individual's complete motivational structure, composed of a complicated network of interrelated subsidation chains and their component attitudes, sentiments, and ergs. (p. 287)

Dynamic trait (Cattell)   A trait that energizes behavior and directs it toward a particular goal. Includes innate ergs, and learned sentiments and attitudes. (p. 285)

Dynamism (Sullivan)   The transformation of physical energy into behavior (overt or covert, conscious or unconscious) that will satisfy a need. (p. 149)

Early recollections (Adler)   Memories of infancy and childhood, which provide important clues about a person's style of life even if they are inaccurate. (p. 99)

Eclectic (eclecticism)   Selecting the best aspects of various theories of personality, and integrating them into a meaningful and interrelated whole. (p. 219)

Economic value (Allport)   A philosophy of life that involves a businesslike concern with the useful and practical. (p. 264)

Effectiveness (Fromm)   A synonym for transcendence.

Ego (Freud)   The logical, self-preservative, problem-solving part of personality that mediates among the demands of the id, the superego, and the external world, delays the discharge of tension until a suitable object can be found, and uses defense mechanisms. The stronger the ego, the healthier the personality. (p. 19)

Ego (Erikson)   Similar to Freud's definition, but possesses important constructive capacities (such as identity and mastery) as well as defenses against illicit id instincts and anxiety. (p. 173)

Ego (Jung)   A complex of conscious ideas that constitutes the center of awareness, and provides feelings of identity ("I am I") and continuity ("I am the same person today that I was yesterday"). (p. 64)

Ego enhancement (Allport)   A synonym for self-esteem.

Ego extension (Allport)   A synonym for self-extension.

Ego ideal (Freud)   The part of the superego that rewards desirable actions, thoughts, and wishes by making the ego feel proud and virtuous. (p. 25)

Ego identity (Erikson)   A synonym for identity.

Ego integrity (Erikson)   Feeling that one's life has been valuable and worthwhile. (p. 180)

Ego psychology (Erikson)   A theory of personality that hews more closely to Freudian psychoanalysis than does the work of Jung, Adler, Horney, Fromm, and Sullivan, but stresses the strengths and capacities of the rational ego and deemphasizes the role of instincts and the irrational id. (p. 167)

Ego strength (Cattell)   The ability to control one's impulses, remain calm, and deal realistically with one's problems. A temperament trait. (p. 289)

Eigenwelt (May)   The world of one's self, potentials, and values ("own-world"). One of the three simultaneous and interrelated modes of being-in-the-world. (p. 239)

Electra complex   A term that Freud preferred not to use for the female Oedipus complex. (p. 28)

Elements (Kelly)   The things described by a personal construct; may be people, inanimate objects, events, or one or both poles of another construct. (p. 351)

Empathy (Rogers)   A reasonably accurate understanding of someone else's experience; putting oneself in another person's shoes. (p. 205)

Enantiodromia (Jung)   The tendency of any characteristic to eventually turn into its opposite. (p. 62)

Encounter group (Rogers)   A group of relatively well-adjusted individuals who meet with a facilitator to pursue further personal growth. Also called T-group. (p. 206)

Epigenetic psychosexual stages (Erikson)   Stages of personality development that unfold according to an innate schedule, are characterized by a specific problem (crisis) that represents a crucial turning point for better or worse, and are influenced much more strongly by parent–child relationships than by instincts. (p. 174)

Erg (Cattell)   An innate dynamic source trait; similar to instinct, but defined by factor analysis. (p. 285)

Ergic tension (Cattell)   The extent to which one is tense, frustrated, and driven (high ergic tension) or relaxed, tranquil, and composed (low ergic tension). A temperament trait. (p. 291)

Eros (Freud)   A synonym for the sexual instinct. (p. 15)

Eros (May)   A passionate striving for self-fulfillment through union with a significant other, including such pleasurable tension increases as thinking of and yearning for the loved one. One of the four components of love. (p. 242)

Erotogenic zone (Freud)   An area of the body that is capable of producing erotic gratification when stimulated. (p. 15)

Esthetic value (Allport)   A philosophy of life that emphasizes the enjoyment of form, beauty, and the artistic. (p. 264)

Euphoria (Sullivan)   A state of total well-being characterized by the absence of any internal needs or noxious external stimuli. (p. 148)

Eupsychian (Maslow)   As psychologically healthy as possible. (p. 230)

Existence (May)   A synonym for being-in-the-world.

Existential psychology   A philosophy of human nature that stresses the ontological charac-teristics (being-in-the-world, anxiety, guilt, intentionality, and love), and the necessity of asserting our being-in-the-world despite the inevitable death that awaits us all. (p. 237)

Expansiveness (Horney)   A synonym for moving against people.

Experience (Rogers)   Everything that is presently within or potentially available to aware-ness, including thoughts, needs, perceptions, and feelings. (p. 199)

Experience corollary (Kelly)   Posits that we frequently revise our system of personal constructs in order to improve its ability to anticipate the future. (p. 350)

Experiential field (Rogers)   A synonym for experience.

Exploitative orientation (Fromm)   A nonproductive frame of orientation that seeks to gain rewards by force or cunning. (p. 136)

Externalization (Horney)   Experiencing intrapsychic processes as occurring outside one-self; similar to projection. (p. 119)

External locus of control   The extent to which one believes that obtaining rewards and avoiding punishment is due to chance, fate, and the actions of other people. (p. 378)

Extinction (Skinner)   (1) Consistently following an operant with no reinforcement, thereby decreasing or eliminating its probability of occurrence. (2) The resulting decrease in frequency or cessation of an operant. (p. 322)

Extraversion (Jung)   An outward flow of libido toward the external world. Extraverts are outgoing, venture forth with careless confidence into the unknown, and are particularly interested in people and events in the environment. *See also* Introversion–extraversion. (p. 71)

Facticity (May)   A synonym for thrownness.

Factor (dimension)   A hypothetical construct designed to simplify our understanding of a larger set of variables, persons, or occasions. (p. 284)

Factor analysis   A statistical/mathematical technique for explaining a set of variables, persons, or occasions in terms of a smaller number of factors. (p. 283)

Factor-analytic trait theory   A theory of personality that uses the statistical technique of factor analysis to determine which of the thousands of traits are most important. (p. 281)

Fantasy (Freud)   Gratifying unfulfilled needs by imagining situations in which they are satisfied; a defense mechanism. Also called daydreaming. (p. 22)

Fear (Sullivan)   An unpleasant tension that feels similar to anxiety, but is caused by a delay in the satisfaction of a need (rather than by anxiety in the mothering one) and is therefore more easily forgotten. (p. 149)

Fear (May)   An unpleasant emotion that feels similar to anxiety, but is not caused by a threat to one's existence or Dasein (is not ontological) and is therefore more easily forgotten. (p. 240)

Feeling (Jung)   *See* Function.

Fictions (Adler)   Unrealistic life goals that influence behavior because the person acts "as if" they were true. (p. 93)

Fidelity (Erikson)   The ability to pledge and maintain loyalty to a cause. The emergence of this ego quality indicates that the crisis of the fifth epigenetic stage has been successfully resolved. (p. 180)

Five-factor theory   *See* "Big Five" personality traits.

Fixation (Freud)   Occurs when libido remains attached to one or more of the pregenital ero-togenic zones. (p. 29)

Fixation   An inability to perceive a problem from a new and better perspective, which makes it difficult or impossible to find the best solution. Types of fixation include functional fixedness and mental sets.

Fixed-interval schedule (FI) (Skinner) Reinforcing the first correct response that occurs after a specified interval of time, measured from the preceding reinforcement. A schedule of intermittent (partial) reinforcement. (p. 318)

Fixed-ratio schedule (FR) (Skinner) Reinforcing the last of a specified number of correct responses, counted from the preceding reinforcement. A schedule of intermittent (partial) reinforcement. (p. 318)

Fixed-role therapy (Kelly) A form of psychotherapy wherein the client tries to enact in everyday life a role designed by a panel of therapists, with the goal of discovering and using more effective personal constructs. (p. 358)

Focus of convenience (Kelly) The particular aspects of behavior for which a personal construct, or a scientific theory, is maximally suited. (p. 345)

Fragmentation corollary (Kelly) Posits that the same person may use contradictory personal constructs at different times. (p. 351)

Frame of orientation (Fromm) A set of principles or personal philosophy that gives meaning to one's life, establishes one's values and goals, and defines one's place in the world; a nonorganic drive. Also called frame of devotion. (p. 133)

Free association (Freud) Saying whatever comes to mind, no matter how silly or embarrassing it may seem. The "fundamental rule" of psychoanalytic therapy, used to bring unconscious material to consciousness. (pp. 16, 40)

Full humanness (Maslow) A synonym for self-actualization.

Fully functioning person (Rogers) An optimally psychologically healthy individual. (p. 203)

Function (Jung) A way of experiencing internal or external stimuli. Sensation establishes that something is there, thinking interprets what is perceived, feeling determines the desirability of what is perceived, and intuition forms hunches or conclusions without the aid of the other functions. (p. 71)

Functional autonomy (Allport) The independence in purpose of adult motives from their childhood counterparts. A means to an end becoming an end in itself, and continuing to influence behavior after the original motive has disappeared. (p. 262)

Functional fixedness Perceiving an object as having only one purpose; being unable to perceive an object in new ways that will solve a problem. (p. 380)

Fundamental postulate (Kelly) Posits that the psychological processes that make up our personality are naturally active, and are molded into patterns by the ways in which we anticipate the future. (p. 346)

Generativity (Erikson) Giving birth to, guiding, and improving the life of future generations. (p. 180)

Genital stage (Freud) The final stage, and goal of, personality development. May be achieved during early adulthood, later adulthood, or not at all. (p. 29)

Genuineness (Rogers) Having an accurate knowledge of one's inner experience and a willingness to share it when appropriate. (p. 205)

Glory (Horney) Grandiose feelings of triumph because one appears to have fulfilled the demands of the idealized image. (p. 119)

"Good-me" personification (Sullivan) How an individual perceives his or her desirable aspects, notably ones that have been rewarded by the parents. Part of the self-system. (p. 151)

Group adherence (Cattell) Being more likely to join and obey a group; the converse of self-sufficiency. A temperament trait. (p. 291)

Growth motive (Maslow) The need to develop one's inner potentials, including the enjoyment of pleasurable drive increases and the giving of B-love to others. Growth motives are relatively independent of the environment and are unique to the individual. Also called being motive, B-motive. (p. 220)

Guided mastery (Bandura)	Methods of psychotherapy that improve clients' perceived self-efficacy by having them perform feared or discouraging tasks. (p. 374)

Guilt (Erikson)	Feeling that it is wrong to want to choose and begin something new, such as an activity or social relationship. The converse of initiative. (p. 177)

Guilt (May)	Regret resulting from the impossibility of fulfilling all of one's innate potentials (a denial of *Eigenwelt*), relating perfectly to others (a denial of *Mitwelt*), and always recognizing our communion with nature (a denial of *Umwelt*). An ontological characteristic. (p. 241)

Guilt (Kelly)	The awareness that "self" has been dislodged from the core role. (p. 354)

Guilt proneness (Cattell)	Being more self-reproaching and apprehensive; the converse of untroubled adequacy. A temperament trait. (p. 290)

Harria (Cattell)	Being more tough-minded and self-reliant; the converse of premsia. A temperament trait. (p. 289)

Having orientation (Fromm)	A nonproductive orientation that regards possessions as extremely important and tends to result in greed. Similar to hoarding orientation.

Helplessness (Horney)	A synonym for moving toward people.

Heritability	The extent to which differences among people can be explained by inherited genetic causes, rather than by learning and the environment. A trait that is more heritable is more strongly influenced by heredity. (p. 294)

Hierarchy of (human) needs (Maslow)	A model of motivation wherein certain needs usually do not become important, or even noticeable, until other lower-level needs have to some extent been satisfied. Includes five levels of needs: physiological (lowest), safety, love, esteem, and self-actualization (highest). (p. 220)

Hoarding orientation (Fromm)	A nonproductive frame of orientation that involves miserliness, compulsive orderliness, and stubbornness. (p. 136)

Holistic (holism)	Treating personality as a unified whole, rather than dividing it into various parts.

Homeostasis	A state of internal equilibrium where the body has no needs and no drives are active; the goal of drive reduction. (p. 15)

Hope (Erikson)	The enduring belief that one's fervent wishes can be attained. The emergence of this ego quality indicates that the crisis of the first epigenetic stage has been successfully resolved. (p. 176)

Hostility (Kelly)	Continued efforts to extort evidence in favor of a social prediction that has proved to be a failure, as when a parent consistently construes a child in unrealistically favorable ways.

Human diminution (Maslow)	A term that Maslow prefers to neurosis, so as to emphasize that psychopathology involves the failure to fulfill one's true, healthy potentials. (p. 228)

Humanistic perspective	Theories of personality that emphasize our inborn potentials for healthy growth and development. Psychopathology occurs when these healthy potentials are blocked by pathogenic environmental forces (such as bad parenting). (p. 193)

Human passion (Fromm)	A synonym for nonorganic drive.

Hysteria (Freud)	A disorder in which psychological problems are unconsciously converted into physical symptoms; such symptoms have no underlying physical cause. Now called conversion disorder. (p. 35)

Id (Freud, Erikson)	The impulsive and childish part of personality that demands immediate pleasure, is chaotic, illogical, and amoral, has no sense of time, and is capable only of producing wish-fulfilling images, but is necessary for survival because it includes all of our innate biological needs (instincts). (p. 18)

Idealized image (Horney)	A grandiose, glorious self-image that conceals one's weak and hated real self. (p. 119)

Ideal self (Rogers)   The self-concept one would most like to possess. (p. 211)

Identification (Freud)   (1) Reducing painful feelings of self-hate by becoming like objects that are illustrious and admired, such as idols, aggressors, or lost loves; a defense mechanism that may be partly or wholly unconscious. (2) The normal, healthy desire to become like one's parents. (p. 24)

Identification with the aggressor (Freud)   Achieving feelings of strength in a demeaning situation by behaving like the cause of one's embarrassment.

Identity (Fromm)   A sense of oneself as a distinct and separate entity; a nonorganic drive. (p. 132)

Identity (Erikson)   A complicated inner state that includes feelings of individuality and uniqueness, a sense of wholeness and indivisibility, an unconscious striving for sameness and continuity, and a sense of solidarity with the ideals and values of some group. (p. 171)

Identity (self-identity) (Allport)   A feeling of inner sameness and continuity. (p. 266)

Identity confusion (Erikson)   The inability to achieve a sense of identity. Involves feelings of inner fragmentation, not knowing where one's life is headed, and not being able to gain support from a social role. (p. 171)

Identity crisis (Erikson)   (1) A synonym for identity confusion. (2) A crucial turning point in the development of personality that occurs during adolescence, and leads to either a sense of identity or identity confusion. (p. 179)

Idiographic approach (Allport)   Studying the single case in order to discover those factors that make a given individual unique. (p. 262)

Id psychology   A synonym for Freudian psychoanalysis. (p. 169)

Imago (Jung)   A synonym for archetype.

Impermeable construct (Kelly)   A construct that is closed to new elements. The converse of permeable construct. (p. 350)

Incongruence (Rogers)   A split between the organismic valuing process and a self-concept burdened by conditions of worth (and, therefore, between the actualizing and self-actualizing tendencies), which results in feelings of tension and confusion. (p. 202)

Individuality corollary (Kelly)   Posits that different people construe (interpret) events differently. (p. 347)

Individual psychology (Adler)   The name Adler gave to his theory of personality. (p. 91)

Individuation (Jung)   The unfolding of one's inherent and unique personality, aided by the transcendent function and leading to the formation of the self. A lifelong task that is rarely if ever completed. (p. 69)

Industry (Erikson)   Taking pride and pleasure in doing important tasks. (p. 177)

Inferiority (Erikson)   The belief that one is incompetent and cannot do important tasks successfully. The converse of industry. (p. 177)

Inferiority complex (Adler)   Exaggerated and pathological feelings of weakness, including the belief that one cannot overcome one's difficulties through appropriate effort. (p. 93)

Inferiority feelings (Adler)   Normal and inevitable feelings of weakness that result from our helplessness during childhood. (p. 93)

Inflation (Jung)   Expansion of the ego beyond its proper limits, resulting in feelings of exaggerated self-importance. Usually compensated for by unconscious feelings of inferiority. (p. 64)

Initiative (Erikson)   The willingness to begin something new, such as an activity or social relationship. (p. 177)

Inner conflict (Horney)   *See* Neurotic conflict.

Insight (Freud)   An emotional and intellectual understanding of the causes and dynamics of one's behavior, achieved by bringing unconscious material to consciousness. (p. 38)

Instinct (Freud)   An innate motivating force that is activated by a physiological need. The two types are sexual and destructive (aggressive). (p. 15)

Instinct (Jung)   An inborn physiological urge. Includes hunger, thirst, sexuality, power, individuation, activity, creativity, morality, and religious needs. (p. 60)

Instinctoid need (Maslow)   An inborn, healthy, but weak instinctual impulse that is easily overwhelmed by the far more powerful forces of learning and culture. (p. 219)

Instinctual drive (Fromm)   A synonym for organic drive.

Instrumental conditioning   A term used by some psychologists, but not by Skinner, as a synonym for operant conditioning.

Intellectualization (Freud)   Unconsciously separating threatening emotions from the associated thoughts or events and reacting on only an intellectual level; a defense mechanism. (p. 23)

Intelligence (Cattell)   The capacity for abstract thinking, sound judgment, and perseverance. An ability trait. (p. 288)

Intention (Allport)   The fusion of an emotional want and a plan to satisfy it that is directed toward some goal. (p. 262)

Intentionality (May)   The capacity of human beings to have a conscious and unconscious sense of purpose. An ontological characteristic. (p. 241)

Intermittent reinforcement (Skinner)   Reinforcement given after some correct responses, but not all. Also called partial reinforcement. The converse of continuous reinforcement. (p. 318)

Internal locus of control   The extent to which one believes that obtaining rewards and avoiding punishment is within one's control and depends on one's own behavior. (p. 378)

Interpersonal security (Sullivan)   A feeling of safety achieved through relationships with other people; the best way to reduce anxiety. (p. 149)

Interpretation (Freud)   The psychoanalyst's explanation of the true meaning of the patient's free associations, resistances, dreams, or other behaviors. (p. 40)

Intimacy (Erikson)   Becoming emotionally close to another person. (p. 180)

Intrapsychic   Occurring within one's own personality (psyche).

Intrapsychic conflict   A clash between two or more parts of one's personality; often unconscious. *See also* Neurotic conflict. (p. 15)

Introjected value (Rogers)   A synonym for condition of worth.

Introjection (Freud)   Unconsciously incorporating another person's values or personal qualities into one's own personality. (p. 24)

Introversion (Jung)   An inward flow of libido toward the depths of the psyche. Characterized by a keen interest in one's own inner world and often preferring to be alone. *See also* Introversion–extraversion. (p. 71)

Introversion–Extraversion   The extent to which one is more sociable and outgoing (extraverted) or more aloof, retiring, reserved, and introspective (introverted). One of the "Big Five" personality traits, and one of Eysenck's three supertraits. *See also* Extraversion; Introversion. (p. 300)

Intuition (Jung)   *See* Function.

In vivo desensitization   A form of behavior therapy wherein clients are placed in the actual situation that they fear, and inhibit the resulting anxiety by practicing previously taught techniques of muscular relaxation. Used with clients who cannot imagine the feared situation vividly enough to benefit from systematic desensitization. (p. 328)

Isolation (Freud)   A synonym for intellectualization. Also called isolation of affect.

Isolation (Erikson)   Remaining emotionally distant from other people because of fears of losing one's identity if one gets too close. The converse of intimacy. (p. 180)

Latency period (Freud) A time during which sexual impulses become deemphasized. Duration is from about age 5 to 12 years. Not a true psychosexual stage. (p. 28)

Latent dream-thoughts (Freud) The unconscious motives, beliefs, emotions, conflicts, and memories that are concealed behind the manifest content of a dream. (p. 32)

L data (Cattell) Personality data obtained by examining life records, such as academic report cards or employer's ratings. (p. 288)

Learned helplessness The belief that one's behavior will have no effect on the environment; a perceived lack of control that may not correspond with reality, and often results from repeated punishments that one cannot avoid. (p. 378)

Learning A long-lasting change in an organism's behavior, or potential to behave, that occurs as a result of experience or practice. Acquiring the capacity to perform new behaviors, although not necessarily demonstrating them at that moment.

Libido (Freud, Erikson) The psychic energy associated with the sexual instinct; sometimes used to refer to both sexual and destructive energy. (p. 16)

Libido (Jung) The psychic energy associated with any of the instincts, including hunger, thirst, sexuality, power, individuation, activity, creativity, morality, and religious needs. (p. 60)

Life cycle (Erikson) The whole of personality development from infancy through childhood, adolescence, and adulthood to old age. (p. 174)

Life style *See* Style of life.

Locus of control *See* External locus of control; Internal locus of control.

Loose construct (Kelly) A construct that leads to varying, contradictory predictions. The converse of tight construct. (p. 355)

Love (Fromm) A sense of responsibility toward humanity that includes caring for others, knowing how others feel, and respecting their right to develop in their own way. Similar to Adler's construct of social interest. (p. 132)

Love (Erikson) The mutuality of devotion that overcomes the conflict between the needs of individuals. The emergence of this ego quality indicates that the crisis of the sixth epigenetic stage has been successfully resolved. (p. 180)

Love (May) A delight in the presence of another person, and a readiness to affirm that person's values and development as much as one's own. An ontological characteristic that always involves a blending of four components, albeit in varying proportions: sex, eros, philia, and agape. (p. 242)

Malevolent transformation (Sullivan) A distortion in personality development, which results in the belief that other people are enemies and have no tenderness or love to give. (p. 155)

Malignant aggression (Fromm) Destructive behavior that serves no rational defensive purpose; a nonorganic drive. One of the three mechanisms of escape. Also called destructiveness. (p. 132)

Mana-personality (Jung) An intense state of inflation or megalomania that may occur when alluring archetypes emerge from the unconscious.

Mandala (Jung) A circular symbol of wholeness and perfection, and therefore of the self. (p. 71)

Manifest content (Freud) The part of a dream that one remembers, or could remember, upon awakening. (p. 32)

Marketing orientation (Fromm) A nonproductive frame of orientation wherein one characterizes oneself as a product that will "sell" in the social marketplace, and tries to become what others want. (p. 136)

Masculine protest (Adler) Behavior motivated by objections to the belief that society regards men as superior to women. (p. 102)

Masochism (Fromm)   A desire to submit to powerful others and inflict pain on oneself. (p. 134)

Mastery (Horney)   A synonym for moving against people.

Mastery (Erikson)   A sense of competence in dealing with the environment. (p. 172)

Mechanism of escape (Fromm)   An undesirable method for resolving threatening feelings of isolation and freedom; similar to nonproductive orientation. Includes authoritarianism, automaton conformity, and malignant aggression. (p. 134)

Mental set   A tendency to approach a problem in only one way, and not necessarily the best way, because this method has been successful in the past. (p. 380)

Metaneeds (metamotives) (Maslow)   The atypical, nonhierarchical needs of those rare individuals who have achieved self-actualization. Metaneeds include the love of beauty, truth, goodness, and justice. (p. 222)

Metapathology (Maslow)   Occurs when an individual has largely satisfied the four lowest need levels, but cannot satisfy his or her metamotives and achieve self-actualization. (p. 228)

Mistrust (Erikson)   The belief that the environment is unpredictable and unlikely to satisfy one's needs. The converse of basic trust. (p. 176)

Mitwelt (May)   The world of relationship to other people ("with-world"). One of the three simultaneous and interrelated modes of being-in-the-world. (p. 239)

Modeling (Bandura)   (1) A synonym for observational learning. (2) A form of behavior therapy wherein the client observes one or more people demonstrating desirable or effective behaviors. (p. 372)

Modulation corollary (Kelly)   Posits that some personal constructs less readily admit new elements to their range of convenience, which limits the extent to which the system can be revised. (p. 350)

Moral anxiety   *See* Anxiety (Freud).

Morbid dependency (Horney)   A synonym for moving toward people.

Morphogenic approach (Allport)   A synonym for idiographic approach.

Morphogenic trait (Allport)   A synonym for personal disposition.

Motivation   A need or a desire that energizes behavior and directs it toward a particular goal.

Moving against people (Horney)   A neurotic attempt to reduce anxiety and gain safety by dominating and mastering other people. (p. 118)

Moving away from people (Horney)   A neurotic attempt to reduce anxiety and gain safety by avoiding other people and trying to be completely self-sufficient. (p. 118)

Moving toward people (Horney)   A neurotic attempt to reduce anxiety and gain safety by being cared for and protected. (p. 118)

Mutuality (Erikson)   The ideal form of human relationship, wherein the partners facilitate the development of each other's healthy potentials. (p. 172)

Narcissism (Freud)   Self-love; the investment of one's own self with libido. (p. 15)

Narcissism (Fromm)   An innate tendency toward self-centeredness (primary narcissism), which may become a nonproductive frame of orientation later in life (secondary narcissism). (p. 132)

Necrophilia (Fromm)   Love of death; the most pathological and dangerous of the nonproductive frames of orientation. (p. 133)

Need   A physiological lack; thus, an activated instinct. Causes feelings of discomfort or tension (a drive) that signal the body's need for sustenance. (p. 15)

Negative reinforcement (Skinner)   *See* Reinforcement.

Negative reinforcer (Skinner)   A stimulus that increases the probability of a response when removed following that response, such as an electric shock or disapproval. Also called aversive stimulus. (p. 315)

Neglect (Adler)   Failing to give a child sufficient care and nurturing, which creates the belief that the world is a cold and unfriendly place. (p. 96)

Neurosis   A form of psychopathology that is characterized by anxiety and efforts to defend against it. No longer used as a classification of mental disorders. (p. 34)

Neurotic anxiety   *See* Anxiety (Freud).

Neurotic conflict (Horney)   An unconscious intrapsychic clash between healthy and neurotic drives, or between opposing neurotic drives. (p. 117)

Neuroticism   The extent to which one is nervous and insecure (emotionally unstable), as opposed to calm and secure (emotionally stable). One of the "Big Five" personality traits, and one of Eysenck's three supertraits. (p. 300)

Neurotic pride (Horney)   A synonym for idealized image.

Nomothetic approach (Allport)   Studying (usually) groups of people in order to discover general principles concerning human behavior. (p. 262)

Nonorganic drive (Fromm)   A noninstinctual, learned motive. Includes relatedness, transcendence, identity, and the need for a frame of orientation. (p. 131)

Nonproductive orientation (Fromm)   A frame of orientation that is undesirable because it involves the surrender of one's innate potentials for healthy growth and self-realization. (p. 136)

"Not-me" personification (Sullivan)   A normally unconscious component of personality, whose emergence into consciousness produces uncanny emotions and the feeling of not being oneself. (p. 153)

Numinosum (Jung)   A profoundly moving experience with spiritual, mystical, and religious aspects. (p. 68)

Object (Freud)   Whatever will satisfy an activated instinct. May be an inanimate object, a person, or even something fanciful and irrational. (p. 21)

Objective anxiety   *See* Anxiety (Freud).

Object-loss anxiety (Freud)   Reducing the pain caused by losing a loved one or thing by behaving like the missing object.

Observational learning (Bandura)   Learning by watching other people's behavior and its consequences for them. Also called social learning, modeling. (p. 372)

Obsessive-compulsive neurosis   A psychological disorder characterized by persistent thoughts (obsessions) and/or actions (compulsions) that are intended to reduce anxiety, but achieve only temporary relief and are therefore repeated frequently. Now called obsessive-compulsive disorder.

Oedipus complex (Freud)   Powerful feelings of love for the parent of the opposite sex and hostile jealousy for the parent of the same sex, together with powerful feelings of love for the parent of the same sex and hostile jealousy for the parent of the opposite sex. The former set of attitudes is usually the stronger. (p. 27)

One-Genus Postulate (Sullivan)   Posits that the similarities among human personalities far exceed the differences. (p. 147)

Ontological characteristics (May)   Those qualities that are distinctively human, including being-in-the-world (*Dasein*), anxiety, guilt, intentionality, and love. (p. 240)

Ontology (May)   The science of existence or being, notably of being human. (p. 240)

Openness to experience (Rogers)   A willingness to accept any experience into awareness without distorting it. (p. 203)

Openness to experience (openness)   The extent to which one is creative and nonconformist (more open) or conventional and down-to-earth (less open). One of the "Big Five" personality traits. (p. 302)

Operant (Skinner)   A type of behavior on which reinforcement is contingent, such as pecking the key in a Skinner box. (p. 315)

Operant conditioning (Skinner)   A form of learning wherein a response operates on the environment to produce a positive reinforcer or to remove a negative reinforcer, and is therefore more likely to recur. (p. 315)

Operant conditioning apparatus (Skinner)   A synonym for Skinner box, which Skinner prefers. (p. 316)

Oral fixation (oral personality) (Freud)   A personality that is dependent on other people, gullible (likely to "swallow anything"), and likely to overdo such pleasures as eating or smoking ("oral-dependent"). If fixation occurs after the teeth have emerged and biting is possible, the personality tends to be more aggressive ("oral-sadistic"), as by using ridicule and sarcasm. (p. 29)

Oral stage (Freud)   The first stage of personality development. Duration is from birth until about age 1½ years, and the primary source of pleasure is the mouth, tongue, and lips. (p. 26)

Organic drive (Fromm)   An instinctual, biological motive. Includes hunger, thirst, sex, and defense through fight (benign aggression) or flight. Also called instinctual drive. (p. 131)

Organ inferiority (Adler)   A significant physiological defect that can cause strong feelings of inferiority, and may lead to an inferiority complex if not effectively compensated. (p. 97)

Organismic valuing process (Rogers)   An innate ability to value positively those experiences that are perceived as actualizing, and to value negatively those that are perceived as nonactualizing. (p. 199)

Organization corollary (Kelly)   Posits that in order to make it easier to anticipate the future, we organize our personal constructs into a hierarchical system. Such hierarchies differ among different individuals. (p. 347)

Overdetermination (Freud)   A term referring to the numerous, complicated causes of most behavior. (p. 17)

Pampering (Adler)   Giving a child excessive attention and protection, which inhibits the development of initiative and independence, creates the impression that the world ones one a living, and leads to an inferiority complex. Also called spoiling. (p. 96)

Parapraxis (Freud)   An apparent accident that is caused by unconscious mental processes, and therefore indicates one's real feelings and beliefs; a "Freudian slip." (p. 16)

Parataxic mode (Sullivan)   A mode of experiencing internal and external stimuli that is characterized by the use of private symbols, and an inability to understand conventional concepts of cause and effect. (p. 150)

Parmia (Cattell)   Being more venturesome and bold; the converse of threctia. A temperament trait. (p. 289)

Partial reinforcement (Skinner)   A synonym for intermittent reinforcement. (p. 318)

Pathogenic   Causing psychological illness.

Pathological primaries (Cattell)   Traits that distinguish psychotics (and neurotics) from more healthy people. (p. 295)

Peak experience (Maslow)   A mystical and awesome experience that represents the highest and healthiest form of human functioning. (p. 226)

Penis envy (Freud)   The girl's jealousy of the boy's protruding sexual organ. (p. 28)

Perceived self-efficacy (Bandura)   The extent to which a person believes that he or she can perform the behaviors required by a particular situation. (p. 370)

Perceptual set   A predisposition to perceive events in one way rather than another. (p. 380)

Peripheral construct (Kelly)   A construct that can be revised without greatly altering any core constructs because it is relatively subordinate. The converse of core construct. (p. 352)

Permeable construct (Kelly)   A construct that readily admits new elements to its range of convenience, and is therefore easily revised in the light of experience. The converse of impermeable construct. (p. 350)

Persona (Jung)   A protective facade that conceals one's true inner nature in order to meet the demands of society; the outward face of personality. (p. 64)

Personal construct (Kelly)   A dichotomous concept that an individual creates in order to predict and interpret, and thereby control, the environment. (p. 346)

Personal disposition (personal trait) (Allport)   Similar in definition to common trait, but unique to a given individual. *See also* Cardinal personal disposition, Central personal dispositions, Secondary personal disposition. (p. 265)

Personality   Important and relatively stable characteristic within a person that account for consistent patterns of behavior. Aspects of personality may be observable or unobservable, and conscious or unconscious. (p. 4)

Personal unconscious (Jung)   The part of personality that includes material that is no longer (or is not yet) at the level of awareness because it has been forgotten, repressed, or perceived subliminally. (p. 65)

Person-centered theory (Rogers)   The name Rogers gave to his theory of personality. (p. 198)

Personification (Sullivan)   An organized perception of another person, which need not (and often does not) correspond well with reality. (p. 151)

Phallic fixation (phallic personality) (Freud)   A personality that is promiscuous or chastely preoccupied with feeling attractive, vain or self-contemptuous, and/or reckless or timid. (p. 31)

Phallic stage (Freud)   The third stage of personality development. Duration is from about age 2 to 5 years, and the primary source of pleasure is the penis or clitoris. The stage during which the Oedipus complex occurs. (p. 27)

Phenomenal field (Rogers)   A synonym for experience.

Philia (May)   Friendship and liking for another person. One of the four components of love. (p. 242)

Phobia   Fear of a specific object that is not dangerous. (p. 37)

Physicochemical need (Sullivan)   A physiological lack that creates a state of psychological tension; includes sexual desire, the need to eliminate bodily wastes, and deficiencies in food, water, oxygen, and body heat. (p. 148)

Play therapy (Erikson)   A form of psychotherapy in which a child creates a scene or story by using toys; the "royal road" to a child's unconscious. (p. 183)

Pleasure principle (Freud)   The goal underlying all human behavior, to achieve pleasure and avoid unpleasure (pain). (p. 18)

Poles (Kelly)   The two opposites that define a personal construct. (p. 349)

Political value (Allport)   A philosophy of life that emphasizes the love of power, not necessarily related to the field of politics. (p. 264)

Positive psychology   An area of psychology that deals with the study of optimal human functioning, including positive feelings of well-being (e.g., happiness), positive character traits (e.g., courage, resilience), and well-functioning organizations and communities. (p. 378)

Positive regard (Rogers)   Warmth, respect, and acceptance from another person; a universal, innate human need. (p. 198)

Positive reinforcement (Skinner)   *See* Reinforcement.

Positive reinforcer (Skinner)   A stimulus that increases the probability of a response when presented following that response, such as food or approval. (p. 315)

Positive self-regard (Rogers)   Accepting and respecting oneself. A learned human need, derived from the need for positive regard. (p. 198)

Praxernia (Cattell)   Being more practical and down-to-earth; the converse of autia. A temperament trait. (p. 289)

Preconscious (Freud)   The part of personality that includes material that is not within one's awareness, but can readily be brought to mind. (p. 17)

Preemptive construct (Kelly)   A construct that prohibits any other constructs from applying to its elements. A converse of propositional construct. (p. 353)

Pregenital stage (Freud)   A psychosexual stage that occurs prior to the final stage of personality development: oral, anal, urethral, or phallic. (p. 29)

Prejudice (Allport)   An irrational hostility toward other people solely because of their presumed membership in a particular group. (p. 270)

Premsia (Cattell)   Being more tender-minded, sensitive, and clinging; the converse of harria. A temperament trait. (p. 289)

Preverbal construct (Kelly)   A construct that is not associated with a verbal label, usually because it was learned prior to the development of language skills, and is therefore difficult to identify and communicate. (p. 355)

Primal scene (Freud)   Observing one's parents' sexual intercourse. (p. 34)

Primary gain (Freud)   The partial discharge of libido provided by neurotic symptoms. (p. 37)

Primary process (Freud)   The chaotic, irrational mode of thought representative of the id. (p. 19)

Primordial image (Jung)   A synonym for archetype.

Principle of entropy (Jung)   The tendency for psychic energy to flow from a more highly valued to a less highly valued part of personality, just as heat flows from a warmer to a colder body. (p. 62)

Principle of equivalence (Jung)   The tendency for psychic energy that is withdrawn from one part of personality to reappear elsewhere within the psyche. (p. 62)

Principle of opposites (Jung)   Posits that personality consists of many contradictory ideas, emotions, and instincts, and the spark of life is created from the tension between these extremes. (p. 62)

Probability of a response (Skinner)   The likelihood that a response will be emitted in the future. (p. 321)

Productive orientation (Fromm)   A healthy frame of orientation that involves the fulfillment of one's positive innate potentials. Characterized by love, biophilia, work that benefits oneself and others, and rational thought. (p. 136)

Programmed instruction (Skinner)   An approach to education wherein specific correct responses are promptly reinforced, often by a teaching machine, in a sequence designed to produce optimal learning. (p. 330)

Progression (Jung)   A forward movement of libido, favoring personal growth and development. (p. 71)

Projection (Freud, Jung)   Unconsciously attributing one's own threatening impulses, emotions, or beliefs to other people or things; a defense mechanism. (p. 22)

Propositional construct (Kelly)   A construct that does not limit other constructs from applying to its elements. The converse of preemptive construct and constellatory construct. (p. 354)

Propriate striving (Allport)   Forming the intentions and goals that give purpose to one's life. (p. 267)

Proprium (Allport)   The unifying core of personality; somewhat similar to self or ego. (p. 266)

Protension (Cattell)   Being more suspicious and (unconsciously) projecting anger onto others; the converse of alaxia. A temperament trait. (p. 289)

Prototaxic mode (Sullivan)   The primitive mode of experiencing internal and external stimuli that is prominent in early infancy, consists of a succession of momentary discrete states, is incapable of such distinctions as before and after or self and others, and cannot be communicated. (p. 150)

Psychic determinism (Freud)   The principle that nothing in the psyche happens by chance; all mental activity has a prior cause. (p. 16)

Psychic energy (Freud, Jung)   The "fuel" that powers all mental activity; an unobservable, abstract construct. (p. 16)

Psychoanalysis (Freud)   (1) The name Freud gave to his theory of personality. (2) The method of psychotherapy devised by Freud. (p. 14)

Psychoanalyst (analyst)   A person who practices psychoanalytic therapy, either Freudian or a modified version.

Psychodynamic perspective   Theories of personality that emphasize the unconscious: many important aspects of personality are beyond our awareness and can be brought to consciousness only with great difficulty, if at all. (p. 1)

Psychology   The science of behavior and mental processes.

Psychology of personal constructs (Kelly)   The name Kelly gave to his theory of personality. (p. 345)

Psychosexual stages (Freud)   Specific periods through which every child's personality develops, each of which is characterized by a particular erotogenic zone that serves as the primary source of pleasure. (p. 26)

Psychosis   A severe form of psychopathology that involves bizarre beliefs and thoughts, major distortions of reality, and an inability to function in society; usually requires hospitalization. (p. 37)

Psychosocial identity (Erikson)   A synonym for identity.

Psychotherapist   A person who treats mental illness using psychological methods, not necessarily psychoanalytic.

Psychoticism (Eysenck)   The extent to which one is egocentric, aggressive, and lacking in concern for the rights and feelings of other people; one of the three supertraits. (p. 300)

Punishment (Skinner)   A procedure designed to reduce the probability of an operant, wherein the operant is followed by the presentation of a negative reinforcer or the removal of a positive reinforcer. The converse of reinforcement. (p. 324)

Purpose (Erikson)   The courage to visualize and pursue valued goals. The emergence of this ego quality indicates that the crisis of the third epigenetic stage has been successfully resolved. (p. 177)

Q data (Cattell)   Personality data obtained through self-reports or questionnaires wherein participants describe themselves. (p. 288)

Q-sort   A method for measuring a person's self-concept. A set of cards, each of which contains a single descriptive phrase ("I set high standards for myself"), is sorted into a 9-point scale with an approximately normal distribution that varies from least descriptive to most descriptive. (p. 209)

Quaternity (Jung)   A four-sided symbol that is similar to the mandala.

Radicalism (Cattell)   Being more liberal, free-thinking, and experimenting; the converse of conservatism of temperament. A temperament trait. (p. 290)

Range corollary (Kelly)   Posits that a personal construct is useful for anticipating only some types of events, and this range of convenience may be narrow or wide. (p. 349)

Range of convenience (Kelly)   The particular aspects of behavior for which a personal construct, or a scientific theory, is generally well suited. (p. 345)

Rationalization (Freud)   Using and believing superficially plausible explanations in order to justify illicit behavior and reduce feelings of guilt; a defense mechanism. (p. 23)

Reaction formation (Freud)   Repressing threatening beliefs, emotions, or impulses and unconsciously replacing them with their opposites; a defense mechanism. (p. 22)

Reality principle (Freud) Delaying the discharge of tension until a suitable object has been found; a function of the ego. (p. 19)

Receptive orientation (Fromm) A nonproductive frame of orientation that seeks to obtain rewards by being loved and cared for. (p. 136)

Reciprocal determinism (Bandura) The continuous interrelationship of behavior, internal personal factors (e.g., thoughts, beliefs, expectations), and environmental influences, any one of which may cause any of the others. (p. 367)

Reciprocal inhibition Using a positive stimulus to inhibit the anxiety caused by an aversive stimulus, with the latter first presented at a considerable distance and gradually brought closer until it can be handled without anxiety. (p. 327)

Regression (Freud) (1) Unconsciously adopting behavior typical of an earlier and safer time in one's life; a defense mechanism. (p. 24) (2) A reverse flow of libido to an object previously abandoned, or to an earlier psychosexual stage. (p. 31)

Regression (Jung) A backward movement of libido to earlier memories or periods of development. May be a creative process that liberates neglected aspects of personality. (p. 71)

Reinforcement (1) In classical conditioning: presenting a conditioned stimulus followed by an unconditioned stimulus. (2) In operant conditioning: following a response with the presentation of a positive reinforcer (positive reinforcement), or with the removal of a negative reinforcer (negative reinforcement), thereby increasing its probability of occurrence. (p. 315)

Reinforcement (Bandura) An increase in the frequency of certain behaviors because of expectations that they will gain rewards or avoid punishment. (p. 368)

Reinforcer (Skinner) Any stimulus that increases the probability of a response when presented (positive reinforcer) or removed (negative reinforcer). (p. 315)

Relatedness (Fromm) A nonorganic drive for interpersonal relationships, which results from feelings of isolation and the physical weakness of the human species. Sometimes called rootedness. (p. 131)

Religious value (Allport) A philosophy of life that emphasizes a mystical desire for unity with some higher reality. (p. 264)

Repetition compulsion (Freud) An inborn unconscious tendency to repeat previous experiences.

Repression (Freud, Erikson) Unconsciously eliminating threatening material from consciousness and using anticathexes to prevent it from regaining consciousness, and therefore being unable to recall it; a defense mechanism. (p. 20)

Repression (Jung) Unconsciously eliminating threatening material from consciousness and relegating it to the personal unconscious. In contrast to Freudian theory, repression is not actively maintained and repressed material may be recovered fairly easily. (p. 64)

Repression (May) Excluding any of the ontological characteristics from consciousness. (p. 241)

Rep test (Kelly) *See* Role Construct Repertory Test.

Resignation (Horney) A synonym for moving away from people.

Resistance (Freud) The patient's unconscious attempts to defeat the purpose of psychoanalytic therapy and preserve illicit id wishes. May take any form that violates the fundamental rule of free association, such as long silences, refusing to talk about certain topics, telling carefully structured stories, or being absent from therapy. (p. 40)

Respondent conditioning A synonym for classical conditioning.

Response (Skinner) (1) A single instance of an operant, such as one peck of the disk in a Skinner box. (2) A synonym for operant. (p. 321)

Response generalization (Skinner)   A change in the probability of a response that has not been conditioned, because it is similar to one that has. (p. 319)

Response induction (Skinner)   A synonym for response generalization.

Response shaping (Skinner)   A synonym for shaping.

Ritualizations (Erikson)   Interpersonal rituals that help the ego to adapt to the standards and demands of society. (p. 180)

Role (Kelly)   A specific pattern of behavior that is determined by construing the personal constructs of other people. (p. 351)

Role confusion (Erikson)   A synonym for identity confusion.

Role Construct Repertory Test (Rep Test) (Kelly)   A measure designed to provide preliminary information about a client's personal constructs and psychological problems, wherein the client forms triads of significant people and devises constructs to describe how two members of each triad are alike yet different from the third. (p. 357)

Role-playing (Kelly)   Behaving according to what one believes another person thinks; putting oneself in another person's shoes. A person who can play various roles (spouse, parent, friend, leader, follower) is more easily anticipated by other people, and is therefore more likely to develop effective interpersonal relationships. (p. 351)

Rootedness (Fromm)   (1) A synonym for relatedness. (2) Feeling that one has a firm place in the world; a nonorganic drive. (p. 131)

Rubricizing (Maslow)   Describing people, events, or experiences by using labels and categories, and therefore ignoring their unique qualities.

Sadism (Fromm)   A desire to dominate and inflict pain on others. (p. 134)

Satiation (Skinner)   (1) Decreasing the probability of an operant by providing reinforcement without requiring the correct response to be made. (2) The resulting decrease in the probability of an operant. (p. 319)

Schedules of reinforcement (Skinner)   Programs of (usually) intermittent reinforcement, including interval schedules, ratio schedules, and various combinations thereof. (p. 318)

Schema   A mental framework for organizing and interpreting information. (p. 379)

Schizophrenia   A severe psychological disorder characterized by bizarre beliefs (delusions), disorganized and fragmented thinking (which may lead to speech that seems to make no sense), hallucinations (usually auditory), and inappropriate emotions. A psychotic disorder that usually requires hospitalization, though there may be periods of remission in some cases.

Secondary gain (Freud)   An incidental advantage provided by neurotic symptoms, such as avoiding unpleasant tasks or receiving sympathy from others. (p. 37)

Secondary personal disposition (secondary personal trait) (Allport)   A personal disposition that influences behavior less strongly, and less frequently, than does a central personal disposition. (p. 266)

Secondary process (Freud)   The logical, self-preservative, problem-solving mode of thought representative of the ego. (p. 19)

Secondary reinforcement (Skinner)   A synonym for conditioned reinforcement. (p. 319)

Selective inattention (Sullivan)   Deliberately, albeit unconsciously, not noticing threatening stimuli in order to reduce anxiety. (p. 151)

Self (Jung)   The new center of personality that results from individuation, unifies the various opposites, and lies between consciousness and the unconscious. (p. 70)

Self (Sullivan)   *See* Self-system.

Self (Rogers)   A synonym for self-concept.

Self-actualization (Rogers)   The tendency to satisfy the demands of the self-concept. If the learned self-actualizing tendency remains unified (congruent) with the inborn actualizing tendency, the individual is psychologically well adjusted. (p. 201)

Self-actualization (Maslow)   Fulfilling one's own innate potentials; the highest and most pleasurable need, but also the most difficult to recognize and satisfy. A growth motive, similar to actualization (*not* self-actualization) in Rogerian theory. (p. 222)

Self-concept (Rogers)   A learned, conscious sense of being separate and distinct from other people and things. (p. 201)

Self-construct (Kelly)   The personal construct that distinguishes those elements that relate to oneself from those that involve other people. (p. 354)

Self-contempt (Horney)   Hating one's true abilities, feelings, and wishes because they seem much worse than the glorious idealized image. (p. 119)

Self-dynamism (Sullivan)   *See* Self-system.

Self-effacement (Horney)   A synonym for moving toward people.

Self-efficacy (Bandura)   *See* Perceived self-efficacy.

Self-esteem (Sullivan)   How favorably an individual's self-personification compares to personifications of important people in his or her life. Very low self-esteem occurs when most or all personifications of other people seem superior to one's self-personification, and is similar to the Adlerian inferiority complex. (p. 157)

Self-esteem (Rogers)   How favorably or unfavorably a person evaluates his or her self-concept. (p. 210)

Self-esteem (Allport)   How favorably or unfavorably a person evaluates his or her self-concept. Also called ego-enhancement. (p. 267)

Self-extension (Allport)   Expanding the sense of self by conceiving of important external objects as "mine." Also called ego-extension. (p. 267)

Self-hate (Horney)   A synonym for self-contempt.

Self-identity (Allport)   *See* Identity.

Self-image (Allport)   The organized perception of one's own self. Should serve as an accurate guide to one's strengths and weaknesses, but may become exaggerated and establish unrealistic and unattainable standards. (p. 267)

Self-realization (Horney)   Developing one's healthy innate potentials and abilities. (p. 117)

Self-reinforcement (Bandura)   Establishing standards of behavior for oneself, and praising or criticizing oneself accordingly. (p. 370)

Self-sentiment integration (Cattell)   The extent to which one is controlled and compulsive (high self-sentiment strength) or lax and impulsive (low self-sentiment strength). A temperament trait. (p. 291)

Self-sufficiency (Cattell)   Being more self-reliant and resourceful; the converse of group adherence. A temperament trait. (p. 291)

Self-system (Sullivan)   The organized perception (personification) of one's own self, including the desirable "good-me" and undesirable "bad-me." Also called self-dynamism. (p. 151)

Sensation (Jung)   *See* Function.

Sentiment (Cattell)   A learned dynamic source trait that is more general than an attitude, and is subsidiary to one or more ergs. (p. 285)

Shadow (Jung)   The primitive, unwelcome side of personality. Contains material that is shameful and unpleasant, but also provides vitality and strength. (p. 65)

Shame and doubt (Erikson)   Feeling ashamed about wanting to be independent and do things one's own way (shame), and uncertain as to whether it is desirable and proper to be independent (doubt). The converse of autonomy. (p. 176)

Shaping (Skinner)   Facilitating learning by reinforcing increasingly more accurate approximations of the desired response. (p. 317)

Shoulds (Horney)   Commands to conform to the idealized image that come from one's own personality, but may be externalized and appear (incorrectly) to be imposed by other people. (p. 121)

Shrewdness (Cattell)   Being more astute and socially aware; the converse of artlessness. A temperament trait. (p. 290)

Significant other (Rogers)   An important source of positive regard, such as a parent. (p. 198)

Sixteen Personality Factor Questionnaire (16 P.F.) (Cattell)   A measure of 15 temperament source traits, and one ability source trait (intelligence). (p. 288)

Sizia (Cattell)   Being more reserved, detached, critical, and aloof; the converse of affectia. A temperament trait, similar to introversion. (p. 288)

Social-cognitive theory (Bandura)   The name Bandura gave to his psychological theory. Also called social learning theory. (p. 365)

Social feeling (Adler)   A synonym for social interest.

Social interest (Adler)   An innate potential to relate to and cooperate with other people. Also called community feeling, social feeling. (p. 92)

Sociality corollary (Kelly)   Posits that in order to relate effectively to another person, we must understand how that person construes the world, but we do not have to use the identical constructs ourselves. (p. 351)

Social learning (Bandura)   A synonym for observational learning.

Social learning theory (Bandura)   A synonym for social-cognitive theory. (p. 365)

Social reinforcers (Skinner)   Reinforcers that consist of human interactions, such as attention, approval, smiles, and hugs. (p. 332)

Social value (Allport)   A philosophy of life that emphasizes a concern for and love of other people. (p. 264)

Somnolent detachment (Sullivan)   A "safety" dynamism that serves the desirable purpose of preventing anxiety from becoming too intense. However, too much detachment can be harmful.

Source trait (Cattell)   A basic element of personality, identifiable only through factor analysis. The converse of surface trait. (p. 285)

Specification equation (Cattell)   A weighted sum of an individual's traits, used to predict what that person will do in a given situation. (p. 291)

Spoiling (Adler)   A synonym for pampering.

Spontaneous recovery (Skinner)   A temporary increase in the probability of an operant that is undergoing extinction, which occurs without any additional reinforcement. (p. 322)

Stability (Eysenck)   The extent to which one is emotionally secure; the converse of neuroticism. (p. 300)

Stagnation (Erikson)   Refusing to care about future generations, and behaving as though one were one's own special child. The converse of generativity. (p. 180)

Stereotype (Sullivan)   A personification that is rigidly and equally applied to a group of people, and obscures the true differences among them. (p. 151)

Stimulus generalization (Skinner)   The occurrence of a conditioned response to a stimulus that resembles the conditioned stimulus, without any further conditioning. (p. 319)

Stimulus induction (Skinner)   A synonym for stimulus generalization.

Striving for self-perfection (perfection, significance) (Adler)   Synonyms for striving for superiority.

Striving for superiority (Adler)   A universal, innate drive to overcome feelings of inferiority by mastering our formidable environment. Healthy strivings for superiority are guided by social interest, whereas pathological strivings for superiority ignore the welfare of others. Also called striving for perfection, striving for self-perfection, striving for significance. (p. 93)

Structural model (Freud)   Defining the structure of personality in terms of id, ego, and superego. (p. 18)

Study of Values, A (Allport)   A questionnaire devised by Allport that measures the relative importance to an individual of the six value orientations. (p. 271)

Style of life (Adler)   A person's chosen life goals and the methods used to achieve them. (p. 98)

Subception (Rogers)   Apprehending stimuli below the level of awareness. Similar to Jung's construct of subliminal perception. (p. 199)

Sublimation (Freud)   Unconsciously channeling illicit instinctual impulses into socially acceptable outlets. A form of displacement, but one that represents ideal behavior. (p. 15)

Sublimation (Sullivan)   The unconscious substitution of a partially satisfying behavior for one that would be more gratifying, but would arouse greater anxiety. (p. 154)

Subliminal perception (Jung)   A sensory impression that influences our behavior, but is not strong enough for us to be aware of it. (p. 65)

Submergence (Kelly)   Difficulty in becoming aware of one pole of a personal construct, usually because it has intolerable implications. (p. 355)

Submissiveness (Cattell)   Being more humble, docile, and accommodating; the converse of dominance. A temperament trait. (p. 289)

Subordinate construct (Kelly)   A personal construct that is included as an element of another (superordinate) construct. (p. 348)

Subsidation chain (Cattell)   The relationship between an attitude, a sentiment, and the erg they are intended to satisfy. The basic unit of a dynamic lattice. (p. 287)

Successive approximations (Method of)   A synonym for shaping. (p. 318)

Superego (Freud, Erikson)   The part of personality that establishes standards of right and wrong and communicates these standards to the ego. (p. 24)

Superego strength (Cattell)   The extent to which one is conscientious and moralistic (high superego strength), or expedient and disregards rules (low superego strength). A temperament trait. (p. 289)

Superiority complex (Adler)   Pathological feelings of power and arrogance that conceal an underlying inferiority complex. (p. 102)

Superordinate construct (Kelly)   A personal construct that includes another (subordinate) construct among its elements. The more constructs that it includes, the more superordinate it is. (p. 348)

Superstitious behavior (Skinner)   Behavior that does not operate on the environment to produce reinforcement, but has been strengthened by poorly designed contingencies. (p. 326)

Supertraits (Eysenck)   Three traits that consistently emerge from factor-analytic studies as the most important: introversion–extraversion, neuroticism, and psychoticism. (p. 300)

Surface trait (Cattell)   A manifest personality characteristic resulting from the combination of two or more source traits. Not a basic element of personality, no matter how fundamental it may appear. (p. 292)

Surgency (Cattell)   Being more happy-go-lucky and enthusiastic; the converse of desurgency. A temperament trait. (p. 289)

Suspension (Kelly)   Difficulty in becoming aware of an element because revisions in one's system have excluded those personal constructs that are capable of interpreting it.

Symbol (Freud, Jung)   An entity which conveys a meaning that is not immediately apparent; a representation of something vague and unknown. The "language" in which dreams occur. (p. 33)

Symbolic language (Fromm)   A mode of expression wherein one entity stands for another; found in dreams, fairy tales, and myths. (p. 137)

Synchronicity (Jung)   A relationship between events that is based on meaningful coincidence, rather than cause and effect. (p. 80)

Syntality (Cattell)   The personality of a group, including the prediction of group behavior through appropriate specification equations. (p. 299)

Syntaxic mode (Sullivan)   The most highly developed form of experiencing internal and external stimuli, characterized by the use of socially understood symbols (such as language) and by an understanding of conventional concepts of cause and effect. (p. 150)

Systematic desensitization   A form of behavior therapy wherein the client imagines a hierarchical sequence of feared stimuli (anxiety hierarchy), and inhibits the resulting anxiety by practicing previously taught techniques of muscular relaxation. *See also* In vivo desensitization. (p. 328)

T data (Cattell)   Personality data obtained through written or other tests. (p. 288)

Teleology   The belief that personality is shaped by our intentions and plans for the future. (p. 63)

Temperament   An inborn tendency to be more relaxed, cheerful, and easygoing or more irritable, tense, and excitable. (p. 389)

Temperament trait (Cattell)   A trait that determines the style with which one strives to reach a particular goal. (p. 288)

Tension (Sullivan)   Feelings of discomfort caused by a physicochemical need, the need for sleep, anxiety, or the need to express maternal tenderness. (p. 148)

T-group (Rogers)   A synonym for encounter group.

Theoretical value (Allport)   A philosophy of life that emphasizes an intellectual desire to discover truth and organize one's knowledge, as by becoming a scientist or philosopher. (p. 263)

Theory   An unproved speculation about certain phenomena, which provides us with descriptions and explanations when more factual information is not available. (p. 4)

Theory of personality   An "educated guess" about important aspects of human behavior, which may be based on clinical observation of empirical research (or both). (p. 5)

Thinking (Jung)   *See* Function.

Threat (Kelly)   The awareness of imminent, widespread changes in one's core constructs. (p. 354)

Threctia (Cattell)   Being more shy and timid; the converse of parmia. A temperament trait. (p. 289)

Thrownness (May)   A term referring to those few aspects of existence into which we are cast by birth and cannot control through our own choices, such as having instinctual needs and a culture with certain expectations. (p. 240)

Tight construct (Kelly)   A construct that leads to unvarying, clear-cut predictions. The converse of loose construct. (p. 356)

Token economy   A form of behavior therapy, based on Skinnerian operant conditioning, wherein desirable behaviors are followed with conditioned positive reinforcers (such as plastic tokens) that can later be exchanged for reinforcers chosen by the client. (p. 327)

Topographic model (Freud)   Defining the structure of personality in terms of the unconscious, preconscious, and conscious; abandoned by Freud as inadequate. (p. 17)

Trait (Allport)   An aspect of personality that initiates and guides consistent forms of behavior. *See also* Common trait, Personal disposition. (p. 265)

Trait (Cattell)   A psychological structure that is relatively stable and predictable, and characterizes an individual's personality. Traits vary in function (dynamic traits, temperament traits, ability traits), origin (innate traits, learned traits), centrality (source traits, surface traits), and uniqueness (common traits, unique traits). (p. 285)

Trait perspective   Theories of personality that emphasize a surface-oriented approach, describe the conscious and concrete aspects of personality in straightforward terms (e.g., "friendliness," "ambitiousness"), and deemphasize the unconscious and abstract explanations of human behavior. (p. 257)

Transcendence (Fromm)   Rising above the animal state and exerting a significant effect on one's environment; a nonorganic drive. Healthy transcendence is characterized by creativity and love, whereas pathological transcendence includes hate and malignant aggression. Similar to Adler's construct of striving for superiority. (p. 132)

Transcendent function (Jung)   A process that joins various opposing forces into a coherent middle ground, and furthers the course of individuation by providing personal lines of development that could not be reached by adhering to collective norms. (p. 63)

Transference (Freud)   An unconscious displacement of emotion or behavior, by the patient, from some other important person (such as a parent) to the psychoanalyst. Produces the attachment that makes positive therapeutic change possible, but may defeat the therapy if it becomes too negative. (p. 40)

Transference neurosis (Freud)   A major intensification of transference, wherein the relationship to the analyst becomes even more important than the problems that originally brought the patient into psychoanalytic therapy. (p. 40)

Transpersonal unconscious (Jung)   A synonym for collective unconscious.

Trust (Erikson)   *See* Basic trust.

Turning against the self (Freud)   A form of displacement in which one unconsciously diverts aggressive or destructive behavior from other, more threatening objects (such as a parent) to oneself.

Umwelt (May)   The world of internal and external objects, which forms our physiological and physical environment ("around-world"). One of the three simultaneous and interrelated modes of being-in-the-world. (p. 239)

Uncanny emotions (Sullivan)   Extremely unpleasant feelings, including dread, horror, and loathing, which involve intense anxiety and often indicate the emergence of the "not-me" personification. (p. 148)

Unconditional positive regard (Rogers)   Accepting and respecting another person's self-concept and feelings; a nonjudgmental and nonpossessive caring for another person. (Does not apply to specific behaviors, which may be valued negatively.) (p. 201)

Unconditional positive self-regard (Rogers)   An ideal state of total self-acceptance, or absence of any conditions of worth. (p. 203)

Unconditioned response   An automatic, unlearned response elicited by an unconditioned stimulus. (p. 311)

Unconditioned stimulus   A stimulus that automatically elicits a particular (unconditioned) response, without any learning or conditioning being necessary. (p. 311)

Unconscious (Freud)   The part of personality that includes material that is not within one's awareness and cannot readily be brought to mind. (p. 17)

Undoing (Freud)   Unconsciously adopting ritualistic behaviors that symbolically negate previous actions or thoughts that cause feelings of guilt; a defense mechanism. (p. 24)

Unique trait (Cattell)   A trait characteristic of a particular individual, but not others. (p. 285)

Untroubled adequacy (Cattell)   Being more secure, self-assured, and serene; the converse of guilt proneness. A temperament trait. (p. 290)

Urethral stage (Freud)   Not clearly distinct from the second (anal) stage of personality development. The primary source of pleasure is the urethra, the canal that carries urine from the bladder. (p. 27)

Value (Jung)   The amount of psychic energy that is invested in a mental event. The greater the value, the more the event is preferred or desired. (p. 61)

Value (value orientation) (Allport)   A unifying philosophy that gives meaning to one's life. Types include theoretical, economic, esthetic, social, political, and religious. (p. 263)

Variable-interval schedule (VI) (Skinner)   Reinforcing the first correct response that occurs after a varying interval of time, measured from the preceding reinforcement, with the series of intervals having a specified mean. A schedule of intermittent (partial) reinforcement. (p. 318)

Variable-ratio schedule (VR) (Skinner)   Reinforcing the last of a varying number of correct responses, counted from the preceding reinforcement, with the series of ratios having a specified mean. A schedule of intermittent (partial) reinforcement. (p. 318)

Vicarious punishment (Bandura)   A decrease in the frequency of certain behaviors, which occurs as the result of seeing others punished for the same actions (i.e., through observational learning). (p. 373)

Vicarious reinforcement (Bandura)   An increase in the frequency of certain behaviors, which occurs as the result of seeing others rewarded for the same actions (i.e., through observational learning). (p. 373)

Will (May)   The conscious capacity to move toward one's self-selected goals. (p. 241)

Will power (Erikson)   The determination to exercise free choice as well as self-control. The emergence of this ego quality indicates that the crisis of the second epigenetic stage has been successfully resolved. (p. 176)

Wisdom (Erikson)   Not fearing death because one has made the most of life. The emergence of this ego quality indicates that the crisis of the eighth epigenetic stage has been successfully resolved. (p. 180)

Wish (Freud)   A synonym for drive.

Wish-fulfillment (Freud)   Forming a mental image of an object that will satisfy a need; a function of the id. (p. 18)

Word association test (Jung)   A procedure for determining the strength of a complex. The tester reads a list of words, one at a time, and the respondent answers with the first word that comes to mind. The stronger the complex, the more likely are unusual responses, hesitations, and physiological changes. (p. 62)

Working through (Freud)   The process by which the patient in psychoanalytic therapy becomes convinced that formerly unconscious material is true, learns to avoid repressing it, and gradually refines this new knowledge into appropriate and effective behavior. (p. 40)

Glossary of Theorists

Note: To help students who may wish to engage in further study, this Glossary includes several personality theorists whose work was not discussed in the text.

Alfred Adler   Like Jung, an early opponent of Freud; unlike Jung (and Freud), he regarded consciously chosen goals as much more important than unconscious processes and argued that personality is always a unified, indivisible whole. See Chapter 4.

Gordon Allport   Using data obtained from empirical research, rather than clinical insight, he devised the trait perspective. See Chapter 12.

Albert Bandura   Argued that Skinner was wrong to reject important inner cognitive causes of behavior and to focus primarily on operant conditioning, which is less important than observational (social) learning. See Chapter 16.

Ludwig Binswanger, Medard Boss   Swiss psychiatrists who were among the first existential psychologists, but whose complicated (and at times virtually untranslatable) constructs pose grave difficulties for most readers.

Raymond Cattell   Tried to ascertain the most important traits by using the statistical technique of factor analysis. See Chapter 13.

John Dollard and Neal Miller   Dollard and Miller were the first to call attention to the importance of social (observational) learning. They also sought to synthesize the contributions of two seemingly irreconcilable theorists, Freud and Pavlov, by applying concepts of conditioning to the study of unconscious processes and inner causes of behavior. Although Dollard and Miller were researchers, they also believed strongly in the benefits of clinical observation. "Outside of psychotherapy, how many subjects have been studied for an hour a day, for five days a week, [and] for from one to three years … [and in a] life situation [which] is vital, [where] the alternatives are years of misery or years of relative peace and success?" (Dollard & Miller, 1950, p. 4; see also Miller & Dollard, 1941.)

Among Dollard and Miller's ideas are that early conflicts become unconscious because the young child cannot use language to label them properly (similar to Kelly's preverbal construct), repression occurs because it is reinforcing not to think about anxiety-provoking material, and neurosis occurs when such repressions prevent us from using thinking and reasoning to solve painful problems. "[The neurotic] is not able to solve his conflict even with the passage of time. Though obviously intelligent in some ways, he is stupid insofar as his neurotic conflict is concerned. This stupidity is not an overall affair, however. It is really a stupid area in the mind of a person who is quite intelligent in other respects" (Dollard & Miller, 1950, p. 14.)

Dollard and Miller's theory has not had much impact on modern psychology. They presented their views in a 1950 book but published nothing in this area thereafter, which is hardly the best way to reconcile such bitterly opposed theoretical camps as behaviorism and psychoanalysis. And they argued in favor of retaining Freudian techniques of psychotherapy, rather than devising the methodological innovations later achieved by the behavior therapists. Dollard and Miller are best known for their work on intrapsychic conflicts: A personality may be torn by approach–approach conflicts (having to choose between two positive alternatives), avoidance–avoidance conflicts (having to choose between two negative alternatives), approach–avoidance conflicts (one goal has both positive and negative qualities, so approaching the goal is threatening but avoiding the goal prevents reinforcement), and multiple approach–avoidance conflicts (having to choose between two or more alternatives, all of which have positive and negative qualities).

Erik Erikson   Became the leader of the psychoanalytic movement by correcting many of Freud's significant errors in ways that did not offend the establishment. Like Horney, Fromm, and Sullivan, he regarded the social determinants of personality as much more important than innate instincts. See Chapter 8.

Hans Eysenck   Like Cattell, he tried to ascertain the most important traits by using the statistical technique of factor analysis, but reached different conclusions. See Chapter 13.

Sigmund Freud   Devised the first theory of personality, psychoanalysis. See Chapter 2.

Erich Fromm   Like Horney, Sullivan, and Erikson, he regarded the social determinants of personality as much more important than innate instincts. His primary areas of interest were pathogenic societal influences and dream interpretation. See Chapter 6.

Heinz Hartmann   One of the first ego psychologists, Hartmann argued in favor of more peaceful intrapsychic functioning than Freud posited. Hartmann characterized such functions as language, memory, motor skills, and thinking as a "conflict-free ego sphere"— somewhat like the peaceful maintenance-oriented center of a nation, which is related to but distinguishable from any wars that may be occurring at its borders. Hartmann's theory failed to prove as popular as Erikson's because it is extremely abstract and metaphysical.

Karen Horney   Split with Freud over the issues of instincts, which she regarded as much less important determinants of personality than parent–child relationships, and female sexuality. Her primary area of interest was neurosis. See Chapter 5.

Carl Jung   Originally a supporter of psychoanalysis, he split with Freud in order to develop his own theoretical views about unconscious processes. See Chapter 3.

George Kelly   Devised an idiosyncratic cognitive theory of personality that does away with virtually all typical constructs and posits that we all behave very much like the research scientist. See Chapter 15.

Kurt Lewin   During the 1940s, Lewin devised a theory of personality based on the mathematical concepts of topology (the properties of space), boundaries (divisions between sectors of the life space that are more or less difficult to cross), vectors (the forces impelling one toward or away from a goal), and valences (the positive or negative values of people and objects) that is no longer popular. Also a social psychologist, Lewin was one of the first to advocate the styles of participatory management that have been used to good effect in countries like Japan, and to call attention to the "sleeper effect" in persuasive messages: a message may initially have no effect because it has been advocated by a questionable or negative source, but is accepted some time later when the source of the message has been forgotten.

Abraham Maslow   Like Rogers, one of the foremost exponents of humanistic psychology; unlike Rogers, he tried to combine the best aspects of various theories of personality (including Freudian psychoanalysis) into a meaningful whole and focused on studying the psychologically healthiest people. See Chapter 10.

Rollo May   Devised a theory of personality based on existential psychology, a philosophy that emphasizes the need to assert our being-in-the-world despite our fears of the inevitable death that awaits us all. See Chapter 11.

Neal Miller   *See* John Dollard and Neal Miller.

Walter Mischel   Showed that behavior is much less consistent across different situations than is commonly believed, a particularly acute problem for trait theory. Using honesty as an example, a person may not steal money that a friend leaves on the table or rob a bank, but may cheat on income tax returns and often drive 15 miles above the speed limit.

Henry Murray   A colleague of Allport's at Harvard, Murray's theory of personality differs in almost every respect. Murray became a devotee of unconscious processes after meeting with Jung in 1925, at age 32. "We talked for hours, sailing down the lake and smoking before the hearth of his Faustian retreat. 'The great floodgates of the wonder-world swung open,' and I saw things that my philosophy had never dreamt of. … and I went off decided on depth psychology. I had *experienced* the unconscious" (Murray, 1940, pp. 152–153; see also Murray, 1951; 1959; 1967; 1968a; Murray & Kluckhohn, 1953; Murray et al., 1938). Murray sought to extend the scope of Freudian psychoanalysis to healthy individuals. "Freud's contribution to man's conceptualized knowledge of himself is the greatest since the works of Aristotle; but his view of human nature is exceptionally—perhaps projectively and inevitably—one-sided. … Were an analyst to be confronted by that much heralded but still missing specimen of the human race—the normal man—he would be struck dumb, for once, through lack of appropriate ideas. … [My theory set forth] a health-oriented extension of, and complement to, the illness-oriented Freudian system" (Murray, 1959, p. 37; 1968a, p. 6; 1951/1968, p. 64).

According to Murray, human motivation involves some 20 needs that may be conscious or unconscious and often operate in complicated combinations. For example, if an unscrupulous politician befriends an informant in order to obtain scandalous facts about an opponent and win an election, the need for affiliation (with the informant) is subsidiary to the need for aggression (against the opponent), which is in turn subsidiary to the need for achievement (to win the election).

Although Murray's name remains a respected one, most of his constructs have had little impact on modern psychology. Perhaps because his terminology is often abstruse and his writings dry and technical, his effort to extend the scope of Freudian psychoanalysis was overshadowed by Erikson's ego psychology. Murray is best known for two ideas: need for achievement and the Thematic Apperception Test.

Need for achievement involves the desire to accomplish something difficult, master a subject, and/or exceed what others have done. As with self-esteem and perceived self-efficacy, those who are high in need for achievement tend to set higher goals and accomplish more. But they may well find it difficult to delegate tasks to subordinates or accept suggestions, because they feel that the task is more likely to be done correctly if they do it themselves and do it their way, or to be interested in any activity where there is no clear-cut measure of success.

The Thematic Apperception Test is designed to measure unconscious processes, and it ranks with the well-known Rorschach inkblot test in popularity. Participants are shown a series of twenty pictures, which are relatively ambiguous with regard to the emotions of the characters and the events taking place, and are asked to make up a story that tells what led up to the events in the picture, what is happening at the moment, and the probable outcome. The underlying rationale is that participants will inevitably (and unconsciously) project their important feelings, motives, and beliefs into the stories. (See Morgan & Murray, 1935; Murray, 1943; Murray et al., 1938.)

Carl Rogers   A humanistic psychologist who strongly objected to Freud's wholly negative view of human nature, and argued that our innate potentials are entirely positive. See Chapter 9.

Julian Rotter   In addition to emphasizing the importance of locus of control (see Chapter 16), Rotter's theory attributes behavior to both expectations and reinforcement value. As in

Bandura's theory, we are more likely to behave in ways that we expect to be reinforced. But we do not base our behavior solely on the expectancy of success, for then we would try only the easiest of tasks. We may well try for reinforcement that is highly valued but relatively unlikely, as when a job seeker applies for a prestigious and high-paying job for which there is keen competition rather than a pedestrian and lower-paying job that is easy to obtain.

William Sheldon   Sheldon believed that personality is determined by bodily characteristics (somatotypes), a theory that he devised during the 1940s. The endomorph has soft roundness throughout the body, the mesomorph is predominantly muscle and bone, and the ectomorph is long and slender with poorly developed muscles. The corpulent detective and gourmand Nero Wolfe is primarily an endomorph, the muscular Arnold Schwarzenegger is primarily a mesomorph, and the lean and wiry Sherlock Holmes is primarily an ectomorph. People rarely belong entirely to one type (Holmes was far from a weakling), so Sheldon evaluated individuals on three 7-point scales regarding the extent to which they matched each of these dimensions. For example, Holmes might be rated as 1-4-7: not endomorphic, moderately mesomorphic, and predominantly ectomorphic.

Sheldon also posited three basic temperaments. Viscerotonia involves a love of comfort, sociability, affection, and gluttony. Somatotonia is reflected by a craving for muscular activity, the lust for power, ruthlessness, and risk-taking. Cerebrotonia is demonstrated by inhibited behavior and avoiding social contact. Sheldon believed that there is a high correlation between bodily characteristics and temperament. But his theory is not popular among modern psychologists, who contend that he greatly overstated the influence of physical characteristics on personality and behavior.

B. F. Skinner   A behaviorist who argued that psychology should deal only with observable behavior, and that operant conditioning is a much more important type of learning than classical conditioning. See Chapter 14.

Harry Stack Sullivan   Like Horney, Fromm, and Erikson, he regarded the social determinants of personality as much more important than innate instincts. His primary areas of interest were personality development and schizophrenia. See Chapter 7.

Bibliography

Adler, A. *The neurotic constitution: Outline of a comparative individualistic psychology and psychotherapy.* Original publication: 1912. Hardcover English edition: New York: Moffat, 1917a.

Adler, A. *Study of organ inferiority and its psychical compensation: A contribution to clinical medicine.* Original publication: 1907. Hardcover English edition: New York: Nervous and Mental Disease Publishing Co., 1917b.

Adler, A. *Understanding human nature.* Original publication: 1927. Hardcover English edition: New York: Greenberg, 1927. Paperback reprint: Greenwich, Conn.: Fawcett, 1957.

Adler, A. *What life should mean to you.* Original publication: 1931. Hardcover English edition: Boston: Little Brown, 1931. Paperback reprint: New York: Capricorn Books, 1958.

Adler, A. *The problem child: The life style of the difficult child as analyzed in specific cases.* Original publication: 1930. Paperback English edition: New York: Capricorn Books, 1963.

Adler, A. *Problems of neurosis.* Original publication: 1929. Hardcover English edition: London: Routledge & Kegan Paul, 1929. Paperback reprint: New York: Harper Torch-Books, 1964a.

Adler, A. *Social interest: A challenge to mankind.* Original publication: 1933. Hardcover English edition: London: Faber & Faber, 1938. Paperback reprint: New York: Capricorn Books, 1964b.

Adler, A. *The science of living.* Original publication: 1929. Hardcover English edition: New York: Greenberg, 1929. Paperback reprint: New York: Anchor Books, 1969.

Adler, A. *The practice and theory of individual psychology.* Original publication: 1920. Hardcover English edition: London: Routledge & Kegan Paul, 1925. Paperback reprint: Totowa, N.J.: Littlefield, Adams & Co., 1973.

Adler, A. Advantages and disadvantages of the inferiority feeling. Original publication: 1933. In H. L. Ansbacher & R. R. Ansbacher (Eds.), *Superiority and social interest: A Collection of Alfred Adler's later writings.* New York: Norton, 1979a, pp. 50–58.

Adler, A. Complex compulsion as part of personality and neurosis. Original publication: 1935. In H. L. Ansbacher & R. R. Ansbacher (Eds.), *Superiority and social interest: A Collection of Alfred Adler's later writings.* New York: Norton, 1979b, pp. 71–80.

Adler, A. Compulsion neurosis. Original publication: 1931. In H. L. Ansbacher & R. R. Ansbacher (Eds.), *Superiority and social interest: A collection of Alfred Adler's later writings.* New York: Norton, 1979c, pp. 112–138.

Adler, A. The death problem in neurosis. Original publication: 1936. In H. L. Ansbacher & R. R. Ansbacher (Eds.), *Superiority and social interest: A collection of Alfred Adler's later writings.* New York: Norton, 1979d, pp. 239–247.

Adler, A. The differences between individual psychology and psychoanalysis. Original publication: 1931. In H. L. Ansbacher & R. R. Ansbacher (Eds.), *Superiority and social interest: A collection of Alfred Adler's later writings.* New York: Norton, 1979e, pp. 205–218.

Adler, A. The neurotic's picture of the world: A case study. Original publication: 1936. In H. L. Ansbacher & R. R. Ansbacher (Eds.), *Superiority and social interest: A collection of Alfred Adler's later writings.* New York: Norton, 1979f, pp. 96–111.

Adler, A. On the origin of the striving for superiority and of social interest. Original publication: 1933. In H. L. Ansbacher & R. R. Ansbacher (Eds.), *Superiority and social interest: A collection of Alfred Adler's later writings.* New York: Norton, 1979g, pp. 29–40.

Adler, A. Religion and individual psychology. Original publication: 1933. In H. L. Ansbacher & R. R. Ansbacher (Eds.), *Superiority and social interest: A collection of Alfred Adler's later writings.* New York: Norton, 1979h, pp. 271–308.

Adler, A. The structure of neurosis. Original publication: 1932. In H. L. Ansbacher & R. R. Ansbacher (Eds.), *Superiority and social interest: A collection of Alfred Adler's later writings.* New York: Norton, 1979i, pp. 83–95.

Adler, A. Typology of meeting life problems. Original publication: 1935. In H. L. Ansbacher & R. R. Ansbacher (Eds.), *Superiority and social interest: A collection of Alfred Adler's later writings.* New York: Norton, 1979j, pp. 66–70.

Ainsworth, M. D. S. Patterns of infant–mother attachments: Antecedents and effects on development. *Bulletin of the New York Academy of Medicine,* 1985, *61:* 771–791.

Allport, G. W. *Personality: A psychological interpretation.* New York: Holt, 1937.

Allport, G. W. *The use of personal documents in psychological science* (Bull. 49). New York: Social Science Research Council, 1942.

Allport, G. W. *The individual and his religion.* New York: Macmillan, 1950.

Allport, G. W. *Becoming: Basic considerations for a psychology of personality.* New Haven: Yale University Press, 1955.

Allport, G. W. *The nature of prejudice.* Reading, Mass.: Addison-Wesley, 1954. Paperback reprint (abridged): New York: Anchor Books, 1958.

Allport, G. W. *Personality and social encounter.* Boston: Beacon Press, 1960.

Allport, G. W. *Pattern and growth in personality.* New York: Holt, Rinehart & Winston, 1961.

Allport, G. W. *Letters from Jenny.* New York: Harcourt, Brace and World, 1965.

Allport, G. W. *The person in psychology: Selected essays.* Boston: Beacon Press, 1968.

Allport, G. W., & Allport, F. H. *The A–S reaction study.* Original publication: 1928. Revised edition: Boston: Houghton Mifflin, 1949.

Allport, G. W., & Postman, L. *The psychology of rumor.* New York: Holt, 1947.

Allport, G. W., & Vernon, P. E. *Studies in expressive movement.* New York: Macmillan, 1933.

Allport, G. W., Vernon, P. E., & Lindzey, G. *A study of values.* Original publication (Allport & Vernon): 1931. Third edition: Boston: Houghton Mifflin, 1960.

American Psychological Association. *Cumulative subject index to Psychological Abstracts 1981–1983.* Washington, D.C.: APA, 1984.

Anastasi, A. *Psychological testing* (4th ed.). New York: Macmillan, 1976.

Arieti, S. *Interpretation of schizophrenia* (Rev. ed.). New York: Basic Books, 1974.

Ayllon, T., & Azrin, N. H. *The token economy: A motivational system for therapy and rehabilitation.* New York: Appleton-Century-Crofts, 1968.

Bachelor, A., & Horvath, A. The therapeutic relationship. In M. A. Hubble, B. L. Duncan, & S. D. Miller (Eds.), *The heart and soul of change: What works in therapy.* Washington, D.C.: American Psychological Association, 1999. pp. 133–178.

Bandura, A. *Principles of behavior modification.* New York: Holt, Rinehart and Winston, 1969.

Bandura, A. (Ed.). *Psychological modeling: Conflicting theories.* Chicago: Aldine Atherton, 1971.

Bandura, A. *Aggression: A social learning analysis.* Englewood Cliffs, N. J.: Prentice-Hall, 1973.

Bandura, A. *Social learning theory.* Englewood Cliffs, N. J.: Prentice-Hall, 1977.

Bandura, A. Self-efficacy: Toward a unifying theory of behavioral change. *Psychological Review,* 1977b, *84:* 181–215.

Bandura, A. The self system in reciprocal determinism. *American Psychologist,* 1978, *33:* 344–358.

Bandura, A. Self-referent thought: A developmental analysis of self-efficacy. In J. H. Flavell & L. Ross (Eds.), *Social cognitive development: Frontiers and possible futures.* Cambridge, England: Cambridge University Press, 1981.

Bandura, A. Self-efficacy mechanism in human agency. *American Psychologist,* 1982a, *37:* 122–147.

Bandura, A. The self and mechanisms of agency. In J. Suls (Ed.), *Psychological perspectives of the self* (Vol. 1). Hillsdale, N.J.: Lawrence Erlbaum Associates, 1982b.

Bandura, A. *Social foundations of thought and action: A social cognitive theory.* Englewood Cliffs, N. J.: Prentice-Hall, 1986.

Bandura, A. Social cognitive theory of moral thought and action. In W. M. Kurtines & J. L. Gewritz (Eds.), *Handbook of moral behavior and development: Vol. 1. Theory.* Hillsdale, N. J.: Lawrence Erlbaum Associates, 1991.

Bandura, A. Exercise of personal and collective efficacy in changing societies. In A. Bandura (Ed.), *Self-efficacy in changing societies.* Cambridge England: Cambridge University Press, 1995.

Bandura, A. *Self-efficacy: The exercise of control.* New York: Freeman, 1997.

Bandura, A., Barbaranelli, C., Caprara, G. V., & Pastorelli, C. Multifaceted impact of self-efficacy beliefs on academic functioning. *Child Development,* 1996, *67:* 1206–1222.

Bandura, A., Ross, D., & Ross, S. A. Transmission of aggression through imitation of aggressive models. *Journal of Abnormal and Social Psychology,* 1961, *63:* 575–582.

Bandura, A., & Walters, R. *Social learning and personality development.* New York: Holt, Rinehart and Winston, 1963.

Bannister, D. (Ed.) *Issues and approaches in personal construct theory.* Orlando, Fla.: Academic Press, 1985.

Baumeister, R. F., & Tice, D. M. Anxiety and social exclusion. *Journal of Social and Clinical Psychology,* 1990, *9:* 165–196.

Baumeister, R. F., Tice, D. M., & Hutton, D. G. Self-presentational motivations and personality differences in self–esteem. *Journal of Personality,* 1989, *57:* 547–579.

Becker, E. *The denial of death*. New York: Free Press, 1973.

Bergin, A. E. The evaluation of therapeutic outcomes. In A. E. Bergin & S. L. Garfield (Eds.), *Handbook of psychotherapy and behavior change: An empirical analysis*. New York: Wiley, 1971.

Bergin, A. E., & Strupp, H. H. *Changing frontiers in the science of psychotherapy*. Chicago: Aldine Atherton, 1972.

Bieber, I. *Cognitive psychoanalysis*. New York: Aronson, 1980.

Bloland, S. E. Fame: The power and cost of a fantasy. *The Atlantic Monthly,* 1999 (Nov.), 51–62.

Blumenthal, R. Scholars seek the hidden Freud in newly emerging letters. *The New York Times,* 18 August 1981, pp. 15–16. (a)

Blumenthal, R. Did Freud's isolation, peer rejection prompt key theory reversal? *The New York Times,* 25 August 1981, pp. 13, 16. (b)

Bottome, P. *Alfred Adler: A portrait from life* (3rd ed.). New York: Vanguard Press, 1957.

Bower, G. H., & Hilgard, E. R. *Theories of learning* (5th ed.). Englewood Cliffs, N.J.: Prentice-Hall, 1981.

Bowlby, J. *Attachment and loss*. New York: Basic Books, 1969.

Bowlby, J. *A secure base: Parent–child attachment and healthy human development*. New York: Basic Books, 1988.

Boy, A. V., & Pine, G. J. *A person-centered foundation for counseling and psychotherapy* (2nd ed.). Springfield, Ill: Charles C. Thomas, 1999.

Breger, L. *Freud's unfinished journey: Conventional and critical perspectives in psychoanalytic theory*. London: Routledge & Kegan Paul, 1981.

Brenner, C. *An elementary textbook of psychoanalysis* (Rev. ed.). New York: International Universities Press, 1973. Paperback reprint: New York: Anchor Books, 1974.

Brome, V. *Jung: Man and myth*. New York: Atheneum, 1978.

Brown, J. D., & Gallagher, F. M. Coming to terms with failure: Private self-enhancement and public self-effacement. *Journal of Experimental Social Psychology,* 1992, *28:* 3–22.

Brown, J. D., & Smart, S. A. The self and social conduct: Linking self-representations to prosocial behavior. *Journal of Personality and Social Psychology,* 1991, *60:* 368–375.

Cain, D. J., & Seeman, J. (Eds.). *Humanistic psychotherapies: Handbook of research and practice*. Washington, D.C.: American Psychological Association, 2002.

Cantril, H., & Allport, G. W. *The psychology of radio*. New York: Harper, 1935.

Carlson, R. Personality. *Annual Review of Psychology,* 1975, *26:* 393–414.

Carlson, R., & Levy, N. Studies of Jungian typology: I. Memory, social perception, and social action. *Journal of Personality,* 1973, *41:* 559–576.

Cassidy, J. Child–mother attachment and the self in six-year-olds. *Child Development,* 1988, *59:* 121–134.

Cattell, R. B. *Description and measurement of personality*. New York: World Book Co., 1946.

Cattell, R. B. Concepts and methods in the measurement of group syntality. *Psychological Review,* 1948, *55:* 48–63.

Cattell, R. B. *Personality: A systematic, theoretical, and factual study*. New York: McGraw-Hill, 1950.

Cattell, R. B. *Factor analysis: An introduction and manual for psychologist and social scientist*. New York: Harper, 1952a.

Cattell, R. B. The three basic factor-analytic research designs—Their interrelations and derivatives. *Psychological Bulletin,* 1952b, *49:* 499–520.

Cattell, R. B. *Personality and motivation structure and measurement*. New York: World Book Co., 1957.

Cattell, R. B. Personality theory growing from multivariate quantitative research. In S. Koch (Ed.), *Psychology: A study of a science* (Vol. 3). New York: McGraw-Hill, 1959, pp. 257–327.

Cattell, R. B. The multiple abstract variance analysis equations and solutions for nature–nurture research on continuous variables. *Psychological Review,* 1960, *67:* 353–372.

Cattell, R. B. *Personality and social psychology*. San Diego: Knapp, 1964.

Cattell, R. B. *The scientific analysis of personality*. London: Penguin, 1965.

Cattell, R. B. (Ed.). *Handbook of multivariate experimental psychology*. Chicago: Rand McNally, 1966.

Cattell, R. B. *Abilities: Their structure, growth, and action*. Boston: Houghton Mifflin, 1971.

Cattell, R. B. *Personality and mood by questionnaire*. San Francisco: Jossey-Bass, 1973.

Cattell, R. B. Autobiography. In G. Lindzey (Ed.), *A history of psychology in autobiography* (Vol. 6). Englewood Cliffs, N.J.: Prentice-Hall, 1974, pp. 61–100.

Cattell, R. B. *Personality and learning theory: Vol. 1. The structure of personality in its environment*. New York: Springer, 1979.

Cattell, R. B. *Personality and learning theory: Vol. 2. A systems theory of maturation and structured learning*. New York: Springer, 1980.

Cattell, R. B. *The inheritance of personality and ability: Research methods and findings*. New York: Academic Press, 1982.

Cattell, R. B., & Child, D. *Motivation and dynamic structure*. New York: Wiley, 1975.

Cattell, R. B., & Dreger, R. N. (Eds.). *Handbook of modern personality theory*. New York: Appleton-Century-Crofts, 1975.

Cattell, R. B., Eber, H. W., & Tatsuoka, M. M. *Handbook for the sixteen personality factor questionnaire*. Champaign, Ill.: Institute for Personality and Ability Testing, 1970.

Cattell, R. B., & Kline, P. *The scientific analysis of personality and motivation*. New York: Academic Press, 1976.

Cattell, R. B., & Scheier, I. H. *The meaning and measurement of neuroticism and anxiety*. New York: Ronald, 1961.

Chomsky, N. Review of Skinner's *Verbal Behavior. Language,* 1959, *35:* 26–58.

Chomsky, N. The case against B. F. Skinner. *New York Review of Books,* 1971, *12/20:* 18–24.

Coles, R. *Erik H. Erikson: The growth of his work*. Boston: Little, Brown, 1970.

Cook, E. W., III, Hodes, R. L., & Lang, P. J. Preparedness and phobia: Effects of stimulus content on human visceral conditioning. *Journal of Abnormal Psychology,* 1986, *95:* 195–207.

Coopersmith, S. *Coopersmith self-esteem inventories*. Palo Alto, Calif.: Consulting Psychologists Press, 1984.

Corsini, R. (Ed.). *Current psychotherapies*. Itasca, Ill.: F. E. Peacock, 1973.

Costa, P. T., Jr., & McCrae, R. R. Personality in adulthood: A six-year longitudinal study of self-reports and spouse ratings on the NEO personality inventory. *Journal of Personality and Social Psychology,* 1988, *54:* 853–863.

Costa, P. T., Jr., & McCrae, R. R. *Revised NEO Personality Inventory (NEO-PI-R) and NEO Five-Factor Inventory (NEO-FFI) professional manual*. Odessa, Fla.: Psychological Assessment Resources, 1992a.

Costa, P. T., Jr., & McCrae, R. R. Trait psychology comes of age. In T. B. Sonderegger (Ed.), *Nebraska symposium on motivation: Psychology and aging*. Lincoln: University of Nebraska Press, 1992b.

Costa, P. T., Jr., & McCrae, R. R. Set like plaster? Evidence for the stability of adult personality. In T. F. Heatherton & J. L. Weinberger (Eds.), *Can personality change?* Washington, D.C.: American Psychological Association, 1994.

Cramer, P. Defense mechanisms in psychology today. *American Psychologist,* 2000, *55:* 637–646.

Cramer, P., & Block, J. Preschool antecedents of defense mechanism use in young adults. *Journal of Personality and Social Psychology,* 1998, *74:* 159–169.

Cramer, P., & Davidson, K. (Eds.). Defense mechanisms in contemporary personality research. *Journal of Personality,* 1998, *66*(6).

Crumbaugh, J. C. Cross-validation of purposes-in-life test based on Frankl's concept. *Journal of Individual Psychology,* 1968, *24:* 74–81.

Davey, G. C. L. Preparedness and phobias: Specific evolved associations or a generalized expectancy bias? *Behavioral and Brain Sciences,* 1995, *18:* 289–297.

Dement, W. Experimental dream studies. In J. Masserman (Ed.), *Science and psychoanalysis: Scientific proceedings of the academy of psychoanalysis* (Vol. 7). New York: Grune & Stratton, 1964.

Dement, W. *Some must watch while some must sleep*. San Francisco: Freeman, 1974.

Digman, J. M. Personality structure: Emergence of the five-factor model. *Annual Review of Psychology,* 1990, *41:* 417–440.

Dollard, J., & Miller, N. E. *Personality and psychotherapy: An analysis in terms of learning, thinking, and culture*. New York: McGraw-Hill, 1950.

Eagle, M. N. Review of P. I. Mahony: *Freud and the Rat Man. Contemporary Psychology,* 1988, *33:* 205–206.

Ellenberger, H. F. *The discovery of the unconscious*. New York: Basic Books, 1970.

Ellenberger, H. F. The story of "Anna O.": A critical review with new data. *The Journal of the History of the Behavior Sciences,* 1972, *8:* 267–279.

Elms, A. C. Skinner's dark year and *Walden Two. American Psychologist,* 1981, *36:* 470–479.

Elms, A. C. Erikson's history. *Contemporary Psychology,* 2001, *46:* 388–391.

Endler, N. S., & Speer, R. L. Personality psychology: Research trends for 1993–1995. *Journal of Personality,* 1998, *66:* 621–669.

Epstein, S. The self-concept: A review and the proposal of an integrated theory of personality. In E. Staub (Ed.), *Personality: Basic aspects and current research*. Englewood Cliffs, N. J.: Prentice-Hall, 1980.

Erikson, E. H. Statement to the committee on privilege and tenure of the University of California concerning the California loyalty oath. *Psychiatry,* 1951, *14:* 243–245.

Erikson, E. H. The dream specimen of psychoanalysis. *Journal of the American Psychoanalytic Association,* 1954, *2:* 5–56.

Erikson, E. H. *Young man Luther: A study in psychoanalysis and history*. New York: Norton, 1958.

Erikson, E. H. *Identity and the life cycle: Selected papers*. New York: International Universities Press, 1959.

Erikson, E. H. *Childhood and society* (2nd ed.). New York: Norton, 1963.

Erikson, E. H. *Insight and responsibility: Lectures on the ethical implications of psychoanalytic insight*. New York: Norton, 1964.

Erikson, E. H. The ontogeny of ritualization. In R. Loewenstein et al. (Eds.), *Psychoanalysis—a general psychology*. New York: International Universities Press, 1966.

Erikson, E. H. *Identity: Youth and crisis*. New York: Norton, 1968.

Erikson, E. H. *Gandhi's truth: On the origins of militant nonviolence*. New York: Norton, 1969.

Erikson, E. H. *In search of common ground: Conversations with Erik H. Erikson and Huey P. Newton.* New York: Norton, 1973.

Erikson, E. H. *Dimensions of a new identity: The 1973 Jefferson lectures in the humanities.* New York: Norton, 1974.

Erikson, E. H. *Life history and the historical moment.* New York: Norton, 1975.

Erikson, E. H. *Toys and reasons.* New York: Norton, 1977.

Erikson, E. H. *The life cycle completed: A review.* New York: Norton, 1982.

Erwin, E. Psychoanalytic therapy: The Eysenck argument. *American Psychologist,* 1980, *35:* 435–443.

Evans, R. I. *Dialogue with Erich Fromm.* New York: Harper & Row, 1966.

Evans, R. I. *B. F. Skinner: The man and his ideas.* New York: E. P. Dutton, 1968.

Evans, R. I. *Dialogue with Erik Erikson.* New York: Harper & Row, 1967. Paperback reprint: New York: E. P. Dutton, 1969.

Evans, R. I. *Gordon Allport: The man and his ideas.* New York: E. P. Dutton, 1970.

Evans, R. I. *Carl Rogers: The man and his ideas.* New York: E. P. Dutton, 1975.

Evans, R. I. *Jung on elementary psychology: A discussion between C. G. Jung and Richard I. Evans* (2nd ed.). New York: E. P. Dutton, 1976.

Ewen, R. B. *An introduction to theories of personality* (1st ed.). New York: Academic Press, 1980.

Ewen, R. B. Personality theories. In W. E. Craighead & C. B. Nemeroff (Eds.), *The Corsini encyclopedia of psychology and behavioral science,* (3rd ed.) New York: Wiley, 2001, pp. 1176–1181.

Eysenck, H. J. *Dimensions of personality.* London: Routledge & Kegan Paul, 1947.

Eysenck, H. J. The effects of psychotherapy: An evaluation. *Journal of Consulting Psychology,* 1952, *16:* 319–324.

Eysenck, H. J. *The effects of psychotherapy. International Journal of Psychiatry,* 1965, *1:* 99–142.

Eysenck, H. J. *The effects of psychotherapy.* New York: International Science Press, 1966.

Eysenck, H. J. *The biological basis of personality.* Springfield, Ill.: Thomas, 1967.

Eysenck, H. J. *The inequality of man.* San Diego, Calif.: Edits Publishers, 1975.

Eysenck, H. J. Development of a theory. In C. D. Spielberger (Ed.), *Personality, genetics, and behavior.* New York: Praeger, 1982.

Eysenck, H. J., & Eysenck, S. B. G. *Manual for the Eysenck personality inventory.* San Diego, Calif.: Educational and Industrial Testing Service, 1968.

Eysenck, H. J., & Eysenck, S. B. G. *Manual of the Eysenck Personality Questionnaire.* San Diego, Calif.: Educational and Industrial Testing Service, 1975.

Fenichel, O. *The psychoanalytic theory of neurosis.* New York: Norton, 1945.

Ferster, C. B., & Skinner, B. F. *Schedules of reinforcement.* New York: Appleton-Century-Crofts, 1957.

Fiedler, F. E. A comparison of therapeutic relationships in psychoanalytic, nondirective, and Adlerian therapy. *Journal of Consulting psychology,* 1950, *14:* 436–445.

Fine, R. Psychoanalysis. In R. Corsini (Ed.), *Current psychotherapies.* Itasca, Ill.: F. E. Peacock, 1973, pp. 1–33.

Fisher, S., & Greenberg, R. P. *The scientific credibility of Freud's theories and therapy.* New York: Basic Books, 1977.

Fisher, S., & Greenberg, R. P. *Freud scientifically reappraised: Testing the theories and therapy.* New York: Wiley, 1996.

Fiske, D. W. *Strategies for personality research.* San Francisco: Jossey-Bass, 1978.

Fordham, F. *An introduction to Jung's psychology.* London Pelican Books, 1966.

Foulkes, D. *The psychology of sleep.* New York: Charles Scribner's Sons, 1966.

Fransella, F. *George Kelly.* London: Sage, 1995.

Freud, A. *The ego and the mechanisms of defense.* Original publication: 1936. Revised edition: New York: International Universities Press, 1966.

Freud, S. *Character and anal erotism.* Original publication: 1908a. Standard edition: London: Hogarth Press, Vol. 9.

Freud, S. *"Civilized" sexual morality and modern nervous illness.* Original publication: 1908b. Standard edition: London: Hogarth Press, Vol. 9.

Freud, S. *Analysis of a phobia in a five-year-old boy.* Original publication: 1909. Standard edition: London: Hogarth Press, Vol. 10.

Freud, S. *A difficulty in the path of psychoanalysis.* Original publication: 1917a. Standard edition: London: Hogarth Press, Vol. 17.

Freud, S. *On the transformation of instincts with special reference to anal erotism.* Original publication: 1917b. Standard edition: London: Hogarth Press, Vol. 17.

Freud, S. *Why war?* Original publication: 1933. Standard edition: London: Hogarth Press, Vol. 22.

Freud, S. *Moses and monotheism.* Original publication: 1939. Standard edition: London: Hogarth Press, Vol. 23.

Freud, S. *Totem and taboo.* Original publication: 1912–1913. Standard edition: London: Hogarth Press, Vol. 13. Paperback reprint: New York: Norton, 1950.

Freud, S. *On dreams.* Original publication: 1901. Standard edition: London: Hogarth Press, Vol. 5. Paperback reprint: New York: Norton, 1952.

Freud, S. *Group psychology and the analysis of the ego.* Original publication: 1921. Standard edition: London: Hogarth Press, Vol. 18. Paperback reprint: New York: Norton, 1959.

Freud, S. *Beyond the pleasure principle.* Original publication: 1920. Standard edition: London: Hogarth Press, Vol. 18. Paperback reprint: New York: Norton, 1961a.

Freud, S. *Civilization and its discontents.* Original publication: 1930. Standard edition: London: Hogarth Press, Vol. 21. Paperback reprint: New York: Norton, 1961b.

Freud, S. *The future of an illusion.* Original publication: 1927. Standard edition: London: Hogarth Press, Vol. 21. Paperback reprint: New York: Norton, 1961c.

Freud, S. *The ego and the id.* Original publication: 1923. Standard edition: London: Hogarth Press, Vol. 19. Paperback reprint: New York: Norton, 1962.

Freud, S. *An autobiographical study.* Original publication: 1925. Standard edition: London: Hogarth Press, Vol. 20. Paperback reprint: New York: Norton, 1963a.

Freud, S. Fragment of an analysis of a case of hysteria. Original publication: 1905. Standard edition: London: Hogarth Press, Vol. 7. Paperback reprint: *Dora: An analysis of a case of hysteria.* New York: Collier, 1963b, pp. 21–144.

Freud, S. Formulations on the two principles of mental functioning. Original publication: 1911. Standard edition: London: Hogarth Press, Vol. 12. Paperback reprint: *General psychological theory.* New York: Collier, 1963c, pp. 21–28.

Freud, S. On narcissism: An introduction. Original publication: 1914. Standard edition: London: Hogarth Press, Vol. 14. Paperback reprint: *General psychological theory.* New York: Collier, 1963d, pp. 56–82.

Freud, S. Instincts and their vicissitudes. Original publication: 1915. Standard edition: London: Hogarth Press, Vol. 14. Paperback reprint: *General psychological theory.* New York: Collier, 1963e, pp. 83–103.

Freud, S. Repression. Original publication: 1915. Standard edition: London: Hogarth Press, Vol. 14. Paperback reprint: *General psychological theory.* New York: Collier, 1963f, pp. 104–115.

Freud, S. The unconscious. Original publication: 1915. Standard Edition: London: Hogarth Press, Vol. 14. Paperback reprint: *General psychological theory.* New York: Collier, 1963g, pp. 116–150.

Freud, S. The economic problem of masochism. Original publication: 1924. Standard edition: London: Hogarth Press, Vol. 19. Paperback reprint: *General psychological theory.* New York: Collier, 1963h, pp. 190–201.

Freud, S. *Jokes and their relation to the unconscious.* Original publication: 1905. Standard edition: London: Hogarth Press, Vol. 8. Paperback reprint: New York: Norton, 1963i.

Freud, S. *Inhibitions, symptoms, and anxiety.* Original publication: 1926. Standard edition: London: Hogarth Press, Vol. 20. Paperback reprint: *The problem of anxiety.* New York: Norton, 1963j.

Freud, S. My views on the part played by sexuality in the etiology of the neuroses. Original publication: 1906. Standard edition: London: Hogarth Press, Vol. 7. Paperback reprint: *Sexuality and the psychology of love.* New York: Collier, 1963k, pp. 11–19.

Freud, S. The psychogenesis of a case of female homosexuality. Original publication: 1920. Standard edition: London: Hogarth Press, Vol. 18. Paperback reprint: *Sexuality and the psychology of love.* New York: Collier, 1963l, pp. 133–159.

Freud, S. Some neurotic mechanisms in jealousy, paranoia, and homosexuality. Original publication: 1922. Standard edition: London: Hogarth Press, Vol. 18. Paperback reprint: *Sexuality and the psychology of love.* New York: Collier, 1963m, pp. 160–170.

Freud, S. The infantile genital organization of the libido: A supplement to the theory of sexuality. Original publication: 1923. Standard edition: London: Hogarth Press, Vol. 19. Paperback reprint: *Sexuality and the psychology of love.* New York: Collier, 1963n, pp. 171–175.

Freud, S. The dissolution of the Oedipus complex. Original publication: 1924. Standard edition: London: Hogarth Press, Vol. 19. Paperback reprint: *Sexuality and the psychology of love.* New York: Collier, 1963o, pp. 176–182.

Freud, S. Some psychological consequences of the anatomical distinction between the sexes. Original publication: 1925. Standard edition: London: Hogarth Press, Vol. 19. Paperback reprint: *Sexuality and the psychology of love.* New York: Collier, 1963p, pp. 183–193.

Freud, S. Female sexuality. Original publication: 1931. Standard edition: London: Hogarth Press, Vol. 21. Paperback reprint: *Sexuality and the psychology of love.* New York, Collier, 1963q, pp. 194–211.

Freud, S. On psychotherapy. Original publication: 1905. Standard edition: London: Hogarth Press, Vol. 7. Paperback reprint: *Therapy and technique.* New York: Collier, 1963r, pp. 63–75.

Freud, S. The future prospects of psychoanalytic therapy. Original publication: 1910. Standard edition: London: Hogarth Press, Vol. 11. Paperback reprint: *Therapy and technique.* New York: Collier, 1963s, pp. 77–87.

Freud, S. Further recommendations on the technique of psychoanalysis. I. On beginning the treatment. Original publication: 1913. Standard edition: London: Hogarth Press, Vol. 12. Paperback reprint: *Therapy and technique.* New York: Collier, 1963t, pp. 135–156.

Freud, S. Further recommendations on the technique of psychoanalysis. II. Recollection, repetition and working through. Original publication: 1914. Standard edition: London: Hogarth Press, Vol. 12. Paperback reprint: *Therapy and technique.* New York: Collier, 1963u, pp. 157–166.

Freud, S. Further recommendations on the technique of psychoanalysis. III. Observations on transference-love. Original publication: 1915. Standard edition: London: Hogarth Press, Vol. 12. Paperback reprint: *Therapy and technique*. New York: Collier, 1963v, pp. 167–179.

Freud, S. Analysis terminable and interminable. Original publication: 1937. Standard edition: London: Hogarth Press, Vol. 23. Paperback reprint: *Therapy and technique*. New York: Collier, 1963w, pp. 233–271.

Freud, S. Constructions in analysis. Original publication: 1937. Standard edition: London: Hogarth Press, Vol. 23. Paperback reprint: *Therapy and technique*. New York: Collier, 1963x, pp. 273–286.

Freud, S. Notes on a case of obsessional neurosis. Original publication: 1909. Standard edition: London: Hogarth Press, Vol. 10. Paperback reprint: *Three case histories*. New York: Collier, 1963y, pp. 15–102.

Freud, S. Psychoanalytic notes on an autobiographical account of a case of paranoia (dementia paranoides). Original publication: 1911. Standard edition: London: Hogarth Press, Vol. 12. Paperback reprint: *Three case histories*. New York: Collier, 1963z, pp. 103–186.

Freud, S. From the history of an infantile neurosis. Original publication: 1918. Standard edition: London: Hogarth Press, Vol. 17. Paperback reprint: *Three case histories*. New York: Collier, 1963aa, pp. 187–316.

Freud, S. *The interpretation of dreams*. Original publication: 1900. Standard edition: London: Hogarth Press, Vol. 4–5. Paperback reprint: New York: Avon Books, 1965a.

Freud, S. *New introductory lectures on psychoanalysis*. Original publication: 1933. Standard edition: London: Hogarth Press, Vol. 22. Paperback reprint: New York: Norton, 1965b.

Freud, S. *The psychopathology of everyday life*. Original publication: 1901. Standard edition: London: Hogarth Press, Vol. 6. Paperback reprint: New York: Norton, 1965c.

Freud, S. *Three essays on the theory of sexuality*. Original publication: 1905. Standard edition: London: Hogarth Press, Vol. 7. Paperback reprint: New York: Avon Books, 1965d.

Freud, S. *Introductory lectures on psychoanalysis* (Rev. ed.). Original publication: 1916–1917. Standard edition: London: Hogarth Press, Vol. 15–16. Paperback reprint: New York: Norton, 1966.

Freud, S. *On the history of the psychoanalytic movement*. Original publication: 1914. Standard edition: London: Hogarth Press, Vol. 14. Paperback reprint: New York: Norton, 1967.

Freud, S. *An outline of psychoanalysis* (Rev. ed.). Original publication: 1940. Standard edition: London: Hogarth Press, Vol. 23. Paperback reprint: New York: Norton, 1969a.

Freud, S. *The question of lay analysis*. Original publication: 1926. Standard edition: London: Hogarth Press, Vol. 20. Paperback reprint: New York: Norton, 1969b.

Freud, S., & Breuer, J. *Studies on hysteria*. Original publication: 1895. Standard edition: London: Hogarth Press, Vol. 2. Paperback reprint: New York: Avon Books, 1966.

Friedman, L. J. *Identity's architect: A biography of Erik H. Erikson*. New York: Scribner, 1999.

Fromm, E. *The forgotten language: An introduction to the understanding of dreams, fairy tales, and myths*. New York: Holt, Rinehart, & Winston, 1951. Paperback reprint: New York: Grove Press, 1957.

Fromm, E. *Marx's concept of man*. New York: Frederick Ungar, 1961.

Fromm, E. *Beyond the chains of illusion: My encounter with Marx and Freud*. New York: Simon & Schuster, 1962a.

Fromm, E. Interview in *The New York Post*, 22 April 1962b.

Fromm, E. *Escape from freedom*. New York: Holt, Rinehart, & Winston, 1941. Paperback reprint: New York: Avon Books, 1965.

Fromm, E. *Psychoanalysis and religion*. New Haven: Yale University Press, 1950. Paperback reprint: New York: Bantam Books, 1967.

Fromm, E. *The crisis of psychoanalysis: Essays on Freud, Marx, and social psychology*. New York: Holt, Rinehart, & Winston, 1970. Paperback reprint: New York: Fawcett, 1971a.

Fromm, E. *The heart of man: Its genius for good or evil*. New York: Harper & Row, 1964. Paperback reprint: New York: Perennial, 1971b.

Fromm, E. *The anatomy of human destructiveness*. New York: Holt, Rinehart, & Winston, 1973.

Fromm, E. *The art of loving*. New York: Harper & Row, 1956. Paperback reprint: New York: Perennial, 1974a.

Fromm, E. *The revolution of hope*. New York: Harper & Row, 1968. Paperback reprint: New York: Perennial, 1974b.

Fromm, E. *Man for himself: An inquiry into the psychology of ethics*. New York: Holt, Rinehart, & Winston, 1947. Paperback reprint: New York: Fawcett, 1976a.

Fromm, E. *The sane society*. New York: Holt, Rinehart, & Winston, 1955. Paperback reprint: New York: Fawcett, 1976b.

Fromm, E. *To have or to be?* New York: Harper & Row, 1976c.

Fromm, E. *Greatness and limitations of Freud's thought*. New York: Harper & Row, 1980.

Fromm, E. *On disobedience: And other essays*. New York: Seabury Press, 1981.

Fromm-Reichmann, F. *Principles of intensive psychotherapy*. Chicago: University of Chicago Press, 1950.

Furtmüller, C. Alfred Adler: A biographical essay. Original prepared: 1946. In H. L. Ansbacher & R. R. Ansbacher (Eds.), *Superiority and social interest* (3rd ed.). New York: Norton, 1979, pp. 311–394.

Garcia, J., & Koelling, R. A. Relation of cue to consequences in avoidance learning. *Psychonomic Science,* 1966, *4:* 123–124.

Garfield, S. Psychotherapy: A 40-year appraisal. *American Psychologist,* 1981, *36:* 174–183.

Gay, P. *Freud: A life for our time.* New York: Norton, 1988.

Gelman, D. Finding the hidden Freud. *Newsweek,* 30 November 1981, pp. 64–70.

Gelman, D. Revival sessions: A resurgence of interest in classic psychoanalysis. *Newsweek,* 25 November 1991, pp. 60–61.

Gendlin, E. T. Carl Rogers (1902–1987). *American Psychologist,* 1988, *43:* 127–128.

Glassman, W. E. *Approaches to psychology.* (3rd ed.) Buckingham, England: Open University Press, 2000.

Goldberg, L. R. An alternative "description of personality:" The Big Five factor structure. *Journal of Personality and Social Psychology,* 1990, *59:* 1216–1229.

Goldberg, L. R. The structure of phenotypic personality traits. *American Psychologist,* 1993, *48:* 26–34.

Goldfried, M. R. Toward the delineation of therapeutic change principles. *American Psychologist,* 1980, *35:* 991–999.

Goldstein, K. *The organism.* New York: American Book Co., 1939.

Goldstein, K. *Human nature in the light of psychopathology.* Cambridge, Mass.: Harvard University Press, 1940.

Goleman, D. As a therapist, Freud fell short, scholars find. *The New York Times,* 6 March 1990, pp. B5, B9.

Graham, W., & Balloun, J. An empirical test of Maslow's need hierarchy theory. *Journal of Humanistic Psychology,* 1973, *13:* 97–108.

Hall, C. S. *The meaning of dreams.* New York: McGraw-Hill, 1966.

Hall, M. H. An interview with B. F. Skinner. *Psychology Today,* 1967a, *1*(5): 21–23; 68–71.

Hall, M. H. An interview with Rollo May. *Psychology Today,* 1967b, *1*(5): 25–29; 72–73.

Hall, M. H. A conversation with Carl Rogers. *Psychology Today,* 1967c *1*(7): 19–21; 62–66.

Hall, M. H. A conversation with Abraham H. Maslow. *Psychology Today,* 1968a, *2*(2): 35–37; 54–57.

Hall, M. H. A conversation with Henry A. Murray. *Psychology Today,* 1968b, *2*(4): 57–63.

Harris, B. Whatever happened to little Albert? *American Psychologist,* 1979, *34:* 151–160.

Harris, B. Ceremonial versus critical history of psychology. *American Psychologist,* 1980, *35:* 218–219.

Harter, S. The perceived competence scale for children. *Child Development,* 1982, *53:* 87–97.

Hartshorne, H., & May, M. A. *Studies in the nature of character: Studies in deceit.* New York: Macmillan, 1928.

Hattie, J. *Self-concept.* Hillsdale, N.J.: Lawrence Erlbaum Associates, 1992.

Heine, R. W. A comparison of patients' reports on psychotherapeutic experiences with psychoanalytic, nondirective, and Adlerian therapists. *American Journal of Psychotherapy,* 1953, *7:* 16–23.

Hetherington, E. M., & McIntyre, C. W. Developmental psychology. *Annual Review of Psychology,* 1975, *26:* 97–136.

Hilgard, E. R., & Bower, G. H. *Theories of learning* (4th ed.). Englewood Cliffs, N.J.: Prentice-Hall, 1975.

Hoffman, E. *The right to be human: A biography of Abraham Maslow.* Los Angeles: Tarcher, 1988.

Horn, J. Raymond Bernard Cattell (1905–1998). *American Psychologist,* 2001, *56:* 71–72.

Horney, K. *The neurotic personality of our time.* New York: Norton, 1937.

Horney, K. *New ways in psychoanalysis.* New York: Norton, 1939.

Horney, K. *Self-analysis.* New York: Norton, 1942.

Horney, K. *Our inner conflicts: A constructive theory of neurosis.* New York: Norton, 1945.

Horney, K. *Neurosis and human growth: The struggle toward self-realization.* New York: Norton, 1950.

Horney, K. *Feminine psychology.* Original publication: 1923–1937. Paperback English edition: New York: Norton, 1967.

Hunt, J. M. Psychological development: Early experience. *Annual Review of Psychology,* 1979, *30:* 103–143.

Jaffé, A. *The myth of meaning: Jung and the expansion of consciousness.* New York: G. P. Putnam's Sons, 1971. Paperback reprint: New York: Penguin Books, 1975.

John, O. P. The "Big Five" factor taxonomy: Dimensions of personality in the natural language and in questionnaires. In L. A. Pervin (Ed.), *Handbook of personality: Theory and research.* New York: Guilford Press, 1990.

Jones, E. Rationalization in everyday life. *Journal of Abnormal Psychology,* 1908, *3:* 161.

Jones, E. *The life and work of Sigmund Freud.* New York: Basic Books, Vol. 1, 1953. Paperback reprint (abridged): New York: Anchor Books, 1963a.

Jones, E. *The life and work of Sigmund Freud.* New York: Basic Books, Vol. 2, 1955. Paperback reprint (abridged): New York: Anchor Books, 1963b.

Jones, E. *The life and work of Sigmund Freud.* New York: Basic Books, Vol. 3, 1957. Paperback reprint (abridged): New York: Anchor Books, 1963c.

Jones, M. C. The elimination of children's fears. *Journal of Experimental Psychology,* 1924a, *7:* 382–390.

Jones, M. C. A laboratory study of fear: The case of Peter. *Journal of Genetic Psychology,* 1924b, *31:* 308–315.

Jung, C. G. The association method. Original publication: 1910. Standard edition: Princeton, N.J.: Princeton University Press, Vol. 2.

Jung, C. G. *Symbols of transformation*. Original publication: 1911–1912. Standard edition: Princeton, N.J.: Princeton University Press, Vol. 5.

Jung, C. G. Commentary on *The secret of the golden flower*. Original publication: 1929. Standard edition: Princeton, N.J.: Princeton University Press, Vol. 13.

Jung, C. G. Some aspects of modern psychotherapy. Original publication: 1930. Standard edition: Princeton, N.J.: Princeton University Press, Vol. 16.

Jung, C. G. Problems of modern psychotherapy. Original publication: 1929. Standard edition: Princeton, N.J.: Princeton University Press, Vol. 16. Paperback reprint (slightly different translation): *Modern man in search of a soul*. New York: Harcourt, Brace & World, 1933a, pp. 28–54.

Jung, C. G. The aims of psychotherapy. Original publication: 1931. Standard edition: Princeton, N.J.: Princeton University Press, Vol. 16. Paperback reprint (slightly different translation): *Modern man in search of a soul*. New York: Harcourt, Brace & World, 1933b, pp. 55–73.

Jung, C. G. Archaic man. Original publication: 1931. Standard edition: Princeton, N.J.: Princeton University Press, Vol. 10. Paperback reprint (slightly different translation): *Modern man in search of a soul*. New York: Harcourt, Brace & World, 1933c, pp. 125–151.

Jung, C. G. Psychotherapists or the clergy. Original publication: 1932. Standard edition: Princeton, N.J.: Princeton University Press. Vol. 11. Paperback reprint (slightly different translation): *Modern man in search of a soul*. New York: Harcourt, Brace & World, 1933d, pp. 221–244.

Jung, C. G. A review of the complex theory. Original publication: 1934a. Standard edition: Princeton, N.J.: Princeton University Press, Vol. 8.

Jung, C. G. Archetypes of the collective unconscious. Original publication: 1934b. Standard edition: Princeton, N.J.: Princeton University Press, Vol. 9, Part 1.

Jung, C. G. The state of psychotherapy today. Original publication: 1934c. Standard edition: Princeton, N.J.: Princeton University Press, Vol. 10.

Jung, C. G. Principles of practical psychotherapy. Original publication: 1935a. Standard edition: Princeton, N.J.: Princeton University Press, Vol. 16.

Jung, C. G. What is psychotherapy? Original publication: 1935b. Standard edition: Princeton, N.J.: Princeton University Press, Vol. 16.

Jung, C. G. Psychological factors determining human behavior. Original publication: 1937. Standard edition: Princeton, N.J.: Princeton University Press, Vol. 8.

Jung, C. G. Psychology and religion (the Terry lectures). Original publication: 1938. Standard edition: Princeton, N.J.: Princeton University Press, Vol. 11. Paperback reprint: New Haven, Conn.: Yale University Press, 1938.

Jung, C. G. The psychology of the child archetype. Original publication: 1940. Standard edition: Princeton, N.J.: Princeton University Press, Vol. 8, Part 1.

Jung, C. G. *Psychology and alchemy*. Original publication: 1944. Standard edition: Princeton, N.J.: Princeton University Press, Vol. 12.

Jung, C. G. *Aion: Researches into the phenomenology of the self*. Original publication: 1951. Standard edition: Princeton, N.J.: Princeton University Press, Vol. 9, Part 2.

Jung, C. G. *Mysterium coniunctionis*. Original publication: 1955–1956. Standard edition: Princeton, N.J.: Princeton University Press, Vol. 14.

Jung, C. G. Flying saucers: A modern myth. Original publication: 1958a. Standard edition: Princeton, N.J.: Princeton University Press, Vol. 10.

Jung, C. G. The undiscovered self (present and future). Original publication: 1957. Standard edition: Princeton, N.J.: Princeton University Press, Vol. 10. Paperback reprint: *The undiscovered self*. New York: Mentor, 1958b.

Jung, C. G. *Memories, dreams, reflections*. New York: Random House, 1961. Paperback reprint: New York: Vintage Books, 1965.

Jung, C. G. (Ed.) *Man and his symbols*. London: Aldus Books, 1964. Paperback reprint: New York: Dell, 1968.

Jung, C. G. On psychic energy. Original publication: 1928. Standard edition: Princeton, N.J.: Princeton University Press, Vol. 8. Paperback reprint: *On the nature of the psyche*. Princeton, N.J.: Princeton University Press, 1969a, pp. 3–66.

Jung, C. G. On the nature of the psyche. Original publication: 1947. Standard edition: Princeton, N.J.: Princeton University Press, Vol. 8. Paperback reprint: *On the nature of the psyche*. Princeton, N.J.: Princeton University Press, 1969b, pp. 69–144.

Jung, C. G. Analytical psychology and education: Three lectures. Original publication: 1926. Standard edition: Princeton, N.J.: Princeton University Press, Vol. 17. Paperback reprint: *Psychology and education*. Princeton, N.J.: Princeton University Press, 1969c, pp. 55–122.

Jung, C. G. Child development and education. Original publication: 1928. Standard edition: Princeton, N.J.: Princeton University Press, Vol. 17. Paperback reprint: *Psychology and education*. Princeton, N.J.: Princeton University Press, 1969d, pp. 39–52.

Jung, C. G. The gifted child. Original publication: 1943. Standard edition: Princeton, N.J.: Princeton University Press, Vol. 17. Paperback reprint: *Psychology and education*. Princeton, N.J.: Princeton University Press, 1969e, pp. 125–135.

Jung, C. G. *The psychology of the transference*. Original publication: 1946. Standard edition: Princeton, N.J.: Princeton University Press, Vol. 16. Paperback reprint: Princeton, N.J.: Princeton University Press, 1969f.

Jung, C. G. Psychological aspects of the mother archetype. Original publication: 1938. Standard edition: Princeton, N.J.: Princeton University Press, Vol. 9, Part 1. Paperback reprint: *Four archetypes*. Princeton, N.J.: Princeton University Press, 1970a, pp. 9–44.

Jung, C. G. Concerning rebirth. Original publication: 1940. Standard edition: Princeton, N.J.: Princeton University Press, Vol. 9, Part 1. Paperback reprint: *Four archetypes*. Princeton, N.J.: Princeton University Press, 1970b, pp. 45–81.

Jung, C. G. The phenomenology of the spirit in fairytales. Original publication: 1945. Standard edition: Princeton, N.J.: Princeton University Press, Vol. 9, Part 1. Paperback reprint: *Four archetypes*. Princeton, N.J.: Princeton University Press, 1970c, pp. 85–132.

Jung, C. G. On the psychology of the trickster-figure. Original publication: 1954. Standard edition: Princeton, N.J.: Princeton University Press, Vol. 9, Part 1. Paperback reprint: *Four archetypes*. Princeton, N.J.: Princeton University Press, 1970d, pp. 135–152.

Jung, C. G. The stages of life. Original publication: 1930–1931. Standard edition: Princeton, N.J.: Princeton University Press, Vol. 8. Paperback reprint: *The portable Jung*. New York: Viking Press, 1971a, pp. 3–22.

Jung, C. G. The structure of the psyche. Original publication: 1927. Standard edition: Princeton, N.J.: Princeton University Press, Vol. 8. Paperback reprint: *The portable Jung*. New York: Viking Press, 1971b, pp. 23–46.

Jung, C. G. Instinct and the unconscious. Original publication: 1919. Standard edition: Princeton, N.J.: Princeton University Press, Vol. 8. Paperback reprint: *The portable Jung*. New York: Viking Press, 1971c, pp. 47–58.

Jung, C. G. Marriage as a psychological relationship. Original publication: 1925. Standard edition: Princeton, N.J.: Princeton University Press, Vol. 17. Paperback reprint: *The portable Jung*. New York: Viking Press, 1971d, pp. 163–177.

Jung, C. G. The transcendent function. Original publication: 1916. Standard edition: Princeton, N.J.: Princeton University Press, Vol. 8. Paperback reprint: *The portable Jung*. New York: Viking Press, 1971e, pp. 273–300.

Jung, C. G. On the relation of analytical psychology to poetry. Original publication: 1922. Standard edition: Princeton, N.J.: Princeton University Press, Vol. 15. Paperback reprint: *The spirit in man, art, and literature*. Princeton, N.J.: Princeton University Press, 1971f, pp. 65–83.

Jung, C. G. Psychology and literature. Original publication: 1930. Standard edition: Princeton, N.J.: Princeton University Press, Vol. 15. Paperback reprint: *The spirit in man, art, and literature*. Princeton, N.J.: Princeton University Press, 1971g, pp. 84–105.

Jung, C. G. Mandalas. Original publication: 1955. Standard edition: Princeton, N.J.: Princeton University Press, Vol. 9, Part 1. Paperback reprint: *Mandala symbolism*. Princeton, N.J.: Princeton University Press, 1972a, pp. 3–5.

Jung, C. G. A study in the process of individuation. Original publication: 1934. Standard edition: Princeton, N.J.: Princeton University Press, Vol. 9, Part 1. Paperback reprint: *Mandala symbolism*. Princeton, N.J.: Princeton University Press, 1972b, pp. 6–70.

Jung, C. G. Concerning mandala symbolism. Original publication: 1950. Standard edition: Princeton, N.J.: Princeton University Press, Vol. 9, Part 1. Paperback reprint: *Mandala symbolism*. Princeton, N.J.: Princeton University Press, 1972c, pp. 71–100.

Jung, C. G. On the psychology of the unconscious. Original publication: 1917. Standard edition: Princeton, N.J.: Princeton University Press, Vol. 7. Paperback reprint: *Two essays on analytical psychology*. Princeton, N.J.: Princeton University Press, 1972d, pp. 3–119.

Jung, C. G. The relations between the ego and the unconscious. Original publication: 1928. Standard edition: Princeton, N.J.: Princeton University Press, Vol. 7. Paperback reprint: *Two essays on analytical psychology*. Princeton, N.J.: Princeton University Press, 1972e, pp. 123–241.

Jung, C. G. New paths in psychology. Original publication: 1912. Standard edition: Princeton, N.J.: Princeton University press, Vol. 7. Paperback reprint: *Two essays on analytical psychology*. Princeton, N.J.: Princeton University Press, 1972f, pp. 245–268.

Jung, C. G. Answer to Job. Original publication: 1952. Standard edition: Princeton, N.J.: Princeton University Press, Vol. 11. Paperback reprint: *Answer to Job*. Princeton, N.J.: Princeton University Press, 1973a.

Jung, C. G. Synchronicity: An acausal connecting principle. Original publication: 1952. Standard edition: Princeton, N.J.: Princeton University Press, Vol. 8. Paperback reprint: *Synchronicity*. Princeton, N.J.: Princeton University Press, 1973b, pp. 3–103.

Jung, C. G. On synchronicity. Original publication: 1951. Standard edition: Princeton, N.J.: Princeton University Press, Vol. 8. Paperback reprint: *Synchronicity*. Princeton, N.J.: Princeton University Press, 1973c, pp. 104–115.

Jung, C. G. General aspects of dream psychology. Original publication: 1916. Standard edition: Princeton, N.J.: Princeton University Press, Vol. 8. Paperback reprint: *Dreams*. Princeton, N.J.: Princeton University Press, 1974a, pp. 23–66.

Jung, C. G. On the nature of dreams. Original publication: 1945. Standard edition: Princeton, N.J.: Princeton University Press, Vol. 8. Paperback reprint: *Dreams*. Princeton, N.J.: Princeton University Press, 1974b, pp. 67–83.

Jung, C. G. The practical use of dream-analysis. Original publication: 1934. Standard edition: Princeton, N.J.: Princeton University Press, Vol. 16. Paperback reprint: *Dreams*. Princeton, N.J.: Princeton University Press, 1974c, pp. 87–109.

Jung, C. G. Individual dream symbolism in relation to alchemy. Original publication: 1936. Standard edition: Princeton, N.J.: Princeton University Press, Vol. 12. Paperback reprint: *Dreams*. Princeton, N.J.: Princeton University Press, 1974d, pp. 115–297.

Jung, C. G. Psychoanalysis and association experiments. Original publication: 1905. Standard edition: Princeton, N.J.: Princeton University Press, Vol. 2. Paperback reprint: *The psychoanalytic years*. Princeton, N.J.: Princeton University Press, 1974e, pp. 3–32.

Jung, C. G. *The psychology of dementia praecox*. Original publication: 1907. Standard edition: Princeton, N.J.: Princeton University Press, Vol. 3. Paperback reprint: Princeton, N.J.: Princeton University Press, 1974f, pp. 3–151.

Jung, C. G. On the psychogenesis of schizophrenia. Original publication: 1939. Standard edition: Princeton, N.J.: Princeton University Press, Vol. 3. Paperback reprint: *The psychology of dementia praecox*. Princeton, N.J.: Princeton University Press, 1974g, pp. 155–171.

Jung, C. G. The theory of psychoanalysis. Original publication: 1913. Standard edition: Princeton, N.J.: Princeton University Press, Vol. 4. Paperback reprint: *Critique of psychoanalysis*. Princeton, N.J.: Princeton University Press, 1975a, pp. 3–144.

Jung, C. G. General aspects of psychoanalysis. Original publication: 1913. Standard edition: Princeton, N.J.: Princeton University Press, Vol. 4. Paperback reprint: *Critique of psychoanalysis*. Princeton, N.J.: Princeton University Press, 1975b, pp. 147–160.

Jung, C. G. Freud and Jung: Contrasts. Original publication: 1929. Standard edition: Princeton, N.J.: Princeton University Press, Vol. 4. Paperback reprint: *Critique of psychoanalysis*. Princeton, N.J.: Princeton University Press, 1975c, pp. 225–232.

Jung, C. G. *Psychological types*. Original publication: 1921. Standard edition: Princeton, N.J.: Princeton University Press, Vol. 6. Paperback reprint: Princeton, N.J.: Princeton University Press, 1976.

Kahn, E. Heinz Kohut and Carl Rogers: A timely comparison. *American Psychologist,* 1985, *40:* 893–904.

Karen, R. Becoming attached. *Atlantic Monthly,* 1990(2), 35–70.

Kazdin, A. E. *The token economy: A review and evaluation*. New York: Plenum Press, 1977.

Kelly, G. A. *The psychology of personal constructs* (2 vols.). New York: Norton, 1955. Paperback reprint (Chapters 1–3 only): *A theory of personality: The psychology of personal constructs*. New York: Norton, 1963.

Kelly, G. A. *Clinical psychology and personality: Selected papers*. (B. Maher, Ed.) New York: Wiley, 1969.

Kelly, G. A. A brief introduction to personal construct theory. In D. Bannister (Ed.), *Perspectives in personal construct theory*. New York: Academic Press, 1970a, pp. 1–29.

Kelly, G. A. Behavior is an experiment. In D. Bannister (Ed.), *Perspectives in personal construct theory*. New York: Academic Press, 1970b, pp. 255–269.

Kelman, H. C. Introduction. In K. Horney, *Feminine psychology*. New York: Norton, 1967.

Kernis, M. H., Brockner, J., & Frankel, B. S. Self-esteem and reactions to failure: The mediating role of overgeneralization. *Journal of Personality and Social Psychology,* 1989, *57:* 707–714.

Kilmann, R. H., & Taylor, V. A. Contingency approach to laboratory learning: Psychological types versus experimental norms. *Human Relations,* 1974, *27:* 891–909.

Lazarus, A. A. Where do behavior therapists take their troubles? *Psychological Reports,* 1971, *28:* 349–350.

Leahy, R. L. Parental practices and the development of moral judgment and self-image disparity during adolescence. *Developmental Psychology,* 1981, *17:* 580–594.

Leahy, R. L., & Huard, C. Role taking and self-image disparity in children. *Developmental Psychology,* 1976, *12:* 504–508.

Leary, M. R. The social and psychological importance of self-esteem. In R. M. Kowalski & M. R. Leary (Eds.), *The social psychology of emotional and behavioral problems*. Washington, D.C.: American Psychological Association, 1999.

Lewis, H. B. *Freud and modern psychology: Vol. 1. The emotional basis of mental illness*. New York: Plenum Press, 1981.

Lippmann, P. *Nocturnes: On listening to dreams*. Hillsdale, N.J.: Analytic Press, 2000.

Locke, E. L. Is "behavior therapy" behavioristic? [An analysis of Wolpe's psychotherapeutic methods]. *Psychological Bulletin,* 1971, *76:* 318–327.

Loehlin, J. C., McCrae, R. R., & Costa, P. T., Jr. Heritabilities of common and measure-specific components of the Big Five personality factors. *Journal of Research in Personality, 1998, 32:* 431–453.

Lowry, R. J. (Ed.). *The journals of A. H. Maslow* (2 Vols.). Monterey, C.A.: Brooks/Cole, 1979.

Luborsky, L., Singer, B., & Luborsky, L. Comparative studies of psychotherapies: Is it true that "Everyone has won and all must have prizes?" *Archives of General Psychiatry, 1975, 32:* 995–1008.

Lyubomirsky, S. Why are some people are happier than others? The role of cognitive and motivational processes in well-being. *American Psychologist, 2001, 56:* 239–249.

MacCorquodale, K. Skinner's *Verbal behavior:* A retrospective appreciation. *Journal of the Experimental Analysis of Behavior, 1969, 12:* 831–841.

MacCorquodale, K. On Chomsky's review of Skinner's *Verbal behavior. Journal of the Experimental Analysis of Behavior, 1970, 13:* 83–100.

Maddux, J. E. Why the little blue engine could: Self-efficacy and the real power of positive thinking. *Contemporary Psychology, 1998, 43:* 601–602.

Maher, B. (Ed.). *See* Kelly, 1969.

Mahony, P. J. *Freud and the Rat Man.* New Haven, Conn.: Yale University Press, 1986.

Manaster, G. J., & Corsini, R. J. *Individual psychology: Theory and practice.* Itasca, Ill.: F. E. Peacock, 1982.

Manktelow, K. I. *Reasoning and thinking.* Hove, England: Psychology Press, 1999.

Marcia, J. E. Development and validation of ego-identity status. *Journal of Personality and Social Psychology, 1966, 3:* 551–558.

Marcia, J. E. Identity in adolescence. In J. Adelson (Ed.), *Handbook of adolescent psychology.* New York: Wiley, 1980, pp. 159–187.

Marcia, J. E. The relational roots of identity, In J. Kroger (Ed.), *Discussions on ego identity.* Hillsdale, N.J.: Lawrence Erlbaum Associates, 1993. pp. 101–120.

Marmor, J., & Woods, S. M. (Eds.). *The interface between the psychodynamic and behavioral therapies.* New York: Plenum, 1980.

Marsh, H. W. A multidimensional, hierarchical self-concept: Theoretical and empirical justification. Educational Psychology Review, 1990, 2: 77–172.

Marsh, H. W. Integrating of self-concept theory and research: A lonely cry of protest from the dust bowl of empiricism. *Contemporary Psychology, 1992, 37:* 1321–1322.

Maslow, A. H. *Eupsychian management: A journal.* Homewood, IL.: Irwin-Dorsey, 1965.

Maslow, A. H. *Toward a psychology of being* (2nd ed.). New York: Van Nostrand Reinhold, 1968.

Maslow, A. H. *The psychology of science: A reconnaissance.* New York: Harper & Row, 1966. Paperback reprint: Chicago: Regnery, 1969.

Maslow, A. H. *Religions, values, and peak-experiences.* Columbus: Ohio State University Press, 1964. Paperback reprint: New York: Viking, 1970a.

Maslow, A. H. *Motivation and personality* (2nd ed.). New York: Harper & Row, 1970b.

Maslow, A. H. *The farther reaches of human nature.* New York: Viking, 1971.

Masters, W. H., & Johnson, V. E. *Human sexual response.* Boston: Little, Brown, 1966.

May, R. (Ed.). Symbolism in religion and literature. New York: Braziller, 1960.

May, R. *The art of counseling.* Nashville: Abingdon-Cokesbury, 1939. Paperback reprint: Nashville: Apex Books, 1967a.

May, R. Contributions of existential psychotherapy. In R. May, E. Angel, & H. F. Ellenberger (Eds.), *Existence: A new dimension in psychiatry and psychology.* New York: Basic Books, 1958. Paperback reprint: New York: Touchstone Books, 1967b, pp. 37–91.

May, R. The origins and significance of the existential movement in psychology. In R. May, E. Angel, & H. F. Ellenberger (Eds.), *Existence: A new dimension in psychiatry and psychology.* New York: Basic Books, 1958. Paperback reprint: New York: Touchstone Books, 1967c, pp. 3–36.

May, R. *Psychology and the human dilemma.* New York: Van Nostrand Reinhold, 1967d.

May, R. The emergence of existential psychology. In R. May (Ed.), *Existential psychology* (2nd ed.). New York: Random House, 1969a.

May, R. Existential bases of psychotherapy. In R. May (Ed.), *Existential psychology* (2nd ed.). New York: Random House, 1969b.

May, R. *Love and will.* New York: Norton, 1969c.

May, R. *Power and innocence: A search for the sources of violence.* New York: Norton, 1972.

May, R. *Man's search for himself.* New York: Norton, 1953. Paperback reprint: New York: Delta, 1973.

May, R. *The courage to create.* New York: Norton, 1975.

May, R. *The meaning of anxiety* (Rev. ed.). New York: Norton, 1977a.

May, R. Reflections and commentary. In C. Reeves, *The psychology of Rollo May.* San Francisco: Jossey-Bass, 1977b, pp. 295–309.

May, R. *Freedom and destiny.* New York: Norton, 1981.

May, R. *My quest for beauty*. Dallas, Texas: Saybrook, 1985.

May, R., & Caligor, L. *Dreams and symbols: Man's unconscious language*. New York: Basic Books, 1968.

McAdams, D. P. The five-factor model in personality: A critical appraisal. *Journal of Personality*, 1992, *60:* 329–361.

McAdams, D. P. *The stories we live by: Personal myths and the making of the self*. New York: William Morrow, 1993.

McAdams, D. P. Can personality change? Levels of stability and growth in personality across the life span. In T. F. Heatherton & J. L. Weinberger (Eds.), *Can personality change?* Washington, D.C.: American Psychological Association, 1994.

McAdams, D. P. Three voices of Erik Erikson. *Contemporary Psychology*, 1997, *42:* 575–578.

McCrae, R. R. (Ed.) The five-factor model: Issues and applications [Special issue]. *Journal of Personality*, 1992, *60*.

McCrae, R. R., & Costa, P. T., Jr. Validation of the five-factor model of personality across instruments and observers. *Journal of Personality and Social Psychology*, 1987, *52:* 81–90.

McCrae, R. R., & Costa, P. T., Jr. *Personality in adulthood*. New York: Guilford Press, 1990.

McCrae, R. R., Costa, P. T., Jr., de Lirna, M. P., Simoes, A., Ostendorf, F., Angleitner, A., Marusic, I., Bratko, D., Caprara, G. V., Barbaranelli, C., Chae, J-H., & Piedmont, R. L. Age differences in personality across the adult life span: Parallels in five cultures. *Developmental Psychology*, 1999, *35:* 466–477.

McCrae, R. R., Costa, P. T., Jr., del Pilar, G. H., Rolland, J. P., & Parker, W. D. Cross-cultural assessment of the five-factor model: The revised NEO personality inventory. *Journal of Cross-Cultural Psychology*, 1998, *29:* 171–188.

McGuire, W. (Ed.). *The Freud/Jung letters*. Princeton, N.J.: Princeton University Press, 1974.

Meltzoff, J., & Kornreich, M. *Research in psychotherapy*. New York: Atherton, 1970.

Menninger, K. A., & Holzman, P. S. *Theory of psychoanalytic technique* (2nd ed.). New York: Basic Books, 1973.

Miller, N. E., & Dollard, J. *Social learning and imitation*. New Haven: Yale University Press, 1941.

Mindess, H. *Makers of psychology: The personal factor*. New York: Human Sciences Press, 1988.

Mischel, W. Toward a cognitive social learning reconceptualization of personality. *Psychological Review*, 1973, *80:* 252–283.

Mischel, W. Convergences and challenges in the search for consistency. *American Psychologist*, 1984, *39:* 351–354.

Mischel, W. Personality dispositions revisited and revised: A view after three decades. In L. A. Pervin (Ed.), *Handbook of personality: Theory and research*. New York: Guilford Press, 1990.

Mischel, W., & Peake, P. K. Beyond déjà vu in the search for cross-situational consistency. *Psychological Review*, 1982, *89:* 730–755.

Morgan, C. D., & Murray, H. A. A method for investigating fantasies. *Archives of Neurological Psychiatry*, 1935, *34:* 289–306.

Mosak, H. H., & Dreikurs, R. Adlerian psychotherapy. In R. Corsini (Ed.), *Current psychotherapies*. Itasca, Ill.: F. E. Peacock, 1973, pp. 35–83.

Murray, H. A. What should psychologists do about psychoanalysis? *Journal of Abnormal and Social Psychology*, 1940, *35:* 150–175.

Murray, H. A. *Thematic Apperception Test manual*. Cambridge, Mass.: Harvard University Press, 1943.

Murray, H. A. (Office of Strategic Services Assessment Staff). *Assessment of men*. New York: Rinehart, 1948.

Murray, H. A. Some basic psychological assumptions and conceptions. *Dialectica*, 1951, *5:* 266–292.

Murray, H. A. Preparations for the scaffold of a comprehensive system. In S. Koch (Ed.), *Psychology: A study of a science* (Vol. 3). New York: McGraw-Hill, 1959, pp. 7–54.

Murray, H. A. Studies of stressful interpersonal disputations. *American Psychologist*, 1963, *18:* 28–36.

Murray, H. A. Autobiography. In E. G. Boring & G. Lindzey (Eds.), *A history of psychology in autobiography* (Vol. 5). New York: Appleton-Century-Crofts, 1967, pp. 283–310.

Murray, H. A. Components of an evolving personological system. In D. L. Sills (Ed.), *International encyclopedia of the social sciences* (Vol. 12). New York: Macmillan and Free Press, 1968a, 5–13.

Murray, H. A. In nomine diaboli. *New England Quarterly*, 1951, *24:* 435–452. Reprinted in *Psychology Today*, 1968b, *2*(4): 64–69.

Murray, H. A., & Kluckhohn, C. Outline of a conception of personality. In C. Kluckhohn, H. A. Murray, & D. M. Schneider (Eds.), *Personality in nature, society, and culture* (2nd ed.). New York: Knopf, 1953, pp. 3–52.

Murray, H. A. et al. *Explorations in personality*. New York: Oxford University Press, 1938.

Myers, D. G. *Psychology*. (6th ed.) New York: Worth, 2001.

Myers, I. B. *The Myers-Briggs Type Indicator*. Princeton, N.J.: Educational Testing Service, 1962.

Myers, I. B. *Introduction to type*. Palo Alto, Calif.: Consulting Psychologists Press, 1993.

Myers, I. B., & McCaulley, M. H. *Manual: A guide to the development and use of the Myers-Briggs Type Indicator*. Palo Alto, Calif.: Consulting Psychologists Press, 1985.

Myers, K. D., & Kirby, L. K. *Introduction to type dynamics and development*. Palo Alto, Calif.: Consulting Psychologists Press, 1994.

Neimeyer, G. J., & Neimeyer, R. A. (Eds.). *Advances in personal construct psychology* (Vol. 1). Greenwich, Conn.: JAI Press, 1990.

Neimeyer, R. A. & Neimeyer, G. J. (Eds.). *Advances in personal construct psychology* (Vol. 2). Greenwich, Conn.: JAI Press, 1992.

Newman, B. M., & Newman, P. R. *Development through life: A psychosocial approach.* (7th ed.) Belmont, Calif.: Brooks/Cole Wadsworth, 1999.

Ohman, A. Face the beast and fear the face: Animal and social fears as prototypes for the evolutionary analyses of emotion. *Psychophysiology,* 1986, *23:* 123–145.

Olson, H. A. (Ed.) *Early recollections: Their use in diagnosis and psychotherapy.* Springfield, Ill.: Charles C. Thomas, 1979.

Oppenheimer, R. Analogy in science. *American Psychologist,* 1956, *11:* 127–135.

Orgler, H. *Alfred Adler: The man and his work.* New York: Liveright, 1963. Paperback reprint: New York: Mentor Books, 1972.

Overall, J. E. Note on the scientific status of factors. *Psychological Bulletin,* 1964, *61:* 270–276.

Paulhus, D. L. Sphere-specific methods of perceived control. *Journal of Personality and Social Psychology,* 1983, *44:* 1253–1265.

Paulhus, D. L., Fridhandler, B., & Hayes, S. Psychological defense: Contemporary theory and research. In R. Hogan, J. Johnson, & S. Briggs (Eds.), *Handbook of personality.* New York: Academic Press, 1997, pp. 544–580.

Pavlov, I. P. The scientific investigations of the psychical faculties or processes in the higher animals. *Science,* 1906, *24:* 613–619.

Pavlov, I. P. *Conditional reflexes: An investigation of the physiological activity of the cerebral cortex.* New York: Oxford University Press, 1927.

Pavlov, I. P. *Lectures on conditioned reflexes.* New York: International Publishers, 1928.

Perry, H. S. *Psychiatrist of America: The life of Harry Stack Sullivan.* Cambridge, Mass.: Belknap/Harvard University Press, 1982.

Pettigrew, T. F. A bold stroke for personality half a century ago. *Contemporary Psychology,* 1990, *35:* 533–536.

Piers, E. V. *Piers–Harris self-concept scale (The way I feel about myself).* Los Angeles, Calif.: Western Psychological Services, 1984.

Progoff, I. *Jung's psychology and its social meaning.* New York: Julian Press, 1953. Paperback reprint (2nd ed.): New York: Anchor Books, 1973.

Quinn, S. *A mind of her own: The life of Karen Horney.* Reading, Mass.: Addison-Wesley, 1988.

Rapaport, D., Gill, M. M., & Schafer, R. *Diagnostic psychological testing* (Rev. ed., edited by R. R. Holt). London: University of London Press, 1970.

Reeves, C. *The psychology of Rollo May.* San Francisco: Jossey-Bass, 1977.

Reik, T. *Listening with the third ear.* New York: Farrar, Straus and Co., 1948. Paperback reprint: New York: Pyramid, 1964.

Rieff, P. *Freud: The mind of the moralist.* New York: Viking, 1959. Paperback reprint: New York: Anchor Books, 1961.

Rieff, P. Introduction. In S. Freud, *Dora: An analysis of a case of hysteria.* New York: Collier, 1963.

Roazen, P. (Ed.). *Sigmund Freud.* Englewood Cliffs, N.J.: Prentice-Hall, 1973.

Roazen, P. *Erik H. Erikson: The power and limits of a vision.* New York: Free Press, 1976a.

Roazen, P. *Freud and his followers.* New York: Knopf, 1975. Paperback reprint: New York: Meridian, 1976b.

Rogers, C. R. *Counseling and psychotherapy: Newer concepts in practice.* Boston: Houghton Mifflin, 1942.

Rogers, C. R. *Client-centered therapy: Its current practice, implications, and theory.* Boston: Houghton Mifflin, 1951.

Rogers, C. R. A theory of therapy, personality, and interpersonal relationships, as developed in the client-centered framework. In S. Koch (Ed.), *Psychology: A study of a science* (Vol. 3). New York: McGraw-Hill, 1959, pp. 184–256.

Rogers, C. R. *On becoming a person: A therapist's view of psychotherapy.* Boston: Houghton Mifflin, 1961.

Rogers, C. R. Client-centered therapy. In E. Shostrom (Ed.), *Three approaches to psychotherapy* (Film No. 1). Orange, California: Psychological Films, 1965 (Transcript reprinted in Rogers & Wood, 1974, pp. 237–253.)

Rogers, C. R. Autobiography. In E. G. Boring & G. Lindzey (Eds.), *A history of psychology in autobiography* (Vol. 5). New York: Appleton-Century-Crofts, 1967, pp. 341–384.

Rogers, C. R. *Freedom to learn: A view of what education might become.* Columbus, Ohio: Charles E. Merrill, 1969.

Rogers, C. R. *Becoming partners: Marriage and its alternatives.* New York: Delta, 1972.

Rogers, C. R. *Carl Rogers on encounter groups.* New York: Harper & Row, 1970. Paperback reprint: New York: Perennial, 1973a.

Rogers, C. R. Some new challenges. *American Psychologist,* 1973b, *28:* 379–387.

Rogers, C. R. In retrospect: Forty-six years. *American Psychologist,* 1974, *29:* 115–123. (Reprinted in Evans, 1975, pp. 121–146.)

Rogers, C. R. *Carl Rogers on personal power.* New York: Delacorte, 1977.

Rogers, C. R. *A way of being*. Boston: Houghton-Mifflin, 1980.

Rogers, C. R. Nuclear war: A personal response. *American Psychological Association Monitor,* 1982, *13*(8): 6–7.

Rogers, C. R. *Freedom to learn for the 80s*. Columbus, Ohio: Merrill, 1983.

Rogers, C. R., & Dymond, R. F. (Eds.). *Psychotherapy and personality change*. Chicago: University of Chicago Press, 1954.

Rogers, C. R., Gendlin, E. T., Kiesler, D. J., & Truax, C. B. *The therapeutic relationship and its impact: A study of psychotherapy with schizophrenics*. Madison: University of Wisconsin Press, 1967.

Rogers, C. R., & Skinner, B. F. Some issues concerning the control of human behavior: A symposium. *Science,* 1956, *124:* 1057–1066. (Reprinted in Evans, 1975, pp. xliv–lxxxviii.)

Rogers, C. R., & Stevens, B. *Person to person: The problem of being human*. Moab, Utah: Real People Press, 1967. Paperback reprint: New York: Pocket Books, 1971.

Rogers, C. R., & Wood, J. K. Client-centered theory: Carl R. Rogers. In A. Burton (Ed.), *Operational theories of personality*. New York: Brunner/Mazel, 1974, pp. 211–258.

Roid, G. H., & Fitts, W. H. *Tennessee self-concept scale: Revised manual*. Los Angeles, Calif.: Western Psychological Services, 1988.

Rosenhan, D. L. On being sane in insane places. *Science,* 1973, *179:* 250–258.

Rotter, J. B. Generalized expectancies for internal versus external control of reinforcement. *Psychological Monographs,* 1966, 80, *1* (Whole No. 609).

Rubins, J. L. *Karen Horney: Gentle rebel of psychoanalysis*. New York: Dial, 1978.

Rutter, M. Maternal deprivation. In M. H. Bornstein (Ed.), *Handbook of parenting: Vol. 4. Applied and practical parenting*. Hillsdale, N.J.: Lawrence Erlbaum Associates, 1995. pp. 3–31.

Rychlak, J. F. The marginalist as alternativist. *Contemporary Psychology,* 1997, *42:* 106–107.

Sagan, C. *The demon-haunted world: Science as a candle in the dark*. New York: Random House, 1996.

Samelson, F. J. B. Watson's Little Albert, Cyril Burt's twins, and the need for a critical science. *American Psychologist,* 1980, *35:* 619–625.

Schiedel, D. G., & Marcia, J. E. Ego identity, intimacy, sex role orientation, and gender. *Journal of Personality and Social Psychology,* 1985, 21, 149–160.

Schulz, R., & Ewen, R. B. *Adult development and aging: Myths and emerging realities* (2nd ed.). New York: Macmillan, 1993.

Schur, M. *Freud: Living and dying*. New York: International Universities Press, 1972.

Searles, H. F. *Collected papers on schizophrenia and related subjects*. New York: International Universities Press, 1965.

Sechrest, L. Personality. *Annual Review of Psychology,* 1976, *27:* 1–27.

Seligman, M. E. P. *Helplessness: On depression, development, and death*. San Francisco: Freeman, 1975.

Seligman, M. E. P. *Learned optimism*. New York: Knopf, 1991.

Seligman, M. E. P. The effectiveness of psychotherapy: The *Consumer Reports* study. *American Psychologist,* 1995, *50:* 965–974.

Shedler, J., Mayman, M., & Manis, M. The *illusion* of mental health. *American Psychologist,* 1993, *48:* 1117–1131.

Shevrin, H., & Dickman, S. The psychological unconscious: A necessary assumption for all psychological theory? *American Psychologist,* 1980, *35:* 421–434.

Shlien, J. M., Mosak, H. H., & Dreikurs, R. Effect of time limits: A comparison of two psychotherapies. *Journal of Counseling Psychology,* 1962, *9:* 31–34.

Shostrom, E. *Personal Orientation Inventory (POI): A test of self-actualization*. San Diego, Calif.: Educational and Industrial Testing Service, 1963.

Shostrom, E. An inventory for the measurement of self-actualization. *Educational and Psychological Measurement,* 1965, *24:* 207–218.

Silverman, L. H. On the role of data from laboratory experiments in the development of the clinical theory of psychoanalysis. *International Review of Psycho-Analysis,* 1975, *2:* 1–22.

Silverman, L. H. Psychoanalytic theory: "The reports of my death are greatly exaggerated." *American Psychologist,* 1976, *31:* 621–637.

Singer, E. *Key concepts in psychotherapy* (2nd ed.). New York: Basic Books, 1970.

Singer, J. L. An updated evaluation of Freud's theories: Will anyone listen? *Contemporary Psychology,* 1997, *42:* 309–310.

Skinner, B. F. *The behavior of organisms: An experimental analysis*. New York: Appleton-Century-Crofts, 1938.

Skinner, B. F. *Walden Two*. New York: Macmillan, 1948.

Skinner, B. F. *Verbal behaviors*. New York: Appleton-Century-Crofts, 1957.

Skinner, B. F. *Science and human behavior*. New York: Macmillan, 1953. Paperback reprint: New York: Free Press, 1965.

Skinner, B. F. Autobiography. In E. G. Boring & G. Lindzey (Eds.), *A history of psychology in autobiography* (Vol. 5). New York: Appleton-Century-Crofts, 1967, pp. 385–413.

Skinner, B. F. *The technology of teaching*. Englewood Cliffs, N.J.: Prentice-Hall, 1968.

Skinner, B. F. *Contingencies of reinforcement: A theoretical analysis*. Englewood Cliffs, N.J.: Prentice-Hall, 1969.

Skinner, B. F. *Beyond freedom and dignity*. New York: Knopf, 1971. Paperback reprint: New York: Bantam, 1972a.

Skinner, B. F. *Cumulative Record: A selection of papers* (3rd ed.). New York: Appleton-Century-Crofts, 1972b.

Skinner, B. F. *About behaviorism*. New York: Knopf, 1974. Paperback reprint: New York: Vintage Books, 1976.

Skinner, B. F. *Particulars of my life*. New York: McGraw-Hill, 1976. Paperback reprint: New York: McGraw-Hill, 1977.

Skinner, B. F. *Reflections on behaviorism and society*. Englewood Cliffs, N.J.: Prentice-Hall, 1978.

Skinner, B. F. *The shaping of a behaviorist: Part two of an autobiography*. New York: Knopf, 1979.

Skinner, B. F. Intellectual self-management in old age. *American Psychologist*, 1983, *38:* 239–244.

Skinner, B. F. The shame of American education. *American Psychologist*, 1984, *39:* 947–954.

Skinner, B. F. What is wrong with daily life in the Western world? *American Psychologist*, 1986, *41:* 568–574.

Skinner, B. F. *Upon further reflection*. Englewood Cliffs, N.J.: Prentice-Hall, 1987.

Skinner, B. F., & Vaughan, M. E. *Enjoy old age: A program of self-management*. New York: Norton, 1983.

Sloane, R. B., Staples, F. R., Cristol, A. H., Yorkston, N.J., & Whipple, K. *Psychotherapy versus behavior therapy*. Cambridge, Mass.: Harvard University Press, 1975.

Stephenson, W. The significance of Q-technique for the study of personality. In M. L. Reymert (Ed.), *Feelings and emotions: The Mooseheart symposium*. New York: McGraw-Hill, 1950.

Stephenson, W. *The study of behavior: Q-technique and its methodology*. Chicago: University of Chicago Press, 1953.

Stern, P. J. *C. G. Jung: The haunted prophet*. New York: Braziller, 1976. Paperback reprint: New York: Delta Books, 1977.

Sternberg, R. J. *Cognitive psychology* (2nd ed.). Fort Worth Texas: Harcourt, 1999.

Sternberg, R. J. *Psychology: In search of the human mind* (3rd ed.). Fort Worth Texas: Harcourt, 2001.

Sternberg, R. J., & Ben-Zeev, T. *Complex cognition: The psychology of human thought*. New York: Oxford University Press, 2001.

Strupp, H. H. Some comments on the future of psychoanalysis. *Journal of Contemporary Psychotherapy*, 1971, *3:* 117–120.

Strupp, H. H. On the technology of psychotherapy. *Archives of General Psychiatry*, 1972, *26:* 270–278.

Strupp, H. H. On the basic ingredients of psychotherapy. *Journal of Consulting and Clinical Psychology*, 1973, *41:* 1–8.

Strupp, H. H., & Bergin, A. E. Some empirical and conceptual bases for coordinated research in psychotherapy: A critical review of issues, trends, and evidence. *International Journal of Psychiatry*, 1969, *7:* 18–90.

Strupp, H. H., & Howard, K. I. A brief history of psychotherapy research. In D. K. Freedheim (Ed.), *History of psychotherapy: A century of change*. Washington, D.C.: American Psychological Association, 1992.

Suinn, R. The terrible twos–Anger and anxiety. *American Psychologist*, 2001, *56:* 27–36.

Sullivan, H. S. Entry in *Current Biography*, 1942.

Sullivan, H. S. *Conceptions of modern psychiatry*. Original publication: 1947. Paperback reprint: New York: Norton, 1953.

Sullivan, H. S. *The interpersonal theory of psychiatry*. Original publication: 1953. Paperback reprint: New York: Norton, 1968.

Sullivan, H. S. *The psychiatric interview*. Original publication: 1954. Paperback reprint: New York: Norton, 1970.

Sullivan, H. S. *The fusion of psychiatry and social science*. Original publication: 1964. Paperback reprint: New York: Norton, 1971.

Sullivan, H. S. *Personal psychopathology*. Originally prepared: 1932–33. New York: Norton, 1972.

Sullivan, H. S. *Clinical studies in psychiatry*. Original publication: 1956. Paperback reprint: New York: Norton, 1973.

Sullivan, H. S. *Schizophrenia as a human process*. Original publication: 1962. Paperback reprint: New York: Norton, 1974.

Sulloway, F. *Born to rebel*. New York: Pantheon, 1996.

Tafarodi, R. W., & Vu, C. Two-dimensional self-esteem and reactions to success and failure. *Personality and Social Psychology Bulletin*, 1997, *23:* 626–635.

Thorne, F. C., & Pishkin, V. The existential study. *Journal of Clinical Psychology*, 1973, *29:* 387–410.

Tice, D. M. Esteem protection or enhancement? Self-handicapping motives and attributions differ by trait self-esteem. *Journal of Personality and Social Psychology*, 1991, *60:* 711–725.

Triandis, H. C. The self and social behavior in differing cultural contexts. *Psychological Review*, 1989a, *96:* 506–520.

Triandis, H. C. Cross-cultural studies of individualism and collectivism. In J. J. Berman (Ed.), *Nebraska symposium on motivation 1989*. Lincoln: University of Nebraska Press, 1989b.

Triandis, H. C. *Culture and social behavior*. New York: McGraw-Hill, 1994a.

Triandis, H. C. Culture and social behavior. In W. J. Lonner & R. S. Malpass (Eds.), *Psychology and culture*. Boston: Allyn & Bacon, 1994b.

VandenBos, G. R. (Ed.). Psychotherapy research [Special Issue]. *American Psychologist,* 1986, *41:* 111–214.

VandenBos, G. R. (Ed.). Outcome assessment of psychotherapy [Special Issue]. *American Psychologist,* 1996, *51:* 1007–1079.

Wachtel, P. L. *Psychoanalysis and behavior therapy: Toward an integration.* New York: Basic Books, 1977.

Wachtel, P. L. Investigation and its discontents: Some constraints on progress in psychological research. *American Psychologist,* 1980, *35:* 399–408.

Wachtel, P. L. *Action and insight.* New York: Guilford Press, 1987.

Wahba, M. A., & Bridwell, L. G. Maslow reconsidered: A review of research on the need hierarchy theory. *Organizational Behavior and Human Performance,* 1976, *15:* 212–240.

Wallerstein, R. S., & Sampson, H. Issues in research in the psychoanalytic process. *International Journal of Psychoanalysis,* 1971, *52:* 11–50.

Waterman, A. S. Identity development from adolescence to adulthood: An extension of theory and a review of research. *Developmental Psychology,* 1982, *18:* 341–358.

Waterman, C. K., Buebel, M. E., & Waterman, A. S. Relationship between resolution of the identity crisis and outcomes of previous psychosocial crises. *Proceedings of the Annual Convention of the American Psychological Association,* 1970, *5:* 467–468.

Watson, J. B. Psychology as the behaviorist views it. *Psychological Review,* 1913, *20:* 158–177.

Watson, J. B. *Behavior from the standpoint of a behaviorist.* Philadelphia: Lippincott, 1919.

Watson, J. B. *Behaviorism.* New York: Norton, 1924.

Watson, J. B., & Rayner, R. Conditioned emotional reactions. *Journal of Experimental Psychology,* 1920, *3:* 1–14.

Watson, J. B., & Watson, R. R. Studies on infant psychology. *Scientific Monthly,* 1921, *13:* 493–515.

Welkowitz, J., Ewen, R. B., & Cohen, J. *Introductory statistics for the behavioral sciences* (5th ed.). New York: Wiley, 2000.

White, M. J. Sullivan and treatment. In P. Mullahy (Ed.), *The contributions of Harry Stack Sullivan.* New York: Hermitage House, 1952, pp. 117–150.

Whitmont, E. C., & Kaufmann, Y. *Analytical psychotherapy.* In R. Corsini (Ed.), *Current psychotherapies.* Itasca, Ill.: F. E. Peacock, 1973, pp. 85–117.

Winter, D. A. *Personal construct psychology in clinical practice: Theory, research and applications.* New York: Routledge, 1992.

Wolpe, J. *Psychotherapy by reciprocal inhibition.* Stanford, CA.: Stanford University Press, 1958.

Wolpe, J. *The practice of behavior therapy* (2nd ed.). New York: Pergamon, 1973.

Wolpe, J., & Lazarus, A. A. *Behavior therapy techniques: A guide to the treatment of neuroses.* New York: Pergamon, 1966.

Wylie, R. C. *The self-concept* (Vol. 1). Lincoln: University of Nebraska Press, 1974.

Wylie, R. C. *The self-concept* (Vol. 2). Lincoln: University of Nebraska Press, 1979.

Wylie, R. C. *Measures of self-concept.* Lincoln, Nebraska: University of Nebraska Press, 1989.

Yalom, I. D., & Lieberman, M. A. A study of encounter group casualties. *Archives of General Psychiatry,* 1971, *25:* 16–30.

Credits

Photos

Figures

8.1. Slightly modified from Children and Society, Second Edition, by Erik H. Erikson, by permission of W. W. Norton & Company, Inc. © 1950, © 1963 by W. W. Norton & Company, Inc. Copyright renewed 1978 by Erik H. Erikson.

12.1. Courtesy of Robert W. Allport.

13.1. Cattell, R. B. The Scientific Analysis of Personality, Penguin, 1965. Adapted from Cattell, R. B. and Kline, P. *The Scientific Analysis of Personality and Motivation,* Elsevier Science 1976, Fig. 9–1, p. 177. Used by permission.

13.2. Ewen, R. B., Personality: A Topical Approach, Lawrence Erlbaum Associates, Inc., 1997, p. 139.

14.1. Courtesy of B. F. Skinner Foundation. Used by permission.

Index